GENDER ROLES

GENDER ROLES
A Handbook of Tests and Measures

CAROLE A. BEERE

GREENWOOD PRESS
New York • Westport, Connecticut • London

Library of Congress Cataloging-in-Publication Data

Beere, Carole A.
    Gender roles : a handbook of tests and measures / Carole A. Beere.
      p. cm.
    ISBN 0–313–26278–0 (lib. bdg. : alk. paper)
    1. Sociometry—Methodology—Handbooks, manuals, etc. 2. Scale
analysis (Psychology)—Handbooks, manuals, etc. 3. Sex role—
Research—Methodology—Handbooks, manuals, etc. 4. Social role—
Research—Methodology—Handbooks, manuals, etc. I. Title.
HM253.B43   1990
305.3'072—dc20   89–17033

British Library Cataloguing in Publication Data is available.

Library of Congress Catalog Card Number: 89–17033
ISBN: 0–313–26278–0

First published in 1990

Greenwood Press, Inc.
88 Post Road West, Westport, Connecticut 06881

Printed in the United States of America

The paper used in this book complies with the
Permanent Paper Standard issued by the National
Information Standards Organization (Z39.48–1984).

10 9 8 7 6 5 4 3 2 1

Contents

Acknowledgments

A project of this magnitude could never be completed by one person working alone. I am indebted to many people for their encouragement and their labors on behalf of this book. Beth Macleod, librarian at Central Michigan University, must be thanked first, because it was she who encouraged me to undertake this project. Second, I want to thank Dr. Deb Poole, who urged me to apply for outside funding to support the project. This project could not have come to fruition without the financial support of Central Michigan University, which provided me with a sabbatical leave, the Rockefeller Foundation, which awarded me a grant to support the project, and the CMU Faculty Research and Creative Endeavors Committee, who provided an initial grant for the literature searches.

Several colleagues contributed expert advice and moral support as I struggled to complete this book. I am grateful to Dr. Dan King and Dr. Lynda King, who were always willing to answer my statistical questions, even when I asked the same questions over and over; and my thanks to Dr. Richard Hartley, my wonderful computer consultant who even helped rescue lost files on a Sunday afternoon. Ruth Helwig and Mary Halfmann, of the Interlibrary Loan Office at CMU, graciously obtained hundreds of articles for me, some on very short notice. I cannot possibly list all of the ways in which the next three people were helpful to me. Librarians Sue Miles, David Ginsburg, and Bill Miles were crucial to the completion of this project. They provided the necessary moral support when I thought I could not keep at it another day; they willingly helped me to find the materials to match an incredible array of incomplete and inaccurate citations; and they answered all sorts of questions regarding everything from grammatical constructions to postal addresses. (I think librarians are the unsung heroes of all authors.) Four students assisted me during various phases of my work; I want to thank Lisa McDonald, Debbie Robb, Carol Ryan, and Nancy Thornton. I could not have done it without their help.

As one reads this book, it is apparent that I exchanged letters with numerous colleagues around the country and was in telephone contact with many of them. Researchers sent me copies of their measures and their published and unpublished articles. Many also took time from their busy professional lives to answer specific questions for me. Because it was necessary to limit the scope of this book, some who took much time and effort to assist me are not even listed in the book. My sincerest thanks to everyone who sent me materials for possible inclusion. Though we have never met, I feel indebted to all of you for the successful completion of this project.

Special thanks are reserved for Mary Cannon, who reviewed every word of the manuscript at least three times, looking for inconsistencies and inaccurate citations. She did a wonderful job, and the book would not have been completed without her help. Special thanks also go to Lucille Berger, my mother. Every time she visited our town, she managed to pitch in and help with this book. She did filing, photocopying, and located materials within the library, even though she retired from her own job several years ago. Her desire to help will always be remembered.

Finally, thanks to my immediate family. Not only did they have to put up with my absences from our home as I spent endless hours at the library, but they contributed their own time to helping me complete the project. I am sure both of my children will long remember their hours searching the library for particular journal articles. Heartfelt thanks go to my son, Jonathan, and my daughter, Jennifer. Most of all, thanks to my husband, Don, who is a wonderful colleague and critic, as well as a wonderful husband and father. I can't imagine a man more supportive and more helpful than he is.

1

Introduction

Slightly over 10 years ago, I wrote *Women and Women's Issues: A Handbook of Tests and Measures* (Beere, 1979) in order to provide researchers with a convenient source of measures to use in research regarding women and women's issues. I hoped the handbook would contribute to gender-related research in several ways: (1) by making it easier for researchers to locate quality instruments appropriate for their research, (2) by discouraging the proliferation of substandard or redundant measures, (3) by setting some minimal standards for measures used in women's research, and (4) by encouraging more research regarding women and women's issues. To achieve these goals, I searched the psychological, sociological, and educational literature from the 1920s through 1977. I identified the best 235 measures and described them in the handbook. The measures were organized into 11 chapters: Sex Roles (59 scales), Sex Stereotypes (25 scales), Sex Role Prescriptions (7 scales), Children's Sex Roles (11 scales), Gender Knowledge (5 scales), Marital and Parental Roles (23 scales), Employee Roles (16 scales), Multiple Roles (20 scales), Attitudes Toward Women's Issues (41 scales), Somatic and Sexual Issues (17 scales), and Unclassified (11 scales).

I was gratified by the feedback I received from users who found the handbook very useful, and I was pleased with the positive reviews the handbook received. The field of women's studies has grown phenomenally within the past decade; however, some older measures have become obsolete, and some new measures have been developed to replace them. More is known about the psychometric properties of some measures that have been used extensively. In addition, new areas of research have been developed, which have led to the development of new measures. A book written in 1979 can no longer provide researchers with up-to-date information regarding the measures used in women's research.

It is within this context that I began work on this handbook. The goals as listed above remained the same, with one exception: I broadened the scope of coverage to include additional women's issues, and I searched for measures regarding men and men's issues. Also, the literature search covered a different period of time; this handbook covers the period from the prior book through the middle of 1988.

Search for Measures

The literature search to identify measures for this handbook centered on two sources: SilverPlatter's PsycLIT and SilverPlatter's ERIC. Both are computer-searchable databases stored on compact discs. The PsycLIT database contains citations and abstracts for all journal articles in *Psychological Abstracts*, and therefore it covers the world's periodicals in psychology and related disciplines. About 1,300 journals are abstracted in PsycLIT. The ERIC database includes the information contained in two sources: *Current Index to Journals in Education (CIJE)*, which abstracts over 740 journals, and *Resources in Education (RIE)*, which abstracts the microfiche collection of the Education Resources Information Center (ERIC).

There was no theoretical framework for determining the terms to use for the search. Rather, by reviewing the thesaurus associated with each database and by some trial-and-error work with the compact discs, I tried to identify all search terms that might lead to relevant articles. Because the indexing terms are different in PsycLIT and ERIC, the two computer searches were conducted with slightly different terms. Listed below are the terms used to search PsycLIT.

amenorrhea	human females	obscenity
androgyny	husbands	ovariectomy
anorexia nervosa	hysterectomy	parental role
appetite disorders	incest	pornography
birth	induced abortion	pregnancy
bulimia	labor-childbirth	premenstrual tension
childbirth training	lesbianism	prostitution
daughters	marital relations	rape
divorce	marriage	sex discrimination
dual career	masculinity	sex role
dysmenorrhea	mastectomy	sexual harassment
family planning	matriarchy	sexual attitude
attitudes	menarche	sisters

family structure	menopause	spontaneous abortion
family violence	menstrual disorders	unwed mothers
fathers	menstrual cycle	widows
femininity	menstruation	wives
feminism	mother-child relations	women's-liberation
gender identity	mothers	movement
housewives	natural childbirth	working women

ERIC was searched using the following terms:

abortion	femininity	pregnancy
anorexia nervosa	feminism	pregnant students
androgyny	gynecology	rape
battered women	homemakers	sex bias
birth	homosexuality	sex education
bulimia	incest	sex fairness
contraception	lesbianism	sex role
daughters	marital satisfaction	sex stereotypes
displaced homemakers	marital status	sexual abuse
divorce	marriage	sexual harassment
employed parents	masculinity	sexual identity
employed women	mother attitudes	sexuality
family attitudes	mothers	sons
family planning	obscenity	spouses
family role	parent role	unwed mothers
family violence	pornography	women's studies
fathers		

Most of the terms in these two lists were used as descriptors; that is, an article was selected by the computer search only if the indexer had keyed the article on that term. Some terms, however, were used for free text searching; the computer searched every word of the abstract as well as the indexed terms, and an article was selected if the term was mentioned in the abstract of the article. Of the 58 terms used to search PsycLIT, 6 were used for free-text searching: *androgyny, dual career, femininity, gender identity, masculinity,* and *sex role.* Of the 49 terms used to search ERIC, 3 were used for free-text searching: *androgyny, femininity,* and *masculinity.*

Using the terms listed, the computer searched the two databases for articles entered into them between January 1978 and December 1988.

References were downloaded directly from SilverPlatter's databases into a database I had created on my own computer. Using a simple computer program, I eliminated duplicate references (there was some overlap between PsycLIT and ERIC), references to foreign language periodicals, and references to articles that used nonhuman subjects. A pool of about 36,000 references remained as potentially relevant; it included about 17,000 references from PsycLIT, about 10,000 references from *CIJE*, and about 9,000 references from *RIE*. At the comparable stage in the preparation of my last handbook, I had identified 8,000 references. The tremendous increase in the number of references is due to both the growth of research in gender-related areas and the increase in topics encompassed by the search.

Unfortunately, the computer could not be used for further screening of articles. Instead, each abstract had to be read in order to determine whether the article reported the results of relevant, empirical research, and if so, whether that research involved the use of a scale that might be appropriate for this handbook.

In addition to searching the two databases, hand searching was done of selected journals. *Sex Roles* and *Psychology of Women Quarterly* are the journals most directly relevant to the focus of this book. Page-by-page searching was done of every post–1977 issue of these two journals to ensure that if any issue of these two publications was inadvertently omitted from PsycLIT (and several were), they would not be overlooked in my search process.

The lag time between the publication of a journal and its inclusion by an indexing or abstracting service is quite variable—sometimes as long as one year. To ensure that recent issues of particularly relevant journals were not overlooked, page-by-page searching was done of the issues not yet abstracted in the PsycLIT or ERIC databases. The journals that were hand searched were: *Adolescence, Behaviour Research and Therapy, Child Development, Developmental Psychology, Family Relations, Journal of Clinical Psychology, Journal of Counseling Psychology, Journal of Marriage and the Family, Journal of Sex Research, Journal of Sex and Marital Therapy, Journal of Social Psychology, Journal of Vocational Behavior, Perceptual and Motor Skills, Personality and Social Psychology Bulletin,* and *Psychological Reports.*

After the abstracts were reviewed, articles judged as not useful were removed from my database. I then read the methods section of the remaining articles and identified the measuring instruments used in each. In order to organize the voluminous amount of information I had, I classified articles and measures into the following categories: gender roles, marital roles, parental roles, employee roles, multiple roles, stereotypes, attitudes toward gender-related issues, family planning (including contraception and abortion), violence, somatic issues, homosexuality, heterosexual relations, eating disorders, selected personality traits (e.g., intimacy, self-disclosure, loneliness), and hetero-social relations. There were some scales that did not fit neatly into one of these categories, and I temporarily labeled those "miscellaneous."

At this point, I retained 6,900 of the original 36,000 references. These 6,900 articles and ERIC documents were published since the mid–1970s and reported the results of empirical research. A total of 1,450 different "measures" were used in this research. At the comparable stage in preparing my last handbook, I had identified approximately 850 measures. Most measures identified for this handbook were mentioned in only one or a handful of articles, and often all of those articles were written by the person who had developed the measure. Of the 1,450 measures in my pool, 992 (68%) of them were cited in only a single article or ERIC document. Only 111 measures (8%) were cited in more than 5 articles and ERIC documents, and only 61 measures (4%) were cited in more than 10 articles.

Beyond a doubt, the most popular measure was the Bem Sex Role Inventory (Bem, 1974), which was used in 973 articles and ERIC documents published since the literature search for my last handbook. The next most popular measure was the Attitudes Toward Women Scale (Spence & Helmreich, 1972) with 321 new citations, followed by the Personal Attributes Questionnaire (Spence, Helmreich, & Stapp, 1974) with 284 citations. There were only two other measures that were used in over 100 studies, and these two measures are not directly related to the focus of this handbook. The Locke-Wallace (1959) Marital Adjustment Test was cited in 263 articles, and Spanier's (1976) Dyadic Adjustment Scale was cited in 193 articles. Although all of these measures were developed prior to 1977, the number of citations listed here is based on a literature search that considered references added to the databases only after 1977.

Earlier I described my system for classifying articles. Based on this system, the most popular area of research was the study of adult gender roles, and the second most popular area was the study of marriage and marital roles. Attitudes toward gender-related issues and sexuality were, respectively, the third and fourth most popular areas for research. Of course, these rankings do not include research conducted without the use of identifiable "measures."

Screening the Measures

The number of different measures in the literature necessitated the establishment of criteria for determining what to include in this handbook. For my previous handbook, a measure had to satisfy only one of the following four criteria: "(1) the construction of the instrument must be empirically or theoretically based and must be explained, (2) data must be available regarding its reliability, (3) data must be available regarding its validity, and (4) it must have been used by a variety of researchers" (Beere, 1979, p. 5). For that handbook, these criteria were adequate to reduce the pool of measures to 235 scales. Now, however, these criteria are not sufficiently stringent. With the almost universal availability of computers, researchers frequently report coefficient alpha for a series of Likert-type items, and according to the criteria for the previous handbook, this would qualify the scale for inclusion.

Therefore, it was necessary to establish another set of criteria for determining which scales to include in this handbook. It was easiest to establish a criterion for the scales that appeared in my last book: any scale described in my previous handbook was retained for this one if it was used again in research published since my previous literature search.

The process of screening the newer measures was more complex. First, if a scale was relevant, *and* there was evidence of its reliability and/or validity, *and* it was used in *more than one* published article or ERIC document, the scale was retained for this handbook. It is presumed that these measures had been indirectly "approved" by more than one set of reviewers. This criterion of multiple use is biased toward including older scales, since a very new scale was unlikely to have been used in more than one published study.

If a scale did not satisfy this first set of criteria but there was an article or ERIC document that focused on the scale's development, the scale was retained. It is likely that scales that met this criterion will be used by other researchers in the future. A few scales that did not meet the criteria were, nevertheless, retained because they were unusual or pertained to a topic that would otherwise receive inadequate coverage in this handbook.

Despite establishing more stringent criteria for including measures in this book, the number of measures retained far exceeded the number that could realistically be described in a single handbook. This is partially due to the fact that there have been many new measures developed in the past decade and partially due to the fact that my literature search covered a wide range of topics. Rather than eliminate a few measures from each of the topics or completely eliminate entire topics, I decided to write two books. One book, *Sex and Gender Issues: A Handbook of Tests and Measures* (Beere, in press), covers a variety of *issues* relating to sex and gender. Included in that book are such topics as abortion, contraception, heterosocial relations, heterosexual relations, pregnancy and childbirth, somatic issues, homosexuality, rape and sexual coercion, spouse abuse and incest, sexual knowledge, sexuality, eating disorders, body image, and selected gender-related personality traits.

This book, *Gender Roles: A Handbook of Tests and Measures*, describes the measures pertaining to gender *roles* and attitudes toward gender-related issues. Gender roles is a broad topic encompassing adults' and children's gender roles, gender stereotypes, marital roles, parental roles, employee roles, and multiple roles. A total of 211 measures satisfied the criteria for inclusion in this book and pertained to the topics just listed. These 211 measures include 67 scales described in my previous handbook.

Sources of Information for Scale Descriptions

Generally the information provided in the scale descriptions was obtained from the published articles and ERIC documents reporting the results of research using the scale. In some instances, where the scale development was undertaken in conjunction with the completion of a doctoral dissertation or master's thesis, I relied on those documents for information. Unless the scale was available in full in a published source, I contacted the authors for a copy of the scale. I also took advantage of that opportunity to ask the authors for other information regarding the scale.

Writing letters to scale authors produced varied responses. My original letters came back with no forwarding address; secretaries answered my letters either indicating a current address or informing me of the impossibility of locating the author; and scale authors sent both short and long letters indicating that their scale was not worth disseminating, was long forgotten, or was borrowed from someone else's research. Many letters elicited no response whatsoever. What is most important for this handbook, however, is that many authors sent me their measures, and many included information that greatly facilitated the task of writing the descriptions. No scale is described in this book unless I was able to review the entire scale.

Format for Scale Descriptions

The scale descriptions follow a standard format that provides the following information:

TITLE. The title of the scale is given first. Whenever the authors gave their scale a title, that is the title I use here. If the authors did not assign a title, I assigned one, generally starting with the authors' names. If the scale's name is customarily abbreviated, the abbreviation is given in parentheses following the title. There are instances in which two or more scales have the same abbreviation.

AUTHORS: Generally the author or authors are listed as they appear on the earliest publication mentioning the scale. In some cases, however, information contained in correspondence I received from the scale authors or in a publication indicated different authors or a different order for the author's names. I used the best information I had to identify the authors.

DATE: The date given is generally the earliest date that the scale was mentioned in a publication. If the scale was revised, the date of the revision is indicated in parentheses following the initial date. If I could identify the earliest date when the scale was used, the use date is given in parentheses following the initial publication date.

VARIABLE: I provide a very brief description of the variable being measured. Rather than strive for consistency across the different scales, I tried to represent the variable as the scale's authors represented it, except that I used the more accurate term *gender role* in place of the more commonly used *sex role*. Of course, the authors' claim as to what a scale measures is not sufficient evidence of the scale's validity. Furthermore, researchers sometimes use a scale to measure a variable different from that intended by the scale's authors. Only the authors' description of the variable measured is given here.

TYPE OF INSTRUMENT: The most common type of measure described in this handbook is the summated rating scale in which the respondent is presented with a statement accompanied by three to seven options. The options generally vary from strong agreement to strong disagreement. Of the 211 scales in this handbook, 126 (60%) are summated rating scales. Also included in this book are: (a) semantic differential scales in which a concept such as "woman" is followed by a list of bipolar adjective pairs with each adjective pair separated by a 7-point scale; respondents rate the concept on each of the adjective scales; (b) forced choice measures in which respondents are presented with pairs of statements and asked to select the one item in each pair which is more true; (c) forced choice picture preference tests in which children are asked to select one item from each pair of pictures; (d) Guttman scales in which respondents indicate which of a series of statements they agree with (Guttman scales are used to assess attitudes, are more difficult to construct than more commonly used attitude measures, and require that the item set represent a continuum from easiest to endorse to most difficult to endorse); (e) Thurstone measures in which respondents are given a series of statements and indicate which ones they endorse (the development of Thurstone scales involves the use of judges to determine scale values for the items on the scale; scoring depends on the scale values of the endorsed items); (f) true/false scales in which respondents judge each item on the scale; (g) multiple choice measures in which respondents are given a series of fixed options for responding to each item on the scale (the response options may be consistent across items or they may vary across items); (h) projective tests in which respondents are given ambiguous verbal or pictorial stimuli and asked to tell stories or draw pictures in response to the stimuli; the assumption is made that respondents are projecting their own needs, feelings, or unconscious desires onto the stimuli; (i) ranking scales in which respondents are asked to rank order a series of stimuli; (j) rating scales in which respondents rate specific stimuli on specific variables; (k) checklists that provide respondents a list, frequently consisting of adjectives, and the respondents check all that apply; (l) toy preference tests in which children select the toys they would most like to play with; and (m) observation schedules, which are generally used by trained observers to rate other persons or media samples.

DESCRIPTION: A general description of the scale is provided, including information regarding the content of the items, the length of the scale, and the response options. Any subscales are also described.

SAMPLE ITEMS: A few items are reproduced from the scale. In most instances where there are subscales, an item is reproduced from each subscale.

PREVIOUS SUBJECTS: A brief description of each group who completed the scale is given. I considered college students as a specific subset of adults and listed them separately. For samples of college students, authors sometimes provided the college major, a description of the class in which the measure was completed, or information regarding the students' academic standing (e.g., undergraduate versus graduate, sophomore versus junior). In general, I did not list this information. If I knew that the scale had been used in foreign countries, I often listed that information. If no country is specified, it can be presumed that the scale has been used in the United States.

APPROPRIATE FOR: A brief description of who might be expected to complete the measure is given. Unless there is a statement to the contrary, a measure is appropriate for both males and females. Since scale authors generally do not provide information on intended respondents, I had to make a judgment about who could complete the measure, and I made that judgment based on the scale's content and apparent difficulty level. Thus, my recommendation should be considered very tentative. Before a scale can be used with any particular group, there should be evidence that the scale is both reliable and valid for that group. My statement of who the scale is appropriate for does not reflect reliability or validity data.

ADMINISTRATION: This line contains information on how the scale is administered and how long it takes to complete the scale. Most scales in this handbook can be self-administered, although some, particularly those for use with young children, require individual administration. Scale authors occasionally provided information on the length of time required to complete their scale. If the authors provided the information, it is included here. Otherwise, the time estimates are my best guess and should be verified before the measure is used in large-scale research.

SCORING: Information is provided on the number of scores, the scoring procedures, the range of scores, and the availability of normative data. For most scales, subscale and total scores are obtained simply by summing item scores. If a scoring key or conversion tables are needed, it is so indicated.

DEVELOPMENT: The theoretical and empirical bases for scale and subscale development are explained here. Generally the information in this section was obtained from articles and paper presentations written by the scale's authors. Occasionally, the information was augmented by correspondence I received from the authors. There is considerable variability in the detail provided in this section; some authors provided specific information regarding the scale's development, and others provided a few general statements. If no information was available regarding the scale's development, I so indicate in this section.

RELIABILITY: Test-retest, alternate form, split-half, and internal consistency reliabilities are presented here. Data regarding item-total correlations are also reported. The most commonly reported form of reliability is coefficient alpha, which reflects the internal consistency of the scale. Because there are rarely alternate forms of a scale, alternate form reliability cannot be computed for most measures. Unfortunately, test-retest reliability is also rarely reported.

The fact that there are data regarding the scale's reliability does not mean the scale is sufficiently reliable. In fact, the reliability coefficients for some scales, and particularly for some subscales, suggest that the measures are not sufficiently reliable. Furthermore, reliability data for one sample do not necessarily generalize to another sample.

I obtained the data regarding reliability from the published articles and ERIC documents listed at the end of the scale's description. Sometimes the authors provided me additional information. The statement "no information was provided" indicates that I was unable to locate any evidence regarding reliability.

VALIDITY: Validating a measure is a never-ending process. At no point can one say, "This scale is valid." A scale is to some extent valid, for a particular purpose, with a particular population, looking at a particular type of validity. There are a variety of ways to provide evidence of a scale's validity. Evidence of construct validity, criterion-related validity, and content validity are included in this section. Content validity reflects whether the items are sufficiently representative of the content domain to be measured. Content validity should be built into the scale as a function of the way the scale is constructed. Criterion-related validity is demonstrated by correlating scale scores with scores on another measure designed to assess the same attribute. Evidence regarding construct validity was generally obtained by hypothesis testing. Sometimes the hypothesis testing involved comparing known groups; often these were groups of males and females or groups presumed to be liberal and conservative. Evidence of construct validity was also acquired by testing whether scores correlated in the predicted direction with other variables. This is known as convergent validity, and the "other variables" may be demographic characteristics or scores on measures hypothesized to correlate with the scale of interest. Data regarding discriminant validity, another aspect of construct validity, are obtained by checking that scores are independent of scores on measures predicted to measure independent traits. Frequently researchers look at correlations with scores on the Marlowe-Crowne Social Desirability Scale (Crowne & Marlowe, 1960); ideally the two sets of scores will be independent. Other evidence of construct validity is obtained by looking at whether "treatments" have the expected impact on scores. Factorial validity also pertains to construct validity. Factorial validity involves the use of factor analysis to determine whether the obtained factors are consistent with the predicted ones.

As is the case with reliability, information contained in this section does not necessarily substantiate the scale's validity. It may in fact provide evidence leading one to question the scale's validity. Sometimes information reported in the section titled "NOTES & COMMENTS" provides additional evidence reflecting on the scale's validity. When I state "no information was provided," it means that neither the scale's authors nor the users of the scale provided any data that shed light on the scale's validity.

ARTICLES LISTED IN BEERE, 1979: This heading is used only for the 67 measures described in my previous handbook (Beere, 1979). Because the references given in that book are not repeated here, the researcher is likely to want to know how many references accompanied the earlier description of the scale. That number is reported here.

NOTES & COMMENTS: This heading provides a catchall for important information that does not conveniently fit into one of the other areas. Results of factor analytic studies are likely to be given here. Information on modifications and foreign language translations of the scale is described. The focus of different research studies using the scale is summarized. If the scale is listed in *The Ninth Mental Measurements Yearbook* or *Tests in Print III*, it is referenced here. My evaluative comments regarding the scale are also included in this section.

AVAILABLE FROM: The purpose of this entry is to provide the prospective researcher with a source from which to obtain a full copy of the scale. If the measure is available in any published source—a book, a journal article, or a published separate—that information is listed. In most cases, if the scale was not available from one of these sources, I contacted the scale authors in order to give them a choice of what to list under this heading. Some authors requested that I provide their address, and I did. Other authors agreed to allow me to deposit their test materials with the National Auxiliary Publication Service (NAPS). In those instances, I have indicated the necessary information for researchers to purchase a copy of the material from NAPS. In a few instances, the authors informed me of another source researchers could use for obtaining the measure. If the authors did not provide me with information regarding the availability of their measures, I listed the authors' address for researchers to use. Before using any scale, a researcher must be certain to obtain permission from the authors. Failure to do so may result in a copyright violation. The fact that a scale can be readily obtained does not mean that researchers have permission to use it. Contacting the scale's authors can also reap unexpected benefits. The author may be able to direct the researcher to current information regarding the scale or even to a revised version of the scale.

USED IN: This section lists the articles and ERIC documents that reported research using the scale. If I serendipitously located doctoral dissertations or master's theses that reported on the use of the scale, I also listed those here, but I did not actively search for dissertations and theses. Scale authors sometimes sent me relevant materials—unpublished manuscripts and in press publications—and these are also listed. Generally, the research described in these various citations was summarized in the NOTES & COMMENTS section. My searching for the period 1977–1988 was quite thorough, and I hope the lists are close to complete for journal articles and ERIC documents; however, the lists of citations are not complete for the period prior to 1977. If the scale was described in my previous handbook, the reader is referred to that source for the older citations. Otherwise researchers must do their own searching to locate older citations.

BIBLIOGRAPHY: Listed here are citations for materials that are referred to in the scale's description but do not report on research using the measure. Sometimes these citations refer to articles that provided the theoretical basis for the scale's development or that are the source for measures used in the validation process.

Two types of descriptions are included in this handbook. Full-length descriptions are given for the 144 scales that were not described in my previous handbook. The full-length descriptions include all of the headings listed above except "ARTICLES LISTED IN BEERE, 1979." Abbreviated descriptions are provided for the 67 scales that were described in my last book. The abbreviated descriptions contain the following information: TITLE, AUTHOR, DATE, VARIABLE, DESCRIPTION, ARTICLES LISTED IN BEERE, 1979, NOTES & COMMENTS, AVAILABLE FROM, USED IN, and BIBLIOGRAPHY. This information should be sufficient for a researcher to determine whether the scale is potentially relevant. For those scales that seem promising, the researcher should consult Beere (1979) to supplement the information provided in these abbreviated descriptions.

Organization of the Scales

The 211 scales described in this handbook are organized into seven chapters. "Gender Roles" contains 39 scales, 15 of which were described in my previous book. Most of the scales in this chapter are used to assess persons' "masculinity" or "femininity" or to assess their adherence to particular gender roles. The chapter includes 5 scales intended for females only, 6 scales intended for males only, and 28 scales intended for both sexes. Three of the measures in this chapter are projective tests that can be used with children as well as adults; the remaining scales are appropriate for older persons. Some of these scales can be used with persons as young as 12 years old, some can be used with high school students and older persons, and some should not be used with persons below age 16 or below age 18.

"Children's Gender Roles" contains 18 scales; 10 of these measures were described in my previous handbook. This is the only chapter that includes such a high percentage of scales from that book. Half of the scales in this chapter assess masculinity and femininity. The chapter also includes scales assessing gender constancy, gender disturbance, gender role flexibility, gender saliency, and approval of gender role behavior. Because these measures are intended for use with children, many of them must be individually administered.

"Stereotypes" includes 18 measures, 5 of which were described in my previous handbook. Half of the measures in this chapter are intended for use with children. One scale in this chapter is used for rating sexism in the media.

"Marital and Parental Roles" includes 26 scales, 7 of which were described in my previous handbook. These 26 scales pertain to three areas: marital roles, with 10 scales that consider such topics as decision making, task allocation, homemaking stress, and attitudes toward traditional versus egalitarian marriages; parenthood motivation and timing, with 7 scales that look at when and why persons become parents; and parental roles, with 9 scales that deal with parental stress, the transition to parenthood, attitudes about parental roles, and several specific maternal issues.

"Employee Roles" includes 24 scales, 4 of them described in my previous handbook. Nine measures in this chapter deal with specific cross-sex-typed careers, for example, male nurses or female police officers. Four measures deal with sexual harassment, and the remaining 11 measures deal with a variety of issues linking gender roles and employee roles.

"Multiple Roles" includes 30 scales dealing with men and/or women in regard to at least two roles—generally the marital/parental and the employee roles. Eleven scales in this chapter focus on role strain or role conflict. Three scales deal specifically with dual career couples, and 16 scales deal with a variety of issues linking gender with more than one role.

"Attitudes Toward Gender Role Issues" is the last chapter in the handbook. It contains the largest number of scales. Fifty-six scales are described in this chapter; 19 of them were described in my previous handbook. The first 7 scales in the chapter focus on issues relating to men; the next 24 scales focus on issues regarding women; and the last 26 measures focus on issues regarding both men and women or both boys and girls. The item content on these scales tends to be heterogeneous.

The organization of the handbook is intended to facilitate browsing so that a researcher can page through a section reviewing related measures. Each chapter begins with an overview of measurement in the area. There are several indexes to facilitate locating measures by subject, title, author or by user. This handbook should be beneficial to researchers as the first place they look for measures; it should never be the last source consulted. The handbook will help a researcher narrow the list of possible measures, but original sources must be consulted for complete information regarding any scale.

Other References

Researchers seeking information about scales not described in this handbook may find it useful to consult one or more of the reference books described here.

Measures for Clinical Practice: A Sourcebook by Corcoran and Fischer (1987) is intended "to provide for practitioners and students a number of instruments that they can use to help them monitor and evaluate their practice. These instruments were specifically selected because they measure most of the common problems seen in clinical practice, they are relatively short, easy to score and administer" (p. xxv). The book includes descriptions and copies of 127 scales organized into three sections: 92 measures for adults, 19 measures for children, and 16 measures for couples and families. In addition to providing information on the specific measures, Corcoran and Fischer include an overview of the principles of measurement and information on how to select a measure.

Sexuality-Related Measures edited by Davis, Yarber, and Davis (1988) includes descriptions of 109 measures organized under the following headings: abortion, aggression, aging, anxiety, arousal/arousability, attitudes, beliefs, contraception, decision making, education, emotions, experience, extramarital, family planning, fantasy, female sexuality, functioning, gender identification, guilt, homophobia, homosexualities, identity, ideology, initiative, involvement, jealousy, knowledge, love, marriage, masculinity, masturbation, medical, premarital rape, satisfaction, sexually transmitted diseases, transsexualism, variations, and vasectomy. Though some of the headings are ambiguous, all of the scales pertain to human sexuality. In addition to providing descriptions of the scales, many scales are reproduced in this book. Unfortunately, there are no indexes to facilitate using the book.

Marriage and Family Assessment: A Sourcebook for Family Therapy edited by Filsinger (1983) contains 14 chapters describing measures that can be used in family therapy or family research. The book includes 5 chapters concerning observational techniques, 5 chapters concerning marital questionnaires, and 4 chapters pertaining to family questionnaires. Twelve of the chapters each discuss a single measuring procedure. Included are the Inventory of Marital Conflict, the Spouse Observation Checklist, the Marital Interaction Coding System, the Couples Interaction Scoring System, the Dyadic Adjustment Scale, the Marital Satisfaction Inventory, the Marital Communication Inventory, the Marital Agendas Protocol, the PREPARE-ENRICH Inventories, the Family Environment Scale, the Family Inventory of Life Events and Changes, and the Family Adaptability and Cohesion Evaluation Scales.

Family Assessment: A Guide to Methods and Measures by Grotevant and Carlson (1989) provides an overview of family assessment techniques including observational measures and self-report measures. The book contains descriptions of 70 family assessment measures; 13 interaction coding schemes, 8 rating scales, 17 self-report measures focusing on whole-family functioning, 9 self-report measures focusing on family stress and coping, and 23 self-report measures focusing on parent-child relationships. The descriptions in the book were written by the book's authors, but a unique feature is that a description is followed by a comment from the scale's author. The comments average about half a page.

Dictionary of Behavioral Assessment Techniques edited by Hersen and Bellack (1988) contains descriptions of 287 behavioral assessment measures, including "behavioral observations, self-reports, parent ratings, staff ratings, sibling ratings, judges' ratings, teacher ratings, therapist ratings, nurses' ratings, physiological assessment, biochemical assessment, biological assessment, structured interviews, semistructured interviews, and analogue tests" (p. xix). Each description is written by a different contributor, often the author of the scale, who provided information regarding the following aspects of each measure: description, purpose, development, psychometric characteristics, clinical use, and future directions. A "User's Guide" that lists scales by topic and an author index facilitate locating scales within the book.

Sourcebook of Measures of Women's Educational Equity by Parks, Bogart, Reynolds, Hamilton, and Finley (1982) includes descriptions of 198 measures "deemed potentially useful for providing information about Women's Educational Equity Act (WEEA)–funded projects and other activities designed to eliminate sex stereotyping in educational programs, policies, and institutions" (p. 3). The measures are organized into nine areas: Attitude Toward Mathematics; Awareness of Sexism and Racism; Career Awareness, Choice, Motivation, Interest; Institutional Sexism; Management and Leadership Characteristics and Skills; Materials Assessment Guidelines; Self-Concept and Self-Esteem; Sex Role Perception; and Other Instruments. Title, subject, population, and author indexes are provided to facilitate locating measures.

Handbook of Family Measurement Techniques by Touliatos, Perlmutter, and Straus (1989) provides descriptions of 976 instruments that have been developed and used over the past 50 years. The descriptions are grouped according to five categories: dimensions of interaction, intimacy and family values, parenthood, roles and power, and adjustment. Relatively detailed information, including several references to research using the measure, is provided for the 504 measures appearing in published reports since 1975. Abbreviated descriptions are provided for the remaining measures. To facilitate using the book, three indexes are provided: author, title, and classification.

Sex and Gender Issues: A Handbook of Tests and Measures by Beere (in press) includes descriptions of measures relating to the following topics: heterosocial relations, heterosexual relations, somatic issues, pregnancy and childbirth, homosexuality, abortion and contraception, rape and sexual coercion, spouse abuse and incest, eating disorders, body image, sexuality-related measures, and gender-related personality traits. The format of the book parallels the format of this handbook.

The books just described were published after 1980. Some older books also provide information on measures that might be useful to researchers: *Sociological Measurement: An Inventory of Scales and Indices* (Bonjean, Hill, & McLemore, 1967), *Measures for Psychological Assessment: A Guide to 3,000 Original Sources and Their Applications* (Chun, Cobb, & French, 1975), *A Sourcebook of Mental Health Measures* (Comrey, Backer, & Glaser, 1973), *Directory of Unpublished Experimental Mental Measures* (Vols. 1–2) (Goldman & Busch, 1978; Goldman & Saunders, 1974), *Tests and Measurements in Child Development: Handbook I* (Johnson & Bommarito, 1971), *Tests and Measurements in Child Development: Handbook II* (Johnson, 1976), *Handbook of Research Design and Social Measurement* (Miller, 1970), *Measures of Occupational Attitudes and Occupational Characteristics* (Robinson, Athanasiou, & Head, 1969), *Measure of Political Attitudes* (Robinson, Rusk, & Head, 1968), *Scales for the Measurement of Attitudes* (Shaw & Wright, 1967), and *Socioemotional Measures for Preschool and Kindergarten Children* (Walker, 1973).

Another source for obtaining information on potentially relevant measures is the Health Instruments File database, an online database service, updated quarterly, containing information on measures "in all health, health-related, and behavioral sciences." The information in the database dates back to 1985 "with selective retrospective coverage," and new measures are continuously being added. The Health Instruments File database is accessible through BRS Information Technologies, 1200 RT 7, Latham, NY 12110 (telephone: 1–800–345–4277).

BIBLIOGRAPHY:

Beere, C. A. (1979). *Women and women's issues: A handbook of tests and measures.* San Francisco: Jossey-Bass.

Beere, C. A. (in press). *Sex and gender issues: A handbook of tests and measures.* Westport, CT: Greenwood Press.

Bem, S. L. (1974). The measurement of psychological androgyny. *Journal of Consulting and Clinical Psychology, 42,* 155–162.

Bonjean, C. M., Hill, R. J., & McLemore, S. D. (1967). *Sociological measurement: An inventory of scales and indices.* San Francisco: Chandler.

Chun, K. T., Cobb, S., & French, J. R. P., Jr. (1975). *Measures for psychological assessment: A guide to 3,000 original sources and their applications.* Ann Arbor: Survey Research Center of the Institute for Social Research.

Comrey, A. L., Backer, T. E., & Glaser, E. M. (1973). *A sourcebook of mental health measures.* Los Angeles: Human Interaction Research Institute.

Corcoran, K., & Fischer, J. (1987). *Measures for clinical practice: A sourcebook.* New York: Free Press.

Crowne, D. P., & Marlowe, D. (1960). A new scale of social desirability independent of psychopathology. *Journal of Consulting Psychology, 24,* 349–354.

Davis, C. M., Yarber, W. L., & Davis, S. L. (Eds). (1988). *Sexuality-related measures: A compendium.* Syracuse: Editors.

Filsinger, E. E. (Ed.). (1983). *Marriage and family assessment: A sourcebook for family therapy.* Beverly Hills: Sage.

Goldman, B. A., & Busch, J. C. (1978). *Directory of unpublished experimental mental measures* (Vol. 2). New York: Human Sciences Press.

Goldman, B. A., & Saunders, J. L. (1974). *Directory of unpublished experimental mental measures* (Vol. 1). New York: Behavioral Publications.

Grotevant, H. D., & Carlson, C. I. (1989). *Family assessment: A guide to methods and measures.* New York: Guilford Press.

Hersen, M., & Bellack, A. S. (Eds.). (1988). *Dictionary of behavioral assessment techniques.* New York: Pergamon Press.

Johnson, O. G. (1976). *Tests and measurements in child development: Handbook II.* San Francisco: Jossey-Bass.

Johnson, O. G., & Bommarito, J. W. (1971). *Tests and measurements in child development: Handbook I.* San Francisco: Jossey-Bass.

Locke, H. J., & Wallace, K. M. (1959). Short marital adjustment and prediction tests: Their reliability and validity. *Journal of Marriage and the Family, 21,* 251–255.

Miller, D. C. (1970). *Handbook of research design and social measurement* (2d ed.). New York: McKay.

Parks, B. J., Bogart, K., Reynolds, D. F., Hamilton, M., & Finley, C. J. (1982). *Sourcebook of measures of women's educational equity.* Palo Alto: American Institutes for Research.

Robinson, J. P., Athanasiou, R., & Head, K. B. (1969). *Measures of occupational attitudes and occupational characteristics.* Ann Arbor: Institute for Social Research, University of Michigan.

Robinson, J. P., Rusk, J. G., & Head, K. B. (1968). *Measures of political attitudes.* Ann Arbor: Institute for Social Research, University of Michigan.

Shaw, M. E., & Wright, J. M. (1967). *Scales for the measurement of attitudes.* New York: McGraw-Hill.

Spanier, G. B. (1976). Measuring dyadic adjustment: New scales for assessing the quality of marriage and similar dyads. *Journal of Marriage and the Family, 38,* 15–28.

Spence, J. T., & Helmreich, R. L. (1972). The Attitudes Toward Women Scale: An objective instrument to measure attitudes toward the rights and roles of women in contemporary society. *Catalog of Selected Documents in Psychology, 2,* 66. (Ms. No. 153)

Spence, J. T., Helmreich, R. L., & Stapp, J. (1974). The Personal Attributes Questionnaire: A measure of sex role stereotypes and masculinity-femininity. *Catalog of Selected Documents in Psychology, 4,* 43–44. (Ms. No. 617)

Touliatos, J., Perlmutter, B. F., & Straus, M. A. (1989). *Handbook of family measurement techniques.* Newbury Park, CA: Sage.

Walker, D. K. (1973). *Socioemotional measures for preschool and kindergarten children.* San Francisco: Jossey-Bass.

2

Measurement

The scales described in this handbook measure personality traits, interests, attitudes, beliefs, and behavior. Measurement of these variables is not easy, and so it is not surprising that there are numerous problems to be considered. In my previous handbook (Beere, 1979), I discussed 10 of these problems: (1) many of the measures referred to in the research literature *cannot be obtained*; (2) there is *too little information* provided about measures referred to in the research literature; (3) there is sometimes a *low correlation* between two scales that claim to measure the same variable; (4) the terms used in gender-related studies are often *not clearly defined*; (5) measures *lack content validity*; (6) often little is known about the *dimensionality* of the measures; (7) the heavy reliance on self-report scales produces *response bias problems*, and the scales are *easily faked*; (8) little is known regarding the *behavioral correlates* of the measures; (9) scales are developed on one population, often college students, but *used with other populations*; and (10) researchers ignore the possibility that scores are *affected by extraneous variables*, such as the sex of the examiner or the composition of the group in which the measure is completed. Not surprisingly, none of the problems has been totally solved, but some problems are less serious than they once were. How have things changed since I wrote the previous handbook?

Measures are still difficult to locate. To obtain copies of scales that might be appropriate for this handbook, I wrote letters to 464 authors who had developed scales I could not locate in the published literature. I received the measures I requested from 121 (26%) of the authors; 59 authors (13%) wrote back indicating that their measure should not be considered for the book because it was not a good one, it was obsolete, it was no longer available, or they had used an existing scale but had failed to identify the measure fully in their article; 9 authors (2%) referred me to an existing book or dissertation; and I was unable to find current addresses for 19 letters (4%) returned to me with no forwarding address. The balance of my letters elicited no response whatsoever. That is, 250 (54%) of the authors I wrote to never answered my letter, and my original letter was not returned to me. I do not know how many of those letters reached the intended recipient who simply decided not to reply and how many never reached their destination. In my letters to scale authors, I indicated that I was writing a book and wanted to consider describing their measure in it. Therefore, my response rates cannot be generalized to situations in which a researcher writes to an author and asks for a scale. Scale authors may be more, or less, willing to send a scale to a researcher than they were to have it considered for a book.

It is still true that too little information is available regarding many measures. The worst situation occurs when a researcher states "A scale was used . . . ," but provides neither the scale name nor data regarding its psychometric properties. Readers and other researchers are unable to evaluate the research, to replicate the research, or to build on it. What kind of scale was used? How and when was it developed? What evidence is there that it was reliable and valid? Sometimes authors include a footnote providing an address from which readers can obtain more information. However, people's addresses change, people leave the academic world, people die, and so forth. Any information not contained in a published article and not available through a document depository should be considered as only temporarily available.

Even when information is provided regarding the psychometric properties of a scale, the information is often insufficient. Frequently the author fails to report the year in which the scale was developed or in which the data were gathered. Both the development and use dates are important to researchers considering using the scale and to readers evaluating the implications of the study. Information regarding the scale's development is often scant and sometimes nonexistent. There may be no mention of the scale's reliability and validity. The topics may be omitted because the author did not empirically determine the reliability and validity of the scale or because relevant data were simply omitted from the article. Because costs associated with publishing have escalated in the past decade, editors work to keep articles as succinct as possible, and information regarding the psychometric properties of the scale is often considered expendable. The lack of published information regarding measures appears to be a bigger problem today than it was when I reviewed the literature for my previous handbook.

A low correlation between two scales that claim to measure the same variable is still a problem. This is particularly true for the measures in Chapter 3, "Gender Roles." There are numerous scales to measure "masculinity" and "femininity," but these measures often do not yield comparable results.

When I wrote my previous handbook, the terms used in gender roles research lacked agreed-on definitions. This problem has declined during the past decade; many of the terms that were previously undefined and used interchangeably and inconsistently are not used as often today. Terms such as *sex role orientation, sex role preference, sex role identification,* and *sex role adoption* used to be common in the literature, particularly in the literature regarding children's gender roles. These terms are no longer common in the literature, probably because the past decade has produced less research on children's gender roles and more research on adults' gender roles. Though there are still no theoretically based definitions for "masculinity" and "femininity," the terms *sex* and *gender* have been clarified. *Sex* refers to whether one is born a male or a female. It is a biologically based distinction. *Gender* refers to personality traits, activities, interests, and behavior. Gender is a socially based distinction that we label with the terms *masculine, feminine,* and *androgynous.* Interestingly, the titles of scales fail to reflect the sex-gender distinction. For example, the most frequently used measure in this book is the Bem Sex Role Inventory (Bem, 1974), which should be titled the Bem Gender Role Inventory. Furthermore, the literature is replete with examples of the two terms being used incorrectly. In fact, the term *sex role* is used more often than the term *gender role* to refer to masculinity and femininity. Thus, while the definitions of *sex* and *gender* have been clarified, their correct usage has, in practice, still not been adopted. Since the term *sex role* implies some biological basis for our roles, it is important that researchers adopt the more appropriate term, *gender roles,* which says nothing regarding the basis for our roles.

The measures I located in the 1970s generally lacked content validity. Since the authors failed initially to specify the content domain for their scale, it was impossible to know to what domain the scores generalized. Based on my literature review for this handbook, it appears that scale authors today are somewhat more concerned with content validity. There are several instances in which the authors had "judges" review their item pool to ensure that it adequately covered the content domain. Overall, however, authors still ignore the issue of content validity.

Authors of scales developed prior to the mid–1970s rarely considered the dimensionality of the scales, probably because the necessary statistical procedures were too complex and computers were not readily available. More recently, however, authors are likely to factor analyze responses to their measures. Overall, factor analysis was involved in the development or later study of about 40% of the 144 scales new to this handbook. As discussed later in this chapter, however, factor analysis is not without its problems.

Most often, the study of gender roles involves the use of self-report scales. In my previous handbook, I described a variety of problems that can reduce the quality of self-report items: items can be double-barreled so that respondents want to agree with one portion of the item and disagree with another portion of it; items may be ambiguous or awkwardly phrased, leaving respondents uncertain of what they are being asked; all items can be phrased in the same direction, thereby encouraging an acquiescent response style. Even when the quality of the items is excellent, the problem of faking cannot be eliminated. On most nonprojective, self-report measures, persons can intentionally present themselves in a certain light; for example, respondents could intentionally portray themselves as liberal or conservative, masculine or feminine. Faking is not necessarily a conscious process. There are numerous social pressures operating in our society, and respondents often give socially desirable responses without being aware that they are misrepresenting themselves. Respondents may have a need to deceive themselves if their real answers are not consistent with their self-perception. Not surprisingly, none of these problems has been eliminated. The quality of items is variable across scales. In selecting scales, researchers should look for ones with well-written items. When administering a scale, researchers should set up the conditions to encourage honest responding. And when interpreting results, researchers should consider whether responses were likely to have been faked or affected by a particular response bias.

In my previous handbook, I pointed out that the relationships between scale scores and behavior were rarely known. For some of the more commonly used scales, such as the Bem Sex Role Inventory (Bem, 1974) and the Personal Attributes Questionnaire (Spence, Helmreich, & Stapp, 1974), there has been research looking at the behavioral concomitants of various scores. In general, however, except for the behavioral measures, researchers are still ignorant of the relationship between scores and behavior. For example, psychologists still do not know whether those who score high on a stereotype measure behave differently from those who score low or which, if any, behaviors can be predicted from scores on most of the attitude measures described in this handbook. The trend seems to be to give greater attention to behavior, but many researchers are still content to look only at scale scores.

As was the case when I wrote my previous handbook, researchers develop measures on one sample, generally college students, and then use the measures with another sample that is often quite different. Researchers must ensure that a scale is understandable, reliable, and valid for the population they are studying. It is not sufficient to show that the scale is psychometrically sound for an educated sample of college students.

As I pointed out in my previous handbook, factors affecting the administration of a measure can affect the scores achieved on that measure. The sex of the examiner might affect responses to gender role measures; the composition of the group completing the measure might have an impact on the scores of the individuals in the group. There has been little attention given to these extraneous factors that can reduce the validity of scores on gender-related measures.

In summary, gender roles research is still plagued by most of the 10 problems I described previously, though there has been some noticeable improvement in certain areas. In addition, there are numerous problems not mentioned in my previous book that researchers working in gender roles research should consider.

Reliability is a major problem associated with the scales used in gender roles research. For some measures, there is no information whatsoever regarding reliability. This is inexcusable. For other scales, coefficient alpha is frequently reported, probably because it requires only a single administration of the test and computers easily handle the computations. But internal consistency is only one aspect of reliability. Test-retest reliability is equally as important, though it requires more effort to obtain the data. Researchers must realize that reporting reliability data is not sufficient. In order to put confidence in research results, the measures have to be sufficiently reliable. The literature search for this handbook revealed numerous instances in which researchers reported full-scale or subscale reliabilities and then ignored the fact that they were unacceptably low. I did not find this to be the case as frequently when writing my previous handbook.

What constitutes sufficient reliability? Certainly, demonstrating that a reliability coefficient is statistically significant does not provide the necessary evidence. Showing that a correlation coefficient is statistically significant simply shows that the correlation is different from zero; with a large enough sample size, almost any correlation will be significantly different from zero. How then should we evaluate a reliability coefficient?

Tests of ability and achievement frequently have reliability coefficients above .90. Unfortunately, personality, interest, and attitude measures rarely have reliability coefficients that high. Instead, a reliability coefficient of .80 and higher is considered sufficient for the measures in this book. Reliability coefficients between .70 and .80 are acceptable in the early stages of scale development, but before the scale is used in much research, more work must be done to refine the scale and raise these reliability coefficients. Reliability coefficients below .70 are unacceptable. If subscale scores are used, the reliability requirements for the subscales are the same as the reliability requirements for the full scale. This is particularly problematic for many measures in this book. The full scale is adequately reliable, but the subscales are not.

Apparently the reliability of measures used with children poses a special problem because the reliability coefficients are often quite low. Unfortunately, this problem may not have a solution. Reliability refers to consistency of measurement, and measurement cannot be consistent if there is no consistency to the trait being measured. Gender roles in children may be too changeable to be measured reliably.

Reliability is a necessary, but not a sufficient, condition for a good measure. Validity is at least equally important; validity indicates whether the scale measures what we want it to measure. At the very least, scale authors need to demonstrate that a scale has convergent validity (it correlates with other measures it should correlate with) and discriminant validity (it is independent of other measures that it should not correlate with). Ideally, there should be evidence of the content validity, criterion-related validity, and construct validity of a measure. The validity data should be relevant to the specific population being studied and the specific purpose for which the scale is being used.

Like many other tools, factor analysis has the potential to be of great value. It can be useful during the scale development process, and it can be useful for establishing factorial validity. Unfortunately, factor analysis is probably being overused by people underqualified to use it. Due to the ready availability of computers and software capable of handling large factor analytic studies, the use of factor analysis has been increasing, but there are several reasons to believe that it is being misused. Factor analysis is a complex procedure requiring a fairly sophisticated statistical background. There is not just one factor analytic procedure nor is there one unique solution when factor analysis is done. In fact, two analyses of the exact same data set can produce different results. When a single article reports the results of a complex factor analytic study and also reports that the reliability coefficients are significantly different from zero, it leads the reader to be suspicious of the researcher's statistical competence. Furthermore, experts on factor analysis are clear that the number of subjects has to be fairly large relative to the number of variables. For example, Nunnally (1978) stated, "A good rule is to have at least 10 times as many subjects as variables" (p. 421), yet researchers describe factor analytic studies in which there are two subjects per variable. One researcher even reported using fewer subjects than variables. Factor analytic studies should be performed only by those who are competent to handle the data and only when the number of subjects is large enough to produce stable results.

Computers have led to an increased use of other complex statistical procedures. For example, compared to 10 years ago, there are now more studies using discriminant analysis and multivariate analysis of variance. It is important that researchers using these statistics are either thoroughly versed in statistics or rely on the help of a good statistical consultant. Though computers facilitate the computations, they do not ensure that the technique is appropriate for the data nor do they interpret the results. Furthermore, the most sophisticated statistical procedure is of no value if the data are obtained from an unreliable and invalid scale. Good statistics do not compensate for poor measures.

The proliferation of research on gender roles does not ensure that we are progressing toward greater understanding of how gender affects people. First, many studies are using a measure that has not been used in any other research study. As stated in Chapter 1, 68% of the 1,450 measures identified as potentially appropriate for this handbook were used in only a single study. Sometimes measures were cited in two, three, or four articles, but all the articles were written by the same researcher. There needs to be greater consistency in the measures used by different researchers. Comparing results from studies using different measures is problematic.

Despite the continuing proliferation of measures, there has also been increasing consistency in the choice of measures. In particular, three measures have been used in a large number of studies: the Bem Sex Role Inventory (Bem, 1974), the Personal Attributes Questionnaire (Spence, Helmreich, & Stapp, 1974), and the Attitudes Toward Women Scale (Spence & Helmreich, 1972). Despite the extensive use of these three scales, it is not clear how much progress researchers are making toward achieving a greater understanding of gender roles and how much researchers are just replicating each other's findings with different samples.

Like many other areas of psychology, college students have served as the primary source for subjects in gender-related research. I estimate that about 60% of gender role research involves studying college students. Given that college students comprise a unique subset of the general population, it seems doubtful that we can generalize findings from college students to adults in general.

Another problem that has surfaced in preparing this handbook is that respondents probably do not understand all of the items presented to them. It is rare for researchers to discuss the difficulty level of their measures, but a study by Antill, Cunningham, Russell, and Thompson (1981) showed that high school students did not understand almost 25% of the 512 items given to them. Jensen, Witcher, and Upton (1987) looked at the reading level of nine measures. They found that the instructions were generally readable by junior high school or senior high school students, but for seven of the scales, the reading level of the items was at the 12th grade or college level. Since reliable and valid results cannot be obtained unless the items are understandable to the respondents, researchers need to verify that a measure is not too difficult for the sample they are testing. This is particularly important when a measure was developed using college students but is used with a noncollege sample.

Most of the measures described in this handbook are used exclusively with English-speaking samples; however, some scales have been translated into other languages. When this is done, it is important that the researchers have the measures back-translated to ensure that the original meanings are preserved.

It is not unusual for researchers to administer many scales to the same sample of respondents; however, it is then impossible to know whether the results obtained from one of the later tests have been affected by the process of completing the earlier tests. Perhaps respondents were sensitized to certain issues or changed in some unpredictable way as a result of completing the earlier tests. Counterbalancing the order of testing can lessen the impact of this problem, but it cannot solve it totally. Ignoring the problem, which is too common, solves nothing.

Although all the scales included in this handbook can be criticized, they are the best ones available. Unfortunately, many researchers interested in gender roles are using their own, untested scales in their research. To be included here, a scale had to have evidence of reliability and/or validity and/or had to be empirically developed. Over 900 "scales" were excluded from this book because they failed to meet the criteria listed. A measure with unknown psychometric properties produces results that are of unknown value. Researchers should be sufficiently sophisticated to avoid writing a few items that are known to have only face validity. Good scale development requires considerable work and consumes considerable time. In the future, researchers are advised to study and refine the existing scales rather than develop new ones overlapping with those already developed.

The best advice for someone considering research in gender role areas is to be knowledgeable. Be knowledgeable about the base on which the research is being built; be knowledgeable about the measures that are available; be knowledgeable about research design, statistics, and measurement theory. Obviously anyone who is reading these words knows that this handbook, along with Beere (in press), can assist with the task of locating appropriate measures. Other potential sources of measures are listed in Chapter 1. Although there are numerous books about research design, *Quasi-Experimentation-Design and Analysis Issues for Field Settings* (Cook & Campbell, 1979) is of particular value. It describes threats to four aspects of validity: internal validity, construct validity of putative causes and effects, external validity, and statistical conclusion validity, which encompasses reliability. A good source for learning about basic testing concepts is *Psychological Testing* (6th edition) by Anastasi (1988). Though Anastasi provides enough information for test users, anyone involved in test development should be familiar with the tenets of psychometric theory. A good source for learning about psychometric theory is Nunnally's (1978) book, *Psychometric Theory*.

Measurement in any of the social sciences presents challenging problems. We cannot solve many of these problems, but by applying what we know about research design, measurement, and statistics, we can minimize their impact.

BIBLIOGRAPHY:

Anastasi, A. (1988). *Psychological testing* (6th ed.). New York: Macmillan.

Antill, J. K., Cunningham, J. D., Russell, G., & Thompson, N. L. (1981). An Australian Sex-Role Scale. *Australian Journal of Psychology, 33*, 169–183.

Beere, C. A. (1979). *Women and women's issues: A handbook of tests and measures.* San Francisco: Jossey-Bass.

Beere, C. A. (in press). *Sex and gender issues: A handbook of tests and measures.* Westport, CT: Greenwood.

Bem, S. L. (1974). The measurement of psychological androgyny. *Journal of Consulting and Clinical Psychology, 42*, 155–162.

Cook, T. D. & Campbell, D. T. (1979). *Quasi-experimentation: Design and analysis issues for field settings.* Chicago: Rand McNally.

Jensen, B. J., Witcher, D. B., & Upton, L. R. (1987). Readability assessment of questionnaires frequently used in sex and marital therapy. *Journal of Sex and Marital Therapy, 13*, 137–141.

Nunnally, J. C. (1978). *Psychometric theory.* New York: McGraw-Hill.

Spence, J. T., & Helmreich, R. L. (1972). The Attitudes Toward Women Scale: An objective instrument to measure attitudes towards the rights and roles of women in contemporary society. *Catalog of Selected Documents in Psychology, 2*, 66. (Ms. No. 153)

Spence, J. T., Helmreich, R. L., & Stapp, J. T. (1974). The Personal Attributes Questionnaire: A measure of sex role stereotypes and masculinity-femininity. *Catalog of Selected Documents in Psychology, 4*, 43–44. (Ms. No. 617)

3

Gender Roles

More has been written on the subject of gender roles and more research has been done with the gender role measures in this chapter than has been the case with any other topic covered in this handbook. Books, book chapters, and a tremendous number of articles have been written on the topic of gender roles. Various aspects of gender role research have been discussed and debated. Are masculinity and femininity opposite ends of a single continuum, or are they independent traits? How should gender role scales be scored? Are masculinity and femininity useful constructs? Is it better to be masculine or androgynous? Is self-esteem related to gender role, or is the relationship an artifact of the measuring procedures? Is there a relationship between the gender typing of our personality traits and the gender typing of our behavior? Is it accurate that gender role research "has produced not cumulative discovery but a pattern of repetition and reification" (Morawski, 1985, p. 196)?

The questions go on and on, and for the most part, the answers are beyond the scope of this book; however, a few observations need to be made. First, the term *sex role* has essentially been replaced by the more accurate term *gender role*. Scale names have not been changed, however, so measures still include *sex role* in their title. This chapter titled "Gender Roles" is analogous to the "Sex Roles" chapter in my previous book (Beere, 1979).

In general, psychologists now agree that masculinity and femininity should be treated as independent traits, not as the ends of a single continuum. Still, some researchers continue to ignore the prevailing viewpoint and act as though masculinity and femininity comprise a bipolar construct.

The prevailing approach for scoring gender role measures is to obtain separate scores for masculinity and femininity and then use a median split procedure to classify subjects into four categories: masculine, feminine, androgynous, and undifferentiated. In the first half of the 1980s, there was a debate about whether androgyny should be scored as a single continuous variable. (See Blackman, 1985; Heilbrun, 1983; Strahan, 1981, 1984.)

This chapter is one of the longest in the handbook, not because it contains the largest number of scales but because some scales in this chapter are accompanied by long listings of articles. This reflects the fact that they have been used extensively in published research.

Before going on to the measures reported in this chapter, let us compare what was included in the previous handbook (Beere, 1979) with what is included here. Previously I described 32 gender role measures appropriate for use with adults: 3 were described in the section on children's gender role measures, 14 were described in full in the section on adult gender role measures, and 15 were described briefly because they were personality inventories yielding several scores, one of which related to gender role. The gender roles chapter in this handbook contains descriptions of 39 measures, 15 of which were described in the last handbook. The three measures that had previously been in the children's gender role chapter are all projective tests. They are briefly described in this handbook because all 3 have been used in additional research since the last literature search was completed. Of the 14 adult gender role measures described in full in the prior book, 8 are briefly described in this book; these 8 have been used in research published since I completed the literature search for the last handbook. The literature search for this handbook failed to locate articles or ERIC documents that reported on the use of the other 6 adult gender role scales, so they are omitted from this book. Of the 15 personality inventories briefly described in the previous handbook, 5 have been used in gender role research since the previous search was completed. These 5 are the Adjective Check List, the California Personality Inventory, the Minnesota Multiphasic Personality Inventory, the Guilford-Zimmerman Temperament Survey, and the Strong Vocational Interest Blank. The first 4 are briefly described in this handbook. To summarize, this chapter contains descriptions of 39 gender role measures: 24 are new to this handbook and are fully described here; 15 were described in my previous book and are only briefly described here. Included in this chapter are measures of gender role identity and gender role behavior, as well as measures of gender disturbance.

There is considerable variability in the scales included in this chapter. The oldest scale is the Attitude Interest Analysis Test (Terman & Miles,

1936), and the newest is Snell's (1988) Extended Masculine Role Inventory. The shortest scale is Stern, Barak, and Gould's (1987) Sexual Identity Scale, which has only 4 items. The longest scales are the Attitude Interest Analysis Test, with over 450 items, and the Sex Role Behavior Scale–2 (Orlofsky, Ramsden, & Cohen, 1982), with 240 items. While most of the scales included in this chapter are self-report measures, there are also two behavioral observation measures in which a trained observer rates the behavior of other persons.

There is considerable variability in the extent to which the scales in this chapter have been used in published research. Six of the measures have been used in only a single published research study, and another 5 measures have been used in only two published research studies. At the other end of the continuum is the Bem Sex Role Inventory (BSRI) (Bem, 1974), which has been used about 1,000 times since it was developed. The bibliography following the description of the BSRI contains over 700 articles published after the completion of the literature search for my previous book. A search for ERIC documents identified another 167 manuscripts that reported on the use of the BSRI. Those citations are not included here. The second most commonly used gender role measure is the Personal Attributes Questionnaire/Extended Personal Attributes Questionnaire (Spence, Helmreich, & Stapp, 1974; Spence, Helmreich, & Holahan, 1979). With 238 articles and 49 ERIC documents reporting on the use of the PAQ or EPAQ, they lag far behind the BSRI. However, the PAQ/EPAQ are the second most popularly used gender role measures in the entire handbook. Excluding the BSRI and the PAQ/EPAQ, 5 scales in this chapter are accompanied by more than 20 citations describing the use of the scales. All 5 were described in my previous handbook: Gough Femininity Scale, California Personality Inventory, figure drawing (a procedure more than a particular scale), Minnesota Multiphasic Personality Inventory, and PRF ANDRO. The fact that these scales were used relatively often may say more about their availability and age than it does about their quality, since none of the gender role measures new to this handbook has been available long enough to have been used as extensively as the older measures.

The majority of the scales in this chapter can be used with both males and females, but 5 are intended for use only with females and another 5 are intended for use only with males. The 5 scales for females are described first, followed by the 5 scales for males, and then the 29 scales for both sexes.

Of the 39 measures described in this chapter, 10 can be used with persons below high school age; this includes the 3 projective tests (figure drawing, Franck Drawing Completion Test [Franck & Rosen, 1949], and May Measure of Gender Identity [May, 1966]) that can be used with young children. The remaining scales can be used either with high school students and older or with college students and older. Some of the scales are intended for use in foreign countries. The Chinese Sex Role Inventory (Keyes, 1983) is intended for use with Cantonese-speaking persons; the Bar-Ilan Sex Role Inventory (Tzuriel, 1984) is intended for use in Israel; the Australian Sex Role Inventory (Drinkwater, 1979) and the Australian Sex Role Scale (Antill, Cunningham, Russell, & Thompson, 1981) are both intended for use in Australia.

A common approach to measuring adult gender roles is to ask persons about their own personality traits. Often these traits are presented as adjectives or adjective phrases, and the respondents' task is either to rate themselves on the traits or to check those traits that are true for them. Sometimes the adjectives are all positive, as is the case with the BSRI (Bem, 1974); other times, there are both positive and negative traits on the measure, as is the case with the Australian Sex Role Scale (Antill et al., 1981). Another common approach used with adult gender role measures is to use a summated rating scale and ask respondents to react to items about their own interests, habits, personality characteristics, attitudes, and behavior. Studying gender role by studying behavior is a fairly recent phenomenon. Two scales in this chapter look at specific gender-typed motor behaviors: the Effeminacy Rating Scale (Schatzberg, Westfall, Blumetti, & Birk, 1975) and the Sex Role Motor Behavior Checklist (Barlow et al., 1979). Other measures ask for self-reports of behavior and behavioral intentions. Examples of these scales are the Robinson Behavioral Inventory (Robinson & Follingstad, 1985) and the Sex Role Behavior Scale—2 (Orlofsky et al., 1982).

A fairly new approach to gender role measurement is to use a modification of the Role Construct Repertory Test (Baldwin, Critelli, Stevens, & Russell, 1986; Mast & Herron, 1986; Ravinder, 1987). The Heilbrun Measure of Sex Role Blending (Heilbrun, 1986) is a somewhat unusual and quite promising scale. It is an adjective ranking test designed to measure the extent to which one has integrated masculine and feminine behaviors. Another unusual measure is Bernard's (1981) Multidimensional Sex Role Inventory—Revised. This scale is unusual because it measures seven aspects of gender role: Aesthetic Interests, Masculine Stereotyped Interests, Anxiety, Feminine Conventions, Boisterousness, Dominance, and Supportiveness.

There are several significant problems regarding the measures of adult gender roles. These problems relate to definitions, development, reliability, validity, and factor analysis. At the time I wrote my previous book, there were no theoretically based definitions for the terms *masculine* and *feminine*. Little progress has been made in this regard, though I think most researchers have finally accepted that "masculinity" and "femininity" are what is measured by masculinity and femininity scales. Accepting these definitions implies accepting that the definitions are culture bound and time bound.

The development of gender role measures frequently involves college students, either as judges rating items or as subjects providing normative data for the researcher to identify items that discriminate between males and females. It may be unreasonable to assume that scales developed with inputs from college students are appropriate for use with other groups such as middle-aged executives or senior citizens.

Because there are rarely alternate forms of gender role measures, there are only two types of reliability that we generally can consider: internal consistency or stability across items and test-retest or stability over time. Internal consistency reliability requires that the scale be administered to a group of subjects on only one occasion. This, combined with the fact that computers simplify the task of computing reliability, has led most scale authors to report some evidence of the scale's internal consistency. Generally the results indicate acceptable levels of internal consistency. However, occasionally the results suggest that the scale is too heterogeneous to produce interpretable scores; frequently, low reliabilities are associated with short subscales. Regardless, low reliabilities should not be ignored; it is not sufficient to report the reliability. If it is low, conclusions from the research are suspect.

Test-retest reliability is not reported nearly as often as internal consistency reliability. When it is reported, the levels are generally acceptable. Perhaps there is a bias here in that researchers may only be reporting test-retest reliability when the results are at an acceptable level.

Validity of a scale is crucially important. A measure is not useful if it is not measuring what we believe it to be measuring. However, researchers often devote insufficient attention to determining the validity of a scale. For gender role measures, the most common approach to validity is to compare results obtained by males and females, with the presumption that the scores of males and females will be significantly different. Several other methods are commonly used to assess the validity of gender role measures: comparing known groups, such as heterosexuals and homosexuals; looking at the relationships between a scale and other gender role measures; and looking at the relationships between a gender role measure and other variables, some of which are expected to correlate with the measure and some of which are expected to be independent of the measure. All of these procedures are helpful in supporting the validity of a measure.

Factor analytic procedures have been used in conjunction with 8 measures in this chapter, sometimes as part of the scale development process and sometimes to provide a better understanding of the scale or to determine its factorial validity. Though factor analysis can produce useful and meaningful information, one needs to be certain that the number of subjects is large relative to the number of items. Otherwise the results of the factor analysis cannot be presumed stable. Furthermore, factor analysis does not yield a unique solution.

It is left to the reader to determine whether the study of gender roles is a fruitful area of research. Those who want to engage in research in this area will find a large number of scales to select from: some new and some well established; some using common methods and some based on creative approaches; some looking at personality and some looking at behavior; some presuming unidimensionality and some emphasizing the multidimensionality of the constructs. There are now enough measures that new measures are not needed; rather existing measures can be improved and refined.

BIBLIOGRAPHY:

Antill, J. K., Cunningham, J. D., Russell, G., & Thompson, N. L. (1981). An Australian Sex-Role Scale. *Australian Journal of Psychology, 33,* 169–183.

Baldwin, A. C., Critelli, J. W., Stevens, L. C., & Russell, S. (1986). Androgyny and sex role measurement: A personal construct approach. *Journal of Personality and Social Psychology, 51,* 1081–1088.

Barlow, D. H., Hayes, S. C., Nelson, R. O., Steele, D. L., Meeler, M. E., & Mills, J. R. (1979). Sex Role Motor Behavior: A behavioral checklist. *Behavioral Assessment, 1,* 119–138.

Beere, C. A. (1979) *Women and women's issues: A handbook of tests and measures.* San Francisco: Jossey-Bass.

Bem, S. L. (1974). The measurement of psychological androgyny. *Journal of Consulting and Clinical Psychology, 42,* 155–162.

Bernard, L. C. (1981). The multidimensional aspects of masculinity—femininity. *Journal of Personality and Social Psychology, 41,* 797–802.

Blackman, S. (1985). Comparisons among methods of scoring androgyny continuously using computer-simulated data. *Psychological Reports, 57,* 151–154.

Drinkwater, B. A. (1979). Social desirability of characteristics of the Bem Sex-Role Inventory. *Australian Psychologist, 14,* 311–317.

Franck, K., & Rosen, F. (1949). A projective test of masculinity-femininity. *Journal of Consulting Psychology, 13,* 247–256.

Heilbrun, A. B., Jr. (1983). Scoring androgyny as a continuous variable: A reply to Blackman. *Psychological Reports, 53,* 398.

Heilbrun, A. B., Jr. (1986). Androgyny as type and androgyny as behavior: Implications for gender schema in males and females. *Sex Roles, 14,* 123–139.

Keyes, S. (1983). Sex differences in cognitive abilities and sex-role stereotypes in Hong Kong Chinese adolescents. *Sex Roles, 9,* 853–870.

Mast, D. L., & Herron, W. G. (1986). The Sex-Role Antecedents Scales. *Perceptual and Motor Skills, 63,* 27–56.

May, R. R. (1966). Sex differences in fantasy patterns. *Journal of Projective Techniques and Personality Assessment, 30,* 576–586.

Morawski, J. G. (1985). The measurement of masculinity and femininity: Engendering categorical realities. *Journal of Personality, 53,* 196–223.

Orlofsky, J. L., Ramsden, M. W., & Cohen, R. S. (1982). Development of the Revised Sex-Role Behavior Scale. *Journal of Personality Assessment, 46,* 632–638.

Ravinder, S. (1987). An empirical investigation of Garnets and Pleck's sex role strain analysis. *Sex Roles, 16*, 165–179.

Robinson, E. A., & Follingstad, D. R. (1985). Development and validation of a behavioral sex-role inventory. *Sex Roles, 13*, 691–713.

Schatzberg, A. F., Westfall, M. P., Blumetti, A. B., & Birk, C. L. (1975). Effeminacy. I. A quantitative rating scale. *Archives of Sexual Behavior, 4*, 31–41.

Snell, W. E., Jr. (1988). *Validation of the Extended Masculine Role Inventory (EMRI)*. Paper presented at the meeting of the Southwestern Psychological Association, Tulsa, OK.

Spence, J. T., Helmreich, R. L., & Holahan, C. K. (1979). Negative and positive components of psychological masculinity and femininity and their relationships to self-reports of neurotic and acting-out behaviors. *Journal of Personality and Social Psychology, 37*, 1673–1682.

Spence, J. T., Helmreich, R. L., & Stapp, J. T. (1974). The Personal Attributes Questionnaire: A measure of sex role stereotypes and masculinity-femininity. *Catalog of Selected Documents in Psychology, 4*, 43–44. (Ms. No. 617)

Stern, B. B., Barak, B., & Gould, S. J. (1987). Sexual Identity Scale: A new self-assessment measure. *Sex Roles, 17*, 503–519.

Strahan, R. F. (1981). Remarks on scoring androgyny as a single continuous variable. *Psychological Reports, 49*, 887–890.

Strahan, R. F. (1984). More on scoring androgyny as a single continuous variable. *Psychological Reports, 55*, 241–242.

Terman, L. M., & Miles, C. C. (1936). *Sex and personality*. New York: McGraw-Hill.

Tzuriel, D. (1984). Sex role typing and ego identity in Israeli, Oriental, and Western adolescents. *Journal of Personality and Social Psychology, 46*, 440–457.

MASCULINE GENDER IDENTITY IN FEMALES (MGI)

AUTHORS: Ray Blanchard and Kurt Freund

DATE: 1983

VARIABLE: Masculine gender identity in females, defined as "a hypothetical factor that accounts for that covariation in male sex-typed behaviors observable within the population of anatomical females" (Blanchard & Freund, 1983, p. 205).

TYPE OF INSTRUMENT: Multiple choice.

DESCRIPTION: There are two parts to the Masculine Gender Identity in Females (MGI) scale: Part A contains 20 items and is administered to all respondents; Part B contains 9 items and is administered to homosexual females only. Nineteen of the items on Part A ask about the respondent's childhood or adolescence. The items pertain to play activities, interests, and fantasies. The items in Part B relate directly to transsexual and homosexual activities and fantasies.

SAMPLE ITEMS: (Scoring weights are given in parentheses)

(Part A) Between the ages of 6 and 12, did you prefer . . . to play with boys (2) . . . to play with girls (0) . . . didn't make any difference (1) . . . not to play with other children (1) . . . don't remember (1).

(Part B) Between the ages of 6 and 12, did you put on men's underwear or clothing . . . once a month or more, for about a year or more (2) . . . (less often, but) several times a year for about 3 years or more (2) . . . very seldom did this during this period (0) . . . never did this during this period (0) . . . don't remember (0).

PREVIOUS SUBJECTS: College women, female nursing students, non-transsexual homosexual females, transsexual homosexual females

APPROPRIATE FOR: Females, ages 18 and older

ADMINISTRATION: Self-administered; about 15 minutes

SCORING: For each item, scoring weights are assigned to each response option. A total score is obtained by summing the appropriate item weights. Total scores on Part A range from 0 to 31. Total scores on Part B range from 0 to 17.

DEVELOPMENT: The development of the scale was based on the assumption that cross-gender identity is "a continuous variable, with the greatest degree of cross-gender identity expected among transsexuals" (Blanchard & Freund, 1983, p. 205). The initial item pool, which included 25 items on Part A and 9 items on Part B, consisted of items that were essentially identical to those used in the development of the Feminine Gender Identity Scale (Freund, Nagler, Langevin, Zajac, & Steiner, 1974) (see separate entry). Wording changes were made to adapt the items for females. The items in Part A pertained to "childhood play and peer preferences, fantasies, and the wish to have been born a male" (Blanchard & Freund, 1983, p. 207). Part B pertained to "cross dressing and items concerning erotic preferences, which presuppose homosexuality" (Blanchard & Freund, 1983, p. 207). The item pool was administered to groups of females including 236 university and nursing students, 50 transsexual homosexuals, and 44 nontranssexual homosexuals. Item-remainder correlations were calculated for each item. For Part A, five items had correlations below .30, and they were eliminated from the scale. No item on Part B had a correlation below .30, so all items were retained.

RELIABILITY: Using the data from the respondents on whom the scale was developed, coefficient alpha for the 20 items on Part A was .89; alpha for Part B was .92.

Alumbaugh (1987) administered the scale to 496 college students and obtained a coefficient alpha of .75 for Part A.

VALIDITY: Total scores on Part A for the three groups—heterosexual, nontranssexual homosexual, and transsexual homosexual—differed significantly and in the predicted direction, with transsexual homosexuals having the highest mean and heterosexuals having the lowest mean score. Subjects were classified using the following criteria: scores below 13 were classified as heterosexuals; scores of 13 to 20 were classified as nontranssexual homosexuals; and scores above 20 were classified as transsexual homosexuals. This system resulted in an overall percentage of correct classifications equal to 69.4%. Part A scores were not significantly correlated with age, but they were significantly correlated with education for the heterosexual group.

As predicted, transsexual homosexuals scored significantly higher than nontranssexual homosexuals on Part B. Part B scores were correlated with age and with education; none of the correlations was significant. Respondents with Part B scores above 8 were classified as transsexual. This system resulted in 95.7% correct classifications.

Full scale scores were not significantly correlated with age or with education.

Alumbaugh (1987) compared scores on the MGI with scores on the Bem Sex Role Inventory (Bem, 1974) (see separate entry) and the Mf scale of the MMPI (see separate entry). Part A scores on the MGI correlated .23 with Bem's masculine scale and −.24 with Bem's feminine scale. The correlation between the Mf scale of the MMPI and Part A scores on the MGI was −.15. These findings suggest that the MGI is measuring something different from what the Bem Sex Role Inventory and the Mf scale of the MMPI measure.

NOTES & COMMENTS: (1) A factor analysis of responses to Part A resulted in three weak factors and one strong factor. A factor analysis of Part B produced one factor, accounting for 56.9% of the total variance.

(2) A comparable scale exists for males: the Feminine Gender Identity Scale for males (see separate entry).

AVAILABLE FROM: Blanchard and Freund, 1983; Davis, Yarber, and Davis, 1988, pp. 141–143.

USED IN:

Alumbaugh, R. V. (1987). Contrast of the gender-identity scale with Bem's sex-role measures and the Mf scale of the MMPI. *Perceptual and Motor Skills*, *64*, 136–138.

Blanchard, R., & Freund, K. (1983). Measuring masculine gender identity in females. *Journal of Consulting and Clinical Psychology*, *51*(2), 205–214.

BIBLIOGRAPHY:

Bem, S. L. (1974). The measurement of psychological androgyny. *Journal of Consulting and Clinical Psychology*, *42*, 155–162.

Davis, C. M., Yarber, W. L., & Davis, S. L. (1988). *Sexuality-related measures* (pp. 140–143). Syracuse: Editors.

Freund, K., Nagler, E., Langevin, R., Zajac, A., & Steiner, B. (1974). Measuring feminine gender identity in homosexual males. *Archives of Sexual Behavior*, *3*(3), 249–260.

ROBINSON BEHAVIORAL INVENTORY (RBI)
AUTHOR: Elizabeth A. Robinson
DATE: 1985
VARIABLE: Enactment of traditional versus nontraditional gender role behaviors in women
TYPE OF INSTRUMENT: Summated rating scale
DESCRIPTION: There are two forms of the Robinson Behavioral Inventory (RBI): one for single females and one for married females. Many of the items on the Married form refer to "spouse," while many items on the Single form refer to "a person of the opposite sex." Furthermore, while some items on the Single form refer to dating, some items on the Married form refer to the division of household responsibilities. Each form consists of 34 items. On both forms, items 1 to 10 and items 26 to 34 are statements of behavioral intentions. Responses to these items are expressed on a 10-point scale ranging from "0 = will definitely not do so" to "9 = will definitely do so." Items 11 to 25 ask about behavior during the previous year. These items have the same focus as the behavioral intention items. Responses to items 11 to 19 are expressed on a scale ranging from "never" to "9 times or more," and responses to items 20 to 25 use a scale from "0%" to "90% or more." About half the items on both forms are phrased to reflect traditional behavior, and half are phrased to reflect nontraditional behavior.
SAMPLE ITEMS: (Single form, behavioral intention) If trying to get your own way, how likely are you to use tears with a person of the opposite sex within the next year at least once?
   (Single form, past behavior) How frequently have you gone out with a person of the opposite sex that you didn't like very much because you didn't know how to say no when asked during the past year?
   (Married form, behavioral intention) Within the next year how likely is your spouse to help with the daily housework on a regular basis (e.g., dishes, cooking, cleaning)?
   (Married form, past behavior) Within the last year, what percent of the time have you, rather than your spouse, initiated sexual intercourse?
PREVIOUS SUBJECTS: College students
APPROPRIATE FOR: Women, ages 18 and older
ADMINISTRATION: Self-administered; about 15–20 minutes
SCORING: Each item is scored on a 9-point scale; responses reflecting nontraditional behavior are assigned the higher points. Total scores can range from 0 (very traditional) to 306 (very nontraditional). Robinson and Follingstad (1985) reported means and standard deviations for two samples of college students: a sample of single women and a sample of married women.
DEVELOPMENT: A pool of items was developed with many of the items "taken from the previously developed sex-role *belief* scales and restated

in *behavioral* terms" (Robinson & Follingstad, 1985, p. 692). The items represented six categories: "Feminist activity," such as attendance at meetings of feminist organizations; "Independence," such as traveling alone; "Assertiveness," including sexual and interpersonal assertiveness; "Positive attitude toward other women," such as considering plans with women to be as significant as plans made with men; "Declining chivalrous attention from males," such as sharing expenses for a date rather than allowing the man to assume the expense; and "Redistributing the traditional division of household labor" (Robinson & Follingstad, 1985, p. 694). A sample of 574 single college women completed a 40-item version of the Single form of the scale, and a sample of 265 married college women completed a 40–item version of the Married form of the scale. A subset of 95 women completed the scale a second time, about 4 weeks later, and another subset of 98 women completed two parallel forms of the behavioral inventory. The responses to these measures were used to compute test-retest reliability, parallel forms reliability, split-half reliability, and item-total correlations for the RBI. Respondents also completed four other measures: the short form of the Attitudes Toward Women Scale (Spence, Helmreich, & Stapp, 1973) (see separate entry), the Political Radicalism-Conservatism Scale (Comrey & Newmeyer, 1965), the Rathus Assertiveness Scale (Rathus, 1973), and the Marlowe-Crowne Social Desirability Scale (Crowne & Marlowe, 1964). RBI scores were correlated with scores from these four measures. Six items on each form of the RBI failed to meet the minimal criteria for item reliability and validity. These items were deleted, leaving two 34-item versions of the RBI. The data collected during this phase of scale development were also used for determining reliability and validity, as reported below.

RELIABILITY: Internal consistency reliability for the Single form was .95; for the Married form, it was .96. Split-half correlations were .83 for the Single form and .92 for the Married form. Test-retest reliability was estimated as .86 for the Single form and .82 for the Married form. By dividing the scale in half, two parallel forms were created. When the two forms were administered at the same time, reliability was .91 for the Single form and .93 for the Married form. When the two forms were administered 4 weeks apart, the reliability was .81 for the Single form and .88 for the Married form.

VALIDITY: For single respondents, age, income, and educational level were all significantly correlated with RBI scores. For married women, only education was significantly correlated with RBI scores. For both the Single and the Married forms, RBI scores were significantly correlated with three of the four other measures: Attitudes Toward Women Scale (r = .56 and .55), Political Radicalism-Conservatism Scale (r = − .46 and − .58), and Rathus Assertiveness Scale (r = .34 and .41). The correlations were in the predicted direction. The Marlowe-Crowne scores were significantly correlated with RBI scores on the Married form, but the correlation was rather low ($r = -.15$). When groups of respondents were compared, the group means were in the predicted direction: Catholic women were the most traditional, and members of the National Organization for Women and consciousness-raising groups were the most nontraditional. RBI scores were significantly correlated with responses to a question regarding agreement or disagreement with the principles of the women's movement.

NOTES AND COMMENTS: The RBI is different from traditional sex role scales that usually focus on attitudes or personality traits. The RBI asks about behavioral intentions and recent behavioral history. It would be interesting to see how these self-reports of prior behavior and behavioral intentions compare with actual observations of behavior.

USED IN:

Robinson, E. A., & Follingstad, D. R. (1985). Development and validation of a behavioral sex-role inventory. *Sex Roles, 13,* 691–713.

BIBLIOGRAPHY:

Comrey, A., & Newmeyer, J. (1965). Measurement of radicalism-conservatism. *Journal of Social Psychology, 67,* 357–369.

Crowne, D. P., & Marlowe, D. (1964). *The approval motive.* New York: Wiley.

Rathus, S. (1973). A 30-item schedule for assessing assertive behavior. *Behavior Therapy, 4,* 398–406.

Spence, J. T., Helmreich, R. L., & Stapp, J. T. (1973). A short version of the Attitudes Toward Women Scale (AWS). *Bulletin of the Psychonomic Society, 2,* 219–220.

ROLE ACCEPTANCE SCALE

AUTHORS: Constance Berry and Frederick L. McGuire

DATE: 1972

VARIABLE: Acceptance of the female role

TYPE OF INSTRUMENT: Alternate choice: true/false

DESCRIPTION: The Role Acceptance Scale consists of 31 statements pertaining to "whether or not a subject likes being a woman, feels positive about having and nursing babies, accepts menstruation as a normal routine, accepts the more dominant social role of men, and has conflicts about sexuality" (Berry & McGuire, 1972, p. 84). According to Watts, Dennerstein, and Horne (1980), 10 items relate to feminine stereotypes, 8 items relate to childbearing and child rearing, 7 items concern sex and masturbation, and 6 items deal with menarche and menses. About two-thirds of the statements are phrased to reflect a negative attitude toward women's roles; the other one-third express a positive attitude. The respondent is to indicate whether each statement is true or false as it pertains to her.

SAMPLE ITEMS: (feminine stereotypes) There are times when I just don't enjoy being a woman.

   (childbearing and child rearing) I want to nurse my babies.

(sex and masturbation) Sexual intercourse is desirable for physical and mental health.

(menarche and menses) When my periods first began I remember feeling quite grown up and proud.

PREVIOUS SUBJECTS: Female patients at a state hospital; women experiencing premenstrual or menstrual distress; women

APPROPRIATE FOR: Females who have gone through puberty

ADMINISTRATION: Self-administered; 10–15 minutes

SCORING: A response indicating acceptance of the female role is assigned 1 point. Item scores are summed to yield a total score that can range from 0 (strongly negative attitude toward women's role) to 31 (strongly positive attitude toward women's role). (See NOTES & COMMENTS for information regarding subscale scores.)

DEVELOPMENT: Very little information was provided regarding the development of the scale. The items were taken from Paulson (1956). Berry and McGuire (1972) determined how each item would be scored.

RELIABILITY: No information was provided.

VALIDITY: Berry and McGuire (1972) tested 100 female patients at a state hospital and compared their scores on the Role Acceptance Scale with their scores on the Menstrual Distress Questionnaire (MDQ) (Moos, 1969) (see Beere, in press). They found significant, though fairly low, negative correlations between scores on the Role Acceptance Scale and scores on four subscales of the MDQ: pain, concentration, autonomic reaction, and control. These correlations, which ranged from $-.16$ to $-.32$, were significant during the premenstrual period and after menstruation started. They also found that severity of cramps during menstruation was significantly and negatively correlated ($r = -.23$) with Role Acceptance Scale scores. Role Acceptance Scale scores were not significantly correlated with four subscales of the MDQ: water retention, arousal, behavioral change, and negative affect.

Watts et al. (1980) used a modified version of the Role Acceptance Scale (see NOTES & COMMENTS) with 67 women: 42 who experienced premenstrual syndrome and 23 controls. When Watts et al. compared the two groups, they found no significant differences on the three subscales that included only items from the original Berry and McGuire Role Acceptance Scale. They did, however, obtain significant differences on the two other subscales: body and genitals, and menarche and menses.

Rangaswamy, Premkumar, and Anatharaman (1982) computed three subscale scores on the Role Acceptance Scale: feminine stereotypes, childbearing and child rearing, and menarche and menses. They found significant negative correlations among all three Role Acceptance Scale scores and scores on the Menstrual Symptom Questionnaire (Chesney & Tasto, 1975) (see Beere, in press). The strongest relationship was with the menarche and menses subscale of the Role Acceptance Scale ($r = -.84$).

NOTES & COMMENTS: (1) Watts et al. (1980) modified the Role Acceptance Scale in two ways. First, they added 10 items to the original set of 31 items; second, they obtained scores for five subscales: feminine stereotypes (10 items), childbearing and child rearing (8 items), body and genitals (8 items, all newly written), sex and masturbation (9 items, including 2 newly written), and menarche and menses (6 items). They did not provide information to explain the rationale or the procedures for making these changes.

(2) More information is needed about this scale. The first and most obvious need is for reliability data. Second, information is needed regarding the subscales. Do they add to or detract from the usefulness of the scale? Third, information is needed on whether there would be consensus on the direction of scoring for each item. For example, does agreement with the following item reflect acceptance or rejection of the female role: "As a girl, I was taught that kissing and necking were wrong"?

(3) Some of the items on this scale are outdated, not surprising given the age of the scale. This fact, in combination with the concerns raised above, suggests that the scale may be of limited value today.

AVAILABLE FROM: Berry and McGuire, 1972

USED IN:

Berry, C., & McGuire, F. L. (1972). Menstrual distress and acceptance of sexual role. *American Journal of Obstetrics and Gynecology, 114,* 83–87.

Rangaswamy, K., Premkumar, R., & Anatharaman, R. N. (1982). A study of menstrual distress. *Journal of Psychological Researches, 26*(2), 84–87.

Watts, S., Dennerstein, L., & Horne, D. J. (1980). The premenstrual syndrome: A psychological evaluation. *Journal of Affective Disorders, 2,* 257–266.

BIBLIOGRAPHY:

Beere, C. A. (in press). *Sex and gender issues: A handbook of tests and measures.* Westport, CT: Greenwood.

Chesney, M. A., & Tasto, D. L. (1975). The development of the Menstrual Symptom Questionnaire. *Behaviour Research and Therapy, 13,* 237–244.

Moos, R. H. (1969). *Menstrual Distress Questionnaire—Preliminary Manual.* Unpublished paper, Department of Psychiatry, Stanford University School of Medicine, Stanford, CA.

Paulson, M. J. (1956). *Psychological concomitants of premenstrual tension.* Unpublished doctoral dissertation, University of Kansas.

TRADITIONAL-LIBERATED SOCIAL STEREOTYPE SCALE (TLSS)/TRADITIONAL-LIBERATED SELF-CONCEPT SCALE (TLSC)

AUTHORS: Rosalind D. Cartwright, Stephen Lloyd, Judith Brown Nelson, and Susan Bass

DATE: 1983
VARIABLE: Gender role
TYPE OF INSTRUMENT: Checklist
DESCRIPTION: The Traditional-Liberated Social Stereotype Scale (TLSS) and the Traditional-Liberated Self-Concept Scale (TLSC) are actually subsets of items from the 300-item Adjective Check List (Gough & Heilbrun, 1965). The TLSS contains 45 items: 15 reflect a "traditional" orientation, and 30 reflect a "liberated" orientation. The TLSC contains 41 items: 34 reflect a traditional self-concept, and 7 reflect a liberated self-concept. Respondents are to check all adjectives that they feel are self-descriptive.
SAMPLE ITEMS: (TLSS—Traditional) Conservative; Considerate
   (TLSS—Liberated) Adventurous; Aggressive
   (TLSC—Traditional) Absent-minded; Affected
   (TLSC—Liberated) Good-natured; Independent
PREVIOUS SUBJECTS: College and adult women
APPROPRIATE FOR: The Adjective Check List is considered appropriate for persons in grade 9 and older. Thus, it is reasonable to assume that TLSS and TLSC scores can be obtained for females in grade 9 and up. However, the scales were developed using data for college-age women and older.
ADMINISTRATION: Self-administered; the 300 items on the Adjective Check List can be completed in 15–20 minutes.
SCORING: For each scale, a count is taken of the number of traditional items that are endorsed, the number of liberated items that are endorsed, and the total number of items endorsed of the 300 items on the scale. Because the scales are oriented so that higher scores indicate greater traditionality, the liberated items are reverse scored. The authors have scoring manuals to convert the raw scores into T scores.
DEVELOPMENT: The development of the TLSS began with 233 women with differing backgrounds, including members of the American Psychological Association, divorced and widowed women, faculty at a nursing school, and college alumnae, who were asked to complete two copies of the Adjective Check List. For one copy, they were to select the adjectives descriptive of the traditional woman; for the other copy, they were to select the adjectives descriptive of the liberated woman. Item analysis procedures were used to identify items that were differentially endorsed for traditional and liberated women. From the differentially endorsed items, the 78 items that were endorsed by at least 100 persons in the total sample were selected for the next stage of scale development. Using these data plus data from an additional 109 college women, further item analyses were performed, and 45 adjectives were selected for the final scale. The selection process was intended to maximize the value of coefficient alpha.

As the first step in the development of the TLSC, 140 women, ages 17–67, completed the Adjective Check List. The women were classified as traditional if they were married and not employed outside the home. They were classified as liberated if they were employed full time and rated themselves as liberated on a self-rating scale. In selecting items, the first step was to eliminate items that were not endorsed by at least 10% of the respondents. Item analysis procedures were then used to determine which items differentiated between the traditional and the liberated women, as defined. This procedure led to 53 items being retained. As was the case in the development of the TLSS, data from 109 college women were added, and further item analyses were performed. These analyses led to the selection of 41 adjectives for the TLSC scale. These items were selected to maximize coefficient alpha.

RELIABILITY: Coefficient alpha was .80 for the TLSS and .84 for the TLSC. Eighty-two college women were tested on two occasions, separated by a 3-week interval. The test-retest reliability for these women was .82 on the TLSS and .79 on the TLSC. Another sample of adult women, ages 30–55, was tested on two occasions, separated by a 6-month interval. Test-retest reliability was .75 for the TLSS and .62 for the TLSC.

VALIDITY: Using data from 106 college women, the correlation between the two scales, TLSS and TLSC, was .65. For 50 married women, the correlation was .61. For 56 women beginning the divorce process, the correlation was .47, and for 50 women divorced within the past year, the correlation was .67. The authors concluded: "It appears that the stereotype scores based on the items judged by a wide range of women to be characteristic of traditional women only account for 22% to 45% of the variance in the traditionality self-concept scores" (Cartwright, Lloyd, Nelson, & Bass, 1983, p. 585), yet the correlations actually are rather substantial. Even higher correlations are found when TLSS scores are related to other androgyny measures. The correlation with Heilbrun's (1976) masculinity scale, also taken from the Adjective Check List (see separate entry), was −.81, and the correlation with the Bem Sex Role Inventory (Bem, 1974) (see separate entry) was .70. The TLSC, on the other hand, did not correlate significantly with either Heilbrun's measure or with the Bem Sex Role Inventory.

Consistent with expectations, women classified as liberated on the self-rating and on employment criteria scored as more liberated on the TLSS when compared with women classified as traditional on the marital and employment criteria. In a group of women undergoing divorce, the TLSC, but not the TLSS, correlated significantly with measures of poor social adjustment, lack of social self-confidence, and measures of depression. In another study, the TLSC was found to be significantly correlated with a measure of depression among divorced women but not among married women. Cartwright et al. (1983) concluded that "women who have traditional self-concepts are uniquely vulnerable to the loss of their status as wives" (p. 586).

NOTES & COMMENTS: (1) Cartwright et al. (1983) correlated scores on the TLSC with the various personality scales on the Adjective Check List and the Bem Sex Role Inventory. Overall they found that the traits associated with the traditional self-concept were not very favorable.

(2) Cartwright et al. (1983) concluded that "the TLSS is less useful in that it seems to be redundant with other recent measures of sex role identity with which it shares social stereotype as the criterion for item selection" (p. 587). They are more favorable in their overall assessment of the usefulness of the TLSC. "The TLSC scale is not based on role expectations or judgments about the characteristics of people at the extremes on this dimension, nor is it based on a theoretic conception of personality traits associated with gender. It is instead an empirically based scale derived from items differentiating the self-conceptions of women occupying different life-styles" (p. 588).

AVAILABLE FROM: The Adjective Check List is published by Consulting Psychologists Press, 577 College Ave., Palo Alto, CA 94306. For the items on the TLSS and TLSC, see Cartwright, Lloyd, Nelson, and Bass, 1983.

USED IN:

Cartwright, R. D., Lloyd, S., Nelson, J. B., & Bass, S. (1983). The traditional-liberated dimension: Social stereotype and self-concept. *Journal of Personality and Social Psychology, 3,* 581–588.

BIBLIOGRAPHY:

Bem, S. L. (1974). The measurement of psychological androgyny. *Journal of Consulting and Clinical Psychology, 42,* 155–162.

Gough, H., & Heilbrun, A. (1965). *The Adjective Check List Manual.* Palo Alto: Consulting Psychologists Press.

Heilbrun, A. (1976). Measurement of masculine and feminine sex role identities as independent dimensions. *Journal of Consulting and Clinical Psychology, 44,* 183–190.

WELLESLEY ROLE ORIENTATION SCALE (WROS)

AUTHOR: Thelma G. Alper

DATE: 1973 (used 1964)

VARIABLE: Gender role preference

DESCRIPTION: The Wellesley Role Orientation Scale (WROS) is a summated rating scale consisting of 24 items. There are 3 filler items plus 7 items on each of three subscales: Feminine Traits, Feminine Role Activities, and Male-Oriented Careers. The six response alternatives range from "strongly agree" to "strongly disagree."

ARTICLES LISTED IN BEERE, 1979: 7

AVAILABLE FROM: Thelma G. Alper, 51 Harvard Avenue, Apt. #1, Brookline, MA 02146

USED IN:
Gralewski, C., & Rodgon, M. M. (1980). Effects of social and intellectual instruction on achievement motivation as a function of role orientation. *Sex Roles,*
6, 301–309.
Rodgon, M. M., & Gralewski, C. (1979). Employment status and sex role attitudes in middle-class suburban mothers. *Journal of Applied Social Psychol-*
ogy, 9, 127–134.
Sellers, E. B., & Keenan, V. C. (1977, May). *A construct validation of fear of success.*
Paper presented at the Rocky Mountain Psychological Association, Albuquerque. (ERIC Document Reproduction Service No. ED 156 685)
Steinberg, C. L., Teevan, R. C., & Greenfeld, N. (1983). Sex-role orientation and
fear of failure in women. *Psychological Reports, 52,* 987–992.
Teglasi, H. (1978). Sex-role orientation, achievement motivation, and causal
attributions of college females. *Sex Roles, 4,* 381–397.
Teglasi, H. (1980). Acceptance of the traditional female role and sex of the first
person drawn on the Draw-A-Person Test. *Perceptual and Motor Skills, 51,*
267–271.
Teglasi, H. (1981). First and third person pronouns in sex role questionnaires.
Psychology of Women Quarterly, 5, 785–789.
Travis, C. B., & Seipp, P. H. (1978). An examination of secondary reinforcement,
operant conditioning, and status envy hypotheses in relation to sex-role
ideology. *Sex Roles, 4,* 525–538.
BIBLIOGRAPHY:
Beere, C. A. (1979). *Women and women's issues: A handbook of tests and measures*
(pp. 145–147). San Francisco: Jossey-Bass.

BOYHOOD GENDER CONFORMITY SCALE (BGCS)

AUTHORS: Stewart L. Hockenberry and Robert E. Billingham
DATE: 1985
VARIABLE: Gender orientation
TYPE OF INSTRUMENT: Summated rating scale
DESCRIPTION: The Boyhood Gender Conformity Scale (BGCS) consists
of 20 statements regarding activities, feelings, or experiences remembered from childhood. Half of the items mention stereotypical masculine
behaviors and self-perceptions, and the other items mention behaviors
and self-perceptions that are not typical for boys. For each item, the
respondent is to indicate the frequency with which the statement was
true of him. Seven response options are provided, ranging from "never
or almost never true" to "always or almost always true." Hockenberry
and Billingham (1987) identified a 13-item subset of the BGCS, as well
as a 5-item subset of the 13-item subset.
SAMPLE ITEMS: As a child I felt like I was similar to or not very different
from other boys my age.
    As a child I liked to read romantic stories.
PREVIOUS SUBJECTS: Homosexual and heterosexual adult males between the ages of 18 and 75

APPROPRIATE FOR: Males, ages 18 and older

ADMINISTRATION: Self-administered; about 5–10 minutes

SCORING: Items are scored on a 7-point scale ranging from 0 to 6. Higher scores are assigned to the responses reflecting typical masculinity. Total scores can range from 0 (extremely effeminate) to 120 (extremely masculine).

DEVELOPMENT: The items on the BGCS were adapted from Part A of the Feminine Gender Identity Scale (Freund, Nagler, Langevin, Zajac, & Steiner, 1974) (see separate entry) and from Whitam's (1977) indicators of homosexuality. Discriminant analysis was used to identify subsets of items that would effectively classify homosexuals and heterosexuals. Two subsets of items were identified: a 13-item subset with discriminant loadings greater than .30 and a 5-item subset with discriminant loadings greater than .40.

RELIABILITY: Test-retest reliability was computed based on a 2-week interval between successive testings. For the 13-item subset, the coefficient of stability was .89; for the 5-item subset, the coefficient of stability was .92.

VALIDITY: Each of the 20 items on the BGCS differentiated between heterosexual and homosexual males. The 13-item and 5-item subsets were both able to classify successfully over 87% of a sample of 54 heterosexual and 57 homosexual males.

The 13-item and 5-item subsets of the BGCS were both significantly correlated with the Feminine Gender Identity Scale and Whitam's indicators of homosexuality. The correlations with the former measure were − .63 for the 13 items and − .67 for the 5 items. The correlations with the latter measure were − .57 for the 13 items and − .62 for the 5 items.

NOTES & COMMENTS: Surprisingly, the psychometric data suggest that the 5-item version of the BGCS is the better scale to use in terms of its reliability and validity. The content of the items relates primarily to typically masculine activities, and heterosexual males endorsed these activities significantly more than did homosexual males.

AVAILABLE FROM: Hockenberry and Billingham, 1987

USED IN:

Billingham, R. E., & Hockenberry, S. L. (1987). Gender conformity, masturbation fantasy, infatuation, and sexual orientation: A discriminant analysis investigation. *Journal of Sex Research, 23,* 368–374.

Hockenberry, S. L. (1985). *Male sexual orientation: The development roles of gender identity, affectional, and erotic cognitions.* Unpublished master's thesis, Indiana University.

Hockenberry, S. L., & Billingham, R. E. (1987). Sexual orientation and boyhood gender conformity: Development of the Boyhood Gender Conformity Scale (BGCS). *Archives of Sexual Behavior, 16,* 475–492.

BIBLIOGRAPHY:
Freund, K., Nagler, E., Langevin, R., Zajac, A., & Steiner, B. (1974). Measuring
    feminine gender identity in homosexual males. *Archives of Sexual Behavior*,
    3, 249–260.
Whitam, F. L. (1977). Childhood indicators of male homosexuality. *Archives of
    Sexual Behavior*, 6, 89–96.

EFFEMINACY RATING SCALE
AUTHORS: Alan F. Schatzberg, Michael P. Westfall, Anthony Blumetti,
and C. Lee Birk
DATE: 1975
VARIABLE: Effeminate behavior in males
TYPE OF INSTRUMENT: Alternate choice: yes/no
DESCRIPTION: The Effeminacy Rating Scale consists of 67 questions
covering 10 areas: speech (22 items), gait (6 items), posture and tonus
(12 items), mouth movements (4 items), upper face and eyes (7 items),
hand gestures (4 items), hand and torso gestures (3 items), body type
(5 items), body narcissism (3 items), and other (1 item). The scale is to
be completed by a trained observer who responds "yes" or "no" to each
item after observing the subject for at least 15 minutes.
SAMPLE ITEMS: (speech) Does he speak with soft tones? (The desig-
nation "soft tones" includes low volume, slurring of consonants, and a
poor definition of word-ending.)
    (gait) Does he move sinuously?
    (posture and tonus) When he sits, does he double cross his legs, that
is, at both the knee and ankle?
    (mouth movements) Does he purse his lips when he speaks?
    (upper face and eyes) Does he flirt with his eyes?
    (hand gestures) Does he use an excessive number of wrist gestures?
    (hand and torso gestures) As he sits does he make sinuous move-
ments?
    (body type) Does he have a noticeably pear-shaped body with large
hips and buttocks?
    (body narcissism) Does he preen his hair?
    (other) Does he take his shoes off during the interview?
PREVIOUS SUBJECTS: Homosexual and heterosexual men; transsexuals
APPROPRIATE FOR: Males, ages 16 and older
ADMINISTRATION: The Effeminacy Rating Scale is to be completed by
a trained observer after having at least 15 minutes to observe the subject.
In order to provide the observer with an opportunity to see a variety of
behaviors, the 15-minute observation time should be spent administering an open-ended or semistructured interview. It takes about 10 minutes to complete the rating scale; the scale is not completed when the
subject is present.

SCORING: The score is the number of items endorsed ("yes" responses) for the subject. Schatzberg, Westfall, Blumetti, and Birk (1975) offered the following guidelines for interpreting scores: 0–5 is "not effeminate"; 5–9 is "mildly effeminate"; 9–13 is "moderately effeminate"; and 13 and over is "markedly effeminate." For the 32 men tested by Schatzberg et al., the range of scores was 0 to 17. Thirty of the 32 men scored positively on at least one item; half of the 32 men were heterosexual.

DEVELOPMENT: Initially a scale was developed for recording gross ratings of effeminacy in four categories: speech, gait, posture-tonus, and gestures. Ratings were established on a scale ranging from 0 to 4 + . Even with experienced raters, interrater reliability was unacceptably low. Therefore, a different approach was taken. Effeminate behavior was observed and its discrete components listed. This resulted in a list of 67 behaviors that comprise the Effeminacy Rating Scale. In constructing the items, attempts were made to minimize the need for subjective judgments. The authors were only partially successful in this regard; many items still require judgment.

RELIABILITY: Based on testing 32 subjects, the interrater reliability for total scores was .94. The percentage of agreement was 54%. When two independent, nonprofessional raters scored videotaped interviews for two samples of 10 subjects, their interrater reliabilities were .93 and .94.

Lutz, Roback, and Hart (1984) reported interrater reliability of .85 for two self-trained raters who observed and scored 5 subjects. Later, when the raters observed 23 subjects and rated their behavior, the interrater reliability was .92.

VALIDITY: In the study by Schatzberg et al. (1975), the sample of 32 men were also scored on dress and grooming. The correlation between the dress-grooming measure and the Effeminacy Rating Scale was .09, showing that the Effeminacy Rating Scale was not merely reflecting dress and grooming; rather it reflected behavior.

Information regarding sexual behavior was taken from the 32 men, and each was assigned a Kinsey number ranging from 0 (completely heterosexual) to 6 (completely homosexual). The correlation between Kinsey numbers and scores on the Effeminacy Rating Scale was .45. The men also completed the Gough Femininity Scale (Gough, 1952), a measure of psychological femininity (see separate entry). The correlation between the Gough scale and the Effeminacy scale was .31.

NOTES & COMMENTS: (1) There are no data to indicate whether scores are related to the length of the observation period. Would scores be higher if observations were made over a longer period of time or if they were based on observations made in several different environments?

(2) As Schatzberg et al. (1975) pointed out, some of the items appear contradictory. For example "prolonged eye contact" and "furtive eye contact" appear inconsistent with each other. However, both are in-

cluded on the scale because both may reflect effeminate behavior, albeit in very different ways.

(3) Schatzberg et al. (1975) tested 32 men and found that 20 items were not endorsed for any of the men rated. Further research needs to be done with larger samples to determine whether these items should be retained on the scale.

(4) Lutz et al. (1984) used the Effeminacy Rating Scale to subdivide a group of homosexual men into two groups: effeminate homosexuals and masculine homosexuals. These two groups, along with two groups who had applied for sex reassignment surgery, were compared on the Feminine Gender Identity Scale (Freund, Nagler, Langevin, Zajac, & Steiner, 1974) (see separate entry) and the Tennessee Self-Concept Scale (Fitts, 1965).

AVAILABLE FROM: Schatzberg, Westfall, Blumetti, and Birk, 1975
USED IN:

Lutz, D. J., Roback, H. B., & Hart, M. (1984). Feminine gender identity and psychological adjustment of male transsexuals and male homosexuals. *Journal of Sex Research*, 20(4), 350–362.
Schatzberg, A. F., Westfall, M. P., Blumetti, A. B., & Birk, C. L. (1975). Effeminacy. I. A quantitative rating scale. *Archives of Sexual Behavior*, 4(1), 31–41.
BIBLIOGRAPHY:
Fitts, W. (1965). *The Tennessee Self-Concept Scale*. Nashville: Counselor Recordings and Tests.
Freund, K., Nagler, E., Langevin, R., Zajac, A., & Steiner, B. (1974). Measuring feminine gender identity in homosexual males. *Archives of Sexual Behavior*, 3, 249–260.
Gough, H. G. (1952). Identify psychological femininity. *Educational and Psychological Measurement*, 12, 427–439.

FEMININE GENDER IDENTITY SCALE
AUTHORS: Kurt Freund, Ernest Nagler, Ronald Langevin, Andrew Zajac, and Betty Steiner
DATE: 1974
VARIABLE: Feminine gender identity in men
DESCRIPTION: Originally the Feminine Gender Identity Scale was a multiple choice measure with 3 to 10 response options per item. Intended for use with males over the age of 18, the test included 19 items. The first 12 items, to be answered by all respondents, dealt primarily with whether the respondent, as a child and adolescent, preferred girls' activities and women's clothing and whether he had wanted to be born a girl. The last 7 items, to be answered only by nontranssexual homosexual males, concerned sexual preferences and the desire to be a woman.

The extended version of the Feminine Gender Identity Scale includes 29 items divided into three parts: A, B, and C. Parts B and C include

items that were on the original Feminine Gender Identity Scale. Part A, which asks questions about the respondent's childhood and adolescence, was expanded from 9 to 19 items. Scoring weights are given for each of the response options accompanying each item on the scale.
ARTICLES LISTED IN BEERE, 1979: 6
NOTES & COMMENTS: (1) Some of the studies listed below relied on portions of the original Feminine Gender Identity Scale, and others used the extended version of the scale.

(2) Blanchard and Freund (1983) developed a comparable scale for females: Masculine Gender Identity in Females (see separate entry). Hockenberry and Billingham (1987) developed the Boyhood Gender Conformity Scale (see separate entry), based to a large extent on Part A of the Feminine Gender Identity Scale, as well as on some items taken from another gender inventory.
AVAILABLE FROM: Freund, Nagler, Langevin, Zajac, and Steiner, 1974, for the original version; Freund, Langevin, Satterberg, and Steiner, 1977, for the expanded version; Davis, Yarber, and Davis, 1988, pp. 146–148, for the expanded version
USED IN:

Freund, K., & Blanchard, R. (1983). Is the distant relationship of fathers and homosexual sons related to the sons' erotic preference for male partners, or to the sons' atypical gender identity, or to both? *Journal of Homosexuality*, 9(1), 7–25.
Freund, K., & Blanchard, R. (1987). Feminine gender identity and physical aggressiveness in heterosexual and homosexual pedophiles. *Journal of Sex and Marital Therapy*, 13(1), 25–34.
Freund, K., Langevin, R., Satterberg, J., & Steiner, B. (1977). Extension of the Gender Identity Scale for Males. *Archives of Sexual Behavior*, 6(6), 507–519.
Freund, K., Nagler, E., Langevin, R., Zajac, A., & Steiner, B. (1974). Measuring feminine gender identity in homosexual males. *Archives of Sexual Behavior*, 3(3), 249–260.
Freund, K., Scher, H., Chan, S., & Ben-Aron, M. (1982). Experimental analysis of pedophilia. *Behaviour Research and Therapy*, 20(2), 105–112.
Freund, K., Steiner, B. W., & Chan, S. (1982). Two types of cross-gender identity. *Archives of Sexual Behavior*, 11(1), 49–63.
Hockenberry, S. L., & Billingham, R. E. (1987). Sexual orientation and boyhood gender conformity: Development of the Boyhood Gender Conformity Scale (BGCS). *Archives of Sexual Behavior*, 16(6), 475–492.
Hooberman, R. E. (1979). Psychological androgyny, feminine gender identity and self-esteem in homosexual and heterosexual males. *Journal of Sex Research*, 15(4), 306–315.
Lutz, D. J., Roback, H. B., & Hart, M. (1984). Feminine gender identity and psychological adjustment of male transsexuals and male homosexuals. *Journal of Sex Research*, 20(4), 350–362.
BIBLIOGRAPHY:
Beere, C. A. (1979). *Women and women's issues: A handbook of tests and measures* (pp. 114–115). San Francisco: Jossey-Bass.

Blanchard, R., & Freund, K. (1983). Measuring masculine gender identity in
    females. *Journal of Consulting and Clinical Psychology*, *51*, 205–214.
Davis, C. M., Yarber, W. L., & Davis, S. L. (1988). *Sexuality-related measures* (pp.
    143–151). Syracuse: Editors.

GENDER ROLE CONFLICT SCALE I (GRCS-I)/GENDER ROLE CONFLICT SCALE II (GRCS-II)

AUTHOR: James M. O'Neil

DATE: 1982

VARIABLE: Gender Role Conflict Scale I (GRCS-I) relates to "men's personal gender-role attitudes, behaviors, and conflicts." Gender Role Conflict Scale II (GRCS-II) relates to "men's gender-role conflicts in specific gender-role conflict situations" (O'Neil, Helms, Gable, David, & Wrightsman, 1986, p. 335).

TYPE OF INSTRUMENT: Summated rating scale

DESCRIPTION: The GRCS-I, also referred to as the Situational Behavior Scale, consists of 37 statements, each accompanied by six response options ranging from "strongly agree" to "strongly disagree." Thirteen of the items pertain to "success, power, and competition"; 10 items relate to "restrictive emotionality"; 8 items deal with "restrictive affectionate behavior between men"; and 6 items relate to "conflict between work and family relations" (O'Neil et al., 1986, p. 340).

The GRCS-II includes 16 items, each describing a situation in which potential conflict relates to gender roles. Each item is followed with a specific question regarding the amount of conflict or discomfort the respondent would experience in the situation. Four response options are provided, ranging from "very much conflict—very uncomfortable" to "no conflict—very comfortable." The items load on four factors: "Factor 1–success, power, competition (6 items); Factor 2—homophobia (4 items); Factor 3—lack of emotional response (3 items); Factor 4—public embarrassment from gender-role deviance (3 items)" (O'Neil et al., 1986, p. 346).

SAMPLE ITEMS: GRCS-I

(success, power, competition) Moving up the career ladder is important to me.

(restrictive emotionality) I have difficulty telling others I care about them.

(restrictive affectionate behavior between men) Verbally expressing my love to another man is difficult for me.

(conflicts between work and family relations) I feel torn between my hectic work schedule and caring for my health.

GRCS-II

Your best friend has lost his job at the factory where you work. He is obviously upset, afraid, and angry but he has these emotions hidden.

How comfortable/uncomfortable are you about responding to your friend's intense emotions and fear about unemployment?

There's a guy you've idolized since grade school. He's three years older than you are. In high school he was the star quarterback, valedictorian, and very active in the Young Methodist Fellowship. Last year he graduated from college. You have just learned he is a homosexual. How much conflict do you feel between your admiration for this person and the fact that he is a homosexual?

PREVIOUS SUBJECTS: College men

APPROPRIATE FOR: Men, ages 18 and older

ADMINISTRATION: Self-administered; each of the two measures requires about 15 minutes

SCORING: Items are individually scored, with a 6-point scale used to score the GRCS-I (1 = strongly disagree, 6 = strongly agree) and a 4-point scale used to score the GRCS-II (1 = no conflict, 4 = very much conflict). Item scores are totaled to yield a total score on each of the two scales. Scores for the four factors on each scale can also be obtained.

DEVELOPMENT: O'Neil (1981) posited six patterns of gender role conflict/strain: "restrictive emotionality, health care problems, obsession with achievement and success, restricted sexual and affectionate behavior, socialized control, power, and competition issues, and homophobia" (p. 206). O'Neil's definitions of these terms and a review of the relevant literature led to the development of 85 items for the GRCS-I and 51 items for the GRCS-II. These initial scales and the Personal Attributes Questionnaire (PAQ) (Spence, Helmreich, & Stapp, 1974) (see separate entry) were administered to 527 undergraduate men. To reduce the number of items on the scales, the following procedures were used. First, items that did not have a standard deviation of at least 1.00 were eliminated because these items did not show sufficient variability to be of much value. Second, items had to correlate at least .30 with other items to be retained. Third, factor analysis was performed, and items were excluded if they did not have a factor loading of at least .35 on one factor or if they had factor loadings greater than .30 on more than one factor. These procedures left 37 items on the GRCS-I and 16 items on the GRCS-II; four factors were identified for each scale.

RELIABILITY: For the GRCS-I, alpha coefficients for the four factor scores ranged from .75 to .85. For the GRCS-II, alpha coefficients for the four factor scores ranged from .51 to .76. Test-retest reliabilities were computed with a 4-week interval between testings. For the GRCS-I, data were available for 17 students, and the test-retest reliabilities ranged from .72 to .86 for the four factors. For the GRCS-II, data were available for 14 students, and the test-retest reliabilities ranged from .78 to .85.

VALIDITY: O'Neil et al. (1986) hypothesized that "subjects with different gender-role orientations, measured by the PAQ, would differ with respect to the degree to which they express patterns of gender-role conflict" (p. 339). Using PAQ scores, they classified respondents as masculine, feminine, androgynous, or undifferentiated. Looking at GRCS-I scores, they found significant differences between the groups on three of the four factors; there were no significant differences on "conflicts between work and family relations." Similar results were obtained for GRCS-II scores in that only one factor—"success, power, and competition"—failed to show significant differences.

NOTES & COMMENTS: (1) Although O'Neil's original theory suggested six gender role patterns and the scale was developed to reflect all six patterns, the factor analyses revealed four factors on each scale, and these factors were somewhat different from those originally suggested.

(2) In earlier writing, O'Neil, David, and Wrightsman (1982) referred to the GRCS-I as the Fear of Femininity Scale.

AVAILABLE FROM: For the GRCS-I, see O'Neil, Helms, Gable, David, and Wrightsman, 1986. For the GRCS-II, contact James O'Neil, Department of Educational Psychology, Box U–64, 249 Glenbrook Road, Storrs, CT 06268

USED IN:

O'Neil, J. M., David, L., & Wrightsman, L. (1982, August). *Fear of Femininity Scale (FOFS): Men's gender role conflict*. Paper presented at the meeting of the American Psychological Association, Washington, DC. (ERIC Document Reproduction Service No. ED 247 480)

O'Neil, J. M., Helms, B. J., Gable, R. K., David, L., & Wrightsman, L. S. (1986). Gender-Role Conflict Scale: College men's fear of femininity. *Sex Roles*, *14*, 335–350.

O'Neil, J. M., Helms, B. J., Gable, R., Stillson, R., David, L., & Wrightsman, L. S. (1984, August). *Data on college men's gender role conflict and strain*. Paper presented at the meeting of the American Psychological Association, Toronto. (ERIC Document Reproduction Service No. ED 248 448)

BIBLIOGRAPHY:

O'Neil, J. M. (1981). Patterns of gender role conflicts and strain: Sexism and fear of femininity in men's lives. *Personnel and Guidance Journal*, *60*, 203–210.

Spence, J. T., Helmreich, R. L., & Stapp, J. T. (1974). The Personal Attributes Questionnaire: A measure of sex-role stereotypes and masculinity-femininity. *Catalog of Selected Documents in Psychology*, *4*, 43–44. (Ms. No. 617)

HYPERMASCULINITY INVENTORY

AUTHORS: Donald L. Mosher and Mark Sirkin

DATE: 1984

VARIABLE: Adoption of the macho personality, including calloused sex attitudes toward women, a conception of violence as manly, and a view of danger as exciting.

TYPE OF INSTRUMENT: Forced choice

DESCRIPTION: The Hypermasculinity Inventory consists of 30 forced-choice pairs. One item of each pair represents endorsement of a "macho" personality characteristic; the other item in the pair does not reflect a macho personality. For each pair, the respondent is to select the one item most descriptive of him.

SAMPLE ITEMS: (Calloused Sex Attitudes Toward Women) A. Get a woman drunk, high, or hot and she'll let you do whatever you want. B. It's gross and unfair to use alcohol and drugs to convince a woman to have sex.

(Conception of Violence as Manly) A. Call me a name and I'll pretend not to hear you. B. Call me a name and I'll call you another.

(View of Danger as Exciting) A. After I've gone through a really dangerous experience my knees feel weak and I shake all over. B. After I've been through a really dangerous experience I feel high.

PREVIOUS SUBJECTS: College men

APPROPRIATE FOR: Men, ages 18 and older

ADMINISTRATION: Self-administered; about 15–20 minutes

SCORING: Items are scored 1 if the keyed (macho) option is selected. Scores can be obtained for each of the three subscales and for the total scale, but it is recommended that only the total score be used unless there is specific justification for using a subscale score.

DEVELOPMENT: A pool of items, including 70 calloused-sex items, 91 violence-as-manly items, and 60 danger-as-exciting items, was administered to 60 college men. Item-subtotal correlations were computed for each of the three sets of items, and the 30 items with the highest correlations were selected for each subscale. This pool of 90 items was then administered to another sample of 135 college men, and item-subtotal correlations were again computed for each subscale. The 10 items with the highest item-subtotal correlations were selected for each of the three scales, giving a final scale with a total of 30 items.

RELIABILITY: Coefficient alpha was computed for the three subscales and the total scale. The results were: calloused sex = .79; violence as manly = .79; danger as exciting = .71; and total scale = .89.

VALIDITY: Scores on the Hypermasculinity Inventory were compared with scores on a variety of other measures using data obtained from the 135 college men who were used for scale development (Mosher & Sirkin, 1984). As expected, Hypermasculinity scores were significantly correlated with the frequency of use of alcohol and drugs, with changes in driving and aggressive behavior following alcohol consumption, and with self-reported delinquency during the high school years. Respondents also completed the Personality Research Form (Jackson, 1974). It was found that Hypermasculinity scores correlated positively and significantly with scores on Play, Impulsivity, Exhibition, Aggression, Autonomy, and Dominance, and they correlated negatively and significantly with Cognitive Structure, Harm Avoidance, Nurturance, Order, Understanding, and Social Desirability.

In other research, Mosher and Anderson (1986) administered the Hypermasculinity Inventory and the Aggressive Sexual Behavior Inventory (Koss & Oros, 1982) to 175 male college sophomores. As expected, scores on the Hypermasculinity Inventory correlated significantly with a history of sexual aggression ($r = .33$, $p < .001$). The Calloused Sex Attitudes subscale showed an even stronger correlation ($r = .53$) with a history of sexual aggression. Mosher and Anderson (1986) found that higher scores on the Hypermasculinity Inventory were "related to experiencing less affective disgust, anger, fear, distress, shame, contempt, and guilt as the men imagined committing a rape" (p. 77).

NOTES & COMMENTS: (1) A factor analysis suggested "the presence of a single, predominant, latent variable that was relatively homogeneous and which was named the macho personality pattern" (Mosher & Sirkin, 1984, p. 154).

(2) Mosher and Sirkin (1984) offered an interesting explanation for the use of the forced-choice format. First, they pointed out that forcing one to choose between the two items in a pair mirrors the choosing that men do in real life. "The nonreflective decision to engage in dangerous, aggressive, or calloused sexual behavior in life, which typify the macho constellation, might be paralleled by the selection of the somewhat undesirable macho alternatives with an amused bravado during the administration of the inventory" (Mosher & Sirkin, 1984, p. 160). Second, the macho answer might appear undesirable unless it was paired with an equally, or perhaps more, undesirable option. That is, "the choice can be compared to being a 'macho' or a 'wimp' " (p. 160).

(3) Smeaton and Byrne (1987) used the Hypermasculinity Inventory to determine whether hypermasculinity has an impact on acquaintance rape proclivity.

AVAILABLE FROM: Mosher and Sirkin, 1984; Davis, Yarber, and Davis, 1988, pp. 226–227.

USED IN:

Mosher, D. L., & Anderson, R. D. (1986). Macho personality, sexual aggression, and reactions to guided imagery of realistic rape. *Journal of Research in Personality, 20,* 77–94.

Mosher, D. L., & Sirkin, M. (1984). Measuring a macho personality constellation. *Journal of Research in Personality, 18,* 150–163.

Smeaton, G., & Byrne, D. (1987). The effects of R-rated violence and erotica, individual differences, and victim characteristics on acquaintance rape proclivity. *Journal of Research in Personality, 21,* 171–184.

BIBLIOGRAPHY:

Davis, C. M., Yarber, W. L., & Davis, S. L. (1988). *Sexuality-related measures* (pp. 225–227). Syracuse: Editors.

Jackson, D. N. (1974). *Personality Research Form—Form E.* Goshen, NY: Research Psychologists Press.

Koss, M. P., & Oros, C. J. (1982). Sexual Experiences Survey: A research instrument investigating sexual aggression and victimization. *Journal of Consulting and Clinical Psychology*, *50*, 455–457.

ADJECTIVE CHECK LIST (ACL)

AUTHOR: Harrison G. Gough

DATE: 1952

VARIABLE: Masculinity/femininity

DESCRIPTION: The Adjective Check List (ACL) provides a list of 300 adjectives, and respondents check those that they feel describe them. Of the 300 adjectives, Gough and Heilbrun found that 54 of them discriminated between feminine college females and masculine college males. Some researchers use this set of 54 items as the measure of masculinity/femininity, and others use the scale in other ways to measure masculinity/femininity. The full ACL yields 37 scores: Number of Adjectives Checked, Number of Favorable Adjectives, Number of Unfavorable Adjectives, Communality, Achievement, Dominance, Endurance, Order, Intraception, Nurturance, Affiliation, Heterosexuality, Exhibition, Autonomy, Aggression, Change, Succorance, Abasement, Deference, Counseling Readiness, Self-Control, Self-Confidence, Personal Adjustment, Ideal Self, Creative Personality, Military Leadership, Masculine Attributes, Feminine Attributes, Critical Parent, Nurturing Parent, Adult, Free Child, Adapted Child, High Origence–Low Intellectence, High Origence–High Intellectence, Low Origence–Low Intellectence, Low Origence–High Intellectence.

NOTES & COMMENTS: (1) The ACL is listed in *Tests in Print III* (entry 116) and in *The Ninth Mental Measurements Yearbook* (entry 52). The ACL was described in Beere (1979).

(2) The ACL is frequently used as a measure of stereotypes. Either the entire set or a subset of the 300 adjectives is used.

(3) Pearson (1980a, 1980b) factor analyzed responses to the ACL, along with responses to the Bem Sex Role Inventory (Bem, 1974) (see separate entry) and the Personal Attributes Questionnaire (Spence, Helmreich, & Stapp, 1974) (see separate entry).

(4) Several researchers have compared results obtained with the ACL to results obtained with other sex role measures (Herron, Goodman, & Herron, 1983; Kelly, Furman, & Young, 1978; Ramanaiah & Martin, 1984; Small, Erdwins, & Gross, 1979; Wilson & Cook, 1984).

AVAILABLE FROM: Consulting Psychologists Press, 577 College Avenue, Palo Alto, CA 94306

USED IN:

Benoist, I. R., & Butcher, J. N. (1977). Nonverbal cues to sex-role attitudes. *Journal of Research in Personality*, *11*, 431–442.

Edwards, J. R., & Williams, J. E. (1980). Sex-trait stereotypes among young children and young adults: Canadian findings and cross-national comparisons. *Canadian Journal of Behavioural Science, 12,* 210–220.

Fioravanti, M., Gough, H. G., & Frere, L. J. (1981). English, French, and Italian adjective check lists: A social desirability analysis. *Journal of Cross Cultural Psychology, 12*(4), 461–472.

Harrington, D. M., & Andersen, S. M. (1980, September). *Creative self-concept, masculinity, femininity and three models of androgyny.* Paper presented at the meeting of the American Psychological Association, Montreal. (ERIC Document Reproduction Service No. ED 194 849)

Harrington, D. M., & Andersen, S. M. (1981). Creativity, masculinity, femininity, and three models of psychological androgyny. *Journal of Personality and Social Psychology, 41,* 744–757.

Hawkins, D., Herron, W. G., Gibson, W., Hoban, G., & Herron, M. J. (1988). Homosexual and heterosexual sex-role orientation on six sex-role scales. *Perceptual and Motor Skills, 66,* 863–871.

Heilbrun, A. B., Jr. (1976). Measurement of masculine and feminine sex role identities as independent dimensions. *Journal of Consulting and Clinical Psychology, 44,* 183–190.

Heilbrun, A. B., Jr. (1978). An exploration of antecedents and attributes of androgynous and undifferentiated sex roles. *Journal of Genetic Psychology, 132,* 97–107.

Heilbrun, A. B., Jr. (1981). Gender differences in the functional linkage between androgyny, social cognition, and competence. *Journal of Personality and Social Psychology, 41,* 1106–1118.

Heilbrun, A. B., Jr. (1984a). Identification with the father and peer intimacy of the daughter. *Family Relations, 33,* 597–605.

Heilbrun, A. B., Jr. (1984b). Sex-based models of androgyny: A further cognitive elaboration of competence differences. *Journal of Personality and Social Psychology, 46,* 216–229.

Heilbrun, A. B., Jr. (1986). Androgyny as type and androgyny as behavior: Implications for gender schema in males and females. *Sex Roles, 14,* 123–139.

Heilbrun, A. B., Jr., & Han, Y. L. (1984). Cost-effectiveness of college achievement by androgynous men and women. *Psychological Reports, 55*(3), 977–978.

Heilbrun, A. B., Jr., & Han, Y. L. (1986). Sex differences in the adaptive value of androgyny. *Psychological Reports, 59,* 1023–1026.

Heilbrun, A. B., Jr., & Mulqueen, C. M. (1987). The second androgyny: A proposed revision in adaptive priorities for college women. *Sex Roles, 17,* 187–207.

Heilbrun, A. B., Jr., & Pitman, D. (1979). Testing some basic assumptions about psychological androgyny. *Journal of Genetic Psychology, 135*(2), 175–188.

Heilbrun, A. B., Jr., & Schwartz, H. L. (1982). Sex-gender differences in level of androgyny. *Sex Roles, 8*(2), 201–214.

Herron, W. G., Goodman, C. K., & Herron, M. J. (1983). Comparability of sex-role measures. *Psychological Reports, 53*(3), 1087–1094.

Humphreys, L. G. (1978). Research on individual differences requires correlational analysis, not ANOVA. *Intelligence, 2*(1), 1–5.

Kelly, J. A., Furman, W., & Young, V. (1978). Problems associated with the typological measurement of sex roles and androgyny. *Journal of Consulting and Clinical Psychology, 46,* 1574–1576.

Komarovsky, M., & Mayer, E. R. (1984). Consistency of female gender attitudes: A research note. *Social Forces, 62,* 1020–1025.

Krasnoff, A. G. (1981). The sex difference in self-assessed fears. *Sex Roles, 7,* 19–23.

Mills, C. J. (1983). Sex-typing and self-schemata effects on memory and response latency. *Journal of Personality and Social Psychology, 45,* 163–172.

Mills, C. J., & Tyrrell, D. J. (1983). Sex-stereotypic encoding and release from proactive interference. *Journal of Personality and Social Psychology, 45(4),* 772–781.

Mimick-Chalmers, C. (1986). A study of college women: Androgyny and perceptions of a feminist therapist. *Sex Roles, 14,* 281–286.

O'Grady, K. E., Freda, J. S., & Mikulka, P. J. (1979). A comparison of the Adjective Check List, BEM Sex Role Inventory, and Personal Attributes Questionnaire masculinity and femininity subscales. *Multivariate Behavioral Research, 14,* 215–225.

Pearson, J. C. (1980a). A factor analytic study of the items in three selected sex-role instruments. *Psychological Reports, 46(3),* 1119–1126.

Pearson, J. C. (1980b, November). *The psychometric adequacy of three selected sex role instruments.* Paper presented at the meeting of the Speech Communication Association, New York. (ERIC Document Reproduction Service No. ED 196 085)

Ramanaiah, N. V., & Martin, H. J. (1984). Convergent and discriminant validity of selected masculinity and femininity scales. *Sex Roles, 10,* 493–504.

Rapin, L. S., & Cooper, M. A. (1980). Images of men and women: A comparison of feminists and nonfeminists. *Psychology of Women Quarterly, 5(2),* 186–194.

Robinson, B. E. (1982). Sex-stereotyped attitudes of male and female preschool teachers as a function of personality characteristics. *Psychological Reports, 50(1),* 203–208.

Robinson, B. E., & Canaday, H. (1978). Sex-role behaviors and personality traits of male day care teachers. *Sex Roles, 4(6),* 853–865.

Schwarz, J. C., & Williams, B. E. (1986). Masculinity and femininity: The role of desirability in the relationships among measures based on self-concept and personality traits. *Sex Roles, 15,* 569–584.

Small, A. C., Erdwins, C., & Gross, R. B. (1979). A comparison of the Bem Sex-Role Inventory and the Heilbrun Masculinity and Femininity Scales. *Journal of Personality Assessment, 43(4),* 393–395.

Small, A. C., Gross, R. B., & Batlis, N. C. (1979). Sexual identity and personality variables in normal and disturbed adolescent girls. *Adolescence, 14,* 31–44.

Tarr, L. H. (1978). Developmental sex-role theory and sex-role attitudes in late adolescents. *Psychological Reports, 42(3),* 807–814.

Urberg, K. A. (1979). Sex role conceptualizations in adolescents and adults. *Developmental Psychology, 15(2),* 90–92.

Urberg, K. A., & Labouvie-Vief, G. (1976). Conceptualizations of sex roles: A life span developmental study. *Developmental Psychology, 12(1),* 15–23.

Ward, C. (1982). Sex trait stereotypes of males and females in Malaysia. *Psychologia*, 25(4), 220–227.

Ward, C., & Williams, J. E. (1982). A psychological needs analysis of male and female sex trait stereotypes in Malaysia. *International Journal of Psychology*, 17, 369–381.

Welsh, G. S., & Baucom, D. H. (1977). Sex, masculinity-femininity, and intelligence. *Intelligence*, 1(2), 218–233.

Wiggins, J. S., & Holzmuller, A. (1978). Psychological androgyny and interpersonal behavior. *Journal of Consulting and Clinical Psychology*, 46, 40–52.

Williams, J. E., Best, D. L., Haque, A., Pandey, J., & Verma, R. K. (1982). Sex-trait stereotypes in India and Pakistan. *Journal of Psychology*, 111(2), 167–181.

Williams, J. E., Daws, J. T., Best, D. L., Tilquin, C., Wesley, F., & Bjerke, T. (1979). Sex-trait stereotypes in France, Germany, and Norway. *Journal of Cross Cultural Psychology*, 10(2), 133–156.

Wilson, F. R., & Cook, E. P. (1984). Concurrent validity of four androgyny instruments. *Sex Roles*, 11, 813–837.

Zimet, S. G., & Zimet, C. N. (1977). Teachers view people: Sex-role stereotyping. *Psychological Reports*, 41, 583–591.

BIBLIOGRAPHY:

Beere, C. A. (1979). *Women and women's issues: A handbook of tests and measures* (pp. 148–150). San Francisco: Jossey-Bass.

Bem, S. L. (1974). The measurement of psychological androgyny. *Journal of Consulting and Clinical Psychology*, 42, 155–162.

Mitchell, J. V., Jr. (Ed.). (1983). *Tests in print III*. Lincoln: Buros Institute of Mental Measurements, University of Nebraska.

Mitchell, J. V., Jr. (Ed.). (1985). *The ninth mental measurements yearbook* (Vol. 1). Lincoln: Buros Institute of Mental Measurements, University of Nebraska.

Spence, J. T., Helmreich, R. L., & Stapp, J. T. (1974). The Personal Attributes Questionnaire: A measure of sex role stereotypes and masculinity-femininity. *Catalog of Selected Documents in Psychology*, 4, 43–44. (Ms. No. 617)

ATTITUDE INTEREST ANALYSIS TEST

AUTHORS: Lewis M. Terman and Catharine Cox Miles

DATE: 1936

VARIABLE: Masculinity/femininity

DESCRIPTION: The Attitude Interest Analysis Test is a very lengthy, multiple choice test intended to measure masculinity/femininity in persons ages 12 and older. There are two forms of the test: Form A has 456 items, and Form B has 454 items. Each form consists of seven subtests, called exercises and titled Word Association, Ink-Blot Association, Information, Emotional and Ethical Response, Interests, Personalities and Opinions, and Introvertive Response.

ARTICLES LISTED IN BEERE, 1979: 65

NOTES & COMMENTS: (1) Given the age of this test, it is not surprising that its use has declined. Whereas Beere (1979) listed 65 articles that used the Attitude Interest Analysis Test, there are only 7 citations listed below, and only 1 of those was published after 1980. LaTorre and Piper (1978) provided more recent information on the psychometric properties of the measure. Their findings should be reviewed by anyone considering using the Attitude Interest Analysis Test.

(2) Some researchers use only a portion of the test.

AVAILABLE FROM: Terman and Miles, 1936

USED IN:

Fisher, S. (1978). Anxiety and sex role in body landmark functions. *Journal of Research in Personality, 12*, 87–99.

Fisher, S., & Greenberg, R. P. (1979). Masculinity-femininity and response to somatic discomfort. *Sex Roles, 5*(4), 483–493.

Kenna, J. C., & Hoenig, J. (1979). Verbal tests and transsexualism. *Acta Psychiatrica Scandinavica, 59*(1), 80–86.

LaTorre, R. A., & Gregoire, P. A. (1977). Gender role in university mental health clients. *Journal of Individual Psychology, 33*(2), 246–249.

LaTorre, R. A., & Piper, W. E. (1978). The Terman-Miles M-F Test: An examination of exercises 1, 2, and 3 forty years later. *Sex Roles, 4*(1), 141–154.

LaTorre, R. A., & Piper, W. E. (1979). Gender identity and gender role in schizophrenia. *Journal of Abnormal Psychology, 88*(1), 68–72.

LaTorre, R. A., Yu, L., Fortin, L., & Marrache, M. (1983). Gender-role adoption and sex as academic and psychological risk factors. *Sex Roles, 9*(11), 1127–1130.

Terman, L. M., & Miles, C. C. (1936). *Sex and personality.* New York: McGraw-Hill.

BIBLIOGRAPHY:

Beere, C. A. (1979). *Women and women's issues: A handbook of tests and measures* (pp. 97–104). San Francisco: Jossey-Bass.

AUSTRALIAN SEX ROLE INVENTORY

AUTHOR: Betty A. Drinkwater

DATE: 1979

VARIABLE: Gender role

TYPE OF INSTRUMENT: Summated rating scale

DESCRIPTION: The Australian Sex Role Inventory includes 20 masculine traits, 20 feminine traits, and 20 sex-neutral traits, giving a total of 60 items that are sequenced randomly. All of the traits on the scale are intended to be socially desirable characteristics. Each item is accompanied by a 5-point rating scale ranging from "not at all true of me" to "extremely true of me."

SAMPLE ITEMS: (masculine) self sufficient; rugged
   (feminine) cries without shame; glamorous
   (neutral) adaptable; biased

PREVIOUS SUBJECTS: Australian college students

APPROPRIATE FOR: High school students and older could understand

and respond to the items on the scale. Since the scale was developed in Australia, its use should generally be restricted to Australia.

ADMINISTRATION: Self-administered; about 20 minutes

SCORING: Items are individually scored on a 5-point scale, with 5 points given to the "extremely true" end of the continuum and 1 point given to the "not true" end of the continuum. The masculinity items are totaled and the femininity items are totaled to yield two subscale scores.

DEVELOPMENT: Eighty-four college students served as raters to evaluate the social desirability of each item in the initial pool of 412 characteristics from which the Bem Sex Role Inventory (BSRI) (Bem, 1974) (see separate entry) was developed. Half of the raters were asked to rate the items on their desirability in an Australian man, and the other half of the raters were asked to rate the items on their desirability in an Australian woman. In rating the items, the judges were to consider how Australian society would rate the item; they were not asked for just their own opinion. A 5-point rating scale accompanied each item; the response options ranged from "(1) not at all desirable" to "(5) very desirable." In analyzing the judgments made by the Australian raters, Drinkwater (1979) found that "all but 3 of the 40 Masculine and Feminine characteristics [from the BSRI] were judged by combined male and female Queensland raters as being significantly more desirable for the category as defined by the BSRI" (p. 314). Nevertheless, Drinkwater identified a subset of items that she felt would comprise a better gender role inventory for use in Australia. She selected items "which Australian men and women rated above the midpoint of social desirability (3.0) for one sex, but below it for the other sex" (p. 316).

RELIABILITY: No information was provided.

VALIDITY: Ho and Zemaitis (1980) administered the Australian Sex Role Inventory and three other measures—Concern Over the Negative Consequences of Success, Measure of Individual Differences in Achieving Tendency, and an anagram task—to college students. They predicted that "femininity would be positively related to concern over the negative consequences of success, and negatively related to achievement motivation, initial expectation of success and quality of performance" (p. 462). None of these hypotheses was confirmed; femininity scores were unrelated to all of these variables. However, for both males and females, masculinity scores were related to the other measures. Specifically, masculinity was negatively related to concern over the negative consequences of success and positively related to achievement motivation, initial expectations of success, and quality of performance. Ho and Zemaitis (1980) suggested that the failure to find significant relations between femininity and the other measured variables may have resulted from the fact that the femininity measure consists of traits "which have nothing to do with achievement or performance on a task" (p. 464).

NOTES & COMMENTS: (1) Of the 60 items on the Australian Sex Role Inventory, 13 masculine items and 9 feminine items overlap items on the BSRI.

(2) The Australian Sex Role Scale (Antill, Cunningham, Russell, & Thompson, 1981) (see separate entry) is quite similar to the Australian Sex Role Inventory: The development of both scales relates to the BSRI. Both are designed for use in Australia, and both ask respondents to provide self-ratings on a series of traits. The two scales differ in terms of number of items, number of response options, and the specific list of traits. The Australian Sex Role Scale includes both positive and negative traits.

AVAILABLE FROM: Drinkwater, 1979

USED IN:

Drinkwater, B. A. (1979). Social desirability of characteristics of the Bem Sex-Role Inventory. *Australian Psychologist, 14*(3), 311–317.

Ho, R., & Zemaitis, R. (1980). Behavioral correlates of an Australian version of the Bem Sex-Role Inventory. *Australian Psychologist, 15*(3), 459–466.

Ho, R., & Zemaitis, R. (1981). Concern over the negative consequences of success. *Australian Journal of Psychology, 33*, 19–28.

Jobson, S., & Watson, J. S. (1984). Sex and age differences in choice behaviour: The object-person dimension. *Perception, 13*, 719–724.

BIBLIOGRAPHY:

Antill, J. K., Cunningham, J. D., Russell, G., & Thompson, N. L. (1981). An Australian Sex-Role Scale. *Australian Journal of Psychology, 33*, 169–183.

Bem, S. L. (1974). The measurement of psychological androgyny. *Journal of Consulting and Clinical Psychology, 42*, 155–162.

AUSTRALIAN SEX ROLE SCALE (ASRS)

AUTHORS: John K. Antill, John D. Cunningham, Graeme Russell, and Norman L. Thompson

DATE: 1981

VARIABLE: Gender role

TYPE OF INSTRUMENT: Summated Rating scale

DESCRIPTION: There are two forms of the Australian Sex Role Scale (ASRS), each with 50 items: 10 positive and 10 negative feminine items, 10 positive and 10 negative masculine items, and 5 positive and 5 negative social desirability items. Each item consists of one or a few words that describe a personality trait. For each item, the respondent uses a 7-point scale to indicate how true the item is for the respondent. The options range from "never or almost never true" to "always or almost always true."

SAMPLE ITEMS: (positive feminine) Loves children

(negative feminine) Dependent

(positive masculine) Firm

(negative masculine) Bossy

(positive social desirability) Interesting
(negative social desirability) Tense

PREVIOUS SUBJECTS: High school students, college students, and adults in Australia

APPROPRIATE FOR: High school students and older could understand and respond to the items on the scale. However, the scale was developed in Australia, and in general, its use should be restricted to Australia. Furthermore, there is evidence to suggest that the scale might be appropriate only for persons in college (Ray & Lovejoy, 1984).

ADMINISTRATION: Self-administered; about 15–20 minutes

SCORING: Individual items are scored on a 7-point scale, with 7 points assigned to the response "always or almost always true" and 1 point assigned to the opposite end of the continuum. Subscale scores can be computed for the positive masculine items (M+), the negative masculine items (M−), the positive feminine items (F+), the negative feminine items (F−), the positive social desirability items (S+), and the negative social desirability items (S−). One can also obtain overall scores on masculinity, femininity, and social desirability. The masculinity and femininity scores can be used to classify persons as masculine, feminine, androgynous, and undifferentiated.

DEVELOPMENT: A pool of 591 items was compiled by eliminating duplicate items from a list compiled from three sources: (1) the items used in developing the Bem Sex Role Inventory (BSRI) (Bem, 1974) (see separate entry); (2) the terms on the Adjective Check List (Gough & Heilbrun, 1965) (see separate entry); and (3) the Sex Role Stereotype Questionnaire (Rosenkrantz, Vogel, Bee, Broverman, & Broverman, 1968) (see separate entry). Long items, synonyms, and negatives (e.g., *irrational* is the negative of *rational*) were eliminated, leaving a pool of 512 items. By separating the odd items and the even items, two parallel forms, each with 256 items, were constructed. Ten versions of the scale were created by using the two forms and developing five different sets of directions for each form. The directions asked persons to: (1) rate themselves; (2) rate the desirability of each characteristic for an Australian male; (3) rate the desirability of each characteristic for an Australian female; (4) rate how typical each characteristic is for an Australian male; or (5) rate how typical each characteristic is for an Australian female.

The 10 different forms were administered to 2,427 subjects: 985 college students, 1,046 high school students, and 396 adults. When completing the scales, respondents were asked to place an X next to any item that was not clear to them. If 10% of the respondents in any of the 10 samples placed an X next to the item, it was deleted from further consideration. This led to the deletion of 55 items from List A and 68 items from List B.

The next step in the scale development involved constructing "parallel forms" of some initial scales. Items more typical of males than females and more desirable in males comprised the M+ scales. Items more typical of females than males and more desirable in females comprised the F+ scales. Items that were more typical of males but undesirable in males comprised the M− scale, and items more typical of females but undesirable in females comprised the F− scale. To reduce the scales' length further, attention was given to obtaining high internal consistency on the individual scales and low correlations between the masculinity and femininity scales. Furthermore, synonyms were eliminated when possible so as to avoid artificially inflating the internal consistency of the scales.

Items that were typical of both males and females were included on the social desirability scales. If the item was desirable for both sexes, it was an S+ item; if the item was undesirable for both sexes, it was an S− item. Using the guidelines described, 50 items were selected from each of the two lists to form the two versions of the scale. The scales were then administered to new samples of 144 male and 138 female high school students to gather data on the reliability and validity of the measures.

RELIABILITY: Using the data from the high school students, Antill, Cunningham, Russell, and Thompson (1981) computed coefficient alpha for each form by sex by subscale combination. For both sexes, on both forms, the coefficients for the S+, S−, and S total scores tended to be quite low. This is not surprising since the scales are very short—five items on each subscale—and there is no real substantive commonality to the items. For the M+, M−, and M total scores, the coefficients ranged from .61 (M+ subscale for Form A, males) to .81 (M total score for Form A, males). For the F+, F−, and F total scores, the coefficients ranged from .39 (F− subscale for Form B, females) to .83 (F+ subscale for Form B, males). The low value of .39 is unacceptably low for an internal consistency coefficient.

Hong, Kavanagh, and Tippett (1983) administered both forms of the ASRS to high school students between the ages of 14 and 18. They obtained similar results in that coefficients for the S scores were lower than the coefficients for the M and F scores, and the coefficient for the F− subscale of Form B was again unacceptably low; alpha was equal to .47.

Russell and Antill (1984) administered both forms of the ASRS to high school and college students. Though the coefficients they obtained tended to be somewhat higher than those already reported, their results were relatively consistent with the results from other studies, particularly in regard to low coefficients for the S subscales and unacceptably low coefficients for the F− scores on Form B: .50 for males and .51 for females.

Farnill and Ball (1985) tested college females and adult males. The alpha coefficients they obtained were consistent with those reported above.

Antill et al. (1981) compared the fourfold classifications that would result from using the median split procedures on Form A and Form B. For males, 65.3% were classified similarly regardless of which form was used; for females, 63% were classified similarly. In defending these findings, Antill et al. (1981) stated: "Although not as high as one might like, they exceed those for any pair of sex-role measures commonly in use" (p. 182). The most common inconsistencies between Form A and Form B classifications were in the undifferentiated and masculine categories for males and in the androgynous and feminine categories for females.

Antill et al. (1981) calculated alternate form reliability, separately for males and females. The S scores tended to have lower reliabilities than did the other scores. Among the M and F scores, the lowest value was for the F− score for females ($r = .49$), and the highest value was for the F+ score for males ($r = .79$). Russell and Antill (1984) also calculated alternate form reliability, separately for males and females. For both sexes, the lowest coefficient was for the S total scores (.41 for males, .39 for females), and the highest coefficient was for the M total scores (.72 for each sex). From their research, Hong et al. (1983) concluded, "The present findings did not support the contention that Forms A and B are parallel forms" (p. 504).

VALIDITY: Testing 144 high school boys and 138 high school girls, Antill et al. (1981) found significant sex differences on both Forms A and B, for M+, M−, M total, F+, F−, and F total. Although these differences were expected and add to the validity of the scale, there were also unexpected and significant sex differences on S− and S total scores for Form A. Hong et al. (1983) performed a similar study with high school students. They also found the expected significant sex differences, except for the M− scores. And, like Antill et al. (1981), they found no significant sex differences on S scores from Form B, but they did find some significant differences on S scores from Form A. Similar results were obtained by Russell and Antill (1984) and by Farnill and Ball (1985), except that Russell and Antill did not find significant differences on any of the S scores.

As would be expected, both sexes endorsed the positive items more often than they endorsed the negative items (Antill et al., 1981; Russell & Antill, 1984).

NOTES & COMMENTS: (1) Several researchers looked at the intercorrelations between the subscale scores. Overall, the correlations tended to be moderate, and in general, the M total and F total scores were not related to each other, suggesting that the two dimensions are independent (Antill et al., 1981; Russell & Antill, 1984). Farnill and Ball (1985), however, obtained a correlation between F total and M total of −.48 for males and −.31 for females. Antill et al. (1981) and Russell and Antill (1984) found low correlations between total S score and total M score or total F score, but the findings of Farnill and Ball (1985) and Hong et al. (1983) did not support these results.

(2) Factor analytic studies of the ASRS were performed by Hong et al. (1983), Farnill and Ball (1985), and Marsh and Myers (1986). Their results are not consistent with each other. Hong et al. (1983) concluded: "The present factor analytic results did not support the assumption that sex-role could be confined within the six sub-scales proposed by Antill, et al." (p. 504). Farnill and Ball (1985), on the other hand, concluded: "The factor structures reported here . . . offer better support for the sub-scale design for the [ASRS]" (p. 212), but they do caution against combining the F+ and F− scores to give an overall F score. Their data suggested that femininity is multidimensional.

(3) As part of the development process, Antill et al. (1981) deleted items that were marked as "not understandable" by at least 10% of any of the 10 samples completing the scale; 123 of 512 items were deleted by this criterion. Considering that the deleted items were taken from existing measures or lists of items used to develop existing measures and keeping in mind that the respondents in this study were high school and college students, these findings should lead one to wonder whether existing scales include items that are not understandable to some respondents, particularly when the scales are used with less educated samples.

(4) Ray and Lovejoy (1984) modified the scale by combining the two forms, omitting the S items, and using antonyms in place of 35 of the 80 items. They found that 44 items did not differentiate between men and women. Using the 36 items that did differentiate between the sexes, they developed two 12-item scales.

(5) Several researchers working in Australia compared ASRS scores with other variables. Harris (1986) compared ASRS Form A scores of college students who had attended single-sex high schools with scores from college students who had attended coeducational high schools. No differences were found. Marsh and Jackson (1986) compared ASRS Form A scores of women athletes and nonathletes. They found that the athletes were more masculine than the nonathletes, but there were no differences in femininity scores. In several studies, ASRS Form A scores were related to scores on measures of self-concept (Marsh, 1987; Marsh & Myers, 1986; Marsh & Smith, 1984).

(6) In a study comparing Australian adolescent girls of Italian descent with those of Anglo descent, Grieve, Rosenthal, and Cavallo (1988) had a sample of 108 Australian girls rate themselves and their ideal selves on the Australian Sex Role Scale.

(7) Another scale, the Australian Sex Role Inventory (Drinkwater,

1979) (see separate entry), is quite similar to the ASRS. The development of both scales relates to the BSRI. Both were developed for use in Australia, and both ask respondents to provide self-ratings on a series of traits. The two scales differ in terms of number of items, number of response options, and the specific list of traits. Furthermore, the Australian Sex Role Inventory includes only positive traits.

AVAILABLE FROM: Antill, Cunningham, Russell, and Thompson, 1981
USED IN:

Antill, J. K., Cunningham, J. D., Russell, G., & Thompson, N. L. (1981). An Australian Sex-Role Scale. *Australian Journal of Psychology, 33*(2), 169–183.

Farnill, D., & Ball, I. L. (1985). Male and female factor structures of the Australian Sex-Role Scale (Form A). *Australian Psychologist, 20*(2), 205–213.

Grieve, N., Rosenthal, D., & Cavallo, A. (1988). Self-esteem and sex-role attitudes. *Psychology of Women Quarterly, 12*, 175–189.

Harris, M. B. (1986). Coeducation and sex roles. *Australian Journal of Education, 30*(2), 117–131.

Hong, S. M., Kavanagh, K., & Tippett, V. (1983). Factor structure of the Australian Sex-Role Scale. *Psychological Reports, 53*(2), 499–505.

Marsh, H. W. (1987). Masculinity, femininity, and androgyny: Their relations with multiple dimensions of self-concept. *Multivariate Behavioral Research, 22*(1), 91–118.

Marsh, H. W., & Jackson, S. A. (1986). Multidimensional self-concepts, masculinity, and femininity as a function of women's involvement in athletics. *Sex Roles, 15*(7/8), 391–415.

Marsh, H. W., & Myers, M. (1986). Masculinity, femininity, and androgyny: A methodological and theoretical critique. *Sex Roles, 14*(7/8), 397–430.

Marsh, H. W., & Smith, I. D. (1984). *Masculinity, femininity and androgyny: Their relations to multiple dimensions of self-concept.* Unpublished manuscript, University of Sydney, Australia. (ERIC Document Reproduction Service No. ED 252 529)

Ray, J. J., & Lovejoy, F. H. (1984). The great androgyny myth: Sex roles and mental health in the community at large. *Journal of Social Psychology, 124*, 237–246.

Russell, G., & Antill, J. (1984). An Australian Sex-Role Scale: Additional psychometric data and correlations with self-esteem. *Australian Psychologist, 19*(1), 13–18.

BIBLIOGRAPHY:

Bem, S. L. (1974). The measurement of psychological androgyny. *Journal of Consulting and Clinical Psychology, 42*, 155–162.

Drinkwater, B. A. (1979). Social desirability of characteristics of the Bem Sex-Role Inventory. *Australian Psychologist, 14*, 311–317.

Gough, H. G., & Heilbrun, A. B. (1965). *Manual for the Adjective Check List and the Need Scales for the ACL.* Palo Alto: Consulting Psychologists Press.

Rosenkrantz, P., Vogel, S., Bee, H., Broverman, I., & Broverman, D. M. (1968). Sex-role stereotypes and self-concepts in college students. *Journal of Consulting and Clinical Psychology, 32*, 287–295.

BAR-ILAN SEX ROLE INVENTORY (BI-SRI)
AUTHOR: David Tzuriel
DATE: 1984
VARIABLE: Masculinity and femininity
TYPE OF INSTRUMENT: Summated rating scale
DESCRIPTION: The Bar-Ilan Sex Role Inventory (BI-SRI) is a modification of the Bem Sex Role Inventory (BSRI) (Bem, 1974) (see separate entry). It contains 20 masculine, 20 feminine, and 20 neutral items, all of them positive traits. Each item is an adjective or adjective phrase that is to be rated on a 7-point scale ranging from "never or almost never true of me" to "always or almost always true of me." Nine masculine items, 9 feminine items, and 8 neutral items on the BI-SRI are identical to items on the BSRI. Three masculine items and 5 feminine items on the BI-SRI are connotatively similar to items on the BSRI. Twenty-six items on the BI-SRI—8 masculine, 6 feminine, and 12 neutral—are new.
SAMPLE ITEMS: (masculine) dynamic; solid
   (feminine) peaceful; romantic
   (neutral) fast; generous
PREVIOUS SUBJECTS: Eleventh and 12th graders in Israel; mothers in Israel
APPROPRIATE FOR: High school ages and older in Israel. The scale could also be completed by persons in the United States, but it was developed using data from Israeli students
ADMINISTRATION: Self-administered; about 20 minutes
SCORING: Items are individually scored on a 7-point scale and summed to yield two scores: a masculinity score and a femininity score. The median split procedure can then be applied to classify respondents as masculine, feminine, androgynous, or undifferentiated.
DEVELOPMENT: A list of 120 traits was developed, including all 60 traits from the BSRI plus 60 additional traits suggested by a sample of students. A different sample of 750 Israeli high school students rated each trait in terms of its social desirability for men or women in Israeli society. Traits were selected for the BI-SRI if they were rated as significantly more desirable for one sex than for the other. Undesirable traits were excluded, and 20 masculine, 20 feminine, and 20 neutral traits were selected for the final version of the BI-SRI.
RELIABILITY: No information was provided.
VALIDITY: As would be expected, males, compared to females, scored significantly higher ($p < .0001$) on the masculine items. Similarly, females compared to males scored significantly higher ($p < .0001$) on the feminine items.
NOTES & COMMENTS: Tzuriel (1984) used the BI-SRI in a study looking

at the relationship between sex role typing and ego identity. Tzuriel and Weller (1986) used the BI-SRI in a study looking at whether breast-feeding behavior in new mothers is related to their gender role.
AVAILABLE FROM: Tzuriel, 1984
USED IN:
Tzuriel, D. (1984). Sex role typing and ego identity in Israeli, Oriental, and Western adolescents. *Journal of Personality and Social Psychology, 46,* 440–457.
Tzuriel, D., & Weller, L. (1986). Social and psychological determinants of breast-feeding and bottle-feeding mothers. *Basic and Applied Social Psychology, 7*(2), 85–100.
BIBLIOGRAPHY:
Bem, S. L. (1974). The measurement of psychological androgyny. *Journal of Consulting and Clinical Psychology, 42,* 155–162.

BAUCOM SEX ROLE INVENTORY
AUTHOR: Donald H. Baucom
DATE: 1976
VARIABLE: Masculinity and femininity
TYPE OF INSTRUMENT: Alternate choice: true/false
DESCRIPTION: The Baucom Sex Role Inventory consists of two sub-scales: a 54-item masculinity subscale (MSC) and a 42-item femininity subscale (FMN). All of the items are taken from the California Psychological Inventory (CPI) (Gough, 1956) (see separate entry). Respondents generally complete the full CPI, but only the MSC and FMN items are scored.
SAMPLE ITEMS: (Masculinity) I think I would enjoy having authority over other people.
   (Femininity) The thought of being in an automobile accident is very frightening to me.
PREVIOUS SUBJECTS: College students; married and cohabiting couples
APPROPRIATE FOR: Ages 13 and older
ADMINISTRATION: Self-administered; the CPI can be completed in about an hour
SCORING: Baucom (1976) provided the information necessary for identifying and scoring the items on the MSC and FMN scales. He also provided means and standard deviations based on responses from those used to develop the scale. In assigning persons to sex types—feminine, masculine, androgynous, and undifferentiated—Baucom (1980) classified a person as high on masculinity and/or femininity only if the person scored in the upper third on that subscale relative to his or her own sex. Similarly, he classified a person as low on masculinity and/or femininity only if he or she scored in the bottom third relative to his or her own sex. Baucom (1980) provided the cutoff scores he used in making assignments to each of the four sex role categories.

DEVELOPMENT: A sample of 159 college men and 128 college women completed the CPI. The sample was divided into four groups: two-thirds of the men, one-third of the men, two-thirds of the women, and one-third of the women. For an item to be included on the MSC, it had to be responded to in the same direction by at least 70% of the males, and 10% fewer of the females had to respond to it in the same direction as the males. Items were added to the MSC if they correlated significantly with MSC scores ($p < .05$) in each of the four sample groups and if they did not correlate significantly with FMN scores. Items were selected for the FMN scale in a fashion analogous to that used to select MSC items. This resulted in a 54-item MSC scale, with 11 items keyed "true" and 43 items keyed "false," and a 42-item FMN scale, with 9 items keyed "true" and 33 items keyed "false."

RELIABILITY: Baucom (1976) reported test-retest reliabilities, with a 3-week interval between testings. For MSC scores, the stability coefficient was .93; for FMN scores, the stability coefficient was .80. Baucom did not report separate test-retest coefficients by sex.

VALIDITY: The objective was to create independent measures of masculinity and femininity. Baucom (1976) found that MSC scores were not significantly correlated with FMN scores in any of the four subgroups he studied.

Baucom (1976) found that males and females scored significantly differently ($p < .001$) on both MSC and FMN scores. He also compared MSC and FMN scores with scores on Fe, the femininity scale traditionally computed from the CPI. Correlations between Fe and MSC were significant and negative: $r = -.32$ for males and $r = -.34$ for females; correlations between Fe and FMN were significant and positive: $r = .60$ for males and $r = .20$ for females. Because the Fe scale overlapped considerably with the MSC and FMN scales, it is not surprising that all of these coefficients were significant.

Baucom and Sanders (1978) compared results obtained with the Baucom Sex Role Inventory with results obtained with the Bem Sex Role Inventory (BSRI) (Bem, 1974) (see separate entry). They found significant correlations between the two measures. For masculinity scores, the correlation was .56; for femininity scores, the correlation was .23. Baucom and Sanders also found that college women with high MSC scores were more profeminist on the Attitudes Toward Women Scale (Spence & Helmreich, 1972) (see separate entry), and members of the National Organization for Women were likely to have high MSC scores.

Baucom (1980) found that the four different sex role types—masculine, feminine, androgynous, and undifferentiated—have different profiles on the CPI. He described the four groups in terms of their CPI scores and their scores on the Adjective Check List (Gough & Heilbrun, 1965). For example, he found that "masculinity included self-confidence, mental alertness, assertiveness, leadership, and poise; femininity included socialization, self-control, development of ethical standards, and emotional sensitivity" (p. 262). Baucom also found that androgynous persons described themselves in favorable terms, but undifferentiated persons generally were unhappy, withdrawn, and distrustful.

Baucom and Danker-Brown (1983) used the Baucom Sex Role Inventory to identify four groups of college students: masculine, feminine, androgynous, and undifferentiated. Each identified student was then rated on the Adjective Check List by a peer selected by the student. Baucom and Danker-Brown found that the four sex role groups were perceived differently by their friends.

NOTES & COMMENTS: (1) The CPI Femininity scale (Fe) is different from the Baucom Sex Role Inventory. The CPI Fe scale is intended to differentiate males from females and is based on the assumption that femininity is bipolar, with femininity at one end of the continuum and masculinity at the other end. Thus, the CPI yields only a single Fe score, whereas the Baucom Sex Role Inventory provides separate scores for masculinity and femininity.

(2) The Baucom Sex Role Inventory was used to divide respondents into four groups—masculine, feminine, androgynous, and undifferentiated—so that the relationship between sex role type and learned helplessness could be explored (Baucom, 1983; Baucom & Danker-Brown, 1979, 1984). The Baucom Sex Role Inventory was used to study the relationship of gender roles, relationship satisfaction, and other relationship characteristics among married and cohabiting couples (Baucom & Aiken, 1984; Burger & Jacobson, 1979; House, 1986). Baucom, Besch, and Callahan (1985) looked at scores on the Baucom Sex Role Inventory, the BSRI, and the Adjective Check List and related them to levels of testosterone in college women.

AVAILABLE FROM: Baucom (1976) specifies which items from the California Psychological Inventory comprise the Baucom Sex Role inventory. The California Psychological Inventory can be purchased from Consulting Psychologists Press, 577 College Avenue, Palo Alto, CA 94306

USED IN:

Baucom, D. H. (1976). Independent masculinity and femininity scales on the California Psychological Inventory. *Journal of Consulting and Clinical Psychology*, 44, 876.

Baucom, D. H. (1980). Independent CPI masculinity and femininity scales: Psychological correlates and a sex-role typology. *Journal of Personality Assessment*, 44(3), 262–271.

Baucom, D. H. (1983). Sex role identity and the decision to regain control among women: A learned helplessness investigation. *Journal of Personality and Social Psychology*, 44(2), 334–353.

Baucom, D. H., & Aiken, P. A. (1984). Sex role identity, marital satisfaction, and response to behavioral marital therapy. *Journal of Consulting and Clinical Psychology*, *52*(3), 438–444.

Baucom, D. H., Besch, P. K., & Callahan, S. (1985). Relation between testosterone concentration, sex role identity, and personality among females. *Journal of Personality and Social Psychology*, *48*, 1218–1226.

Baucom, D. H., & Danker-Brown, P. (1979). Influence of sex roles on the development of learned helplessness. *Journal of Consulting and Clinical Psychology*, *47*, 928–936.

Baucom, D. H., & Danker-Brown, P. (1983). Peer ratings of males and females possessing different sex role identities. *Journal of Personality Assessment*, *47*(5), 494–506.

Baucom, D. H., & Danker-Brown, P. (1984). Sex role identity and sex-stereotyped tasks in the development of learned helplessness in women. *Journal of Personality and Social Research*, *46*(2), 422–430.

Baucom, D. H., & Sanders, B. S. (1978). Masculinity and femininity as factors in feminism. *Journal of Personality Assessment*, *42*, 378–384.

Burger, A. L., & Jacobson, N. S. (1979). The relationship between sex role characteristics, couple satisfaction and couple problem-solving skills. *American Journal of Family Therapy*, *7*(4), 52–60.

House, E. A. (1986). Sex role orientation and marital satisfaction in dual- and one-provider couples. *Sex Roles*, *14*, 245–259.

Klions, D. E., Sanders, K. S., Hudak, M. A., Dale, J. A., & Klions, H. I. (1987). Facial action patterns, electromyography, and moods in response to an insoluble task as a function of sex and sex-role differences. *Perceptual and Motor Skills*, *65*, 495–502.

BIBLIOGRAPHY:

Bem, S. L. (1974). The measurement of psychological androgyny. *Journal of Consulting and Clinical Psychology*, *42*, 155–162.

Gough, H. G. (1956). *California Psychological Inventory manual*. Palo Alto: Consulting Psychologists Press.

Gough, H. G., & Heilbrun, A. B. (1965). *The Adjective Check List manual*. Palo Alto: Consulting Psychologists Press.

Spence, J. T., & Helmreich, R. L. (1972). The Attitudes Toward Women Scale: An objective instrument to measure attitudes toward the rights and roles of women in contemporary society. *Catalog of Selected Documents in Psychology*, *2*, 66. (Ms. No. 153)

BEM SEX ROLE INVENTORY (BSRI)

AUTHOR: Sandra Bem

DATE: 1974

VARIABLE: Masculinity and femininity

DESCRIPTION: The Bem Sex Role Inventory (BSRI) consists of 60 adjectives or adjective phrases: 20 masculine, 20 feminine, and 20 neutral. Each adjective is accompanied by a 7-point rating scale ranging from 1, "never or almost never true," to 7, "always or almost always true." The scale yields scores on Masculinity and Femininity and is frequently used to classify people as masculine, feminine, androgynous, or undifferentiated.

The Short BSRI contains 10 masculine, 10 feminine, and 10 neutral items. Items were selected for the Short BSRI so as to maximize internal consistency on the Masculinity and Femininity scales and also to maximize the independence of the two scales. The item selection procedures resulted in the omission of several items that had previously been considered as somewhat negative traits; also the traits "masculine" and "feminine" were omitted from the Short BSRI. Overall, "the Femininity and Masculinity scales of the Short BSRI consist of items that represent the most desirable personality characteristics for a given sex, and the variances of their social desirability ratings are comparable" (Bem, 1981a, p. 14).

ARTICLES LISTED IN BEERE, 1979: 82

NOTES & COMMENTS: (1) The BSRI is by far the most commonly used measure in all areas of gender-related research. The literature search for this book identified 795 articles and 167 ERIC documents that used the BSRI. None of these overlaps the references listed in Beere (1979). Only the articles are listed here.

(2) Numerous researchers have modified the BSRI. Some modifications are not sufficient to label the revised instrument as a "new measure" (e.g., Antill & Russell, 1980; Lorr & Diorio, 1978; Rao, Gupta, & Murthy, 1982; Wheeless & Dierks-Stewart, 1981). Other modifications are sufficiently extensive to be called "new" measures. Five scales in this book are actually modifications of the BSRI: Drinkwater (1979) developed the Australian Sex Role Inventory, and Antill, Cunningham, Russell, and Thompson (1981) developed the Australian Sex Role Scale; both are modifications for use in Australia. Tzuriel (1984) constructed the Bar-Ilan Sex Role Inventory (BI-SRI), a modified BSRI for use in Israel. Thomas and Robinson (1981) constructed a modification of the BSRI, the Adolescent Sex Role Inventory (ASRI), and Kurdek and Siesky (1980) constructed one for children and titled it Children's Sex-Role Self-Concept Inventory.

Users of the BSRI have also modified the scale by asking respondents to use the BSRI to rate someone or something other than "self."

(3) College students comprise the groups most often tested with the BSRI. About 65% of the published studies using the BSRI tested college students. Homosexuals and transsexuals are frequently tested with the BSRI. The BSRI has also been given to athletes, physicians, attorneys, hotel employees, married couples, adolescents, infertile couples, parents-to-be, parents, senior citizens, college faculty, women awaiting trial, counselors in training, public school administrators and educators, medical, dental, and dental hygiene students, incarcerated criminals, women with gynecological problems, anorexics and bulimics, middle

managers, ministerial students and ministers, nursing students, psychiatric inpatients, meditators, teachers, psychotherapists, high school and college athletes, homosexual fathers, patients, physicians, career counseling clients, juvenile delinquents, physical educators, clinical psychologists, university faculty, police cadets, athletic administrators, health professionals, accountants, museum visitors, women receiving abortions, social workers, prostitutes, alcoholics, and schizophrenics. The BSRI has been used with Asian-Americans and Hispanic-Americans. It has been used in numerous foreign countries, sometimes in English and sometimes after translation into the native language. The countries have included Germany, New Zealand, Australia, Israel, India, West Indies, Ireland, Sweden, South Africa, Canada, Mexico, Saudi Arabia, Malaysia, and Finland.

(4) Some researchers have replicated, with and without modification, the item selection procedures Bem used to develop the BSRI. Item selection studies have been reported by Edwards and Ashworth (1977), Heerboth and Ramanaiah (1985), Ramanaiah and Hoffman (1984), Walkup and Abbott (1978), and Ward and Sethi (1986).

(5) There was considerable debate in the literature on the appropriate procedures for scoring gender role scales. Though most of the issues have now been resolved, researchers might be interested in articles that focus on the scoring of the BSRI. Some of the issues are discussed by Bryan, Coleman, and Ganong (1981), Faulkender (1987), Motowidlo (1981), Myers and Sugar (1979), and Orlofsky, Aslin, and Ginsburg (1977).

(6) The BSRI has frequently been compared to other gender role scales. Following is a list of the authors who compared the BSRI to at least one other gender role scale. Also listed are the scales to which the BSRI was compared. With the exception of the De Cecco-Shively Social Sex-Role Inventory (Shively, Rudolph, & De Cecco, 1978), the scales are all described in this book. The articles comparing scales include: Alumbaugh (1987): Masculine Gender Identity Scale and MMPI Mf scale; Betz and Bander (1980): MMPI Mf, CPI Fe, and PAQ; Bohannon and Mills (1979): CPI Fe; Cunningham and Antill (1980): PAQ, PRF ANDRO, CPI Fe, and Comrey Personality Scales; Edwards and Norcross (1980): PRF ANDRO; Gaa and Liberman (1981): PAQ; Gaa, Liberman, and Edwards (1979): PAQ; Gross, Batlis, Small, and Erdwins (1979): PAQ; Hawkins, Herron, Gibson, Hoban, and Herron (1988): PAQ, PRF ANDRO, and ACL; Herron, Goodman, and Herron (1983): PAQ, PRF ANDRO, and ACL; Kelly, Furman, and Young (1978): PAQ, PRF ANDRO, and ACL; Larsen and Seidman (1986): PRF ANDRO; Marsh and Myers (1986): Comrey Personality Scales and Australian Sex Role Scale; O'Grady, Freda, and Mikulka (1979): PAQ and ACL; Pearson (1980a): PAQ and ACL; Ramanaiah and Martin (1984): ACL and PRF ANDRO; Small, Erdwins, and Gross

(1979): ACL; Smith (1983): De Cecco-Shively Sex-Role Inventory and PAQ; Spence and Helmreich (1980): PAQ; Volentine (1981): MMPI Mf; and Wilson and Cook (1984): PAQ, ACL, and PRF ANDRO.

(7) Many researchers have looked at the factor analytic structure of the BSRI. Included among them are: Antill and Cunningham (1982a), Antill and Russell (1982), Belcher, Crocker, and Algina (1984), Bledsoe (1983b), Bohannon and Mills (1979), Carlsson (1981), Collins, Waters, and Waters (1979), Feather (1978), Gaa, Liberman, and Edwards (1979), Gross, Batlis, Small, and Erdwins (1979), Gruber and Powers (1982), Kimlicka, Wakefield, and Friedman (1980), Larsen and Seidman (1986), Lorr and Diorio (1978), Marsh and Myers (1986), Martin and Ramanaiah (1988), Pearson (1980a), Ratliff and Conley (1981), Ruch (1984), Sassenrath and Yonge (1979), Thompson and Melancon (1986), Waters, Waters, and Pincus (1977), and Waters and Popovich (1986).

(8) Issues of social desirability were the focus of articles by Puglisi (1980) and Taylor (1981). Issues regarding response styles were the focus of studies by Liberman and Gaa (1980, 1986) and Millimet and Votta (1979). Aspects of the scale's validity were studied by Carlsson and Magnusson (1980), Hinrichsen and Stone (1978), Myers and Gonda (1982), Schmitt and Millard (1988), Taylor (1984), and Uleman and Weston (1986). The stability of BSRI scores over time was studied by Yanico (1985).

(9) There have been cross-cultural studies using the BSRI. Included among them are Reed-Sanders, Dodder, and Webster (1985), Ross (1983a), and Rowland (1977).

(10) For general articles that deal with the psychometric properties of the BSRI, see Larsen and Seidman (1986), Pedhazur and Tetenbaum (1979), Rowland (1980), Sines and Russell (1978), Wheeless and Dierks-Stewart (1981), and Williamson and Holman (1980).

(11) According to Jensen, Witcher, and Upton (1987), the BSRI instructions require a ninth-grade reading level; the items on the BSRI require college level reading ability.

(12) The BSRI is listed in the *Ninth Mental Measurements Yearbook* (entry 137).

AVAILABLE FROM: Consulting Psychologists Press, 577 College Avenue, Palo Alto, CA 94306

USED IN:

Abbott, M. W., & Koopman Boyden, P. G. (1981). Expectations and predictors of the division of labour within marriage. *New Zealand Psychologist, 10*(1), 24–32.

Abrahams, B., Feldman, S. S., & Nash, S. C. (1978). Sex role self-concept and sex role attitudes: Enduring personality characteristics or adaptations to changing life situations? *Developmental Psychology, 14*(4), 393–400.

Adams, C. H., & Sherer, M. (1982). Sex-role orientation and psychological adjustment: Comparison of MMPI profiles among college women and housewives. *Journal of Personality Assessment, 46*(6), 607–613.

Adams, C. H., & Sherer, M. (1985). Sex-role orientation and psychological adjustment: Implications for the masculinity model. *Sex Roles, 12,* 1211–1218.

Al Qataee, A. (1984). The effect of exposure to Western cultures on the sex-role identity of Saudi Arabians. *Contemporary Educational Psychology, 9*(3), 303–312.

Allgeier, E. R. (1981). The influence of androgynous identification on heterosexual relations. *Sex Roles, 7*(3), 321–330.

Alperson, B. L., & Friedman, W. J. (1983). Some aspects of the interpersonal phenomenology of heterosexual dyads with respect to sex-role stereotypes. *Sex Roles, 9*(4), 453–474.

Alter, R. C. (1984). Abortion outcome as a function of sex-role identification. *Psychology of Women Quarterly, 8,* 211–233.

Alumbaugh, R. V. (1987). Contrast of the gender-identity scale with Bem's sex-role measures and the MF scale of the MMPI. *Perceptual and Motor Skills, 64,* 136–138.

Ames, M., & Kidd, A. H. (1979). Machiavellianism and women's grade point averages. *Psychological Reports, 44*(1), 223–228.

Amstey, F. H., & Whitbourne, S. K. (1981). Continuing education, identity, sex role, and psychosocial development in adult women. *Sex Roles, 7*(1), 49–58.

Andersen, M. B., & Williams, J. M. (1987). Gender role and sport competition anxiety: A re-examination. *Research Quarterly for Exercise and Sport, 58,* 52–56.

Andersen, S. M., & Bem, S. L. (1981). Sex typing and androgyny in dyadic interaction: Individual differences in responsiveness to physical attractiveness. *Journal of Personality and Social Psychology, 41*(1), 74–86.

Anderson, K. L. (1986). Androgyny, flexibility, and individualism. *Journal of Personality Assessment, 50*(2), 265–278.

Anderson, L. R. (1987). Correlates of self-monitoring, sex role typing, and social skills in New Zealand and the United States. *Journal of Social Psychology, 127*(6), 677–679.

Antill, J. K. (1983). Sex role complementarity versus similarity in married couples. *Journal of Personality and Social Psychology, 45*(1), 145–155.

Antill, J. K., & Cotton, S. (1988). Factors affecting the division of labor in households. *Sex Roles, 18*(9/10), 531–553.

Antill, J. K., Cotton, S., & Tindale, S. (1983). Egalitarian or traditional: Correlates of the perception of an ideal marriage. *Australian Journal of Psychology, 35*(2), 245–257.

Antill, J. K., & Cunningham, J. D. (1979). Self-esteem as a function of masculinity in both sexes. *Journal of Consulting and Clinical Psychology, 47*(4), 783–785.

Antill, J. K., & Cunningham, J. D. (1980). The relationship of masculinity, femininity, and androgyny to self-esteem. *Australian Journal of Psychology, 32*(3), 195–207.

Antill, J. K., & Cunningham, J. D. (1982a). Comparative factor analyses of the

Personal Attributes Questionnaire and the Bem Sex-Role Inventory. *Social Behavior and Personality*, *10*(2), 163–172.

Antill, J. K., & Cunningham, J. D. (1982b). A critical appraisal of the PRF AN-DRO scale. *Current Psychological Research*, *2*(4), 223–230.

Antill, J. K., & Cunningham, J. D. (1982c). Sex differences in performance on ability tests as a function of masculinity, femininity, and androgyny. *Journal of Personality and Social Psychology*, *42*(4), 718–728.

Antill, J. K., & Russell, G. (1980). A preliminary comparison between two forms of the Bem Sex-Role Inventory. *Australian Psychologist*, *15*(3), 427–435.

Antill, J. K., & Russell, G. (1982). The factor structure of the Bem Sex-Role Inventory: Method and sample comparisons. *Australian Journal of Psychology*, *34*(2), 183–193.

Appelgryn, A. E., & Plug, C. (1981). Application of the theory of relative deprivation to occupational discrimination against women. *South African Journal of Psychology*, *11*(4), 143–147.

Arkin, R. M., & Johnson, K. S. (1980). Effects of increased occupational participation by women on androgynous and nonandrogynous individuals' ratings of occupational attractiveness. *Sex Roles*, *6*(4), 593–605.

Arkkelin, D., & Simmons, R. (1985). The "good manager": Sex-typed, androgynous, or likable? *Sex Roles*, *12*, 1187–1198.

Ashford, B., Collins, J. K., & McCabe, M. P. (1979). Sex role and age as variables in hypnotic susceptibility. *Australian Journal of Clinical and Experimental Hypnosis*, *7*(2), 125–133.

Astley, S. L., & Downey, R. G. (1980). Sex role consequences: Depends on the point of view. *Journal of College Student Personnel*, *21*, 419–426.

Auten, P. D., Hull, D. B., & Hull, J. H. (1985). Sex role orientation and Type A behavior pattern. *Psychology of Women Quarterly*, *9*(2), 288–290.

Avery, A. W. (1982). Escaping loneliness in adolescence: The case for androgyny. *Journal of Youth and Adolescence*, *11*(6), 451–459.

Babl, J. D. (1979). Compensatory masculine responding as a function of sex role. *Journal of Consulting and Clinical Psychology*, *47*(2), 252–257.

Babladelis, G. (1978). Sex-role concepts and flexibility on measures of thinking, feeling, and behaving. *Psychological Reports*, *42*(1), 99–105.

Bailey, W. C., Hendrick, C., & Hendrick, S. S. (1987). Relation of sex and gender role to love, sexual attitudes, and self-esteem. *Sex Roles*, *16*(11/12), 637–648.

Baldwin, A. C., Critelli, J. W., Stevens, L. C., & Russell, S. (1986). Androgyny and sex role measurement: A personal construct approach. *Journal of Personality and Social Psychology*, *51*(5), 1081–1088.

Bancroft, J., Axworthy, D., & Ratcliffe, S. (1982). The personality and psychosexual development of boys with 47 XXY chromosome constitution. *Journal of Child Psychology and Psychiatry and Allied Disciplines*, *23*(2), 169–180.

Bander, R. S., & Betz, N. E. (1981). The relationship of sex and sex role to trait and situationally specific anxiety types. *Journal of Research in Personality*, *15*(3), 312–322.

Banikiotes, P. G., Kubinski, J. A., & Pursell, S. A. (1981). Sex role orientation, self-disclosure, and gender-related perceptions. *Journal of Counseling Psychology*, *28*(2), 140–146.

Banikiotes, P. G., & Merluzzi, T. V. (1981). Impact of counselor gender and counselor sex role orientation on perceived counselor characteristics. *Journal of Counseling Psychology*, *28*(4), 342–348.

Banikiotes, P. G., Neimeyer, G. J., & Lepkowsky, C. (1981). Gender and sex-role orientation effects on friendship choice. *Personality and Social Psychology Bulletin*, *7*(4), 605–610.

Bankart, C. P., & Wittenbraker, J. E. (1980). Sex-role orientation of perceivers and targets as variables in the person perception process. *Psychological Record*, *30*(2), 143–153.

Barak, A., Golan, E., & Fisher, W. A. (1988). Effects of counselor gender and gender-role orientation on client career choice traditionality. *Journal of Counseling Psychology*, *34*(3), 287–293.

Basow, S. A., & Crawley, D. M. (1982). Helping behavior: Effects of sex and sex-typing. *Social Behavior and Personality*, *10*, 69–72.

Basow, S. A., & Medcalf, K. L. (1988). Academic achievement and attributions among college students: Effects of gender and sex typing. *Sex Roles*, *19*, 555–567.

Bassoff, E. S. (1984). Relationships of sex-role characteristics and psychological adjustment in new mothers. *Journal of Marriage and the Family*, *46*, 449–454.

Batlis, N., & Small, A. (1982). Sex roles and Type A behavior. *Journal of Clinical Psychology*, *38*(2), 315–316.

Batlis, N., Small, A., Erdwins, C., & Gross, R. (1981). Sex-role and need configuration. *Multivariate Experimental Clinical Research*, *5*(2), 53–65.

Baucom, D. H., Besch, P. K., & Callahan, S. (1985). Relation between testosterone concentration, sex role identity, and personality among females. *Journal of Personality and Social Psychology*, *48*(5), 1218–1226.

Baucom, D. H., & Sanders, B. S. (1978). Masculinity and femininity as factors in feminism. *Journal of Personality Assessment*, *42*(4), 378–384.

Baumrind, D. (1982). Are androgynous individuals more effective persons and parents? *Child Development*, *53*(1), 44–75.

Baxter, L. A., & Shepard, T. L. (1978). Sex role identity, sex of other, and affective relationship as determinants of interpersonal conflict-management Styles. *Sex Roles*, *4*, 813–825.

Beauvais, C., & Spence, J. T. (1987). Gender, prejudice, and categorization. *Sex Roles*, *16*(1/2), 89–100.

Beckham, J. C., Carbonell, J. L., & Gustafson, D. J. (1988). Are there sex differences in problem solving? An investigation of problem context and sex role type. *Journal of Psychology*, *122*, 21–32.

Beckman, L. J. (1978). Sex-role conflict in alcoholic women: Myth or reality. *Journal of Abnormal Psychology*, *87*(4), 408–417.

Bedeian, A. G., & Hyder, J. L. (1977). Sex-role attitude as a moderator in the relationship between locus of control and achievement. *Psychological Reports*, *41*(3), 1172–1174.

Belcher, M. J., Algina, J., & Crocker, L. (1985). Comparing self-report and desirability ratings in sex role assessment. *Educational and Psychological Research*, *5*(2), 117–129.

Belcher, M. J., Crocker, L. M., & Algina, J. (1984). Can the same instrument be used to measure sex-role perceptions of males and females? *Measurement and Evaluation in Guidance, 17*(1), 15–23.

Bell, G. C., & Schaffer, K. F. (1984). The effects of psychological androgyny on attributions of causality for success and failure. *Sex Roles, 11,* 1045–1055.

Bell, N. J., Avery, A. W., Jenkins, D., Feld, J., & Schoenrock, C. J. (1985). Family relationships and social competence during late adolescence. *Journal of Youth and Adolescence, 14*(2), 109–119.

Bell, N. J., McGhee, P. E., & Duffey, N. S. (1986). Interpersonal competence, social assertiveness and the development of humour. *British Journal of Developmental Psychology, 4*(1), 51–55.

Bell, N. J., Schoenrock, C. J., Young, M., Avery, A. W., Croft, C. A., & Lane, S. (1985). Family constellation, social competence, and sex-role development. *Journal of Genetic Psychology, 146*(2), 273–275.

Bem, S. L. (1979). Theory and measurement of androgyny: A reply to the Pedhazur-Tetenbaum and Locksley-Colten critiques. *Journal of Personality and Social Psychology, 37*(6), 1047–1054.

Bem, S. L. (1981a). *Bem Sex-Role Inventory: Professional manual.* Palo Alto: Consulting Psychologists Press.

Bem, S. L. (1981b). Gender schema theory: A cognitive account of sex typing. *Psychological Review, 88*(4), 354–364.

Bennett, B. W., & Grosser, G. S. (1981). Movement toward androgyny in college females through experimental education. *Journal of Psychology, 107*(2), 177–183.

Bennett, S. M. (1984). Family environment for sexual learning as a function of fathers' involvement in family work and discipline. *Adolescence, 19*(75), 609–627.

Benson, B. A. (1981). Personality correlates of self-punitive behavior. *Journal of Abnormal Psychology, 90*(2), 183–185.

Benz, C. R., Pfeiffer, I., & Newman, I. (1981). Sex role expectations of classroom teachers, Grades 1–12. *American Educational Research Journal, 18*(3), 289–302.

Bernard, J. L., & Bernard, M. L. (1985). Courtship violence and sex-typing. *Family Relations, 34,* 573–576.

Bernard, L. C. (1980). Multivariate analysis of new sex role formulations and personality. *Journal of Personality and Social Psychology, 38*(2), 323–336.

Bernard, L. C. (1982). Sex-role factor identification and sexual preference of men. *Journal of Personality Assessment, 46*(3), 292–299.

Bernard, L. C., & Epstein, D. J. (1978a). Androgyny scores of matched homosexual and heterosexual males. *Journal of Homosexuality, 4*(2), 169–178.

Bernard, L. C., & Epstein, D. J. (1978b). Sex role conformity in homosexual and heterosexual males. *Journal of Personality Assessment, 42*(5), 505–511.

Bernstein, B. L., Hofmann, B., & Wade, P. (1987). Preferences for counselor gender: Students' sex role, other characteristics, and type of problem. *Journal of Counseling Psychology, 34*(1), 20–26.

Betz, N. E., & Bander, R. S. (1980). Relationships of MMPI Mf and CPI Fe scales of fourfold sex role classifications. *Journal of Personality and Social Psychology, 39,* 1245–1248.

Betz, N. E., & Hackett, G. (1983). The relationship of mathematics self-efficacy expectations to the selection of science-based college majors. *Journal of Vocational Behavior, 23*(3), 329–345.

Birdsall, P. (1980). A comparative analysis of male and female managerial communication style in two organizations. *Journal of Vocational Behavior, 16,* 183–196.

Black, K. N., & Stevenson, M. R. (1984). The relationship of self-reported sex-role characteristics and attitudes toward homosexuality. *Journal of Homosexuality, 10,* 83–93.

Blackman, S. (1986). The masculinity-femininity of women who study college mathematics. *Sex Roles, 15,* 33–41.

Blakemore, J. E. (1981). Age and sex differences in interaction with a human infant. *Child Development, 52*(1), 386–388.

Blanchard-Fields, F., & Friedt, L. (1988). Age as a moderator of the relation between three dimensions of satisfaction and sex role. *Sex Roles, 18*(11/12), 759–768.

Bledsoe, J. C. (1983a). Comparison of selected methods of transformations of proportions. *Perceptual and Motor Skills, 57*(2), 423–426.

Bledsoe, J. C. (1983b). Factorial validity of the BEM Sex-Role Inventory. *Perceptual and Motor Skills, 56*(1), 55–58.

Bledsoe, J. C. (1983c). Female teachers' classroom interactions with boys and girls as predictors of their self-definition of sex-role type. *Psychological Reports, 52*(3), 993–994.

Bledsoe, J. C. (1983d). Sex differences in female teachers' approval and disapproval behaviors as related to their self-definition of sex-role type. *Psychological Reports, 53*(3), 711–714.

Bohannon, W. E., & Mills, C. J. (1979). Psychometric properties and underlying assumptions of two measures of masculinity/femininity. *Psychological Reports, 44*(2), 431–450.

Boyd, D. A., & Parish, T. S. (1984). An investigation of father loss and college students' androgyny scores. *Journal of Genetic Psychology, 145*(2), 279–280.

Boyden, T., Carroll, J. S., & Maier, R. A. (1984). Similarity and attraction in homosexual males: The effects of age and masculinity-femininity. *Sex Roles, 10,* 939–948.

Bradbury, T. N., & Fincham, F. D. (1988). Individual difference variables in close relationships: A contextual model of marriage as an integrative framework. *Journal of Personality and Social Psychology, 54,* 713–721.

Branscombe, N. R., Deaux, K., & Lerner, M. S. (1985). Individual differences and the influence of context on categorization and prejudice. *Representative Research in Social Psychology, 15,* 25–35.

Bray, J. H., & Howard, G. S. (1980). Interaction of teacher and student sex and sex role orientations and student evaluations of college instruction. *Contemporary Educational Psychology, 5*(3), 241–248.

Brehony, K. A., & Geller, E. S. (1981). Relationships between psychological androgyny, social conformity, and perceived locus of control. *Psychology of Women Quarterly, 6*(2), 204–217.

Brems, C., & Schlottmann, R. S. (1988). Gender-bound definitions of mental health. *Journal of Psychology, 122,* 5–14.

Brewer, M. B., & Blum, M. W. (1979). Sex-role androgyny and patterns of causal attribution for academic achievement. *Sex Roles, 5*(6), 783–796.

Bridges, J. S. (1978). Correlates of sex role and attitudes toward women. *Psychological Reports, 43*(3), 1279–1282.

Bridges, J. S. (1981). Sex-typed may be beautiful but androgynous is good. *Psychological Reports, 48*(1), 267–272.

Briere, J., Ward, R., & Hartsough, W. R. (1983). Sex-typing and cross-sex-typing in "androgynous" subjects. *Journal of Personality Assessment, 47*(3), 300–302.

Brodzinsky, D. M., Barnet, K., & Aiello, J. R. (1981). Sex of subject and gender identity as factors in humor appreciation. *Sex Roles, 7*, 561–573.

Brooks-Gunn, J., & Fisch, M. (1980). Psychological androgyny and college students' judgments of mental health. *Sex Roles, 6*(4), 575–580.

Brouse, S. H. (1985). Effect of gender role identity on patterns of feminine and self-concept scores from late pregnancy to early postpartum. *Advances in Nursing Science, 7*(3), 32–48.

Bruch, M. A., Heisler, B. D., & Conroy, C. G. (1981). Effects of conceptual complexity on assertive behavior. *Journal of Counseling Psychology, 28*(5), 377–385.

Bryan, L., Coleman, M., & Ganong, L. (1981). Geometric mean as a continuous measure of androgyny. *Psychological Reports, 48*(3), 691–694.

Burchardt, C. J., & Servin, L. A. (1982). Psychological androgyny and personality adjustment in college and psychiatric populations. *Sex Roles, 8*, 835–851.

Burda, P. C., Vaux, A., & Schill, T. (1984). Social support resources: Variation across sex and sex role. *Personality and Social Psychology Bulletin, 10*(1), 119–126.

Burge, P. L. (1983). Sex-role identity and work perceptions of nontraditional vocational graduates. *Journal of Vocational Education Research, 8*(2), 41–54.

Buriel, R., & Saenz, E. (1980). Psychocultural characteristics of college-bound and noncollege-bound Chicanas. *Journal of Social Psychology, 110*(2), 245–251.

Burke, K. L. (1986). Comparison of psychological androgyny within a sample of female college athletes who participate in sports traditionally appropriate and traditionally inappropriate for competition by females. *Perceptual and Motor Skills, 63*, 779–782.

Bussey, K., & Maughan, B. (1982). Gender differences in moral reasoning. *Journal of Personality and Social Psychology, 42*(4), 701–706.

Butt, D. S. (1985). Psychological motivation and sports performance in world class women field hockey players. *International Journal of Women's Studies, 8*(4), 328–337.

Butterfield, D. A., & Powell, G. N. (1981). Convergent validity in students' perceptions of Jimmy Carter, Ted Kennedy, and the ideal president. *Perceptual and Motor Skills, 52*(1), 51–56.

Callan, V. J. (1982). How do Australians value children? A review and research update using the perceptions of parents and voluntarily childless adults. *Australian and New Zealand Journal of Sociology, 18*(3), 384–398.

Callan, V. J. (1983a). Childlessness and partner selection. *Journal of Marriage and the Family, 45*(1), 181–186.

Callan, V. J. (1983b). Factors affecting early and late deciders of voluntary childlessness. *Journal of Social Psychology, 119*(2), 261–268.

Callan, V. J. (1985). Comparisons of mothers of one child by choice with mothers wanting a second birth. *Journal of Marriage and the Family, 47*(1), 155–164.

Callan, V. J., & Gallois, C. (1985). Sex-role attitudes and attitudes to marriage among urban Greek-Australian and Anglo-Australian youth. *Journal of Comparative Family Studies, 16*(3), 345–356.

Calway-Fagen, N., Wallston, B. S., & Gabel, H. (1979). The relationship between attitudinal and behavioral measures of sex preference. *Psychology of Women Quarterly, 4*(2), 274–280.

Cano, L., Solomon, S., & Holmes, D. S. (1984). Fear of success: The influence of sex, sex-role identity, and components of masculinity. *Sex Roles, 10*, 341–346.

Capurso, R. J., & Blocher, D. H. (1985). The effects of sex-role consistent and inconsistent information on the social perceptions of complex, noncomplex, androgynous, and sex-typed women. *Journal of Vocational Behavior, 26*(1), 79–91.

Card, A. L., Jackson, L. A., Stollak, G. E., & Ialongo, N. S. (1986). Gender role and person-perception accuracy. *Sex Roles, 15*, 159–171.

Cardell, M., Finn, S., & Marecek, J. (1981). Sex-role identity, sex-role behavior, and satisfaction in heterosexual, lesbian, and gay male couples. *Psychology of Women Quarterly, 5*(3), 488–494.

Carlson, H. M., & Baxter, L. A. (1984). Androgyny, depression, and self-esteem in Irish homosexual and heterosexual males and females. *Sex Roles, 10*, 457–467.

Carlson, H. M., & Steuer, J. (1985). Age, sex-role categorization, and psychological health in American homosexual and heterosexual men and women. *Journal of Social Psychology, 125*(2), 203–211.

Carlsson, M. (1981). Note on the factor structure of the Bem Sex-Role Inventory. *Scandinavian Journal of Psychology, 22*(2), 123–127.

Carlsson, M., & Magnusson, E. (1980). Construct validation of the Bem Sex Role Inventory. *Scandinavian Journal of Psychology, 21*(1), 27–31.

Caron, S. L., Carter, D. B., & Brightman, L. A. (1985). Sex-role orientation and attitudes towards women: Differences among college athletes and nonathletes. *Perceptual and Motor Skills, 61*(3), 803–806.

Carr, G. D., & Wilson, C. P. (1983). The use of the Bem Sex-Role Inventory and other data. *Journal of Business Education, 58*, 214–217.

Carsrud, A. L., & Carsrud, K. B. (1979). The relationship of sex role and levels of defensiveness to self-reports of fear and anxiety. *Journal of Clinical Psychology, 35*(3), 573–575.

Carter, D. B. (1985). Relationships between cognitive flexibility and sex-role orientation in young adults. *Psychological Reports, 57*(3), 763–766.

Cash, T. F., & Kilcullen, R. N. (1985). The aye of the beholder: Susceptibility to sexism and beautyism in the evaluation of managerial applicants. *Journal of Applied Social Psychology, 15*(7), 591–605.

Cash, T. F., & Smith, E. (1982). Physical attractiveness and personality among American college students. *Journal of Psychology, 111*(2), 183–191.

Cegala, D. J. (1984). Affective and cognitive manifestations of interaction involvement during unstructured and competitive interactions. *Communication Monographs, 51*(4), 320–338.

Chalip, L., Villiger, J., & Duignan, P. (1980). Sex-role identity in a select sample of women field hockey players. *International Journal of Sport Psychology, 11*(4), 240–248.

Chernovetz, M. E., Jones, W. H., & Hansson, R. O. (1979). Predictability, attentional focus, sex role orientation, and menstrual-related stress. *Psychosomatic Medicine, 41*(5), 383–391.

Clarey, J. H. (1985). Resocialization: A strategy for moving beyond stereotypes. *Journal of Counseling and Development, 64*(3), 195–197.

Clarey, J. H., & Sanford, A. (1982). Female career preference and androgyny. *Vocational Guidance Quarterly, 30*(3), 258–264.

Clark, M. L. (1986). Predictors of scientific majors for black and white college students. *Adolescence, 21*, 205–213.

Clark-Stedman, M., & Wolleat, P. L. (1979). A nonsexist group-counseling intervention: Moving toward androgyny. *School Counselor, 27*(2), 110–118.

Clingman, J. M. (1983). The double standard of age. *Journal of Psychology, 115*(2), 281–290.

Cohen, D., & Schmidt, J. P. (1979). Ambiversion: Characteristics of midrange responders on the introversion-extraversion continuum. *Journal of Personality Assessment, 43*(5), 514–516.

Coleman, K. H., Weinman, M. L., & Hsi, B. P. (1980). Factors affecting conjugal violence. *Journal of Psychology, 105*(2), 197–202.

Coleman, M., & Ganong, L. H. (1985). Love and sex role stereotypes: Do macho men and feminine women make better lovers? *Journal of Personality and Social Psychology, 49*(1), 170–176.

Colley, A., Roberts, N., & Chipps, A. (1985). Sex-role identity, personality and participation in team and individual sports by males and females. *International Journal of Sport Psychology, 16*(2), 103–112.

Collins, J., Reardon, M., & Waters, L. K. (1980). Occupational interest and perceived personal success: Effects of gender, sex-role orientation, and the sexual composition of the occupation. *Psychological Reports, 47*(3), 1155–1159.

Collins, M., Waters, C. W., & Waters, L. K. (1979). Factor analysis of sex-typed items from the BEM Sex-Role Inventory: A replication. *Psychological Reports, 44*(2), 517–518.

Collins, M., Waters, L. K., & Waters, C. W. (1979). Relationships between sex-role orientation and attitudes toward women as managers. *Psychological Reports, 45*(3), 828–830.

Conley, J. J. (1978). Sex differences and androgyny in fantasy content. *Journal of Personality Assessment, 42*(6), 604–610.

Cooper, K., Chassin, L. A., & Zeiss, A. (1985). The relation of sex-role self-concept and sex-role attitudes to the marital satisfaction and personal adjustment of dual-worker couples with preschool children. *Sex Roles, 12*, 227–241.

Costos, D. (1986). Sex role identity in young adults: Its parental antecedents and relation to ego development. *Journal of Personality and Social Psychology, 50*(3), 602–611.

Covell, K., & Turnbull, W. (1982). The long-term effects of father absence in childhood on male university students' sex-role identity and personal adjustment. *Journal of Genetic Psychology, 141*(2), 271–276.

Crombie, G. (1983). Women's attribution patterns and their relation to achievement: An examination of within-sex differences. *Sex Roles, 9*(12), 1171–1182.

Cunningham, A., & Saayman, G. S. (1984). Effective functioning in dual-career families: An investigation. *Journal of Family Therapy, 6*(4), 365–380.

Cunningham, J. D., & Antill, J. K. (1980). A comparison among five masculinity-femininity-androgyny instruments and two methods of scoring androgyny. *Australian Psychologist, 15*(3), 437–448.

Cunningham, J. D., & Antill, J. K. (1984). Changes in masculinity and femininity across the family life cycle: A reexamination. *Developmental Psychology, 20*(6), 1135–1141.

Currant, E. P., Dickson, A. L., Anderson, H. N., & Faulkender, P. J. (1979). Sex-role stereotyping and assertive behavior. *Journal of Psychology, 101*(2), 223–228.

Dailey, D. M. (1979). Adjustment of heterosexual and homosexual couples in pairing relationships: An exploratory study. *Journal of Sex Research, 15*(2), 143–157.

Dailey, D. M. (1983). Androgyny, sex-role stereotypes, and clinical judgment. *Social Work Research and Abstracts, 19*(1), 20–24.

Dailey, D. M., & Rosenzweig, J. (1988). Variations in men's psychological sex role self-perception as a function of work, social and sexual life roles. *Journal of Sex and Marital Therapy, 14*(3), 225–240.

Daitzman, R., & Zuckerman, M. (1980). Disinhibitory sensation seeking, personality and gonadal hormones. *Personality and Individual Differences, 1*(2), 103–110.

Davis, W. E., Pursell, S. A., & Burnham, R. A. (1979). Alcoholism, sex-role orientation and psychological distress. *Journal of Clinical Psychology, 35*(1), 209–212.

de Fronzo, J., & Boudreau, F. (1977). An alternative procedure for assessing effects of psychological androgyny. *Psychological Reports, 41*(3), 1059–1062.

de Fronzo, J., & Boudreau, F. (1979). Further research into antecedents and correlates of androgyny. *Psychological Reports, 44*(1), 23–29.

Deaux, K., Kite, M. E., & Lewis, L. L. (1985). Clustering and gender schemata: An uncertain link. *Personality and Social Psychology Bulletin, 11*(4), 387–397.

Deaux, K., & Major, B. (1977). Sex-related patterns in the unit of perception. *Personality and Social Psychology Bulletin, 3*(2), 297–300.

DeGregorio, E., & Carver, C. S. (1980). Type A behavior pattern, sex role orientation, and psychological adjustment. *Journal of Personality and Social Psychology, 39*(2), 286–293.

della Selva, P. C., & Dusek, J. B. (1984). Sex role orientation and resolution of Eriksonian crises during the late adolescent years. *Journal of Personality and Social Psychology, 47*(1), 204–212.

DeLucia, J. L. (1987). Gender role identity and dating behavior: What is the relationship? *Sex Roles, 17,* 153–161.

Denmark, F. L., Shaw, J. S., & Ciali, S. D. (1985). The relationship among sex roles, living arrangements, and the division of household responsibilities. *Sex Roles, 12,* 617–625.

DePaulo, B. M. (1978). Accepting help from teachers—when the teachers are children. *Human Relations, 31*(5), 459–474.

Dicken, C. (1982). Sex-role orientation and smoking. *Psychological Reports, 51*(2), 483–489.

Dillon, K. M., Wolf, E., & Katz, H. (1985). Sex roles, gender, and fear. *Journal of Psychology, 119*(4), 355–359.

Doerfler, M. C., & Kammer, P. P. (1986). Workaholism, sex, and sex role stereotyping among female professionals. *Sex Roles, 14,* 551–560.

Doherty, P. A., & Schmidt, M. R. (1978). Sex-typing and self-concept in college women. *Journal of College Student Personnel, 19*(6), 493–497.

Donio, D., & Lester, D. (1985). Factors affecting the sex of one's friends. *Psychological Reports, 57*(3), 1040.

Doolittle, T. M., Wolfe, J. A., & Hart, P. P. (1983). CAPS members as an androgynous population: Evaluation of a self report questionnaire. *Journal of Psychology and Christianity, 2*(1), 19–26.

Dorgan, M., Goebel, B. L., & House, A. E. (1983). Generalizing about sex role and self-esteem: Results or effects? *Sex Roles, 9*(6), 719–724.

Downey, A. M. (1984a). The relationship of sex-role orientation to death anxiety in middle-aged males. *Omega Journal of Death and Dying, 14*(4), 355–367.

Downey, A. M. (1984b). The relationship of sex-role orientation to self-perceived health status in middle-aged males. *Sex Roles, 11,* 211–225.

Downing, N. E., & Nevill, D. D. (1983). Conceptions of psychological health: The role of gender and sex-role identity. *British Journal of Social Psychology, 22*(2), 171–173.

Drinkwater, B. A. (1979). Social desirability of characteristics of the Bem Sex-Role Inventory. *Australian Psychologist, 14*(3), 311–317.

Duhon, M. D., & Brown, B. B. (1987). Self-disclosure as an influence strategy: Effects of machiavellianism, androgyny, and sex. *Sex Roles, 16,* 109–123.

Dunn, P. K., & Ondercin, P. (1981). Personality variables related to compulsive eating in college women. *Journal of Clinical Psychology, 37*(1), 43–49.

Edwards, A. L., & Ashworth, C. D. (1977). A replication study of item selection for the Bem Sex Role Inventory. *Applied Psychological Measurement, 1*(4), 501–507.

Edwards, K. J., & Norcross, B. N. (1980). A comparison of two sex-role androgyny measures in a study of sex-role identity for incarcerated delinquent and nondelinquent females. *Sex Roles, 6*(6), 859–870.

Edwards, S. W., Gordin, R. D., & Henschen, K. P. (1984). Sex-role orientations of female NCAA championship gymnasts. *Perceptual and Motor Skills, 58*(2), 625–626.

Ekhardt, B. N., & Goldsmith, W. M. (1984). Personality factors of men and women pastoral candidates: I. Motivational profiles. *Journal of Psychology and Theology, 12*(2), 109–118.

Elpern, S., & Karp, S. A. (1984). Sex-role orientation and depressive symptomatology. *Sex Roles, 10*, 987–992.

Epstein, N., & Jayne, C. (1981). Perceptions of cotherapists as a function of therapist sex roles and observer sex roles. *Sex Roles, 7*(5), 497–509.

Erdwins, C., Small, A. C., & Gross, R. (1980). The relationship of sex role to self-concept. *Journal of Clinical Psychology, 36*(1), 111–115.

Erdwins, C. J., Tyer, Z. E., & Mellinger, J. C. (1980). Personality traits of mature women in student versus homemaker roles. *Journal of Psychology, 105*(2), 189–195.

Erdwins, C. J., Tyer, Z. E., & Mellinger, J. C. (1983). A comparison of sex role and related personality traits in young, middle-aged, and older women. *International Journal of Aging and Human Development, 17*(2), 141–152.

Erkut, S. (1983). Exploring sex differences in expectancy, attribution, and academic achievement. *Sex Roles, 9*(2), 217–231.

Etaugh, C., & Weber, S. (1982). Perceptions of sex roles of young and middle-aged women and men. *Perceptual and Motor Skills, 55*, 559–562.

Evans, R. G. (1982). Defense mechanisms in females as a function of sex-role orientation. *Journal of Clinical Psychology, 38*(4), 816–817.

Evans, R. G. (1984). Hostility and sex guilt: Perceptions of self and others as a function of gender and sex-role orientation. *Sex Roles, 10*, 207–215.

Evans, R. G., & Dinning, W. D. (1982). MMPI correlates of the Bem Sex Role Inventory and Extended Personal Attributes Questionnaire in a male psychiatric sample. *Journal of Clinical Psychology, 38*(4), 811–815.

Falbo, T., Graham, J. S., & Gryskiewicz, S. S. (1978). Sex roles and fertility in college women. *Sex Roles, 4*(6), 845–851.

Farmer, H. S. (1980). Environmental, background, and psychological variables related to optimizing achievement and career motivation for high school girls. *Journal of Vocational Behavior, 17*(1), 58–70.

Farmer, H. S. (1985). Model of career and achievement motivation for women and men. *Journal of Counseling Psychology, 32*(3), 363–390.

Farmer, H. S., & Fyans, L. J. (1983). Married women's achievement and career motivation: The influence of some environmental and psychological variables. *Psychology of Women Quarterly, 7*(4), 358–372.

Faulkender, P. J. (1985). Relationship between Bem Sex-Role Inventory groups and attitudes of sexism. *Psychological Reports, 57*(1), 227–235.

Faulkender, P. J. (1987). Validity of using Bem Sex-Role Inventory norms on other samples: Analysis of a southern sample. *Psychological Reports, 60*, 399–406.

Feather, N. T. (1978). Factor structure of the Bem Sex-Role Inventory: Implications for the study of masculinity, femininity, and androgyny. *Australian Journal of Psychology, 30*(3), 241–254.

Feather, N. T. (1984). Masculinity, femininity, psychological androgyny, and the structure of values. *Journal of Personality and Social Psychology, 47*(3), 604–620.

Feather, N. T., O'Driscoll, M. P., & Nagel, T. (1979). Conservatism, sex-typing, and the use of titles: Miss, Mrs, or Ms? *European Journal of Social Psychology, 9*(4), 419–426.

Feather, N. T., & Said, J. A. (1983). Preference for occupations in relation to masculinity, femininity, and gender. *British Journal of Social Psychology,* 22(2), 113–127.

Feinberg, R. A., & Workman, J. E. (1981). Sex-role orientation and cognitive complexity. *Psychological Reports, 49*(1), 246.

Feldman, S. S., & Aschenbrenner, B. (1983). Impact of parenthood on various aspects of masculinity and femininity: A short-term longitudinal study. *Developmental Psychology, 19*(2), 278–289.

Feldman, S. S., Biringen, Z. C., & Nash, S. C. (1981). Fluctuations of sex-related self-attributions as a function of stage of family life cycle. *Developmental Psychology, 17*(1), 24–35.

Feldman, S. S., & Nash, S. C. (1978). Interest in babies during young adulthood. *Child Development, 49*(3), 617–622.

Feldman, S. S., & Nash, S. C. (1979). Sex differences in responsiveness to babies among mature adults. *Developmental Psychology, 15*(4), 430–436.

Feldman, S. S., Nash, S. C., & Aschenbrenner, B. G. (1983). Antecedents of fathering. *Child Development, 54*(6), 1628–1636.

Feldstein, J. C. (1980). Empathic responses of counselors-in-training to typical and atypical female clients. *Journal of Counseling Services, 4*(1), 27–33.

Fischer, J. L., & Narus, L. R. (1981a). Sex roles and intimacy in same sex and other sex relationships. *Psychology of Women Quarterly, 5*(3), 444–455.

Fischer, J. L., & Narus, L. R., Jr. (1981b). Sex-role development in late adolescence and adulthood. *Sex Roles, 7*(2), 97–106.

Fischer, J. L., & Narus, L. R., Jr. (1982). Strong but not silent: A reexamination of expressivity in the relationships of men. *Sex Roles, 8*(2), 150–168.

Fitzpatrick, M. A., & Indvik, J. (1982). The instrumental and expressive domains of marital communication. *Human Communication Research, 8*(3), 195–213.

Flagg, K. (1984). Psychological androgyny and self-esteem in clergywomen. *Journal of Psychology and Theology, 12*(3), 222–229.

Flaherty, J. F., & Dusek, J. B. (1980). An investigation of the relationship between psychological androgyny and components of self-concept. *Journal of Personality and Social Psychology, 38*(6), 984–992.

Flake-Hobson, C., Robinson, B. E., & Skeen, P. (1981). Relationship between parental androgyny and early child-rearing ideals and practices. *Psychological Reports, 49*(2), 667–675.

Fleck, J. R., Fuller, C. C., Malin, S. Z., Miller, D. H., & Acheson, K. R. (1980). Father psychological absence and heterosexual behavior, personal adjustment and sex-typing in adolescent girls. *Adolescence, 15*, 847–860.

Fleming, M. Z., Jenkins, S. R., & Bugarin, C. (1980). Questioning current definitions of gender identity: Implications of the Bem Sex-Role Inventory for transsexuals. *Archives of Sexual Behavior, 9*(1), 13–26.

Fong, M. L., & Borders, L. D. (1985). Effect of sex role orientation and gender on counseling skills training. *Journal of Counseling Psychology, 32*(1), 104–110.

Fong, M. L., Borders, L. D., & Neimeyer, G. J. (1986). Sex role orientation and self-disclosure flexibility in counselor training. *Counselor Education and Supervision, 25*(3), 210–221.

Forbes, G. B., & King, S. (1983). Fear of success and sex-role: There are reliable relationships. *Psychological Reports, 53*(3), 735–738.

Forisha, B. L. (1978). Creativity and imagery in men and women. *Perceptual and Motor Skills, 47*(3), 1255–1264.

Frable, D. E. (1987). Sex-typed execution and perception of expressive movement. *Journal of Personality and Social Psychology, 53*(2), 391–396.

Frable, D. E., & Bem, S. L. (1985). If you are gender schematic, all members of the opposite sex look alike. *Journal of Personality and Social Psychology, 49*(2), 459–468.

Francis, P. L., Lombardo, J. P., & Simon, L. J. (1987). Relation of sex and sex role to adults' ability to decode infants' emotions. *Perceptual and Motor Skills, 65,* 595–600.

Frank, D. I., Downard, E., & Lang, A. R. (1986). Androgyny, sexual satisfaction, and women. *Journal of Psychosocial Nursing and Mental Health Services, 24*(7), 10–15.

Frodi, A. M., Lamb, M. E., Frodi, M., Hwang, C., Forsstrom, B., & Corry, T. (1982). Stability and change in parental attitudes following an infant's birth into traditional and nontraditional Swedish families. *Scandinavian Journal of Psychology, 23*(1), 53–62.

Frost, R. O., Sher, K. J., & Geen, T. (1986). Psychopathology and personality characteristics of nonclinical compulsive checkers. *Behaviour Research and Therapy, 24*(2), 133–143.

Fyfe, B. (1979). Effects of a sexual enhancement workshop on young adults. *Journal of Clinical Psychology, 35*(4), 873–875.

Gaa, J. P., & Liberman, D. (1981). Categorization agreement of the Personality Attributes Questionnaire and the Bem Sex Role Inventory. *Journal of Clinical Psychology, 37*(3), 593–601.

Gaa, J. P., Liberman, D., & Edwards, T. A. (1979). A comparative factor analysis of the Bem Sex Role Inventory and the Personality Attributes Questionnaire. *Journal of Clinical Psychology, 35*(3), 592–598.

Gabrenya, W. K., & Arkin, R. M. (1980). Self-Monitoring Scale: Factor structure and correlates. *Personality and Social Psychology Bulletin, 6*(1), 13–22.

Gackenbach, J. I. (1978). A perceptual defense approach to the study of gender sex related traits, stereotypes, and attitudes. *Journal of Personality, 46*(4), 645–676.

Gackenbach, J. (1981). Sex-role identity across two cultures. *Psychological Reports, 49*(2), 677–678.

Gackenbach, J. (1982). Collegiate swimmers: Sex differences in self-reports and indices of physiological stress. *Perceptual and Motor Skills, 55*(2), 555–558.

Gackenback, J. I., Heretick, D. M. L., Alexander, D. (1979). The effects of unipolar sex-role identities and situational determinants on components of fear of success. *Journal of Vocational Behavior, 15*(3), 347–366.

Galambos, N. L., Petersen, A. C., Richards, M., & Gitelson, I. B. (1985). The Attitudes Toward Women Scale for Adolescents (AWSA): A study of reliability and validity. *Sex Roles, 13,* 343–356.

Galejs, I., & King, A. (1983). Sex-role perceptions of traditional and nontraditional college women. *Journal of Psychology, 113*(2), 257–263.

Gannon, L., Heiser, P., & Knight, S. (1985). Learned helplessness versus reactance: The effects of sex-role stereotypy. *Sex Roles, 12,* 791–806.

Ganong, L. H., & Coleman, M. (1985). Sex, sex roles, and emotional expressiveness. *Journal of Genetic Psychology, 146*(3), 405–411.

Ganong, L. H., & Coleman, M. (1987a). Sex roles and yielded/expressed self-control. *Sex Roles, 16*(7/8), 401–408.

Ganong, L. H., & Coleman, M. M. (1987b). Sex, sex roles, and familial love. *Journal of Genetic Psychology, 148*(1), 45–52.

Garcia, L. T. (1982). Sex-role orientation and stereotypes about male-female sexuality. *Sex Roles, 8*(8), 863–876.

Gauthier, J., & Kjervik, D. (1982). Sex-role identity and self-esteem in female graduate nursing students. *Sex Roles, 8*(1), 45–56.

Gayton, W. F., Havu, G., Baird, J. G., & Ozman, K. (1983). Psychological androgyny and assertiveness in females. *Psychological Reports, 52*(1), 283–285.

Gayton, W. F., Havu, G., Barnes, S., Ozman, K. L., & Bassett, J. S. (1978). Psychological androgyny and fear of success. *Psychological Reports, 42*(3), 757–758.

Gayton, W. F., Havu, G. F., Ozman, K. L., & Tavormina, J. (1977). A comparison of the Bem Sex Role Inventory and the PRF ANDRO Scale. *Journal of Personality Assessment, 41*(6), 619–621.

Gerber, G. L. (1988). Leadership roles and the gender stereotype traits. *Sex Roles, 18*(11/12), 649–668.

Gerdes, E. P., Gehling, J. D., & Rapp, J. N. (1981). The effects of sex and sex-role concept on self-disclosure. *Sex Roles, 7*(10), 989–998.

Gerson, M. J. (1980). The lure of motherhood. *Psychology of Women Quarterly, 5*(2), 207–218.

Gerson, M. J. (1983). A scale of motivation for parenthood: The Index of Parenthood Motivation. *Journal of Psychology, 113*(2), 211–220.

Gerson, M. J. (1984). Feminism and the wish for a child. *Sex Roles, 11,* 389–399.

Gerson, M. J., & Lewis, K. L. (1984). Sex role identification and the clinical psychology student. *Professional Psychology Research and Practice, 15*(4), 601–607.

Gianakos, I., & Subich, L. M. (1986). The relationship of gender and sex-role orientation to vocational undecidedness. *Journal of Vocational Behavior, 29*(1), 42–50.

Gibb, G. D., & Lambirth, T. T. (1982). Who are the Equal Rights Amendment defenders and opposers? *Psychological Reports, 51*(3), 1239–1242.

Gilbert, L. A. (1979). An approach to training sex-fair mental health workers. *Professional Psychology, 10*(3), 365–372.

Gilbert, L. A., Deutsch, C. J., & Strahan, R. F. (1978). Feminine and masculine dimensions of the typical, desirable, and ideal woman and man. *Sex Roles, 4*(5), 767–778.

Gilbert, L. A., Waldroop, J. A., & Deutsch, C. J. (1981). Masculine and feminine stereotypes and adjustment: A reanalysis. *Psychology of Women Quarterly, 5*(5), 790–794.

Gillen, B. (1981). Physical attractiveness: A determinant of two types of goodness. *Personality and Social Psychology Bulletin, 7*(2), 277–281.

Gilroy, F. D., Talierco, T. M., & Steinbacher, R. (1981). Impact of maternal employment on daughters' sex-role orientation and fear of success. *Psychological Reports, 49*(3), 963–968.

Glass, C. R., & Biever, J. L. (1981). Sex-roles and social skill: A cognitive-behavioral analysis. *Behavioral Counseling Quarterly, 1*(4), 244–260.

Glass, C. R., Merluzzi, T. V., Biever, J. L., & Larsen, K. H. (1982). Cognitive assessment of social anxiety: Development and validation of a self-statement questionnaire. *Cognitive Therapy and Research, 6,* 37–55.

Glazebrook, C. K., & Munjas, B. A. (1986). Sex roles and depression. *Journal of Psychosocial Nursing and Mental Health Services, 24*(12), 9–12.

Glazer, C. A., & Dusek, J. B. (1985). The relationship between sex-role orientation and resolution of Eriksonian developmental crises. *Sex Roles, 13,* 653–661.

Goff, D. G., & Lehrer, S. K. (1980). Sex-role portrayals of selected female television characters. *Journal of Broadcasting, 24*(4), 467–478.

Goktepe, J. R., & Schneier, C. E. (1988). Sex and gender effects in evaluating emergent leaders in small groups. *Sex Roles, 19*(1/2), 29–36.

Gold, D., Reis, M., & Berger, C. (1979). Male teachers and development of nursery-school children. *Psychological Reports, 44*(2), 457–458.

Goldberg, S., Blumberg, S. L., & Kriger, A. (1982). Menarche and interest in infants: Biological and social influences. *Child Development, 53*(6), 1544–1550.

Golding, J. M., & Singer, J. L. (1983). Patterns of inner experience: Daydreaming styles, depressive moods, and sex roles. *Journal of Personality and Social Psychology, 45*(3), 663–675.

Goldsmith, W. M., & Ekhardt, B. N. (1984). Personality factors of men and women pastoral candidates: II. Sex-role preferences. *Journal of Psychology and Theology, 12*(3), 211–221.

Gonzalez, C. T., & Williams, K. E. (1981). Relationship between locus of control and sex-role stereotyping. *Psychological Reports, 49*(1), 70.

Good, P. R., & Smith, B. D. (1980). Menstrual distress and sex-role attributes. *Psychology of Women Quarterly, 4*(4), 482–491.

Goodman, S. H., & Kantor, D. (1983). Influence of sex-role identity on two indices of social anxiety. *Journal of Research in Personality, 17*(4), 443–450.

Green, R., Mandel, J. B., Hotvedt, M. E., Gray, J., & Smith, L. (1986). Lesbian mothers and their children: A comparison with solo parent heterosexual mothers and their children. *Archives of Sexual Behavior, 15*(2), 167–184.

Greenblatt, L., Hasenauer, J. E., & Freimuth, V. S. (1980). Psychological sex type and androgyny in the study of communication variables: Self-disclosure and communication apprehension. *Human Communication Research, 6*(2), 117–129.

Gregson, J. F., & Colley, A. (1986). Concomitants of sport participation in male and female adolescents. *International Journal of Sport Psychology, 17*(1), 10–22.

Grimm, L. G., & Yarnold, P. R. (1985). Sex typing and the coronary-prone behavior pattern. *Sex Roles, 12,* 171–178.

Gross, R., Batlis, N. C., Small, A. C., & Erdwins, C. (1979). Factor structure of the Bem Sex-Role Inventory and the Personal Attributes Questionnaire. *Journal of Consulting and Clinical Psychology, 47*(6), 1122–1124.

Grossman, F. K., Pollack, W. S., & Golding, E. (1988). Fathers and children: Predicting the quality and quantity of fathering. *Developmental Psychology*, 24(1), 82–91.

Gruber, K. J., & Powers, W. A. (1982). Factor and discriminant analysis of the Bem Sex-Role Inventory. *Journal of Personality Assessment*, 46(3), 284–291.

Gulanick, N. A., & Howard, G. S. (1979). Evaluation of a group program designed to increase androgyny in feminine women. *Sex Roles*, 5(6), 811–827.

Gunter, B., & Furnham, A. F. (1985). Androgyny and the perception of television violence as perpetrated by males and females. *Human Relations*, 38(6), 535–549.

Gutek, B. A., & Stevens, D. A. (1979). Effects of sex of subject, sex of stimulus cue, and androgyny level on evaluations in work situations which evoke sex role stereotypes. *Journal of Vocational Behavior*, 14(1), 23–32.

Guy, R. F., Rankin, B. A., & Norvell, M. J. (1980). The relation of sex role stereotyping to body image. *Journal of Psychology*, 105(2), 167–173.

Haber, S. (1980). Cognitive support for the career choices of college women. *Sex Roles*, 6(1), 129–138.

Hackett, G. (1985). Role of mathematics self-efficacy in the choice of math-related majors of college women and men: A path analysis. *Journal of Counseling Psychology*, 32(1), 47–56.

Hainline, L., & Feig, E. (1978). The correlates of childhood father absence in college-aged women. *Child Development*, 49(1), 37–42.

Hamby, C. L. (1982a). Dental hygiene students: Stereotypically feminine. *Psychological Reports*, 50(3), 1237–1238.

Hamby, C. L. (1982b). The role of psychological androgyny in female students' dental career choices. *Journal of Dental Education*, 46(9), 537–540.

Hamby, C. L., & Shapiro, S. (1982). Females in dentistry: Variations in psychological androgyny. *Psychological Reports*, 51(3), 863–866.

Hamby, C. L., & Shapiro, S. (1983). An assessment of the sex-role status of dental hygienists located in three states. *Psychological Reports*, 53(2), 635–638.

Hamby, R. (1978). Effects of gender and sex-role on tension and satisfaction in small groups. *Psychological Reports*, 42(2), 403–410.

Hamilton, M. A. (1984). The evidence of sex-typed behaviors in professional Jamaican men and women. *Sex Roles*, 11, 1009–1019.

Handal, P. J., & Salit, E. D. (1985). Gender-role classification and demographic relationships: A function of type of scoring procedures. *Sex Roles*, 12, 411–419.

Hansen, G. L. (1982). Androgyny, sex-role orientation, and homosexism. *Journal of Psychology*, 112(1), 39–45.

Hansson, R. O., Jones, W. H., & Chernovetz, M. E. (1979). Contraceptive knowledge: Antecedents and implications. *Family Coordinator*, 28(1), 29–34.

Hansson, R. O., Knopf, M. F., Downs, E. A., Monroe, P. R., Stegman, S. E., & Wadley, D. S. (1984). Femininity, masculinity, and adjustment to divorce among women. *Psychology of Women Quarterly*, 8(3), 248–260.

Harackiewicz, J. M., & DePaulo, B. M. (1982). Accuracy of person perception:

A component analysis according to Cronbach. *Personality and Social Psychology Bulletin, 8*(2), 247–256.

Harren, V. A., & Biscardi, D. L. (1980). Sex roles and cognitive styles as predictors of Holland Typologies. *Journal of Vocational Behavior, 17*(2), 231–241.

Harren, V. A., Kass, R. A., Tinsley, H. E., & Moreland, J. R. (1978). Influence of sex role attitudes and cognitive styles on career decision making. *Journal of Counseling Psychology, 25*(5), 390–398.

Harren, V. A., Kass, R. A., Tinsley, H. E., & Moreland, J. R. (1979). Influence of gender, sex-role attitudes, and cognitive complexity on gender-dominant career choices. *Journal of Counseling Psychology, 26*(3), 227–234.

Harrington, D. M., & Anderson, S. M. (1981). Creativity, masculinity, femininity, and three models of psychological androgyny. *Journal of Personality and Social Psychology, 41*(4), 744–757.

Harris, R. M. (1983). Changing women's self-perceptions: Impact of a psychology of women course. *Psychological Reports, 52*(1), 314.

Harris, T. L., & Schwab, R. (1979). Personality characteristics of androgynous and sex-typed females. *Journal of Personality Assessment, 43*(6), 614–616.

Hartman, S. J., Griffeth, R. W., Miller, L., & Kinicki, A. J. (1988). The impact of occupation, performance, and sex on sex role stereotyping. *Journal of Social Psychology, 128*(4), 451–463.

Hassler, M., Birbaumer, N., & Feil, A. (1985). Musical talent and visual-spatial abilities: A longitudinal study. *Psychology of Music, 13*(2), 99–113.

Hatzenbuehler, L. C., & Joe, V. C. (1981). Stress and androgyny: A preliminary study. *Psychological Reports, 48*(1), 327–332.

Hawkins, D., Herron, W. G., Gibson, W., Hoban, G., & Herron, M. J. (1988). Homosexual and heterosexual sex-role orientation on six sex-role scales. *Perceptual and Motor Skills, 66*, 863–871.

Heerboth, J. R., & Ramanaiah, N. V. (1985). Evaluation of the BSRI masculine and feminine items using desirability and stereotype ratings. *Journal of Personality Assessment, 49*(3), 264–270.

Henschen, K. P., Edwards, S. W., & Mathinos, L. (1982). Achievement motivation and sex-role orientation of high school female track and field athletes versus nonathletes. *Perceptual and Motor Skills, 55*(1), 183–187.

Herron, W. G., Goodman, C. K., & Herron, M. J. (1983). Comparability of sex-role measures. *Psychological Reports, 53*(3), 1087–1094.

Hess, E. P., Bridgwater, C. A., Bornstein, P. H., & Sweeney, T. M. (1980). Situational determinants in the perception of assertiveness: Gender-related influences. *Behavior Therapy, 11*(1), 49–58.

Highlen, P. S., & Russell, B. (1980). Effects of counselor gender and counselor and client sex role on females' counselor preference. *Journal of Counseling Psychology, 27*(2), 157–165.

Hiller, D. V., & Philliber, W. W. (1985). Internal consistency and correlates of the Bem Sex Role Inventory. *Social Psychology Quarterly, 48*(4), 373–380.

Hinrichsen, J. J., Follansbee, D. J., & Ganellen, R. (1981). Sex-role-related differences in self-concept and mental health. *Journal of Personality Assessment, 45*(6), 584–592.

Hinrichsen, J. J., & Stone, L. (1978). Effects of three conditions of administration on Bem Sex Role Inventory scores. *Journal of Personality Assessment*, 42(5), 512.

Hirschowitz, R. (1987). Behavioral and personality correlates of a need for power in a group of English-speaking South African women. *Journal of Psychology*, 121, 575–590.

Ho, R., & Zemaitis, R. (1981). Concern over the negative consequences of success. *Australian Journal of Psychology*, 33(1), 19–28.

Hoch, Z., Safir, M. P., Peres, Y., & Shepher, J. (1981). An evaluation of sexual performance: Comparison between sexually dysfunctional and functional couples. *Journal of Sex and Marital Therapy*, 7(3), 195–206.

Hoferek, M. J. (1980). Psychological sex-role and choice in women's physical education. *Journal of Physical Education and Recreation*, 51(9), 71–72.

Hoferek, M. J. (1982). Sex-role prescriptions and attitudes of physical educators. *Sex Roles*, 8(1), 83–98.

Hoffman, D. M., & Fidell, L. S. (1979). Characteristics of androgynous, undifferentiated, masculine, and feminine middle-class women. *Sex Roles*, 5(6), 765–781.

Hoffman, S. R., & Levant, R. F. (1985). A comparison of childfree and child-anticipated married couples. *Family Relations*, 34(2), 197–203.

Hogan, H. W. (1977). The measurement of psychological androgyny: An extended replication. *Journal of Clinical Psychology*, 33(4), 1009–1013.

Hogan, H. W. (1979). German and American responses to the Bem Sex Role Inventory. *Journal of Social Psychology*, 109(1), 141–142.

Hogan, H. W., & McWilliams, J. M. (1978). Factors related to self-actualization. *Journal of Psychology*, 100(1), 117–122.

Holleran, P. R., & Lopez, L. C. (1984). Predictors of sextypical and asextypical career choice in college undergraduates. *Journal of Employment Counseling*, 21(4), 182–184.

Holleran, P. R., Staszkiewicz, M., & Lopez, L. C. (1983). Self-reported social desirability in sex-stereotyped and androgynous individuals. *Counseling and Values*, 28(1), 31–41.

Holmbeck, G. N., & Bale, P. (1988). Relations between instrumental and expressive personality characteristics and behaviors: A test of Spence and Helmreich's theory. *Journal of Research in Personality*, 22, 37–59.

Hooberman, R. E. (1979). Psychological androgyny, feminine gender identity and self-esteem in homosexual and heterosexual males. *Journal of Sex Research*, 15(4), 306–315.

Hoppe, C. M. (1979). Interpersonal aggression as a function of subject's sex, subject's sex role identification, opponent's sex, and degree of provocation. *Journal of Personality*, 47(2), 317–329.

Hornick, J. P., Devlin, M. C., Downey, M. K., & Baynham, T. (1986). Successful and unsuccessful contraceptors: A multivariate typology. *Journal of Social Work and Human Sexuality*, 4, 17–31.

Houser, B. B., & Garvey, C. (1985). Factors that affect nontraditional vocational enrollment among women. *Psychology of Women Quarterly*, 9(1), 105–117.

Hudson, M. P. (1983). Polarizations of personality: A factor explanation. *Psychological Reports*, 53(3), 1095–1100.

Hughes, B. C., & Warner, P. D. (1984). Sex-role perception and depression in college women. *College Student Journal, 18*(4), 406–415.

Hughes, R. N. (1979). Bem Sex-Role Inventory performance in students: Comparisons between New Zealand, Australian and American samples. *New Zealand Psychologist, 8*(2), 61–66.

Hughes, R. N. (1981). Sex differences in Group Embedded Figures Test performance in relation to sex-role, state and trait anxiety. *Current Psychological Research, 1*(4), 227–234.

Hungerford, J. K., & Sobolew-Shubin, A. P. (1987). Sex-role identity, gender identity, and self-schemata. *Psychology of Women Quarterly, 11*(1), 1–10.

Hyde, J. S., & Phillis, D. E. (1979). Androgyny across the lifespan. *Developmental Psychology, 15*(3), 334–336.

Ickes, W., & Barnes, R. D. (1978). Boys and girls together—and alienated: On enacting stereotyped sex roles in mixed-sex dyads. *Journal of Personality and Social Psychology, 36*(7), 669–683.

Inderlied, S. D., & Powell, G. (1979). Sex-role identity and leadership style: Different labels for the same concept? *Sex Roles, 5*(5), 613–625.

Indvik, J., & Fitzpatrick, M. A. (1982). "If you could read my mind, love . . . ," Understanding and misunderstanding in the marital dyad. *Family Relations, 31*(1), 43–51.

Intons-Peterson, M. J., & Samuels, A. K. (1978). The cultural halo effect: Black and white women rate black and white men. *Bulletin of the Psychonomic Society, 11*(5), 309–312.

Ireland-Galman, M. M., & Michael, W. B. (1983). The relationship of a measure of the fear of success construct to scales representing the locus of control and sex-role orientation constructs for a community college sample. *Educational and Psychological Measurement, 43*(4), 1217–1225.

Irvine, J. J., & Robinson, C. (1982). The relationships among sex role orientations, general attitudes toward women, and specific attitudes toward women in managerial roles. *Journal of Educational Equity and Leadership, 2*(3), 196–204.

Jackson, A. D. (1982). Militancy and black women's competitive behavior in competitive versus noncompetitive conditions. *Psychology of Women Quarterly, 6*(3), 342–353.

Jackson, L. A. (1983). The perception of androgyny and physical attractiveness: Two is better than one. *Personality and Social Psychology Bulletin, 9*(3), 405–413.

Jackson, L. A. (1985). Self-conceptions and gender role: The correspondence between gender-role categorization and open-ended self-descriptions. *Sex Roles, 13*, 549–566.

Jackson, L. A. (1987). Gender and distributive justice: The influence of gender-related characteristics on allocations. *Sex Roles, 17*(1/2), 73–91.

Jackson, L. A., & Cash, T. F. (1985). Components of gender stereotypes: Their implications for inferences on stereotypic and nonstereotypic dimensions. *Personality and Social Psychology Bulletin, 11*(3), 326–344.

Jackson, L. A., Ialongo, N., & Stollak, G. E. (1986). Parental correlates of gender role: The relations between parents' masculinity, femininity, and child-rearing behaviors and their children's gender roles. *Journal of Social and Clinical Psychology, 4*(2), 204–224.

Jackson, L. A., Messe, L. A., & Hunter, J. E. (1985). Gender role and distributive justice behavior. *Basic and Applied Social Psychology, 6*(4), 329–343.

Jackson, L. A., Sullivan, L. A., & Hymes, J. S. (1987). Gender, gender role, and physical appearance. *Journal of Psychology, 121*, 51–56.

Jackson, L. A., Sullivan, L. A., & Rostker, R. (1988). Gender, gender role, and body image. *Sex Roles, 19*(7/8), 429–443.

Jacobson, N. S., Follette, W. C., & Pagel, M. (1986). Predicting who will benefit from behavioral marital therapy. *Journal of Consulting and Clinical Psychology, 54*(4), 518–522.

Jamison, W., & Signorella, M. L. (1980). Sex-typing and spatial ability: The association between masculinity and success on Piaget's water-level task. *Sex Roles, 6*(3), 345–353.

Jensen, B. J., Witcher, D. B., & Upton, L. R. (1987). Readability assessment of questionnaires frequently used in sex and marital therapy. *Journal of Sex and Marital Therapy, 13*(2), 137–141.

Jensen, M. P. (1987). Gender, sex roles, and attitudes toward war and nuclear weapons. *Sex Roles, 17*(5/6), 253–267.

Johnson, D. H. (1978). Students' sex preferences and sex role expectancies for counselors. *Journal of Counseling Psychology, 25*(6), 557–562.

Johnson, M. (1988). Influences of gender and sex role orientation on help-seeking attitudes. *Journal of Psychology, 122*, 237–241.

Johnson, S. J., & Black, K. N. (1981). The relationship between sex-role identity and beliefs in personal control. *Sex Roles, 7*(4), 425–431.

Jones, G. P., & Jacklin, C. N. (1988). Changes in sexist attitudes toward women during introductory women's and men's studies courses. *Sex Roles, 18*(9/10), 611–622.

Jones, W. H., Chernovetz, M. E., & Hansson, R. O. (1978). The enigma of androgyny: Differential implications for males and females? *Journal of Consulting and Clinical Psychology, 46*(2), 298–313.

Jose, P. E., & McCarthy, W. J. (1988). Perceived agentic and communal behavior in mixed-sex group interactions. *Personality and Social Psychology Bulletin, 14*(1), 57–67.

Juni, S., Rahamim, E. L., & Brannon, R. (1985). Sex role development as a function of parent models and oedipal fixation. *Journal of Genetic Psychology, 146*(1), 89–99.

Kabacoff, R. I., Marwit, S. J., & Orlofsky, J. L. (1985). Correlates of sex role stereotyping among mental health professionals. *Professional Psychology Research and Practice, 16*(1), 98–105.

Kachel, D. W. (1979). Locus of control, sex-role identity, and academic achievement of female college students. *Journal of the NAWDAC, 42*(3), 22–26.

Kagel, S. A., & Schilling, K. M. (1985). Sexual identification and gender identity among father-absent males. *Sex Roles, 13*, 357–370.

Kahn, S. E. (1982). Sex-role attitudes: Who should raise consciousness? *Sex Roles, 8*(9), 977–985.

Kahn, S. E., & Richardson, A. (1983). Evaluation of a course in sex roles for secondary school students. *Sex Roles, 9*(4), 431–440.

Kalin, R. (1979). Method for scoring androgyny as a continuous variable. *Psychological Reports*, *44*(3), 1205–1206.

Kalin, R., & Lloyd, C. A. (1985). Sex role identity, sex-role ideology and marital adjustment. *International Journal of Women's Studies*, *8*(1), 32–39.

Kane, M. J. (1982). The influence of level of sport participation and sex-role orientation on female professionalization of attitudes toward play. *Journal of Sport Psychology*, *4*(3), 290–294.

Kapalka, G. M., & Lachenmeyer, J. R. (1988). Sex-role flexibility, locus of control, and occupational status. *Sex Roles*, *19*(7/8), 417–427.

Kaplan, B. J., & Plake, B. S. (1981). The effects of sex-role orientation and cognitive skill on mathematics achievement. *Educational Studies*, *7*(2), 123–131.

Katz, P. A., & Boswell, S. (1986). Flexibility and traditionality in children's gender roles. *Genetic, Social and General Psychology Monographs*, *112*(1), 103–147.

Kav-Venaki, S., & Zakham, L. (1983). Psychological effects of hysterectomy in premenopausal women. *Journal of Psychosomatic Obstetrics and Gynaecology*, *2*(2), 76–80.

Kearney, M. (1982). Are masculine trait-factors in women a help or a hindrance in dealing with fear of success? *Psychological Reports*, *51*(2), 558.

Kelly, J. A., Caudill, M. S., Hathorn, S., & O'Brien, C. G. (1977). Socially undesirable sex-correlated characteristics: Implications for androgyny and adjustment. *Journal of Consulting and Clinical Psychology*, *45*(6), 1185–1186.

Kelly, J. A., Furman, W., & Young, V. (1978). Problems associated with the typological measurement of sex roles and androgyny. *Journal of Consulting and Clinical Psychology*, *46*(6), 1574–1576.

Kelly, J. A., O'Brien, G. G., & Hosford, R. (1981). Sex roles and social skills considerations for interpersonal adjustment. *Psychology of Women Quarterly*, *5*(5), 758–766.

Kelly, J. A., Wildman, H. E., & Urey, J. R. (1982). Gender and sex role differences in group decision-making social interactions: A behavioral analysis. *Journal of Applied Social Psychology*, *12*(2), 112–127.

Kemp, A. E. (1985). Psychological androgyny in musicians. *Bulletin of the Council for Research in Music Education*, *85*, 102–108.

Kenrick, D. T., Stringfield, D. O., Wagenhals, W. L., Dahl, R. H., & Ransdell, H. J. (1980). Sex differences, androgyny, and approach responses to erotica: A new variation on the old volunteer problem. *Journal of Personality and Social Psychology*, *38*(3), 517–524.

Keys, D. E. (1985). Gender, sex role, and career decision making of certified management accountants. *Sex Roles*, *13*, 33–46.

Kiecolt-Glaser, J. K., & Dixon, K. (1984). Postadolescent onset male anorexia. *Journal of Psychosocial Nursing and Mental Health Services*, *22*(1), 11–20.

Kihlstrom, J. F., Diaz, W. A., McClellan, G. E., Ruskin, P. M., Pistole, D. D., & Shor, R. E. (1980). Personality correlates of hypnotic susceptibility: Needs for achievement and autonomy, self-monitoring, and masculinity-femininity. *American Journal of Clinical Hypnosis*, *22*(4), 225–230.

Kimlicka, T., Cross, H., & Tarnai, J. (1983). A comparison of androgynous, feminine, masculine, and undifferentiated women on self-esteem, body satisfaction, and sexual satisfaction. *Psychology of Women Quarterly, 7*(3), 291–294.

Kimlicka, T. M., Wakefield, J. A., & Friedman, A. F. (1980). Comparison of factors from the Bem Sex-Role Inventory for male and female college students. *Psychological Reports, 46*(3), 1011–1017.

Kimlicka, T. M., Wakefield, J. A., & Goad, N. A. (1982). Sex-roles of the ideal opposite sexed persons for college males and females. *Journal of Personality Assessment, 46*(5), 519–521.

Kirkpatrick, S. W. (1979). Sex-role classifications of adolescents: Relationship to actual and perceived parental types. *Journal of Genetic Psychology, 135*(2), 237–244.

Kleinke, C. L., & Hinrichs, C. A. (1983). College adjustment problems and attitudes toward drinking reported by feminine, androgynous, and masculine college women. *Psychology of Women Quarterly, 7*(4), 373–382.

Knowles, G. A., & Martin, R. E. (1982). Teacher sex role perceptions and male enrollment patterns in home economics programs. *Canadian Vocational Journal, 18*(1), 27–31.

Koffman, S., & Lips, H. M. (1980). Sex differences in self-esteem and performance expectancies in married couples. *Social Behavior and Personality, 8*(1), 57–63.

Koopman-Boyden, P. G., & Abbott, M. (1985). Expectations for household task allocation and actual task allocation: A New Zealand study. *Journal of Marriage and the Family, 47*(1), 211–219.

Korabik, K. (1982a). The effects of sex-typed trait descriptions of judgments of likableness. *Social Behavior and Personality, 10*(2), 157–161.

Korabik, K. (1982b). Sex-role orientation and impressions: A comparison of differing genders and sex roles. *Personality and Social Psychology Bulletin, 8*(1), 25–30.

Korabik, K. (1982c). Sex-role orientation and leadership style. *International Journal of Women's Studies, 5*(4), 329–337.

Kozma, C., & Zuckerman, M. (1983). An investigation of some hypotheses concerning rape and murder. *Personality and Individual Differences, 4*(1), 23–29.

Kranau, E. J., Green, V., & Valencia-Weber, G. (1982). Acculturation and the Hispanic woman: Attitudes toward women, sex-role attribution, sex-role behavior, and demographics. *Hispanic Journal of Behavioral Sciences, 4*(1), 21–40.

Kravetz, D., & Jones, L. E. (1981). Androgyny as a standard of mental health. *American Journal of Orthopsychiatry, 51*(3), 502–509.

Kriss, R. T., & Kraemer, H. C. (1986). Efficacy of group therapy for problems with postmastectomy self-perception, body image, and sexuality. *Journal of Sex Research, 22*(4), 438–451.

Kulik, J. A., & Harackiewicz, J. M. (1979). Opposite-sex interpersonal attraction as a function of the sex roles of the perceiver and the perceived. *Sex Roles, 5*(4), 443–452.

Kumar, D., & Kapila, A. (1987). Problem solving as a function of extraversion and masculinity. *Personality and Individual Differences, 8*(1), 129–132.

Kurdek, L. A. (1987). Sex role self schema and psychological adjustment in coupled homosexual and heterosexual men and women. *Sex Roles, 17*(9/ 10), 549–562.

Kurdek, L. A., & Blisk, D. (1983). Dimensions and correlates of mothers' divorce experiences. *Journal of Divorce, 6*(4), 1–24.

Kurdek, L. A., & Schmitt, J. P. (1986). Interaction of sex role self-concept with relationship quality and relationship beliefs in married, heterosexual cohabiting, gay, and lesbian couples. *Journal of Personality and Social Psychology, 51*(2), 365–370.

Kurdek, L. A., & Schmitt, J. P. (1986). Relationship quality of partners in heterosexual married, heterosexual cohabiting, and gay and lesbian relationships. *Journal of Personality and Social Psychology, 51*(4), 711–720.

Kurdek, L. A., & Schmitt, J. P. (1987). Partner homogamy in married, heterosexual cohabiting, gay, and lesbian couples. *Journal of Sex Research, 23*(2), 212–232.

Kurdek, L. A., & Siesky, A. E. (1980). Sex role self-concepts of single divorced parents and their children. *Journal of Divorce, 3*(3), 249–261.

Kweskin, S. L., & Cook, A. S. (1982). Heterosexual and homosexual mothers' self-described sex-role behavior and ideal sex-role behavior in children. *Sex Roles, 8*(9), 967–975.

LaFrance, M., & Carmen, B. (1980). The nonverbal display of psychological androgyny. *Journal of Personality and Social Psychology, 38*(1), 36–49.

Lamb, M. E., Frodi, A. M., Hwang, C., Frodi, M., & Steinberg, J. (1982). Mother- and father-infant interaction involving play and holding in traditional and nontraditional Swedish families. *Developmental Psychology, 18*(2), 215–221.

Lamke, L. K. (1982a). Adjustment and sex-role orientation in adolescence. *Journal of Youth and Adolescence, 11*(3), 247–259.

Lamke, L. K. (1982b). The impact of sex-role orientation on self-esteem in early adolescence. *Child Development, 53*(6), 1530–1535.

Lamke, L. K., & Bell, N. J. (1982). Sex-role orientation and relationship development in same-sex dyads. *Journal of Research in Personality, 16*(3), 343– 354.

Lamke, L. K., Bell, N. J., & Murphy, C. (1980). Sibling constellation and androgynous sex role development. *Journal of Psychology, 105*(1), 139–144.

Lamke, L. K., & Filsinger, E. E. (1983). Parental antecedents of sex role orientation. *Adolescence, 18*(70), 429–432.

Lara-Cantu, M. A., & Navarro-Arias, R. (1986). Positive and negative factors in the measurement of sex roles: Findings from a Mexican sample. *Hispanic Journal of Behavioral Sciences, 8*(2), 143–155.

Lara-Cantu, M., & Suzan-Reed, M. (1988). How valid is the social desirability scale of Bem's Sex Role Inventory. *Psychological Reports, 62*, 553–554.

Larsen, R. J., & Seidman, E. (1986). Gender schema theory and sex role inventories: Some conceptual and psychometric considerations. *Journal of Personality and Social Psychology, 50*(1), 205–211.

LaTorre, R. A. (1978). Gender role and psychological adjustment. *Archives of Sexual Behavior, 7*(2), 89–96.

LaTorre, R. A., & Gregoire, P. A. (1977). Gender role in university mental health clients. *Journal of Individual Psychology, 33*(2), 246–249.

LaTorre, R. A., & Piper, W. E. (1979). Gender identity and gender role in schizophrenia. *Journal of Abnormal Psychology, 88*(1), 68–72.

Lavine, L. O., & Lombardo, J. P. (1984). Self-disclosure: Intimate and nonintimate disclosures to parents and best friends as a function of Bem Sex-
Role category. *Sex Roles, 11*, 735–744.

Leahy, R. L., & Eiter, M. (1980). Moral judgment and the development of real
and ideal androgynous self-image during adolescence and young adulthood. *Developmental Psychology, 16*(4), 362–370.

Leak, G. K., Millard, R. J., Perry, N. W., & Williams, D. E. (1985). An investigation of the nomological network of social interest. *Journal of Research
in Personality, 19*(2), 197–207.

Leary, M. R., & Snell, W. E. (1988). The relationship of instrumentality and
expressiveness to sexual behavior in males and females. *Sex Roles, 18*(9/
10), 509–522.

Lee, A. G. (1982). Psychological androgyny and social desirability. *Journal of
Personality Assessment, 46*(2), 147–152.

Lee, A. G., & Scheurer, V. L. (1983). Psychological androgyny and aspects of
self-image in women and men. *Sex Roles, 9*(3), 289–306.

Lee, S. S. (1987). Attributions and performance: The effects of sex role identity
and sex-typed tasks. *Journal of Social Psychology, 127*(2), 151–157.

Lemkau, J. P. (1983). Women in male-dominated professions: Distinguishing
personality and background characteristics. *Psychology of Women Quarterly,
8*(2), 144–165.

Lemkau, J. P. (1984). Men in female-dominated professions: Distinguishing personality and background features. *Journal of Vocational Behavior, 24*(1), 110–
122.

Lenz, E. R., Soeken, K. L., Rankin, E. A., & Fischman, S. H. (1985). Sex-role
attributes, gender, and postpartal perceptions of the marital relationship.
Advances in Nursing Science, 7(3), 49–62.

Lester, D. (1984a). The fear of death, sex and androgyny: A brief note. *Omega
Journal of Death and Dying, 15*(3), 271–274.

Lester, D. (1984b). Sex differences in self-reported psychophysiological activity:
Physique versus personality. *Research Communications in Psychology, Psychiatry and Behavior, 9*(2), 269–272.

Lester, D., Brazill, N., Ellis, C., & Guerin, T. (1984). Correlates of romantic
attitudes toward love: Androgyny and self-disclosure. *Psychological Reports, 54*(2), 554.

Lester, D., Gronau, F., & Wondrack, K. (1982). The personality and attitudes
of female police officers: Needs, androgyny, and attitudes toward rape.
Journal of Police Science and Administration, 10(3), 357–360.

Lester, P., & Chu, L. (1981). Women administrators: Feminine, masculine or
androgynous? *Journal of Educational Equity and Leadership, 1*(3), 171–179.

Levant, R. F., Slattery, S. C., & Loiselle, J. E. (1987). Fathers' involvement in
housework and child care with school-aged daughters. *Family Relations,
36*, 152–157.

Levine, R., Gillman, M. J., & Reis, H. (1982). Individual differences for sex
differences in achievement attributions? *Sex Roles, 8*(4), 455–466.

Lewis, E. T., & McCarthy, P. R. (1988). Perceptions of self-disclosure as a function of gender-linked variables. *Sex Roles, 19*(1/2), 547–565.

Liberman, D., & Gaa, J. P. (1980). Response tendency on the Bem Sex Role Inventory. *Journal of Psychology, 106*(2), 259–263.

Liberman, D., & Gaa, J. P. (1986). The effect of response style on the validity of the BSRI. *Journal of Clinical Psychology, 42*(6), 905–908.

Lippa, R. (1978). The naive perception of masculinity-femininity on the basis of expressive cues. *Journal of Research in Personality, 12*(1), 1–14.

Lippa, R. (1983). Sex typing and the perception of body outlines. *Journal of Personality, 51*(4), 667–682.

Lippa, R., & Beauvais, C. (1983). Gender jeopardy: The effects of gender, assessed femininity and masculinity, and false success/failure feedback on performance in an experimental quiz. *Journal of Personality and Social Psychology, 44*(2), 344–353.

Lippa, R., Valdez, E., & Jolly, A. (1983). The effects of self-monitoring on the expressive display of masculinity-femininity. *Journal of Research in Personality, 17*(3), 324–338.

Lobel, T. E., & Winch, G. L. (1986). Different defense mechanisms among men with different sex role orientations. *Sex Roles, 15*(3/4), 215–220.

Logan, D. D., & Kaschak, E. (1980). The relationship of sex, sex role, and mental health. *Psychology of Women Quarterly, 4*(4), 573–580.

Lohr, J. M., & Nix, J. (1982). Relationship of assertiveness and the short form of the Bem Sex-Role Inventory: A replication. *Psychological Reports, 50*(1), 114.

Lombardo, J. P. (1986). Interaction of sex and sex role in response to violations of preferred seating arrangements. *Sex Roles, 15*(3/4), 173–183.

Lombardo, J. P., & Lavine, L. O. (1981). Sex-role stereotyping and patterns of self-disclosure. *Sex Roles, 7*(4), 403–411.

Long, V. O. (1982). Ending the perpetuation of sex-role stereotypes in our schools: A possible consequence of psychological androgyny. *Psychology in the Schools, 19*(2), 250–254.

Long, V. O. (1986). Relationship of masculinity to self-esteem and self-acceptance in female professionals, college students, clients, and victims of domestic violence. *Journal of Consulting and Clinical Psychology, 54*(3), 323–327.

Lorr, M., & Diorio, M. (1978). Analysis and abbreviation of Bem's Sex-Role Inventory. *Psychological Reports, 43*(3), 879–882.

Lorr, M., & Manning, T. T. (1978). Personality correlates of the sex role types. *Journal of Clinical Psychology, 34*(4), 884–888.

Lubinski, D. (1983). The androgyny dimension: A comment on Stokes, Childs, and Fuehrer. *Journal of Counseling Psychology, 30*(1), 130–133.

Lubinski, D., Tellegen, A., & Butcher, J. N. (1981). The relationship between androgyny and subjective indicators of emotional well-being. *Journal of Personality and Social Psychology, 40*(4), 722–730.

Lubinski, D., Tellegen, A., & Butcher, J. N. (1983). Masculinity, femininity, and androgyny viewed and assessed as distinct concepts. *Journal of Personality and Social Psychology, 44*(2), 428–439.

Lueger, R. J., & Evans, R. G. (1981). Emotional expressivity and sex-role perceptions of repressors and sensitizers. *Journal of Personality Assessment*, 45(3), 288–294.

Luessenheide, D., & Vandever, J. (1978). Independence of sex-role and gender identity. *Psychological Reports*, 42(3), 821–822.

Lukken, K. M. (1987). Androgyny and the career choices of allied health professions students. *Journal of Allied Health*, 16(1), 49–58.

Lutes, C. J. (1981). Early marriage and identity foreclosure. *Adolescence*, 16, 809–815.

Lyons, D. S., & Green, S. B. (1988). Sex role development as a function of college experiences. *Sex Roles*, 18(1/2), 31–40.

Macdonald, N. E., Ebert, P. D., & Mason, S. E. (1987). Marital status and age as related to masculine and feminine personality dimensions and self-esteem. *Journal of Social Psychology*, 127(3), 289–298.

Mack, D., Williams, J. G., & Kremer, J. M. (1979). Perception of a simulated other player and behavior in the reiterated Prisoner's Dilemma game. *Psychological Record*, 29(1), 43–48.

Maiuro, R. D., Trupin, E. W., & James, J. (1983). Sex-role differentiation in a female juvenile delinquent population: Prostitute vs. control samples. *American Journal of Orthopsychiatry*, 53(2), 345–352.

Major, B. (1979). Sex-role orientation and fear of success: Clarifying an unclear relationship. *Sex Roles*, 5(1), 63–70.

Malchon, M. J., & Penner, L. A. (1981). The effects of sex and sex-role identity on the attribution of maladjustment. *Sex Roles*, 7(4), 363–378.

Maloney, P., Wilkof, J., & Dambrot, F. (1981). Androgyny across two cultures: United States and Israel. *Journal of Cross Cultural Psychology*, 12(1), 95–102.

Markus, H., Crane, M., Bernstein, S., & Siladi, M. (1982). Self-schemas and gender. *Journal of Personality and Social Psychology*, 42(1), 38–50.

Markus, H., Smith, J., & Moreland, R. L. (1985). Role of the self-concept in the perception of others. *Journal of Personality and Social Psychology*, 49(6), 1494–1512.

Marsh, H. W., & Myers, M. (1986). Masculinity, femininity, and androgyny: A methodological and theoretical critique. *Sex Roles*, 14(7/8), 397–430.

Marshall, S. J., & Wijting, J. P. (1980). Relationships of achievement motivation and sex-role identity to college women's career orientation. *Journal of Vocational Behavior*, 16(3), 299–309.

Martin, C. L. (1987). A ratio measure of sex stereotyping. *Journal of Personality and Social Psychology*, 52(3), 489–499.

Martin, C. L., & Paulhus, D. L. (1985). Bipolar-biasing effects of sex-role extremity on memory for traits. *Sex Roles*, 13, 463–474.

Martin, H., & Ramanaiah, N. (1988). Confirmatory factor analysis of the Bem Sex-Role Inventory. *Psychological Reports*, 62, 343–350.

Martin, R. E., & Light, H. K. (1984). Sex-role orientation of university students. *Psychological Reports*, 54(1), 316.

Marwit, S. J. (1981). Assessment of sex-role stereotyping among male and female psychologist practitioners. *Journal of Personality Assessment*, 45(6), 593–599.

Mast, D. L., & Herron, W. G. (1986). The Sex-role Antecedents Scales. *Perceptual and Motor Skills*, 63(1), 27–56.

Matteo, S. (1986). The effect of sex and gender-schematic processing on sport participation. *Sex Roles, 15*(7/8), 417–432.

McCabe, M. P. (1982). The influence of sex and sex role on the dating attitudes and behavior of Australian youth. *Journal of Adolescent Health Care, 3*(1), 29–36.

McCabe, M. P., & Collins, J. K. (1979). Sex role and dating orientation. *Journal of Youth and Adolescence, 8*(4), 407–425.

McCauley, E. A., & Ehrhardt, A. A. (1977). Role expectations and definitions: A comparison of female transsexuals and lesbians. *Journal of Homosexuality, 3*(2), 137–147.

McCauley, E. A., & Ehrhardt, A. A. (1984). Follow-up of females with gender identity disorders. *Journal of Nervous and Mental Disease, 172*(6), 353–358.

McGraw, K. M., & Bloomfield, J. (1987). Social influence on group moral decisions: The interactive effects of moral reasoning and sex role orientation. *Journal of Personality & Social Psychology, 53*, 1080–1087.

McLean, B. K., & Payne, R. B. (1982). Sex, sex role, and psychomotor reminiscence. *Acta Psychologica, 51*(2), 115–122.

McMahan, E. M., & Stacks, D. W. (1984). The relationship between androgyny and cognitive complexity: An exploratory investigation. *Southern Speech Communication Journal, 49*(3), 229–240.

McPherson, K. S., & Spetrino, S. K. (1983). Androgyny and sex-typing: Differences in beliefs regarding gender polarity in ratings of ideal men and women. *Sex Roles, 9*(4), 441–451.

Mednick, M. T. S. (1981). Factors influencing role-innovative career striving in black and white college women: The effect of expectancies, causal attribution, sex role self concept and achievement related motives. *Catalog of Selected Documents in Psychology, 11*, 54. (Ms. No. 2299)

Melancon, J. G., & Thompson, B. (1985). Selected correlates of computer arcade game play. *Perceptual and Motor Skills, 61*(3), 1123–1129.

Mellinger, J. C., & Erdwins, C. J. (1985). Personality correlates of age and life roles in adult women. *Psychology of Women Quarterly, 9*(4), 503–514.

Merluzzi, T. V., & Merluzzi, B. (1981). Androgyny, stereotypy and the perception of female therapists. *Journal of Clinical Psychology, 37*(2), 280–284.

Mertensmeyer, C., & Coleman, M. (1987). Correlates of inter-role conflict in young rural and urban parents. *Family Relations, 36*, 425–429.

Mezydlo, L. S., & Betz, N. E. (1980). Perceptions of ideal sex roles as a function of sex and feminist orientation. *Journal of Counseling Psychology, 27*(3), 282–285.

Milgram, R. M., Yitzhak, V., & Milgram, N. A. (1977). Creative activity and sex-role identity in elementary school children. *Perceptual and Motor Skills, 45*(2), 371–376.

Millard, R. J., Habler, B. L., & List, J. (1984). Sex-role orientation and career indecision. *Journal of Psychology, 117*(2), 217–220.

Millham, J., & Weinberger, L. E. (1977). Sexual preference, sex role appropriateness, and restriction of social access. *Journal of Homosexuality, 2*(4), 343–357.

Millimet, C. R., & Votta, R. P. (1979). Acquiescence and the Bem Sex-Role Inventory. *Journal of Personality Assessment, 43*(2), 164–165.

Mills, C. J. (1981). Sex roles, personality, and intellectual abilities in adolescents. *Journal of Youth and Adolescence, 10*(2), 85–112.

Mills, C. J., & Bohannon, W. E. (1983). Personality, sex-role orientation, and psychological health in stereotypically masculine groups of males. *Sex Roles, 9*(12), 1161–1169.

Mills, C. J., & Tyrrell, D. J. (1983). Sex-stereotypic encoding and release from proactive interference. *Journal of Personality and Social Psychology, 45*(4), 772–781.

Mimick-Chalmers, C. (1986). A study of college women: Androgyny and perceptions of a feminist therapist. *Sex Roles, 14,* 281–286.

Mindingall, M. P. (1985). Characteristics of female clients that influence preference for the socially intimate and nonintimate female psychotherapists. *Journal of Clinical Psychology, 41*(2), 188–197.

Mitchack, J. A. (1978). Occupational sex role stereotypes and social desirability among counselor trainees. *Journal of Counseling Psychology, 25*(2), 172–175.

Montgomery, C. L., & Burgoon, M. (1977). An experimental study of the interactive effects of sex and androgyny on attitude change. *Communication Monographs, 44*(2), 130–135.

Moore, D., & Nuttall, J. R. (1981). Perceptions of the male sex role. *Personality and Social Psychology Bulletin, 7*(2), 320–325.

Moore, S. M., & Rosenthal, D. A. (1980). Sex-roles: Gender, generation, and self-esteem. *Australian Psychologist, 15*(3), 467–477.

Moreland, J. R., Harren, V. A., Krimsky-Montague, E., & Tinsley, H. E. (1979). Sex role self-concept and career decision making. *Journal of Counseling Psychology, 26*(4), 329–336.

Morse, C., & Dennerstein, L. (1985). Infertile couples entering an in vitro fertilisation programme: A preliminary survey. *Journal of Psychosomatic Obstetrics and Gynaecology, 4*(3), 207–219.

Motowidlo, S. J. (1981). A scoring procedure for sex-role orientation based on profile similarity indices. *Educational and Psychological Measurement, 41*(3), 735–745.

Motowidlo, S. J. (1982). Sex role orientation and behavior in a work setting. *Journal of Personality and Social Psychology, 42*(5), 935–945.

Mulig, J. C., Haggerty, M. E., Carballosa, A. B., Cinnick, W. J., & Madden, J. M. (1985). Relationships among fear of success, fear of failure, and androgyny. *Psychology of Women Quarterly, 9*(2), 284–287.

Murstein, B. I., & Williams, P. D. (1983). Sex roles and marriage adjustment. *Small Group Behavior, 14*(1), 77–94.

Murstein, B. I., & Williams, P. D. (1985). Assortative matching for sex-role and marriage adjustment. *Personality and Individual Differences, 6*(2), 195–201.

Myers, A. M., & Finn, P. (1985). The utility of an open-ended measure of self-concept in assessing androgyny and self-esteem research. *International Journal of Women's Studies, 8*(5), 505–511.

Myers, A. M., & Gonda, G. (1982). Empirical validation of the Bem Sex-Role Inventory. *Journal of Personality and Social Psychology, 43*(2), 304–318.

Myers, A. M., & Lips, H. M. (1978). Participation in competitive amateur sports as a function of psychological androgyny. *Sex Roles, 4*(4), 571–578.

Myers, A. M., & Sugar, J. (1979). A critical analysis of scoring the BSRI: Implications for conceptualization. *Catalog of Selected Documents in Psychology, 9,* 24. (Ms. No. 1833)

Myrsten, A. L., Lundberg, U., & Frankenhaeuser, M., Ryan, G., Dolphin, C., & Cullen, J. (1984). Sex-role orientation as related to psychological and physiological responses during achievement and orthostatic stress. *Motivation and Emotion, 8*(3), 243–258.

Nadler, A., Maler, S., & Friedman, A. (1984). Effects of helper's sex, subjects' androgyny, and self-evaluation on males' and females' willingness to seek and receive help. *Sex Roles, 10,* 327–339.

Nash, S. C., & Feldman, S. S. (1980). Responsiveness to babies: Life-situation specific sex differences in adulthood. *Sex Roles, 6*(5), 751–758.

Neimeyer, G. J., Banikiotes, P. G., & Merluzzi, T. V. (1981). Cognitive mediation of sex-role orientation. *Social Behavior and Personality, 9*(1), 49–52.

Newman, J. L., Attig, M., & Kramer, D. A. (1983). Do sex-role appropriate materials influence the Piagetian task performance of older adults? *Experimental Aging Research, 9*(3), 197–202.

Nezu, A. M., & Nezu, C. M. (1987). Psychological distress, problem solving, and coping reactions: Sex role differences. *Sex Roles, 16,* 205–214.

Ngan Ling Chow, E. (1987). The influence of sex-role identity and occupational attainment on the psychological well-being of Asian American women. *Psychology of Women Quarterly, 11*(1), 69–82.

Nicholson, S. I., & Antill, J. K. (1981). Personal problems of adolescents and their relationship to peer acceptance and sex-role identity. *Journal of Youth and Adolescence, 10*(4), 309–325.

Nix, J., & Lohr, J. M. (1981). Relationship between sex, sex-role characteristics and coronary-prone behavior in college students. *Psychological Reports, 48*(3), 739–744.

Nix, J., Lohr, J. M., & Mosesso, L. (1984). The relationship of sex-role characteristics to self-report and role-play measures of assertiveness in women. *Behavioral Assessment, 6*(1), 89–93.

Nix, J., Lohr, J. M., & Stauffacher, R. (1980). Relationship of sex, sex-role orientation and a self-report measure of assertiveness in college students. *Psychological Reports, 47*(3), 1239–1244.

Nordholm, L. A., & Westbrook, M. T. (1982a). Job attributes preferred by female health professionals, before and after entering the work force. *Personnel Psychology, 35*(4), 853–863.

Nordholm, L. A., & Westbrook, M. T. (1982b). Longitudinal data on the BEM Sex Role Inventory. *Australian Psychologist, 17*(1), 97–98.

Obstfeld, L. S., Lupfer, M. B., & Lupfer, S. L. (1985). Exploring the relationship between gender identity and sexual functioning. *Journal of Sex and Marital Therapy, 11*(4), 248–258.

O'Grady, K. E., Freda, J. S., & Mikulka, P. J. (1979). A comparison of the Adjective Check List, BEM Sex Role Inventory, and Personal Attributes Questionnaire masculinity and femininity subscales. *Multivariate Behavioral Research, 14*(2), 215–225.

Oldham, S., Farnill, D., & Ball, I. (1982). Sex-role identity of female homosexuals. *Journal of Homosexuality, 8*(1), 41–46.

Olejnik, A. B. (1982). Sex differences, sex-role orientation, and reward allocations. *Sex Roles, 8*(7), 711–719.

O'Neil, J. M., Ohlde, C., Barke, C., Gelwick, B. P., & Garfield, N. (1980). Research on a workshop to reduce the effects of sexism and sex role socialization on women's career planning. *Journal of Counseling Psychology, 27*(4), 355–363.

Orlofsky, J. L. (1979). Parental antecedents of sex-role orientation in college men and women. *Sex Roles, 5*(4), 495–512.

Orlofsky, J. L. (1981). A comparison of projective and objective fear-of-success and sex-role orientation measures as predictors of women's performance on masculine and feminine tasks. *Sex Roles, 7*(10), 999–1018.

Orlofsky, J. L. (1982). Psychological androgyny, sex-typing, and sex-role ideology as predictors of male-female interpersonal attraction. *Sex Roles, 8*(10), 1057–1073.

Orlofsky, J. L., Aslin, A. L., & Ginsburg, S. D. (1977). Differential effectiveness of two classification procedures on the Bem Sex Role Inventory. *Journal of Personality Assessment, 41*(4), 414–416.

Orlofsky, J. L., & Windle, M. T. (1978). Sex-role orientation, behavioral adaptability and personal adjustment. *Sex Roles, 4*(6), 801–811.

Otto, M. W., & Dougher, M. J. (1985). Sex differences and personality factors in responsivity to pain. *Perceptual and Motor Skills, 61*(2), 383–390.

Overton, W. F., & Meehan, A. M. (1982). Individual differences in formal operational thought: Sex role and learned helplessness. *Child Development, 53*(6), 1536–1543.

Owie, I. (1981). Influence of sex-role standards in sport competition anxiety. *International Journal of Sport Psychology, 12*(4), 289–292.

Palkovitz, R. (1984). Parental attitudes and fathers' interactions with their 5-month-old infants. *Developmental Psychology, 20*(6), 1054–1060.

Paludi, M. A. (1978). Machover revisited: Impact of sex-role orientation on sex sequence on the Draw-A-Person Test. *Perceptual and Motor Skills, 47*(3), 713–714.

Paludi, M. A. (1984). Impact of androgynous and traditional sex-role orientations on evaluations of successful performance. *Psychology of Women Quarterly, 8*(4), 370–375.

Paul, M. J., & Fischer, J. L. (1980). Correlates of self-concept among black early adolescents. *Journal of Youth and Adolescence, 9*(2), 163–173.

Paulhus, D. L., & Martin, C. L. (1988). Functional flexibility: A new conception of interpersonal flexibility. *Journal of Personality and Social Psychology, 55*, 88–101.

Payne, F. D. (1987). "Masculinity," "femininity," and the complex construct of adjustment. *Sex Roles, 17*(7/8), 359–374.

Payne, F. D., & Futterman, J. R. (1983). "Masculinity," "femininity," and adjustment in college men. *Journal of Research in Personality, 17*(1), 110–124.

Pearson, J. C. (1980a). A factor analytic study of the items in three selected sex-role instruments. *Psychological Reports, 46*(3), 1119–1126.

Pearson, J. C. (1980b). Sex roles and self-disclosure. *Psychological Reports, 47*(2), 640.

Pedersen, D. M., & Bond, B. L. (1985). Shifts in sex-role after a decade of cultural change. *Psychological Reports, 57*(1), 43–48.

Pedhazur, E. J., & Tetenbaum, T. J. (1979). Bem Sex Role Inventory: A theoretical and methodological critique. *Journal of Personality and Social Psychology, 37*(6), 996–1016.

Peevers, B. H. (1979). Androgyny on the TV screen? An analysis of sex-role portrayal. *Sex Roles, 5*(6), 797–809.

Pendleton, L. (1982). Attraction responses to female assertiveness in heterosexual social interactions. *Journal of Psychology, 111*(1), 57–65.

Petersen, A. C. (1984). The early adolescence study: An overview. *Journal of Early Adolescence, 4*(2), 103–106.

Petry, R. A., & Thomas, J. R. (1986). The effect of androgyny on the quality of psychotherapeutic relationships. *Psychotherapy, 23*(2), 249–251.

Pettinati, H. M., Franks, V., Wade, J. H., & Kogan, L. G. (1987). Distinguishing the role of eating disturbance from depression in the sex role self-perceptions of anorexic and bulimic inpatients. *Journal of Abnormal Psychology, 96*(3), 280–282.

Phillips, W. M., & Phillips, A. M. (1980). Gender, sex-role identity and avoidance confrontation of existential issues for psychiatric inpatients. *Psychological Reports, 46*(3), 967–972.

Phye, G. D., & Sola, J. L. (1984). Stability of expressive and instrumental traits in an adolescent female population. *Journal of Genetic Psychology, 145*(2), 179–184.

Pidano, A. E., & Tennen, H. (1985). Transient depressive experiences and their relationship to gender and sex-role orientation. *Sex Roles, 12*, 97–110.

Pillard, R. C., Poumadere, J., & Carretta, R. A. (1982). A family study of sexual orientation. *Archives of Sexual Behavior, 11*(6), 511–520.

Plake, B. S., Kaplan, B. J., & Steinbrunn, J. (1986). Sex role orientation, level of cognitive development and mathematics performance in late adolescence. *Adolescence, 21*, 607–613.

Popiel, E. M., & de Lisi, R. (1984). An examination of spatial ability in relation to factors from the Bem Sex-Role Inventory. *Perceptual and Motor Skills, 59*(1), 131–136.

Porter, N., Geis, F. L., Cooper, E., & Newman, E. (1985). Androgyny and leadership in mixed-sex groups. *Journal of Personality and Social Psychology, 49*(3), 808–823.

Powell, G. N. (1982). Sex-role identity and sex: An important distinction for research on women in management. *Basic and Applied Social Psychology, 3*(1), 67–79.

Powell, G. N. (1986). Effects of sex role identity and sex on definitions of sexual harassment. *Sex Roles, 14*, 9–19.

Powell, G. N., & Butterfield, D. A. (1979). The "good manager": Masculine or androgynous? *Academy of Management Journal, 22*, 395–403.

Powell, G. N., & Butterfield, D. A. (1981). A note on sex-role identity effects on managerial aspirations. *Journal of Occupational Psychology, 54*(4), 299–301.

Powell, G. N., & Butterfield, D. A. (1984). If "good managers" are masculine, what are "bad managers"? *Sex Roles, 10*, 477–484.

Powell, G. N., Butterfield, D. A., & Mainiero, L. A. (1981). Sex-role identity and sex as predictors of leadership style. *Psychological Reports, 49*(3), 829–830.

Powell, G. N., & Posner, B. Z. (1983). Stereotyping by college recruiters. *Journal of College Placement, 44*(1), 63–65.

Prager, K. J., & Bailey, J. M. (1985). Androgyny, ego development, and psychosocial crisis resolution. *Sex Roles, 13,* 525–536.

Pratt, M. W., Golding, G., & Hunter, W. J. (1984). Does morality have a gender? Sex, sex role, and moral judgment relationships across the adult lifespan. *Merrill Palmer Quarterly, 30*(4), 321–340.

Pratt, M. W., & Royer, J. M. (1982). When rights and responsibilities don't mix: Sex and sex-role patterns in moral judgment orientation. *Canadian Journal of Behavioural Science, 14*(3), 190–204.

Price-Bonham, S., & Skeen, P. (1982). Black and white fathers' attitudes toward children's sex roles. *Psychological Reports, 50*(3), 1187–1190.

Pryor, J. B. (1987). Sexual harassment proclivities in men. *Sex Roles, 17*(5/6), 269–290.

Puglisi, J. T. (1980). Equating the social desirability of Bem Sex-Role Inventory masculinity and femininity subscales. *Journal of Personality Assessment, 44*(3), 272–276.

Puglisi, J. T. (1983). Self-perceived age changes in sex role self concept. *International Journal of Aging and Human Development, 16*(3), 183–191.

Puglisi, J. T., & Jackson, D. W. (1981). Sex role identity and self esteem in adulthood. *International Journal of Aging and Human Development, 12*(2), 129–138.

Pursell, S. A., & Banikiotes, P. G. (1978). Androgyny and initial interpersonal attraction. *Personality and Social Psychology Bulletin, 4*(2), 235–239.

Pursell, S., Banikiotes, P. G., & Sebastian, R. J. (1981). Androgyny and the perception of marital roles. *Sex Roles, 7*(2), 201–215.

Radin, N. (1981). Childrearing fathers in intact families: I. Some antecedents and consequences. *Merrill Palmer Quarterly, 27*(4), 489–514.

Radin, N., & Goldsmith, R. (1985). Caregiving fathers of preschoolers: Four years later. *Merrill Palmer Quarterly, 31*(4), 375–383.

Ramanaiah, N. V., & Hoffman, S. C. (1984). Effects of instructions and rating scales on item selection for the BSRI Scales. *Journal of Personality Assessment, 48*(2), 145–152.

Ramanaiah, N. V., & Martin, H. J. (1984). Convergent and discriminant validity of selected masculinity and femininity scales. *Sex Roles, 10,* 493–504.

Rancer, A. S., & Dierks-Stewart, K. J. (1985). The influence of sex and sex-role orientation on trait argumentativeness. *Journal of Personality Assessment, 49*(1), 69–70.

Range, L. M., Anderson, H. N., & Wesley, A. L. (1982). Personality correlates of multiple choice answer-changing patterns. *Psychological Reports, 51*(2), 523–527.

Rao, S., Gupta, G. R., & Murthy, V. N. (1982). B.S.R.I. (A): An Indian adaptation of the Bem Sex Role Inventory. *Personality Study and Group Behaviour, 2*(1), 1–10.

Ratliff, E. S., & Conley, J. (1981). The structure of masculinity-femininity: Multidimensionality and gender differences. *Social Behavior and Personality*, *9*(1), 41–47.

Rea, J. S., & Strange, C. C. (1983). The experience of cross-gender majoring among male and female undergraduates. *Journal of College Student Personnel*, *24*(4), 356–363.

Reed-Sanders, D., Dodder, R. A., & Webster, L. (1985). The Bem Sex Role Inventory across three cultures. *Journal of Social Psychology*, *125*(4), 523–525.

Reiser, C., & Troost, K. M. (1986). Gender and gender-role identity influences upon self- and other-reports of communicative competence. *Sex Roles*, *14*(7/8), 431–443.

Rendely, J. G., Holmstrom, R. M., & Karp, S. A. (1984). The relationship of sex-role identity, life style, and mental health in suburban American home-makers: I. Sex role, employment and adjustment. *Sex Roles*, *11*, 839–848.

Repetti, R. L. (1984). Determinants of children's sex stereotyping: Parental sex-role traits and television viewing. *Personality and Social Psychology Bulletin*, *10*(3), 457–468.

Resnick, M. D., & Blum, R. W. (1985). Developmental and personological correlates of adolescent sexual behavior and outcome. *International Journal of Adolescent Medicine and Health*, *1*, 293–313.

Richardson, A. G. (1986). Sex-role orientation of Caribbean adolescents. *Perceptual and Motor Skills*, *63*, 1113–1114.

Richmond, P. G. (1984). An aspect of sex-role identification with a sample of twelve year olds and sixteen year olds. *Sex Roles*, *11*, 1021–1032.

Rickel, A. U., & Anderson, L. R. (1981). Name ambiguity and androgyny. *Sex Roles*, *7*(10), 1057–1066.

Ridley, C. A., Lamke, L. K., Avery, A. W., & Harrell, J. E. (1982). The effects of interpersonal skills training on sex-role identity of premarital dating partners. *Journal of Research in Personality*, *16*(3), 335–342.

Rim, Y. (1980). Sex-typing and means of influence in marriage. *Social Behavior and Personality*, *8*(1), 117–119.

Robins, C. J. (1986). Sex role perceptions and social anxiety in opposite-sex and same-sex situations. *Sex Roles*, *14*(7/8), 383–395.

Robinson, B. E., & Skeen, P. (1982). Sex-role orientation of gay fathers versus gay nonfathers. *Perceptual and Motor Skills*, *55*(3), 1055–1059.

Robinson, B. E., Skeen, P., & Flake-Hobson, C. (1982). Sex role endorsement among homosexual men across the life span. *Archives of Sexual Behavior*, *11*(4), 355–359.

Roddy, J. M., Klein, H. A., Stericker, A. B., & Kurdek, L. A. (1981). Modification of stereotypic sex-typing in young children. *Journal of Genetic Psychology*, *139*(1), 109–118.

Rodgon, M. M., & Gralewski, C. (1979). Employment status and sex role attitudes in middle-class suburban mothers. *Journal of Applied Social Psychology*, *9*(2), 127–134.

Roe, M. D., & Prange, M. E. (1982). On quantifying the magnitude of sex-role endorsement. *Journal of Personality Assessment*, *46*, 300–303.

Romberg, D. L., & Shore, M. F. (1986). A test of two hypotheses of fear of success. *Sex Roles*, *14*, 163–180.

Rooney, G. S. (1983). Distinguishing characteristics of the life roles of worker, student, and homemaker for young adults. *Journal of Vocational Behavior, 22*(3), 324–342.

Roosa, M. W. (1988). The effect of age in the transition to parenthood: Are delayed childbearers a unique group? *Family Relations, 37,* 322–327.

Rosen, A. C., Rekers, G. A., & Brigham, S. L. (1982). Gender stereotypy in gender-dysphoric young boys. *Psychological Reports, 51*(2), 371–374.

Rosenthal, K. R., Gesten, E. L., & Shiffman, S. (1986). Gender and sex role differences in the perception of social support. *Sex Roles, 14,* 481–499.

Rosenwasser, S. M., Adams, V., & Tansil, K. (1983). Visual attention as a function of sex and apparel of stimulus object: Who looks at whom? *Social Behavior and Personality, 11*(2), 11–15.

Rosenwasser, S. M., Gonzales, M. H., & Adams, V. (1985). Perceptions of a housespouse: The effects of sex, economic productivity, and subject background variables. *Psychology of Women Quarterly, 9*(2), 258–264.

Ross, M. W. (1983a). Femininity, masculinity, and sexual orientation: Some cross-cultural comparisons. *Journal of Homosexuality, 9*(1), 27–36.

Ross, M. W. (1983b). Societal relationships and gender role in homosexuals: A cross-cultural comparison. *Journal of Sex Research, 19*(3), 273–288.

Ross, L., Anderson, D. R., & Wisocki, P. A. (1982). Television viewing and adult sex-role attitudes. *Sex Roles, 8*(6), 589–592.

Rotberg, H. L., Brown, D., & Ware, W. B. (1987). Career self-efficacy expectations and perceived range of career options in community college students. *Journal of Counseling Psychology, 34*(2), 164–170.

Rotheram, M. J., & Weiner, N. (1983). Androgyny, stress, and satisfaction: Dual-career and traditional relationships. *Sex Roles, 9*(2), 151–158.

Rotter, N. G., & O'Connell, A. N. (1982). The relationships among sex-role orientation, cognitive complexity, and tolerance for ambiguity. *Sex Roles, 8*(12), 1209–1220.

Rowland, R. (1977). The Bem Sex-Role Inventory. *Australian Psychologist, 12*(1), 83–88.

Rowland, R. (1980). The Bem Sex-Role Inventory and its measurement of androgyny. *Australian Psychologist, 15*(3), 449–457.

Ruch, L. O. (1984). Dimensionality of the Bem Sex Role Inventory: A multidimensional analysis. *Sex Roles, 10,* 99–117.

Russell, G. (1978). The father role and its relation to masculinity, femininity, and androgyny. *Child Development, 49*(4), 1174–1181.

Russell, G., Antill, J., & Cunningham, J. (1978). The measurement of masculinity, femininity and androgyny: A reply to Rowland (1977). *Australian Psychologist, 13*(1), 41–50.

Russell, M. A., & Sines, J. O. (1978). Further evidence that M-F is bipolar and multidimensional. *Journal of Clinical Psychology, 34*(3), 643–649.

Ryan, G., Dolphin, C., Lundberg, U., & Myrsten, A. L. (1987). Sex role patterns in an Irish student sample as measured by the Bem Sex Role Inventory (comparisons with an American Sample). *Sex Roles, 17*(1/2), 17–29.

Sadd, S., Miller, F. D., & Zeitz, B. (1979). Sex roles and achievement conflicts. *Personality and Social Psychology Bulletin, 5*(3), 352–355.

Safir, M. P., Yochanan, P., Lichenstein, M., Hoch, Z., & Sherpher, J. (1982).

Psychological androgyny and sexual adequacy. *Journal of Sex and Marital Therapy, 8*(3), 228–240.

Sahoo, F. M., Rout, J., & Rout, A. K. (1985). Androgyny and psychological rigidity. *Psychological Studies, 30*(2), 111–115.

Sassenrath, J. M., & Yonge, G. D. (1979). The Bem Sex-Role Inventory reexamined. *Psychological Reports, 45*(3), 935–941.

Sattem, L., Savells, J., & Murray, E. (1984). Sex-role stereotypes and commitment of rape. *Sex Roles, 11,* 849–860.

Saunders, D. M., Fisher, W. A., Hewitt, E. C., & Clayton, J. P. (1985). A method for empirically assessing volunteer selection effects: Recruitment procedures and responses to erotica. *Journal of Personality and Social Psychology, 49*(6), 1703–1712.

Savin-Williams, R. C., Bolger, N., & Spinola, S. M. (1986). Social interactions of adolescent girls during sports activity: Age and sex role influences. *Journal of Early Adolescence, 6*(1), 67–75.

Schenk, J., & Heinisch, R. (1986). Self-descriptions by means of sex-role scales and personality scales: A critical evaluation of recent masculinity and femininity scales. *Personality and Individual Differences, 7*(2), 161–168.

Scher, D. (1984). Sex-role contradictions: Self-perceptions and ideal perceptions. *Sex Roles, 10,* 651–656.

Schiedel, D. G., & Marcia, J. E. (1985). Ego identity, intimacy, sex role orientation, and gender. *Developmental Psychology, 21*(1), 149–160.

Schiff, E., & Koopman, E. J. (1978). The relationship of women's sex-role identity to self-esteem and ego development. *Journal of Psychology, 98*(2), 299–305.

Schmitt, B. H., & Millard, R. T. (1988). Construct validity of the Bem Sex Role Inventory (BSRI): Does the BSRI distinguish between gender-schematic and gender aschematic individuals? *Sex Roles, 19,* 581–588.

Schneider, J., & Schneider-Duker, M. (1984). Sex roles and nonverbal sensitivity. *Journal of Social Psychology, 122*(2), 281–282.

Scida, J., & Vannicelli, M. (1979). Sex-role conflict and women's drinking. *Journal of Studies on Alcohol, 40*(1), 28–44.

Segal, M., & Richman, S. (1978). The Bem Sex-Role Inventory: A North-South comparison. *Psychological Reports, 43*(1), 183–186.

Selkow, P. (1985). Male/female differences in mathematical ability: A function of biological sex or perceived gender role? *Psychological Reports, 57*(2), 551–557.

Senneker, P., & Hendrick, C. (1983). Androgyny and helping behavior. *Journal of Personality and Social Psychology, 45*(4), 916–925.

Sethi, A. S., & Bala, N. (1983). Relationship between sex-role orientation and self-esteem in Indian college females. *Psychologia, An International Journal of Psychology in the Orient, 26*(2), 124–127.

Shapiro, D. H., Shapiro, J., Walsh, R. N., & Brown, D. (1982). Effects of intensive meditation on sex-role identification: Implications for a control model of psychological health. *Psychological Reports, 51*(1), 44–46.

Shapiro, J., McGrath, E., & Anderson, R. C. (1983). Patients', medical students', and physicians' perceptions of male and female physicians. *Perceptual and Motor Skills, 56*(1), 179–190.

Shavelson, E., Biaggio, M. K., Cross, H. H., & Lehman, R. E. (1980). Lesbian women's perceptions of their parent-child relationships. *Journal of Homosexuality, 5*(3), 205–215.

Shaw, J. S. (1982). Psychological androgyny and stressful life events. *Journal of Personality and Social Psychology, 43*(1), 145–153.

Shaw, J. S., & Rodriguez, W. (1981). Birth order and sex-type. *Psychological Reports, 48*(2), 387–390.

Sherer, M., & Adams, C. H. (1983). Construct validation of the Self-Efficacy Scale. *Psychological Reports, 53*(3), 899–902.

Shichman, S., & Cooper, E. (1984). Life satisfaction and sex-role concept. *Sex Roles, 11*, 227–240.

Shueman, S. A., & Sedlacek, W. E. (1977). An evaluation of a women's studies program. *Journal of the NAWDAC, 41*(1), 7–12.

Siegel, R. G., Galassi, J. P., & Ware, W. B. (1985). A comparison of two models for predicting mathematics performance: Social learning versus math aptitude-anxiety. *Journal of Counseling Psychology, 32*(4), 531–538.

Siegel, S. J. (1986). The effect of culture on how women experience menstruation: Jewish women and Mikvah. *Women and Health, 10*(4), 63–74.

Signorella, M. L. (1984). Cognitive consequences of personal involvement in gender identity. *Sex Roles, 11*, 923–939.

Signorella, M. L., & Jamison, W. (1978). Sex differences in the correlations among field dependence, spatial ability, sex role orientation, and performance on Piaget's water-level task. *Developmental Psychology, 14*(6), 689–690.

Silvern, L. E., & Ryan, V. L. (1979). Self-rated adjustment and sex-typing on the Bem Sex-Role Inventory: Is masculinity the primary predictor of adjustment? *Sex Roles, 5*(6), 739–763.

Silvern, L. E., Ryan, V. L. (1983). A reexamination of masculine and feminine sex-role ideals and conflicts among ideals for the man, woman, and person. *Sex Roles, 9*(12), 1223–1248.

Sines, J. O., & Russell, M. A. (1978). The BSRI M, F, and androgyny scores are bipolar. *Journal of Clinical Psychology, 34*(1), 53–56.

Sinnott, J. D. (1982). Correlates of sex roles of older adults. *Journal of Gerontology, 37*(5), 587–594.

Sinnott, J. D. (1984). Older men, older women: Are their perceived sex roles similar? *Sex Roles, 10*, 847–856.

Sinnott, J. D., Block, M. R., Grambs, J. D., Gaddy, C. D., & Davidson, J. L. (1981). Sex roles in mature adults: Antecedents and correlates. *Catalog of Selected Documents in Psychology, 11*, 82. (Ms. No. 2368)

Skrapec, C., & MacKenzie, K. R. (1981). Psychological self-perception in male transsexuals, homosexuals, and heterosexuals. *Archives of Sexual Behavior, 10*(4), 357–370.

Small, A. C., Erdwins, C., & Gross, R. B. (1979). A comparison of the Bem Sex-Role Inventory and the Heilbrun Masculinity and Femininity Scales. *Journal of Personality Assessment, 43*(4), 393–395.

Small, A., Erdwins, C., Gross, R., & Gessner, T. (1979). Cognitive correlates of sex-role identification. *Perceptual and Motor Skills, 49*(2), 373–374.

Small, A., Gessner, T., & Ferguson, T. (1984). Sex role and dysphoric mood. *Sex Roles, 11*, 627–638.

Small, A., Gross, R., Erdwins, C. J., & Gessner, T. (1979). Social attitude correlates of sex role. *Journal of Psychology, 101*(1), 115–121.

Small, A., Teagno, L., & Selz, K. (1980). The relationship of sex role to physical
and psychological health. *Journal of Youth and Adolescence, 9*(4), 305–314.

Smith, K. E. (1981). Male teachers in early childhood education: Sex-role perceptions. *Humanist Educator, 20*(2), 58–64.

Smith, K. E. (1986). Sex-typed occupational roles and self-image among teachers.
Psychological Reports, 58(1), 73–74.

Smith, S. G. (1983). A comparison among three measures of social sex-role.
Journal of Homosexuality, 9(1), 99–107.

Snow, L. J., & Parsons, J. L. (1983). Sex role orientation and female sexual
functioning. *Psychology of Women Quarterly, 8*(2), 133–143.

Snyder, M., & Skrypnek, B. J. (1981). Testing hypotheses about the self: Assessments of job suitability. *Journal of Personality, 49*(2), 193–211.

Sollie, D. L., & Fischer, J. L. (1985). Sex-role orientation, intimacy of topic, and
target person differences in self-disclosure among women. *Sex Roles, 12,*
917–929.

Spanos, N. P., Stam, H. J., Radtke, H. L., & Nightingale, M. E. (1980). Ab-
sorption in imaginings, sex-role orientation, and the recall of dreams by
males and females. *Journal of Personality Assessment, 44*(3), 277–282.

Spence, J. T., & Helmreich, R. L. (1980). Masculine instrumentality and feminine
expressiveness: Their relationships with sex role attitudes and behaviors.
Psychology of Women Quarterly, 5(2), 147–163.

Spencer, S. L., & Zeiss, A. M. (1987). Sex roles and sexual dysfunction in college
students. *Journal of Sex Research, 23*(2), 338–347.

St. Lawrence, J. S., Hansen, D. J., Cutts, T. F., Tisdelle, D. A., & Irish, J. D.
(1985). Sex role orientation: A superordinate variable in social evaluations
of assertive and unassertive behavior. *Behavior Modification, 9*(3), 387–396.

Steinman, D. L., Wincze, J. P., Sakheim, B. A., Barlow, D. H., & Mavissakalian,
M. (1981). A comparison of male and female patterns of sexual arousal.
Archives of Sexual Behavior, 10(6), 529–547.

Stephens, N., & Day, H. D. (1979). Sex-role identity, parental identification,
and self-concept of adolescent daughters from mother-absent, father-
absent, and intact families. *Journal of Psychology, 103*(2), 193–202.

Stern, B. B., Barak, B., & Gould, S. J. (1987). Sexual Identity Scale: A new self-
assessment measure. *Sex Roles, 17*(9/10), 503–519.

Stevens, M. J., Pfost, K. S., & Ackerman, M. D. (1984). The relationship between
sex-role orientation and the Type A behavior pattern: A test of the main
effect hypothesis. *Journal of Clinical Psychology, 40*(6), 1338–1341.

Steward, M. S., Bryant, B. K., & Steward, D. S. (1979). Adolescent women's
developing identity: A study of self-definition in the context of family
relationships. *Journal of Youth and Adolescence, 8*(2), 209–222.

Steward, M. S., Steward, D. S., & Dary, J. A. (1983). Women who choose a
man's career: A study of women in ministry. *Psychology of Women Quarterly, 8*(2), 166–173.

Stockton, N., Berry, J., Shepson, J., & Utz, P. (1980). Sex-role and innovative
major choice among college students. *Journal of Vocational Behavior, 16*(3),
360–366.

Stokes, J. (1983). Androgyny as an interactive concept: A reply to Lubinski. *Journal of Counseling Psychology, 30*(1), 134–136.

Stokes, J., Childs, L., & Fuehrer, A. (1981). Gender and sex roles as predictors of self-disclosure. *Journal of Counseling Psychology, 28*(6), 510–514.

Stokes, K., Kilmann, P. R., & Wanlass, R. L. (1983). Sexual orientation and sex role conformity. *Archives of Sexual Behavior, 12*(5), 427–433.

Stoppard, J. M., & Paisley, K. J. (1987). Masculinity, femininity, life stress, and depression. *Sex Roles, 16*(9/10), 489–496.

Strange, C. C., & Rea, J. S. (1983). Career choice considerations and sex role self-concept of male and female undergraduates in nontraditional majors. *Journal of Vocational Behavior, 23*(2), 219–226.

Straub, C. A., & Rodgers, R. F. (1986). An exploration of Chickering's theory and women's development. *Journal of College Student Personnel, 27*(3), 216–224.

Street, S. (1985). Sex roles, feedback and self-concept. *High School Journal, 69*(1), 70–80.

Swenson, E. V., & Ragucci, R. (1984). Effects of sex-role stereotypes and androgynous alternatives on mental health judgments of psychotherapists. *Psychological Reports, 54*(2), 475–481.

Taylor, D. (1981). Social desirability and the Bem Sex-Role Inventory. *Psychological Reports, 48*(2), 503–506.

Taylor, D. (1984). Concurrent validity of the Bem Sex Role Inventory: A person-environment approach. *Sex Roles, 10*, 713–723.

Taylor, S. E., & Falcone, H. (1982). Cognitive bases of stereotyping: The relationship between categorization and prejudice. *Personality and Social Psychology Bulletin, 8*(3), 426–432.

Teri, L. (1982). Effects of sex and sex-role style on clinical judgment. *Sex Roles, 8*(6), 639–649.

Thomas, S., & Robinson, M. (1981). Development of a measure of androgyny for young adolescents. *Journal of Early Adolescence, 1*(2), 195–209.

Thompson, B., & Melancon, J. G. (1986). Factor structure of the Bem Sex Role Inventory. *Measurement and Evaluation in Counseling and Development, 19*(2), 77–83.

Tiberia, V. (1977). The feminine component of the masculine psyche as anima projection. *International Journal of Symbology, 8*(1), 1–16.

Tice, D. M., & Baumeister, R. F. (1985). Masculinity inhibits helping in emergencies: Personality does predict the bystander effect. *Journal of Personality and Social Psychology, 49*(2), 420–428.

Tieger, T. (1981). Self-rated likelihood of raping and the social perception of rape. *Journal of Research in Personality, 15*(2), 147–158.

Tinsley, E. G., Sullivan-Guest, S., & McGuire, J. (1984). Feminine sex role and depression in middle-aged women. *Sex Roles, 11*, 25–32.

Tinsley, H. E., Kass, R. A., Moreland, J. R., & Harren, V. A. (1983). A longitudinal study of female college students' occupational decision making. *Vocational Guidance Quarterly, 32*(2), 89–102.

Tobacyk, J. J., & Thomas, C. (1980). Correlations of masculinity and femininity to sensation seeking. *Psychological Reports, 47*(3), 1339–1343.

Trujillo, C. M. (1983). The effect of weight training and running exercise intervention programs on the self-esteem of college women. *International Journal of Sport Psychology, 14*(3), 162–173.

Tucker, C. M., James, L. M., & Turner, S. M. (1985). Sex roles, parenthood, and marital adjustment: A comparison of blacks and whites. *Journal of Social and Clinical Psychology, 3*(1), 51–61.

Tunnell, G. (1981). Sex role and cognitive schemata: Person perception in feminine and androgynous women. *Journal of Personality and Social Psychology, 40*(6), 1126–1136.

Turner, R. G., Scheier, M. F., Carver, C. S., & Ickes, W. (1978). Correlates of self-consciousness. *Journal of Personality Assessment, 42*(3), 285–289.

Turner, R. L., Jr. (1980). Femininity and the librarian—another test. *College and Research Libraries, 41*(3), 235–241.

Tyer, Z. E., & Erdwins, C. J. (1979). Relationship of sex role to male- and female-dominated professions. *Psychological Reports, 44*(3), 1134.

Tzuriel, D. (1984). Sex role typing and ego identity in Israeli, Oriental, and Western adolescents. *Journal of Personality and Social Psychology, 46*, 440–457.

Uguccioni, S. M., & Ballantyne, R. H. (1980). Comparison of attitudes and sex roles for female athletic participants and nonparticipants. *International Journal of Sport Psychology, 11*(1), 42–48.

Uleman, J. S., & Weston, M. (1986). Does the BSRI inventory sex-roles? *Sex Roles, 15*(1/2), 43–62.

Vance, B. K., & Green, V. (1984). Lesbian identities: An examination of sexual behavior and sex role attribution as related to age of initial same-sex sexual encounter. *Psychology of Women Quarterly, 8*(3), 293–307.

Vandever, J. (1977). Sex-typing and androgyny: An empirical study. *Psychological Reports, 40*(2), 602.

Vandever, J. (1978). Nursing students: Stereotypically feminine. *Psychological Reports, 43*(1), 10.

Vazquez-Nuttall, E., Romero-Garcia, I., & De Leon, B. (1987). Sex roles and perceptions of femininity and masculinity of Hispanic women. *Psychology of Women Quarterly, 11*, 409–425.

Vedovato, S., & Vaughter, R. M. (1980). Psychology of women courses changing sexist and sex-typed attitudes. *Psychology of Women Quarterly, 4*(4), 587–590.

Voelz, C. J. (1985). Effects of gender role disparity on couples' decision-making processes. *Journal of Personality and Social Psychology, 49*(6), 1532–1540.

Volentine, S. Z. (1981). The assessment of masculinity and femininity: Scale 5 of the MMPI compared with the BSRI and the PAQ. *Journal of Clinical Psychology, 37*(2), 367–374.

von Baeyer, C. L., Sherk, D. L., & Zanna, M. P. (1981). Impression management in the job interview: When the female applicant meets the male (chauvinist) interviewer. *Personality and Social Psychology Bulletin, 7*(1), 45–51.

Waddell, F. T. (1983). Factors affecting choice, satisfaction, and success in the female self-employed. *Journal of Vocational Behavior, 23*(3), 294–304.

Waldron, H., & Routh, D. K. (1981). The effect of the first child on the marital relationship. *Journal of Marriage and the Family, 43*(4), 785–788.

Walfish, S., & Myerson, M. (1980). Sex role identity and attitudes toward sexuality. *Archives of Sexual Behavior, 9*(3), 199–203.

Walkup, H., & Abbott, R. D. (1978). Cross-validation of item selection on the Bem Sex Role Inventory. *Applied Psychological Measurement, 2*(1), 63–71.

Ward, C. (1980). Psychological androgyny and attitudes toward women. *Representative Research in Social Psychology, 11*(1), 44–47.

Ward, C., & Sethi, R. R. (1986). Cross-cultural validation of the Bem Sex Role Inventory. *Journal of Cross-Cultural Psychology, 17*(3), 300–314.

Warfel, K. A. (1984). Gender schemas and perceptions of speech style. *Communication Monographs, 51*(3), 253–267.

Wark, K. A., & Wittig, A. F. (1979). Sex role and sport competition anxiety. *Journal of Sport Psychology, 1*(3), 248–250.

Waterman, A. S., & Whitbourne, S. K. (1982). Androgyny and psychosocial development among college students and adults. *Journal of Personality, 50*(2), 121–133.

Waters, C. W., Waters, L. K., & Pincus, S. (1977). Factor analysis of masculine and feminine sex-typed items from the Bem Sex-Role Inventory. *Psychological Reports, 40*(2), 567–570.

Waters, L., & Popovich, P. (1986). Factor analysis of sex-typed items from the Bem Sex-Role Inventory. *Psychological Reports, 59*, 1323–1326.

Watson, P. J., Taylor, D., & Morris, R. J. (1987). Narcissism, sex roles, and self-functioning. *Sex Roles, 16*(7/8), 335–350.

Wech, B. A. (1983). Sex-role orientation, stress, and subsequent health status demonstrated by two scoring procedures for Bem's scale. *Psychological Reports, 52*(1), 69–70.

Weener, P., & Van Blerkom, M. (1982). Dichhaptic laterality and field dependence. *Brain and Cognition, 1*(3), 323–330.

Wehr, J. V., & Gilroy, F. D. (1986). Sex-role orientation as a predictor of preferential cognitive response style. *Journal of Clinical Psychology, 42*(1), 82–86.

Weinberger, L. E., & Millham, J. (1979). Attitudinal homophobia and support of traditional sex roles. *Journal of Homosexuality, 4*, 237–246.

Weinstein, J. B., & Bobko, P. (1980). The relationship between creativity and androgyny when moderated by an intelligence threshold. *Gifted Child Quarterly, 24*(4), 162–166.

Weiss, R. W., & Russakoff, S. (1978). The sex role identity of male drug abusers. *Journal of Clinical Psychology, 34*(4), 1010–1013.

Welch, R. (1979). Androgyny and derived identity in married women with varying degrees of non-traditional role involvement. *Psychology of Women Quarterly, 3*(3), 308–315.

Welch, R. L., & Huston, A. C. (1982). Effects of induced success/failure and attributions on the problem-solving behavior of psychologically androgynous and feminine women. *Journal of Personality, 50*(1), 81–97.

Welkowitz, J., Lish, J. D., & Bond, R. N. (1985). The Depressive Experiences Questionnaire: Revision and validation. *Journal of Personality Assessment, 49*(1), 89–94.

Wells, K. (1980). Gender-role identity and psychological adjustment in adolescence. *Journal of Youth and Adolescence, 9*(1), 59–73.

Wells, M. A., Peltier, S., & Glickauf-Hughes, C. (1982). The analysis of the sex role orientation of gifted male and female adolescents. *Roeper Review, 4*(4), 46–48.

Westbrook, M. T., & Nordholm, L. A. (1984). Characteristics of women health professionals with vertical, lateral, and stationary career plans. *Sex Roles, 10,* 743–756.

Wheelan, S. A. (1978). The effect of personal growth and assertive training classes on female sex-role self-concept. *Group and Organization Studies, 3*(2), 239–244.

Wheeless, V. E., & Dierks-Stewart, K. (1981). The psychometric properties of the Bem Sex-Role Inventory: Questions concerning reliability and validity. *Communication Quarterly, 29*(3), 173–186.

Wheeless, V. E., & Duran, R. L. (1982). Gender orientation as a correlate of communicative competence. *Southern Speech Communication Journal, 48*(1), 51–64.

White, K. M., Speisman, J. C., Jackson, D., Bartis, S., & Costas, D. (1986). Intimacy maturity and its correlates in young married couples. *Journal of Personality and Social Psychology, 50*(1), 152–162.

Widom, C. S. (1979). Female offenders: Three assumptions about self-esteem, sex-role identity, and feminism. *Criminal Justice and Behavior, 6*(4), 365–382.

Wiggins, J. S., & Holzmuller, A. (1978). Psychological androgyny and interpersonal behavior. *Journal of Consulting and Clinical Psychology, 46*(1), 40–52.

Wiggins, J. S., & Holzmuller, A. (1981). Further evidence on androgyny and interpersonal flexibility. *Journal of Research in Personality, 15*(1), 67–80.

Wildman, B. G., & Clementz, B. (1986). Assertive, empathic assertive, and conversational behavior: Perceptions of likability, effectiveness, and sex role. *Behavior Modification, 10*(3), 315–331.

Williams, D., Leak, G., & Millard, R. (1984). Relationship between androgyny and self-monitoring. *Psychological Reports, 55*(1), 197–198.

Williams, D. G. (1982a). Relationships between the Bem Sex-Role Inventory and the Eysenck Personality Questionnaire. *Personality and Individual Differences, 3*(2), 223–224.

Williams, D. G. (1982b). Weeping by adults: Personality correlates and sex differences. *Journal of Psychology, 110*(2), 217–226.

Williams, J. M., & Miller, D. M. (1983). Sex-role orientation and athletic administration. *Sex Roles, 9*(11), 1137–1148.

Williams, S. W., & McCullers, J. C. (1983). Personal factors related to typicalness of career and success in active professional women. *Psychology of Women Quarterly, 7*(4), 343–357.

Williamson, A. M., & Holman, J. (1980). Sex roles: Personal choice or societal expectations. *Australian Psychologist, 15*(3), 499–501.

Wilson, F. R., & Cook, E. P. (1984). Concurrent validity of four androgyny instruments. *Sex Roles, 11,* 813–837.

Wilson, J. B. (1986). Perceived influence of male sex role identity on female partner's life choices. *Journal of Counseling and Development, 65*(2), 74–77.

Windle, M. (1986). Sex role orientation, cognitive flexibility, and life satisfaction among older adults. *Psychology of Women Quarterly, 10*(3), 263–273.

Windle, M., & Sinnott, J. D. (1985). A psychometric study of the Bem Sex Role Inventory with an older adult sample. *Journal of Gerontology, 40*(3), 336–343.

Winstead, B. A., Derlega, V. J., & Wong, P. T. (1984). Effects of sex-role orientation on behavioral self-disclosure. *Journal of Research in Personality, 18*(4), 541–553.

Wisner, B. L., Lombardo, J. P., & Catalano, J. F. (1988). Rotary pursuit performance as a function of sex, sex-role, and intertrial interval. *Perceptual and Motor Skills, 66*, 443–452.

Wittig, A. F. (1984). Sport competition anxiety and sex role. *Sex Roles, 10*, 469–473.

Wolfe, L. K., & Betz, N. E. (1981). Traditionality of choice and sex-role identification as moderators of the congruence of occupational choice in college women. *Journal of Vocational Behavior, 18*(1), 43–55.

Wolff, L., & Taylor, S. E. (1979). Sex, sex-role identification, and awareness of sex-role stereotypes. *Journal of Personality, 47*(1), 177–184.

Wolff, S., & Watson, C. G. (1983). Personality adjustment differences in the Bem Masculinity and Femininity Scales. *Journal of Clinical Psychology, 39*(4), 543–550.

Wong, P. T., Kettlewell, G. E., & Sproule, C. F. (1985). On the importance of being masculine: Sex role, attribution, and women's career achievement. *Sex Roles, 12*, 757–769.

Wood, D. R. (1986). Self-perceived masculinity between bearded and non-bearded males. *Perceptual and Motor Skills, 62*(3), 769–770.

Woods, D. J., & Launius, A. L. (1979). Type of menstrual discomfort and psychological masculinity in college women. *Psychological Reports, 44*(1), 257–258.

Wrisberg, C. A., Draper, M. V., & Everett, J. J. (1988). Sex role orientations of male and female collegiate athletes from selected individual and team sports. *Sex Roles, 19*(1/2), 81–90.

Yanico, B. J. (1981). Sex-role self-concept and attitudes related to occupational daydreams and future fantasies of college women. *Journal of Vocational Behavior, 19*(3), 290–301.

Yanico, B. J. (1982). Androgyny and occupational sex-stereotyping of college students. *Psychological Reports, 50*(3), 875–878.

Yanico, B. J. (1985). BSRI scores: Stability over four years for college women. *Psychology of Women Quarterly, 9*(2), 277–283.

Yanico, B. J., & Hardin, S. I. (1981). Sex-role self-concept and persistence in a traditional vs. nontraditional college major for women. *Journal of Vocational Behavior, 18*(2), 219–227.

Yanico, B. J., Hardin, S. I., & McLaughlin, K. B. (1978). Androgyny and traditional versus nontraditional major choice among college freshmen. *Journal of Vocational Behavior, 12*(3), 261–269.

Yarnold, P. R. (1984). Note on the multidisciplinary scope of psychological androgyny theory. *Psychological Reports, 54*(3), 936–938.

Yelsma, P., & Brown, C. T. (1985). Gender roles, biological sex, and predisposition to conflict management. *Sex Roles, 12*, 731–747.

Yogev, S., & Shadish, W. R. (1982). A method for monitoring the impact of sex-

role stereotypes on the therapeutic behavior of beginning psychotherapists. *American Journal of Orthopsychiatry, 52*(3), 545–548.

Zeff, S. B. (1982). A cross-cultural study of Mexican American, black American,
and white American women at a large urban university. *Hispanic Journal
of Behavioral Sciences, 4*(2), 245–261.
Ziegler, C., & Dusek, J. B. (1985). Perceptions of child rearing and adolescent
sex role development. *Journal of Early Adolescence, 5*(2), 215–227.
Ziegler, C. B., Dusek, J. B., & Carter, D. B. (1984). Self-concept and sex-role
orientation: An investigation of multidimensional aspects of personality
development in adolescence. *Journal of Early Adolescence, 4*(1), 25–39.
Zuroff, D. C., Moskowitz, D. S., Wieglus, M. S., Powers, T. A., & Franko, D. L.
(1983). Construct validation of the dependency and self-criticism scales
of the Depressive Experiences Questionnaire. *Journal of Research in Per-
sonality, 17*(2), 226–241.
BIBLIOGRAPHY:
Antill, J. K., Cunningham, J. D., Russell, G., & Thompson, N. L. (1981). An
Australian Sex-Role Scale. *Australian Journal of Psychology, 33*(2), 169–183.
Beere, C. A. (1979). *Women and women's issues: A handbook of tests and measures*
(pp. 104–113). San Francisco: Jossey-Bass.
Mitchell, J. V., Jr. (Ed.). (1985). *The ninth mental measurements yearbook* (Vol. 1).
Lincoln: Buros Institute of Mental Measurements, University of Nebraska.
Shively, M. G., Rudolph, J. R., & De Cecco, J. P. (1978). The identification of
the social sex-role stereotypes. *Journal of Homosexuality, 3*, 225–234.

CALIFORNIA PSYCHOLOGICAL INVENTORY (CPI)

AUTHOR: Harrison G. Gough

DATE: 1956

VARIABLE: Femininity

DESCRIPTION: The California Psychological Inventory (CPI) is a lengthy
personality inventory that yields scores on femininity (Fe) and 17 other
traits: dominance, capacity for status, sociability, social presence, self-
acceptance, sense of well-being, responsibility, socialization, self-
control, tolerance, good impression, communality, achievement via con-
formance, achievement via independence, intellectual efficiency, psychological mindedness, and flexibility. Six additional scores can be
obtained when the responses are scored by the publisher: empathy,
independence, managerial interests, work orientation, leadership, and
social maturity. The test is available in French, German, Italian, and
Spanish as well as English.

NOTES & COMMENTS: (1) The Fe scale of the CPI is a 38-item subset
of the 58-item Gough Femininity Scale (Gough, 1952) (see separate entry).

(2) Two studies compare results obtained with the CPI to results obtained with other sex role scales (Betz & Bander, 1980; Cunningham &
Antill, 1980).

(3) There is a separate entry in this book for Baucom's version of the CPI Femininity scale titled the Baucom Sex Role Inventory.

(4) The CPI is listed in *Tests In Print III* (entry 354) and in *The Ninth Mental Measurements Yearbook* (entry 182). The CPI was described briefly in Beere (1979).

AVAILABLE FROM: Consulting Psychologists Press, 577 College Avenue, Palo Alto, CA 94306

USED IN:

Antill, J. K., & Cunningham, J. D. (1980). The relationship of masculinity, femininity, and androgyny to self-esteem. *Australian Journal of Psychology, 32*(3), 195–207.

Antill, J. K., & Cunningham, J. D. (1982). Sex differences in performance on ability tests as a function of masculinity, femininity, and androgyny. *Journal of Personality and Social Psychology, 42*(4), 718–728.

Babl, J. D. (1979). Compensatory masculine responding as a function of sex role. *Journal of Consulting and Clinical Psychology, 47*(2), 252–257.

Barglow, P., Vaughn, B. E., & Molitor, N. (1987). Effects of maternal absence due to employment on the quality of infant-mother attachment in a low-risk sample. *Child Development, 58*, 945–954.

Barnes, M. L., & Buss, D. M. (1985). Sex differences in the interpersonal behavior of married couples. *Journal of Personality and Social Psychology, 48*(3), 654–661.

Beckman, L. J. (1978). Sex-role conflict in alcoholic women: Myth or reality. *Journal of Abnormal Psychology, 87*(4), 408–417.

Bernard, L. C. (1981). The multidimensional aspects of masculinity-femininity. *Journal of Personality and Social Psychology, 41*(4), 797–802.

Betz, N. E., & Bander, R. S. (1980). Relationships of MMPI Mf and CPI Fe scales of fourfold sex role classifications. *Journal of Personality and Social Psychology, 39*(6), 1245–1248.

Bohannon, W. E., & Mills, C. J. (1979). Psychometric properties and underlying assumptions of two measures of masculinity/femininity. *Psychological Reports, 44*(2), 431–450.

Buhrich, N., & McConaghy, N. (1979). Tests of gender feelings and behavior in homosexuality, transvestism and transsexualism. *Journal of Clinical Psychology, 35*(1), 187–191.

Bunt, D. D., & Armstrong, N. (1976). Teacher's perceptions of eighth grade students' likability and motivation as related to sex, femininity, ability, and achievement. *Journal of the Association for the Study of Perception, 11*(1), 9–13.

Butt, D. S., & Schroeder, M. L. (1980). Sex-role adaptation, socialization and sport participation in women. *International Journal of Sport Psychology, 11*(2), 91–99.

Cunningham, J. D., & Antill, J. K. (1980). A comparison among five masculinity-femininity-androgyny instruments and two methods of scoring androgyny. *Australian Psychologist, 15*(3), 437–448.

Erdwins, C. J., Tyer, Z. E., & Mellinger, J. C. (1980). Personality traits of mature women in student versus homemaker roles. *Journal of Psychology, 105*(2), 189–195.

Erdwins, C. J., Tyer, Z. E., & Mellinger, J. C. (1983). A comparison of sex role and related personality traits in young, middle-aged, and older women. *International Journal of Aging and Human Development, 17*(2), 141–152.

Fisher, S. (1978). Anxiety and sex role in body landmark functions. *Journal of Research in Personality, 12*(1), 87–99.

Fisher, S., & Greenberg, R. P. (1979). Masculinity-femininity and response to somatic discomfort. *Sex Roles, 5*(4), 483–493.

Goebel, B., & Harris, E. (1977). Impact of sex-role values on cognitive performance. *Psychological Reports, 41*(3), 1251–1256.

Humphreys, L. G. (1978). Research on individual differences requires correlational analysis, not ANOVA. *Intelligence, 2,* 1–5.

Illingworth, D. J., & Syme, G. J. (1977). Birthdate and femininity. *Journal of Social Psychology, 103*(1), 153–154.

Irvine, R. W. (1979). Structure of school, personality and high school dropouts. *Journal of Negro Education, 48*(1), 67–72.

Mayes, B., & Klugh, H. E. (1978). Birthdate psychology: A look at some new data. *Journal of Psychology, 99*(1), 27–30.

Medini, G., Lomranz, J., Rosenberg, E. H., & Bisker, E. (1982). Femininity and therapist success and potential. *Journal of Social Psychology, 117*(1), 57–62.

Mendelsohn, G. A., Weiss, D. S., & Feimer, N. R. (1982). Conceptual and empirical analysis of the typological implications of patterns of socialization and femininity. *Journal of Personality and Social Psychology, 42*(6), 1157–1170.

Mills, C. J. (1980, April). *A factor-analytic comparison of two measures of masculinity-femininity in post and early adolescent populations.* Paper presented at the meeting of the Eastern Psychological Association, Hartford, CT. (ERIC Document Reproduction Service No. ED 189 495)

Mills, C. J. (1981). Sex roles, personality, and intellectual abilities in adolescents. *Journal of Youth and Adolescence, 10*(2), 85–112.

Montross, J. F., Neas, F., Smith, C. L., & Hensley, J. H. (1988). The effects of role-playing high gender identification on the California Psychological Inventory. *Journal of Clinical Psychology, 44*(2), 160–164.

Moran, P., & Barclay, A. (1988). Effect of fathers' absence on delinquent boys: Dependency and hypermasculinity. *Psychological Reports, 62,* 115–121.

Newcombe, N., & Bandura, M. M. (1982, April). *Pubertal timing and personality in early adolescent girls.* Paper presented at the meeting of the Southeastern Conference on Human Development, Baltimore. (ERIC Document Reproduction Service No. ED 217 991)

Newcombe, N., & Bandura, M. M. (1983). Effect of age at puberty on spatial ability in girls: A question of mechanism. *Developmental Psychology, 19*(2), 215–224.

Newman, R. C., & Carney, R. E. (1981). Cross-validation of sex-role measures for children with correlation of sex-role measures for children and parents. *Perceptual and Motor Skills, 52*(3), 883–890.

Pillard, R. C., Poumadere, J., & Carretta, R. A. (1982). A family study of sexual orientation. *Archives of Sexual Behavior, 11*(6), 511–520.

Pitariu, H. (1981). Validation of the CPI Femininity Scale. *Journal of Cross Cultural Psychology, 12*(1), 111–117.

Russell, G. W., Bullock, J. L., & Corenblum, B. S. (1977). Personality correlates of concrete and symbolic precautionary behaviours. *International Review of Applied Psychology, 26*(1), 51–61.

Savage, J. E., Jr., Stearns, A. D., & Friedman, P. (1979). Relationship of internal-external locus of control, self-concept, and masculinity-femininity to fear of success in black freshman and senior college women. *Sex Roles, 5,* 373–383.

Slade, P., & Jenner, F. A. (1980). Attitudes to female roles, aspects of menstruation and complaining of menstrual symptoms. *British Journal of Social and Clinical Psychology, 19*(2), 109–113.

Small, A. C., Biller, H. B., Gross, R. B., & Prochaska, J. O. (1977). Congruency of sex-role identification in normal and disturbed adolescent males. *Psychological Reports, 41*(1), 39–46.

Small, A. C., Gross, R. B., & Batlis, N. C. (1979). Sexual identity and personality variables in normal and disturbed adolescent girls. *Adolescence, 14,* 31–44.

Stamp, P. (1979). Girls and mathematics: Parental variables. *British Journal of Educational Psychology, 49*(1), 39–50.

Streitmatter, J. L. (1985). Cross-sectional investigation of adolescent perceptions of gender roles. *Journal of Adolescence, 8*(2), 183–193.

Teicholz, J. G. (1978, March). *Psychological correlates of voluntary childlessness in married women.* Paper presented at the meeting of the Eastern Psychological Association, Washington, DC. (ERIC Document Reproduction Service No. ED 163 316)

Welsh, G. S., & Baucom, D. H. (1977). Sex, masculinity-femininity, and intelligence. *Intelligence, 1*(2), 218–233.

BIBLIOGRAPHY:

Beere, C. A. (1979). *Women and women's issues: A handbook of tests and measures* (pp. 151–153). San Francisco: Jossey-Bass.

Gough, H. G. (1952). Identifying psychological femininity. *Educational and Psychological Measurement, 12,* 427–439.

Mitchell, J. V., Jr. (Ed.). (1985). *The ninth mental measurements yearbook* (Vol. 1). Lincoln: NE: Buros Institute of Mental Measurements, University of Nebraska.

Mitchell, J. V., Jr. (Ed.). (1985). *Tests in print III.* Lincoln, NE: Buros Institute of Mental Measurements, University of Nebraska.

CHINESE SEX-ROLE INVENTORY (CSRI)

AUTHOR: Susan Keyes

DATE: 1983

VARIABLE: Gender role

TYPE OF INSTRUMENT: Summated rating scale

DESCRIPTION: The Chinese Sex-Role Inventory (CSRI), which is in Cantonese, consists of 51 items listing character traits (9 male typed, 9 female typed, and 9 sex neutral), activities (6 male typed, 6 female typed, and 3 sex neutral), and school subjects (3 male typed and 6 sex neutral). Respondents use a 7-point scale to rate how accurately each character trait describes them or how frequently they engage in each activity listed.

School subjects are presented in groups of three, and respondents select the one in each set that they would most like to excel in. Keyes's (1983, 1984) work with the scale led her to use only the character traits in data analyses.

SAMPLE ITEMS: (male character traits) active; ambitious
   (female character traits) kind and approachable; lively
   (neutral character traits) clever; sympathetic
   (male activities) ballgames; soccer
   (female activities) minding children; singing
   (neutral activities) badminton; reading
   (male school subjects) math; science
   (neutral school subjects) Chinese history; domestic science

PREVIOUS SUBJECTS: Cantonese-speaking Chinese students, ages 12–13 and 15–16 living in Kowloon Peninsula; Chinese women undergoing hysterectomies

APPROPRIATE FOR: Cantonese-speaking Chinese persons, ages 12 and over

ADMINISTRATION: Self-administered; about 15–20 minutes

SCORING: Several different scores can be obtained from the scale. Total scores can be found for the male-typed items, the female-typed items, and the neutral items, and a difference score can be obtained by subtracting the total of the female-typed items from the total of the male-typed items. Furthermore, the median split procedure can be used to classify persons as masculine, feminine, androgynous, and undifferentiated.

DEVELOPMENT: Scale development began by asking Chinese students to prepare four lists: activities and/or school subjects that boys should excel in, activities and/or school subjects that girls should excel in, character traits that boys should possess, and character traits that girls should possess. From these lists, an item pool of 68 character traits and 36 activity/school subject terms was constructed. Two age groups of students, 13 year olds and 14 year olds, were then asked to rate the items in terms of how important each was for a girl or for a boy; no student rated terms for both sexes. Following the procedures of Bem (1974), an item was considered male typed if both sexes judged it as more desirable for boys than for girls; a term was judged female typed if both sexes judged it as more desirable for girls than for boys; and a term was judged neutral if it was no more desirable for one sex than the other. From the terms that satisfied these criteria for judges at both age levels, 27 character traits, 15 activity items, and 3 school subjects were selected for the final scale. Six other school subjects were added to the scale. Further analyses of data gathered with the CSRI revealed large variability on ratings of activities. Given this variability and given that the school subjects were not balanced in terms of male typed, female typed, and sex neutral, Keyes (1984) used only the character traits in further analyses.

RELIABILITY: Separate alpha coefficients were computed for boys and for girls for the male, female, and neutral items. The coefficients ranged from .63 (girls' responses to neutral character traits) to .85 (girls' responses to male school subjects) (Keyes, 1984). However, when the CSRI was used as a self-rating instrument, the alpha coefficients for the activity ratings were unacceptably low.

VALIDITY: Keyes (1984) pointed out "that the terms provide a fair reflection of culturally relevant stereotypes was supported by observations, interviews, and conversations with students and friends throughout the fieldwork period" (p. 138).

As would be expected, when boys and girls were compared on their ratings of male- and female-typed terms, it was found that boys scored significantly higher than girls on the male-typed terms, and girls scored significantly higher than boys on the female-typed terms. Somewhat surprisingly, the girls scored slightly higher on the male-typed terms, though the differences were probably not significant.

When the median split method was used to classify individuals into masculine, feminine, androgynous, and undifferentiated groups, the resulting distribution was quite similar to that found with samples in the United States. Furthermore, consistent with expectation, younger children were more likely to be classified as undifferentiated than were older children.

NOTES & COMMENTS: Tsoi, Ho, and Poon (1984) administered the 27 character trait items to 20 Chinese women undergoing hysterectomies. They found no significant relationship between the CSRI scores and measures of general health and hypochondriasis.

AVAILABLE FROM: For English translations of the items, see Keyes, 1983, 1984.

USED IN:

Keyes, S. (1983). Sex differences in cognitive abilities and sex-role stereotypes in Hong Kong Chinese adolescents. *Sex Roles*, 9(8), 853–870.

Keyes, S. (1984). Measuring sex-role stereotypes: Attitudes among Hong Kong Chinese adolescents and the development of the Chinese Sex-Role Inventory. *Sex Roles*, 10(1/2), 129–140.

Tsoi, M. M., Ho, P. C., & Poon, R. S. M. (1984). Pre-operation indicators and post-hysterectomy outcome. *British Journal of Clinical Psychology*, 23, 151–152.

BIBLIOGRAPHY:

Bem, S. L. (1974). The measurement of psychological androgyny. *Journal of Consulting and Clinical Psychology*, 42, 155–162.

COMREY PERSONALITY SCALES
AUTHOR: Andrew L. Comrey
DATE: 1970

VARIABLE: Masculinity/femininity

APPROPRIATE FOR: Ages 16 and over

NOTES & COMMENTS: The instrument yields nine other scores: trust versus defensiveness, orderliness versus lack of compulsion, social conformity versus rebelliousness, activity versus lack of energy, emotional stability versus neuroticism, extraversion versus introversion, empathy versus egocentrism, validity check, and response bias.

AVAILABLE FROM: Educational and Industrial Testing Service, P.O. Box 7234, San Diego, CA 92107

USED IN:

Antill, J. K., & Cunningham, J. D. (1982). Sex differences in performance on ability tests as a function of masculinity, femininity, and androgyny. *Journal of Personality and Social Psychology*, 42(4), 718–728.

Comrey, A. L., & Schiebel, D. (1983). Personality test correlates of psychiatric outpatient status. *Journal of Consulting and Clinical Psychology*, 51(5), 757–762.

Cunningham, J. D., & Antill, J. K. (1980). A comparison among five masculinity-femininity-androgyny instruments and two methods of scoring androgyny. *Australian Psychologist*, 15(3), 437–448.

Levin, J., Montag, I., & Comrey, A. (1983). Comparison of multitrait-multimethod, factor, and smallest space analysis on personality scale data. *Psychological Reports*, 53, 591–596.

Marsh, H. W. (1985). The structure of masculinity/femininity: An application of confirmatory factor analysis to higher-order factor structures and factorial invariance. *Multivariate Behavioral Research*, 20(4), 427–449.

Marsh, H. W., & Myers, M. (1982). Masculinity, femininity, and androgyny: A methodological and theoretical critique. *Sex Roles*, 14(7/8), 397–430.

McCreary, C. P., & Gershen, J. A. (1982). Changes in personality among male and female dental graduates. *Journal of Dental Education*, 46(5), 279–283.

Stoner, S. B., & Panek, P. E. (1985). Age and sex differences with the Comrey Personality Scale. *Journal of Psychology*, 119(2), 137–142.

Thomas, D. A., & Reznikoff, M. (1984). Sex role orientation, personality structure, and adjustment in women. *Journal of Personality Assessment*, 48(1), 28–36.

FIGURE DRAWING

DATE: 1948

VARIABLE: Sex role identification

DESCRIPTION: Figure drawing is a general procedure used to measure sex role orientation or identification. There have been variations in the procedures used, but the most common figure drawing procedure is the Draw-A-Person test in which a person is asked to draw a picture of a whole person. The person drawing the picture is often asked to indicate the sex of the figure drawn. Sometimes the person is asked to draw a person of the opposite sex after the first drawing is complete. Scoring procedures vary.

ARTICLES LISTED IN BEERE, 1979: 71

NOTES & COMMENTS: (1) Though the test has been used extensively, it has also been the subject of criticism (e.g., Farylo & Paludi, 1985; Paludi, 1978).

(2) The figure drawing technique is most often used with preschoolers, though it has also been used with college students, adults, and special populations, including children referred for gender problems, transsexuals, transvestites, and alcoholics. The figure drawing technique is used most often in the United States, but it has also been used in Nigeria, Mexico, and Israel.

(3) The citations listed warrant a few comments. In two studies (Downs & Langlois, 1988; Seegmiller, 1977), preschool children were tested with several measures including the Draw-A-Person, and scores on the various measures were compared. Fleming, Cohen, and Salt (1981), unlike most other researchers using drawing techniques, asked persons to draw pictures of animals. The subjects for their study were college students. Troll's (1976) study used the Goodenough-Harris Test, a figure drawing measure that assesses intellectual functioning. Troll tested children ages 11 to 13 and concluded that the test was not useful because scoring was based on outdated notions about women.

AVAILABLE FROM: No source is necessary

USED IN:

Bancroft, J., Axworthy, D., & Ratcliffe, S. (1982). The personality and psychosexual development of boys with 47 XXY chromosome constitution. *Journal of Child Psychology and Psychiatry and Applied Disciplines*, 23(2), 169–180.

Bentler, P. M., Rekers, G. A., & Rosen, A. C. (1979). Congruence of childhood sex-role identity and behaviour disturbances. *Child Care, Health, and Development*, 5, 267–283.

Buhrich, N., & McConaghy, N. (1979). Tests of gender feelings and behavior in homosexuality, transvestism, and transsexualism. *Journal of Clinical Psychology*, 35(1), 187–191.

Cole, H. J., Zucker, K. J., & Bradley, S. J. (1982). Patterns of gender-role behaviour in children attending traditional and non-traditional day-care centres. *Canadian Journal of Psychiatry*, 27, 410–414.

Delatte, J. G., Jr. (1985). Significance of femininity in human figure drawings of girls. *Psychological Reports*, 56, 165–166.

Downs, A. C., & Langlois, J. H. (1988). Sex typing: Construct and measurement issues. *Sex Roles*, 18(1/2), 87–100.

Drake, C. T., & McDougall, D. (1977). Effects of the absence of a father and other male models on the development of boys' sex roles. *Developmental Psychology*, 13(5), 537–538.

Drotar, D., Owens, R., & Gotthold, J. (1980). Personality adjustment of children and adolescents with hypopituitarism. *Child Psychiatry and Human Development*, 11(1), 59–66.

Farylo, B., & Paludi, M. A. (1985). Research with the Draw-A-Person Test: Conceptual and methodological issues. *Journal of Psychology*, 119(6), 575–580.

Fleming, M., Cohen, D., & Salt, P. (1981). Use of animal and opposite drawings in assessment of gender identity of young adults. *Psychological Reports, 49*, 987–993.

Fleming, M., Koocher, G., & Nathans, J. (1979). Draw-A-Person Test: Implications for gender identification. *Archives of Sexual Behavior, 8*(1), 55–61.

Gold, D., & Berger, C. (1978). Problem-solving performance of young boys and girls as a function of task appropriateness and sex identity. *Sex Roles, 4*(2), 183–193.

Green, R. (1978). Sexual identity of 37 children raised by homosexual or transsexual parents. *American Journal of Psychiatry, 135*(6), 692–697.

Grossman, B. (1977, August). *Children's "ideal self"—which sex? Drawings from two Mexican subcultures.* Paper presented at the meeting of the American Psychological Association, San Francisco. (ERIC Document Reproduction Service No. ED 159 514)

Jaffe, Y., & Rosenfeld, H. (1982). Field dependence, handling of hostility, and sexual identification in posttraumatic Yom Kippur war veterans. *Series in Clinical and Community Psychology Stress and Anxiety, 8*, 177–188.

Johnson, H., O'Connell, A., & Siiter, R. (1983, April). *Sex-role concepts and gender identity in children's drawings.* Paper presented at the meeting of the Eastern Psychological Association, Philadelphia. (ERIC Document Reproduction Service No. ED 241 164)

Koff, E., Rierdan, J., & Silverstone, E. (1978). Changes in representation of body image as a function of menarcheal status. *Developmental Psychology, 14*(6), 635–642.

LaTorre, R. A., & Gregoire, P. A. (1977). Gender role in university mental health clients. *Journal of Individual Psychology, 33*, 246–249.

McCauley, E. A., & Ehrhardt, A. A. (1977). Role expectations and definitions: A comparison of female transsexuals and lesbians. *Journal of Homosexuality, 3*(2), 137–147.

Paludi, M. A. (1978). Machover revisited: Impact of sex-role orientation on sex sequence on the Draw-A-Person test. *Perceptual and Motor Skills, 47*, 713–714.

Pfeffer, K. (1985). Sex-identification and sex-typing in some Nigerian children's drawings. *Social Behavior and Personality, 13*(1), 69–72.

Rierdan, J., & Koff, E. (1980). The psychological impact of menarche: Integrative versus disruptive changes. *Journal of Youth and Adolescence, 9*(1), 49–58.

Scida, J., & Vannicelli, M. (1979). Sex-role conflict and women's drinking. *Journal of Studies on Alcohol, 40*(1), 28–44.

Seegmiller, B. R. (1977, April). *Measuring sex role development: A comparison of two methods.* Paper presented at the meeting of the Eastern Psychological Association, Boston. (ERIC Document Reproduction Service No. ED 144 985)

Seegmiller, B. R. (1980). Sex-role differentiation in preschoolers: Effects of maternal employment. *Journal of Psychology, 104*, 185–189.

Seegmiller, B. R., & Dunivant, N. (1981). A comparison of two methods of measuring sex-role differentiation in preschoolers. *Journal of Psychology, 108*, 137–147.

Seegmiller, B. R., Suter, B., & Dunivant, N. (1978). *Personal, socioeconomic, and sibling influences on sex-role differentiation.* Unpublished manuscript, Hunter College, New York. (ERIC Document Reproduction Service No. ED 176 895)

Seegmiller, B. R., Suter, B., & Dunivant, N. (1979). *Sex-role socialization in the nursery school: Background, design, methods, and subjects.* Unpublished manuscript, Hunter College, New York. (ERIC Document Reproduction Service No. ED 178 167)

Seegmiller, B. R., Suter, B., Dunivant, N., & Baldemor, D. (1979). The effects of tester sex on sex-typed responses of preschoolers. *Journal of Psychology, 102,* 215–224.

Suter, B., Seegmiller, B. R., & Dunivant, N. (1980). *Age, sex, and income level effects on sex-role differentiation in preschoolers.* Unpublished manuscript, New York. (ERIC Document Reproduction Service No. ED 183 249)

Suter, B., Seegmiller, B. R., & Dunivant, N. (1980). Effects of age, sex, and income level on sex-role differentiation in preschoolers. *Journal of Psychology, 104,* 217–220.

Teglasi, H. (1980). Acceptance of the traditional female role and sex of the first person drawn on the Draw-A-Person Test. *Perceptual and Motor Skills, 51,* 267–271.

Troll, E. W. (1976, September). *The Barbee doll mentality and the Goodenough-Harris Drawing Test.* Paper presented at the meeting of the American Psychological Association, Washington, DC. (ERIC Document Reproduction Service No. ED 164 546)

Zucker, K. J., Bradley, S. J., Doering, R. W., & Lozinski, J. A. (1985). Sex-typed behavior in cross-gender-identified children: Stability and change at a one-year follow-up. *Journal of the American Academy of Child Psychiatry, 24,* 710–719.

Zucker, K. J., Doering, R. W., Bradley, S. J., & Finegan, J. K. (1981, April). *Sex-typed play and behavior in cross-gender identified children: A one-year follow-up.* Paper presented at the meeting of the Society for Research in Child Development, Boston. (ERIC Document Reproduction Service No. ED 202 608)

Zucker, K. J., Finegan, J. K., Doering, R. W., & Bradley, S. J. (1983). Human figure drawings of gender-problem children: A comparison to sibling, psychiatric, and normal controls. *Journal of Abnormal Child Psychology, 11*(2), 287–298.

Zucker, K. J., Finegan, J. K., Doering, R. W., & Bradley, S. J. (1984). Two subgroups of gender-problem children. *Archives of Sexual Behavior, 13*(1), 27–39.

BIBLIOGRAPHY:

Beere, C. A. (1979). *Women and women's issues: A handbook of tests and measures* (pp. 41–48). San Francisco: Jossey-Bass.

FRANCK DRAWING COMPLETION TEST (FDCT)
AUTHOR: Kate Franck
DATE: 1949
VARIABLE: Unconscious gender identity

DESCRIPTION: The Franck Drawing Completion Test (FDCT) is a projective drawing test in which the respondent is presented with a series of 36 simple, abstract line drawings, each placed inside a square 2¼ inches on a side. Respondents are instructed to complete each drawing in any manner they choose. Scoring requires considerable skill.

ARTICLES LISTED IN BEERE, 1979: 72

NOTES & COMMENTS: (1) Based on the citations listed below, the scale has been given to children, adolescents, and college students, to adolescents and men in Israel, to women alcoholics and women with emotional or psychiatric disorders, to transvestites and men seeking sex-change operations, to disturbed and normal adolescent girls, and to predelinquent, psychiatric, and normal adolescents.

(2) Two studies listed below looked at the psychometric properties of the scale. Berg (1985) looked at test-retest reliability over a 7-year period and at correlations between FDCT scores and socioeconomic status and intelligence. Harkey (1982) looked at the validity of the scale for children in grades 2, 4, 6, 8, 10, and 12 and college students.

(3) The FDCT is listed in *Tests in Print III* (entry 917).

AVAILABLE FROM: Australian Council for Educational Research, P.O. Box 210, Hawthorn, Victoria, 3122, Australia

USED IN:

Anderson, S. C. (1980). Patterns of sex-role identification in alcoholic women. *Sex Roles, 6*(2), 231–243.

Beckman, L. J. (1978). Sex-role conflict in alcoholic women: Myth or reality. *Journal of Abnormal Psychology, 87*(4), 408–417.

Berg, R. (1985). The Franck Test for gender identity: Correlation with occupation and long-term stability of score in normal men. *Social Behavior and Personality, 13*(1), 83–89.

Berg, R., & Berg, G. (1983). Penile malformation, gender identity, and sexual orientation. *Acta Psychiatrica Scandinavica, 68*(3), 154–166.

Buhrich, N., & McConaghy, N. (1979). Tests of gender feelings and behavior in homosexuality, transvestism, and transsexualism. *Journal of Clinical Psychology, 35*(1), 187–191.

Harkey, N. J. (1982). The Franck Drawing Completion Test: A tool for research in sex-role identification. *Journal of Personality Assessment, 46*(1), 32–43.

Kagel, S. A., & Schilling, K. M. (1985). Sexual identification and gender identity among father-absent males. *Sex Roles, 13*(5/6), 357–370.

Klein, M. M., & Shulman, S. (1981). Adolescent masculinity-femininity in relation to parental models of masculinity-femininity and marital adjustment. *Adolescence, 16*, 45–48.

Shea, J. D. C. (1983). Sex typing in Australian children as a function of social class, sex and age. *Australian Psychologist, 18*(2), 243–250.

Small, A. C., Biller, H. B., Gross, R. B., & Prochaska, J. O. (1977). Congruency of sex-role identification in normal and disturbed adolescent males. *Psychological Reports, 41*, 39–46.

Small, A. C., Gross, R. B., & Batlis, N. C. (1979). Sexual identity and personality variables in normal and disturbed adolescent girls. *Adolescence, 14*, 31–44.

Snarey, J., & Son, L. (1986). Sex-identity development among Kibbutz-born
    males: A test of the Whiting hypothesis. *Ethos, 14*(2), 99–119.
Teicholz, J. G. (1978, March). *Psychological correlates of voluntary childlessness in
    married women.* Paper presented at the meeting of the Eastern Psycholog-
    ical Association, Washington, DC. (ERIC Document Reproduction Service
    No. ED 163 316)
BIBLIOGRAPHY:
Beere, C. A. (1979). *Women and women's issues: A handbook of tests and measures*
    (pp. 48–54). San Francisco: Jossey-Bass.
Mitchell, J. V., Jr. (Ed.). (1983). *Tests in print III.* Lincoln, NE: Buros Institute of
    Mental Measurements, University of Nebraska.

GOUGH FEMININITY SCALE
AUTHOR: Harrison G. Gough
DATE: 1952
VARIABLE: Femininity
DESCRIPTION: The Gough Femininity Scale is a true/false measure ap-
propriate for persons over the age of 12. The scale consists of 58 items
covering a broad range of topics, including interests, self-perceptions,
feelings, and thoughts.
ARTICLES LISTED IN BEERE, 1979: 34
NOTES & COMMENTS: (1) A subset of 38 of these items comprises the
Femininity scale on the California Psychological Inventory (Gough, 1956)
(see separate entry). Some researchers use these 38 items and refer to
them as a short form of the Gough Femininity Scale.

(2) Baldwin (1984) looked at the stability of Gough Femininity scores
over a period of 11 years and found little change in test scores over that
period; that is, semester after semester, introductory psychology students seem to obtain relatively consistent scores.
AVAILABLE FROM: Gough, 1952
USED IN:

Baldwin, R. O. (1984). Stability of masculinity-femininity scores over an eleven-
    year period. *Sex Roles, 10*(3/4), 257–260.
Berg, R., & Berg, G. (1983). Penile malformation, gender identity, and sexual
    orientation. *Acta Psychiatrica Scandinavica, 68*, 154–166.
Chasia, S., & Eyo, I. E. (1977). Locus of control and traditional/non-traditional
    sex-role orientations in a sample of British female undergraduates. *Psy-
    chological Reports, 41*, 1015–1019.
Goldberg, C. (1977). The current effects of age, sex, and social class on con-
    formity. *International Journal of Intercultural Relations, 1*(3), 103–117.
Gough, H. G. (1952). Identifying psychological femininity. *Educational and Psy-
    chological Measurement, 12*, 427–439.
Lester, D., McLaughlin, S., Cohen, R., & Dunn, L. (1977). Sex-deviant hand-
    writing, femininity, and homosexuality. *Perceptual and Motor Skills, 45*,
    1156.
Mannarino, A. P., & Marsh, M. E. (1978). The relationship between sex role

identification and juvenile delinquency in adolescent girls. *Adolescence*, *13*, 643–652.

Savage, J. E., Jr., & Stearns, A. D. (1979). Relationship of internal-external locus of control, self-concept, and masculinity-femininity to fear of success in black freshmen and senior college women. *Sex Roles*, *5*, 373–383.

Siegelman, M. (1978). Psychological adjustment of homosexual and heterosexual men: A cross-national replication. *Archives of Sexual Behavior*, *7*(1), 1–11.

Siegelman, M. (1981). Parental backgrounds of homosexual and heterosexual men: A cross national replication. *Archives of Sexual Behavior*, *10*(6), 505–513.

Vess, J. D., Jr., Schwebel, A. I., & Moreland, J. (1983). The effects of early parental divorce on the sex role development of college students. *Journal of Divorce*, *7*(1), 83–95.

BIBLIOGRAPHY:

Beere, C. A. (1979). *Women and women's issues: A handbook of tests and measures* (pp. 121–126). San Francisco: Jossey-Bass.

Gough, H. G. (1956). *California Psychological Inventory Manual*. Palo Alto: Consulting Psychologists Press.

GUILFORD-ZIMMERMAN TEMPERAMENT SURVEY

AUTHORS: J. P. Guilford and Wayne S. Zimmerman

DATE: 1949

VARIABLE: Masculinity

DESCRIPTION: The Guilford-Zimmerman Temperament Survey is a personality test that has been used to measure masculinity. The scale yields nine other scores: general activity, restraint, ascendance, sociability, emotional stability, objectivity, friendliness, thoughtfulness, and personal relations.

NOTES & COMMENTS: The Guilford-Zimmerman Temperament Survey is listed in *Tests in Print III* (entry 1046) and in *The Ninth Mental Measurements Yearbook* (entry 460). It was described briefly in Beere (1979).

AVAILABLE FROM: Sheridan Psychological Services, Inc., P.O. Box 6101, Orange, CA 92667

USED IN:

Bernard, L. C. (1981). The multidimensional aspects of masculinity-femininity. *Journal of Personality and Social Psychology*, *41*(4), 797–802.

BIBLIOGRAPHY:

Beere, C. A. (1979). *Women and women's issues: A handbook of tests and measures* (p. 155). San Francisco: Jossey-Bass.

Mitchell, J. V., Jr. (Ed.). (1983). *Tests in print III*. Lincoln: Buros Institute of Mental Measurements, University of Nebraska.

Mitchell, J. V., Jr. (Ed.). (1985). *The ninth mental measurements yearbook* (Vol. 1). Lincoln: Buros Institute of Mental Measurements, University of Nebraska.

HEILBRUN MEASURE OF SEX ROLE BLENDING
AUTHOR: Alfred B. Heilbrun, Jr.
DATE: 1979
VARIABLE: Sex role blending, defined as "the integration of masculine and feminine behaviors within a discrete social situation" (Heilbrun, 1986, p. 123).
TYPE OF INSTRUMENT: Adjective ranking task
DESCRIPTION: The Heilbrun Measure of Sex Role Blending consists of a list of eight interpersonal situations, each accompanied by a list of 20 adjectives presented in alphabetical order. Half of the adjectives are masculine traits, and half are feminine traits. The respondents' task is to rank order the adjectives in terms of how well each adjective would characterize their behavior in the given interpersonal situation. Thus, with eight situations, the respondents are required to create eight rank orderings of the adjectives, with each rank ordering going from the most characteristic trait to the least characteristic trait. Two forms of the scale are available: a male form and a female form that differ in terms of some of the adjectives to be rank ordered.
SAMPLE ITEMS: (interpersonal situations) With someone in whom you are sexually interested; with an acquaintance you don't care much about
   (masculine items on both forms) aggressive; assertive; deliberate
   (feminine items on both forms) dependent; excitable; helpful
PREVIOUS SUBJECTS: College students
APPROPRIATE FOR: High school students and older
ADMINISTRATION: Self-administered; about 40 minutes
SCORING: For each situation, a score is obtained by finding the difference between the sum of the ranks assigned to the masculine terms and the sum of the ranks assigned to the feminine terms. The scale score is the sum of the absolute value of the eight difference scores. If masculine and feminine traits are interspersed in a situation, the sum of the ranks for the two subsets of items will be quite similar, and the difference between the ranks will be small. If, on the other hand, all the feminine traits are given high ranks and all the masculine traits are given low ranks, the two sums will be quite different, and the difference score will be high. Thus, low scores indicate blending of masculine and feminine behaviors, and high scores indicate sex-typed behavior. The range of scores reported for one study (Heilbrun & Mulqueen, 1987) was 116 to 800.
DEVELOPMENT: This measure is an adaptation of one developed by Block (1961). The set of eight interpersonal measures was adapted from Block's measure. The sets of adjectives were selected from the Adjective Check List (Gough & Heilbrun, 1980) (see separate entry). To ensure that the masculine and feminine terms were correctly sex typed

and were similar in social desirability, Heilbrun (1986) relied on ratings reported in a study by Williams and Best (1982).

RELIABILITY: Split-half reliability coefficients ranged from .66 to .93 (Schwartz, 1983, as reported in Heilbrun & Mulqueen, 1987).

VALIDITY: Heilbrun (1981) compared scores on this measure of sex role blending with scores on another measure. He obtained similar results with the two measures.

As predicted, females consistently showed more sex role blending than did males (Heilbrun, 1981, 1986; Heilbrun & Han, 1986; Heilbrun & Pitman, 1979; Schwartz, 1983, as reported in Heilbrun, 1986).

NOTES & COMMENTS: (1) Heilbrun used the Heilbrun Measure of Sex Role Blending in several studies. Heilbrun and Pitman (1979) compared sex role blending with the masculinity/femininity of laboratory behavior in several different situations. Results were compared for males and females. Heilbrun and Mulqueen (1987) used the scale to classify college women as blenders and nonblenders. Those scoring in the lowest third on the scale were considered androgynous blenders; the remaining two-thirds of the respondents were considered nonblenders. The nonblenders were further classified into three groups: balanced androgynous, masculine, and feminine. The researchers then compared the four groups in terms of daily stress symptoms, Type A characteristics, menstrual distress, and eating disorders. Heilbrun (1986) separately compared males' and females' sex role blending with their performance on a gender schema task. Heilbrun and Han (1986) compared scores on the blending measure with scores on the Masculinity and Femininity scales of the Adjective Check List.

(2) The Heilbrun Measure of Sex Role Blending is a creative measure, differing from the typical gender role scale described in this chapter. The Heilbrun Measure of Sex Role Blending should prove useful for other researchers.

AVAILABLE FROM: Heilbrun, 1986.

USED IN:

Heilbrun, A. B., Jr. (1981). *Human sex-role behavior*. New York: Pergamon.

Heilbrun, A. B., Jr. (1986). Androgyny as type and androgyny as behavior: Implications for gender schema in males and females. *Sex Roles, 14*(3/4), 123–139.

Heilbrun, A. B., Jr., & Han, Y. L. (1986). Sex differences in the adaptive value of androgyny. *Psychological Reports, 59*(3), 1023–1026.

Heilbrun, A. B., Jr., & Mulqueen, C. M. (1987). The second androgyny: A proposed revision in adaptive priorities for college women. *Sex Roles, 17*(3/4), 187–207.

Heilbrun, A. B., Jr., & Pitman, D. (1979). Testing some basic assumptions about psychological androgyny. *Journal of Genetic Psychology, 135*(2), 175–188.

Schwartz, H. L. (1983). Sex differences in social competence among androgyne:

The influence of sex-role blending nonverbal information processing and social cognition. (Doctoral dissertation, Emory University, 1982). *Dissertation Abstracts International, 43*, 3375B.

BIBLIOGRAPHY:

Block, J. (1961). Ego identity, role variability, and adjustment. *Journal of Consulting Psychology, 25*(5), 392–397.

Gough, H. G., & Heilbrun, A. B. (1980). *The Adjective Check List manual.* Palo Alto: Consulting Psychologists Press.

Williams, J. E., & Best, D. L. (1982). *Measuring sex stereotypes: A thirty-nation study.* Beverly Hills: Sage.

JOHNSON'S EXPRESSIVENESS AND INSTRUMENTALITY

AUTHORS: Miriam M. Johnson, Jean Stockard, Joan Acker, and Claudeen Naffziger

DATE: 1975

VARIABLE: Expressiveness, instrumentality, and autonomy

TYPE OF INSTRUMENT: Summated rating scale

DESCRIPTION: Johnson's Expressiveness and Instrumentality scale includes 23 adjectives indicative of expressiveness, instrumentality, and autonomy. Each adjective is accompanied by four response options: "very true of me, somewhat true of me, somewhat untrue of me, very untrue of me."

SAMPLE ITEMS: (expressiveness) sympathetic
   (instrumentality) thorough
   (autonomy) assertive

PREVIOUS SUBJECTS: High school students, college students, and nurses

APPROPRIATE FOR: High school students and older

ADMINISTRATION: Self-administered; about 10 minutes

SCORING: Item scores range from 1 (very untrue of me) to 4 (very true of me). Scale scores are obtained by averaging the item scores for the items contributing to the particular scale. Scores can be obtained for as many as five scales: expressiveness (7 items), instrumental-industrious (4 items), instrumental-analytical (3 items), autonomy-forceful (7 items), and autonomy-adventurous (2 items). Gill, Stockard, Johnson, and Williams (1987) provided means and standard deviations, separately for males and females, for each of the five scales.

DEVELOPMENT: Scale development began with a theoretical approach and continued empirically. The instrumental orientation was defined "as concern with the attainment of goals external to the interaction process, while an expressive orientation gives primacy to facilitating the interaction process itself. . . . Expressiveness involves what is now called 'interdependence' and 'relationality.' . . . Expressiveness does not imply a lack of instrumental competence, nor does competence in instrumental activities preclude the ability to relate expressively" (Gill et al., 1987). Four women with PhDs and three male graduate students sorted the adjectives on Gough's Adjective Check List (Gough, 1965) into seven categories: "positive expressive, negative expressive, positive instrumental, negative instrumental, active and/or independent, and passive and/or dependent, and a residual category for words that could not be placed in any of these six" (Johnson, Stockard, Acker, & Naffziger, 1975, p. 627). Forty-six adjectives that were classified the same by three of the four female judges and two of the three male judges were retained.

Approximately 400 college students were asked to rate themselves on the 46 adjectives. Their responses were subjected to both factor analysis and cluster analysis, and the results were combined to select items for the next version of the scale (Johnson et al., 1975). The scale was administered to high school and college students in 1982, to nurses in 1983, and to other college students in 1984 (Gill et al., 1987). The 1983 and 1984 replications included only the positive items, giving a scale of 23 items. Furthermore, on the scale given to nurses, a few other items were altered. The data obtained from each of these samples were factor analyzed and the results used to identify the five factors for which scores can be obtained.

RELIABILITY: Alpha coefficients were computed, by sex, for each group tested. For the expressiveness subscale, the coefficients ranged from .74 to .83. For the instrumental-industrious subscale, the coefficients ranged from .54 to .77. The instrumental-analytical subscale with only 3 items had lower alpha coefficients; they ranged from .39 to .69. The autonomy-forceful subscale had coefficients ranging from .63 to .76. No coefficient was computed for the autonomy-adventurous subscale because only 2 items are on that scale.

VALIDITY: Gill et al. (1987) reported the intercorrelations between the scales. The correlations were generally positive and moderate in size, supporting their contention that the scales represent distinct dimensions and those dimensions were not opposites to each other; that is, a person could be both expressive and instrumental.

The only consistent sex difference was that women in every group and time period rated themselves significantly higher than men on the expressiveness subscale.

NOTES & COMMENTS: (1) Gill et al. (1987) recommended that their scales be used as an alternative to the "typical" androgyny scales, such as the Bem Sex Role Inventory (Bem, 1974) (see separate entry) and the Personal Attributes Questionnaire (Spence, Helmreich, & Stapp, 1974) (see separate entry). They contended that "the only single dimension along which groups of males and females consistently differ, through time and across groups, is expressiveness, or a relational orientation, with men less relational than women. *We suggest that this dimension is the one researchers should focus upon in examining gender difference*" (Gill et al. 1987, p. 397).

(2) Given the low reliabilities for some of the subscales and the lack

of any real evidence of validity, this scale should be used with extreme caution.

AVAILABLE FROM: Gill, Stockard, Johnson, and Williams, 1987.

USED IN:

Gill, S., Stockard, J., Johnson, M., & Williams, S. (1987). Measuring gender differences: The expressive dimension and critique of androgyny scales. *Sex Roles*, 17(7/8), 375–400.

Johnson, M. M., Stockard, J., Acker, J., & Naffziger, C. (1975). Expressiveness reevaluated. *School Review*, 83(4), 617–644.

BIBLIOGRAPHY:

Bem, S. L. (1974). The measurement of psychological androgyny. *Journal of Consulting and Clinical Psychology*, 42, 155–162.

Gough, H. G. (1965). *The Adjective Check List*. Palo Alto: Consulting Psychologists Press.

Spence, J. T., Helmreich, R. L., & Stapp, J. T. (1974). The Personal Attributes Questionnaire: A measure of sex role stereotypes and masculinity-femininity. *Catalog of Selected Documents in Psychology*, 4, 43–44. (Ms. No. 617)

MARKE-GOTTFRIES ATTITUDE INTEREST SCHEDULE

AUTHORS: Sven Marke and Ingrid Gottfries

DATE: 1967 (used 1963)

VARIABLE: Masculinity/femininity

DESCRIPTION: The Marke-Gottfries Attitude Interest Schedule is a lengthy multiple choice measure of masculinity/femininity. Forty to 60 minutes are required to complete the scale, which consists of 10 subscales: Occupations, Hobbies, Books, Drawings, Plays, Animals, Disgust, Pity, Fear, and Ethics.

ARTICLES LISTED IN BEERE, 1979: 5

NOTES & COMMENTS: Collins (1985) modified the scale to obtain separate masculinity and femininity scores.

AVAILABLE FROM: Marke and Gottfries, 1967

USED IN:

Collins, A. (1985). Interaction of sex-related psychological characteristics and psychoneuroendocrine stress responses. *Sex Roles*, 12, 1219–1230.

Marke, S., & Gottfries, I. (1967). Measurement of masculinity-femininity. *Psychological Research Bulletin*, 7, 1–51.

BIBLIOGRAPHY:

Beere, C. A. (1979). *Women and women's issues: A handbook of tests and measures* (pp. 126–129). San Francisco: Jossey-Bass.

MASCULINE ROLE INVENTORY (MRI)/EXTENDED
MASCULINE ROLE INVENTORY (EMRI)

AUTHOR: William E. Snell, Jr.

DATE: 1986 for MRI; 1988 for EMRI

VARIABLE: Adherence to the masculine role

TYPE OF INSTRUMENT: Summated rating scale

DESCRIPTION: The Masculine Role Inventory (MRI) contains 30 items, 25 of which load on three factors: Factor I, the Success Preoccupation subscale, with 5 items; Factor II, the Restrictive Emotionality subscale, with 13 items; and Factor III, the Inhibited Affection subscale, with 7 items. Each statement on the scale is accompanied by a 5-point scale ranging from "strongly disagree" through "strongly agree."

The Extended Masculine Role Inventory (EMRI) contains 20 items with 5 items on each of four subscales: Success Dedication, Restrictive Emotionality, Inhibited Affection, and Control Obsession. Each item is accompanied by five response options: "agree, slightly agree, neither agree nor disagree, slightly disagree, disagree."

SAMPLE ITEMS: (MRI—Success Preoccupation) Close relationships can detract from career developments.

(MRI—Restrictive Emotionality) I avoid discussing my feelings because others might think I am weak.

(MRI—Inhibited Affection) I don't devote too much time to personal relationships.

(EMRI—Success Dedication) I spend a great deal of my time pursuing a highly successful career.

(EMRI—Restrictive Emotionality) I don't usually discuss my feelings and emotions with others.

(EMRI—Inhibited Affection) I don't devote much time to intimate relationships.

(EMRI—Control Obsession) I try to be in control of everything in my life.

PREVIOUS SUBJECTS: College students

APPROPRIATE FOR: College students and adults

ADMINISTRATION: Self-administered; about 10–15 minutes for each scale

SCORING: On the MRI, item scores range from $+2$ for "strongly agree" to 0 for "neither agree nor disagree" to -2 for "strongly disagree." Subscale scores are obtained by taking the average of the scores on the relevant items. Higher scores mean more of the trait; for example, a higher score means more restricted emotionality, more preoccupation with success, and more inhibition of affection.

On the EMRI, item scores again range from $+2$ to -2, with positive scores again reflecting agreement with the item and negative scores reflecting disagreement with the item. Subscale scores are obtained by summing the items on the subscale. With five items on each subscale, subscale scores can range from -10 (not engaging in typical masculine behaviors) to $+10$ (definitely engaging in typical masculine behaviors).

DEVELOPMENT: Scale development of the MRI began with the definitions of three aspects of the masculine role. "Restrictive Emotionality" was defined as having difficulty expressing one's own feelings and dealing with other's emotional expressiveness. "Success Preoccupation" concerns the tendency to be so goal directed regarding success, eminence, and accomplishment that interpersonal relationships and commitments are largely ignored. "Inhibited Affection" is the tendency to inhibit feelings of love and affection for others. Thirty items, representing these three areas and listed in random order, were administered to four groups of college students over a 3-year period from 1980 through 1982. The data from all four groups were combined and factor analyzed. Three factors, matching the three areas defined, were extracted. All items on the Success Preoccupation subscale had loadings over .40; all items on the Restrictive Emotionality factor had loadings over .50; and all items on the Inhibited Affection subscale had loadings over .45. In selecting items for the subscales, items with the highest loadings on a factor were retained as long as they did not load on a second factor with a loading equal to or greater than .30.

In developing the EMRI, Snell extensively revised the MRI subscales and added a fourth subscale measuring Control Obsession, defined as "the tendency to be preoccupied with having and maintaining control over one's life" (Snell, 1988, p. 5). The new and revised items focused on behavioral tendencies. Snell selected the 5 best items for each subscale but did not indicate his criteria for determining which items were "best." RELIABILITY: Using data from three of the four samples that completed the MRI, alpha coefficients were computed on each subscale. For the Success Preoccupation subscale, alpha ranged from .71 to .80; for the Restrictive Emotionality subscale, alpha ranged from .78 to .88; and for the Inhibited Affection subscale, alpha ranged from .71 to .79.

A sample of over 400 students completed the EMRI; many students completed the scale a second time, four weeks later. Internal consistency reliability, as measured by coefficient alpha, was .87 for Success Dedication, .89 for Restrictive Emotionality, .89 for Inhibited Affection, and .69 for Control Obsession. Test-retest reliabilities were .62 for Success Dedication, .70 for Restrictive Emotionality, .65 for Inhibited Affection, and .48 for Control Obsession.

VALIDITY: In comparing men's and women's responses on the MRI, Snell (1986b) found that women scored significantly lower than men on the Restrictive Emotionality subscale and the Inhibited Affection subscale. No significant differences were found on the Success Preoccupation subscale.

Snell (1986b) hypothesized that subscale scores on the MRI would correlate negatively with self-disclosure. He further predicted that this would be more true for the Restrictive Emotionality and Inhibited Affection subscales than for the Success Preoccupation subscale. In general, his findings supported the hypotheses. That is, he found that for men, higher scores on the Inhibited Affection subscale were associated with less self-disclosure, and for women, greater preoccupation with success was associated with less willingness to self-disclose. The strongest support for his hypothesis came from the clear-cut finding that for both men and women, higher scores on the Restrictive Emotionality subscale were associated with less willingness to self-disclose.

As further evidence of the validity of the MRI, Snell (1986a) compared MRI scores with scores on the Male-Female Relations Questionnaire (MFRQ) (Spence, Helmreich, & Sawin, 1980) (see Beere, in press), the Jenkins Activity Survey (JAS) (Jenkins, 1978), and the Extended Personal Attributes Questionnaire (EPAQ) (Spence, Helmreich, & Holahan, 1979) (see separate entry). As expected, positive relations were found between scores on the MRI and the MFRQ, a measure of gender role behaviors and preferences, and between the MRI and JAS, a measure of Type A behavior patterns. Also as predicted, few significant correlations were found between the MRI scores and scores on the EPAQ.

In order to confirm that the 20 items on the EMRI comprise four subscales, Snell (1988) factor analyzed responses from about 400 college students. The factors and item loadings were consistent with predictions. That is, four factors were identified, each with the anticipated 5 items. Factor I included the Restrictive Emotionality items with factor loadings ranging from .55 to .86 on this factor. Factor II included the Success Dedication items with factor loadings ranging from .56 to .85. Factor III included the Inhibited Affection items with factor loadings ranging from .52 to .83. Factor IV included the Control Obsession items with factor loadings ranging from .38 to .69.

Male-female comparisons on the EMRI showed significant differences on all four subscales. Males scored higher on Success Dedication, Restrictive Emotionality, and Inhibited Affection, and females scored higher on Control Obsession.

In addition to using the EMRI, Snell (1988) administered the Personal Attributes Questionnaire (PAQ) (Spence & Helmreich, 1978) (see separate entry) to college students. Correlations between scores on the two measures showed that instrumental personality characteristics as measured by the PAQ were positively related to Success Dedication and Control Obsession and negatively related to Restrictive Emotionality for females and Inhibited Affection for both sexes. Expressive personality attributes as measured by the PAQ were positively correlated with Success Dedication for males and negatively correlated with Restrictive Emotionality and Inhibited Affection for each sex.

NOTES & COMMENTS: (1) On the MRI, the intercorrelations among the three subscales, computed separately for each of three samples, ranged from .35 to .51. Although these correlations were all statistically significant, Snell (1986b) concluded that "there was evidence that the three subscales are not excessively redundant, but instead assess different aspects of the masculine role" (p. 450).

(2) The low test-retest reliabilities for the EMRI subscales should not be overlooked.

(3) Belk, Martin, and Snell (1982) and Belk and Snell (in press) related scores on the MRI to the choice of strategies college students used in order to avoid being influenced by others. Snell, Belk, and Hawkins (1986a) examined the relationship among scores on the three subscales of the MRI and the impact that stress had on the respondents. Snell, Belk, and Hawkins (1987) studied how scores on the MRI related to the use of drugs and alcohol during periods of high stress.

(4) Intercorrelations for the subscales on the EMRI were computed separately for each sex (Snell, 1988). The strongest correlations were between the Inhibited Affection and Restrictive Emotionality subscales and between the Control Obsession and Success Dedication subscales. Statistically significant but relatively low correlations were obtained between the Control Obsession and Restrictive Emotionality subscales and between the Control Obsession and the Inhibited Affection subscales.

AVAILABLE FROM: Order from NAPS c/o Microfiche Publications, P.O. Box 3513, Grand Central Station, New York, NY 10163–3513; NAPS document no. 04709; for microfiche, in U.S. remit $4.00 with order.

USED IN:

Belk, S. S., Martin, H. P., & Snell, W. E., Jr. (1982, April). *Avoidance strategies in intimate relationships*. Paper presented at the meeting of the Southwestern Psychological Association, Dallas. (ERIC Document Reproduction Service No. ED 229 698)

Belk, S. S., & Snell, W. E., Jr. (1988). Avoidance strategy use in intimate relationships. *Journal of Social and Clinical Psychology, 7,* 80–96.

Snell, W. E., Jr. (1986a). *Convergent and discriminant validity of the masculine role inventory*. Paper presented at the meeting of the Southwestern Psychological Association, Fort Worth.

Snell, W. E., Jr. (1986b). The Masculine Role Inventory: Components and correlates. *Sex Roles, 15*(7/8), 443–455.

Snell, W. E., Jr. (1988). *Validation of the Extended Masculine Role Inventory (EMRI)*. Paper presented at the meeting of the Southwestern Psychological Association, Tulsa.

Snell, W. E., Jr., Belk, S. S., & Hawkins, R. C., II. (1986a). The masculine role as a moderator of stress-distress relationships. *Sex Roles, 15*(7/8), 359–366.

Snell, W. E., Jr., Belk, S. S., & Hawkins, R. C., II. (1986b). The Stereotypes About Male Sexuality Scale (SAMSS): Components, correlates, antecedents, consequences and counselor bias. *Social and Behavioral Science Documents, 16*(1), 9. (Ms. No. 2746)

Snell, W. E., Jr., Belk, S. S., & Hawkins, R. C., II. (1987). Alcohol and drug use in stressful times: The influence of the masculine role and sex-related personality attributes. *Sex Roles, 16*(7/8), 359–373.

BIBLIOGRAPHY:
Beere, C. A. (in press). *Sex and gender issues: A handbook of tests and measures.* Westport, CT: Greenwood.
Jenkins, C. D. (1978). A comparative review of the interview and questionnaire methods in the assessment of the coronary-prone behavior pattern. In T. N. Dembroski, S. M. Weiss, J. L. Shields, S. Haynes, & M. Feinleib (Eds.), *Coronary-prone behavior.* New York: Springer.
Spence, J. T., & Helmreich, R. L. (1978). *Masculinity and femininity: Their psychological dimensions, correlates, and antecedents.* Austin: University of Texas Press.
Spence, J. T., Helmreich, R. L., & Holahan, C. K. (1979). Negative and positive components of psychological masculinity and femininity and their relationships to self-reports of neurotic and acting-out behaviors. *Journal of Personality and Social Psychology, 37,* 1673–1682.
Spence, J. T., Helmreich, R. L., & Sawin, L. L. (1980). The Male-Female Relations Questionnaire: A self-report inventory of sex role behaviors and preferences, and its relationships to masculine and feminine personality traits, sex role attitudes, and other measures. *Catalog of Selected Documents in Psychology, 10,* 87. (Ms. No. 2123)

MAY MEASURE OF GENDER IDENTITY
AUTHOR: Robert R. May
DATE: 1966
VARIABLE: Gender identity
DESCRIPTION: The May Measure of Gender Identity is a projective storytelling instrument in which respondents tell a story in response to two pictures: a man and a woman shown in mid-air doing a trapeze act and a bullfighter standing alone in the ring. The measure can be group or individually administered; stories can be communicated orally or in writing.
ARTICLES LISTED IN BEERE, 1979: 8
NOTES & COMMENTS: The measure has been used with children, adolescents, and adults. The trapeze picture seems to be used consistently by researchers, but the bullfighter picture is either omitted or replaced.
AVAILABLE FROM: May, 1966 (pictures not included)
USED IN:
Cramer, P. (1975). The development of play and fantasy in boys and girls: Empirical studies. *Psychoanalysis and Contemporary Science, 4,* 529–567.
Cramer, P. (1980). The development of sexual identity. *Journal of Personality Assessment, 44*(6), 604–612.
Cramer, P. (1986). Fantasies of college men: Then and now. *Psychoanalytic Review, 73*(4), 567–578.
Cramer, P., & Carter, T. (1978). The relationship between sexual identification and the use of defense mechanisms. *Journal of Personality Assessment, 42*(1), 63–73.

Drotar, D., Owens, R., & Gotthold, J. (1980). Personality adjustment of children and adolescents with hypopituitarism. *Child Psychiatry and Human Development, 11*(1), 59–66.

Drotar, D., Owens, R., & Gotthold, J. (1981). Personality adjustment of children and adolescents with hypopituitarism. *Annual Progress in Child Psychiatry and Child Development*, 306–314.

Fakouri, M. E. (1979). Relationship among differences in fantasy pattern, IQ, and sex-role adoption. *Psychological Reports, 44*(3), 775–781.

Kagel, S. A., & Schilling, K. M. (1985). Sexual identification and gender identity among father-absent males. *Sex Roles, 13*(5/6), 357–370.

May, R. R. (1966). Sex differences in fantasy patterns. *Journal of Projection Techniques and Personality Assessment, 30*, 576–586.

BIBLIOGRAPHY:

Beere, C. A. (1979). *Women and women's issues: A handbook of tests and measures* (pp. 77–79). San Francisco: Jossey-Bass.

MINNESOTA MULTIPHASIC PERSONALITY INVENTORY (MMPI)

AUTHORS: Starke R. Hathaway and J. Charnley McKinley

DATE: 1943

VARIABLE: Masculinity/femininity

DESCRIPTION: The Minnesota Multiphasic Personality Inventory (MMPI) is a lengthy scale that yields a masculinity/femininity score (Mf) on a bipolar continuum, four validity scores, and nine other clinical scores: hypochondriasis, depression, hysteria, psychopathic deviate, paranoia, psychasthenia, schizophrenia, hypomania, and social introversion.

NOTES & COMMENTS: (1) The MMPI is listed in *Tests in Print III* (entry 1498) and in *The Ninth Mental Measurements Yearbook* (entry 715). The MMPI was described briefly in Beere (1979).

(2) Until the mid–1970s, the MMPI Mf scale was one of the most commonly used measures of masculinity/femininity. Its use declined as researchers turned to using measures that provided two scores: a masculinity score and a femininity score.

(3) Three of the studies listed below compared the Mf score of the MMPI with other gender role measures (Evans & Dinning, 1982; Russell & Sines, 1978; Volentine, 1981).

AVAILABLE FROM: NCS-Professional Assessment Services, 5605 Green Circle Drive, Minnetonka, MN 55343; telephone: 1–800–627–7271

USED IN:

Bernard, L. C. (1981). The multidimensional aspects of masculinity-femininity. *Journal of Personality and Social Psychology, 41*(4), 797–802.

Bernknopf, L. A. (1980). Responses of adolescents on a masculinity-femininity scale and a stereotyping questionnaire. *Exceptional Children, 47*(1), 59–61.

Betz, N. E., & Bander, R. S. (1980). Relationships of MMPI Mf and CPI Fe scales of fourfold sex role classifications. *Journal of Personality and Social Psychology*, *39*, 1245–1248.

Burchardt, C. J., & Servin, L. A. (1982). Psychological androgyny and personality adjustment in college and psychiatric populations. *Sex Roles*, *8*(8), 835–851.

Elmore, P. B., & Vasu, E. S. (1979, April). *Math anxiety: Its impact on graduate level statistics achievement*. Paper presented at the meeting of the American Educational Research Association, San Francisco. (ERIC Document Reproduction Service No. ED 178 331)

Elmore, P. B., & Vasu, E. S. (1980). Relationship between selected variables and statistics achievement: Building a theoretical model. *Journal of Educational Psychology*, *72*(4), 457–467.

Elmore, P. B., & Vasu, E. S. (1986). A model of statistics achievement using spatial ability, feminist attitudes, and mathematics-related variables as predictors. *Educational and Psychological Measurement*, *46*(1), 215–222.

Evans, R. G., & Dinning, W. D. (1982). MMPI correlates of the Bem Sex Role Inventory and Extended Personal Attributes Questionnaire in a male psychiatric sample. *Journal of Clinical Psychology*, *38*(4), 811–815.

Freund, K., Langevin, R., Satterberg, J., & Steiner, B. (1977). Extension of the Gender Identity Scale for Males. *Archives of Sexual Behavior*, *6*(6), 507–519.

Humphreys, L. G. (1978). Research on individual differences requires correlational analysis, not ANOVA. *Intelligence*, *2*(1), 1–5.

Kirkpatrick, C. S. (1980). Sex roles and sexual satisfaction in women. *Psychology of Women Quarterly*, *4*(4), 444–459.

LaTorre, R. A., & Piper, W. E. (1979). Gender identity and gender role in schizophrenia. *Journal of Abnormal Psychology*, *88*(1), 68–72.

Leventhal, G. (1977). Female criminality: Is "women's lib" to blame? *Psychological Reports*, *41*(3), 1179–1182.

Levin, J., Montag, I., & Comrey, A. L. (1983). Comparison of multitrait-multimethod, factor, and smallest space analyses on personality scale data. *Psychological Reports*, *53*(2), 591–596.

Montag, I., & Comrey, A. L. (1982). Comparison of certain MMPI, Eysenck, and Comrey personality constructs. *Multivariate Behavioral Research*, *17*(1), 93–97.

Reviere, R., & Posey, T. B. (1978). Correlates of two measures of fear of success in women. *Psychological Reports*, *42*(2), 609–610.

Russell, M. A., & Sines, J. O. (1978). Further evidence that M-F is bipolar and multidimensional. *Journal of Clinical Psychology*, *34*(3), 643–649.

Simono, R. B. (1978). Careers in the clergy: The myth of femininity. *Educational and Psychological Measurement*, *38*(2), 507–511.

Sines, J. O. (1977). M-F: Bipolar and probably multidimensional. *Journal of Clinical Psychology*, *33*(4), 1038–1041.

Steffenhagen, R. A., McCann, H. G., & McAree, C. P. (1976). Personality and drug use: A study of the usefulness of the Mf Scale of the MMPI in measuring creativity and drug use. *Journal of Alcohol and Drug Education*, *21*(3), 8–16.

Stromborg, M. F. (1976). Relationship of sex role identity to occupational image of female nursing students. *Nursing Research*, *25*(5), 363–369.

Tarr, L. H. (1978). Developmental sex-role theory and sex-role attitudes in late adolescents. *Psychological Reports, 42*(3), 807–814.

Torki, M. A. (1985). Achievement motivation in college women in an Arab culture. *Psychological Reports, 56*(1), 267–271.

Volentine, S. Z. (1981). The assessment of masculinity and femininity: Scale 5 of the MMPI compared with the BSRI and the PAQ. *Journal of Clinical Psychology, 37*(2), 367–374.

Welsh, G. S., & Baucom, D. H. (1977). Sex, masculinity-femininity, and intelligence. *Intelligence, 1*(2), 218–233.

Wong, M. R. (1984). MMPI Scale Five: Its meaning, or lack thereof. *Journal of Personality Assessment, 48*(3), 279–284.

Zetenyi, T., & Lukacs, D. (1985). Masculinity-femininity and perceptual style on the Circles Test. *Perceptual and Motor Skills, 60*(2), 361–362.

BIBLIOGRAPHY:

Beere, C. A. (1979). *Women and women's issues: A handbook of tests and measures* (pp. 156–158). San Francisco: Jossey-Bass.

Mitchell, J. V., Jr. (Ed.). (1985). *The ninth mental measurements yearbook* (Vol. 2). Lincoln: Buros Institute of Mental Measurements, University of Nebraska.

Mitchell, J. V., Jr. (Ed.). (1983). *Tests in print III*. Lincoln: Buros Institute of Mental Measures, University of Nebraska.

MULTIDIMENSIONAL SEX ROLE INVENTORY—REVISED (MSRI-R)

AUTHOR: Larry C. Bernard

DATE: 1981

VARIABLE: Gender role identification

TYPE OF INSTRUMENT: Summated rating scale

DESCRIPTION: The Multidimensional Sex Role Inventory—Revised (MSRI-R) consists of 51 items representing seven factors: (1) Aesthetic Interests is "an *interest* scale reflecting enjoyment of fine arts, humanities, and related occupations" (11 items); (2) Masculine Stereotyped Interests is "an *interest* scale reflecting activities which involve physical labor, work with the hands, and traditionally male occupations" (7 items); (3) Anxiety is "a *personality* scale that is similar to Cattell's source trait of Anxiety . . . and Eysenck's . . . Neuroticism factor" (7 items); (4) Feminine Conventions is "an *interpersonal style* scale that reflects self-endorsement of items that are historically stereotypically feminine" (6 items); (5) Boisterousness is "an *interpersonal style* scale that reflects a noisy exuberance characterized by a preference for loud fun, parties, joke-playing, boasting, and begging" (6 items); (6) Dominance is "a scale reflecting a socially-desirable *interpersonal style* of dominant and assertive leadership" (7 items); and (7) Supportiveness is "a scale reflecting a socially-desirable *interpersonal style* of active and supportive involvement" (7 items) (Bernard & Wood, undated, pp. 11–12). Each item is a short sentence generally including a phrase such as, "I am," "I feel,"

"I think," "I like." For each item, respondents are to select one of seven response options, ranging from "NEVER or almost never true" to "AL-WAYS or almost always true."

SAMPLE ITEMS: (Aesthetic Interests) Disregarding salary or any other considerations, I would like the work of a sculptor.

(Masculine Stereotyped Interests) I like mechanics magazines.

(Anxiety) I get very tense and anxious when I think other people are disapproving of me.

(Feminine Conventions) I would like to be a nurse.

(Boisterousness) I like to be with a crowd who play jokes on one another.

(Dominance) I am forceful.

(Supportiveness) I am compassionate.

PREVIOUS SUBJECTS: Undergraduate college students

APPROPRIATE FOR: High school students and older

ADMINISTRATION: Self-administered; about 20–25 minutes

SCORING: Items are individually scored and then averaged to yield scores on each of the seven factors.

DEVELOPMENT: The development of the MSRI-R was based on the development of the Multidimensional Sex Role Inventory (MSRI), so it is important to describe first the development of the MSRI. A total of 375 undergraduate students completed a questionnaire that included items from the Minnesota Multiphasic Personality Inventory Mf scale (see separate entry), the California Psychological Inventory Fe scale (see separate entry), the Guilford-Zimmerman M scale (see separate entry), and the Strong Vocational Interest Blank MF scale (Bernard, 1981). Each item was accompanied by a 7-point response scale ranging from "never or almost never true of me" to "always or almost always true of me." The 147 nonoverlapping items from the scales were factor analyzed, and five factors were retained: Aesthetic Interests, Manual and Physical Interests, Hypersensitivity, Timidity and Sentimentality, and Temerity. In the next step in scale development (Bernard, 1984), 207 students completed a questionnaire including 63 items that had factor loadings greater than .40 in the prior study. This included items from all five factors: Aesthetic Interests, 15 items; Manual and Physical Interests, 11 items; Hypersensitivity, 12 items; Timidity and Sentimentality, 14 items; and Temerity, 11 items. In addition, 7 masculinity items and 7 femininity items from the Bem Sex Role Inventory (BSRI) (Bem, 1974) (see separate entry) were added to the questionnaire, giving a total of 77 items. These 14 BSRI items, labeled Instrumental-Agentic and Expressive-Communal, were selected because they had loaded on masculinity and femininity in three previously published factor analytic studies of the BSRI. A factor analysis was performed using responses to the 63 items from the prior study. Five factors were again retained, and the factors were similar to those in the first study. Then all 77 items were factor analyzed, and seven factors were retained: the five already identified plus two factors from the bidimensional BSRI. Ten items considered weak because they had loadings below .30 or because they loaded equivalently on more than one factor were deleted, and the factor analysis was repeated. The results were basically the same, with seven factors retained. These 66 items comprise the MSRI. Test-retest reliabilities for these factor scores ranged from .81 to .94, and alpha coefficients ranged from .70 to .86 (Bernard & Wood, undated).

To develop the MSRI-R, the MSRI was administered to 125 undergraduate students, and their responses were factor analyzed. The factor structure was basically the same as that obtained earlier, except that some items loaded differently in the two studies. These items were deleted, and the remaining 51 items were administered to a new sample of 251 undergraduate students. The factor analysis was repeated and the same seven independent factors were identified, but 1 item from the Feminine Conventions subscale and 3 items from the Boisterousness subscale loaded more heavily on another factor. As a result, Bernard and Wood (undated) concluded that these two subscales should be "interpreted cautiously at this stage" (p. 14).

RELIABILITY: The MSRI-R was administered to 197 college students on two occasions, separated by a 2-week interval. The test-retest correlations for the subscale scores ranged from .84 to .93 with a median of .88. Alpha coefficients ranged from .52 to .87 with a median of .76. The lowest coefficients were for Boisterousness and Feminine Conventions, and Bernard and Wood (undated) concluded: "It is apparent that these two scales are stable, but only moderately homogenous" (p. 17).

VALIDITY: The MSRI-R was administered to 36 college students who also completed the 16PF (Cattell, Eber, & Tatsuoka, 1970) and to another sample of 24 college students who also completed the Neuroticism, Extraversion, and Openness Inventory (Costa & McCrae, 1985). The data were analyzed using multiple regression procedures, and Bernard and Wood (undated) concluded: "Overall, these relationships were logical and supported the construct validity of the MSRI-R scales" (p. 18).

A sample of 197 students completed the MSRI-R and the Career Assessment Inventory (Johansson, 1982). The Aesthetic Interests score on the MSRI-R correlated .86 with the Artistic-Theme subscale on the Career Assessment Inventory, and the Aesthetic Interests score correlated .74 with the Arts/Crafts Basic Interest Area subscale. The Masculine Stereotyped Interests score from the MSRI-R also had strong correlations with two subscales from the Career Assessment Inventory. The correlation was .81 with the Mechanical/Fixing Basic Interest Area subscale and .76 with the Realistic-Theme subscale. These correlations provided further evidence for the construct validity of the Aesthetic Interests factor score and the Masculine Stereotyped Interests factor score.

Looking at sex differences, Bernard and Wood (undated) found that females scored significantly higher on Aesthetic Interests, Feminine Conventions, and Supportiveness, while males scored significantly higher on Masculine Stereotyped Interests and Boisterousness. These differences were in the expected direction. Somewhat surprisingly, there was not a significant sex difference on Dominance. Bernard and Wood also looked at the relationship between MSRI-R scores and college major. The results were in the predicted direction for five of the seven factor scores.

NOTES & COMMENTS: Whereas the early conceptions of gender role presumed that masculinity and femininity were opposite ends of a single continuum and newer conceptions portrayed masculinity and femininity as separate, independent traits, Bernard and Wood (undated) showed that gender role is a multidimensional trait. Their repeated factor analyses were remarkably stable. As Bernard and Wood point out, "The MSRI-R includes the factors of sex role identification that have been important in the assessment of sex role identification historically and more recently. Rather than discarding these factors, it incorporates them in a single device, producing a profile" (p. 6).

AVAILABLE FROM: Order from NAPS c/o Microfiche Publications, P.O. Box 3513, Grand Central Station, New York, NY 10163–3513; NAPS document no. 04708; for microfiche, in U.S. remit $4.00 with order.

USED IN:

Bernard, L. C. (1981). The multidimensional aspects of masculinity-femininity. *Journal of Personality and Social Psychology*, 41(4), 797–802.

Bernard, L. C. (1984). The multiple factors of sex role identification: Rapprochement of unidimensional and bidimensional assessment. *Journal of Clinical Psychology*, 40(4), 986–991.

Bernard, L. C., & Wood, J. (undated). *Profile analysis of sex role identification: The Multidimensional Sex Role Inventory—Revised*. Unpublished manuscript, Loyola Marymount University, Los Angeles.

BIBLIOGRAPHY:

Bem, S. L. (1974). The measurement of psychological androgyny. *Journal of Consulting and Clinical Psychology*, 42, 155–162.

Cattell, R. B., Eber, H. W., & Tatsuoka, M. M. (1970). *Handbook for the Sixteen Personality Factor Questionnaire*. Champaign, IL: Institute for Personality and Ability Testing.

Costa, P. T., & McCrae, R. R. (1985). *The NEO Personality Inventory*. Odessa, FL: Psychological Assessment Resources.

Johansson, C. (1982). *Manual for the Career Assessment Inventory* (2nd ed.). Minneapolis: National Computer Systems.

PERSONAL ATTRIBUTES QUESTIONNAIRE (PAQ)/
EXTENDED PERSONAL ATTRIBUTES QUESTIONNAIRE (EPAQ)

AUTHORS: Janet T. Spence, Robert Helmreich, and Joy Stapp for the PAQ; Janet T. Spence, Robert Helmreich, and Carole K. Holahan for the EPAQ

DATE: 1974 for the PAQ; 1979 for the EPAQ

VARIABLE: Gender role

DESCRIPTION: The original version of the Personal Attributes Questionnaire (PAQ) consists of 55 bipolar adjective scales. Each adjective scale is a 5-point rating scale with the endpoints labeled with brief descriptive phrases that are opposite to each other in meaning. Respondents rate themselves on each adjective rating scale. In developing the PAQ, traits were selected for the Masculinity (M) subscale if they were socially desirable in both sexes but more common in men; traits were selected for the Femininity (F) subscale if they were socially desirable in both sexes but more common in women; and traits were selected for the Masculinity-Femininity (M-F) subscale if they were more desirable in one sex than in the other. Of the 55 items, 18 comprise the F subscale, 23 comprise the M subscale, and 13 comprise the M-F subscale. The total of the subscales is 54 (1 item does not contribute to any of the subscales).

A short version of the PAQ is most often used. The short version includes 8 items from each of the three subscales: M, F, and M-F. Items were selected for the short form of the PAQ primarily on the basis of item-total correlations. Internal consistency reliabilities for the subscales on the short form were .85, .82, and .78 for M, F, and M-F, respectively (Spence & Helmreich, 1978). Correlations between the corresponding subscales on the full-length and short form of the PAQ were .93, .93, and .91 for M, F, and M-F, respectively.

The Extended Personal Attributes Questionnaire (EPAQ) contains the 24 items on the short form of the PAQ plus an additional 16 items that represent negative traits (Spence, Helmreich, & Holahan, 1979). The new M scale, called negative M or M^-, contains 8 items that are considered socially undesirable in both sexes but more common in males. The items are "arrogant, boastful, egotistical, greedy, dictatorial, cynical, unprincipled, and hostile," all of which are considered negative, instrumental traits. The EPAQ also contains 8 items that are considered socially undesirable in both sexes but more common in females. Four of the items form the F_C^- scale, or "communion" scale; these traits are "servile, spineless, gullible, and subordinates self to others." The other 4 items form the F_{VA}^- scale and are verbally aggressive items: "whiny, complaining, nagging, and fussy."

ARTICLES LISTED IN BEERE, 1979: 9

NOTES & COMMENTS: (1) The PAQ and EPAQ are commonly used measures of gender role, second only to the Bem Sex Role Inventory (Bem, 1974) (see separate entry) in terms of frequency of use during the past decade. Although there were only 9 references for the PAQ in Beere (1979), an additional 238 articles and 49 ERIC documents have reported on research using the PAQ/EPAQ during the past 12 years. The articles, but not the ERIC documents, are listed at the end of this description.

(2) Hall and Halberstadt (1980) developed a variation of the PAQ. Titled the Children's Personal attributes Questionnaire (CPAQ) (see separate entry), it contains 51 items and is appropriate for children in kindergarten through sixth grade. Spence, Helmreich, and Holahan (1978) also developed a children's version of the PAQ. Intended for use with children in kindergarten through fourth grade, the measure has 14 items.

(3) College students have most often been the subjects of research using the PAQ; they have been used in about two-thirds of the studies. The PAQ has also been used with many other groups, including high school students, high school athletes, married and unmarried adults, soon-to-be parents, dental and medical students, transsexuals, persons suffering from agoraphobia, twins, middle school students, executives, personnel administrators, bulimics, homosexuals, parents, U.S. military cadettes, medical patients, engineers, teachers, male homosexual and lesbian couples, members of missing-in-action families, wives of naval aviators, fifth graders, gifted and talented adolescents, distance runners, alcoholics, psychiatric patients, beginning nurses, and Hispanic-Americans. The PAQ has been used in several countries outside the United States, including Mexico, Canada, Great Britain, Germany, Australia, Yugoslavia, France, Tunisia, Fiji, Norway, and Italy.

(4) Many studies have compared the PAQ to other gender role measures. The studies are listed here, along with the gender role measures being compared with the PAQ. With the exception of the De Cecco–Shively Social Sex-Role Inventory (Shively, Rudolph, & De Cecco, 1978), all of the other gender role measures are described in this book. The studies comparing the PAQ or EPAQ to other gender role measures include: Betz and Bander (1980): BSRI, MMPI Mf, and CPI Fe; Cunningham and Antill (1980): BSRI, CPI Fe, PRF ANDRO, and Comrey Personality Scales; Gaa and Liberman (1981): BSRI; Gaa, Liberman, and Edwards (1979): BSRI; Hawkins, Herron, Gibson, Hoban, and Herron (1988): BSRI, PRF ANDRO, and ACL; Herron, Goodman, and Herron (1983): BSRI, PRF ANDRO, and ACL; Kelly, Furman, and Young (1978): BSRI, PRF ANDRO, and ACL; O'Grady, Freda, and Mikulkla (1979): BSRI and ACL; Pearson (1980): BSRI and ACL; Smith (1983): De Cecco-Shively Social Sex-Role Inventory and BSRI; Volentine (1981): BSRI and MMPI Mf; Whitley (1988a): Sex-Role Behavior Scale–2; and Wilson and Cook (1984): BSRI, PRF ANDRO, and ACL.

(5) Several studies have involved factor analysis of the PAQ or EPAQ: Antill and Cunningham (1982a), Gaa, Liberman, and Edwards (1979), Gross, Batlis, Small, and Erdwins (1979), Helmreich, Spence, and Wilhelm (1981), Pearson (1980), and Wilson and Cook (1984).

(6) Schwarz and Williams (1986) studied the impact of trait desirability on PAQ scores. Hortin and Parish (1981) provided normative data for

the PAQ. Yoder, Rice, Adams, Priest, and Prince (1982) provided data regarding the reliability of the PAQ.

(7) Helmreich, Spence, and Wilhelm (1981) provided a good overview of the psychometric properties of both the PAQ and EPAQ.

(8) The PAQ/EPAQ have been used with nonstandard instructions. For example, respondents have been asked to rate themselves, an ideal man, and an ideal woman using the scale.

AVAILABLE FROM: Spence, Helmreich, and Stapp, 1974, for the PAQ; Spence and Helmreich, 1978, for the short form PAQ; Spence, Helmreich, and Holahan, 1979, for the EPAQ

USED IN:

Adams, J. (1984). Women at West Point: A three-year perspective. *Sex Roles*, *11*, 525–541.

Adler, J. D., & Boxley, R. L. (1985). The psychological reactions to infertility: Sex roles and coping styles. *Sex Roles*, *12*, 271–279.

Ajdukovic, D., & Kljaic, S. (1984). Personal attributes, self-esteem, and attitude towards women: Some cross-cultural comparisons. *Studia Psychologica*, *26*(3), 193–198.

Alagna, S. W. (1982). Sex role identity, peer evaluation of competition, and the responses of women and men in a competitive situation. *Journal of Personality and Social Psychology*, *43*(3), 546–554.

Alagna, S. W., & Morokoff, P. J. (1986). Beginning medical school: Determinants of male and female emotional reactions. *Journal of Applied Social Psychology*, *16*(4), 348–360.

Alain, M., & Lussier, Y. (1988). Sex-role attitudes and divorce experience. *Journal of Social Psychology*, *128*(2), 143–152.

Alley, T. R., & Kolker, J. I. (1988). Psychological gender, hand preferences, and sex differences in book-carrying styles. *Perceptual and Motor Skills*, *66*, 815–822.

Almeida Acosta, E., Rodriguez de Arizmendi, G., Mercado Corona, D., Rivero Weber, M., & Sanchez de Almeida, M. E. (1983). Psychological characteristics of male and female students and the status of women in Mexico. *International Journal of Psychology*, *18*, 67–81.

Almeida Acosta, E., & Sanchez de Almeida, M. E. (1983). Psychological factors affecting change in women's roles and status: A cross-cultural study. *International Journal of Psychology*, *18*, 3–35.

Alsaker, F. D., Hovland, O. J., & Vollmer, F. (1985). Sex-role related personality traits and irrationality. *Scandinavian Journal of Psychology*, *26*(2), 187–189.

Antill, J. K., & Cunningham, J. D. (1979). Self-esteem as a function of masculinity in both sexes. *Journal of Consulting and Clinical Psychology*, *47*(4), 783–785.

Antill, J. K., & Cunningham, J. D. (1980). The relationship of masculinity, femininity, and androgyny to self-esteem. *Australian Journal of Psychology*, *32*(3), 195–207.

Antill, J. K., & Cunningham, J. D. (1982a). Comparative factor analyses of the Personal Attributes Questionnaire and the Bem Sex-Role Inventory. *Social Behavior and Personality*, *10*(2), 163–172.

Antill, J. K., & Cunningham, J. D. (1982b). A critical appraisal of the PRF AN-DRO Scale. *Current Psychological Research, 2*(4), 223–230.

Antill, J. K., & Cunningham, J. D. (1982c). Sex differences in performance on ability tests as a function of masculinity, femininity, and androgyny. *Journal of Personality and Social Psychology, 42*(4), 718–728.

Archer, J. (1986). Adolescent gender stereotypes: A comment on Keyes. *British Journal of Social Psychology, 25*(1), 71–72.

Arnold, S. T. (1981). Attitudes of counselors-in-training toward career goals of a male client. *Vocational Guidance Quarterly, 29*(3), 221–228.

Atkinson, J., & Huston, T. L. (1984). Sex role orientation and division of labor early in marriage. *Journal of Personality and Social Psychology, 46*(2), 330–345.

Babladelis, G., Deaux, K., Helmreich, R. L., & Spence, J. T. (1983). Sex-related attitudes and personal characteristics in the United States. *International Journal of Psychology, 18*, 111–123.

Baker, D. R. (1984). Masculinity, femininity and androgyny among male and female science and non-science college majors. *School Science and Mathematics, 84*(6), 459–467.

Barker, C., & Lemle, R. (1984). The helping process in couples. *American Journal of Community Psychology, 12*(3), 321–336.

Barnes, M. L., & Buss, D. M. (1985). Sex differences in the interpersonal behavior of married couples. *Journal of Personality and Social Psychology, 48*(3), 654–661.

Barth, R. J., & Kinder, B. N. (1988). A theoretical analysis of sex differences in same-sex friendships. *Sex Roles, 19*(5/6), 349–363.

Basow, S. A. (1984a). Cultural variations in sex-typing. *Sex Roles, 10*, 577–585.

Basow, S. A. (1984b). Ethnic group differences in educational achievement in Fiji. *Journal of Cross Cultural Psychology, 15*(4), 435–451.

Basow, S. A. (1986). Correlates of sex-typing in Fiji. *Psychology of Women Quarterly, 10*(4), 429–442.

Beauvais, C., & Spence, J. T. (1987). Gender, prejudice, and categorization. *Sex Roles, 16*(1/2), 89–100.

Bebeau, M. J., & Loupe, M. J. (1984). Masculine and feminine personality attributes of dental students and their attitudes toward women's roles in society. *Journal of Dental Education, 48*(6), 309–314.

Belk, S. S., & Snell, W. E., Jr. (1986). Beliefs about women: Components and correlates. *Personality and Social Psychology Bulletin, 12*(4), 403–413.

Belk, S. S., & Snell, W. E., Jr. (in press). Avoidance strategy use in intimate relationships. *Journal of Social and Clinical Psychology.*

Belsky, J., Lang, M., & Huston, T. L. (1986). Sex typing and division of labor as determinants of marital change across the transition to parenthood. *Journal of Personality and Social Psychology, 50*(3), 517–522.

Benson, P. L., & Vincent, S. (1980). Development and validation of the Sexist Attitudes Toward Women Scale (SATWS). *Psychology of Women Quarterly, 5*(2), 276–291.

Berg, J. H., & Peplau, L. A. (1982). Loneliness: The relationship of self-disclosure and androgyny. *Personality and Social Psychology Bulletin, 8*(4), 624–630.

Betz, N. E., & Bander, R. S. (1980). Relationships of MMPI Mf and CPI Fe scales of fourfold sex role classifications. *Journal of Personality and Social Psychology, 39,* 1245–1248.

Black, K. N., & Stevenson, M. R. (1984). The relationship of self-reported sex-role characteristics and attitudes toward homosexuality. *Journal of Homosexuality, 10,* 83–93.

Blakemore, J. E. O., Baumgardner, S. R., & Keniston, A. H. (1988). Male and female nurturing: Perceptions of style and competence. *Sex Roles, 18*(7/8), 449–459.

Blascovich, J., Major, B., & Katkin, E. S. (1981): Sex-role orientation and Type A behavior. *Personality and Social Psychology Bulletin, 7*(4), 600–604.

Boss, P. G. (1980). The relationship of psychological father presence, wife's personal qualities and wife/family dysfunction in families of missing fathers. *Journal of Marriage and the Family, 42*(3), 541–549.

Bridges, J. S. (1988). Sex differences in occupational performance expectations. *Psychology of Women Quarterly, 12,* 75–90.

Bridges, J. S., & Bower, M. S. (1985). The effects of perceived job availability for women on college women's attitudes toward prestigious male-dominated occupations. *Psychology of Women Quarterly, 9*(2), 265–276.

Bugen, L. A., & Humenick, S. S. (1983). Instrumentality, expressiveness, and gender effects upon parent-infant interaction. *Basic and Applied Social Psychology, 4*(3), 239–251.

Burgoon, M., Dillard, J. P., & Doran, N. E. (1983). Friendly or unfriendly persuasion: The effects of violations of expectations by males and females. *Human Communication Research, 10*(2), 283–294.

Butler, T., Giordano, S., & Neren, S. (1985). Gender and sex-role attributes as predictors of utilization of natural support systems during personal stress events. *Sex Roles, 13,* 515–524.

Cano, L., Solomon, S., & Holmes, D. S. (1984). Fear of success: The influence of sex, sex-role identity, and components of masculinity. *Sex Roles, 10,* 341–346.

Cash, T. F., Rissi, J., & Chapman, R. (1985). Not just another pretty face: Sex roles, locus of control, and cosmetics use. *Personality and Social Psychology Bulletin, 11*(3), 246–257.

Cate, R., & Sugawara, A. (1986). Sex role orientation and dimensions of self-esteem among middle adolescents. *Sex Roles, 15,* 145–158.

Chaiken, S., & Pliner, P. (1987). Women, but not men, are what they eat: The effect of meal size and gender on perceived femininity and masculinity. *Personality and Social Psychology Bulletin, 13*(2), 166–176.

Chambless, D. L., & Mason, J. (1986). Sex, sex-role stereotyping and agoraphobia. *Behaviour Research and Therapy, 24*(2), 231–235.

Colker, R., & Widom, C. S. (1980). Correlates of female athletic participation: Masculinity, femininity, self-esteem, and attitudes toward women. *Sex Roles, 6*(1), 47–58.

Cooper, K., Chassin, L. A., & Zeiss, A. (1985). The relation of sex-role self-concept and sex-role attitudes to the marital satisfaction and personal adjustment of dual-worker couples with preschool children. *Sex Roles, 12,* 227–241.

Cota, A. A., & Dion, K. L. (1986). Salience of gender and sex composition of ad hoc groups: An experimental test of distinctiveness theory. *Journal of Personality and Social Psychology, 50*(4), 770–776.

Coutts, J. S. (1987). Masculinity-femininity of self-concept: Its effect on the achievement behavior of women. *Sex Roles, 16,* 9–17.

Cunningham, J. D., & Antill, J. K. (1980). A comparison among five masculinity-femininity-androgyny instruments and two methods of scoring androgyny. *Australian Psychologist, 15*(3), 437–448.

Dambrot, F. H., Reep, D. C., & Bell, D. (1988). Television sex roles in the 1980s: Do viewers' sex and sex role orientation change the picture? *Sex Roles, 19*(5/6), 387–401.

del Rey, P., & Sheppard, S. (1981). Relationship of psychological androgyny in female athletes to self-esteem. *International Journal of Sport Psychology, 12*(3), 165–175.

DePaulo, B. M. (1978). Accepting help from teachers—when the teachers are children. *Human Relations, 31*(5), 459–474.

Desertrain, G. S., & Weiss, M. R. (1988). Being female and athletic: A cause for conflict. *Sex Roles, 18*(9/10), 567–582.

Downs, A. C., & Engleson, S. A. (1982). The Attitudes Toward Men Scale (AMS): An analysis of the role and status of men and masculinity. *Catalog of Selected Documents in Psychology, 12*(4), 45. (Ms. No. 2503)

Dykens, E. M., & Gerrard, M. (1986). Psychological profiles of purging bulimics, repeat dieters, and controls. *Journal of Consulting and Clinical Psychology, 54*(3), 283–288.

Edwards, V. J., & Spence, J. T. (1987). Gender-related traits, stereotypes, and schemata. *Journal of Personality and Social Psychology, 53*(1), 146–154.

Eisenberg, N., Schaller, M., Miller, P. A., Fultz, J., Fabes, R. A., & Shell, R. (1988). Gender-related traits and helping in a nonemergency situation. *Sex Roles, 19,* 605–618.

Eisler, R. M., Skidmore, J. R., & Ward, C. H. (1988). Masculine gender-role stress: Predictor of anger, anxiety, and health-risk behaviors. *Journal of Personality Assessment, 52,* 133–141.

Erdwins, C. J., Small, A. C., Gessner, T., & Gross, R. (1978). Sex-role stereotypes and their relationship to respondents' age and sex. *Psychological Reports, 43*(3), 1343–1346.

Espin, O. M., & Warner, B. (1982). Attitudes towards the role of women in Cuban women attending a community college. *International Journal of Social Psychiatry, 28*(3), 233–239.

Evans, R. G., & Dinning, W. D. (1982). MMPI correlates of the Bem Sex Role Inventory and Extended Personal Attributes Questionnaire in a male psychiatric sample. *Journal of Clinical Psychology, 38*(4), 811–815.

Falbo, T. (1982). PAQ types and power strategies used in intimate relationships. *Psychology of Women Quarterly, 6*(4), 399–405.

Feather, N. T. (1984). Masculinity, femininity, psychological androgyny, and the structure of values. *Journal of Personality and Social Psychology, 47*(3), 604–620.

Feather, N. T. (1985). Masculinity, femininity, self-esteem, and subclinical depression. *Sex Roles, 12,* 491–500.

Fleming, M. Z., MacGowan, B. R., & Salt, P. (1984). Female-to-male transsexualism and sex roles: Self and spouse ratings on the PAQ. *Archives of Sexual Behavior*, *13*(1), 51–57.

Flett, G. L., Vredenburg, K., Pliner, P., & Krames, L. (1985). Sex roles and depression: A preliminary investigation of the direction of causality. *Journal of Research in Personality*, *19*(4), 429–435.

Foushee, H. C., Davis, M. H., & Archer, R. L. (1979). Empathy, masculinity, and femininity. *Catalog of Selected Documents in Psychology*, *9*, 85. (Ms. No. 1974)

Friedman, M. P., Catalano, J. F., & Lombardo, J. P. (1985). Relationship between sex-role and acquisition of motor skill. *Perceptual and Motor Skills*, *61*(2), 659–668.

Friedman, W. J., Robinson, A. B., & Friedman, B. L. (1987). Sex differences in moral judgments? A test of Gilligan's theory. *Psychology of Women Quarterly*, *11*(1), 37–46.

Gaa, J. P., & Liberman, D. (1981). Categorization agreement of the Personality Attributes Questionnaire and the Bem Sex Role Inventory. *Journal of Clinical Psychology*, *37*(3), 593–601.

Gaa, J. P., Liberman, D., & Edwards, T. A. (1979). A comparative factor analysis of the Bem Sex Role Inventory and the Personality Attributes Questionnaire. *Journal of Clinical Psychology*, *35*(3), 592–598.

Gaa, J. P., Sanchez, S., & Liberman, D. (1986). Ethnic and gender concerns in sex-role identity: An illustration of problems in cross-cultural research. *Journal of Educational Equity and Leadership*, *6*(2), 93–104.

Gaeddert, W. P. (1985). Sex and sex role effects on achievement strivings: Dimensions of similarity and difference. *Journal of Personality*, *53*(2), 286–305.

Gerber, G. L. (1984). Attribution of feminine and masculine traits to opposite-sex dyads. *Psychological Reports*, *55*, 907–918.

Gerdes, E. P., & Kelman, J. H. (1981). Sex discrimination: Effects of sex-role incongruence, evaluator sex, and stereotypes. *Basic and Applied Social Psychology*, *2*(3), 219–226.

Goldman, J. A., Olczak, P. V., & Tripp, M. H. (1980). Sex-role identity as a moderator of the polarization effect in person perception. *Journal of Research in Personality*, *14*(3), 321–328.

Grigsby, J. P., & Weatherley, D. (1983). Gender and sex-role differences in intimacy of self-disclosure. *Psychological Reports*, *53*(3), 891–897.

Gross, R., Batlis, N. C., Small, A. C., & Erdwins, C. (1979). Factor structure of the Bem Sex-Role Inventory and the Personal Attributes Questionnaire. *Journal of Consulting and Clinical Psychology*, *47*(6), 1122–1124.

Grotevant, H. D., & Thorbecke, W. L. (1982). Sex differences in styles of occupational identity formation in late adolescence. *Developmental Psychology*, *18*(3), 396–405.

Haimo, S., & Blitman, F. (1985). The effects of assertive training on sex role concept in female agoraphobics. *Women and Therapy*, *4*(2), 53–61.

Halberstadt, A. G., Hayes, C. W., & Pike, K. M. (1988). Gender and gender role differences in smiling and communication consistency. *Sex Roles*, *19*, 589–604.

Hall, J. A., & Halberstadt, A. G. (1980). Masculinity and femininity in children:

Development of the Children's Personal Attributes Questionnaire. *Developmental Psychology, 16,* 270–280.

Hans, V. P., & Eisenberg, N. (1985). The effects of sex-role attitudes and group composition on men and women in groups. *Sex Roles, 12,* 477–490.

Harris, D. V., & Jennings, S. E. (1977). Self-perceptions of female distance runners. *Annals of the New York Academy of Sciences, 301,* 808–815.

Harry, J. (1983). Defeminization and adult psychological well-being among male homosexuals. *Archives of Sexual Behavior, 12*(1), 1–19.

Hatzenbuehler, L. C., & Joe, V. C. (1981). Stress and androgyny: A preliminary study. *Psychological Reports, 48*(1), 327–332.

Hawkins, D., Herron, W. G., Gibson, W., Hoban, G., & Herron, M. J. (1988). Homosexual and heterosexual sex-role orientation on six sex-role scales. *Perceptual and Motor Skills, 66,* 863–871.

Hawkins, R. C., Turell, S., & Jackson, L. J. (1983). Desirable and undesirable masculine and feminine traits in relation to students' dieting tendencies and body image dissatisfaction. *Sex Roles, 9*(6), 705–718.

Heiser, P., & Gannon, L. R. (1984). The relationship of sex-role stereotypy to anger expression and the report of psychosomatic symptoms. *Sex Roles, 10,* 601–611.

Helgeson, V. S., & Sharpsteen, D. J. (1987). Perceptions of danger in achievement and affiliation situations: An extension of the Pollak and Gilligan vs. Benton et al. debate. *Journal of Personality and Social Psychology, 53,* 727–733.

Helmreich, R. L., Spence, J. T., & Holahan, C. K. (1979). Psychological androgyny and sex role flexibility: A test of two hypotheses. *Journal of Personality and Social Psychology, 37*(10), 1631–1644.

Helmreich, R. L., Spence, J. T., & Wilhelm, J. A. (1981). A psychometric analysis of the Personal Attributes Questionnaire. *Sex Roles, 7*(11), 1097–1108.

Herron, M. J., Herron, W. G., & Schultz, C. L. (1983). Sexual dominance/submission, gender and sex-role identification. *Perceptual and Motor Skills, 56*(3), 931–937.

Herron, W. G., Goodman, C. K., & Herron, M. J. (1983). Comparability of sex-role measures. *Psychological Reports, 53*(3), 1087–1094.

Hertsgaard, D., & Light, H. K. (1984). Adolescent females' perceived parental sex-role attributes. *Psychological Reports, 55*(1), 253–254.

Hingst, A. G., Regan, K. R., & Sexton, T. L. (1985). The relationship between parental bonding and sex role identification of adult males. *Australian Journal of Sex, Marriage and Family, 6*(4), 201–209.

Hirschman, E. C. (1983). Psychological sexual identity and hemispheric orientation. *Journal of General Psychology, 108*(2), 153–168.

Hirschman, E. C. (1984). Leisure motives and sex roles. *Journal of Leisure Research, 16*(3), 209–223.

Hirschman, E. C. (1985). Sexual identity and the acquisition of rational, absorbing, escapist, and modeling experiences. *Journal of Social Psychology, 125*(1), 63–73.

Hochstetler, S. A., Rejeski, W. J., & Best, D. L. (1985). The influence of sex-role orientation on ratings of perceived exertion. *Sex Roles, 12,* 825–835.

Holahan, C. K., & Gilbert, L. A. (1979). Interrole conflict for working women: Careers versus jobs. *Journal of Applied Psychology, 64*(1), 86–90.

Holahan, C. K., & Holahan, C. J. (1979). The relationship of psychological masculinity and femininity and gender to personalization and social emphasis in environmental schematization. *Personality and Social Psychology Bulletin, 5*(2), 231–235.

Holahan, C. K., & Spence, J. T. (1980). Desirable and undesirable masculine and feminine traits in counseling clients and unselected students. *Journal of Consulting and Clinical Psychology, 48*(2), 300–302.

Hollinger, C. L. (1983). Counseling the gifted and talented female adolescent: The relationship between social self-esteem and traits of instrumentality and expressiveness. *Gifted Child Quarterly, 27*(4), 157–161.

Hollinger, C. L. (1984). The impact of gender schematic processing on the self directed search responses of gifted and talented female adolescents. *Journal of Vocational Behavior, 24*(1), 15–27.

Hollinger, C. L. (1985). The stability of self perceptions of instrumental and expressive traits and social self esteem among gifted and talented female adolescents. *Journal for the Education of the Gifted, 8*(2), 107–126.

Hollinger, C. L., & Fleming, E. S. (1984). Internal barriers to the realization of potential: Correlates and interrelationships among gifted and talented female adolescents. *Gifted Child Quarterly, 28*(3), 135–139.

Hollinger, C. L., & Fleming, E. S. (1985). Social orientation and the social self-esteem of gifted and talented female adolescents. *Journal of Youth and Adolescence, 14*(5), 389–399.

Holmbeck, G. N., & Bale, P. (1988). Relations between instrumental and expressive personality characteristics and behaviors: A test of Spence and Helmreich's theory. *Journal of Research in Personality, 22*, 37–59.

Holms, V. L., & Esses, L. M. (1988). Factors influencing Canadian high school girls' career motivation. *Psychology of Women Quarterly, 12*, 313–328.

Hortin, J. A., & Parish, T. S. (1981). The Personal Attribute Inventory: A report on normative data. *Perceptual and Motor Skills, 52*(3), 794.

Horwitz, A. V., & White, H. R. (1987). Gender role orientations and styles of pathology among adolescents. *Journal of Health and Social Behavior, 28*(2), 158–170.

Hungerford, J. K., & Sobolew-Shubin, A. P. (1987). Sex-role identity, gender identity, and self-schemata. *Psychology of Women Quarterly, 11*(1), 1–10.

Jackson, L. A., & Cash, T. F. (1985). Components of gender stereotypes: Their implications for inferences on stereotypic and nonstereotypic dimensions. *Personality and Social Psychology Bulletin, 11*(3), 326–344.

Jagacinski, C. M. (1987). Androgyny in a male-dominated field: The relationship of sex-typed traits to performance and satisfaction in engineering. *Sex Roles, 17*(9/10), 529–547.

Johnson, M. E. (1988). Influences of gender and sex role orientation on help-seeking attitudes. *Journal of Psychology, 122*, 237–241.

Jones, R. W., & de Cecco, J. P. (1982). The femininity and masculinity of partners in heterosexual and homosexual relationships. *Journal of Homosexuality, 8*(2), 37–44.

Jones, S. L., & Lamke, L. K. (1985). The relationship between sex role orientation, self esteem, and sex-typed occupational choice of college women. *Psychology of Women Quarterly, 9*(1), 145–152.

Jose, P. E., & McCarthy, W. J. (1988). Perceived agentic and communal behavior in mixed-sex group interactions. *Personality and Social Psychology Bulletin, 14*(1), 57–67.

Katzman, M. A., & Wolchik, S. A. (1984). Bulimia and binge eating in college women: A comparison of personality and behavioral characteristics. *Journal of Consulting and Clinical Psychology, 52*(3), 423–428.

Kelly, J. A., Furman, W., & Young, V. (1978). Problems associated with the typological measurement of sex roles and androgyny. *Journal of Consulting and Clinical Psychology, 46*(6), 1574–1576.

Keyes, S. (1984). Gender stereotypes and personal adjustment: Employing the PAQ, TSBI and GHQ with samples of British adolescents. *British Journal of Social Psychology, 23*(2), 173–180.

Keyes, S. (1986). Reply to Archer. *British Journal of Social Psychology, 25*(1), 73–74.

Keyes, S., & Coleman, J. (1983). Sex-role conflicts and personal adjustment: A study of British adolescents. *Journal of Youth and Adolescence, 12*(6), 443–459.

Kinney, C. D. (1985). A reexamination of nursing role conceptions. *Nursing Research, 34*(3), 170–176.

Klein, H. M., & Willerman, L. (1979). Psychological masculinity and femininity and typical and maximal dominance expression in women. *Journal of Personality and Social Psychology, 37*(11), 2059–2070.

Klonsky, B. G. (1985). Gender-role and sex differences in recreation. *Psychological Reports, 56*(2), 480–482.

Kranau, E. J., Green, V., & Valencia-Weber, G. (1982). Acculturation and the Hispanic woman: Attitudes toward women, sex-role attribution, sex-role behavior, and demographics. *Hispanic Journal of Behavioral Sciences, 4*(1), 21–40.

Krueger, J., & Rothbart, M. (1988). Use of categorical and individuating information in making inferences about personality. *Journal of Personality and Social Psychology, 55*, 187–195.

Kurdek, L. A. (1988). Correlates of negative attitudes toward homosexuals in heterosexual college students. *Sex Roles, 18* (11/12), 727–738.

LaBarbera, J. D. (1984). Seductive father-daughter relationships and sex roles in women. *Sex Roles, 11*, 941–951.

Lamke, L. K. (1982a). Adjustment and sex-role orientation in adolescence. *Journal of Youth and Adolescence, 11*(3), 247–259.

Lamke, L. K. (1982b). The impact of sex-role orientation on self-esteem in early adolescence. *Child Development, 53*(6), 1530–1535.

LaTorre, R. A., & Wendenburg, K. (1983). Psychological characteristics of bisexual, heterosexual and homosexual women. *Journal of Homosexuality, 9*(1), 87–97.

Leaper, C. (1987). Agency, communion, and gender as predictors of communication style and being liked in adult male-female dyads. *Sex Roles, 16*, 137–149.

Lubinski, D., Tellegen, A., & Butcher, J. N. (1983). Masculinity, femininity, and androgyny viewed and assessed as distinct concepts. *Journal of Personality and Social Psychology, 44*(2), 428–439.

Mable, H. M., Balance, W. D. G., & Galgan, R. J. (1986). Body-image distortion and dissatisfaction in university students. *Perceptual and Motor Skills, 63,* 907–911.

Macdonald, N. E., Ebert, P. D., & Mason, S. E. (1987). Marital status and age as related to masculine and feminine personality dimensions and self-esteem. *Journal of Social Psychology, 127*(3), 289–298.

Martin, C. L. (1987). A ratio measure of sex stereotyping. *Journal of Personality and Social Psychology, 52*(3), 489–499.

Maslach, C., Santee, R. T., & Wade, C. (1987). Individuation, gender role, and dissent: Personality mediators of situational forces. *Journal of Personality and Social Psychology, 53,* 1088–1093.

Massad, C. M. (1981). Sex role identity and adjustment during adolescence. *Child Development, 52*(4), 1290–1298.

Mast, D. L., & Herron, W. G. (1986). The Sex-Role Antecedents Scales. *Perceptual and Motor Skills, 63*(1), 27–56.

McCrady, B. S., & Sand, K. S. (1985). Age differences and patterns of sex-role conflict among alcoholics. *Journal of Abnormal Psychology, 94*(2), 237–239.

McHale, S. M., & Huston, T. L. (1984). Men and women as parents: Sex role orientations, employment, and parental roles with infants. *Child Development, 55*(4), 1349–1361.

McIlwraith, R. D., & Schallow, J. R. (1983). Adult fantasy life and patterns of media use. *Journal of Communication, 33*(1), 78–91.

Metzler-Brennan, E., Lewis, R. J., & Gerrard, M. (1985). Childhood antecedents of adult women's masculinity, femininity, and career role choices. *Psychology of Women Quarterly, 9*(3), 371–381.

Mitchell, C. L. (1987). Relationship of femininity, masculinity, and gender to attribution of responsibility. *Sex Roles, 16,* 151–163.

Moore, M., & Gilroy, F. (1986). Is dissonance a factor in the relationship between sex-role orientation and attitudes towards women's roles. *Psychological Reports, 59,* 859–865.

Moore, S. M., & Rosenthal, D. A. (1984). Balance versus main effects androgyny: Their relationship to adjustment in three ethnic groups. *Psychological Reports, 54*(3), 823–831.

Muldrow, T. W., & Bayton, J. A. (1979). Men and women executives and processes related to decision accuracy. *Journal of Applied Psychology, 64*(2), 99–106.

Murphy, L. O., & Ross, S. M. (1987). Gender differences in the social problem-solving performance of adolescents. *Sex Roles, 16*(5/6), 251–264.

Nadelson, C. C., Salt, P., & Norman, M. T. (1983). Evidence of physician adaptability during the medical training period. *Journal of Psychiatric Education, 7*(3), 167–182.

Nettles, E. J., & Loevinger, J. (1983). Sex role expectations and ego level in relation to problem marriages. *Journal of Personality and Social Psychology, 45*(3), 676–687.

Newcombe, N., & Bandura, M. M. (1983). Effect of age at puberty on spatial ability in girls: A question of mechanism. *Developmental Psychology, 19*(2), 215–224.

Niemi, P. (1985). The role of gender-related self-schemata in the attributions of social interaction. *Scandinavian Journal of Psychology, 26*(2), 170–180.

Nigro, G., & Galli, I. (1985). Sex-role identity and machiavellianism. *Psychological Reports, 56*(3), 863–866.

Nyquist, L., Slivken, K., Spence, J. T., & Helmreich, R. L. (1985). Household responsibilities in middle-class couples: The contribution of demographic and personality variables. *Sex Roles, 12*, 15–34.

O'Connor, K., Mann, D. W., & Bardwick, J. M. (1978). Androgyny and self-esteem in the upper-middle class: A replication of Spence. *Journal of Consulting and Clinical Psychology, 46*(5), 1168–1169.

O'Grady, K. E., Freda, J. S., & Mikulka, P. J. (1979). A comparison of the Adjective Check List, BEM Sex Role Inventory, and Personal Attributes Questionnaire masculinity and femininity subscales. *Multivariate Behavioral Research, 14*(2), 215–225.

Olds, D. E., & Shaver, P. (1980). Masculinity, femininity, academic performance, and health: Further evidence concerning the androgyny controversy. *Journal of Personality, 48*(3), 323–341.

O'Neil, J. M., Helms, B. J., & Gable, R. K. (1986). Gender-Role Conflict Scale: College men's fear of femininity. *Sex Roles, 14*, 335–350.

Orlofsky, J. L. (1981). Relationship between sex role attitudes and personality traits and the Sex Role Behavior Scale–1: A new measure of masculine and feminine role behavior. *Journal of Personality and Social Psychology, 40*(5), 927–940.

Orlofsky, J. L., Cohen, R. S., & Ramsden, M. W. (1985). Relationship between sex-role attitudes and personality traits and the Revised Sex-Role Behavior Scale. *Sex Roles, 12*, 377–391.

Orlofsky, J. L., & O'Heron, C. A. (1987a). Development of a short-form Sex-Role Behavior Scale. *Journal of Personality Assessment, 51*(2), 267–277.

Orlofsky, J. L., & O'Heron, C. A. (1987b). Stereotypic and nonstereotypic sex role trait and behavior orientations: Implications for personal adjustment. *Journal of Personality and Social Psychology, 52*(5), 1034–1042.

Orlofsky, J. L., & Stake, J. E. (1981). Psychological masculinity and femininity: Relationship to striving and self-concept in the achievement and interpersonal domains. *Psychology of Women Quarterly, 6*(2), 218–233.

Parsons, J. E., Adler, T. F., & Kaczala, C. M. (1982). Socialization of achievement attitudes and beliefs: Parental influences. *Child Development, 53*(2), 310–321.

Pasquella, M. J., Mednick, M. T., & Murray, S. R. (1981). Causal attributions for achievement outcomes: Sex-role identity, sex and outcome comparisons. *Psychology of Women Quarterly, 5*(4), 586–590.

Patterson, J. M., & McCubbin, H. I. (1984). Gender roles and coping. *Journal of Marriage and the Family, 46*(1), 95–104.

Payne, F. D. (1987). "Masculinity," "femininity," and the complex construct of adjustment. *Sex Roles, 17*(7/8), 359–374.

Payne, T. J., Connor, J. M., & Colletti, G. (1987). Gender-based schematic processing: An empirical investigation and reevaluation. *Journal of Personality and Social Psychology, 52*(5), 937–945.

Pearson, J. C. (1980). A factor analytic study of the items in three selected sex-role instruments. *Psychological Reports, 46*(3), 1119–1126.

Perlmutter, J. C., & Wampler, K. S. (1985). Sex role orientation, wife's employment, and the division of household labor. *Home Economics Research Journal, 13*(3), 237–245.

Prager, K. J. (1983). Identity status, sex-role orientation, and self-esteem in late adolescent females. *Journal of Genetic Psychology, 143*(2), 159–167.

Pratt, M. W., Golding, G., & Hunter, W. J. (1984). Does morality have a gender? Sex, sex role, and moral judgment relationships across the adult lifespan. *Merrill Palmer Quarterly, 30*(4), 321–340.

Pryor, J. B. (1987). Sexual harassment proclivities in men. *Sex Roles, 17*(5/6), 269–290.

Reis, H. T., Wheeler, L., Kernis, M. H., & Spiegel, N. (1985). On specificity in the impact of social participation on physical and psychological health. *Journal of Personality and Social Psychology, 48*(2), 456–471.

Rejeski, W. J., & Sanford, B. (1984). Feminine-typed females: The role of affective schema in the perception of exercise intensity. *Journal of Sport Psychology, 6*(2), 197–207.

Remland, M., Jacobson, C., & Jones, T. (1983). Effects of psychological gender and sex-incongruent behavior on evaluations of leadership. *Perceptual and Motor Skills, 57*(3), 783–789.

Roos, P. E., & Cohen, L. H. (1987). Sex roles and social support as moderators of life stress adjustment. *Journal of Personality and Social Psychology, 52*(3), 576–585.

Rosenbaum, A. (1986). Of men, macho, and marital violence. *Journal of Family Violence, 1*(2), 121–129.

Rowe, D. C. (1982). Sources of variability in sex-linked personality attributes: A twin study. *Developmental Psychology, 18*(3), 431–434.

Ruback, R. B., & Simerly, D. E. (1983). Occupational sex-typing using two unipolar scales. *Psychological Documents, 13*(1), 7. (Ms. No. 2540)

Ruble, T. L. (1983). Sex stereotypes: Issues of change in the 1970s. *Sex Roles, 9*(3), 397–402.

Runge, T. E., Frey, D., Gollwitzer, P. M., Helmreich, R. L., & Spence, J. T. (1981). Masculine (instrumental) and feminine (expressive) traits: A comparison between students in the United States and West Germany. *Journal of Cross Cultural Psychology, 12*(2), 142–162.

Rust, J. O., & McCraw, A. (1984). Influence of masculinity-femininity on adolescent self-esteem and peer acceptance. *Adolescence, 19*, 359–366.

Schenk, J., & Heinisch, R. (1986). Self-descriptions by means of sex-role scales and personality scales: A critical evaluation of recent masculinity and femininity scales. *Personality and Individual Differences, 7*(2), 161–168.

Schullo, S. A., & Alperson, B. L. (1984). Interpersonal phenomenology as a function of sexual orientation, sex, sentiment, and trait categories in long-term dyadic relationships. *Journal of Personality and Social Psychology, 47*(5), 983–1002.

Schwarz, J. C., & Williams, B. E. (1986). Masculinity and femininity: The role of desirability in the relationships among measures based on self-concept and personality traits. *Sex Roles, 15*(11/12), 569–584.

Serafini, D. M., & Pearson, J. C. (1984). Leadership behavior and sex role socialization: Two sides of the same coin. *Southern Speech Communication Journal*, 49(4), 396–405.

Sexton, T. L., Hingst, A. G., & Regan, K. R. (1985). The effect of divorce on the relationship between parental bonding and sexrole identification of adult males. *Journal of Divorce*, 9(1), 17–31.

Sharp, C., & Post, R. (1980). Evaluation of male and female applicants for sex-congruent and sex-incongruent jobs. *Sex Roles*, 6(3), 391–401.

Sipps, G. J., & Janeczek, R. G. (1986). Expectancies for counselors in relation to subject gender traits. *Journal of Counseling Psychology*, 33(2), 214–216.

Smith, S. G. (1983). A comparison among three measures of social sex-role. *Journal of Homosexuality*, 9(1), 99–107.

Snell, W. E., Jr., Belk, S. S., & Hawkins, R. C., II. (1986a). The Masculine and Feminine Self-Disclosure Scale: The politics of masculine and feminine self-preservation. *Sex Roles*, 15, 249–267.

Snell, W. E., Jr., Belk, S. S., & Hawkins, R. C., II. (1986b). The Stereotypes About Male Sexuality Scale (SAMSS): Components, correlates, antecedents, consequences and counselor bias. *Social and Behavioral Science Documents*, 16(1), 9. (Ms. No. 2746)

Snell, W. E., Jr., Belk, S. S., & Hawkins, R. C., II. (1987). Alcohol and drug use in stressful times: The influence of the masculine role in sex-related personality attributes. *Sex Roles*, 16(7/8), 359–373.

Snodgrass, S. E., & Rosenthal, R. (1984). Females in charge: Effects of sex of subordinate and romantic attachment status upon self-ratings of dominance. *Journal of Personality*, 52(4), 355–371.

Spence, J. T., & Helmreich, R. L. (1978). *Masculinity and femininity: Their psychological dimensions, correlates, and antecedents*. Austin: University of Texas Press.

Spence, J. T., & Helmreich, R. L. (1979a). Comparison of masculine and feminine personality attributes and sex-role attitudes across age groups. *Developmental Psychology*, 15(5), 582–583.

Spence, J. T., & Helmreich, R. L. (1979b). On assessing "androgyny." *Sex Roles*, 5(6), 721–738.

Spence, J. T., & Helmreich, R. L. (1980). Masculine instrumentality and feminine expressiveness: Their relationships with sex role attitudes and behaviors. *Psychology of Women Quarterly*, 5(2), 147–163.

Spence, J. T., Helmreich, R. L., & Holahan, C. K. (1978, April). *Psychological masculinity and femininity in children and its relationship to trait stereotypes and toy preferences*. Paper presented at the meeting of the Western Psychological Association, San Francisco. (ERIC Document Reproduction Service No. ED 162 184)

Spence, J. T., Helmreich, R. L., & Holahan, C. K. (1979). Negative and positive components of psychological masculinity and femininity and their relationships to self-reports of neurotic and acting out behavior. *Journal of Personality and Social Psychology*, 37(10), 1673–1682.

Spence, J. T., Helmreich, R. L., & Sawin, L. L. (1980). The Male-Female Relations Questionnaire: A self-report inventory of sex role behaviors and preferences and its relationships to masculine and feminine. *Catalog of Selected Documents in Psychology, 10*, 87. (Ms. No. 2123)

Spence, J. T., Helmreich, R. L., & Stapp, J. T. (1974). The Personal Attributes Questionnaire: A measure of sex role stereotypes and masculinity-femininity. *Catalog of Selected Documents in Psychology, 4*, 43–44. (Ms. No. 617)

Stake, J. E., & Orlofsky, J. L. (1981). On the use of global and specific measures in assessing the self-esteem of males and females. *Sex Roles, 7*(6), 653–662.

Stevenson, M. R., & Black, K. N. (1988). Paternal absence and sex-role development: A meta-analysis. *Child Development, 59*, 793–814.

Storms, M. D. (1979). Sex role identity and its relationships to sex role attributes and sex role stereotypes. *Journal of Personality and Social Psychology, 37*(10), 1779–1789.

Storms, M. D. (1980). Theories of sexual orientation. *Journal of Personality and Social Psychology, 38*(5), 783–792.

Sztaba, T. I., & Colwill, N. L. (1988). Secretarial and management students: Attitudes, attributes, and career choice considerations. *Sex Roles, 19*, 651–665.

Taylor, A. (1983). Conceptions of masculinity and femininity as a basis for stereotypes of male and female homosexuals. *Journal of Homosexuality, 9*(1), 37–53.

Tesch, S. A. (1984). Sex-role orientation and intimacy status in men and women. *Sex Roles, 11*, 451–465.

Thomas, D. A., & Reznikoff, M. (1984). Sex role orientation, personality structure, and adjustment in women. *Journal of Personality Assessment, 48*(1), 28–36.

Thorbecke, W., & Grotevant, H. D. (1982). Gender differences in adolescent interpersonal identity formation. *Journal of Youth and Adolescence, 11*(6), 479–492.

Vaughn, B. E., Black, J. H., & Black, J. (1988). Parental agreement on child rearing during early childhood and the psychological characteristics of adolescents. *Child Development, 59*, 1020–1033.

Vazquez-Nuttall, E., Romero-Garcia, I., & De Leon, B. (1987). Sex roles and perceptions of femininity and masculinity of Hispanic women. *Psychology of Women Quarterly, 11*, 409–425.

Vess, J. D., Schwebel, A. I., & Moreland, J. R. (1983). The effects of early parental divorce on the sex role development of college students. *Journal of Divorce, 7*(1), 83–95.

Volentine, S. Z. (1981). The assessment of masculinity and femininity: Scale 5 of the MMPI compared with the BSRI and the PAQ. *Journal of Clinical Psychology, 37*(2), 367–374.

Vollmer, F. (1986). Why do men have higher expectancy than women? *Sex Roles, 14*(7/8), 351–362.

Vredenburg, K., O'Brien, E., & Krames, L. (1988). Depression in college students: Personality and experiential factors. *Journal of Counseling Psychology, 34*(4), 419–425.

Wheeler, L. (1988). My year in Hong Kong: Some observations about social behavior. *Personality and Social Psychology Bulletin, 14*(2), 410–420.

Wheeler, L., Reis, H., & Nezlek, J. B. (1983). Loneliness, social interaction, and sex roles. *Journal of Personality and Social Psychology, 45*(4), 943–953.

Whitley, B. E., Jr. (1987). The relationship of sex-role orientation to heterosexuals' attitudes toward homosexuals. *Sex Roles, 17*(1/2), 103–113.

Whitley, B. E., Jr. (1988a). Masculinity, femininity, and self-esteem: A multitrait-multimethod analysis. *Sex Roles, 18*(7/8), 419–431.

Whitley, B. E., Jr. (1988b). The relation of gender-role orientation to sexual experience among college students. *Sex Roles, 19*, 619–638.

Wicker, F. W., Lambert, F. B., Groves, K., & Morgan, R. D. (1987). Convergent evidence for basic motivational dimensions. *Journal of Psychology, 121*, 429–440.

Willemsen, E. (1987). Sex-role orientation, self-esteem, and uniqueness: An exploration of the undifferentiated category. *Psychological Reports, 60*, 859–866.

Williams, D. G. (1985). Gender, masculinity-femininity, and emotional intimacy in same-sex friendship. *Sex Roles, 12*, 587–600.

Williams, D., Swicegood, G., Clark, M. P., & Bean, F. D. (1980). Masculinity-femininity and the desire for sexual intercourse after vasectomy: A longitudinal study. *Social Psychology Quarterly, 43*(3), 347–352.

Wilson, F. R., & Cook, E. P. (1984). Concurrent validity of four androgyny instruments. *Sex Roles, 11*, 813–837.

Wittenberg, M. T., & Reis, H. T. (1986). Loneliness, social skills, and social perception. *Personality and Social Psychology Bulletin, 12*(1), 121–130.

Yoder, J. D., Rice, R. W., Adams, J., Priest, R. F., & Prince, H. T., II. (1982). Reliability of the Attitudes Toward Women Scale (AWS) and the Personal Attributes Questionnaire (PAQ). *Sex Roles, 8*(6), 651–657.

Zeldow, P. B., Clark, D., & Daugherty, S. R. (1985). Masculinity, femininity, Type A behavior, and psychosocial adjustment in medical students. *Journal of Personality and Social Psychology, 48*(2), 481–492.

Zeldow, P. B., Clark, D. C., Daugherty, S. R., & Eckenfels, E. J. (1985). Personality indicators of psychosocial adjustment in first-year medical students. *Social Science and Medicine, 20*(1), 95–100.

Zeldow, P. B., Daugherty, S. R., & Clark, D. C. (1987). Masculinity, femininity, and psychosocial adjustment in medical students: A 2-year follow-up. *Journal of Personality Assessment, 51*(1), 3–14.

Zuckerman, M., DeFrank, R. S., Spiegel, N. H., & Larrance, D. T. (1982). Masculinity-femininity and encoding of nonverbal cues. *Journal of Personality and Social Psychology, 42*(3), 548–556.

BIBLIOGRAPHY:

Beere, C. A. (1979). *Women and women's issues: A handbook of tests and measures* (pp. 133–136). San Francisco: Jossey-Bass.

Bem, S. L. (1974). The measurement of psychological androgyny. *Journal of Consulting and Clinical Psychology, 42*, 155–162.

Shively, M. G., Rudolph, J. R., & De Cecco, J. P. (1978). The identification of the social sex-role stereotypes. *Journal of Homosexuality, 3*, 225–234.

PRF ANDRO

AUTHORS: Juris I. Berzins, Martha A. Welling, and Robert E. Wetter

DATE: 1974

VARIABLE: Masculinity, femininity, androgyny

DESCRIPTION: The PRF ANDRO is a 56-item, true/false measure that can be used with persons over the age of 13. The items on the scale are a subset of the 400 items on the Personality Research Form (PRF). The masculine subscale consists of 29 items dealing with "social and intellectual ascendancy, autonomy, and an orientation toward risk"; the feminine subscale consists of 27 items relating to "nurturance, affiliative-expressive concerns, and self-subordination." Separate scores are obtained for masculinity and femininity, and the median split method can be used to classify people as masculine, feminine, androgynous, or undifferentiated.

Many of the citations listed refer to the Interpersonal Disposition Inventory (IDI), which includes the 56-item PRF ANDRO, 20 items assessing self-esteem, 5 items designed to detect careless responding, and 4 filler items.

ARTICLES LISTED IN BEERE, 1979: 9

NOTES & COMMENTS: Several of the citations provide information on the psychometric properties of the PRF ANDRO or demonstrate the relationship between it and other gender role measures (Antill & Cunningham, 1982; Cunningham & Antill, 1980; Gayton, Havu, Ozmon, & Tavormina, 1977; Hawkins, Herron, Gibson, Hoban, & Herron, 1988; Herron, Goodman, & Herron, 1983; Ramanaiah & Martin, 1984; Wilson & Cook, 1984).

AVAILABLE FROM: Juris Berzins, Department of Psychology, University of Kentucky, Lexington, KY 40506

USED IN:

Antill, J. K., & Cunningham, J. D. (1979). Self-esteem as a function of masculinity in both sexes. *Journal of Consulting and Clinical Psychology*, 47(4), 783–785.

Antill, J. K., & Cunningham, J. D. (1980). The relationship of masculinity, femininity, and androgyny to self-esteem. *Australian Journal of Psychology*, 32(3), 195–207.

Antill, J. K., & Cunningham, J. D. (1982a). A critical appraisal of the PRF ANDRO scale. *Current Psychological Research*, 2(4), 223–230.

Antill, J. K., & Cunningham, J. D. (1982b). Sex differences in performance on ability tests as a function of masculinity, femininity, and androgyny. *Journal of Personality and Social Psychology*, 42(4), 718–728.

Barnett, L. R., & Nietzel, M. T. (1979). Relationship of instrumental and affectional behaviors and self-esteem to marital satisfaction in distressed and nondistressed couples. *Journal of Consulting and Clinical Psychology*, 47(5), 946–957.

Berzins, J. I., & Wetter, R. E. (1979, March). *Androgynous vs. traditional sex roles in the light of biographical variables*. Paper presented at the meeting of the Southeastern Psychological Association, New Orleans. (ERIC Document Reproduction Service No. ED 204 669)

Berzins, L. G. (1982, August). *Feeling threatened intellectually: The role of gender, sex role, self-esteem*. Paper presented at the meeting of the American Psychological Association, Washington, DC. (ERIC Document Reproduction Service No. ED 226 305)

Campbell, M., Steffen, J. J., & Langmeyer, D. (1981). Psychological androgyny and social competence. *Psychological Reports, 48*(2), 611–614.

Cunningham, J. D., & Antill, J. K. (1980). A comparison among five masculinity-femininity-androgyny instruments and two methods of scoring androgyny. *Australian Psychologist, 15*(3), 437–448.

Douglas, J., & Nutter, C. P. (1986). Treatment-related change in sex roles of addicted men and women. *Journal of Studies on Alcohol, 47*(3), 201–206.

Edwards, K. J., & Norcross, B. N. (1980). A comparison of two sex-role androgyny measures in a study of sex-role identity for incarcerated delinquent and nondelinquent females. *Sex Roles, 6*(6), 859–870.

Fisher, P. A. (1977, May). *Sex roles and political attitudes and behavior*. Paper presented at the meeting of the Midwestern Psychological Association, Chicago. (ERIC Document Reproduction Service No. ED 145 309)

Ford, M. R., & Lowery, C. R. (1986). Gender differences in moral reasoning: A comparison of the use of justice and care orientations. *Journal of Personality and Social Psychology, 50*(4), 777–783.

Frank, S. J., McLaughlin, A. M., & Crusco, A. (1984). Sex role attributes, symptom distress, and defensive style among college men and women. *Journal of Personality and Social Psychology, 47*(1), 182–192.

Frank, S. J., Towell, P. A., & Huyck, M. (1985). The effects of sex-role traits on three aspects of psychological well-being in a sample of middle-aged women. *Sex Roles, 12*(9/10), 1073–1087.

Frisch, M. B., & McCord, M. (1987). Sex role orientation and social skill: A naturalistic assessment of assertion and conversational skill. *Sex Roles, 17*(7/8), 437–448.

Gaddy, C. D., Arnkoff, D. B., & Glass, C. R. (1985). A study of the Scales for Investigation of the Dual-Career Family. *Measurement and Evaluation in Counseling and Development, 18*(3), 120–127.

Gaddy, C. D., Glass, C. R., & Arnkoff, D. B. (1983). Career involvement of women in dual-career families: The influence of sex role identity. *Journal of Counseling Psychology, 30*(3), 388–394.

Gayton, W. F., Havu, G. F., Ozmon, K. L., & Tavormina, J. (1977). A comparison of the Bem Sex Role Inventory and the PRF ANDRO Scale. *Journal of Personality Assessment, 41*(6), 619–621.

Hall, E. G., Durborow, B., & Progen, J. L. (1986). Self-esteem of female athletes and nonathletes relative to sex role type and sport type. *Sex Roles, 15* (7/8), 379–390.

Hawkins, D., Herron, W. G., Gibson, W., Hoban, G., & Herron, M. J. (1988). Homosexual and heterosexual sex-role orientation on six sex-role scales. *Perceptual and Motor Skills, 66*, 863–871.

Herron, W. G., Goodman, C. K., & Herron, M. J. (1983). Comparability of sex-role measures. *Psychological Reports, 53*(3), 1087–1094.

Hoferek, M. J., Kenworthy, J. A., & Weitzman, S. (1978). *Bem Sex Role Inventory and Jackson's personality rating factors scores on students in tennis and fencing classes*. Unpublished paper, National Center for Research in Vocational Education, Ohio State University. (ERIC Document Reproduction Service No. ED 211 533)

Johnson, C. H. (1984, March). *Effects of personality correlates on achievement motivation in traditional and reentry college women.* Paper presented at the meeting of the Southeastern Psychological Association, New Orleans. (ERIC Document Reproduction Service No. ED 250 646)

Kantner, J. E., & Ellerbusch, R. C. (1980). Androgyny and occupational choice. *Psychological Reports, 47*(3), 1289–1290.

Kelly, J. A., Furman, W., & Young, V. (1978). Problems associated with the typological measurement of sex roles and androgyny. *Journal of Consulting and Clinical Psychology, 46*(6), 1574–1576.

Kondo, C. Y., Powell, B. J., & Penick, E. C. (1978). Clinical correlates of the PRF androgyny scale in an alcoholic population. *Journal of Personality Assessment, 42*(6), 611–612.

Lapp, J. E., & Pihl, R. O. (1985). Sex typing and the perception of disturbance. *International Journal of Women's Studies, 8*(2), 149–157.

Larsen, R. J., & Seidman, E. (1986). Gender schema theory and sex role inventories: Some conceptual and psychometric considerations. *Journal of Personality and Social Psychology, 50*(1), 205–211.

Mitchell, C. L. (1987). Relationship of femininity, masculinity, and gender to attribution of responsibility. *Sex Roles, 16*(3/4), 151–163.

Mitchell, C. L. (1988). Attributions of responsibility for problem cause and problem solution: Their relationship to self-esteem. *Journal of Personality, 122*, 511–518.

Newcomb, M. D. (1986). Notches on the bedpost: Generational effects of sexual experience. *Psychology: A Quarterly Journal of Human Behavior, 23*, 37–46.

Payne, F. D., & Futterman, J. R. (1983). "Masculinity," "femininity," and adjustment in college men. *Journal of Research in Personality, 17*(1), 110–124.

Penick, E. C., Powell, B. J., & Read, M. R. (1984). Sex-role affiliation among male alcoholics. *Journal of Clinical Psychology, 40*(1), 359–363.

Penick, E. C., Powell, B. J., Read, M. R., & Mahoney, D. (1980). Sex-role typing: A methodological note. *Psychological Reports, 47*(1), 143–146.

Powell, B. J., Penick, E. C., & Read, M. R. (1980). Psychological adjustment and sex-role affiliation in an alcoholic population. *Journal of Clinical Psychology, 36*(3), 801–805.

Ramanaiah, N. V., & Martin, H. J. (1984). Convergent and discriminant validity of selected masculinity and femininity scales. *Sex Roles, 10*(7/8), 493–504.

Rodriguez, R., Nietzel, M. T., & Berzins, J. I. (1980). Sex role orientation and assertiveness among female college students. *Behavior Therapy, 11*(3), 353–366.

Rusbult, C. E., Zembrodt, I. M., & Iwaniszek, J. (1986). The impact of gender and sex-role orientation on responses to dissatisfaction in close relationships. *Sex Roles, 15*, 1–20.

Schwarz, K., & Robins, C. J. (1987). Psychological androgyny and ego development. *Sex Roles, 16*, 71–81.

Wilson, F. R., & Cook, E. P. (1984). Concurrent validity of four androgyny instruments. *Sex Roles, 11*, 813–837.

BIBLIOGRAPHY:
Beere, C. A. (1979). *Women and women's issues: A handbook of tests and measures* (pp. 138–141). San Francisco: Jossey-Bass.

SEX REP TEST

AUTHORS: The Role Construct Repertory Test was originally developed by George Kelly. Described below are two variations: one by Shashi Ravinder, and one by Amy C. Baldwin, Joseph W. Critelli, Larry Charles Stevens, and Sue Russell

DATE: 1986

VARIABLE: Gender role

TYPE OF INSTRUMENT: Role construct repertory test

DESCRIPTION: There have been two different approaches to the Sex Rep Test. Ravinder (1987a, 1987b) provided respondents with a list of 14 role titles, one of which is "self." Examples of other role titles are "father" and "mother." For each role listed, respondents first supplied the name of a person they knew. These 14 persons were then presented in triads, with "self" always being one of the persons in the triad. For each triad, the respondent was first to think of a personality trait characteristic of two of the persons in the triad and not characteristic of the third person. In other words, the respondent was asked to think of a way in which two persons were alike and the third one was different. Respondents then wrote down their own characteristic in regard to the trait they just thought of. For example, a respondent might have said that two of the persons were loud and one was quiet. The respondent then wrote down either "loud" or "quiet" as a self-descriptor. The self-descriptors were recorded in duplicate (carbon paper was used). As the last step, the respondent reviewed the 12 self-descriptors and rated each one as "(a) more descriptive of females than males, (b) more descriptive of males than females, or (c) equally descriptive of both sexes" (Ravinder, 1987a, p. 171). The self-ratings of the 12 self-descriptors provided the data for scoring the test.

Baldwin, Critelli, Stevens, and Russell (1986) used a slightly different procedure. They asked respondents to compare "three people whom you consider very feminine, three people whom you consider very masculine, [and] self, mother, father, boyfriend or girlfriend, happiest person you know personally, and the most unsuccessful person you know personally" (Baldwin et al., 1986, p. 1083). As in the Ravinder procedure, names were presented in triads, but Baldwin et al. always used two masculine or two feminine persons in each comparison, whereas Ravinder included the self in each comparison. The respondent was "instructed to describe a feminine way in which two of the designated feminine people were alike and yet different from a third person" (p. 1083). Using these procedures, 6 feminine and 6 masculine constructs were elicited from the respondent. The respondent was then asked to rate each of the 12 persons, including self, on each of the 12 constructs. A respondent rated each person in terms of each trait and then rated the desirability of each trait.

PREVIOUS SUBJECTS: College students in India and Australia completed the Ravinder measure; college students and adult women completed the Baldwin et al. measure

APPROPRIATE FOR: College students and older

ADMINISTRATION: Administered individually or in small groups; less than 30 minutes

SCORING: The Ravinder measure yielded three scores: femininity, masculinity, and transcendence. The scores were determined by how the respondent rated each self-descriptor. If the respondent labeled at least seven self-descriptors as "equally descriptive of both sexes," he or she was classified as "sex role transcendent." Other respondents were classified as masculine, feminine, or androgynous depending on whether they endorsed, respectively, more masculine traits, more feminine traits, or essentially equal numbers of masculine and feminine traits.

Specific information on scoring of the Baldwin et al. measure was not provided, but the scale yielded both an M and an F score that could be used to classify persons as masculine, feminine, androgynous, or undifferentiated.

DEVELOPMENT: The measures described here are based on the work of Kelly (1955).

RELIABILITY: No information was provided.

VALIDITY: Ravinder (1987a, 1987b) reported that females from both Australia and India had higher femininity scores than did the males, and males from both Australia and India had higher masculinity scores than did the females.

Baldwin et al. (1986) reported that the Sex Rep Test discriminated between males and females, with males scoring significantly higher on masculinity and lower on femininity and females scoring significantly higher on femininity and lower on masculinity. Interestingly, they found that the Sex Rep Test classified persons differently from the Bem Sex Role Inventory (BSRI) (Bem, 1974) (see separate entry) classified them. In a discriminant analysis, Baldwin et al. found that both Sex Rep Test scores and BSRI scores significantly predicted sex. Thus, both measures were related to sex but in nonoverlapping ways.

NOTES & COMMENTS: (1) Role Construct Repertory Tests are not new; they have been around since the 1950s; however, the techniques have been used to measure sex role only fairly recently. These approaches have the advantage of allowing the respondent to provide his or her own definition of masculinity and femininity, and they avoid the problems associated with norm-based measures that are culture bound or time bound. Baldwin et al. (1986) presented data and arguments to support the superiority of the Sex Rep approach over the traditional approach used by Bem.

(2) There are also disadvantages to the Role Construct approach. It is a very complicated procedure and lacks the simplicity of typical paper-and-pencil measures. Furthermore, the approach does not deal with problems of social desirability or response bias. In the Ravinder measure, for example, the respondent was asked to label 12 traits as masculine, feminine, or both, after having just indicated that the traits were self-descriptors.

AVAILABLE FROM: Shashi Ravinder, University of Wollongong, New South Wales, Australia; Amy C. Baldwin, Department of Psychology, Northern Arizona University, Flagstaff, AZ 86011

USED IN:

Baldwin, A. C., Critelli, J. W., Stevens, L. C., & Russell, S. (1986). Androgyny and sex role measurement: A personal construct approach. *Journal of Personality and Social Psychology, 51,* 1081–1088.

Ravinder, S. (1987a). An empirical investigation of Garnet's and Pleck's sex role strain analysis. *Sex Roles, 16,* 165–179.

Ravinder, S. (1987b). Androgyny: Is it really the product of educated, middle-class Western societies? *Journal of Cross-Cultural Psychology, 18,* 208–220.

BIBLIOGRAPHY:

Bem, S. L. (1974). The measurement of psychological androgyny. *Journal of Consulting and Clinical Psychology, 42,* 155–162.

Kelly, G. A. (1955). *The psychology of personal constructs.* New York: Norton.

SEX ROLE ANTECEDENTS SCALES
AUTHORS: Dinah Levant Mast and William G. Herron
DATE: 1982
VARIABLE: Gender role of self and parents
TYPE OF INSTRUMENT: Checklist
DESCRIPTION: The Sex Role Antecedents Scales consist of 11 masculine, 11 feminine, and 6 sex-neutral traits interspersed with each other and placed to the left of three columns headed "Self, Mother, Father." For each trait, respondents may mark one or two columns indicating who is most closely associated with the named trait. The respondent is not to mark all three columns for any trait.
SAMPLE ITEMS: (masculine) Self-reliant; willing to take risks
    (feminine) Warm; gentle
    (neutral) Helpful; truthful
PREVIOUS SUBJECTS: College students
APPROPRIATE FOR: Ages 16 and older
ADMINISTRATION: Self-administered; about 15 minutes
SCORING: Respondent's gender role is a function of the responses in

the Self column. Endorsing at least six traits on the Masculine scale and fewer than six on the Feminine scale leads to a classification of masculine. Similarly, endorsing at least six traits on the Feminine scale and fewer than six on the Masculine scale leads to a classification of feminine. Endorsing at least six traits on both the Masculine and Feminine scales leads to the classification of androgynous, and endorsing fewer than six traits on both the Masculine and Feminine scales leads to a classification of undifferentiated. Perceived parental gender role can be classified in an analogous manner.

DEVELOPMENT: In order to develop the Sex Role Antecedents Scales, a rep grid technique (Kelly, 1955) was used, including the 60 adjectives from the Bem Sex Role Inventory (BSRI) (Bem, 1974) (see separate entry), expressed in a bipolar fashion, and three role figures: Self, Mother, Father. A sample of 275 college students participated in the development phase. Their responses to the rep grid were used to select the traits for the Sex Role Antecedents Scales. Specifically, the selected traits for the M and F scales showed "significant differences between the perceived parental identifications of (a) sex-typed men and sex-typed women, (b) sex-typed men and androgynous persons of either sex, (c) sex-typed women and androgynous persons of either sex" (Mast & Herron, 1986, p. 35). The 6 neutral items were randomly selected from the 20 neutral items on the BSRI.

RELIABILITY: Internal consistency reliability for male respondents was .73 on the M scale and .73 on the F scale. For female respondents, the reliabilities were .79 and .70. Combining data from males and females produced reliabilities of .76 and .72 for the M and F scales, respectively.

A sample of 50 college men and 50 college women completed the scale on two occasions, with a 3-week interval between testings. For males, the test-retest reliability was .82 and .81 for the M and F scales, respectively. For females, the test-retest reliability was .87 and .81 for the M and F scales, respectively, and when data from both sexes were combined, the test-retest reliability was .85 and .82 for the M and F scales, respectively.

VALIDITY: Overall, fathers were classified as masculine and mothers as feminine. Androgynous respondents were as likely to classify their fathers as undifferentiated as they were to classify them as masculine. However, no other respondents consistently classified their parents in other than sex-typed categories.

In general, there was a relationship between respondents' own sex typing and their identification with their parents. For example, masculine men and women tended to identify with their fathers, and feminine men and women tended to identify with their mothers.

The Personal Attributes Questionnaire (PAQ) (Spence, Helmreich, & Stapp, 1975) (see separate entry) is another gender role measure. A sample of 300 college students completed the PAQ for themselves, and also used it to report their perceptions of their mothers and their perceptions of their fathers. Correlations between scores on the Sex Role Antecedents Scales and scores on the PAQ were moderate and significant for self-ratings, as well as for ratings of Mother and Father. The correlations for Self ranged from .31 to .49; the correlations for perceptions of Mother ranged from .52 to .60; and the correlations for perceptions of Father ranged from .63 to .70.

NOTES & COMMENTS: The M and F scales are essentially independent. Mast and Herron (1986) reported correlations between M and F scales of .01 and − .06 for men and women, respectively.

AVAILABLE FROM: Mast and Herron, 1986

USED IN:

Mast, D. L. (1983). The Self-Parent Identification Scale: A test construction study. (Doctoral dissertation, St. John's University, 1982). *Dissertation Abstracts International*, 44, 317B.

Mast, D. L., & Herron, W. G. (1986). The Sex-Role Antecedents Scales. *Perceptual and Motor Skills*, 63, 27–56.

BIBLIOGRAPHY:

Bem, S. L. (1974). The measurement of psychological androgyny. *Journal of Consulting and Clinical Psychology*, 42, 155–162.

Kelly, G. A. (1955). *The psychology of personal constructs*. New York: Norton.

Spence, J. T., Helmreich, R. L., & Stapp, J. T. (1975). Ratings of self and peers on sex-role attributes and their relation to self-esteem and conceptions of masculinity and femininity. *Journal of Personality and Social Psychology*, 32, 29–39.

SEX ROLE BEHAVIOR SCALE–2 (SRBS–2)/SEX ROLE BEHAVIOR SCALE—SHORT FORM

AUTHORS: The Sex Role Behavior Scale–1 was developed by Jacob L. Orlofsky. The Sex Role Behavior Scale–2 was developed by Jacob L. Orlofsky, Mark W. Ramsden, and Ralph S. Cohen. The Short Form of the Sex Role Behavior Scale was developed by Jacob L. Orlofsky and Connie A. O'Heron.

DATE: SRBS–1: 1981; SRBS–2: 1982; Short Form: 1987

VARIABLE: Gender role interests and behavior

TYPE OF INSTRUMENT: Summated rating scale

DESCRIPTION: The 240-item Sex Role Behavior Scale–2 (SRBS–2) contains male-valued items (80 M items that are considered desirable in both males and females but are more typical of males), female-valued items (80 F items that are considered desirable in both males and females but are more typical of females), and sex-specific items (80 MF items that are more typical for one sex and also more desirable in that sex). Of the 80 sex-specific items, 45 are MF-male items and 35 are MF-female items. The 240 items pertain to four areas of gender role interests and behavior: "recreational activities, vocational interests, social interaction, and marital or primary relationship behavior" (Orlofsky, Cohen, & Ramsden, 1985, p. 381). Recreational Activities include 13 sports activities and 27 items that are "aptitudes, interests, hobbies, and leisure activities." Vocational Interests include 48 occupations, varying in the level of education they require. Social Interaction includes 46 behaviors that may or may not be exhibited in social and dating situations. For these first three areas, respondents are asked to use a 5-point scale to rate themselves on each item. The response options range from "not at all characteristic of me" to "extremely characteristic of me." The fourth area, Marital Relationships, is divided into five sections: "Relationship" (21 items), "Sexual Relationship" (9 items), "Family Finances" (22 items), "Household Responsibilities" (24 items), and "Childcare" (30 items). There are again five response options, this time ranging from "much more characteristic of my spouse" to "much more characteristic of me." The instructions for the last section direct married persons to answer in terms of their current lives, and unmarried persons are directed to answer in terms of their expectations for the future.

The short form of the SRBS–2 consists of a subset of 96 items from the SRBS–2: 24 items from each of the four content areas. Of the 96 items, 32 are male valued (M), 32 are female valued (F), and 32 are sex typed (MF), with half of those 32 more desirable in females and half more desirable in males.

SAMPLE ITEMS: (These sample items are on both the full-length form and the short form of the SRBS–2.)

(Recreational Activities) (sports) Football; (aptitudes, interests, hobbies, and leisure activities) Neat in habits

(Vocational Interests) Art teacher; Optician

(Social Interaction) Complimenting one's date on their appearance; Preferring to avoid premarital sex

(Marital Relationships) (Relationship) Having an occasional night out with same-sex friends; (Sexual Relationship) Being the one to initiate sexual interactions; (Family Finances) Working at a more enjoyable job though it pays less than a less enjoyable one; (Household Responsibilities) Housework; (Childcare) Getting the children breakfast in the morning.

PREVIOUS SUBJECTS: College students

APPROPRIATE FOR: College students and adults

ADMINISTRATION: The long form takes about an hour to complete; the short form can be completed in about half that time.

SCORING: On the SRBS–2, a variety of scores can be obtained: an overall score for all items, a score for each of the four content areas, and a score for each of the three item types (M, F, MF). For most items, a score of 5 is assigned to the extreme response. The exception is in scoring the sex-specific items, where the female items (MF-f) are reverse scored; that is, the extreme choice is scored as 1. It has been recommended (Orlofsky et al., 1985) that total scores be expressed as averages of the item scores because differing numbers of items contribute to the different scores. Using the median split procedure, respondents can be classified as feminine, masculine, androgynous, or undifferentiated.

The procedures for scoring the short form of the SRBS are the same as for scoring the full-length form; however, because the internal consistency estimates for the content areas are low, it is suggested that those subscale scores not be used; that is, the subscale scores for Recreational Activities, Vocational Interests, Social Interaction, and Marital Behaviors should not be used.

Orlofsky, Ramsden, and Cohen (1982) provided means and standard deviations by sex for each of the content areas divided into M, F, and MF subscales and for the overall scores on M, F, and MF. Orlofsky and O'Heron (1987a) provided the same data for scores on the short form of the SRBS–2.

DEVELOPMENT: The SRBS–2 is an extension of the SRBS–1, which was developed by the following procedures. First, Orlofsky (1981) and his colleagues developed several hundred items, covering "(a) leisure and recreational activities and interests, (b) vocational preferences, (c) social and dating behaviors, and (d) marital behaviors (including child-rearing and household responsibilities)" (p. 929). Because of the limited size of machine-readable answer sheets, the pool was reduced to 239 items. The item pool was administered to three groups of college students. One group was asked to rate each item on a 5-point scale indicating whether the item was more typical of women or more typical of men; another group was asked to rate how desirable each item was for men and for women (half the respondents rated men first; the other half rated women first); the third group was asked to rate themselves on the items. The ratings made by the first two groups were used to select items for the scale. Thirty-two items that were considered equally desirable in both sexes but were seen as more typical of females and 51 items that were equally desirable in both sexes but were seen as more typical of males comprise the F and M items on the SRBS–1. In addition, 46 items more desirable and more typical for males as well as 31 items more desirable and more typical for females are the sex-specific items, MF-m and MF-f, on the SRBS–1. Orlofsky (1981) reported means and standard deviations for the SRBS–1 and its various subscales, along with internal consistency coefficients and correlations with the Personal Attributes Questionnaire (PAQ) (Spence, Helmreich, & Stapp, 1975) (see separate entry) and the Attitudes Toward Women Scale (AWS) (Spence, Helmreich, & Stapp, 1973) (see separate entry).

The development of the SRBS–2 was undertaken to correct some of the deficiencies in the SRBS–1. "One important weakness lies in the uneven number of items on the area subscales. . . . Secondly, internal consistency of the overall M, F, and MF scales was found to be generally adequate . . . however, several of the area subscales were quite deficient in this respect" (Orlofsky et al. 1982, p. 633). Thus, the first step in developing the SRBS–2 was to increase the number of items on the SRBS–1. The procedure followed was basically the same as that used in developing the SRBS–1. A pool of 216 items was administered to three groups of college students, with each group being given a different set of directions, as described above. "Typical" and "desirable" ratings were again used to select items. Altogether, 49 items met the criteria for male-valued items, 60 items met the criteria for female-valued items, and 18 items met the criteria for the sex-specific scales. Thus, 127 items could be added to the 160 items on the SRBS–1. The goal was to retain an item set no larger than 240 items so that responses could be recorded on a single machine-scorable answer sheet. Forty-seven items were eliminated based on their impact on the internal reliabilities of the scales. This left the desired 240 items.

Little information was provided on the development of the short form of the SRBS. Orlofsky and O'Heron (1987a) stated: "A short-form of the SRBS was derived . . . by selecting 96 items from the long form that were broadly representative of each behavior area. Eight items were chosen from each of the 12 behavior area subscales, a procedure that resulted in 32 items in each overall (M, F, and MF) scale" (p. 270).

RELIABILITY: Using data from 520 college students, Orlofsky, Ramsden, and Cohen (undated) obtained alpha coefficients of .93 for the male-valued items, .92 for the female-valued items, and .97 for the sex-specific items. Slightly lower coefficients were obtained when the data for males and females were considered separately. The alpha coefficients for the content-area subscales were all greater than .70. The following internal consistency reliabilities were obtained for the short form of the SRBS–2: male-valued items = .83; female-valued items = .84; and sex-specific items = .92 (Orlofsky & O'Heron, 1987a).

VALIDITY: The SRBS–2 was completed by 520 college students (Orlofsky et al., 1982). As expected, college men scored significantly higher than college women on the M scale and the MF scale, and college women obtained significantly higher scores than college men on the F scale. The only exception was on the Vocational Interests subscale, where there was not a significant difference between the sexes.

Orlofsky et al. (1985) administered the SRBS–2 along with the PAQ and the AWS to 200 college students. When PAQ scores were used to classify students into four categories (masculine, feminine, androgynous, and undifferentiated), fairly large differences were obtained on the scores from the SRBS–2. As would be expected, masculine and androgynous men and women scored higher on both the M and MF scales of the SRBS–2. Similarly, men and women classified as feminine scored higher on the F scale of the SRBS–2. It is important to note, however, that sex—male or female—was a more powerful predictor of gender role interests and behaviors than were gender role traits—masculine or feminine. When SRBS–2 scores were compared with AWS scores, "correlations between AWS scores and both male-valued and female-valued behaviors were generally weak or absent, while somewhat stronger, more consistent relationships were found between AWS scores and most of the sex-specific behavior areas" (Orlofsky et al., 1985, p. 389).

Orlofsky and O'Heron (1987a) compared scores on the long and short forms of the SRBS–2. For the M scale, the correlation was .95 for men and .95 for women. For the F scale, the correlation was .96 for men and .94 for women. On the MF scale, the correlation was .91 for men and .90 for women. All of these values were very high, suggesting that for these three subscales, the short form of the SRBS–2 is an adequate substitute for the long form of the scale. Furthermore, when Orlofsky and O'Heron compared the short form scores on the SRBS–2 with scores on the PAQ and the AWS, they obtained results that were quite similar to those they obtained with the long form of the scale.

Whitley (1988a) administered the short form of the SRBS–2 to over 200 college students. He also administered the PAQ, a trait measure of gender role orientation. The correlations between the behavioral measure and the trait measure were generally low: .32 and .28 for men and women on masculinity and .38 and .17 for men and women on femininity.

NOTES & COMMENTS: (1) Unless evidence to the contrary can be obtained, it is reasonable to assume that the items pertaining to marital behaviors are not measuring the same construct in married and in unmarried persons. For married persons, the respondent is asked to indicate whether each item is more characteristic of the spouse or more characteristic of the respondent. Presumably these items tap something about the marital relationship, which obviously is a function of the behavior of two persons: the respondent and the spouse. Unmarried persons are asked to respond to the items in terms of how they expect they will be when married. The unmarried respondents are therefore answering in terms of their own wishes without having to take into account the needs or behavior of another person. How one expects to act in the future may not be a good indicator of how one actually will act. How one acts in the present within the context of a relationship reflects more than just the wishes/beliefs/desires of the respondent.

(2) Orlofsky et al. (1982) also looked at the intercorrelations among the M, F, and MF scores on the four content areas, a total of 12 scores. For both sexes considered together, they found moderate and statistically significant correlations for all possible comparisons. The highest corre-

lations were on the MF subscales, where the correlations ranged from .66 to .82. When correlations were figured separately for men and for women, the values were lower, with a few not reaching significance. From these analyses, they concluded, "the overall scales have utility as general indices of individuals' adherence to sex-stereotyped behaviors. However, the small magnitude of some of these inter-area relationships suggests that sex-role behaviors are certainly not unidimensional. Thus, the area subscales can and should be used separately as well as collectively" (Orlofsky et al., 1982, p. 637).

(3) Blackman (1986) used the SRBS–2 along with the Bem Sex Role Inventory (Bem, 1974) and the AWS to compare college women in math courses with college women not taking math classes. She used only the first three sections of the scale, omitting the Marital Relations items because a substantial proportion of the subjects were not married. Chomak and Collins (1987) also used an abridged form of the SRBS–2, omitting the Marital Relations items on the grounds that the college students participating in their research were generally unmarried. The focus of Chomak and Collins's study was to compare gender role behaviors with drinking habits, as measured by the Drinking Habits Questionnaire (Cahalan, Cisin, & Crossley, 1969).

(4) Orlofsky and O'Heron (1987b) tested over 400 college students and compared scores on the SRBS–2 with scores on measures of self-esteem and social adjustment. Whitley (1988a) compared scores on the short form of the SRBS–2 to measures of self-esteem. Whitley (1989b) looked at the relationships among gender, gender role, and sexual behavior of college students. He used three measures of gender role, including the SRBS.

(5) Whitley (1987) tested college students to determine the relationship between gender role beliefs (as measured by the AWS) and Doyle & Moore's (1978) Attitudes Toward the Male's Role Scale (see separate entry), gender role self-concept (as measured by the PAQ), gender role behavior pattern (as measured by the short form of the SRBS–2) and attitudes toward homosexuals (as measured by Larsen, Reed, & Hoffman's [1980] Heterosexual Attitudes Toward Homosexuality Scale [see Beere, in press] and Hudson & Ricketts' [1980] Index of Homophobia [see Beere, in press]).

AVAILABLE FROM: Tests in Microfiche, Educational Testing Service, Princeton, NJ 08541. Order #015994 for the regular scale; order #015930 for the short form; or order from NAPS c/o Microfiche Publications, P.O. Box 3513, Grand Central Station, New York, NY 10163–3513; NAPS document no. 04709; for microfiche, in U.S. remit $4.00 with order.
USED IN:
Blackman, S. (1986). The masculinity-femininity of women who study college mathematics. *Sex Roles*, *15*(1/2), 33–41.

Chomak, S., & Collins, L. (1987). Relationship between sex-role behaviors and alcohol consumption in undergraduate men and women. *Journal of Studies on Alcohol, 48*(3), 194–201.

Orlofsky, J. L. (1981). Relationship between sex role attitudes and personality traits and the Sex Role Behavior Scale–1: A new measure of masculine and feminine role behaviors and interests. *Journal of Personality and Social Psychology, 40*(5), 927–940.

Orlofsky, J. L., Cohen, R. S., & Ramsden, M. W. (1985). Relationship between sex-role attitudes and personality traits and the Revised Sex-Role Behavior Scale. *Sex Roles, 12*(3/4), 377–391.

Orlofsky, J. L., & O'Heron, C. A. (1987a). Development of a short-form Sex Role Behavior Scale. *Journal of Personality Assessment, 51*(2), 267–277.

Orlofsky, J. L., & O'Heron, C. A. (1987b). Stereotypic and nonstereotypic sex role trait behavior orientations: Implications for personal adjustment. *Journal of Personality and Social Psychology, 52*(5), 1034–1042.

Orlofsky, J. L., Ramsden, M., & Cohen, R. (undated). *Development of the Sex-Role Behavior Scale–2: Appendix: Item analysis and construction of the SRBS–2.* Unpublished manuscript.

Orlofsky, J. L., Ramsden, M. W., & Cohen, R. S. (1982). Development of the Revised Sex-Role Behavior Scale. *Journal of Personality Assessment, 46*(6), 632–638.

Whitley, B. E., Jr. (1987). The relationship of sex-role orientation to heterosexuals' attitudes toward homosexuals. *Sex Roles, 17*(1/2), 103–113.

Whitley, B. E., Jr. (1988a). Masculinity, femininity, and self-esteem: A multitrait-multimethod analysis. *Sex Roles, 18*(7/8), 419–431.

Whitley, B. E., Jr. (1988b). The relation of gender-role orientation to sexual experience among college students. *Sex Roles, 19*, 619–638.

BIBLIOGRAPHY:

Beere, C. A. (in press). *Sex and gender issues: A handbook of tests and measures.* Westport, CT: Greenwood.

Bem, S. L. (1974). The measurement of psychological androgyny. *Journal of Consulting and Clinical Psychology, 42*, 155–162.

Cahalan, D., Cisin, I. H., & Crossley, H. (1969). *American drinking practices: A national study of drinking behavior and attitudes* (Rutgers Center of Alcohol Studies Monograph No. 6). New Brunswick, NJ.

Doyle, J. A., & Moore, R. J. (1978). Attitudes Toward the Male's Role Scale: An objective instrument to measure attitudes toward the male's sex role in contemporary society. *Catalog of Selected Documents in Psychology, 8*, 35. (Ms. No. 1678)

Hudson, W. W., & Ricketts, W. A. (1980). A strategy for the measurements of homophobia. *Journal of Homosexuality, 5*, 357–372.

Larsen, K. S., Reed, M., & Hoffman, S. (1980). Attitudes of heterosexuals toward homosexuality: A Likert-type scale and construct validity. *Journal of Sex Research, 16*, 245–257.

Spence, J. T., & Helmreich, R. L. (1972). The Attitudes Toward Women Scale: An objective instrument to measure attitudes toward the rights and roles of women in contemporary society. *Catalog of Selected Documents in Psychology, 2*, 66. (Ms. No. 153)

Spence, J. T., & Helmreich, R. L. (1978). *Masculinity and femininity: Their psy-chological dimensions, correlates, and antecedents.* Austin: University of Texas Press.

Spence, J. T., Helmreich, R. L., & Stapp, J. (1973). A short version of the At-titudes Toward Women Scale (AWS). *Bulletin of the Psychonomic Society, 2,* 219–220.

Spence, J. T., Helmreich, R., & Stapp, J. (1975). Ratings of self and peers on sex-role attributes and their relations to self-esteem and conceptions of masculinity and femininity. *Journal of Personality and Social Psychology, 32,* 29–39.

SEX ROLE IDENTITY SCALE (SRIS)

AUTHOR: Michael D. Storms

DATE: 1979

VARIABLE: Gender role identity defined as "a global self-concept of one's masculinity and femininity" (Storms, 1979, p. 1782)

TYPE OF INSTRUMENT: Rating scale

DESCRIPTION: The Sex Role Identity Scale (SRIS) consists of six direct questions that ask respondents to rate their personality, behavior, and overall self in terms of masculinity and again in terms of femininity. Each item is accompanied by a 31-point scale, with the endpoints labeled "not at all masculine" (or feminine) to "extremely masculine" (or feminine).

SAMPLE ITEM: How masculine is your personality?

PREVIOUS SUBJECTS: College students

APPROPRIATE FOR: High school students and older

ADMINISTRATION: Self-administered; less than 5 minutes

SCORING: The three masculine items are scored with the "not at all masculine" end of the continuum scored as 0 points and the "extremely masculine" end scored as 30 points. The three feminine items are scored in the reverse direction. The overall score is the average of the six item scores. Thus, the scores can range from 0 (least masculine/most feminine) to 30 (most masculine/least feminine).

DEVELOPMENT: The SRIS was designed to include face-valid questions consistent with the definition of gender role identity: "a global self-concept of one's masculinity and femininity" (Storms, 1979, p. 1782).

RELIABILITY: When the SRIS was completed by 110 college men and 110 college women (Storms, 1979), the intercorrelations of the masculine items exceeded .68 for women and .66 for men; the intercorrelations of the feminine items exceeded .70 for women and .80 for men.

VALIDITY: As would be expected, scores for the 110 college men and the 110 college women were significantly different; in fact, the differences were quite large. The mean for men was 24.43; the mean for women was 7.9.

Also consistent with expectations, scores on the SRIS related to scores on the Personal Attributes Questionnaire (PAQ) (Spence, Helmreich, & Stapp, 1974) (see separate entry), a measure of gender role attributes. However, this was true only for men on the Masculinity scale of the PAQ, for women on the Femininity scale of the PAQ, and for both sexes on the Masculinity-Femininity scale. When PAQ scores were used to classify respondents into four groups—masculine, feminine, androgynous, and undifferentiated—it was found that there were significant differences between the SRIS scores of the four groups. Again it was found that "sex role identity was related only to masculine attributes for men and only to feminine attributes for women" (Storms, 1979, p. 1785).

NOTES & COMMENTS: (1) Storms (1979) used the data from the college students to test two theories of gender role identity: Kagan's theory and Kohlberg's theory. His results offered partial support for both theories.

(2) Storms's (1979) results (see VALIDITY) led to the conclusion that gender role identity influences same sex-typed attributes but not the development of opposite sex-typed attributes. Hungerford and Sobolew-Shubin (1987) provided further support for this conclusion by testing 80 college students and correlating their scores on the SRIS with scores on the Bem Sex Role Inventory (Bem, 1974) (see separate entry) and the PAQ.

(3) The SRIS treats masculinity and femininity as opposite ends of a single continuum. The prevailing view today is that masculinity and femininity are separate traits.

AVAILABLE FROM: Storms, 1979

USED IN:

Hungerford, J. K., & Sobolew-Shubin, A. P. (1987). Sex-role identity, gender identity, and self-schemata. *Psychology of Women Quarterly*, 11(1), 1–10.

Storms, M. D. (1979). Sex role identity and its relationships to sex role attributes and sex role stereotypes. *Journal of Personality and Social Psychology*, 10, 1779–1789.

BIBLIOGRAPHY:

Bem, S. L. (1974). The measurement of psychological androgyny. *Journal of Consulting and Clinical Psychology*, 42, 155–162.

Spence, J. T., Helmreich, R. L., & Stapp, J. T. (1974). The Personal Attributes Questionnaire: A measure of sex role stereotypes and masculinity-femininity. *Catalog of Selected Documents in Psychology*, 4, 43–44. (Ms. No. 617)

SEX ROLE MOTOR BEHAVIOR CHECKLIST

AUTHOR: David H. Barlow

DATE: 1973 (used 1971)

VARIABLE: Masculinity and femininity of behaviors related to standing, walking, and sitting

TYPE OF INSTRUMENT: Checklist based on behavioral observation

DESCRIPTION: The Sex Role Motor Behavior Checklist looks at behaviors relating to standing, sitting, and walking. The walking and sitting behaviors are divided into upper body movements and lower body movements. The Checklist includes five aspects of standing: (1) feet apart is masculine; (2) arm movements originating from the shoulder are masculine; (3) a firm wrist is masculine; (4) hands in pocket or tucked into belt loops is masculine; and (5) frequent or exaggerated arm movements are feminine. Three items assess walking in terms of the movement of the lower body: (1) long strides are masculine; (2) minimal hip movements are masculine; and (3) feet spread apart when walking is masculine. The Checklist also includes three items assessing walking in terms of the movement of the upper body: (1) arm movements originating from the shoulder are masculine; (2) a firm wrist is masculine; and (3) arms hanging loosely from the body are masculine. The Checklist includes three items assessing sitting behaviors in terms of the lower body: (1) buttocks away from the back of the chair is masculine; (2) legs uncrossed and apart is masculine; and (3) legs crossed with ankle on knee is masculine. Finally, the Checklist includes three items assessing sitting behaviors in terms of the upper body: (1) precise, graceful hand motions are feminine; (2) arm movements originating from the shoulder are masculine; and (3) a firm wrist is masculine. Barlow, Hayes et al. (1979) provided more complete descriptions for determining whether a behavior should be keyed masculine or feminine.

PREVIOUS SUBJECTS: College students, transsexuals

APPROPRIATE FOR: Observations of college students; additional research is needed to determine the validity of the scale for other age groups (e.g., children, adolescents, senior citizens).

ADMINISTRATION: The Sex Role Motor Behavior Checklist is a behavioral observation technique in which observations are made by trained observers. A very brief behavior sample is sufficient, as long as the subject is observed walking, sitting, and standing. The Checklist can be applied unobtrusively; the subject does not need to know he or she is participating in research.

SCORING: Items are individually scored following instructions in Barlow, Hayes et al. (1979) or in Hayes, Nelson, Steele, Meeler, and Barlow (1984). Items are summed to yield a masculine score and a feminine score. The total feminine score can range from 0 to 17; the total masculine score can range from 0 to 16.

DEVELOPMENT: In order to identify motor behaviors that differentiated between the sexes, men and women were observed in natural environments.

RELIABILITY: Barlow, Hayes et al. (1979) reported interrater reliability (percentage agreement) for each item and for the overall scale. For individual items, interrater reliability ranged from .58 to .96; overall, interrater agreement was .80. Barlow (1977) reported 92.5% agreement on

ratings of walking behavior, 100% agreement on ratings of sitting behavior, and 97.45% agreement on ratings of standing behavior.

Perkins (1986) looked at the reliability of the measure and concluded
that overall there was good interrater agreement. For all but three items,
the agreement was initially greater than .80.

VALIDITY: In a study by Barlow, Hayes et al. (1979), two college men,
naive as to the purpose of their activity, walked around campus and
rated students on masculinity/femininity. Based on their ratings, masculine and feminine females and masculine and feminine males were
invited to participate in the research. Barlow, Hayes et al. found that
both masculine and feminine females had higher feminine scores on the
Sex Role Motor Behavior Checklist than did masculine and feminine
males. They also found that males had higher masculine scores than
did females, and masculine females had higher masculine scores than
did feminine females. Thus, the Sex Role Motor Behavior Checklist discriminated between biological males and females and between masculine
and feminine females. It did not, however, discriminate between masculine and feminine males.

Barlow, Mills, Agras, and Steinman (1980) compared eight presurgical
male-to-female transsexuals with an equal number of women selected
because they appeared particularly feminine. They found that the female
subjects compared to the transsexuals emitted a greater percentage of
feminine gender role motor behaviors but a smaller actual number of
feminine behaviors. Specifically, of the rated behaviors, 95% of the females' behaviors and 85% of the transsexuals' behaviors were classified
as feminine; for the female subjects, 55 feminine behaviors were observed, and for the transsexuals, 80 feminine behaviors were observed.

Hayes et al. (1984) conducted a study in which they demonstrated
that, in general, persons can change the gender role typing of their
motor behavior; that is, masculine persons can, when asked, display
more feminine gender role motor behavior, and feminine persons can,
when asked, display more masculine gender role motor behavior. The
subjects in the study were not able to modify all of their gender role
motor behaviors, however. This may have been due to the way in which
persons were selected to participate in the research. The male and female
participants in the study were selected on the basis of demonstrating
extreme masculinity or extreme femininity to naive observers.

Perkins (1986) looked at the validity of the scale for a sample of 600
persons in a London subway station. She found that only six items
discriminated between men and women, and she found that behaviors
were influenced by extraneous variables, such as age, dress, and activity.

Barlow, Hayes et al. (1979) found that subjects showed less feminine
behavior when they were aware of being observed than they showed
when they were not aware their behaviors were being observed.

NOTES & COMMENTS: Barlow, Reynolds, and Agras (1973) and Barlow, Abel, and Blanchard (1979) used the Sex Role Motor Behavior Checklist in research designed to change the gender identity of transsexuals.

AVAILABLE FROM: Barlow, Hayes, Nelson, Steele, Meeler, and Mills, 1979; Hayes, Nelson, Steele, Meeler, and Barlow, 1984

USED IN:

Barlow, D. H. (1977). Assessment of sexual behavior. In A. R. Ciminero, K. S. Calhoun, & H. E. Adams (Eds.), *Handbook of behavioral assessment* (pp. 461–508). New York: Wiley & Sons.

Barlow, D. H., Abel, G. G., & Blanchard, E. B. (1979). Gender identity change in transsexuals. *Archives of General Psychiatry, 36,* 1001–1007.

Barlow, D. H., Hayes, S. C., Nelson, R. O., Steele, D. L., Meeler, M. E., & Mills, J. R. (1979). Sex role motor behavior: A behavioral checklist. *Behavioral Assessment, 1,* 119–138.

Barlow, D. H., Mills, J. R., Agras, W. S., & Steinman, D. L. (1980). Comparison of sex-typed motor behavior in male-to-female transsexuals and women. *Archives of Sexual Behavior, 9*(3), 245–253.

Barlow, D. H., Reynolds, J., & Agras, W. S. (1973). Gender identity change in a transsexual. *Archives of General Psychiatry, 28,* 569–576.

Hayes, S. C., Nelson, R. O., Steele, D. L., Meeler, M. E., & Barlow, D. H. (1984). Instructional control of sex-related motor behavior in extremely masculine or feminine adults. *Sex Roles, 11*(3/4), 315–331.

Perkins, R. E. (1986). The Checklist of Sex Role Motor Behavior applied to a European population in a natural setting. *Behavioral Assessment, 8,* 285–300.

SEXUAL IDENTITY SCALE (SIS)

AUTHORS: Barbara B. Stern, Benny Barak, and Stephen J. Gould

DATE: 1987 (used 1985)

VARIABLE: Self-perceived gender identity; that is, how masculine or feminine a person appears to himself or herself

TYPE OF INSTRUMENT: Summated self-rating scale

DESCRIPTION: The Sexual Identity Scale (SIS) is a very brief measure, consisting of four items that ask respondents to rate themselves in terms of how they feel, look, do things, and their interests. The ratings are made on a 5-point scale ranging from "very masculine" to "very feminine."

SAMPLE ITEMS: I FEEL as though I am . . .

   My INTERESTS are mostly those of a person who is . . .

PREVIOUS SUBJECTS: Adults

APPROPRIATE FOR: Ages 13 and above

ADMINISTRATION: Self-administered; a couple of minutes

SCORING: Individual items are scored from 100 (very masculine) to 500 (very feminine). The overall SIS score is the average of the scores assigned to the four items.

DEVELOPMENT: The development of the SIS rests on two assumptions: that researchers can determine a person's gender role identity by overtly asking the person about his or her gender role identity and that a person's gender role identity is multidimensional. Stern, Barak, and Gould (1987) justified these assumptions by relating them to the relevant literature.

The specific dimensions included on the SIS were based on an existing measure of subjective age. This measure, titled "Cognitive Age," was "tested on several large-scale heterogeneous nonstudent samples..., and found to be a multicomponent, reliable, valid instrument" (Stern et al., 1987, p. 507). Stern et al. elected to use a bipolar masculinity/femininity continuum for recording responses, because regardless of the professionals' debate concerning the relationship between masculinity and femininity, the general public—that is, persons who would be completing the scale—perceive that masculinity and femininity are opposites.

RELIABILITY: Stern et al. (1987) obtained data from 380 adult men and 380 adult women. They calculated alpha coefficients of .96 for the total sample, .85 for the women, and .87 for the men. Analyses using LISREL VI confirmed that the scale was internally consistent.

VALIDITY: Correlations between biological sex and each item of the SIS were statistically significant; they ranged from $-.70$ to $-.81$. Similarly, the correlation between biological sex and total SIS score was significant ($r = -.81$). These correlations showed, to no surprise, that women typically see themselves as feminine and men typically see themselves as masculine.

Respondents completed a Femininity Trait Index and a Masculinity Trait Index, both excerpted from the Bem Sex Role Inventory (Bem, 1974) (see separate entry). Correlations between scores on these measures and scores on the SIS were significant but rather low: $r = .24$ for the Femininity Trait Index and $r = -.28$ for the Masculinity Trait Index. This suggests a relationship between the two measures, but the SIS is definitely measuring something different.

NOTES & COMMENTS: (1) The title of the scale may be misleading because it suggests something about one's sexuality. A better title might be "Gender Role Identity Scale."

(2) Stern et al. (1987) correctly concluded that "the SIS, relying as it does on a respondent's direct self-evaluations, may be particularly useful in an era when rapidly evolving definitions of masculinity and femininity render previous sex role categorizations obsolete" (p. 514).

AVAILABLE FROM: Stern, Barak, and Gould, 1987

USED IN:
Stern, B. B., Barak, B., & Gould, S. J. (1987). Sexual Identity Scale: A new self-
    assessment measure. *Sex Roles*, *17*(9/10), 503–519.
BIBLIOGRAPHY:
Bem, S. L. (1974). The measurement of psychological androgyny. *Journal of Con-
    sulting and Clinical Psychology*, *42*, 155–162.

4

Children and Gender

The 18 scales in this chapter pertain to children and gender. Half of the measures assess gender role; they yield either a single masculinity/femininity score or separate scores on masculinity and femininity. The latter are often used to classify children into four gender role categories: masculine, feminine, androgynous, and undifferentiated. While gender role measures used with adults generally focus on personality traits (i.e., respondents are asked about their own personality traits), gender role measures for children have historically focused on the children's preferences for games, toys, objects, or activities. Recently, however, children's scales have been developed that are similar to the adult scales. Four gender role scales in this chapter ask children about their own personality traits: the Adolescent Sex Role Inventory (Thomas & Robinson, 1981) and the Children's Sex-Role Self-Concept Inventory (Kurdek & Siesky, 1980), which are variations of the adult-level Bem Sex Role Inventory (BSRI) (Bem, 1974) (see separate entry); the Children's Androgyny Scale (Ritchie, Villiger, & Duignan, 1977), which is a scale similar to the BSRI; and the Children's Personal Attributes Questionnaire (Hall & Halberstadt, 1980), which is a variation of the adult-level Personal Attributes Questionnaire (Spence, Helmreich, & Stapp, 1974) (see separate entry).

In addition to gender role measures for children, this chapter contains two scales measuring whether a child possesses the concept of gender constancy, two scales dealing with gender disturbances in children, one scale dealing with gender role flexibility, one assessing gender saliency, one dealing with a variety of gender role concepts, and one measuring whether persons approve or disapprove of gender role–appropriate and gender role–inappropriate behaviors. Most of the scales are completed by the children themselves, and some of the scales are appropriate for children as young as 2 years. Measures used with young children must be individually administered. In fact, of the 18 measures in this chapter, 11 of them require individual administration. Some of the measures can be administered to small groups of children. Two are to be completed by adults rating children.

Many of these 18 scales have been employed for over a decade; however, many scales that were used in the 1960s and 1970s are no longer used today. Of the 30 children's gender role measures described in my previous handbook (Beere, 1979), 20 are not included in this book because they have not been used in published research articles or ERIC documents since my previous literature search was completed. In general, the amount of gender role research regarding children has declined during the past 10 years, and the amount of adult gender role research has increased.

The two oldest measures used to assess children's gender roles are described in Chapter 3 because the measures can also be used with adolescents and adults. These are the Franck Drawing Completion Test (Franck & Rosen, 1949) and the figure drawing procedure, used since 1948. The It Scale for Children (Brown, 1956), the oldest and most commonly used measure exclusively for children, is obsolete; fortunately, its use in recent years has declined considerably. The second most frequently employed measure in this chapter is the Slaby-Frey Gender Concept Test (Slaby & Frey, 1975). It has been used in research reported in over 20 publications. It has even been used in Belize, Kenya, Nepal, American Samoa, and Egypt.

A significant problem affecting many scales in this chapter is reliability. There is often too little information about it, and when there is information, it often shows that the scale is not sufficiently reliable. As in other chapters in this book, internal consistency reliability is reported more often than test-retest reliability; however, when any type of reliability is reported for children's gender role measures, the coefficients tend to be low. Perhaps better scales or longer scales are needed. It is also possible that young children are not reliable reporters, even when reporting information about their own preferences and traits. Furthermore, the self-perceptions, interests, and preferences of some children may be in constant flux. Another possible explanation for the low reliabilities is that the children do not understand the task or the items. Antill, Cunningham, Russell, and Thompson (1981) worked with high school students and discovered that 123 of 512 items failed to meet their criterion for understandability. If high school students do not understand almost 25% of the items given to them, it is likely that young children do not understand a portion of the items they are given. And if the children do not understand the items, they are likely to exhibit random responding, which is not reliable. More work needs to be done to determine whether more reliable scales can be developed for use with children. As the first step, there needs to be evidence that the children understand the task and the items.

Researchers studying gender constancy need to be aware that children may adopt a "pretend" mode when responding to questions of gender constancy. The child may know that a boy cannot become a girl, but it can be fun to pretend that he can. Therefore, gender constancy tests tend to underestimate the number of children who have the concept of gender constancy.

All of the measures in this chapter pertain to children. There are other measures pertaining to children elsewhere in this handbook. Measures intended for use with children but measuring stereotypes are in Chapter 5, "Stereotypes." Three chapters—Chapter 6, "Marital and Parental Roles," Chapter 8, "Multiple Roles," and Chapter 9, "Attitudes toward Gender Role Issues"—also include measures about children. The gender role scales in Chapter 3 include three projective measures that can be used with persons of all ages, including young children: the Franck Drawing Completion Test, the figure drawing procedure, and the May Measure of Gender Identity (May, 1966).

Young children's gender role preferences are also measured by systematic observational techniques (none is included in this book). Various aspects of children's behavior have been recorded, including their toy preferences, activity preferences, sex of playmates, and aspects of their interactions with adults. Although no observational measure satisfied the criteria for inclusion in this handbook, the procedures are still worth pursuing because they provide a behavioral indicator of children's gender roles.

BIBLIOGRAPHY:

Antill, J. K., Cunningham, J. D., Russell, G., & Thompson, N. L. (1981). An Australian Sex-Role Scale. *Australian Journal of Psychology*, 33(2), 169–183.

Beere, C. A. (1979). *Women and women's issues: A handbook of tests and measures*. San Francisco: Jossey-Bass.

Bem, S. L. (1974). The measurement of psychological androgyny. *Journal of Consulting and Clinical Psychology*, 42, 155–162.

Brown, D. G. (1956). Sex role preference in young children. *Psychological Monographs*, 70 (entire issue).

Franck, K., & Rosen, F. (1949). A projective test of masculinity-femininity. *Journal of Consulting Psychology*, 13, 247–256.

Hall, J. A., & Halberstadt, A. G. (1980). Masculinity and femininity in children: Development of the Children's Personal Attributes Questionnaire. *Developmental Psychology*, 16(4), 270–280.

Kurdek, L. A., & Siesky, A. E., Jr. (1980). Sex role self-concepts of single divorced parents and their children. *Journal of Divorce*, 3, 249–261.

May, R. R. (1966). Sex differences in fantasy patterns. *Journal of Projective Techniques and Personality Assessment, 30,* 576–586.

Ritchie, J., Villiger, J., & Duignan, P. (1977). Sex role differentiation in children: A preliminary investigation. *Australian and New Zealand Journal of Sociology, 13*(2), 142–145.

Slaby, R. G., & Frey, K. S. (1975). Development of gender constancy and selective attention to same-sex models. *Child Development, 46,* 849–856.

Spence, J. T., Helmreich, R. L., & Stapp, J. T. (1974). The Personal Attributes Questionnaire: A measure of sex role stereotypes and masculinity-femininity. *Catalog of Selected Documents in Psychology, 4,* 43–44. (Ms. No. 617)

Thomas, S., & Robinson, M. (1981). Development of a measure of androgyny for young adolescents. *Journal of Early Adolescence, 1,* 195–209.

ADOLESCENT SEX ROLE INVENTORY (ASRI)

AUTHORS: Susan Thomas and Mary Robinson

DATE: 1981

VARIABLE: Gender role

TYPE OF INSTRUMENT: Summated rating scale

DESCRIPTION: The Adolescent Sex Role Inventory (ASRI) is a 60-item measure consisting of 20 masculine, 20 feminine, and 20 neutral items. Each item is an adjective or adjective phrase, and respondents use a 5-point scale to indicate the extent to which the statement is true for them. Response options range from "never" to "always."

SAMPLE ITEMS: (masculine) Able to take care of yourself; stand up for your own ideas

  (feminine) Giving in; can feel how another person feels

  (neutral) Care about the things you do; someone you can't count on

PREVIOUS SUBJECTS: Adolescents in grades 6–12; college students

APPROPRIATE FOR: Ages 10–14

ADMINISTRATION: Self-administered; about 20–30 minutes

SCORING: Items are individually scored and summed to yield a masculinity score and a femininity score. The two scores can be used to classify persons as masculine, feminine, androgynous, or undifferentiated.

DEVELOPMENT: Thirty child development majors were given the list of 60 stimulus words/phrases from the Bem Sex Role Inventory (BSRI) (Bem, 1974) (see separate entry) and asked, for each stimulus, to write synonymous words or phrases that would be understandable to adolescents. An inventory was developed in which each BSRI stimulus was used as a stem followed by its three most commonly mentioned synonyms. A sample of 50 child development majors were given this inventory and asked to mark the synonym that most correctly matched each stimulus. Their responses were used to develop the first version of the ASRI, which was later modified based on college students' responses to both the ASRI and BSRI.

RELIABILITY: Thomas and Robinson (1981) administered the ASRI to two groups of college students. Alpha coefficients for masculinity were .86 and .83; for femininity, they were .76 for both groups; for the neutral items, coefficient alpha was .45 and .42; and for the total scale, alpha was .84 and .80. These coefficients were quite similar to those obtained with the BSRI, even to the extent that both scales have unacceptably low reliabilities for the neutral items. However, since the neutral items do not contribute to the fourfold classification of respondents, the low reliability is not a problem.

Denny and Thomas (1986) tested 222 adolescents and obtained an alpha coefficient of .95 for the masculinity scale. They did not score the femininity or neutral scales.

VALIDITY: Thomas and Robinson (1981) factor analyzed college students' responses to the BSRI and to the ASRI. They found four similar factors for the two measures, suggesting considerable overlap in what is measured by the two scales. Furthermore, Thomas and Robinson looked at the BSRI and ASRI scores and their relationship to three other measures: a measure of self-esteem, a measure of locus of control, and a measure of assertiveness. The BSRI and ASRI had similar patterns of relationships to the three personality measures.

Thomas and Robinson (1981) found that masculinity and femininity on the ASRI were essentially independent ($r = -.05$).

NOTES & COMMENTS: Handley and Morse (1984) looked at the relationships between science achievement/science attitudes and a variety of personality traits, including masculinity and femininity as measured by the ASRI. Scott (1984) used the ASRI as one measure to assess the effectiveness of a year-long program developed to "increase sex role flexibility, decision making, and achievement" (p. 369) in 6th-, 7th-, and 8th-grade students. Denny and Thomas (1986) used scores on the masculinity subscale of the ASRI to determine whether adolescents who are effective problem solvers are more masculine than adolescents who are ineffective problem solvers.

AVAILABLE FROM: Thomas and Robinson, 1981

USED IN:

Denny, B. M., & Thomas, S. (1986). The relationship of proportional reasoning ability to self-concept: A cognitive developmental approach. *Journal of Early Adolescence, 6,* 45–54.

Handley, H. M., & Morse, L. W. (1984). Two-year study relating adolescents' self-concept and gender role perceptions to achievement and attitudes toward science. *Journal of Research in Science Teaching, 21,* 599–607.

Scott, K. P. (1984). Effects of an intervention on middle school pupils' decision making, achievement, and sex role flexibility. *Journal of Educational Research, 77,* 369–375.

Thomas, S., & Robinson, M. (1981). Development of a measure of androgyny for young adolescents. *Journal of Early Adolescence, 1,* 195–209.

BIBLIOGRAPHY:
Bem, S. L. (1974). The measurement of psychological androgyny. *Journal of Consulting and Clinical Psychology*, 42, 155–162.

CHILDREN'S ANDROGYNY SCALE
AUTHORS: Jane Ritchie, John Villiger, and Paul Duignan
DATE: 1977
VARIABLE: Gender role orientation
TYPE OF INSTRUMENT: Summated rating scale
DESCRIPTION: The Children's Androgyny Scale consists of 10 traits previously judged as masculine and 10 traits previously judged as feminine. Each trait is presented in the context of a sentence phrased in the first person. Masculine and feminine items are alternated, and each item is accompanied by three response options: "hardly ever, sometimes, often."
SAMPLE ITEMS: (masculine item) I am strong.
   (feminine item) I like sewing.
PREVIOUS SUBJECTS: Children ages 8–11 in Australia and New Zealand
APPROPRIATE FOR: The scale was developed for children ages 9–12 in New Zealand
ADMINISTRATION: Self-administered; about 10 minutes
SCORING: Items are individually scored and then totaled to yield separate scores on the masculine items and the feminine items. Using a median split procedure, children are then classified as masculine, feminine, androgynous, or undifferentiated.
DEVELOPMENT: A list of 63 adjectives and adjective phrases was given to 54 children, average age of 12.63 years, with directions to indicate whether each word or phrase was more descriptive of girls or boys. Analyzing their responses produced 12 "masculine" items and 23 "feminine" items. Because the authors felt that their intended respondents should be given no more than 20 items, they selected 10 masculine items and 10 feminine items from those showing significant differences. No information was given regarding how the final 20 items were selected from the pool of 35 significant items.
RELIABILITY: Kuder-Richardson reliability coefficients were calculated using the data from 77 females and 71 males, with an average age of 10.08. These were not the same respondents used for scale development. The reliability for the feminine scale was .63; for the masculine scale, it was .55. Given the brevity of the two scales, Ritchie, Villiger, and Duignan (1977) were satisfied with the reliability.
VALIDITY: The scale differentiated among the children, producing a fourfold classification following "the same pattern of sex-role categorisation as is found in adults" (Ritchie et al., 1977, p. 145).
   Contrary to prediction, Ritchie et al. (1977) did not find that andro-

gynous children were less anxious than masculine-typed or feminine-typed children.

NOTES & COMMENTS: (1) Although Ritchie et al. (1977) were correct that short scales are likely to have lower reliability coefficients, this does not mean that researchers can apply lower standards to interpreting reliability coefficients from short scales. Given the low reliabilities reported, it is necessary that the subscales be lengthened and their psychometric properties be reexamined before the scale is used again.

(2) Ho (1981) varied the Children's Androgyny Scale by using a 24-item version, with 12 masculine and 12 feminine items, and by using a 5-point response scale. Overall, his data supported his hypothesis that problem solving in children is differentially related to their sex typing. It would be interesting to have reliability data from Ho's study. He lengthened the scale from 20 to 24 items and increased the response options from three choices to five choices. Both changes were likely to contribute to higher reliability.

AVAILABLE FROM: Ritchie, Villiger, and Duignan, 1977

USED IN:

Ho, R. (1981). Sex, sex-role typing, and children's problem-solving behavior. *Journal of Social Psychology, 115*(2), 219–226.

Ritchie, J., Villiger, J., & Duignan, P. (1977). Sex role differentiation in children: A preliminary investigation. *Australian and New Zealand Journal of Sociology, 13*(2), 142–145.

CHILDREN'S PERSONAL ATTRIBUTES QUESTIONNAIRE (CPAQ)

AUTHORS: Judith A. Hall and Amy G. Halberstadt

DATE: 1980

VARIABLE: Masculinity, femininity, and androgyny in children

TYPE OF INSTRUMENT: Summated rating scale

DESCRIPTION: The Children's Personal Attributes Questionnaire (CPAQ) consists of 51 items: 20 on the Masculine scale, 18 on the Feminine scale, and 13 on the Feminine-Masculine scale. Each item is a brief self-descriptive statement, and respondents rate each item on a 4-point scale using the options "very true of me, mostly true of me, a little true of me, not at all true of me." About half of the items are phrased so that the sex-typed response is "very true," and about half are phrased in the reverse direction. There is also a short form of the CPAQ with 21 items: 8 on the Masculine scale, 8 on the Feminine scale, and 5 on the Masculine-Feminine scale.

SAMPLE ITEMS: (Masculine) It is hard for me to make up my mind about things.

(Feminine) My artwork and my ideas are creative and original.

(Masculine-Feminine) It is hard to hurt my feelings.

PREVIOUS SUBJECTS: Grades K–6; mothers rating their elementary school children

APPROPRIATE FOR: Grades K–6

ADMINISTRATION: Individually administered for younger children; self-administered after about 3rd grade. Administration of the long form takes about 20–30 minutes per child; administration of the short form takes about 10–15 minutes per child. Hall and Halberstadt (1980) reported using an audiotape that read each item aloud as the children completed the scale.

SCORING: Items are individually scored on a 4-point scale. After the scoring is reversed for particular items, the item scores are totaled to yield three scores: Masculine, Feminine, and Masculine-Feminine.

DEVELOPMENT: The CPAQ was developed by rephrasing 51 of the items on the Personal Attributes Questionnaire, (PAQ), a 55-item gender role scale developed by Spence, Helmreich, and Stapp (1974) (see separate entry). Halberstadt and Hall (1978) stated: "Three attributes in the PAQ were dropped from the pool of items due to their inappropriateness for children. These were 'skill in business,' 'knowledge of the way of the world,' and 'interest in sex' " (p. 30). A fourth item, "nonconforming to social expectations," was also dropped. The format of the items was changed from the PAQ, which expresses items as bipolar opposites separated by a 5-point scale. For example, the item on the PAQ pertaining to adventurousness consists of the phrases "not at all adventurous" and "very adventurous" placed at opposite ends of a continuum and separated by a 5-point response scale. The comparable item on the CPAQ states, "I would rather be safe than have an adventure," and is followed by four response options ranging from "very true of me" to "not at all true of me."

The 21-item short form of the CPAQ was developed by selecting from each subscale those items that correlated most highly with the subscale total.

RELIABILITY: Hall and Halberstadt (1980) tested 45 boys and 44 girls in grades 3 through 6. They reported alpha coefficients of .64 for the Masculine scale, .62 for the Feminine scale (reported as .68 in Halberstadt & Hall, 1978), and .53 for the Feminine-Masculine scale. After 1 year, they retested 50 children and obtained test-retest correlations of .47 for the Masculine scale, .39 for the Feminine scale, and .46 for the Feminine-Masculine scale.

In a footnote, Hall and Halberstadt (1980) reported the results of some long-term test-retest reliability studies. Test-retest correlations for students in grades 5 through 7 who were retested after a 2-year lapse were as follows: Masculine scale = .62, Feminine scale = .35, and Masculine-Feminine scale = .24.

Hall and Halberstadt (1980) tested another sample, this time 159 children, ages 9–12, who completed the short form of the CPAQ. The alpha coefficients were: Masculine scale = .66, Feminine scale = .72, and Masculine-Feminine scale = .40.

VALIDITY: Thirty college students completed the CPAQ and the comparable items from the PAQ (Hall & Halberstadt, 1980). The correlations were .80 for the Masculine scale, .86 for the Feminine scale, and .86 for the Masculine-Feminine scale. Another group of 55 college students completed the short forms of the PAQ and the CPAQ. Unlike their full-length counterparts, these two scales do not contain items that have identical content because both scales were developed by selecting items with high item-total correlations on the relevant subscale. Thus, the short form of the CPAQ has a different subset of items than is found on the short form of the PAQ; about half the items on the CPAQ correspond to items on the PAQ. Nevertheless, the correlations between the two scales were .73 for the Masculine scale, .72 for the Feminine scale, and .45 for the Masculine-Feminine scale.

The data from 55 children were used to correlate short form CPAQ scores with scores from the full-length scale. The correlations were .58 for the Masculine scale, .61 for the Feminine scale, and .57 for the Masculine-Feminine scale (Hall & Halberstadt, 1980).

Hall and Halberstadt (1980) provided considerable evidence pertaining to the construct validity of the scale, though not all of the evidence was supportive. Mothers rated their children on the CPAQ, and the children's self-ratings correlated positively with the mother's ratings. Differences in scores obtained by boys and by girls were generally in the predicted direction and were rather similar to gender differences obtained by college students on the PAQ. When CPAQ scores were used to classify children into the categories of androgynous, undifferentiated, masculine, and feminine, the proportion falling into each category was similar to the proportions obtained when high school students were tested. Generally low correlations were obtained between CPAQ scores and intellectual functioning, although girls with high masculine scores did perform better. More masculine responding on the part of girls was associated with higher self-concept scores. A sample of children responding to the CPAQ was rated by their camp counselors. More masculine responding on the CPAQ was associated with greater assertiveness and less dependency.

NOTES & COMMENTS: (1) The low reliabilities on the CPAQ, both coefficient alpha and test-retest reliability, should not be overlooked. Some changes will need to be made in the scale in order to produce acceptable reliabilities.

(2) Gaa, Sanchez, and Liberman (1986) used the CPAQ to compare Anglo, black, and Chicano children in grades 4 and 5. Jose (1986) tested children in kindergarten through grade 4 and related their scores on the

CPAQ to scores on a measure of Type A behavior, including leadership and aggressiveness factor scores. Jose also related CPAQ scores to results of a sociometric measure of being liked/disliked. Silvern and Katz (1986) worked with children in grades 4 through 6 and tested them using a 10-item version of the CPAQ and several other gender role measures, including a bipolar adjective measure, a play preferences measure, and a ratings measure. They also assessed the children's verbal ability using the vocabulary subscale of the Wechsler Intelligence Scale for Children— Revised (WISC-R) and they had the children's teachers rate them on a variety of personality and behavioral indicators.

AVAILABLE FROM: Order from NAPS c/o Microfiche Publications, P.O. Box 3513, Grand Central Station, New York, NY 10163–3513; NAPS document no. 04708; for microfiche, in U.S. remit $4.00 with order.

USED IN:

Brody, L. R. (1987, April). *Both boys and girls are more scared of boys than of girls.* Paper presented at the meeting of the Society for Research in Child Development, Baltimore. (ERIC Document Service Reproduction No. ED 282 645)

Gaa, J. P., Sanchez, S., & Liberman, D. (1986). Ethnic and gender concerns in sex-role identity: An illustration of problems in cross-cultural research. *Journal of Educational Equity and Leadership, 6*(2), 93–104.

Halberstadt, A. G., & Hall, J. A. (1978). The Children's Personal Attributes Questionnaire: Children's gender roles in relations to cognitive ability and socially desirable attributes. *Probe, 1*(8), 28–41.

Hall, J. A., & Halberstadt, A. G. (1980). Masculinity and femininity in children: Development of the Children's Personal Attributes Questionnaire. *Developmental Psychology, 16*(4), 270–280.

Jose, P. E. (1986, August). *Effects of sex-roles and Type A behavior on children's friendship choices.* Paper presented at the meeting of the American Psychological Association, Washington, DC. (ERIC Document Reproduction Service No. ED 283 611)

Silvern, L. E., & Katz, P. A. (1986). Gender roles and adjustment in elementary-school children: A multidimensional approach. *Sex Roles, 14*(3/4), 181–202.

BIBLIOGRAPHY:

Spence, J. T., Helmreich, R. L., & Stapp, J. (1974). The Personal Attributes Questionnaire: A measure of sex-role stereotypes and masculinity-femininity. *Catalog of Selected Documents in Psychology, 4*, 43. (Ms. No. 617)

CHECKLIST OF GAMES AND PLAY ACTIVITIES

AUTHORS: B. G. Rosenberg and Brian Sutton-Smith

DATE: 1959 (revised 1964)

VARIABLE: Masculinity/femininity

DESCRIPTION: The Checklist of Games and Play Activities is a lengthy listing of games and play activities. Children indicate which ones they dislike and which they like. Games and activities that are unfamiliar are ignored. There are three versions of the scale, differing in length.

ARTICLES LISTED IN BEERE, 1979: 20
AVAILABLE FROM: Each of the references that follows describes a slightly different version of the Checklist: Rosenberg and Sutton-Smith, 1959; Rosenberg and Sutton-Smith, 1964; and Sutton-Smith and Rosenberg, 1971.
USED IN:
Gardiner, S. F. A. (1983). *Children's sex role preferences and their like-dislike ratings and comprehension of sex-stereotyped reading content.* Unpublished master's thesis, University of Saskatchewan, Canada. (ERIC Document Reproduction Service No. ED 236 569)
Marlowe, M., Algozzine, B., Lerch, H. A., & Welch, P. D. (1978). The games analysis intervention as a method of decreasing feminine play patterns of emotionally disturbed boys. *Research Quarterly, 49*(4), 484–490.
Rosenberg, B. G., & Sutton-Smith, B. (1959). The measurement of masculinity and femininity in children. *Child Development, 30*, 373–380.
Rosenberg, B. G., & Sutton-Smith, B. (1964). The measurement of masculinity and femininity in children: An extension and revalidation. *Journal of Genetic Psychology, 104*, 259–264.
Sutton-Smith, B., & Rosenberg, B. G. (1971). Sixty years of historical change in the game preferences of American children. In R. E. Herron & B. Sutton-Smith (Eds.), *Child's Play*. New York: Wiley.
BIBLIOGRAPHY:
Beere, C. A. (1979). *Women and women's issues: A handbook of tests and measures* (pp. 31–34). San Francisco: Jossey-Bass.

CHILDREN'S SEX-ROLE SELF-CONCEPT INVENTORY
AUTHORS: Lawrence A. Kurdek and Albert E. Siesky, Jr.; modified by Anne B. Stericker and Lawrence A. Kurdek
DATE: 1980
VARIABLE: Gender role
TYPE OF INSTRUMENT: Summated rating scale
DESCRIPTION: The Children's Sex-Role Self-Concept Inventory consists of 20 masculine, 20 feminine, and 20 neutral items, each of which is a phrase that elaborates on an item on the Bem Sex Role Inventory (BSRI) (Bem, 1974) (see separate entry). Each item is accompanied by four response options: "never, sometimes, often, always." Respondents rate the frequency with which each item is true of them.
SAMPLE ITEMS: (masculine) Can do things through your own efforts; stand up for what you think is right
    (feminine) Are ready to go along with what others want; smile and laugh a lot
    (neutral) Help other people; feel real happy one day and sad the next
PREVIOUS SUBJECTS: Ages 8–19
APPROPRIATE FOR: Ages 8 and older
ADMINISTRATION: Self-administered to children who can read the

items and orally administered to groups of children who cannot; about 30 minutes.

SCORING: Items are individually scored on a 4-point scale and summed to yield a masculinity and a femininity score. The median split procedures can be used to classify respondents into four groups: masculine, feminine, androgynous, and undifferentiated.

DEVELOPMENT: Kurdek and Siesky (1980) constructed a preliminary version of the Children's Sex-Role Self-Concept Inventory, which was later modified by Stericker and Kurdek (1982). Items on the BSRI were translated into simpler behavioral terms, and the number of response options was reduced from seven to four.

RELIABILITY: Using the earlier version of the Children's Sex-Role Self-Concept Inventory and a 7-point response scale, Kurdek and Siesky (1980) obtained alpha coefficients of .74 for the Masculinity scale and .71 for the Femininity scale.

Stericker and Kurdek (1982) administered the scale to fourth, sixth, and ninth graders on two occasions, separated by about 6 weeks. The average test-retest reliability for the individual items was .42. Alpha coefficients were .71 for the Masculine scale and .66 for the Feminine scale.

VALIDITY: Kurdek and Siesky (1980) administered the Children's Sex-Role Self-Concept Inventory and the BSRI to 25 college students. The average correlation between corresponding items from the two forms was .55. Stericker and Kurdek (1982) conducted the same test with a different sample of students and a slightly modified scale. The average correlation between corresponding items on the two forms was .52. Unfortunately, in neither case did the authors report the correlation between subscale scores.

Stericker and Kurdek (1982) factor analyzed responses to the 60 items. Their results provided weak support for the Masculinity and Femininity scales. "The first factor was loaded on highest by 12 feminine and 12 neutral items; the second factor by 18 masculine, 3 feminine, and 1 neutral item; and the third factor by 7 neutral, 5 feminine, and 2 masculine items" (Stericker & Kurdek, 1982, p. 921).

NOTES & COMMENTS: The items included on the Children's Sex-Role Self-Concept Inventory are adaptations of items from a scale developed for adults: the BSRI. It is likely that a different set of traits/behaviors would be included on the Children's Inventory if scale development had begun by asking children to determine which of a series of traits/behaviors are more desirable in boys and which are more desirable in girls. In other words, if the procedures used to develop the BSRI had been used to develop the Children's Sex-Role Self-Concept Inventory, it is likely that a different set of items would have been identified for the scale.

AVAILABLE FROM: Stericker and Kurdek, 1982

USED IN:
Kurdek, L. A., & Siesky, A. E., Jr. (1980). Sex role self-concepts of single divorced parents and their children. *Journal of Divorce*, 3, 249–261.
Stericker, A. B., & Kurdek, L. A. (1982). Dimensions and correlates of third through eighth graders' sex-role self-concepts. *Sex Roles*, 8, 915–929.
BIBLIOGRAPHY:
Bem, S. L. (1974). The measurement of psychological androgyny. *Journal of Consulting and Clinical Psychology*, 42, 155–162.

FAULS-SMITH ACTIVITY PREFERENCE TEST
AUTHORS: Lydia Boyce Fauls and Walter D. Smith
DATE: 1956
VARIABLE: Masculinity/femininity
DESCRIPTION: The Fauls-Smith Activity Preference Test is a picture preference test used primarily with preschool children. This brief test asks children to make choices on three pairs of pictures, each showing a masculine activity paired with a feminine activity. There are two forms of the test: one with a boy as the central figure and the other with a girl as the central figure.
ARTICLES LISTED IN BEERE, 1979: 1
AVAILABLE FROM: Fauls and Smith, 1956
USED IN:
Albert, A. A., & Porter, J. R. (1982). Children's perception of parental sex-role expectations. *Journal of Genetic Psychology*, 140, 145–146.
Fauls, L. B., & Smith, W. D. (1956). Sex role learning of five-year-olds. *Journal of Genetic Psychology*, 89, 105–117.
BIBLIOGRAPHY:
Beere, C. A. (1979). *Women and women's issues: A handbook of tests and measures* (pp. 37–39). San Francisco: Jossey-Bass.

IT SCALE FOR CHILDREN (ITSC)
AUTHOR: Daniel G. Brown
DATE: 1956
VARIABLE: Gender role preference
DESCRIPTION: The It Scale for Children (ITSC) is a semiprojective, picture preference test consisting of three sections. In the first section, children make choices among eight pairs of drawings, each with one male-typed toy paired with one female-typed toy. In the second section, children make choices among eight pairs of objects or people; again, a male-typed drawing is paired with a female-typed drawing. In the third part, children select one of four drawings: a male, a female, a male dressed as a female, or a female dressed as a male. The test is considered semiprojective because in its original form, the directions ask children to make choices for an ambiguous-looking figure named "It."
ARTICLES LISTED IN BEERE, 1979: 99
NOTES & COMMENTS: (1) There have been numerous variations in the

directions. For example, children have been asked to make choices for themselves; they have been asked to make choices for an androgynous-looking face (no body); the It figure has been kept in an envelope so the children never see it; in place of the It figure, children have been asked to make choices for a blank white card.

(2) Several researchers have compared ITSC responses with responses on other scales designed to measure children's gender role orientation, among them, Downs and Langlois (1988), Goldman, Smith, and Keller (1982), Seegmiller and Dunivant (1981), and Suter, Seegmiller, and Dunivant (1980a, 1980b).

(3) Although there are many references given below, most are from the late 1970s or the early 1980s. The pictures on the test are quite outdated.

(4) The ITSC is listed in *Tests in Print III* (entry 1201).

AVAILABLE FROM: Psychological Test Specialists, Box 9229, Missoula, MT 59807

USED IN:

Bentler, P. M., Rekers, G. A., & Rosen, A. C. (1979). Congruence of childhood sex-role identity and behaviour disturbances. *Child Care, Health, and Development, 5,* 267–283.

Burge, P. L. (1982). The relationship between sex-role identity and self-concept of preschool children. *Child Study Journal, 12*(4), 249–257.

Cappella, R. (1980, September). *Variables and methodological considerations associated with children's sex role preferences.* Paper presented at the meeting of the American Psychological Association, Montreal. (ERIC Document Reproduction Service No. ED 195 341)

Coonrod, D. (1974). *Four selected paternal child-rearing practices and their relationship to sex-role preferences of four-year-old nursery school children.* Unpublished paper, Indiana University, Bloomington. (ERIC Document Reproduction Service No. ED 157 633)

Coonrod, D. (1981). *Fathering: The effect of father-absence and inadequate fathering on children's personality development.* Unpublished paper, Debcon, Inc., Bloomington, IN. (ERIC Document Reproduction Service No. ED 200 317)

Dixit, R. C., & Gupta, S. (1977). Sex-role preferences among young children of rural and urban social groups. *Psychologia, 20,* 111–119.

Downs, A. C., & Langlois, J. H. (1988). Sex typing: Construct and measurement issues. *Sex Roles, 18*(1/2), 87–100.

Edelbrock, C., & Sugawara, A. I. (1978). Acquisition of sex-typed preferences in preschool-aged children. *Developmental Psychology, 14*(6), 614–623.

Feldman-Rotman, S., Vallacher, R. R., & Leifer, M. (1981, August). *The dual-profession family and children's sex-role preferences.* Paper presented at the meeting of the American Psychological Association, Los Angeles. (ERIC Document Reproduction Service No. ED 207 722)

Fu, V. R., & Leach, D. J. (1980). Sex-role preferences among elementary school children in rural America. *Psychological Reports, 46,* 555–560.

Gold, D., & Berger, C. (1978). Problem-solving performance of young boys and girls as a function of task appropriateness and sex identity. *Sex Roles*, *4*(2), 183–193.

Goldman, J. A., Smith, J., & Keller, E. D. (1982). Sex-role preference in young children: What are we measuring? *Journal of Genetic Psychology*, *141*, 83–92.

Koblinsky, S. A., & Sugawara, A. I. (1979). Effects of non-sexist curriculum intervention on children's sex role learning. *Home Economics Research Journal*, *7*(6), 399–406.

Koblinsky, S. A., & Sugawara, A. I. (1984). Nonsexist curricula, sex of teacher, and children's sex-role learning. *Sex Roles*, *10*(5/6), 357–367.

Lanktree, C. B., & Hamilton, M. L. (1980). Sex-typed instructions and sex-role preference in young children's task performance. *Sex Roles*, *6*(3), 463–474.

Paludi, M. A. (1981). Sex role discrimination among girls: Effect on IT Scale for Children scores. *Developmental Psychology*, *17*(6), 851–852.

Paludi, M. A. (1982). A comment on the misuse of the chi-square statistic in research with the It Scale for Children. *Sex Roles*, *8*(7), 791–793.

Paludi, M. A., Geschke, D., Smith, M., & Strayer, L. A. (1984). The development of a measure of preschoolers' knowledge of sex-determined role standards. *Child Study Journal*, *14*(3), 171–183.

Radin, N. (1978, September). *Childrearing fathers in intact families with preschoolers*. Paper presented at the meeting of the American Psychological Association, Toronto. (ERIC Document Reproduction Service No. ED 194 850)

Radin, N. (1981). Childrearing fathers in intact families, I: Some antecedents and consequences. *Merrill-Palmer Quarterly*, *27*(4), 489–514.

Reis, M., & Gold, D. (1977). Relation of paternal availability to problem solving and sex-role orientation in young boys. *Psychological Reports*, *40*, 823–829.

Seegmiller, B. R. (1977, April). *Measuring sex role development: A comparison of two methods*. Paper presented at the meeting of the Eastern Psychological Association, Boston. (ERIC Document Reproduction Service No. ED 144 985)

Seegmiller, B. R. (1979). *Effects of maternal employment on sex-role differentiation in preschoolers*. Unpublished manuscript, Hunter College, New York. (ERIC Document Reproduction Service No. ED 175 579)

Seegmiller, B. R. (1980). Sex-role differentiation in preschoolers: Effects of maternal employment. *Journal of Psychology*, *104*, 185–189.

Seegmiller, B. R., & Dunivant, N. (1981). A comparison of two methods of measuring sex-role differentiation in preschoolers. *Journal of Psychology*, *108*, 137–147.

Seegmiller, B. R., Suter, B., & Dunivant, N. (1978). *Personal, socioeconomic, and sibling influences on sex-role differentiation*. Unpublished manuscript, Hunter College, New York. (ERIC Document Reproduction Service No. ED 176 895)

Seegmiller, B. R., Suter, B., & Dunivant, N. (1979). *Sex-role socialization in the nursery school: Background, design, methods, and subjects*. Unpublished manuscript, Hunter College, New York. (ERIC Document Reproduction Service No. ED 178 167)

Seegmiller, B. R., Suter, B., Dunivant, N., & Baldemor, D. (1979). The effects of tester sex on sex-typed responses of preschoolers. *Journal of Psychology,* *102,* 215–224.

Smith, J. E., Goldman, J. A., & Keller, E. D. (1979, March). *Sex-role preference: What are we measuring?* Paper presented at the meeting of the Society for Research in Child Development, San Francisco. (ERIC Document Reproduction Service No. ED 175 546)

Sultemeier, B. (1979, February). *Assessing sex role development of kindergarten Mexican-American boys.* Paper prepared for the meeting of the Southwest Educational Association, Houston. (ERIC Document Reproduction Service No. ED 188 803)

Suter, B., Seegmiller, B. R., & Dunivant, N. (1980a). *Age, sex, and income level effects on sex-role differentiation in preschoolers.* Unpublished manuscript, New York. (ERIC Document Reproduction Service No. ED 183 249)

Suter, B., Seegmiller, B. R., & Dunivant, N. (1980b). Effects of age, sex, and income level on sex-role differentiation in preschoolers. *Journal of Psychology, 104,* 217–220.

BIBLIOGRAPHY:

Beere, C. A. (1979). *Women and women's issues: A handbook of tests and measures* (pp. 64–74). San Francisco: Jossey-Bass.

Mitchell, J. V., Jr. (Ed.). (1983). *Tests in print III.* Lincoln: Buros Institute of Mental Measurements, University of Nebraska.

LAOSA-BROPHY TOY PREFERENCE TEST

AUTHORS: Luis M. Laosa and Jere E. Brophy

DATE: 1971

VARIABLE: Gender role preference

DESCRIPTION: The Laosa-Brophy Toy Preference Test includes nine pictures of toys: three feminine toys, three masculine toys, and three sex-neutral toys. The pictures, cut from catalogs and glued to black construction paper, are shown to the child, who is asked to choose the one he or she would like to play with. The procedure is repeated until the child has made five choices.

ARTICLES LISTED IN BEERE, 1979: 3

AVAILABLE FROM: Laosa and Brophy, 1972

USED IN:

Laosa, L. M., & Brophy, J. E. (1972). Effects of sex and birth order on sex role development and intelligence among kindergarten children. *Developmental Psychology, 6,* 409–415.

Mullis, R. L., & Bornhoeft, D. M. (1983). Sex-role orientation and cognitive functioning in young children. *Journal of Psychology, 113*(1), 17–23.

BIBLIOGRAPHY:

Beere, C. A. (1979). *Women and women's issues: A handbook of tests and measures* (pp. 74–75). San Francisco: Jossey-Bass.

MICHIGAN GENDER IDENTITY TEST (MIGIT)

AUTHOR: University of Michigan Personality and Language Behavior Research Project

DATE: 1973
VARIABLE: Gender identity
DESCRIPTION: The Michigan Gender Identity Test (MIGIT) is intended for use with preschool children and has been used with children as young as 16 months. The test must be individually administered. After some trials to determine that the child can competently handle an identification task, the child is shown cartoonlike drawings of a boy and a girl and asked to label them. The child is then shown photographs of boys and girls and asked to identify which are boys and which are girls. Finally, the child is shown photographs of boys, photographs of girls, and a photograph of himself or herself. Again, the child is asked to identify the boys and the girls.
ARTICLES LISTED IN BEERE, 1979: 2
AVAILABLE FROM: Dull, Guiora, Paluszny, Beit-Hallahmi, Catford, and Cooley, 1975, provides a description and the rationale for the test.
USED IN:
Abelson, A. G. (1981). The development of gender identity in the autistic child. *Child Care, Health, and Development, 7,* 347–356.
Abelson, A. G., & Paluszny, M. (1978). Gender identity in a group of retarded children. *Journal of Autism and Childhood Schizophrenia, 8*(4), 403–411.
Dull, C. Y., Guiora, A. Z., Paluszny, M., Beit-Hallahmi, B., Catford, J. C., & Cooley, R. E. (1975). The Michigan Gender Identity Test (MIGIT). *Comprehensive Psychiatry, 16,* 581–592.
BIBLIOGRAPHY:
Beere, C. A. (1979). *Women and women's issues: A handbook of tests and measures* (pp. 253–255). San Francisco: Jossey-Bass.

THE TOY PREFERENCE TEST
AUTHOR: Lenore A. DeLucia
DATE: 1963
VARIABLE: Gender role identification
DESCRIPTION: The Toy Preference Test is a forced-choice picture preference measure appropriate for children ages 4 to 9 years. The test consists of 24 pairs of black and white photographs of toys previously rated in terms of their degree of masculinity or femininity. Ten pairs of pictures include two masculine-typed toys, 10 pairs of pictures include two feminine-typed toys, and 4 pairs include one feminine-typed and one masculine-typed toy. The pictures are placed on a flannel board, one pair at a time, and the child selects the one in each pair that he or she would prefer to play with. When the scale is scored, the child receives 1 point for each sex-appropriate choice; that is, boys receive 1 point when they select the more masculine toy and girls receive 1 point when they select the more feminine toy.
ARTICLES LISTED IN BEERE, 1979: 3
NOTES & COMMENTS: (1) Several researchers have modified the scale,

so it cannot be presumed that all of the references listed used the scale as DeLucia originally constructed it.

(2) Seegmiller (1977) compared children's responses on the Toy Preference Test with their responses on other measures of gender role identification.

AVAILABLE FROM: DeLucia, 1963

USED IN:

Callan, V. J., & Liddy, L. (1982). Sex-role preference in Australian aboriginal and white children. *Journal of Social Psychology, 117,* 147–148.

DeLucia, L. A. (1963). The Toy Preference Test: A measure of sex role identification. *Child Development, 34,* 107–117.

Lanktree, C. B., & Hamilton, M. L. (1980). Sex-typed instructions and sex-role preference in young children's task performance. *Sex Roles, 6*(3), 463–474.

Newman, R. C., II. (1977). Development and standardization of instruments measuring four aspects of sex-roles in primary grade children. *Journal of Personality Assessment, 41,* 164–169.

Newman, R. C., II., & Carney, R. E. (1981). Cross-validation of sex-role measures for children with correlation of sex-role measures for children and parents. *Perceptual and Motor Skills, 52,* 883–890.

Seegmiller, B. R. (1977, April). *Measuring sex role development: A comparison of two methods.* Paper presented at the meeting of the Eastern Psychological Association, Boston. (ERIC Document Reproduction Service No. ED 144 985)

Seegmiller, B. R. (1979). *Effects of maternal employment on sex-role differentiation in preschoolers.* Unpublished manuscript, Hunter College, New York. (ERIC Document Reproduction Service No. ED 175 579)

Seegmiller, B. R. (1980). Sex-role differentiation in preschoolers: Effects of maternal employment. *Journal of Psychology, 104,* 185–189.

Seegmiller, B. R., Suter, B., & Dunivant, N. (1978). *Personal, socioeconomic, and sibling influences on sex-role differentiation.* Unpublished manuscript, Hunter College, New York. (ERIC Document Reproduction Service No. ED 176 895)

Seegmiller, B. R., Suter, B., & Dunivant, N. (1979). *Sex-role socialization in the nursery school: Background, design, methods, and subjects.* Unpublished manuscript, Hunter College, New York. (ERIC Document Reproduction Service No. ED 178 167)

Seegmiller, B. R., Suter, B., Dunivant, N., & Baldemor, D. (1979). The effects of tester sex on sex-typed responses of preschoolers. *Journal of Psychology, 102,* 215–224.

Serbin, L. A., & Sprafkin, C. (1982). Measurement of sex-typed play: A comparison between laboratory and naturalistic observation procedures. *Behavioral Assessment, 4,* 225–235.

Suter, B., Seegmiller, B. R., & Dunivant, N. (1980). *Age, sex, and income level effects on sex-role differentiation in preschoolers.* Unpublished manuscript, New York. (ERIC Document Reproduction Service No. ED 183 249)

BIBLIOGRAPHY:

Beere, C. A. (1979). *Women and women's issues: A handbook of tests and measures* (pp. 92–94). San Francisco: Jossey-Bass.

BOY-GIRL IDENTITY TASK
AUTHORS: Walter Emmerich and Karla S. Goldman
DATE: 1972
VARIABLE: Gender constancy
TYPE OF INSTRUMENT: Structured interview
DESCRIPTION: The Boy-Girl Identity Task consists of two parallel tasks, each with five questions pertaining to whether certain changes can lead a child of one sex to become a child of the opposite sex. In the first task, the respondent is shown a drawing of a long-haired girl, Janie, wearing a dress. The drawing is cut horizontally at the neck so that hypothetical changes can be shown visually as the examiner reads a question. For example, when the examiner asks whether Janie would be a girl or boy if she put on boys' clothes, the examiner flips the lower portion of the picture, thereby revealing the body of a child dressed in boys' clothing. The head is still long-haired Janie. In the second task, the child is shown a drawing of a short-haired boy, Johnny, wearing trousers. Again the drawing is cut at the neck so that changes can be shown as questions are asked. The pictures of both the boy and the girl should be visible to the child at the same time. Then when a question is asked and a picture is flipped, it is very apparent that the newly shown portion now matches the appearance of the opposite-sex figure. The five questions in each task pertain to wishes to be of the opposite sex and changes in activities, hair style, and clothing.
SAMPLE ITEMS: If Janie really *wants to be* a boy, can she be?

If Janie has her *hair cut short* like this and *wears boy clothes* like this, what would she be? Would she be a girl, or would she be a boy?
PREVIOUS SUBJECTS: Ages 4–8
APPROPRIATE FOR: Ages 2–8
ADMINISTRATION: Individually administered; about 5 minutes. The examiner needs training to be certain that he or she is able to probe when answers are ambiguous. The examiner must be careful to avoid any response that could be construed as positive or negative feedback.
SCORING: Responses reflecting gender constancy are scored 1, and those reflecting lack of constancy are scored 0. If the response is ambiguous, it is scored 0.5. Emmerich and Goldman (1972) recommended obtaining three subscores: the sum of the first item across the two tasks, the sum of items 2 through 5 on Task I, and the sum of items 2 through 5 on Task II. Emmerich and Goldman specifically recommended against summing items 1 through 5 on each of the two tasks, but their recommendation has not always been followed by users of the measure.

In addition to obtaining a numerical score, Emmerich, Goldman, Kirsh, and Sharabany (1977) performed a content analysis on the justifications children provided for their answers. They defined 17 categories of responses, which they condensed into 3 major categories for classifying responses. The users of the scale, listed below, have not used the content analysis portion of the scoring.

DEVELOPMENT: According to Emmerich and Goldman (1972), the Boy-Girl Identity Task "is a refinement of the technique introduced by Kohlberg (1966) and used by De Vries (1969). . . . Technical improvements were designed to make the task easier than these earlier versions" (p. 27). The use of three subscale scores on the Boy-Girl Identity Task is based on empirical work showing that the two tasks do not each constitute a unidimensional measure of the gender constancy construct.

RELIABILITY: Emmerich and Goldman (1972) reported alpha coefficients for the three scores for children tested in two successive years. In year 1, alpha was .62, .59, and .63 for the three scores. In year 2, alpha was .81, .49, and .59 for the same three scores. These reliabilities were based on scores from very short subscales. The first score was based on only two items, and the remaining two scores were each based on four items.

VALIDITY: Consistent with theory, the correlation between the two parallel scores (items 2–5 on Task I and items 2–5 on Task II) increased between years 1 and 2.

Emmerich and Goldman (1972) predicted that the two parallel scores would decrease developmentally before they increase developmentally. Based on preliminary evidence, their prediction was supported.

In general, correlations between scores on the Boy-Girl Identity Task and measures of general information and Piagetian measures were low. The first subscale, based on the two items relating to wishing to be the opposite sex, tended to show the strongest correlation with the other measures.

Martin and Halverson (1983) tested children between the ages of 53 months and 78 months. They used both the Boy-Girl Identity Task, which they labeled a perceptual task, and the Slaby-Frey Gender Concept Test (Slaby & Frey, 1975) (see separate entry), which they labeled a verbal task. Using a criterion of 100% accuracy in responding, 23% of the children showed gender constancy on the Boy-Girl Identity Task, and 64% showed gender constancy on the Slaby-Frey Gender Concept Test. Statistical tests supported that many children did better on the verbal test than on the perceptual test. Martin and Halverson discovered that many children adopt a "pretend" mode when responding to questions regarding gender constancy. As a result, they appear to lack the concept of gender constancy, but in fact they are not responding in a "real" mode. The findings from the Martin and Halverson study are particularly important for anyone conducting research regarding gender constancy.

NOTES & COMMENTS: (1) The reliabilities are unacceptably low. Research is needed to identify the best approach for increasing reliability.

(2) Emmerich and Goldman (1972) reported intercorrelations among all 10 items across the two tasks. They also reported the intercorrelations for the three subscores, both within and between two successive testing years.

(3) In interpreting scores, Emmerich and Goldman (1972) suggested that the first subscale score, based on the two wishing items, "may index the beginnings of sex-role constancy based upon concrete operational thought" (p. 34), while the other two subscales may reflect "preoperational sex-role beliefs and attitudes" (p. 34).

(4) Marcus and Overton (1978) used four variations of the Boy-Girl Identity Task: they administered the scale in the usual fashion; they modified the scale by using a photograph of the subject's own face in place of the drawing of the head of the same-sex figure; they used a live model of a child along with enlarged drawings; and they asked the subject to serve as the live model.

AVAILABLE FROM: Emmerich and Goldman, 1972
USED IN:

Baruch, G. K., & Barnett, R. C. (1986). Fathers' participation in family work and children's sex-role attitudes. *Child Development, 57*, 1210–1223.

Emmerich, W., & Goldman, K. S. (1972). Boy-Girl Identity Task: Technical report 1. In V. Shipman (Ed.), *Disadvantaged children and their first school experiences*. Unpublished paper, Educational Testing Service, Princeton, NJ.

Emmerich, W., Goldman, K. S., Kirsh, B., & Sharabany, R. (1977). Evidence for a transitional phase in the development of gender constancy. *Child Development, 48*, 930–936.

Marcus, D. E., & Overton, W. F. (1978). The development of cognitive gender constancy and sex role preferences. *Child Development, 19*, 434–444.

Martin, C. L., & Halverson, C. F., Jr. (1983). Gender constancy: A methodological and theoretical analysis. *Sex Roles, 9*, 775–790.

BIBLIOGRAPHY:

De Vries, R. (1969). Constancy of generic identity in the years three to six. *Monograph of the Society for Research in Child Development, 34*(3, Serial No. 127).

Kohlberg, L. (1966). *Stages in children's conceptions of physical and social objects in the years four to eight*. Unpublished manuscript.

Slaby, R. G., & Frey, K. S. (1975). Development of gender constancy and selective attention to same-sex models. *Child Development, 46*, 849–856.

SLABY-FREY GENDER CONCEPT TEST

AUTHORS: Ronald G. Slaby and Karin S. Frey
DATE: 1975
VARIABLES: Knowledge of gender identity, gender stability over time, gender consistency across situations
DESCRIPTION: The Slaby-Frey Gender Concept Test is used to measure gender knowledge in young children. The test contains 14 questions: 9 assessing knowledge of gender identity, 2 assessing knowledge of gen-

der stability over time, and 3 assessing gender consistency across situations. Each of the questions is followed by a counter-question. For example, the child is shown a doll and asked, "Is this a boy or a girl?" After the child answers, the examiner asks, "Is this a [opposite sex of child's response]?" The test, which must be individually administered, requires a man doll, a woman doll, a boy doll, a girl doll, and several photographs.

ARTICLES LISTED IN BEERE, 1979: 2

NOTES & COMMENTS: (1) Researchers frequently made minor modifications to the scale. Among the other modifications, researchers modified the scale for use in Belize, Kenya, Nepal, American Samoa, and Egypt.

(2) Martin and Halverson (1983) compared results obtained with the Slaby-Frey Gender Concept Test with results obtained using the Boy-Girl Identity Task (Emmerich & Goldman, 1972) another measure of gender constancy (see separate entry). Siegal and Robinson (1987) looked at the effect of reversing the order of the questions on the test.

(3) Martin and Halverson (1983) discovered that many children adopt a "pretend" mode when responding to questions regarding gender constancy. As a result, they appear to lack the concept of gender constancy, when in fact they are not responding in a "real" mode. The findings from the Martin and Halverson study are particularly important for research regarding gender constancy.

AVAILABLE FROM: Slaby and Frey, 1975

USED IN:

Brenes, M. E., Eisenberg, N., & Helmstadter, G. C. (1985). Sex role development of preschoolers from two-parent and one-parent families. *Merrill-Palmer Quarterly*, *31*(1), 33–46.

Bussey, K., & Bandura, A. (1984). Influence of gender constancy and social power on sex-linked modeling. *Journal of Personality and Social Psychology*, *47*(6), 1292–1302.

Coker, D. R. (1984). The relationships among gender concepts and cognitive maturity in preschool children. *Sex Roles*, *10*(1/2), 19–31.

Dickerscheid, J. D., Schwarz, P. M., Noir, S., & El-Taliawy, M. S. T. (1988). Gender concept development of preschool-aged children in the United States and Egypt. *Sex Roles*, *18*(11/12), 669–677.

Downs, A. C., & Langlois, J. H. (1988). Sex typing: Construct and measurement issues. *Sex Roles*, *18*(1/2), 87–100.

Eaton, W. O., & Von Bargen, D. (1981). Asynchronous development of gender understanding in preschool children. *Child Development*, *52*, 1020–1027.

Eaton, W. O., Von Bargen, D., & Keats, J. G. (1981). Gender understanding and dimensions of preschooler toy choice: Sex stereotype versus activity level. *Canadian Journal of Behavioural Science*, *13*(3), 203–209.

Fagot, B. I. (1985). Changes in thinking about early sex role development. *Developmental Review*, *5*, 83–98.

Gold, D., & Berger, C. (1978). Problem-solving performance of young boys and girls as a function of task appropriateness and sex identity. *Sex Roles*, 4(2), 183–193.

Gold, D., Reis, M., & Berger, C. (1977). *Male teachers and the development of nursery-school children*. Unpublished paper, Concordia University, Montreal. (ERIC Document Reproduction Service No. ED 145 965)

Katz, P. A., & Rank, S. A. (1981, April). *Gender constancy and sibling status*. Paper presented at the meeting of the Society for Research in Child Development, Boston. (ERIC Document Reproduction Service No. ED 203 992)

Kuhn, D., Nash, S. C., & Brucken, L. (1978). Sex role concepts of two- and three-year-olds. *Child Development*, 49, 445–451.

Martin, C. L., & Halverson, C. F., Jr. (1983). Gender constancy: A methodological and theoretical analysis. *Sex Roles*, 9(7), 775–790.

Munroe, R. H., & Munroe, R. L. (1980, December). *The development of sex-gender constancy among children in four cultures*. Unpublished paper, Pitzer College, Claremont, CA. (ERIC Document Reproduction Service No. ED 196 744)

Munroe, R. H., Shimmin, H. S., & Munroe, R. L. (1984). Gender understanding and sex role preference in four cultures. *Developmental Psychology*, 20(4), 673–682.

Ruble, D. N., Balaban, T., & Cooper, J. (1981). Gender constancy and the effects of sex-typed televised toy commercials. *Child Development*, 52, 667–673.

Serbin, L. A., & Sprafkin, C. (1986). The salience of gender and the process of sex typing in three- to seven-year-old children. *Child Development*, 57, 1188–1199.

Siegal, M., & Robinson, J. (1987). Order effects in children's gender-constancy responses. *Developmental Psychology*, 23(2), 283–286.

Slaby, R. G., & Frey, K. S. (1975). Development of gender constancy and selective attention to same-sex models. *Child Development*, 46, 849–856.

Smetana, J. G., & Letourneau, K. J. (1984). Development of gender constancy and children's sex-typed free play behavior. *Developmental Psychology*, 20(4), 691–696.

Urberg, K. (1979, March). *Sex role concepts*. Paper presented at the meeting of the Society for Research in Child Development, San Francisco. (ERIC Document Reproduction Service No. ED 183 244)

BIBLIOGRAPHY:

Beere, C. A. (1979). *Women and women's issues: A handbook of tests and measures* (pp. 255–256). San Francisco: Jossey-Bass.

Emmerich, W., & Goldman, K. S. (1972). Boy-Girl Identity Task: Technical report 1. In V. Shipman (Ed.), *Disadvantaged children and their first school experiences*. Unpublished paper, Educational Testing Service, Princeton, NJ.

GAMES INVENTORY

AUTHORS: John E. Bates and Peter M. Bentler

DATE: 1973

VARIABLE: Gender disorders in children

DESCRIPTION: The Games Inventory is a three-part checklist with 64 items. The first part consists of 30 games and play activities that are considered appropriate for girls or for preschoolers; the second part consists of 22 masculine, nonathletic games; and the third part consists of 12 competitive athletic games. The checklist is to be completed by a parent who indicates "yes" if his or her child regularly plays the game or engages in the listed activity or "no" if the child rarely or never plays the game or engages in the activity.

ARTICLES LISTED IN BEERE, 1979: 1

NOTES & COMMENTS: (1) Some users have modified the measure. For example, it has been used as a self-report scale in which children answer for themselves.

(2) Meyer-Bahlburg, Feldman, and Ehrhardt (1985) showed that the scale is useful with both boys and girls up to the age of 13 and that it can be used as a self-report measure.

(3) The measure has also been called the Child Game Participation Questionnaire.

AVAILABLE FROM: Bates and Bentler, 1973

USED IN:

Bates, J. E., & Bentler, P. M. (1973). Play activities of normal and effeminate boys. *Developmental Psychology, 9,* 20–27.

Bentler, P. M., Rekers, G. A., & Rosen, A. C. (1979). Congruence of childhood sex-role identity and behaviour disturbances. *Child Care, Health, and Development, 5*(4), 267–283.

Doering, R. W. (1982). Parental reinforcement of gender-typed behaviours in boys with atypical gender identity. (Doctoral dissertation, University of Toronto, 1981). *Dissertation Abstracts International, 42,* 4189B.

Hargreaves, D., Stoll, L., Farnworth, S., & Morgan, S. (1981). Psychological androgyny and ideational fluency. *British Journal of Social Psychology, 20*(1), 53–55.

Klein, A. R., & Bates, J. E. (1980). Gender typing of game choices and qualities of boys' play behavior. *Journal of Abnormal Child Psychology, 8*(2), 201–212.

Meyer-Bahlburg, H. F. L., Feldman, J. F., & Ehrhardt, A. A. (1985). Questionnaires for the assessment of atypical gender role behavior: A methodological study. *Journal of the American Academy of Child Psychiatry, 24*(6), 695–701.

Rekers, G. A., Crandall, B. F., Rosen, A. C., & Bentler, P. M. (1979). Genetic and physical studies of male children with psychological gender disturbances. *Psychological Medicine, 9*(2), 373–375.

Zucker, K. J., Bradley, S. J., Doering, R. W., & Lozinski, J. A. (1985). Sex-typed behavior in cross-gender-identified children: Stability and change at a one-year follow-up. *Journal of the American Academy of Child Psychiatry, 24*(6), 710–719.

Zucker, K. J., Doering, R. W., Bradley, S. J., & Finegan, J. K. (1981, April). *Sex-typed play and behavior in cross-gender identified children: A one-year follow-up.* Paper presented at the meeting of the Society for Research in Child Development, Boston. (ERIC Document Reproduction Service No. ED 202 608)

Zucker, K. J., Finegan, J. K., Doering, R. W., & Bradley, S. J. (1984). Two subgroups of gender-problem children. *Archives of Sexual Behavior, 13*(1), 27–39.
BIBLIOGRAPHY:
Beere, C. A. (1979). *Women and women's issues: A handbook of tests and measures* (pp. 56–57). San Francisco: Jossey-Bass.

GENDER BEHAVIOR INVENTORY FOR BOYS
AUTHORS: John E. Bates, Peter M. Bentler, and Spencer K. Thompson
DATE: 1973
VARIABLE: Gender disturbance
DESCRIPTION: The Gender Behavior Inventory for Boys, also called the Child Behavior and Attitude Questionnaire, consists of 55 items representing four factors: Feminine Behavior (18 items), Extraversion (14 items), Behavior Disturbance (17 items), and Mother's Boy (6 items). Parents rate their children on each of the 55 items.
ARTICLES LISTED IN BEERE, 1979: 2
NOTES & COMMENTS: (1) Researchers (Doering, 1981; Zucker, Bradley, Corter, Doering, & Finegan, 1980; and Zucker, Finegan, Doering, & Bradley, 1984) have used a 48-item revised version of the questionnaire. This version includes four factor analytically derived scales: a masculine behavior factor, two feminine behavior factors, and a factor measuring orientation to mother and concern for neatness.
AVAILABLE FROM: Bates, Bentler, and Thompson, 1973
USED IN:

Bates, J. E., Bentler, P. M., & Thompson, S. K. (1973). Measurement of deviant gender development in boys. *Child Development, 44*, 591–598.
Doering, R. W. (1981). *Parental reinforcement of gender-typed behaviours in boys with atypical gender identity.* Unpublished doctoral dissertation, University of Toronto.
Meyer-Bahlburg, H. F. L., Feldman, J. F., & Ehrhardt, A. A. (1985). Questionnaires for the assessment of atypical gender role behavior: A methodological study. *Journal of the American Academy of Child Psychiatry, 24*(6), 695–701.
Zucker, K. J., Bradley, S. J., Corter, C. M., Doering, R. W., & Finegan, J. K. (1980). Cross-gender behavior in very young boys: A normative study. In J. Samson (Ed.), *Childhood and sexuality.* Montreal: Editions Etudes Vivantes.
Zucker, K. J., Bradley, S. J., Doering, R. W., & Lozinski, J. A. (1985). Sex-typed behavior in cross-gender-identified children: Stability and change at a one-year follow-up. *Journal of the American Academy of Child Psychiatry, 24*(6), 710–719.
Zucker, K. J., Doering, R. W., Bradley, S. J., & Finegan, J. K. (1981, April). *Sex-typed play and behavior in cross-gender identified children: A one-year follow-up.* Paper presented at the meeting of the Society for Research in Child

Development, Boston. (ERIC Document Reproduction Service No. ED 202 608)

Zucker, K. J., Finegan, J. K., Doering, R. W., & Bradley, S. J. (1984). Two subgroups of gender-problem children. *Archives of Sexual Behavior*, *13*(1), 27–39.

BIBLIOGRAPHY:

Beere, C. A. (1979). *Women and women's issues: A handbook of tests and measures* (pp. 58–59). San Francisco: Jossey-Bass.

FEINMAN MEASURE OF APPROVAL OF APPROPRIATE SEX ROLE AND APPROPRIATE AGE ROLE BEHAVIOR/ FEINMAN MEASURE OF APPROVAL OF CROSS-SEX AND CROSS-AGE BEHAVIOR

AUTHOR: Saul Feinman

DATE: 1977

VARIABLE: Reactions to appropriate/inappropriate gender role and age role behavior

DESCRIPTION: Each of the two Feinman measures consists of 45 items, 40 relevant items and 5 filler items. The Feinman Measure of Approval of Appropriate Sex Role and Appropriate Age Role Behavior includes 10 statements describing a boy who is engaged in behavior typical for his sex and 10 statements describing a boy who is engaged in behavior typical for his age, along with 10 statements describing a girl who is engaged in behavior typical for her sex and 10 statements describing a girl who is engaged in behavior typical for her age. Using an 11-point rating scale, respondents indicate whether they approve or disapprove of the behavior in each statement. The Feinman Measure of Approval of Cross-Sex and Cross-Age Behavior is similar except that the 40 items describe behavior that is not appropriate for the person's sex or the person's age.

ARTICLES LISTED IN BEERE, 1979: 2

NOTES & COMMENTS: Feinman (1981) used a modification of the Measure of Approval of Cross-Sex and Cross-Age Behavior.

AVAILABLE FROM: Saul Feinman, University of Wyoming, Box 3434 University Station, Laramie, WY 82071

USED IN:

Cole, H. J., Zucker, K. J., & Bradley, S. J. (1982). Patterns of gender-role behaviour in children attending traditional and nontraditional day-care centres. *Canadian Journal of Psychiatry*, *27*(5), 410–414.

Feinman, S. (1981). Why is cross-sex-role behavior more approved for girls than for boys? A status characteristic approach. *Sex Roles*, *7*(3), 289–300.

BIBLIOGRAPHY:

Beere, C. A. (1979). *Women and women's issues: A handbook of tests and measures* (pp. 239–246). San Francisco: Jossey-Bass.

GENDER SALIENCE TEST

AUTHORS: Lisa A. Serbin, Carol Sprafkin, and Judith Gulko

DATE: 1985

VARIABLE: Children's use of gender as a basis for categorizing and making affiliation choices

TYPE OF INSTRUMENT: Picture choice

DESCRIPTION: There are two parts to the Gender Salience Test: the classification portion and the affiliation portion. The classification portion, administered first, consists of 12 items measuring the extent to which children use gender as a basis for classification. Each item consists of a stimulus drawing and three other drawings that serve as the response options. For each item, the child is presented with a stimulus drawing that shows either a boy or a girl engaged in some activity. The child is then shown the set of three "response option" pictures and asked to select the one that "goes with" the stimulus picture. For all items, the three response options follow the same pattern (though not always in the same order). One option is a same-sex child engaged in a different activity or displaying a different posture; one option is an opposite-sex child engaged in a related activity or displaying a posture similar to the person in the stimulus picture; and one option is an opposite-sex child engaged in an unrelated activity. Stated differently, one option matches the stimulus drawing in terms of sex only, the second option matches in terms of activity only, and the third option offers no match. This last option is included to detect random responding.

The affiliation portion of the test includes six items measuring children's tendency to make affiliation choices on the basis of gender when a second, attractive choice is available. There are two forms of this portion: a male form and a female form. Prior to administering this portion, the child's sex preference is ascertained by showing the child eight pairs of pictures; within each pair, the pictures are identical except for the sex of the person in the picture. The child is to select the preferred person in each pair. Children who select a majority of one sex are considered to prefer that sex and accordingly are given that version of the affiliation measure. Children who select an equal number of males and females are assigned to the same-sex version of the affiliation measure.

In each of the six items of the affiliation measure, the child is asked a specific question, such as, "Who would you like to go to the zoo with?" The child is then shown a set of three pictures and asked to select one of the three. The three options include a child of the preferred sex who has a blank expression on his or her face, a child of the nonpreferred sex who has a blank expression on his or her face, and a child of the nonpreferred sex who is engaged in an interesting activity or is holding an interesting toy.

PREVIOUS SUBJECTS: Ages 3–12

APPROPRIATE FOR: The classification portion is appropriate for ages 3 through 8 years; the affiliation portion is appropriate for ages 3 through 10 years.

ADMINISTRATION: The test is individually administered and takes 5 to 10 minutes. Each stimulus drawing is placed on a separate page; each set of three response options is placed on a page together. The original Gender Salience Test used photographs, but the later version relies on drawings.

The classification portion is administered first, followed by the sex preferences and then the affiliation preferences. A fourth part, labeled "prop awareness," is administered next. This portion is given solely to determine whether the child is capable of matching on the basis of the activities shown in the pictures. Each of the six items in this part consists of a page with a stimulus picture and a page with three response options. Each set of three response options contains all persons of the same sex; one drawing matches the activity shown in the stimulus picture, and the other two drawings are unrelated. Thus, activity is the only basis for making a choice, and there are "right" answers on these items.

SCORING: For the classification measure, the examiner counts the number of choices that are gender matches, the number that are activity matches, and the number that are random. The three numbers should total to 12 (the total number of items on this part of the test). A child responding randomly would be expected to select four "random" responses; thus, if a child selects more than four random responses, that child's responses are eliminated on the grounds that they are not meaningful. A child's responses can be eliminated if the child made fewer than four correct matches on the final portion of the test (the part designed to determine whether the child is capable of matching on the basis of the activities shown).

For the affiliation measure, the examiner counts the number of choices that reflect gender preference, the number of preferences that reflect activity preference, and the number of random choices. The three numbers should total to six (the number of items on this part of the test).

DEVELOPMENT: To develop the original version of the test, pilot testing was done to identify classification items that produced approximately 50% gender-based responding in 3 year olds. For both sections of the test, items were selected because they contributed to increased reliability. In the later version of the test, line drawings were used rather than photographs "in order to overcome certain limitations of the photographs, such as variations between photographs in quality, and in attractiveness of the people depicted" (Serbin, Sprafkin, & Gulko, 1985–86, p. 6). The newer version also differs from the original version in other ways. The older version used pictures of adults, while the newer version uses pictures of children; the older version included five affiliation preference items, and the newer version includes four of those five items plus two additional items.

RELIABILITY: Reliability data were reported based on pilot testing done with 79 children, ages 3 to 6, who completed the original version of the scale. Internal consistency reliability was .80 for the classification portion and .66 for the affiliation portion. Test-retest reliability, with a 3-week interval between testings, was estimated in a sample of 21 children, ages 3 to 5. The reliability was .88 for the classification items and .68 for the affiliation items. For a sample of 147 children, ages 4 to 7, who completed the original version, the internal consistency was .82 for the classification items and .64 for the affiliation items.

A sample of children 5 to 12 years old completed the photographs and drawings forms of the test. Internal consistency on the photographs form was .93 for the classification items and .60 for the affiliation items. For the drawings version, the values were .92 and .62.

VALIDITY: Serbin and Sprafkin (1986) tested 147 children, ages 3 to 7, with the original version of the Gender Salience Test and with numerous other measures. Many of their conclusions shed light on the validity of the Gender Salience Test. They found that, regardless of age, brighter children were less likely to use gender as a basis for making choices; this finding was upheld on both the classification task and the affiliation task. Gender-based responding on the classification items decreased with increasing age. That is, younger children were more likely than older children to use gender as the basis for making their choices on the classification task. On the affiliation items, age interacted with sex. Boys increased their number of gender-based affiliation choices as their ages increased; girls showed no changes across the different age groups. Scores on the classification items did not correlate significantly with any of three measures of gender role adoption included in the study. However, as predicted, scores on the affiliation items did correlate positively with all three measures of gender role adoption. Gender constancy did not predict results on either the classification or the affiliation items.

NOTES & COMMENTS: (1) The authors of the Gender Salience Test recommended using the line drawing version of the scale, particularly because they felt that pictures of children are more appropriate for the test than are pictures of adults.

(2) The internal consistency of the affiliation items was low. The authors acknowledged this problem and concluded, "Children are asked to choose preferences from among several dimensions; the relative attractiveness of one dimension over another may shift from item to item. This task may, therefore, be sensitive to individual idiosyncrasies concerning preferences, and thus may yield less consistent responding" (Serbin et al., 1985–86, p. 7). Given this situation, it is important that caution be used in interpreting results from any single child, and it is

unlikely that scores would be useful for making predictions about individuals.

(3) Serbin and Sprafkin (1986) found a nonsignificant correlation between scores on the classification items and scores on the affiliation items ($r = .03$).

AVAILABLE FROM: Order from NAPS c/o Microfiche Publications, P.O. Box 3513, Grand Central Station, New York, NY 10163–3513; NAPS document no. 04709; for microfiche, in U.S. remit $4.00 with order.

USED IN:

Serbin, L. A., & Sprafkin, C. (1986). The salience of gender and the process of sex typing in three- to seven-year-old children. *Child Development, 57,* 1188–1199.

Serbin, L. A., Sprafkin, C., & Gulko, J. (1985–86). *The Gender Salience Test: Background information and administration manual.* Unpublished manuscript, Concordia University, Center for Research in Human Development, Department of Psychology, Montreal.

KATZ SEX-ROLE FLEXIBILITY QUESTIONNAIRE

AUTHOR: Phyllis A. Katz

DATE: 1986 (used 1981)

VARIABLE: Gender role flexibility in children

TYPE OF INSTRUMENT: Summated rating scale

DESCRIPTION: The Katz Sex-Role Flexibility Questionnaire consists of 64 items divided into two subscales. The Cross-Gender Flexibility subscale consists of four sets of preference items, and the Tolerance for Flexibility in Others subscale consists of four sets of tolerance items. The four preference sets on the Cross-Gender Flexibility subscale are Toy Preferences, Activity Preferences, Future Occupational Preferences, and Future Domestic Chore Preferences. Each set consists of four male-typed items and four female-typed items; thus, regardless of the sex of the child, there are four same-sex items and four opposite-sex items within each set. For each of the items on the Cross-Gender Flexibility subscale, children are to mark the response showing how much they would like the item. Each item is accompanied by five response options ranging from "not at all" to "a lot." The four sets of items on the Tolerance for Flexibility in Others subscale are Tolerance for Flexibility in Boys, in Girls, in Men, and in Women. Again each set consists of eight items— four male typed and four female typed. The instructions direct the children to indicate how much they would like it if a boy (or girl, or man, or woman, depending on the particular item set) wanted to do each of the activities listed. Five response options, ranging from "not at all" to "a lot," are provided.

SAMPLE ITEMS:

(Preference items)

(toys) Make-up kit; Gobots

(activities) Playing hopscotch; Skateboarding

(jobs) Secretary; Airplane pilot

(domestic chores) Cooking meals; Washing the family car

(Tolerance items)

(boy) Sewing

(girl) Playing kickball

(man) Preschool teacher

(woman) Carpenter

PREVIOUS SUBJECTS: Grades 1–6

APPROPRIATE FOR: Grades 1–6

ADMINISTRATION: Administered in small groups of five or six children; for the younger children, the items should be read aloud, but older children can read them to themselves; about 20–25 minutes

SCORING: The Katz Sex-Role Flexibility Questionnaire yields two scores: a cross-gender flexibility score and a tolerance for flexibility in others score. The first score is obtained by summing the 4 cross-gender items in each set of 8 preference items. Thus, 16 items contribute to the total score, which then undergoes a simple arithmetic transformation so that girls' and boys' scores are reported on a comparable scale (P. A. Katz, personal communication, January 1989). There are 16 cross-gender items among the 32 tolerance items. These 16 items are summed to yield a "tolerance for flexibility in others" score.

DEVELOPMENT: According to P. A. Katz, "A large number of items for each subscale have been piloted and used in research over the past seven years. Those with the best psychometric characteristics have been retained" (personal communication, January, 1989).

RELIABILITY: On the Cross-Gender Flexibility subscale, coefficient alpha was .76 for girls and .72 for boys. On the Tolerance for Flexibility in Others subscale, coefficient alpha was .88 for girls and .86 for boys (P. A. Katz, personal communication, January 1989).

VALIDITY: In response to a request for information regarding the Katz Sex-Role Flexibility Questionnaire, P. A. Katz provided the following statement: "The direction of stereotyping of all items has been demonstrated by extensive piloting and drawing on the work of other researchers. The content covers a number of relevant domains, and the utility of the scales has been demonstrated by their relationship to actual gender-relevant behavior" (personal communication, January 1989).

NOTES & COMMENTS: (1) According to P. A. Katz (personal communication, January, 1989), factor analysis has shown that the two subscale scores "tap a somewhat different domain of gender-role flexibility."

(2) Two parallel forms of the scale are available.

(3) According to Katz, the preference scales can also be used to measure same-sex preferences.

(4) The measure described here is the most current version of the Katz scales, but the references listed below did not all use this current version. AVAILABLE FROM: Phyllis A. Katz, Institute for Research on Social Problems, 520 Pearl Street, Boulder, CO 80302; telephone, (303) 449–7782.
USED IN:

Katz, P. A. (1979, March). *Determinants of sex-role flexibility in children.* Paper presented at the meeting of the Society for Research in Child Development, San Francisco. (ERIC Document Reproduction Service No. ED 179 290)

Katz, P. A., & Boswell, S. L. (1981). *Final progress report, sex-role development and the single child family* (National Institute for Child Health and Human Development, Contract No. NO1-HD92820). Boulder, CO: Institute for Research on Social Problems.

Katz, P. A., & Boswell, S. L. (1983). *Final progress report, concomitants of gender-role orientation in childhood and adolescence* (National Institute for Child Health and Human Development, Contract No. RO1-HD16218). Boulder, CO: Institute for Research on Social Problems.

Katz, P. A., & Boswell, S. L. (1984). Sex-role development and the one-child family. In T. Falbo (Ed.), *The single-child family.* New York: Guilford Press.

Katz, P. A., & Boswell, S. L. (1986). Flexibility and traditionality in children's gender roles. *Genetic, Social, and General Psychology Monographs, 112*(1), 103–147.

Katz, P. A., & Coulter, D. (1987). *Final progress report, modification of gender-stereotyped behavior in children* (National Science Foundation, Contract No. BNS–8316047). Boulder, CO: Institute for Research on Social Problems.

SEX ROLE LEARNING INDEX (SERLI)

AUTHORS: Craig Edelbrock and Alan I. Sugawara
DATE: 1978
VARIABLE: Three variables are measured: (1) gender role discrimination, which means knowledge of the "correct" way to stereotype activities (this could also be termed "knowledge of stereotypes"); (2) gender role preference, which refers to the desire to adhere to commonly held stereotypes; and (3) gender role confirmation, which refers to the desire to adhere to one's own ideas of what is gender role appropriate.
TYPE OF INSTRUMENT: Picture sorting
DESCRIPTION: There are two forms of the Sex Role Learning Index (SERLI): one for boys and one for girls. The boys' form uses pictures of males only; the girls' form uses pictures of females only. Each form consists of 30 black and white drawings divided into three sections: child figures, adult figures, and objects. Each of the first two sections, child figures and adult figures, contains 5 pictures of a person (child or adult) engaged in masculine activities and 5 pictures of a person (child or adult) engaged in feminine activities. The objects portion consists of 20 pictures

of objects relating to the 10 activities shown in the child figures portion and the 10 activities shown in the adult figures portion.

When the test is administered, three boxes are placed on the table in front of the child. The child is told that one box is for girls, one box is for boys, and the middle box is for both girls and boys. The child is then shown each picture in the objects section and asked, "Who would use a/an [object name] to [activity name], boys? girls? or both boys and girls?" (Edelbrock & Sugawara, 1978, p. 616). After the child responds verbally, the child is encouraged to put the picture into the box corresponding to his or her answer. After all 20 pictures are classified, the pictures in the "both" box are removed, and the child is asked, "These things are for both boys and girls, but who would use a/an [object name] to [activity] more, boys? or girls?" (p. 617). In the next portion of the test, the child is shown the pictures in the child figures section and is asked to select the activity that he or she would most like to do. The child's choice is removed, and the question is repeated until all 10 pictures have been sequenced according to the child's preference. The administration of the adult figures section is next; the procedures parallel those used for the administration of the child figures portion.

SAMPLE ITEMS:
   (masculine stereotype, child activity) picture shows child hammering
   (masculine stereotype, adult activity) picture shows man sawing
   (masculine stereotype, object) picture of hammer and nails
   (feminine stereotype, child activity) picture shows child ironing
   (feminine stereotype, adult activity) picture shows woman as teacher
   (feminine stereotype, object) picture of desk and books

PREVIOUS SUBJECTS: Ages 27 months to 9 years

APPROPRIATE FOR: Ages 27 months to 9 years. Since the measure has been used with this wide range of ages, it is difficult to say that it cannot be used with these ages. However, the task may be difficult for children below the age of 2½ years, and the task may be boring for children as old as 9 years.

ADMINISTRATION: Individually administered; about 10 minutes

SCORING: Six scores are computed from the SERLI: own and opposite gender role discrimination, gender role preference in the child figures and in the adult figures, and gender role confirmation in the child figures and in the adult figures. The own gender role discrimination score is the percentage agreement between the child's classification of the 10 objects stereotyped for his or her own sex; for example, if a girl correctly classifies 7 of the 10 feminine-typed objects, her own gender role discrimination score is 70. The opposite gender role discrimination score is found in an analogous fashion using the child's classification of the 10 pictures typed for the opposite sex.

In scoring for gender role preference, gender role stereotypes define what is sex appropriate; in scoring for gender role confirmation, the child's classification of the objects determines what is sex appropriate. The computation of these scores for both the child figures and the adult figures depends on the order in which the sex-appropriate and -inappropriate choices are made. A sex-inappropriate choice made as the second choice will reduce the score more than a sex-inappropriate choice made as the fifth choice. Edelbrock and Sugawara (undated) provided tables for calculating the scores for these portions of the test.

Edelbrock and Sugawara (1978) provided normative data that can provide guidelines for interpreting scores.

DEVELOPMENT: Little information was provided on the development of the SERLI. Edelbrock and Sugawara (1978) stated: "The items were chosen on the basis of content analyses of previous measures of sex role acquisition as well as pilot studies with an initial pool of 200 items. Items were selected that offered a range of activities and roles that are common in children's play constructions and stories and that children view as relatively desirable" (p. 616). Neutral items were intentionally omitted.

RELIABILITY: Eighteen boys and 18 girls were tested on two occasions, 3 weeks apart, for the purpose of computing test-retest correlations. The reliabilities were highest for gender role preference scores: .90 for child figures and .84 for adult figures. For gender role discrimination scores, the reliabilities were .69 for own sex and .65 for opposite sex. The reliabilities for gender role confirmation scores were .69 for child figures and .51 for adult figures. Reliabilities for children tested by opposite-sex experimenters were consistently lower than reliabilities for children tested by same-sex experimenters (Edelbrock & Sugawara, 1978).

VALIDITY: As would be expected, older children scored higher than younger children on gender role discrimination scores, and children scored higher on their own gender role discrimination scale compared to the gender role discrimination scale for the opposite sex.

Edelbrock and Sugawara (1978) administered both the SERLI and the It Scale for Children (Brown, 1956), a measure of gender role preference (see separate entry), to 39 boys and 30 girls. For boys, several scores on the SERLI were significantly related to It Scale scores, but for girls, there was no relationship between SERLI scores and It Scale scores.

Research with the SERLI partially supported an earlier finding that boys adhere more closely to the masculine role than girls do to the feminine role (Edelbrock & Sugawara, 1978).

NOTES & COMMENTS: (1) The SERLI is unique in assessing children's adherence to stereotypes, not only in terms of culturally agreed upon stereotypes but also in terms of the child's own stereotypes.

(2)Results obtained with the SERLI vary according to the sex of the examiner. Both boys and girls make more sex-appropriate choices when tested by an opposite-sex examiner.

(3) Of the children's measures developed during the past 10 years, the SERLI appears to be the most frequently used. Koblinsky and Sugawara (1979, 1984) used the SERLI to evaluate one possible outcome of a nonsexist preschool program. MacKinnon, Stoneman, and Brody (1984) looked at the relationship between gender role discrimination and mother's divorce/employment status. Sugawara, Andrews, Adduci, and Cate (1986) used the SERLI to look at various aspects of gender role learning and compared scores with children's self-concept scores. Serbin and Sprafkin (1986) looked at gender salience from a developmental perspective and considered the relationship between gender role development and gender salience. Levy and Carter (1987) used a portion of the SERLI to test parts of two theories: cognitive development theory and gender schematic processing theory. Stoneman, Brody, and MacKinnon (1986) related SERLI scores to results on a sex-typing analysis of the child's bedroom. Martin and Halverson (1983) and List, Collins, and Westby (1983) used a portion of the SERLI and related results to children's ability to remember sex-typed information. Callan and Liddy (1982) compared the SERLI scores of Australian aboriginal children with those of urban white children. Cann and Newbern (1984) used the SERLI as a pretest to select children showing different levels of stereotyping to serve as subjects in other research. Carter and Levy (1988) used the SERLI and numerous other measures in a study exploring the relationships among various aspects of children's sex role development.

AVAILABLE FROM: Tests in Microfiche, Test Collection, Educational Testing Service, Princeton, NJ 08541 (order #013562)

USED IN:

Callan, V. J., & Liddy, L. (1982). Sex-role preference in Australian aboriginal and white children. *Journal of Social Psychology, 117*(1), 147–148.

Cann, A., & Newbern, S. R. (1984). Sex stereotype effects in children's picture recognition. *Child Development, 55*(3), 1085–1090.

Carter, D. B., & Levy, G. D. (1988). Cognitive aspects of early sex-role development: The influence of gender schemas on preschoolers' memories and preferences for sex-typed toys and activities. *Child Development, 59,* 782–792.

Carter, D. B., Levy, G. D., & Cappabianca, J. M. (1985, April). *Stereotype knowledge, flexibility, and gender constancy: Applications of gender schema theory to sex-typing by preschoolers.* Paper presented at the meeting of the Society for Research in Child Development, Toronto. (ERIC Document Reproduction Service No. ED 256 481)

Edelbrock, C., & Sugawara, A. I. (undated). *The Sex Role Learning Index (SERLI): Examiner's manual.* Unpublished paper, National Institute of Mental Health, Bethesda, MD.

Edelbrock, C., & Sugawara, A. I. (1978). Acquisition of sex-typed preferences in preschool-aged children. *Developmental Psychology, 14*(6), 614–623.

Koblinsky, S. A., & Sugawara, A. I. (1979). Effects of non-sexist curriculum intervention on children's sex role learning. *Home Economics Research Journal*, 7(6), 399–406.

Koblinsky, S. A., & Sugawara, A. I. (1984). Nonsexist curricula, sex of teacher, and children's sex-role learning. *Sex Roles*, 10(5/6), 357–367.

Levy, G. D., & Carter, D. B. (1987, April). *Gender schema, gender constancy, and sex-stereotype knowledge: The roles of cognitive factors in sex-stereotype attributions*. Paper presented at the meeting of the Society for Research in Child Development, Baltimore. (ERIC Document Reproduction Service No. ED 280 621)

List, J. A., Collins, W. A., & Westby, S. D. (1983). Comprehension and inferences from traditional and nontraditional sex-role portrayals on television. *Child Development*, 54(6), 1579–1587.

MacKinnon, C. E., Stoneman, Z., & Brody, G. H. (1984). The impact of maternal employment and family form on children's sex-role stereotypes and mothers' traditional attitudes. *Journal of Divorce*, 8(1), 51–60.

Martin, C. L., & Halverson, C. F. (1983). The effects of sex-typing schemas on young children's memory. *Child Development*, 54(3), 563–574.

Serbin, L. A., & Sprafkin, C. (1986). The salience of gender and the process of sex typing in three- to seven-year-old children. *Child Development*, 57(5), 1188–1199.

Stoneman, Z., Brody, G. H., & MacKinnon, C. E. (1986). Same-sex and cross-sex siblings: Activity choices, roles, behavior, and gender stereotypes. *Sex Roles*, 15(9/10), 495–511.

Sugawara, A., Andrews, D., Adduci, V., & Cate, R. (1986). Self-concept and sex-role learning among preschool children. *Home Economics Research Journal*, 15(2), 97–104.

BIBLIOGRAPHY:

Brown, D. G. (1956). *It Scale for Children*. Missoula, MT: Psychological Test Specialists.

5

Stereotypes

This chapter contains descriptions of 18 scales. Nine scales are intended for use with children; these are listed first, alphabetically by scale name. These 9 scales are followed by 8 scales appropriate for use with adults; again the measures are listed alphabetically by scale name. Finally, there is 1 scale that looks at sexism in the media. It is used by individuals trained to rate media samples.

Measures of stereotypes are often difficult to distinguish from measures of gender role attitudes. As Brannon (1981) pointed out, people often assume that " 'stereotypes are what you get when groups are rated with an adjective check-list' [and] data obtained with Likert items is usually referred to as 'attitudes' " (p. 621). Obviously this method of differentiating measures of stereotypes and measures of attitudes is not very sophisticated nor does it rest on any theoretical underpinnings.

Perhaps definitions of "stereotypes" and "attitudes" can help us to differentiate measures of stereotypes from measures of gender role attitudes. Stereotypes are defined as "perceptions of persons, objects, activities, or concepts that are based on relatively rigid, oversimplified, and over-generalized beliefs or assumptions regarding the characteristics of males and females" (Beere, 1979, p. 164). An attitude is defined as "a set of affective reactions toward the attitude object, derived from the concepts or beliefs that the individual has concerning the object, and predisposing the individual to behave in a certain manner toward the attitude object" (Shaw & Wright, 1967, p. 13). Clearly stereotypes and attitudes are inextricably interwoven. Stereotypes affect attitudes, and attitudes affect stereotypes, and even with definitions of the terms, it is still difficult to determine whether a scale is assessing attitudes or stereotypes. In other words, Brannon's earlier statement may be lacking in theory, but it may be the best we can do.

To some extent, Brannon's "rule" prevails, and the type of measure differentiates the scales in this chapter from the scales contained in Chapter 9, "Attitudes toward Gender Role Issues." Many of the scales described in this chapter ask respondents to assign a sex to an object, activity, occupation, and so forth. Also included are two semantic differential scales and two ratings scales. All of these measures are clearly distinct from those in Chapter 9. This chapter also includes five summated rating scales. Because summated rating scales typically measure attitudes, these measures are similar to the scales in Chapter 9, and including the five scales in this chapter violates Brannon's guidelines for differentiating stereotype measures from measures of gender role attitudes. However, four of these summated rating scales include the word *stereotype* in their title: the Frye Dietz Attitude Toward Stereotypes of Women (Frye & Dietz, 1973), the Self-Administered Survey of Sex Stereotypes (Trent, Crandell, Higgins, & Vild, 1979), the Sex Role Stereotyping Scale (Burt, 1980) and Stereotypes About Male Sexuality Scale (Snell, Belk, & Hawkins, 1986). The authors of the fifth scale, the Beliefs About Women Scale (Belk & Snell, 1983), made it clear that their scale was designed to measure stereotypes.

Nine of the measures in this chapter are intended for use with children. Many of these require individual administration. In general, the scales for children seek to determine children's stereotypes regarding occupations, work and work-related activities, school-related objects and activities, play-related objects and activities, and personality traits. A common procedure is to ask a child to indicate whether each of a series of items or activities is appropriate for males, for females, or for both males and females. The wording of the response options (boys or men or males) and the form of the response options (pictorial, written, verbal, or a combination) vary across the different scales, but conceptually the tasks are similar on the different measures. The specific number of options varies among scales, but if the measure is to be used with young children, say preschoolers or those in early elementary grades, more than three options may confuse the respondents. Regardless of the age of respondents, fewer than three options may force the respondent into a position of sex stereotyping even though he or she may wish to express nonstereotyped responses.

There is some overlap in the scales described in this chapter and those described in my previous handbook (Beere, 1979). Specifically, 5 of the 18 scales in this chapter were described in the other book. It is interesting to note that 19 of the sex stereotype measures described in that handbook are not included in this current one. This means they have not been used in research articles or ERIC documents published since 1978. In other words, most of the sex stereotype measures have not withstood the test of time. It is also interesting that the most frequently used stereotype measure is the Sex Role Stereotype Questionnaire (Rosenkrantz, Vogel, Bee, Broverman, & Broverman, 1968), first published in 1968 and described in my previous handbook. The Sex Role Stereotype Questionnaire has been used in over 50 articles and ERIC documents published after the literature search for my previous handbook was completed. The second most frequently used stereotype scale is the Sex Stereotype Measure/Sex Stereotype Measure II (Williams, Bennett, & Best, 1975; Williams & Best, 1976). First published in 1973 and revised in 1977, the scales have been used in 17 published articles and ERIC documents since the publication of my previous book.

Two approaches have been used for scoring sex stereotype measures: scores are either assigned to individuals, as they are with most other measures, or scores are assigned to items. For example, with a measure of occupational stereotyping, the score may reflect the extent to which the respondent stereotypes occupations, the extent to which the respondent is aware of prevailing occupational stereotypes, or the extent to which a particular occupation is stereotyped by a group of respondents. In the first two examples, scores are assigned to respondents; in the last example, scores are assigned to items.

Although the sex stereotype measures included in this chapter were selected because they were the best found in the literature, they are not without their problems. For example, there is no information regarding the reliability of three of the children's measures and one of the adult measures. Thus, researchers need to be careful about using these measures in their own research.

Another criticism of stereotype measures pertains to validity. There seems to have been little, if any, concern given to the relationship between responses on a stereotype measure and respondents' behavior. In many studies, researchers have been content to measure stereotypes solely for the purpose of measuring and describing self-reported stereotypes.

Researchers also need to be clear about what they are measuring. "Who should...," "Who does...," and "Who can...," are all likely to elicit different responses. Respondents will give different answers if asked to state their own beliefs or if asked to state the beliefs of others. "Who do you think should..." can elicit different responses from "Who do most people think should..." Knowledge of prevailing stereotypes is not equivalent to knowledge of facts or to endorsement of stereotypes. The wording of the directions can have a significant impact on the responses elicited.

In addition to the measures described in this chapter, researchers should be aware of other procedures commonly used to assess stereotypes. Of course, the fact that they are commonly used does not address the issue of their quality. As alluded to earlier, adjective checklists are frequently used to measure sex stereotypes. As an example, the stimulus "woman" or "ideal woman" or "lesbian" may be followed by a series of adjectives; the adjectives may be taken from the Adjective Check List (Gough, 1952) (see separate listing) or the Bem Sex Role Inventory (Bem, 1974) (see separate listing), or they may be compiled, perhaps ad hoc, by the researcher. Similarly, semantic differential scales have frequently been used to measure sex stereotypes. The bipolar adjective pairs comprising the semantic differential may be taken from an existing scale or developed by the researcher. The concepts to be rated are likely to be similar to those rated with adjective checklists. Rothbaum (1977) utilized an intriguing and promising approach for measuring children's stereotypes. He asked children to tell stories about dominant adult characters and about nurturant adult characters. He then looked at the relative mention of male and female characters. Although he was using this approach to reflect gender role orientation, the approach seems promising for measuring sex stereotypes. It is more subtle, and thus less fakeable, than the measures included in this chapter. It might prove interesting to relate results obtained by this less obvious technique with results obtained on the more traditional measures.

BIBLIOGRAPHY:

Beere, C. A. (1979). *Women and women's issues: A handbook of tests and measures.* San Francisco: Jossey-Bass.

Belk, S. S., & Snell, W. E., Jr. (1983). *The Beliefs about Women Scale (BAWS): Scale development and validation.* Paper presented at the meeting of the Southwestern Psychological Association, San Antonio.

Bem, S. L. (1974). The measurement of psychological androgyny. *Journal of Consulting and Clinical Psychology, 42,* 155–162.

Brannon, R. (1981). Current methodological issues in paper-and-pencil measuring instruments. *Psychology of Women Quarterly, 5,* 618–627.

Burt, M. R. (1980). Cultural myths and supports for rape. *Journal of Personality and Social Psychology, 38,* 217–230.

Frye, V. H., & Dietz, S. C. (1973). Attitudes of high school students toward traditional views of women workers. *Journal of the Student Personnel Association for Teacher Education, 11,* 102–108.

Gough, H. (1952). *Adjective Check List.* Palo Alto: Consulting Psychologists.

Rosenkrantz, P., Vogel, S., Bee, H., Broverman, I., & Broverman, D. M. (1968). Sex role stereotypes and self-concepts in college students. *Journal of Consulting and Clinical Psychology, 32,* 287–295.

Rothbaum, F. (1977). Developmental and gender differences in the sex stereotyping of nurturance and dominance. *Developmental Psychology, 13,* 531–532.

Shaw, M. E., & Wright, J. M. (1967). *Scales for the measurement of attitudes.* New York: McGraw-Hill.

Snell, W. E., Jr., Belk, S. S., & Hawkins, R. C., II. (1986). The Stereotypes about Male Sexuality Scale (SAMSS): Components, correlates, antecedents, consequences and counselor bias. *Social and Behavioral Science Documents*, *16*(1), 9. (Ms. No. 2746)

Trent, E. R., Crandell, J. E., Higgins, K. R., & Vild, L. C. (1979). *Modifying attitudes toward sex stereotypes in vocational education (MASSIVE)* (Final Report). Columbus: Ohio State Department of Education, Division of Guidance and Testing. (ERIC Document Reproduction Service No. ED 176 047)

Williams, J. E., Bennett, S. M., & Best, D. L. (1975). Awareness and expression of sex stereotypes in young children. *Developmental Psychology*, *11*, 635–642.

Williams, J. E., & Best, D. L. (1976). *Sex Stereotype Measure II and Sex Attitude Measure: General information and manual of directions*. Unpublished manuscript, Wake Forest University, Winston-Salem, NC.

BACON-LERNER VOCATIONAL ROLE INDEX

AUTHORS: Carolyn Bacon and Richard M. Lerner

DATE: 1975

VARIABLE: Tendency to sex stereotype occupations

DESCRIPTION: The Bacon-Lerner Vocational Role Index is an individually administered scale intended for use with children in grades 2 through 6. The scale includes 10 occupations, half stereotypically masculine and half stereotypically feminine. For each occupation, the child is asked whether the occupation is appropriate for women, for men, or for both men and women.

ARTICLES LISTED IN BEERE, 1979: 3

AVAILABLE FROM: Bacon and Lerner, 1975

USED IN:

Bacon, C., & Lerner, R. M. (1975). Effects of maternal employment status on the development of vocational role perception in females. *Journal of Genetic Psychology*, *126*, 187–193.

Lavine, L. O. (1982). Parental power as a potential influence on girls' career choice. *Child Development*, *53*, 658–663.

BIBLIOGRAPHY:

Beere, C. A. (1979). *Women and women's issues: A handbook of tests and measures* (pp. 169–171). San Francisco: Jossey-Bass.

CHILDREN'S PERCEPTIONS OF SEX STEREOTYPING IN ELEMENTARY SCHOOL

AUTHOR: E. Marcia Sheridan

DATE: 1978 (used 1976)

VARIABLE: Children's perceptions of sex stereotyping in the schools

TYPE OF INSTRUMENT: Multiple choice with pictorial response options

DESCRIPTION: The Children's Perceptions of Sex Stereotyping in Elementary School consists of 18 questions, each asking about some aspect of children's perceptions of the school environment. The questions pertain to six areas: domestic tasks, strength and mechanical tasks, good behavior, negative teacher treatment, positive teacher treatment, and intelligence. To respond to each item, children mark one of five pictures: one shows a girl and is labeled "only girls"; the next one shows two girls and a boy and is labeled "mostly girls"; the third picture shows a boy and a girl and is labeled "both"; a picture with two boys and a girl is labeled "mostly boys"; and a picture with only one boy is labeled "only boys."

SAMPLE ITEMS: Which students move desks, chairs, and other furniture?

Which students behave best on the playground?

PREVIOUS SUBJECTS: Grades 2–6

APPROPRIATE FOR: Grades 2–6

ADMINISTRATION: It is recommended that the scale be administered in small groups, although older children can probably complete it in a large group setting; about 30 minutes

SCORING: Sheridan (1978) did not provide directions for scoring. However, a single score can be obtained by assigning 5 points to the most stereotyped response and 1 point to the least stereotyped response. Alternatively, scores can be assigned to individual items or to clusters of items.

DEVELOPMENT: In a workshop session, teachers produced a list of 40 stereotypic classroom behaviors. As a result of pilot testing, the list was reduced to 18 items.

RELIABILITY: No information was provided.

VALIDITY: According to Parks, Bogart, Reynolds, Hamilton, and Finley (1982), "Content validity was established during a conference held at AIR [American Institutes for Research] in the fall of 1978" (p. 52).

NOTES & COMMENTS: (1) The response options differ not only in terms of sex but also in terms of quantity. Each option includes one, two, or three children. Could this extraneous variable be affecting responses? Would the scale produce different results if all options showed three children?

(2) Kaminski and Sheridan (1984) used a 20-item version of the scale that included two additional questions pertaining to perceptions of greater intelligence in the areas of reading and math. Kaminski and Sheridan compared responses obtained in 1980 with responses obtained in 1975. Sheridan and Short (1984) used only three items from Kaminski and Sheridan's (1984) version. Sheridan and Short looked at stereotypes of intelligence, reading, and math in a sample of 3rd and 6th graders.

AVAILABLE FROM: The questions are given in Sheridan, 1978; the pictures are show in Parks, Bogart, Reynolds, Hamilton, and Finley, 1982.

USED IN:

Kaminski, D., & Sheridan, E. M. (1984). Children's perceptions of sex stereotyping: A five-year study. *International Journal of Women's Studies, 7,* 24–36.

Parks, B. J., Bogart, K., Reynolds, D. F., Hamilton, M., & Finley, C. J. (1982). *Sourcebook of measures of women's educational equity* (pp. 51–53). Washington, DC: Women's Educational Equity Act.

Sheridan, E. M. (1978, March). *Children's perception of sex stereotyping in elementary school*. Unpublished manuscript. (ERIC Document Reproduction Service No. ED 159 262)

Sheridan, E. M. & Short, E. J. (1984). A chauvinistic model of beliefs: Perceptions of sex differences in reading and math. *International Journal of Women's Studies, 7*, 423–429.

CHILDREN'S SEX STEREOTYPES OF ADULT OCCUPATIONS

AUTHORS: Candace Garrett Schau and Lynne Kahn

DATE: 1977

VARIABLE: Tendency to sex stereotype occupational ability

DESCRIPTION: The Children's Sex Stereotypes of Adult Occupations consists of 21 occupations: 7 masculine occupations, 7 feminine occupations, and 7 neutral occupations. Each occupation is briefly defined, and respondents, generally children in grades 1 through 5, are directed either to indicate who "can" perform each job or who "should" perform each job. Each item is accompanied by five response options that are represented both verbally and pictorially. The options are: "only women, more women than men, about the same number of women and men, more men than women, only men."

ARTICLES LISTED IN BEERE, 1979: 4

NOTES & COMMENTS: Schau, Kahn, and Tremaine (1977) used a different version of the measure.

AVAILABLE FROM: Schau, 1976; Tests in Microfiche, Test Collection, Educational Testing Service, Princeton, NJ 08541 (order #008879)

USED IN:

Kurilich, K. R. (1981, May). *Occupational stereotyping in elementary school children*. Unpublished master's thesis, San Francisco State University. (ERIC Document Reproduction Service No. ED 219 132)

Peterson, C., & McDonald, L. (1980). Children's occupational sex-typing. *Journal of Genetic Psychology, 136*, 145–146.

Schau, C. G. (1978, March). *Evaluating the use of sex-role-reversed stories for changing children's stereotypes*. Paper presented at the meeting of the American Educational Research Association, Toronto. (ERIC Document Reproduction Service No. ED 159 494)

Schau, C. G., & Kahn, L. (1976). *Broadening children's stereotypes about sex-requirements for adult occupations: A small grant intervention strategy*. Unpublished manuscript, University of New Mexico. (ERIC Document Reproduction Service No. ED 188 770)

Schau, C. G., & Kahn, L. (1978). *Children's sex-stereotypes of adult occupations*. Unpublished manuscript, University of New Mexico. (ERIC Document Reproduction Service No. ED 160 641)

Schau, C. G., Kahn, L., & Tremaine, L. (1977). *Effects of stories on elementary-school children's gender-stereotyped attitudes toward adult occupations.* Unpublished manuscript, University of New Mexico. (ERIC Document Reproduction Service No. ED 160 208)

Stericker, A. B., & Kurdek, L. A. (1982). Dimensions and correlates of third through eighth graders' sex-role self-concepts. *Sex Roles, 8*(8), 915–929.

BIBLIOGRAPHY:

Beere, C. A. (1979). *Women and women's issues: A handbook of tests and measures* (pp. 171–174). San Francisco: Jossey-Bass.

GENDER-STEREOTYPED ATTITUDE SCALE FOR CHILDREN (GASC)

AUTHORS: Margaret L. Signorella and Lynn S. Liben

DATE: 1980

VARIABLE: Sex stereotyping in children

TYPE OF INSTRUMENT: Multiple choice with pictorial response options

DESCRIPTION: The Gender-Stereotyped Attitude Scale for Children (GASC) consists of 14 masculine-typed items, 14 feminine-typed items, and 7 neutral items. The masculine-typed items include 13 activities and 1 occupation; the feminine-typed items include 9 activities and 5 occupations; the neutral items are all activities. The child is offered three response options with each item: a picture of two women, a picture of two men, and a picture of one man and one woman. When an item is presented, it is prefaced with the phrase, "Show me who can . . ." When the GASC is individually administered, one set of three response options can be provided for the child to point to the answer for each item. When the scale is self-administered, three pictures must accompany each item.

SAMPLE ITEMS: (masculine typed) mow the lawn; doctor

(feminine typed) cook in a kitchen; ballet dancer

(neutral) work a hard puzzle; ride a bicycle

PREVIOUS SUBJECTS: Grades K–4

APPROPRIATE FOR: Grades K–4; younger students would likely have difficulty with some of the vocabulary; older children would likely find the scale boring

ADMINISTRATION: With young respondents, it is often advisable to administer the GASC on an individual basis, but older respondents, such as 4th graders, could complete it in a self-administered form. The GASC takes about 10 minutes per child when individually administered; it takes about 15 minutes to administer to a group of children.

SCORING: The score is a count of "both" responses given to the masculine-typed and feminine-typed items. The neutral items do not contribute to the score. If children are to be divided into "stereotyped" and "nonstereotyped," one method is to divide them at the median on the stereotyping score. For the Liben and Signorella (1980) study, the median was 7 for boys and 8 for girls.

DEVELOPMENT: In designing their measure, Signorella and Liben (1985) gave special consideration to four factors. First, they wanted to ensure that children would be free to give nonstereotyped responses as well as stereotyped answers. Therefore they had to provide more than the answers "male" or "female." They had to include a response that allowed the child to say "both male *and* female." Second, based on other published research, Signorella and Liben concluded that giving more than three response options could serve to confuse younger children; therefore, they provided only three options. Third, in designing the question, Signorella and Liben concluded that the phrasing "Who usually does..." asks more about knowledge of stereotypes than it asks about agreement with stereotypes. Since the researchers were more interested in the latter, they chose to phrase the question in terms of "Who can do...?" Fourth, Signorella and Liben gave consideration to the item content. Published research led them to conclude that young children are better able to understand activities and familiar occupations than they are to understand traits. Thus, the GASC includes activities and occupations. The activities and occupations were selected from items used by Flerx, Ridler, and Rogers (1976) and by Nadelman (1970), and some were selected based on ratings made by 27 female and 16 male college students. All of the items were selected because there was consensus among adult judges that the items were sex typed. Census data regarding who really is employed in the occupations were not taken into account.

RELIABILITY: Signorella and Liben (1985) administered the GASC to four groups of children, ranging from kindergarten through 4th grade. The researchers computed internal consistency reliabilities ranging from .83 to .95 for the four samples. Liben and Signorella (1980) tested 1st and 2nd graders and reported a Kuder-Richardson reliability of .83.

VALIDITY: In responding to the items, children made few errors; that is, they rarely responded with the male option if the item had been prejudged as female, and vice-versa. When errors did occur, they were most likely to be on the items "make a hat" and "cook in a restaurant." When these items were eliminated, 82% of the children made no errors at all. This suggests that the task was certainly understandable to the children.

Consistent with expectations, Signorella and Liben (1985) found that the children were more likely to give the "both" response to the neutral items. This finding suggests that the children were not responding capriciously.

Based on other research, one could expect to find less endorsement of stereotyping as children get older. Data from the GASC supported this expectation (Signorella & Liben, 1985).

Signorella and Liben (1985) gave a second stereotyping measure to the children in one of their samples. They found that 69% of the children received the same classification on both measures.

As further evidence of validity, Signorella and Liben (1985) offer the fact that the classification assigned to children, based on their GASC data, was related to children's memories for pictures of traditional and nontraditional gender role behavior.

NOTES & COMMENTS: (1) Signorella and Liben (1985) differentiate between knowledge of gender stereotypes and attitudes toward gender stereotypes. The former concept increases as age increases. The latter concept might be more appropriately termed "agreement with gender stereotypes." It decreases as age increases.

(2) Signorella and Liben (1984) combined results from the GASC with results obtained from a measure adapted from Williams, Bennett, and Best (1975) (see separate entry for Sex Stereotype Measure). Using the data from both measures, a single stereotyping score was obtained for each child.

AVAILABLE FROM: Signorella and Liben, 1985
USED IN:
Cann, A., & Newbern, S. R. (1984). Sex stereotype effects in children's picture recognition. *Child Development*, *55*(3), 1085–1090.
Liben, L. S., & Signorella, M. L. (1980). Gender-related schemata and constructive memory in children. *Child Development*, *51*, 11–18.
Signorella, M. L., & Liben, L. S. (1984). Recall and reconstruction of gender-related pictures: Effects of attitude, task difficulty, and age. *Child Development*, *55*, 393–405.
Signorella, M. L., & Liben, L. S. (1985). Assessing children's gender-stereotyped attitudes. *Psychological Documents*, *15*, 7. (Ms. No. 2685)
BIBLIOGRAPHY:
Flerx, V. C., Fidler, D. S., & Rogers, R. W. (1976). Sex role stereotypes: Developmental aspects and early intervention. *Child Development*, *47*, 998–1007.
Nadelman, L. (1970). Sex identity in London children: Memory, knowledge and preference tests. *Human Development*, *13*, 28–42.
Williams, J. E., Bennett, S. M., & Best, D. L. (1975). Awareness and expression of sex stereotypes in young children. *Developmental Psychology*, *11*, 635–642.

SEX-ROLE QUESTIONNAIRE (SRQ)

AUTHORS: Catherine A. Emihovich and Eugene L. Gaier
DATE: 1983
VARIABLE: Gender role stereotypes
TYPE OF INSTRUMENT: Alternate choice
DESCRIPTION: There are two 11-item forms of the Sex-Role Questionnaire (SRQ), one giving prescriptions for girls' behavior and the other prescriptions for boys' behavior. Each item starts with the phrase "I think" and is accompanied by the response options "yes" and "no."

About half of the items are phrased in the stereotyped direction, but the stereotyped and nonstereotyped items are not alternated.

SAMPLE ITEMS: (girls) I think it is all right for girls to play on the same sports team with boys.

(boys) I think it is all right for boys to play sometimes with dolls.

PREVIOUS SUBJECTS: Children in grades 5–8; fathers and their sons, average age of 11.7 years

APPROPRIATE FOR: Grades 4 and older

ADMINISTRATION: Self-administered; about 5–10 minutes

SCORING: Stereotyped responses are given 1 point; nonstereotyped answers are given 0 points. Item scores are summed to yield a total score on each form; thus, there is a male stereotype score and a female stereotype score. These scores can each range from 0 (no stereotyping) to 11 (complete stereotyping).

DEVELOPMENT: A 24-item scale was developed based on a search of the relevant literature concerning sex role differences. The scale was pretested for readability and comprehension; this led to the elimination of 2 items and the creation of two 11-item forms: a girls' stereotype measure and a boys' stereotype measure.

RELIABILITY: No information was provided.

VALIDITY: No information was provided.

NOTES & COMMENTS: Emihovich and Gaier (1983) related scores on the SRQ to sex, age, grade, parental occupation, favorite activity, and attitudes toward the women's movement. Emihovich, Gaier, and Cronin (1984) administered the male items (plus one additional male item) to fathers and their elementary school–age sons. The fathers completed the measure twice: first, as they thought their sons would answer, and second, as they would like their sons to answer. The sons answered the questions according to their own beliefs.

AVAILABLE FROM: Emihovich and Gaier, 1983

USED IN:

Emihovich, C. A., & Gaier, E. L. (1983). Women's liberation and preadolescent sex role stereotypes. *Adolescence*, *18*, 637–647.

Emihovich, C. A., Gaier, E. L., & Cronin, N. C. (1984). Sex-role expectations changes by fathers for their sons. *Sex Roles*, *11*(9/10), 861–868.

SEX STEREOTYPE MEASURE (SSM)/SEX STEREOTYPE MEASURE II (SSM II)

AUTHORS: John E. Williams, Susan M. Bennett, and Deborah L. Best

DATE: 1973 (revised 1977)

VARIABLE: Awareness of adult-defined sex stereotypes

DESCRIPTION: The original Sex Stereotype Measure (SSM) consists of 24 brief stories, each describing a person who possesses a sex-stereotyped characteristic. Half are stereotypically male traits, and half are stereotypically female traits. Each story ends with a question regarding who the story is about. The child has to select an adult male's picture or an adult female's picture as the response to the question.

The Sex Stereotype Measure II (SSM II) consists of 32 stories, half highlighting a stereotypically male trait and half highlighting a stereotypically female trait. The response options for the SSM II are male and female silhouettes. The SSM and SSM II can be used with children between the ages of 4 and 12, but the scales must be individually administered to the younger children.

ARTICLES LISTED IN BEERE, 1979: 6

NOTES & COMMENTS: (1) The SSM has been administered in France, Germany, Norway, the Netherlands, Italy, Canada, Korea, Malaysia, England, and Ireland.

(2) Several researchers have modified or adapted the SSM for their work (Coker, 1984; Davis, Williams, & Best, 1982; Harris & Satter, 1981; Leahy & Shirk, 1984; Reis & Wright, 1982; and Roddy, Klein, Stericker, & Kurdek, 1981).

AVAILABLE FROM: Williams and Best, 1976

USED IN:

Best, D. L., Williams, J. E., Cloud, J. M., Davis, S. W., Robertson, L. S., Edwards, J. R., Giles, H., & Fowles, J. (1977). Development of sex-trait stereotypes among young children in the United States, England, and Ireland. *Child Development, 48*, 1375–1384.

Coker, D. R. (1984). The relationships among gender concepts and cognitive maturity in preschool children. *Sex Roles, 10*(1/2), 19–31.

Davidson, E. S., Yasuna, A., & Tower, A. (1979). The effects of television cartoons on sex-role stereotyping in young girls. *Child Development, 50*(2), 597–600.

Davis, S. W., Williams, J. E., & Best, D. L. (1982). Sex-trait stereotypes in the self- and peer descriptions of third grade children. *Sex Roles, 8*(3), 315–331.

Edwards, J. R., & Williams, J. E. (1980). Sex-trait stereotypes among young children and young adults: Canadian findings and cross-national comparisons. *Canadian Journal of Behavioural Science, 12*(3), 210–220.

Etaugh, C., & Riley, S. (1979). Knowledge of sex stereotypes in preschool children. *Psychological Reports, 44*(3), 1279–1282.

Harris, M. B., & Satter, B. J. (1981). Sex-role stereotypes of kindergarten children. *Journal of Genetic Psychology, 138*(1), 49–61.

Lamie, M., Lenzer, I., Street, P., Smith, G., & Stewart, R. (1988). Sex-differences in sex-role attitudes in children of women professionals. *Psychological Reports, 62*, 947–950.

Leahy, R. L., & Shirk, S. R. (1984). The development of classificatory skills and sex-trait stereotypes in children. *Sex Roles, 10*(3/4), 281–292.

Lee, J. Y., & Sugawara, A. I. (1982). Awareness of sex-trait stereotypes among Korean children. *Journal of Social Psychology, 117*(2), 161–170.

McGhee, P. E., & Frueh, T. (1980). Television viewing and the learning of sex-role stereotypes. *Sex Roles, 6*(2), 179–188.

Reis, H. T., & Wright, S. (1982). Knowledge of sex-role stereotypes in children ages 3 to 5. *Sex Roles, 8*(10), 1049–1056.

Roddy, J. M., Klein, H. A., Stericker, A. B., & Kurdek, L. A. (1981). Modification of stereotypic sex-typing in young children. *Journal of Genetic Psychology, 139*(1), 109–118.

Sugawara, A., Andrews, D., Adduci, V., & Cate, R. (1986). Self-concept and sex-role learning among preschool children. *Home Economics Research Journal, 15*(2), 97–104.

Tarrier, N., & Gomes, L. F. (1981). Knowledge of sex-trait stereotypes: Effects of age, sex, and social class on Brazilian children. *Journal of Cross Cultural Psychology, 12*(1), 81–93.

Ward, C. (1985). Sex trait stereotypes in Malaysian children. *Sex Roles, 12*(1/2), 35–45.

Williams, J. E., & Best, D. L. (1976). *Sex Stereotype Measure II and Sex Attitude Measure: General Information and manual of directions*. Unpublished manuscript, Wake Forest University, Winston-Salem, NC. (ERIC Document Reproduction Service No. ED 163 021)

Williams, J. E., Best, D. L., Voss, H. G., Tilquin, C., Bjerke, T., Keller, H., & Baarda, B. (1981). Traits associated with men and women: Attribution by young children in France, Germany, Norway, the Netherlands, and Italy. *Journal of Cross Cultural Psychology, 12*(3), 327–346.

BIBLIOGRAPHY:

Beere, C. A. (1979). *Women and women's issues: A handbook of tests and measures* (pp. 203–206). San Francisco: Jossey-Bass.

SHEPARD HESS STEREOTYPES OF OCCUPATIONS AND ACTIVITIES

AUTHORS: Winifred O. Shepard and David T. Hess

DATE: 1975

VARIABLE: Liberality in terms of stereotypes of occupations and activities

TYPE OF INSTRUMENT: Multiple Choice

DESCRIPTION: The scale consists of 43 occupations and work-related activities. The task of the respondent is to indicate whether each one should be performed by a male, a female, or either.

SAMPLE ITEMS: Wash the dishes

Be a soldier

PREVIOUS SUBJECTS: Kindergartners; children in grades 5, 8, and 11; college students and adults

APPROPRIATE FOR: Grades kindergarten and older

ADMINISTRATION: Younger children are individually interviewed, which may take up to 30 minutes; those past the 5th grade can self-administer the scale in about 20 minutes

SCORING: Shepard and Hess (1975) recommended finding a liberality score by counting the number of times the respondent selects an answer that differs from the traditional (stereotyped) response. Archer (1984)

found a liberality score by counting the number of "either" responses. Both methods yield scores ranging from 0 (very traditional) to 43 (very liberal).

DEVELOPMENT: A set of 44 occupations and activities was given to 50 college men and 50 college women. The college students were asked to indicate for each item whether the traditional American viewpoint would recommend it for a man, for a woman, or for both. Using the criterion that at least 60% of the male and 60% of the female judges had to agree on the categorization of the item, 43 items were retained on the scale. In fact, there was at least 90% agreement on 28 of the items.

RELIABILITY: No information was provided.

VALIDITY: Significant sex differences were found for the 8th graders, college students, and adults. In all three cases, females were more liberal. Overall, 8th graders were more liberal than kindergartners, and college students were the most liberal of the three groups (Shepard & Hess, 1975).

Archer (1984) found significant sex differences at the kindergarten level only; the difference was in the predicted direction. She also found significant age differences, with more liberal scores associated with increasing age; that is, 11th graders were more liberal than 5th graders, who were more liberal than kindergartners.

NOTES & COMMENTS: (1) Both Shepard and Hess (1975) and Archer (1984) provided information on the responses given to each item by particular groups of subjects. The former tested kindergartners, 8th graders, college students, and adult samples; the latter tested kindergartners, 5th graders, and 11th graders.

(2) Shepard and Hess (1975) suggested that an item be labeled as C (conservative) if more than 60% of the respondents selected the traditional response; if more than 60% of the respondents selected the liberal response, the item would be labeled L. The data from the kindergarten sample revealed no L items, but kindergartners had at least 20 C items for each sex. Eighth graders, college students, and adults, on the other hand, had only one C item. Adult men classified "iron" as female. These three older groups—8th graders, college students, and adults—had many L items.

AVAILABLE FROM: Archer, 1984; Shepard and Hess, 1975

USED IN:

Archer, C. J. (1984). Children's attitudes toward sex-role division in adult occupational roles. *Sex Roles*, *10*(1/2), 1–10.

Shepard, W. O., & Hess, D. T. (1975). Attitudes in four age groups toward sex role division in adult occupations and activities. *Journal of Vocational Behavior*, *6*(1), 27–39.

SILVERN SEX ROLE SCALE
AUTHOR: Louise E. Silvern
DATE: 1976

VARIABLE: Sex role stereotypes and social desirability of sex-typed traits
DESCRIPTION: The Silvern Sex Role Scale consists of two parts. The first part, consisting of 46 traits and activities, measures sex role stereotypes. The respondent is to indicate whether "most people think" the trait is more true of boys or of girls. The second part measures the social desirability of the traits. For each of the 46 traits, the child is shown a set of five stick figures that represent varying degrees of the trait. Verbal descriptors are given to serve as anchors. For each trait, the child is to select one stick figure to indicate which "kid you would like best."
ARTICLES LISTED IN BEERE, 1979: 2
NOTES & COMMENTS: As a result of research using the Silvern Sex Role Scale, Silvern (1978) and Silvern and Katz (1986) developed a 22-item measure of masculine-feminine self-concept for use with elementary school children.
AVAILABLE FROM: Silvern, 1977
USED IN:
Rust, J. O., & Lloyd, M. W. (1982) Sex-role attitudes and preferences of junior high school age adolescents. *Adolescence, 17,* 37–43.
Silvern, L. E. (1977). Children's sex role preferences: Stronger among girls than boys. *Sex Roles, 3,* 159–171.
BIBLIOGRAPHY:
Beere, C. A. (1979). *Women and women's issues: A handbook of tests and measures* (pp. 208–210). San Francisco: Jossey-Bass.
Silvern, L. E. (1978). Masculinity-femininity in children's self-concepts: The relationship to teachers' judgements of social adjustment and academic ability, classroom behaviors, and popularity. *Sex Roles, 4*(6), 929–949.
Silvern, L. E., & Katz, P. A. (1986). Gender roles and adjustment in elementary-school children: A multidimensional approach. *Sex Roles, 14*(3/4), 181–202.

TRYON SEX STEREOTYPES OF COMPETENCE
AUTHOR: Bette Whitelock Tryon
DATE: 1980
VARIABLE: Sex stereotypes of boys' and girls' competence
TYPE OF INSTRUMENT: Multiple choice
DESCRIPTION: The Tryon Sex Stereotypes of Competence scale consists of 40 pictures, each displaying an object children might play with. Ten pictures show objects that are sex typed for girls, 10 pictures show objects that are sex typed for boys, and 20 pictures show objects that are sex neutral. The respondent is shown one picture at a time and asked to indicate "who you think is *really good* at using it." Stick figures of a girl, a boy, and a girl and boy together are provided to facilitate the child's expressing an answer.
SAMPLE ITEMS: (female items) sewing machine, makeup
    (male items) tools, boxing gloves
    (neutral items) clay, puppets
PREVIOUS SUBJECTS: Kindergartners, second graders

APPROPRIATE FOR: Ages 4–8

ADMINISTRATION: The scale must be individually administered; about 15 minutes must be allowed for testing because it is desirable for the administrator to establish rapport with the child before beginning the actual testing.

SCORING: Three scores are obtained: a score for the male items, one for the female items, and one for the neutral items. Each score is a count of the number of items correctly answered in that category. In other words, the female score indicates the number of female items that the child correctly classifies as female.

DEVELOPMENT: A sample of 40 children—10 boys and 10 girls in kindergarten and in second grade—were involved in the test development phase of the research. Each child was tested separately and shown a series of 57 pictures. For each picture, the child was asked to indicate whether the toy in the picture would be appealing for a girl, a boy, or both. The directions stated: "When I show you a picture I want you to tell me who you think would like to play with it—the girl, the boy, or both the girl and the boy." Stick figures were provided to allow the child to point to the preferred response. Children's responses were tallied, and items were classified as female typed if 70% or more of the children labeled the toy for a girl; the items were classified as male typed if 70% or more of the children labeled the toy for a boy; and the items were classified as neutral if 70% or more of the children labeled the toy for both boys and girls. These criteria led to 21 items classified as neutral, 13 items classified as male typed, and 16 items classified as female typed. Each set of items was listed in order by the percentage of children agreeing to the classification of the items. The test is composed of the top 10 female-typed items, the top 10 male-typed items, and the top 20 neutral items.

RELIABILITY: A sample of 30 children was tested on two occasions with an unspecified interval between testings. The test-retest reliability was 51 for the combined items. Internal consistency reliability, based on testing 30 girls and 30 boys in kindergarten and in sixth grade, was .81.

VALIDITY: No information was provided.

NOTES & COMMENTS: Tryon (1980) used the scale to determine whether grade level, sex of subject, and sex appropriateness of the item affect the competence choices of early elementary age children. She found that sex of subject made no difference in responses but grade level did; second graders made more choices that were consistent with sex stereotypes than did kindergartners. Furthermore, Tryon found that, in general, girls were judged as more competent with female-typed toys and boys were judged as more competent with male-typed toys. The results for the neutral items were more complex.

AVAILABLE FROM: Tryon, 1980

USED IN:
Tryon, B. W. (1980). Beliefs about male and female competence held by kindergartners and second graders. *Sex Roles*, *6*(1), 85–97.

BELIEFS ABOUT WOMEN SCALE (BAWS)
AUTHORS: Sharyn S. Belk and William E. Snell, Jr.
DATE: 1986
VARIABLE: Stereotypes about women
TYPE OF INSTRUMENT: Summated rating scale
DESCRIPTION: The Beliefs About Women Scale (BAWS) consists of 75
items, with 5 items representing each of 15 stereotypes. Most of the
stereotypes pertain to personality traits of women; for example, women
(compared to men) are less dominant, more passive, more vulnerable,
and less decisive. The phrasing of 61 items is consistent with existing
stereotypes; the phrasing of 14 items is not consistent with existing
stereotypes. Each item is accompanied by five response options:
"strongly agree, slightly agree, neither agree nor disagree, slightly disagree, strongly disagree."
SAMPLE ITEMS: Men want power more than women do.
   Women usually threaten to cry if they can't have their own way.
PREVIOUS SUBJECTS: College students
APPROPRIATE FOR: High school students and older
ADMINISTRATION: Self-administered; about 30 minutes
SCORING: Items are individually scored on a 5-point scale ranging from
-2 to $+2$. Negative scores represent disagreement with the stereotypes
about women; positive scores indicate agreement. The scale yields 15
subscale scores, each representing a stereotype about women. Each subscale score is obtained by averaging the scores of the items representing
that particular stereotype. Thus, subscale scores can range from -2
(disagreement with the stereotypes) to $+2$ (agreement with the stereotypes).
DEVELOPMENT: From a review of the literature regarding women, 15
stereotypes of women were identified. A series of items relating to these
stereotypes were written, and the authors selected the five "best" items
for each stereotype. It is not clear how the authors decided which items
were best.
RELIABILITY: Alpha coefficients were computed for the 15 subscales.
The coefficients ranged from .41 to .81, with an average coefficient of
.62 (Belk & Snell, 1986). Belk and Snell (1983) reported corrected split-
half reliabilities ranging from .57 to .90, with an average of .76.
VALIDITY: It was predicted that BAWS scores would be independent
of social desirability. The authors correlated BAWS scores with scores
on the Marlowe-Crowne Social Desirability Scale (Crowne & Marlowe,
1960) and obtained significant correlations ($p < .05$) for two of the sub-

scales. The correlations, however, were quite low ($r = -.19$ for both subscales).

As predicted, males showed significantly more support for stereotypes than did females. Examination of subscale scores showed significant sex differences on seven subscales: "less career-interested, less intelligent, less decisive, less sexual, sillier, manipulative, and debilitated by menstruation" (Belk & Snell, 1986, p. 410). The fact that college men scored higher on these subscales does not mean that the men endorsed these stereotypes; rather it means that they did not reject these particular stereotypes as strongly as the college women rejected them.

Belk and Snell (1986) compared scores on the BAWS with scores on the Attitudes Toward Women Scale (Spence, Helmreich, & Stapp, 1973) (see separate entry) and with two subscales of the Male-Female Relations Questionnaire (Spence, Helmreich, & Sawin, 1980) (see Beere, in press): the Social Interaction Scale, and the Marital Roles Scale. The results were partially supportive of the hypothesis that "individuals who adhere to traditional, nonfeminist stereotypes about women . . . will also have traditional beliefs about the rights and roles of women . . . and endorse traditional sex role preferences and behaviors" (Belk & Snell, 1986, p. 404).

As predicted, Belk and Snell (1986) found no significant relationship between BAWS scores and scores on the Extended Personal Attributes Questionnaire (Spence, Helmreich, & Holahan, 1979) (see separate entry).

NOTES & COMMENTS: (1) By comparing subscale scores with zero, the neutral value, Belk and Snell (1986) were able to determine how many stereotypes are endorsed by each sex. Females supported four of the stereotypes: "women are less dominating, have more emotional insight, are more interpersonal, and are more moral than men" (Belk & Snell, 1986, p. 408). Males endorsed five of the stereotypes: "women are less dominating, more vulnerable, have more emotional insight, and are more interpersonally oriented than men. . . . [And] women are sexual teases" (p. 408).

(2) Belk and Snell (1986) concluded that the "reliability coefficients were all sufficiently high to justify the use of the BAWS in further analyses" (p. 406). In reality, the alpha values, ranging from .41 to .81, were rather low for reliability coefficients. Similarly, many of the split-half coefficients were unacceptably low.

(3) Belk and Snell (1983) factor analyzed responses to the BAWS and identified two factors.

AVAILABLE FROM: Order from NAPS c/o Microfiche Publications, P.O. Box 3513, Grand Central Station, New York, NY 10163–3513; NAPS document no. 04708; for microfiche, in U.S. remit $4.00 with order.

USED IN:

Belk, S. S., & Snell, W. E., Jr. (1983). *The Beliefs About Women Scale (BAWS): Scale development and validation.* Paper presented at the meeting of the Southwestern Psychological Association, San Antonio.

Belk, S. S., & Snell, W. E., Jr. (1986). Beliefs about women: Components and correlates. *Personality and Social Psychology Bulletin, 12*(4), 403–413.

BIBLIOGRAPHY:

Beere, C. A. (in press). *Sex and gender issues: A handbook of tests and measures.* Westport, CT: Greenwood.

Crowne, D. P., & Marlowe, D. (1960). A new scale of social desirability independent of psychopathology. *Journal of Consulting Psychology, 24,* 349–354.

Spence, J. T., Helmreich, R. L., & Holahan, C. K. (1979). Negative and positive components of psychological masculinity and femininity and their relationships to self-reports of neurotic and acting out behaviors. *Journal of Personality and Social Psychology, 37,* 1673–1682.

Spence, J. T., Helmreich, R. L., & Sawin, L. L. (1980). The Male-Female Relations Questionnaire: A self-report inventory of sex role behaviors and preferences and its relationships to masculine and feminine personality traits, sex role attitudes, and other measures. *Catalog of Selected Documents in Psychology, 10,* 87. (Ms. No. 2123)

Spence, J. T., Helmreich, R. L., & Stapp, J. (1973). A short version of the Attitudes Toward Women Scale (AWS). *Bulletin of the Psychonomic Society, 2,* 219–220.

BERRYMAN-FINK ATTRIBUTIONS FOR FEMINIST

AUTHORS: Cynthia Berryman-Fink and Kathleen S. Verderber

DATE: 1985 (used 1979)

VARIABLE: Attributions for the term *feminist*

TYPE OF INSTRUMENT: Semantic differential

DESCRIPTION: The Berryman-Fink Attributions for Feminist is a semantic differential scale consisting of 54 pairs of bipolar adjectives. There are five dimensions on the scale: General Evaluation (22 items), Behavior (20 items), Political Orientation (7 items), Sexual Preference (3 items), and Gender (2 items). The term to be rated is *feminist*, and there are 7 points on the scale between each pair of bipolar adjectives.

SAMPLE ITEMS: (General Evaluation) Logical . . . Illogical

(Behavioral) Aggressive . . . Nonaggressive

(Political Orientation) Against reform . . . For reform

(Sexual Preference) Homosexual . . . Heterosexual

(Gender) Female . . . Male

PREVIOUS SUBJECTS: College students

APPROPRIATE FOR: High school students and older, but the authors caution that the factor analytic results that led to the identification of the five dimensions may not generalize to noncollege populations.

ADMINISTRATION: Self-administered; about 20–25 minutes

SCORING: Because this measure is intended to provide an understanding of persons' perceptions of the term *feminist*, scores are assigned to the term, not to individuals completing the scale. Berryman-Fink and Verderber (1985) provided group means for each item on the semantic differential.

DEVELOPMENT: Ninety-six college students were asked to indicate what comes to mind when they think of the word *feminist*. The words, phrases, and statements that they generated were tallied, and items that appeared frequently were listed on the first version of the scale. There were 91 bipolar adjective pairs on the first version.

The semantic differential was administered to 768 college students, and their responses were factor analyzed. Five factors were identified with eigenvalues greater than 1.0 and at least three items with loadings greater than .30. For an item to be assigned to a factor, it had to have a loading greater than .30.

RELIABILITY: No information was provided.

VALIDITY: The authors verified the reliability of the factor structure by conducting another factor analysis using each half of the sample. They concluded that "the factor structure obtained through two different factorings and two different rotation methods replicates very closely on the first three factors" (Berryman-Fink & Verderber, 1985, p. 55).

Berryman-Fink and Verderber (1985) computed an overall score for males and for females and computed factor scores for all males and for all females. Rather surprisingly, there were no significant sex differences on the total score or on the factor scores. This finding suggests that the sample was in some way atypical. It is to be expected that females would have more positive attributions for the term than would males.

NOTES & COMMENTS: (1) The three bipolar adjective pairs comprising Factor IV seem very redundant: "homosexual...heterosexual," "straight...gay," and "always a lesbian...never a lesbian." It is not surprising that they load on the same factor. Similarly, Factor V is comprised of "female...male" and "woman...man."

(2) Though the authors specified that each factor had to have at least three items loading on it, the last factor has only two items on it.

AVAILABLE FROM: Berryman-Fink and Verderber, 1985

USED IN:

Berryman-Fink, C., & Verderber, K. S. (1985). Attributions of the term feminist: A factor analytic development of a measuring instrument. *Psychology of Women Quarterly, 9*(1), 51–64.

DEAUX LEWIS GENDER STEREOTYPES SCALE
AUTHORS: Kay Deaux and Laurie L. Lewis
DATE: 1983

VARIABLE: Tendency to stereotype in terms of physical characteristics, role behaviors, occupations, and personality traits

TYPE OF INSTRUMENT: Probabilistic rating scale

DESCRIPTION: The Deaux Lewis Gender Stereotypes Scale consists of 44 items divided as follows: 4 female-typed and 4 male-typed physical characteristics, 4 male-typed and 4 female-typed role behaviors, 6 male-typed and 6 female-typed occupations, and 8 male-typed and 8 female-typed personality traits. Each item is accompanied by a 100-point rating scale, marked at intervals of 5 points. Five anchor points are provided: "extremely unlikely, moderately unlikely, neither likely nor unlikely, moderately likely, extremely likely." A stimulus, a word such as man, person, or homosexual male, is given, and the respondent is asked to rate the stimulus on each of the 44 scales.

SAMPLE ITEMS: (male typed physical characteristic) tall
   (female-typed physical characteristic) soft voice
   (male-typed role behavior) financial provider
   (female-typed role behavior) tends the house
   (male-typed occupation) telephone installer
   (female-typed occupation) speech pathologist
   (male-typed traits) independent
   (female-typed traits) emotional

PREVIOUS SUBJECTS: College students

APPROPRIATE FOR: High school students and older

ADMINISTRATION: Self-administered; about 10 minutes per stimulus

SCORING: Eight scores are obtained: one for each component by sex combination. A score is the sum of the ratings assigned to the items comprising the component.

DEVELOPMENT: As the first step in scale development, 20 females and 19 males were asked to list their associations to one of the following four terms: "feminine, masculine, male sex role, and female sex role" (Deaux & Lewis, 1983, p. 2). Examination of the responses suggested that they could be classified according to the following categories: "personality traits; physical appearance; role behaviors, occupations, and activities; sexual orientation; specific gender references; and a miscellaneous category" (p. 2). By far, the most common response was in the personality traits category. "The results of this preliminary study verify the importance of personality traits to gender stereotypes. At the same time, however, they suggest that other characteristics such as physical appearance, role behaviors, and occupations may also be salient" (p. 4). Thus four components of gender stereotypes—personality traits, physical appearance, role behaviors, and occupations—were identified for further scale development.

A 91-item scale was prepared including 25 physical characteristics, 25 role behaviors, 25 occupations, and the 16 items from the expressive and instrumental scales of the Personal Attributes Questionnaire (PAQ) (Spence, Helmreich, & Stapp, 1974) (see separate entry). The physical characteristics and the role behaviors were drawn primarily from the pretest. The pretest did not produce a long enough list of occupations, so additional occupations were selected from listings of occupational titles. A sample of 195 college students were asked to complete the scale for one of three stimuli: a man, a woman, or a person with sex unspecified.

Using the results from the college students, the item set was reduced. Items were selected for the physical appearance component and the role behaviors component if there was a statistically significant difference in the ratings of male and female stimulus persons and a large absolute difference (generally at least 20 points) in the ratings of male and female stimulus persons. Preference was given to items with a standard deviation of 25 points or less. Furthermore, items were selected if a factor analysis showed that they loaded on the appropriate factor. Two additional criteria were applied in the selection of items for the occupational component: occupations of equal status were selected for male-typed and female-typed scales, and consideration was given to the actual percentage of males and females in the occupations chosen. The trait component contained all 16 items from the instrumental and expressive scales of the PAQ.

RELIABILITY: Alpha coefficients were computed for each of the eight scores by three stimulus person combinations. In other words, eight values of alpha were computed for each stimulus: man, person, and woman. The values ranged from a low of .66 (male roles for the stimulus "man") to a high of .97 (male occupations for the stimulus "person").

VALIDITY: No information was provided.

NOTES & COMMENTS: (1) Deaux and Lewis (1983) reported the intercorrelations between the scores for both a male stimulus person and a female stimulus person. In general, for both the male-typed and female-typed items, "roles, occupations, and physical characteristics show moderately strong correlations with each other, and either low negative or nonsignificant correlations with comparable . . . characteristics [on the opposite-sex scale]" (p. 20). An exception was the case of occupations, where the male and female components were significantly correlated with each other ($r = .43$ for a female stimulus person and $r = .45$ for a male stimulus person).

(2) Deaux and Lewis (1984) conducted several studies to determine how information regarding one of the components affects assumptions made about a stimulus person's standing on the other components.

(3) Kite and Deaux (1987) used the Deaux Lewis Gender Stereotypes Scale to examine the stereotypes of male and female homosexuals.

AVAILABLE FROM: Deaux and Lewis, 1983

USED IN:

Deaux, K., & Lewis, L. L. (1983). Assessment of gender stereotypes: Methodology and components. *Psychological Documents*, *13*, 25. (Ms. No. 2583)

Deaux, K., & Lewis, L. L. (1984). Structure of gender stereotypes: Interrelationships among components and gender label. *Journal of Personality and Social Psychology*, *46*(5), 991–1004.

Kite, M. E., & Deaux, K. (1987). Gender belief systems: Homosexuality and the implicit inversion theory. *Psychology of Women Quarterly*, *11*, 83–96.

BIBLIOGRAPHY:

Spence, J. T., Helmreich, R. L., & Stapp, J. (1974). The Personal Attributes Questionnaire: A measure of sex-role stereotypes and masculinity-femininity. *Catalog of Selected Documents in Psychology*, *4*, 43. (Ms. No. 617)

FRYE DIETZ ATTITUDES TOWARD STEREOTYPES OF WOMEN

AUTHORS: Virginia H. Frye and Siegfried C. Dietz

DATE: 1973

VARIABLE: Attitudes toward traditional views of women workers

TYPE OF INSTRUMENT: Summated rating scale

DESCRIPTION: The Frye Dietz Attitudes Toward Stereotypes of Women scale consists of 20 statements, all phrased in the stereotyped direction. According to Frye and Dietz (1973), 8 items pertain to women's role, and 12 items pertain to women workers. An examination of item content, however, fails to substantiate this distinction. The 12 items intended to measure attitudes toward women workers deal primarily with the cognitive and affective competence of women. Nine of these 12 items make a direct comparison between men and women. The 8 items intended to measure attitudes toward women's role cover several topics, including the relative importance of the wife and mother roles, the desirability of male and female supervisors, and the traits that attract men to women. Items are accompanied by either a 2-point agree/disagree scale or a 4-point response scale with options ranging from "strongly agree" to "strongly disagree."

SAMPLE ITEMS: (women's role) The most important work for a woman is that of wife and mother.

(women workers) Men are better in math and mechanical subjects, and jobs requiring these skills are better suited to men than to women.

PREVIOUS SUBJECTS: Eighth graders, high school students, and college women

APPROPRIATE FOR: Grades 7 and older

ADMINISTRATION: Self-administered; about 10 minutes

SCORING: Most of the users of the scale (Frye and Dietz, 1973; Ditkoff, 1979; Thornburg, 1979) reported results for each item rather than obtaining summary scores for individuals. Chandler, Sawicki, and Stryffeler (1981) reported results for individual items, and they also computed two summary scores: one score for women's role and one for women workers.

DEVELOPMENT: Very little information was provided. Frye and Dietz (1973) stated: "Ambiguities and time requirements were determined by administering the questionnaire to a small (n = 8) sample of high school students. Following the trial test, the instrument was prepared in final form" (p. 103).

RELIABILITY: Chandler et al. (1981) reported coefficient alpha based on testing 225 8th-grade boys and 213 8th-grade girls. Alpha for the women's role score was .65; alpha for the women workers score was .86.

VALIDITY: Frye and Dietz (1973) looked at responses from 123 high school boys and 74 high school girls. The researchers found that over 50% of the boys agreed with 19 of the 20 statements on the Frye Dietz Attitudes Toward Stereotypes of Women scale; in contrast, over 50% of the girls *disagreed* with 13 of the 20 items on the scale.

Thornburg (1979) predicted that college students compared to high school students would be more accepting of working women and would adhere less to stereotypes. After testing 189 college women with the Frye Dietz Attitudes Toward Stereotypes of Women scale, Thornburg compared his findings with data reported by Frye and Dietz (1973). Thornburg did not find the predicted differences.

Ditkoff (1979) predicted that her sample of high school students would be less accepting of stereotypes than was the high school sample tested by Frye and Dietz (1973). The data supported her prediction for some items but not for others. Ditkoff did find that males compared to females were more accepting of 18 of the 20 statements.

Chandler et al. (1981) tested 8th graders and found significant sex differences on a summary score based on the women's role items and on a summary score based on the women workers items; males were more accepting of stereotyped views. Chandler et al. predicted that 8th graders compared to 11th graders would be more likely to agree with the stereotypes. Their prediction was supported for some items but not for others.

Chandler et al. (1981) related scores on the Frye Dietz Attitudes Toward Stereotypes of Women scale to current maternal employment. They found a significant, albeit somewhat low, correlation between attitudes toward women's role and current employment of mothers (r = .26).

NOTES & COMMENTS: (1) Frye and Dietz (1973), Thornburg (1979), Ditkoff (1979), and Chandler et al. (1981) all used a 20-item scale to assess sex stereotypes of occupations, along with using the Frye Dietz Attitudes Toward Stereotypes of Women scale.

(2) Some of the items on the scale are double-barreled; that is, they contain more than a single idea—for example, "Men are more aggressive

and better suited to leadership positions than are women." How should respondents answer the item if they agree with the first portion of the statement, "men are more aggressive," but they disagree with the balance of the item?

(3) It is not surprising that coefficient alpha for the women's role items was quite low. There are few items on the subscale, and the content for those items is quite diverse. Given the low reliability, researchers should probably avoid the use of subscale scores.

AVAILABLE FROM: Frye and Dietz, 1973; Thornburg, 1979; Ditkoff, 1979; and Chandler, Sawicki, and Stryffeler, 1981.

USED IN:

Chandler, T. A., Sawicki, R. F., & Stryffeler, J. M. (1981). Relationship between adolescent sexual stereotypes and working mothers. *Journal of Early Adolescence, 1*(1), 72–83.

Ditkoff, G. S. (1979). Stereotypes of adolescents toward the working woman. *Adolescence, 14,* 277–282.

Frye, V. H., & Dietz, S. C. (1973). Attitudes of high school students toward traditional views of women workers. *Journal of the Student Personnel Association for Teacher Education, 11*(3), 102–108.

Thornburg, H. D. (1979, April). *Adolescent attitudes toward working women.* Paper presented at the meeting of the Rocky Mountain Psychological Association, Las Vegas. (ERIC Document Reproduction Service No. ED 177 425)

SELF-ADMINISTERED SURVEY OF SEX STEREOTYPES (SASSS)

AUTHORS: E. Roger Trent, Janet E. Crandell, Kenneth R. Higgins, and Louis C. Vild

DATE: 1979

VARIABLE: Attitudes toward males and females

TYPE OF INSTRUMENT: Summated rating scale

DESCRIPTION: The Self-Administered Survey of Sex Stereotypes (SASSS) consists of 60 items representing six areas: "level of employment and decision-making responsibilities" (14 items), "importance or purpose of employment" (8 items), "type of employment" (14 items), "how well individuals function in a work setting" (11 items), "an individual's basic abilities" (7 items), and "beliefs about what should exist" (6 items) (Trent, Crandell, Higgins, & Vild, 1979, p. 13). Each item is accompanied by five response options: "strongly agree, agree, neutral, disagree, strongly disagree."

SAMPLE ITEMS: (level of employment and decision-making responsibilities) Important decisions should be made by men.

(importance or purpose of employment) Married women work to keep from being bored at home.

(type of employment) Women who work generally prefer passive jobs.

(how well individuals function in a work setting) Jobs requiring skills in caring for other people are performed best by women.

(an individual's basic abilities) Boys are smarter than girls in science and math as proved by comparing their test scores.

(beliefs about what should exist) Women as well as men should be prepared to support their families financially.

PREVIOUS SUBJECTS: Vocational teachers, counselors, and teacher educators

APPROPRIATE FOR: High school students and older

ADMINISTRATION: Self-administered; about 20–30 minutes

SCORING: Items are individually scored on a 5-point scale, with lower scores assigned to the response showing less sex bias. Item scores are summed to yield six subscale scores and an overall total score.

DEVELOPMENT: The procedure for developing the SASSS was quite complex, involving inputs from "an ad hoc committee including teachers, counselors, administrators, students enrolled in nontraditional programs, and business and industry personnel" (Trent et al., 1979, p. 6). Thirty-one dimensions, expressed as bipolar adjective pairs, and one general area (vocational choice) provided a framework for generating 266 items. A variety of procedures, involving both qualitative judgments and quantitative assessments, was used to reduce the pool to 106 items; these items still represented the 31 dimensions and 1 general area. A sample of 96 men and 58 women from vocational school districts and career centers responded to the 106-item version of the scale. Using their responses, various statistical analyses were performed. Again quantitative and qualitative approaches were used to reduce the scale to 60 items. Trent et al. provided a detailed description of the scale's development.

RELIABILITY: After the SASSS was used as a pretest measure with 114 male teachers and 89 female teachers, coefficient alpha was computed for each of the subscales and the total scores. The estimates ranged from .65 to .93 for the subscales, with the lowest reliability being associated with the last subscale—beliefs about what should exist. For the total score, coefficient alpha was .97. When the SASSS was given as a posttest, coefficient alpha ranged from .68 to .96 for the subscales; it was .98 for the total score. The last subscale had the lowest reliability.

Test-retest reliabilities were computed by looking at the pretest and posttest scores for the control group, which had 67 male teachers and 40 female teachers. The two testings were separated by about 2 weeks. The following reliabilities were computed: level of employment and decision making = .79; importance or purpose of employment = .77; type of employment = .67; how well individuals function in work setting = .74; an individual's basic abilities = .73; beliefs about what should exist = .67; and total score = .80.

VALIDITY: As predicted, Trent et al. (1979) found that males compared to females received significantly higher scores—that is, scores showing more sex bias.

Trent et al. (1979) used a pretest-posttest, with control group, design to determine whether sex bias could be reduced by administering a particular intervention program. Using the SASSS as both the pretest and posttest measure, they found that the scores for those in the experimental group were significantly lower, showing less bias, on the posttest as compared to the pretest. For the control group, there was essentially no change in scores when pretest and posttest scores were compared. When these results were examined for males and females separately, it was found that the scores for females in the treatment group did not change over time, but the scores for the males showed less bias after the treatment.

NOTES & COMMENTS: (1) For the pretest, the correlations between subscale scores and total scores ranged from .55 to .96 for males and from .21 to .97 for females. Scale 6, beliefs about what should exist, had the weakest relationship to the total score. This was also the shortest subscale and the subscale with the lowest reliability. Similar results were obtained when posttest scores were correlated.

(2) Trent et al. (1979) reported the correlations between subscale scores.

(3) Based on a factor analytic study, Trent et al. (1979) concluded, "The findings from this analysis suggest that scale scores (except for Scale 6) do not provide much diagnostic information which is not already available from the total score" (p. 36).

AVAILABLE FROM: Trent, Crandell, Higgins, and Vild, 1979
USED IN:

Trent, E. R., Crandell, J. E., Higgins, K. R., & Vild, L. C. (1979). *Modifying attitudes toward sex stereotypes in vocational education (MASSIVE)* (Final Report). Columbus: Ohio State Department of Education, Division of Guidance and Testing. (ERIC Document Reproduction Service No. ED 176 047)

SEX ROLE STEREOTYPE QUESTIONNAIRE

AUTHORS: Paul Rosenkrantz, Susan R. Vogel, Helen Bee, Inge K. Broverman, and Donald M. Broverman
DATE: 1968
VARIABLE: Perceptions of sex role stereotypes; gender role self-concept
DESCRIPTION: The Sex Role Stereotype Questionnaire is a semantic differential scale consisting of pairs of bipolar adjectives or adjective phrases. There are three standard versions of the instrument: a 122-item version, an 82-item version, and a 38-item version. There is considerable variability in the concept(s) to be rated using the semantic differential

scales; frequently a respondent is asked to rate "self" and "ideal self" or "man," "woman," and "adult."
ARTICLES LISTED IN BEERE, 1979: 69
NOTES & COMMENTS: Researchers frequently modify the scale. Common modifications include altering the scale so that it is easier for children to use, changing the number of items on the scale, or changing the directions to the respondents. Some of the citations listed used only a few of the adjective pairs from the Sex Role Stereotype Questionnaire.
AVAILABLE FROM: Inge K. Broverman, Department of Psychology, Fielding Institute, 2112 Santa Barbara Street, Santa Barbara, CA 93105
USED IN:

Barnett, R. C. (1981). Parental sex-role attitudes and child-rearing values. *Sex Roles*, 7(8), 837–846.

Baruch, G. K., & Barnett, R. C. (1979, August). *Involvement in multiple roles and the well-being of adult women*. Paper presented at the meeting of the American Sociological Association, Boston. (ERIC Document Reproduction Service No. ED 187 608)

Baruch, G. K., & Barnett, R. C. (1981). Fathers' participation in the care of their preschool children. *Sex Roles*, 7(10), 1043–1055.

Bernknopf, L. A. (1980). Responses of adolescents on a masculinity-femininity scale and a stereotyping questionnaire. *Exceptional Children*, 47(1), 59–61.

Bond, L. A. (1981). Perceptions of sex-role deviations: An attributional analysis. *Sex Roles*, 7(2), 107–115.

Boyden, T., Carroll, J. S., & Master, R. A. (1984). Similarity and attraction in homosexual males: The effects of age and masculinity-femininity. *Sex Roles*, 10(11/12), 939–948.

Callan, V. J., & Gallois, C. (1985). Sex-role attitudes and attitudes to marriage among urban Greek-Australian and Anglo-Australian youth. *Journal of Comparative Family Studies*, 16(3), 345–356.

Canty, E. M. (1977, August). *Effects of women's studies courses on women's attitudes and goals*. Paper presented at the meeting of the American Psychological Association, San Francisco. (ERIC Document Reproduction Service No. ED 150 490)

Curry, J. F., & Hock, R. A. (1981). Sex differences in sex role ideals in early adolescence. *Adolescence*, 16, 779–789.

Downing, N. E. (1978, March). *The Broverman study revisited: Implications of androgyny*. Paper presented at the meeting of the Southeastern Psychological Association, Atlanta. (ERIC Document Reproduction Service No. ED 160 920)

Downing, N. E., & Nevill, D. D. (1983). Conceptions of psychological health: The role of gender and sex-role identity. *British Journal of Social Psychology*, 22(2), 171–173.

Dreman, S. B. (1978). Sex-role stereotyping in mental health standards in Israel. *Journal of Clinical Psychology*, 34(4), 961–966.

Freeman, H. R. (1985). Somatic attractiveness: As in other things, moderation is best. *Psychology of Women Quarterly*, 9(3), 311–321.

Gerber, G. L. (1977). The effect of competition on stereotypes about sex-role and marital satisfaction. *Journal of Psychology*, 97(2), 297–308.

Hainline, L., & Feig, E. (1978). The correlates of childhood father absence in college-aged women. *Child Development, 49*(1), 37–42.

Hamilton, M. L. (1977). Ideal sex roles for children and acceptance of variation from stereotypic sex roles. *Adolescence, 12*, 89–96.

Haskell, S. D. (1979, March). *Marital adjustment correlates in young couples.* Paper presented at the meeting of the Southeastern Psychological Association, New Orleans. (ERIC Document Reproduction Service No. ED 174 897)

Hayes, K. E., & Wolleat, P. L. (1978). Effects of sex in judgments of a simulated counseling interview. *Journal of Counseling Psychology, 25*(2), 164–168.

Hochstein, L. M. (1986). Pastoral counselors: Their attitudes toward gay and lesbian clients. *Journal of Pastoral Care, 40*(2), 158–165.

Hock, R. A., & Curry, J. F. (1983). Sex-role identification of normal adolescent males and females as related to school achievement. *Journal of Youth and Adolescence, 12*(6), 461–470.

Huth, C. M. (1978). Married women's work status: The influence of parents and husbands. *Journal of Vocational Behavior, 13*(3), 272–286.

Lii, S. Y., & Wong, S. Y. (1982). A cross-cultural study on sex-role stereotypes and social desirability. *Sex Roles, 8*(5), 481–491.

Lord, L. K. (1986). A comparison of male and female peace officers' stereotypic perceptions of women and women peace officers. *Journal of Police Science and Administration, 14*(2), 83–97.

McDonald, G. J., & Moore, R. J. (1978). Sex-role self-concepts of homosexual men and their attitudes toward both women and male homosexuality. *Journal of Homosexuality, 4*(1), 3–14.

O'Malley, K. M., & Richardson, S. S. (1985). Sex bias in counseling: Have things changed? *Journal of Counseling and Development, 63*(5), 294–299.

Page, S., & Yee, M. (1985). Conception of male and female homosexual stereotypes among university undergraduates. *Journal of Homosexuality, 12*(1), 109–118.

Perloff, R. M. (1977). Some antecedents of children's sex-role stereotypes. *Psychological Reports, 40*(2), 463–466.

Petro, C. S., & Putnam, B. A. (1979). Sex-role stereotypes: Issues of attitudinal changes. *Sex Roles, 5*(1), 29–39.

Phillips, R. D. (1985). The adjustment of men and women: Mental health professionals' views today. *Academic Psychology Bulletin, 7*(2), 253–260.

Phillips, R. D., & Gilroy, F. D. (1985). Sex-role stereotypes and clinical judgments of mental health: The Brovermans' findings reexamined. *Sex Roles, 12*(1/2), 179–193.

Poole, D. A., & Tapley, A. E. (1988). Sex roles, social roles, and clinical judgments of mental health. *Sex Roles, 19*(5/6), 265–272.

Romer, N. (1977). Sex-related differences in the development of the motive to avoid success, sex role identity, and performance in competitive and noncompetitive conditions. *Psychology of Women Quarterly, 1*(3), 260–272.

Romer, N., & Cherry, D. (1980). Ethnic and social class differences in children's sex-role concepts. *Sex Roles, 6*(2), 245–263.

Sellers, E. B., & Keenan, V. C. (1977, May). *A construct validation of fear of success.* Paper presented at the Rocky Mountain Psychological Association, Albuquerque. (ERIC Document Reproduction Service No. ED 156 685)

Smith, R. L., & Bradley, D. W. (1979). Factor validation and refinement of the sex-role questionnaire and its relationship to the Attitudes Toward Women Scale. *Psychological Reports, 44*(3), 1155–1174.

Smith, R. L., & Bradley, D. W. (1980). In defense of the Attitudes Toward Women Scale: An affirmation of validity and reliability. *Psychological Reports, 47*(2), 511–522.

Smyth, M., & McFarlane, G. (1985). Sex-role stereotyping by psychologists and psychiatrists: A further analysis. *International Journal of Women's Studies, 8*(2), 130–139.

Stevens, G., & Gardner, S. (1983). Women's study courses: Do they change attitudes? *Psychological Reports, 53*(1), 81–82.

Stevens, G., Gardner, S., & Barton, E. (1984). Factor analyses of two "attitude toward gender role" questionnaires. *Journal of Personality Assessment, 48*(3), 312–316.

Steward, M. S., Bryant, B. K., & Steward, D. S. (1979). Adolescent women's developing identity: A study of self-definition in the context of family relationships. *Journal of Youth and Adolescence, 8*(2), 209–222.

Thomas, C. (1985). The age of androgyny: The new views of psychotherapists. *Sex Roles, 13*(7/8), 381–392.

Thornton, W. E. (1982). Gender traits and delinquency involvement of boys and girls. *Adolescence, 17*, 749–768.

Tilby, P. J., & Kalin, R. (1979). Effects of sex role deviance in disturbed male adolescents on the perception of psychopathology. *Canadian Journal of Behavioural Science, 11*(1), 45–52.

Tilby, P. J., & Kalin, R. (1980). Effects of sex-role deviant life-styles in otherwise normal persons on the perception of maladjustment. *Sex Roles, 6*(4), 581–592.

Walsh, R. T., & Schallow, J. R. (1977). The experimenter as a sex-role model in sex-role stereotyping. *Canadian Journal of Behavioural Science, 9*(4), 305–314.

Wetmore-Foshay, A. A., O'Neill, P., & Foster, J. A. (1981). Sex role stereotyping among school counsellors. *Canadian Counsellor, 15*(4), 180–184.

Wildner, G., & Ryan, T. T. (1979). A note on the effect of community psychology graduate training on sex-role stereotyping. *Journal of Community Psychology, 7*(4), 360–361.

Wilson, L. K., & Gallois, C. (1985). Perceptions of assertive behavior: Sex combination, role appropriateness, and message type. *Sex Roles, 12*(1/2), 125–141.

Wise, E., & Rafferty, J. (1982). Sex bias and language. *Sex Roles, 8*(12), 1189–1196.

Wise, G. W. (1978). The relationship of sex-role perception and levels of self-actualization in public school teachers. *Sex Roles, 4*(4), 605–617.

Woolever, R. (1974). *What do teachers really want? Sex-role stereotyping and the elementary classroom teacher*. Unpublished manuscript, University of North Carolina at Chapel Hill. (ERIC Document Reproduction Service No. ED 207 975)

BIBLIOGRAPHY:

Beere, C. A. (1979). *Women and women's issues: A handbook of tests and measures* (pp. 196–203). San Francisco: Jossey-Bass.

SEX ROLE STEREOTYPING SCALE
AUTHOR: Martha R. Burt
DATE: 1980 (used 1977)
VARIABLE: Endorsement of traditional sex role stereotypes
TYPE OF INSTRUMENT: Summated rating scale
DESCRIPTION: The Sex Role Stereotyping Scale consists of nine statements; seven of the statements reflect traditional sex role stereotypes, and two express a contemporary view. Eight of the statements pertain to women; one pertains to men. Each item is accompanied by a 7-point response scale ranging from "strongly agree" to "strongly disagree."
SAMPLE ITEMS: A man should fight when the woman he's with is insulted by another man.
   It is acceptable for the woman to pay for the date.
PREVIOUS SUBJECTS: College students; adults, ages 18 and older; convicted rapists; child molesters
APPROPRIATE FOR: High school students and older
ADMINISTRATION: Self-administered (though it has been administered in an interview format); about 5 minutes
SCORING: Items are individually scored on a 7-point scale, with 7 points assigned to the more stereotyped or traditional response, which is "strongly agree" for seven of the items and "strongly disagree" for two of the items. Item scores are totaled to yield an overall score that can range from 7 (very contemporary) to 63 (very stereotyped). For a sample of 598 adults, aged 18 and over, the mean score was 37.6, with a standard deviation of 10.5 (Burt, 1980).
DEVELOPMENT: The Sex Role Stereotyping Scale was developed concurrently with four other scales: Adversarial Sexual Beliefs, Sexual Conservatism, Acceptance of Interpersonal Violence, and Rape Myth Acceptance Scale. (These measures are described in Beere, in press.) Pretesting involving a large item pool was conducted, and based on the results, about twice the number of items to be included on each of the final scales was included on an interview form. The interview was administered to 598 adults in Minnesota, and item analyses were performed on their responses. Based on these analyses, the "best items" were selected for the scale.
RELIABILITY: Coefficient alpha, based on testing 589 adults, was .80.
VALIDITY: Burt (1980) looked at the relationship between Sex Role Stereotyping scores and Rape Myth Acceptance scores. As predicted, persons who were more stereotyped in their beliefs were more accepting of rape myths.
   Check and Malamuth (1983) gave college students the Sex Role Stereotyping Scale and correlated their scores with scores on the Rape Myth Acceptance Scale, the Acceptance of Interpersonal Violence scale, the Adversarial Sexual Beliefs scale, and the Sexual Conservatism scale. The

Sex Role Stereotyping Scale correlated with the other scales as follows: Rape Myth Acceptance Scale = .54, Acceptance of Interpersonal Violence scale = .39, Adversarial Sexual Beliefs scale = .46, and Sexual Conservatism scale = .49.

Check and Malamuth (1983) tested a large sample of college students with the Sex Role Stereotyping Scale and with the Attitudes Toward Women Scale (Spence & Helmreich, 1972) (see separate entry). There was a significant correlation in the predicted direction ($r = -.73$).

College students were asked to read and react to one of three sexual depictions: stranger rape, acquaintance rape, and consenting intercourse (Check & Malamuth, 1983). As predicted, their reactions were mediated by scores on the Sex Role Stereotyping Scale.

A sample of 598 adults heard a description of a scene involving a man and a woman. The scene varied according to the degree of violence described (three levels) and the intimacy of the relationship between the man and woman (strangers, acquaintances, and married persons). The respondents were asked to rate the violence, rate the man in the story, and indicate what the woman did to deserve the violence. In addition, respondents completed several attitude scales, including the Sex Role Stereotyping Scale. It was found that, among the general population, persons scoring high on the Sex Role Stereotyping Scale perceived the stories as less violent (Burt, 1983).

NOTES & COMMENTS: (1) Koss (1985) and Koss, Leonard, Beezley, and Oros (1985) used 37 items from Burt's five scales in research looking at the characteristics of rape victims who never reported their assault (Koss, 1985) and sexual offenders who were never detected (Koss et al., 1985). When these researchers factor analyzed responses to the 37 items, they identified five factors that were quite comparable to the scales Burt developed. Koss (1985) and Koss et al. (1985) labeled their factors "Acceptance of Sexual Aggression; Conservative Attitudes Toward Female Sexuality; Rejection of Rape Myths; Heterosexual Relationships as Game-playing; and Unacceptability of Aggression" (Koss, 1985, p. 198).

(2) Burt (1980) computed item-total correlations based on testing 598 adults. She reported values ranging from .35 to .63. Burt also looked at the relationship between Rape Myth Acceptance scores and a variety of attitude measures, personality characteristics, and personal experiences with rape or rape victims. The attitude measures included the Sex Role Stereotyping Scale.

(3) Rapaport and Burkhart (1984) investigated the relationship between college men's coercive sexual behaviors and their responses on a variety of measures, including the Sex Role Stereotyping Scale. Overholser and Beck (1986) compared incarcerated rapists, incarcerated child molesters, and three control groups on a variety of measures, including the Sex

Role Stereotyping Scale. Pryor (1987) studied college men and compared their scores on a measure of their likelihood to commit sexual harassment with their scores on a variety of other measures, including the Sex Role Stereotyping Scale. Malamuth (1988) used the Sex Role Stereotyping Scale as one of several measures in a study designed to identify the variables that predict men's laboratory aggression against both male and female victims.

(4) Mayerson and Taylor (1987) conducted a study with 98 college women. They used eight items from the Sex Role Stereotyping Scale and selected those females scoring in the highest third and in the lowest third on stereotyping. Mayerson and Taylor then compared these two groups in terms of how pornography affects them. More specifically, they looked at how pornographic depictions, which varied in degree of consent and degree of sexual arousal, affected the two groups of women's scores on 13 items of the Rape Myth Acceptance Scale, 5 items of the Acceptance of Interpersonal Violence scale, 7 items of the Adversarial Sexual Beliefs scale, the Texas Social Behavior Inventory (Spence & Helmreich, 1978), and a measure of body image.

AVAILABLE FROM: Burt, 1980, 1983

USED IN:

Burt, M. R. (1980). Cultural myths and supports for rape. *Journal of Personality and Social Psychology, 38*(2), 217–230.

Burt, M. R. (1983). Justifying personal violence: A comparison of rapists and the general public. *Victimology: An International Journal, 8*(3/4), 131–150.

Check, J. V. P., & Malamuth, N. M. (1983). Sex role stereotyping and reactions to depictions of stranger versus acquaintance rape. *Journal of Personality and Social Psychology, 45*(2), 344–356.

Koss, M. P. (1985). The hidden rape victim: Personality, attitudinal, and situational characteristics. *Psychology of Women Quarterly, 9*, 193–212.

Koss, M. P., Leonard, K. E., Beezley, D. A., & Oros, C. J. (1985). Nonstranger sexual aggression: A discriminant analysis of the psychological characteristics of undetected offenders. *Sex Roles, 12*, 981–992.

Malamuth, N. M. (1988). Predicting laboratory aggression against female and male targets: Implications for sexual aggression. *Journal of Research in Personality, 22*, 474–495.

Mayerson, S. E., & Taylor, D. A. (1987). The effects of rape myth pornography on women's attitudes and the mediating role of sex role stereotyping. *Sex Roles, 17*(5/6), 321–338.

Overholser, J. C., & Beck, S. (1986). Multimethod assessment of rapists, child molesters, and three control groups on behavioral and psychological measures. *Journal of Consulting and Clinical Psychology, 54*(5), 682–687.

Pryor, J. B. (1987). Sexual harassment proclivities in men. *Sex Roles, 17*(5/6), 269–290.

Rapaport, K., & Burkhart, B. R. (1984). Personality and attitudinal characteristics of sexually coercive college males. *Journal of Abnormal Psychology, 93*(2), 216–221.

BIBLIOGRAPHY:
Beere, C. A. (in press). *Sex and gender issues: A handbook of tests and measures.* Westport, CT: Greenwood.
Spence, J. T., & Helmreich, R. (1972). The Attitudes Toward Women Scale: An objective instrument to measure attitudes toward the rights and roles of women in contemporary society. *Catalog of Selected Documents in Psychology*, 2, 66. (Ms. No. 153)
Spence, J. T., & Helmreich, R. (1978). *Masculinity and femininity.* Austin: University of Texas Press.

STEREOTYPES ABOUT MALE SEXUALITY SCALE (SAMSS)

AUTHORS: William E. Snell, Jr., Sharyn S. Belk, and Raymond C. Hawkins II

DATE: 1986

VARIABLE: Stereotypes of 10 aspects of male sexuality

TYPE OF INSTRUMENT: Summated rating scale

DESCRIPTION: The Stereotypes About Male Sexuality Scale (SAMSS) consists of 60 statements, with 6 statements pertaining to each of 10 stereotypes of male sexuality. The stereotypes, based on discussions by Zilbergeld (1978), are: men should not have, or at least they should not express, certain feelings; a man's sexuality is defined in terms of his sexual performance; men are responsible to initiate and direct the course of heterosexual activities; men are perpetually eager for sex; for men, physical contact with a woman should always lead to sex; for men, the important part of sex is sexual intercourse; men must always have an erection to enjoy any sexual interactions; men only enjoy sex when it continually escalates in excitement and terminates in orgasm; men's sexual behavior is natural and spontaneous; men are knowledgeable about sex. Each of the 60 statements is accompanied by a 5-point scale with the endpoints labeled "agree" and "disagree."

SAMPLE ITEMS: (Inexpressiveness) Men should not ask to be held.

(Sex Equals Performance) Men are almost always concerned with their sexual performance.

(Males Orchestrate Sex) Men generally want to be the guiding participant in sexual behavior.

(Always Ready for Sex) Most men are ready to have sex at any time.

(Touching Leads to Sex) Most men desire physical contact only as a prelude for sex.

(Sex Equals Intercourse) The ultimate sexual goal in men's mind is intercourse.

(Sex Requires Erection) Lack of an erection will always spoil sex for a man.

(Sex Requires Orgasm) From a man's perspective, good sex usually has an "earthshaking" aspect to it.

(Spontaneous Sex) Men don't really like to plan their sexual experiences.

(Sexually Aware Men) Most men are sexually well-adjusted.

PREVIOUS SUBJECTS: College students

APPROPRIATE FOR: College students and older

ADMINISTRATION: Self-administered; about 30 minutes

SCORING: Items are scored on a 5-point scale with 5 points assigned to the "agree" end of the continuum. Subscale scores can be obtained by summing the six items pertaining to each stereotype; subscale scores range from 6 to 36. An overall total score is obtained by summing across all the item scores; the total score can range from 60 to 360. Snell, Belk, and Hawkins (1986) reported means and standard deviations for each of the 10 subscales.

DEVELOPMENT: Items were generated to measure each of the 10 stereotypes. Based on item-total correlations, 6 items were selected to measure each of the stereotypes; this produced a 60-item scale.

RELIABILITY: Alpha coefficients for the 10 subscales ranged from .63 to .93. The average alpha coefficient was .80, and only one coefficient was below .70.

VALIDITY: Significant sex differences were found on two subscales: men scored significantly higher on Inexpressiveness and on Males Orchestrate Sex.

In order to determine the convergent and divergent validity, Snell et al. (1986) administered the SAMSS and nine other measures to a sample of college students. The other measures were: the Mosher Sex Guilt Inventory (Mosher, 1966) (see Beere, in press), the Sex Anxiety Inventory (Janda & O'Grady, 1980) (see Beere, in press), the Jenkins Activity Survey (Jenkins, 1978), the Masculine Role Inventory (Snell, 1983) (see separate entry), the Male-Female Relations Inventory (Spence, Helmreich, & Sawin, 1980) (see Beere, in press), the Extended Personal Attributes Questionnaire (Spence, Helmreich, & Holahan, 1979) (see separate entry), the Irrational Beliefs Test (Jones, 1968), the Self-Consciousness Scale (Fenigstein, Scheier, & Buss, 1975), and the Body-Consciousness Scale (Miller, Murphy, & Buss, 1981) (see Beere, in press). Snell et al. (1986) reported all of the possible correlations separately for males and for females. Observation of the correlation matrices suggests that some subscales on the SAMSS were significantly correlated with some of the subscales on the other measures. The pattern of significant correlations was different for males and females. In other words, the results might appropriately be labeled as mixed. In summarizing the voluminous amount of data, Snell et al. concluded: "Overall, then, there was considerable support for the convergent and divergent validity of the Stereotypes About Male Sexuality Scale (SAMSS)" (Snell et al., 1986, p. 30).

NOTES & COMMENTS: (1) Snell et al. (1986) reported the results of a factor analysis of the subscale scores. All of the subscales except Sexually Aware Men had loadings above .30 on a single factor. They also reported the intercorrelations among the subscales. Not surprisingly, most of them were statistically significant and at least moderately high.

(2) Snell et al. (1986) used the SAMSS in a study designed to identify the parental child-rearing antecedents of stereotypes about male sexuality. SAMSS has been used to look at the relationship between men's and women's uses of power and avoidance strategies and their support for the stereotypes about male sexuality (Snell et al., 1986; Snell, Hawkins, & Belk, 1988). Snell et al. (1986) used the SAMSS in a study designed to determine whether support for stereotypes regarding male sexuality moderates the relationship between stress and personal satisfaction. They also used the SAMSS to determine whether male and female counselors in training have different beliefs about the ways healthy men and healthy women would complete the SAMSS. According to Snell et al. (1986), the findings of these various studies using the SAMSS provided further evidence of the predictive validity of the scale.

AVAILABLE FROM: Snell, Belk, and Hawkins, 1986; or order from NAPS c/o Microfiche Publications, P.O. Box 3513, Grand Central Station, New York, NY 10163–3513; NAPS document no. 04708; for microfiche, in U.S. remit $4.00 with order.

USED IN:

Snell, W. E., Jr., Belk, S. S., & Hawkins, R. C., II. (1986). The Stereotypes About Male Sexuality Scale (SAMSS): Components, correlates, antecedents, consequences and counselor bias. *Social and Behavioral Science Documents*, *16*(1), 9. (Ms. No. 2746)

Snell, W. E., Jr., Hawkins, R. C., II, & Belk, S. S. (1988). Stereotypes about male sexuality and the use of social influence strategies in intimate relationships. *Journal of Social and Clinical Psychology*, *7*, 42–48.

BIBLIOGRAPHY:

Beere, C. A. (in press). *Sex and gender issues: A handbook of tests and measures*. Westport, CT: Greenwood.

Fenigstein, A., Scheier, M. F., & Buss, A. H. (1975). Public and private self-consciousness: Assessment and theory. *Journal of Counseling and Clinical Psychology*, *43*, 522–527.

Janda, L. H., & O'Grady, K. E. (1980). Development of a sex anxiety inventory. *Journal of Consulting and Clinical Psychology*, *48*, 169–175.

Jenkins, C. D. (1978). A comparative review of the interview and questionnaire methods in the assessment of the coronary-prone behavior pattern. In T. N. Dembroski, S. M. Weiss, J. L. Shields, S. Haynes, & M. Feinleib (Eds.), *Coronary-prone behavior*. New York: Springer.

Jones, R. G. (1968). A factored measure of Ellis' irrational belief system with personality and maladjustment correlates. (Doctoral dissertation, Texas Technological College, 1968). *Dissertation Abstracts International*, *29*, 4379.

Miller, L. C., Murphy, R., & Buss, A. H. (1981). Consciousness of body: Private and public. *Journal of Personality and Social Psychology, 41,* 397–406.

Mosher, D. L. (1966). The development and multitrait-multimethod matrix analysis of three measures of three aspects of guilt. *Journal of Consulting Psychology, 30,* 25–29.

Snell, W. E., Jr. (1983, April). *The Masculine Role Inventory: Components and correlates.* Paper presented at the annual meeting of the Southwestern Psychological Association, San Antonio, TX.

Spence, J. T., Helmreich, R. L., & Holahan, C. K. (1979). Negative and positive components of psychological masculinity and femininity and their relationships to self-reports of neurotic and acting out behaviors. *Journal of Personality and Social Psychology, 37,* 1673–1682.

Spence, J. T., Helmreich, R. L., & Sawin, L. L. (1980). The Male-Female Relations Questionnaire: A self-report inventory of sex-role behaviors and preferences and its relationship to masculine and feminine personality traits, sex role attitudes, and other measures. *Catalog of Selected Documents in Psychology, 10,* 87. (Ms. No. 2123)

Zilbergeld, B. (1978). *Male sexuality.* Boston: Little, Brown.

SCALE FOR SEXISM IN THE MEDIA

AUTHORS: Matilda Butler and William Paisley

DATE: 1974

VARIABLE: Sexism in the media

TYPE OF INSTRUMENT: Rating scale

DESCRIPTION: The Scale for Sexism in the Media provides a 5-point scale for rating media samples of women. Level I is assigned to samples that suggest that "woman is a two-dimensional, nonthinking decoration" (Pingree, Hawkins, Butler, & Paisley, 1976, p. 194). At this level, women are often shown as decorative objects; in advertising, for example, the woman has no relationship to the product. Level II is assigned to samples that show that a "woman's place is in the home or in womanly occupations" (Pingree et al., 1976, p. 194). At this level, women's traditional strengths are revealed; they may be shown as successful wives, mothers, secretaries, teachers, or nurses. The key here is that their competence is limited to traditional areas, and if they strive for success in nontraditional roles, they are shown in a negative fashion. Level II also includes examples showing women and men in romantic situations, since "romance is a very appropriate status quo setting for a woman" (Pingree et al., 1976, p. 196). Level III is assigned when the "woman may be a professional, but first place is home" (p. 194). For example, the woman may be a successful lawyer, but she is shown serving dinner to her family. There is often the implicit suggestion that her home comes before her career; perhaps her career is like a special hobby. Level IV is assigned when the media sample shows "women and men must be equals" (p. 194). "The important distinction between this level and Level III, which also allows women to be professionals, is that Level IV images do not remind us that housework and mothering are non-negotiably the woman's work as well" (p. 195). Level V is assigned when the samples show "women and men as individuals" (p. 194). "Individual women and men are viewed as superior to each other in some respects, inferior in other respects" (p. 195).

PREVIOUS SUBJECTS: The scale has been used by college students to rate magazine advertisements.

APPROPRIATE FOR: The scale can be used by persons ages 16 and older who have been trained to use it. Any media samples could be rated.

SCORING: The only scoring per se is the assignment of a "level" to a media sample.

DEVELOPMENT: No information was provided.

RELIABILITY: Eleven pairs of college students, usually one male and one female, independently rated magazine advertisements. Of 447 magazine advertisements that were rated, two independent raters disagreed on only 15.

VALIDITY: Pingree et al. (1976) stated: "If the scale is a valid way of tapping sexism in the media, then *Ms.* should have relatively more high-level advertisements than the other magazines and *Playboy* relatively more low-level ads, with *Time* and *Newsweek* falling in between" (p. 196). They also hypothesized that *Time* and *Newsweek* would have high concentrations of Level II, status quo, advertisements. As predicted, *Playboy* had the highest concentration of Level I ads, and *Ms.* had the highest concentration of Level IV and V ads. Furthermore, *Time* and *Newsweek* had the highest concentration of Level II ads. Overall, the greatest percentage of ads were Level II ads followed by Level I ads.

NOTES & COMMENTS: Though the scale was developed for rating the image of women in the media, Pingree et al. (1976) suggest a comparable scale for rating the media's image of men. Levels I, II, and III are analogous to the categories on the women's scale. That is, Level I is "man is a two-dimensional decoration"; Level II is "man's place is at work or at manly activities at home"; and Level III is "man may help out competently at home, but first place is work" (p. 199). Levels IV and V are identical on the men's and women's scale.

AVAILABLE FROM: Pingree, Hawkins, Butler, and Paisley, 1976
USED IN:

Pingree, S., Hawkins, R. P., Butler, M., & Paisley, W. (1976). A scale for sexism. *Journal of Communication, 26*(4), 193–200.

6

Marital and Parental Roles

The 26 scales described in this chapter include 7 scales described in my previous handbook (Beere, 1979) and 19 scales new to this handbook. These measures relate to three areas: marital roles (10 scales), parenthood motivation and timing (7 scales), and parental roles (9 scales). The marital roles scales pertain to such topics as decision making, task allocation, homemaking stress, and attitudes toward traditional versus egalitarian marriages. The chapter includes two unusual scales: the Interpersonal Influence Survey (Wilson, 1984) measures the extent to which the male partner influences the life decisions of the female partner, and the Hoskins Dominance-Accommodation Scale (Hoskins, 1986) measures the balance between dominance and accommodation within the marriage.

Four of the 10 marital roles scales are appropriate only for married persons or those living as though married. The other scales can be used with unmarried persons; in most cases, the respondents should be at least high school age in order to understand the items.

Of the 10 marital roles scales, 2 are more accurately described as "procedures" rather than specific scales. In the 1950s, Blood and Wolfe (1960) developed a measure of marital decision making and a measure of marital task allocation, both described in my last book. Over the past decade, both of these scales have been used in many research studies, but often the scales have been modified dramatically. As a result of the extensive alterations in the scales, I have labeled the 2 scales as "procedures." Some of the 30 references that follow the Blood-Wolfe Marital Decision Making Scale and some of the 74 references that follow the Blood-Wolfe Marital Task Allocation Scale used the original Blood and

Wolfe scales; other references report the use of a modified version of one of the scales.

Following the marital roles scales are 7 scales dealing with parenthood motivation and the process by which people arrive at a decision about having children. All 7 of these scales are new to this handbook, though some were developed as early as the 1960s.

The last 9 scales in the chapter deal with the parental role. They consider parental stress, the transition to parenthood, attitudes about maternal and paternal roles, and specific maternal issues, including self-definition, separation anxiety, and social support. One looks at lone parenthood. These 9 scales are also new to this handbook. Six of the scales are intended for use with parents.

Other than the two Blood and Wolfe procedures, no scale in this chapter includes as many as 20 references. The Scanzoni Scales (Scanzoni, 1975), which deal with marital roles, come closest, with 18 references. Seven of the 26 scales in this chapter include only one citation.

The scales in this chapter are generally older than those in the rest of the handbook. Seventeen of the scales in this chapter were first mentioned in the literature before 1980; six date back to the 1950s.

The most common type of scale in this chapter is the summated rating scale. Twenty of the 26 scales are classified as summated rating scales. Their length varies from 3 to 103 items. The average length is 38 items, suggesting that overall the scales in this chapter are longer than the scales of other chapters.

There is little information on the test-retest reliability of these scales. Of the 19 scales new to this handbook, test-retest reliability data are available for only 3, and the reliability coefficient is low for 1 of these. There is more information on the internal consistency reliability of the 19 scales. Data are provided for 15 of the scales, and the coefficients are sufficiently high for 9 of those 15. Nevertheless, we have no information on the internal consistency reliability of 4 scales; 3 scales are not sufficiently reliable; and 3 scales are on the borderline between sufficiently and not sufficiently reliable. None of the measures included in this chapter is available in equivalent forms; therefore, there is no information on the alternate form reliability of these scales.

The validity of many of these scales is also questionable. While there is generally information regarding the scales' validity, it is often minimal. For most scales, more evidence is needed to support the scale's validity.

Although there are only nine marital roles scales in this chapter, researchers should not conclude that there are few measures regarding marriage. Rather, there are few scales that deal specifically with marital roles. There are a large number of scales that deal with other aspects of marriage, and many have been used repeatedly.

The area of marital research that has received the most attention is that of marital adjustment or marital satisfaction. Two scales in this area are used far more often than other marital scales. The Locke-Wallace Marital Adjustment Test (Locke & Wallace, 1959) has been used in over 250 studies published during the past 12 years, and the Dyadic Adjustment Scale (Spanier, 1976) has been used in over 150 studies published during the past 12 years. Other scales used in this area include Snyder's (1979) Marital Satisfaction Inventory, the Marital Instability Index (Booth, Johnson, & Edwards, 1983), the Kansas Marital Satisfaction Scale (Schumm, Nichols, Schectman, & Grigsby, 1983), the Marital Happiness Scale (Azrin, Naster, & Jones, 1973), the Marital Satisfaction Scale (Roach, Frazier, & Bowden, 1981), and the Marital Status Inventory (Weiss & Cerreto, 1980). Researchers have also devoted considerable effort to researching the areas of marital communication and marital conflict. In the marital communication area, the most frequently used scales are the Marital Interaction Coding System (Hops, Wills, Patterson, & Weiss, 1972), the Marital Communication Inventory (Bienvenu, 1970), the Primary Communication Inventory (Navran, 1967), the Spouse Communication Apprehension measure (Powers & Hutchinson, 1979), and the Dyadic Interaction Scoring Code (Filsinger, 1983). There are also scales for studying aspects of divorce—for example, the Divorce Adjustment Scale (Fisher, 1977) and the Divorce Reaction Inventory (Brown & Reimer, 1984).

In the marital conflict area, the most commonly used scales are the Conflict Resolution Inventory (McFall & Lillesand, 1971), the Conflict Tactics Scale (Straus, 1979), the Marital Problem Solving Scale (Baugh, Avery, & Sheets-Haworth, 1982), the Areas of Change Questionnaire (Weiss & Birchler, 1975; also see Margolin, Talovic, & Weinstein, 1983), and the Inventory of Marital Conflicts (Olson & Ryder, 1970). An extreme expression of marital conflict is physical and/or psychological abuse. Measures of spouse abuse are described in Beere (in press).

Researchers interested in more information regarding measures used in marital research should consult the Handbook of Family Measurement Techniques (Touliatos, Perlmutter, & Straus, 1989), Family Assessment: A Guide to Methods and Measures (Grotevant & Carlson, 1989), and Sabatelli's (1988) article in Journal of Marriage and the Family.

BIBLIOGRAPHY:

Azrin, N., Naster, B., & Jones, R. (1973). Reciprocity counseling: A rapid learning-based procedure for marital counseling. Behavior Research and Therapy, 11, 365–382.

Baugh, C. W., Avery, A. W., & Sheets-Haworth, K. L. (1982). Marital Problem-Solving Scale: A measure to assess relationship conflict negotiation ability. Family Therapy, 9, 43–51.

Beere, C. A. (1979). Women and women's issues: A handbook of test and measures. San Francisco: Jossey-Bass.

Beere, C. A. (in press). *Sex and gender issues: A handbook of tests and measures.* Westport, CT: Greenwood Press.

Bienvenu, M. J., Sr. (1970). Measurement of marital communication. *Family Coordinator, 19,* 26–31.

Blood, R. O., Jr., & Wolfe, D. M. (1960). *Husbands and wives: The dynamics of married living.* Glencoe, IL: Free Press.

Booth, A., Johnson, D. R., & Edwards, J. N. (1983). Measuring marital instability. *Journal of Marriage and the Family, 45,* 387–393.

Brown, S. D., & Reimer, D. A. (1984). Assessing attachment following divorce: Development and psychometric evaluation of the Divorce Reaction Inventory. *Journal of Counseling Psychology, 31,* 521–532.

Filsinger, E. E. (1983). A machine-aided marital observation technique: The Dyadic Interaction Scoring Code. *Journal of Marriage and the Family, 45,* 623–632.

Fisher, B. F. (1977). Identifying and meeting needs of formerly married people through a divorce adjustment seminar. (Doctoral dissertation, University of Northern Colorado, 1977). *Dissertation Abstracts International, 37,* 7036A.

Grotevant, H. D., & Carlson, C. I. (1989). *Family Assessment: A guide to methods and measures.* New York: Guilford Press.

Hops, H., Wills, T. A., Patterson, G. R., & Weiss, R. L. (1972). *Marital Interaction Coding System.* Unpublished manuscript, University of Oregon.

Hoskins, C. N. (1986). Measuring perceived dominance-accommodation: Development of a scale. *Psychological Reports, 58,* 627–642.

Locke, H. J., & Wallace, K. M. (1959). Short marital adjustment and prediction tests: Their reliability and validity. *Journal of Marriage and the Family, 21,* 251–255.

Margolin, G., Talovic, S., & Weinstein, C. D. (1983). Areas of Change Questionnaire: A practical approach to marital assessment. *Journal of Consulting and Clinical Psychology, 51,* 920–931.

McFall, R. M., & Lillesand, D. B. (1971). Behavior rehearsal with modeling and coaching in assertion training. *Journal of Abnormal Psychology, 77,* 313–323.

Navran, L. (1967). Communication and adjustment in marriage. *Family Process, 6,* 173–180.

Olson, D. H., & Ryder, R. G. (1970). Inventory of Marital Conflicts (IMC): An experimental interaction procedure. *Journal of Marriage and Family Living, 32,* 443–448.

Powers, W. G., & Hutchinson, K. (1979). The measurement of communication apprehension in the marriage relationship. *Journal of Marriage and the Family, 41,* 89–95.

Roach, A. J., Frazier, L. P., & Bowden, S. R. (1981). The Marital Satisfaction Scale: Development of a measure for intervention research. *Journal of Marriage and the Family, 43,* 537–546.

Sabatelli, R. M. (1988). Measurement issues in marital research: A review and critique of contemporary survey instruments. *Journal of Marriage and the Family, 50,* 891–916.

Scanzoni, J. H. (1975). *Sex roles, life-styles, and childbearing: Changing patterns in marriage and the family.* New York: Free Press.

Schumm, W. R., Nichols, C. W., Schectman, K. I., & Grigsby, C. C. (1983).

Characteristics of responses to the Kansas Marital Satisfaction Scale by a sample of 84 married mothers. *Psychological Reports, 53,* 567–572.

Snyder, D. K. (1979). Multidimensional assessment of marital satisfaction. *Journal of Marriage and the Family, 41,* 813–823.

Spanier, G. B. (1976). Measuring dyadic adjustment: New scales for assessing the quality of marriage and similar dyads. *Journal of Marriage and the Family, 38,* 15–28.

Straus, M. A. (1979). Measuring intrafamily conflict and violence: The Conflict Tactics (CT) Scale. *Journal of Marriage and the Family, 41,* 75–88.

Touliatos, J., Perlmutter, B. F., & Straus, M. A. (1989). *Handbook of family measurement techniques.* Newbury Park, CA: Sage.

Weiss, R., & Birchler, G. (1975). *Areas of Change.* Unpublished manuscript, University of Oregon.

Weiss, R. L., & Cerreto, M. C. (1980). The Marital Status Inventory: Development of a measure of dissolution potential. *American Journal of Family Therapy, 8,* 80–86.

Wilson, J. B. (1984). Perceptions of male partner's influences on female partner's life choices. *New Jersey Journal of Professional Counseling, 47*(1), 2–5.

ATTITUDES TOWARD THE ROLE OF HUSBAND AND WIFE IN MARRIAGE

AUTHOR: Alver Hilding Jacobson

DATE: 1950

VARIABLE: Support for egalitarian marital roles

DESCRIPTION: The Attitudes Toward the Role of Husband and Wife in Marriage is a summated rating scale consisting of 28 items relating to the marital roles of husbands and wives. The items cover a variety of topics such as decision making, responsibility for home and family tasks, and social freedom. Items are accompanied by five response options ranging from "strongly agree" to "strongly disagree."

ARTICLES LISTED IN BEERE, 1979: 13

NOTES & COMMENTS: Ojha and Singh (1985) used a Hindi version of the scale.

AVAILABLE FROM: Jacobson, 1951

USED IN:

Chia, R. C., Chong, C. J., & Cheng, B. S. (1986). Relationship of modernization and marriage role attitude among Chinese college students. *Journal of Psychology, 120,* 599–605.

Chia, R. C., Chong, C. J., Cheng, B. S., Castellow, W., Moore, C. H., & Hayes, M. (1986). Attitude toward marriage roles among Chinese and American college students. *Journal of Social Psychology, 126*(1), 31–35.

Jacobson, A. H. (1951). Conflict in attitudes toward the marital roles of husband and wife. *Washington State University Research Studies, 19,* 103–106.

Meredith, G. M., & Ching, D. R. (1977). Marriage-role attitudes among Japanese-American and Caucasian-American college students. *Psychological Reports, 40,* 1285–1286.

Ojha, H., & Singh, R. R. (1985). Relationship of marriage-role attitude with dependence proneness and insecurity in university students. *Psychologia*, *28*, 249–253.
BIBLIOGRAPHY:
Beere, C. A. (1979). *Women and women's issues: A handbook of tests and measures* (pp. 266–269). San Francisco: Jossey-Bass.

BLOOD-WOLFE MARITAL DECISION MAKING SCALE
AUTHORS: Robert O. Blood, Jr. and Donald M. Wolfe
DATE: 1958 (used 1955)
VARIABLE: Marital power
DESCRIPTION: The Blood-Wolfe Marital Decision Making Scale asks respondents to identify which spouse has the responsibility for making decisions in eight areas: husband's job selection, car purchase, purchase of life insurance, choice of a vacation spot, selection of house or apartment, wife's employment, use of a doctor, and food budget. The response options are: husband always, husband more than wife, husband and wife exactly the same, wife more than husband, and wife always.
ARTICLES LISTED IN BEERE, 1979: 44
NOTES & COMMENTS: (1) Though some studies listed below relied on Blood and Wolfe's original scale, other studies used modifications of the scale, and the modifications ranged from minor to significant. In fact, some studies used totally different items for ascertaining which spouse had the greater responsibility for decision making. Given all of the modifications of Blood and Wolfe's scale, it is probably most accurate to describe the citations listed as relying on Blood and Wolfe's strategy for assessing marital power rather than saying they used Blood and Wolfe's actual scale.

(2) Some researchers (e.g., Grauerholz, 1987; Ting-Toomey, 1982) used decision-making items appropriate for dating couples rather than married couples.
AVAILABLE FROM: Blood and Wolfe, 1960
USED IN:
Allen, C. M., & Straus, M. A. (1984). "Final say" measures of marital power: Theoretical critique and empirical findings from five studies in the United States and India. *Journal of Comparative Family Studies*, *15*(3), 329–344.
Bean, F. D., Curtis, R. L., Jr., & Marcum, J. P. (1977). Familism and marital satisfaction among Mexican Americans: The effects of family size, wife's labor force participation, and conjugal power. *Journal of Marriage and the Family*, *39*(4), 759–766.
Beckman, L. J., & Houser, B. B. (1979). The more you have, the more you do: The relationship between wife's employment, sex-role attitudes, and household behavior. *Psychology of Women Quarterly*, *4*(2), 160–174.
Blood, R. O., Jr., & Wolfe, D. M. (1960). *Husbands and wives: The dynamics of married living*. Glencoe, IL: Free Press.

Burge, P. L. (1983). Triple roles of Appalachian farm women: Household, farm, and wage-earning. *Research in Rural Education*, 2(2), 69–72.

Burr, W. R., Ahern, L., & Knowles, E. M. (1977). An empirical test of Rodman's theory of resources in cultural context. *Journal of Marriage and the Family*, 39(3), 505–514.

Cooney, R. S., Rogler, L. H., Hurrell, R. M., & Ortiz, V. (1982). Decision making in intergenerational Puerto Rican families. *Journal of Marriage and the Family*, 44(3), 621–631.

Cromwell, V. L., & Cromwell, R. E. (1978). Perceived dominance in decision-making and conflict resolution among Anglo, Black, and Chicano couples. *Journal of Marriage and the Family*, 40(4), 749–759.

Filiatrault, P., & Ritchie, J.R.B. (1980). Joint purchasing decisions: A comparison of influence structure in family and couple decision-making units. *Journal of Consumer Research*, 7, 131–140.

Grauerholz, E. (1987). Balancing the power in dating relationships. *Sex Roles*, 17(9/10), 563–571.

Gray-Little, B. (1982). Marital quality and power processes among black couples. *Journal of Marriage and the Family*, 44(3), 633–646.

Katz, R., & Peres, Y. (1985). Is resource theory equally applicable to wives and husbands? *Journal of Comparative Family Studies*, 16(1), 1–10.

Krausz, S. L. (1986). Sex roles within marriage. *Social Work*, 31(6), 457–464.

Kurdek, L. A., & Schmitt, J. P. (1986). Relationship quality of partners in heterosexual married, heterosexual cohabiting, and gay and lesbian relationships. *Journal of Personality and Social Psychology*, 51(4), 711–720.

Lundgren, D. C., Jergens, V. H., & Gibson, J. L. (1980). Marital relationships, evaluations of spouse and self, and anxiety. *Journal of Psychology*, 106, 227–240.

Lyson, T. A. (1985). Husband and wife work roles and the organization and operation of family farms. *Journal of Marriage and the Family*, 47(3), 759–764.

Madden, M. E. (1982, April). *Women's and men's marriages: Marital satisfaction, perceived control, and attitudes toward women*. Paper presented at the meeting of the Eastern Psychological Association, Baltimore. (ERIC Document Reproduction Service No. ED 223 932)

Mashal, M. M. (1985). Marital power, role expectations and marital satisfaction. *International Journal of Women's Studies*, 8(1), 40–46.

Meyer, R. J., & Lewis, R. A. (1976). New wine from old wineskins: Marital power research. *Journal of Comparative Family Studies*, 7(3), 397–407.

Monroe, P. A., Bokemeier, J. L., Kotchen, J. M., & McKean, H. (1985). Spousal response consistency in decision-making research. *Journal of Marriage and the Family*, 47(3), 733–738.

Radin, N. (1981). Childrearing fathers in intact families, I: Some antecedents and consequences. *Merrill-Palmer Quarterly*, 27(4), 489–514.

Rogler, L. H., & Procidano, M. E. (1986). The effect of social networks on marital roles: A test of the Bott hypothesis in an intergenerational context. *Journal of Marriage and the Family*, 48, 693–701.

Rosen, D. L., & Granbois, D. H. (1983). Determinants of role structure in family financial management. *Journal of Consumer Research*, 10, 253–258.

Schaninger, C. M., & Buss, W. C. (1986). A longitudinal comparison of consumption and finance handling between happily married and divorced
couples. *Journal of Marriage and the Family, 48,* 129–136.

Schumm, W. R., Bollman, S. R., & Jurich, A. P. (1981). Validity of Edmond's
Marital Conventionalization Scale. *Journal of Psychology, 109,* 65–71.

Spitze, G. D., & Huber, J. (1981, August). *The division of household labor.* Paper
presented at the meeting of the American Sociological Association, Toronto. (ERIC Document Reproduction Service No. ED 208 193)

Szinovacz, M. E. (1977). Role allocation, family structure, and female employment. *Journal of Marriage and the Family, 39*(4), 781–791.

Szinovacz, M. E. (1978). Another look at normative resource theory: Contri-
butions from Austrian data—a research note. *Journal of Marriage and the
Family, 40*(2), 413–421.

Szinovacz, M. E. (1980). Role allocation, family structure, and female employment. *Advances in Family Psychiatry, 2,* 481–498.

Ting-Toomey, S. (1982, October). *Communication of love and decision-making power
in dating relationships.* Paper presented at the meeting of the Communication, Language, and Gender Conference, Athens, OH. (ERIC Document
Reproduction Service No. ED 224 066)

Willis, F. M. (1976). *Options for life styles of university women.* Unpublished manuscript, American Association of University Women, Washington, DC.
(ERIC Document Reproduction Service No. ED 179 119)

BIBLIOGRAPHY:

Beere, C. A. (1979). *Women and women's issues: A handbook of tests and measures*
(pp. 269–274. San Francisco: Jossey-Bass.

BLOOD-WOLFE MARITAL TASK ALLOCATION SCALE

AUTHORS: Robert O. Blood, Jr. and Donald M. Wolfe

DATE: 1958 (used 1955)

VARIABLE: Division of family-oriented tasks among husbands and
wives

DESCRIPTION: The original Blood-Wolfe Marital Task Allocation Scale
asks spouses to identify who has major responsibility for each of the
following tasks: making necessary repairs around the house, mowing
the lawn, shoveling the sidewalk, doing the grocery shopping, getting
the husband's breakfast on workdays, straightening the living room for
company, doing the evening dishes, and keeping track of the money
and bills. Of the eight tasks, three are typically masculine, four are
typically feminine, and one is sex neutral. For each item, the spouse
selects one of five response options: "husband always, husband more
than wife, husband and wife exactly the same, wife more than husband,
wife always."

ARTICLES LISTED IN BEERE, 1979: 19

NOTES & COMMENTS: The Blood-Wolfe Marital Task Allocation Scale
has been modified in so many different ways that it is probably best to
refer to it as a procedure or a strategy for determining marital task

allocation. The most frequent change has been to revise the list of tasks on the scale. The scale has also been changed by asking adolescents how they hope their marriage will be in the future, by asking children who they think should perform each task, and by asking children and adolescents to report their perceptions of their parents' marriage. Another scale modification has been to ask husbands and wives to indicate the amount of time they spend engaged in each task. Some of the researchers listed below acknowledge that their measure is based on the Blood-Wolfe Marital Task Allocation Scale; others may have been unaware of the Blood-Wolfe scale when they developed their measure, but all are listed here because they include a list of tasks as the stimulus and the objective of the measure is to determine marital task allocation.
AVAILABLE FROM: Blood and Wolfe, 1960
USED IN:

Aguren, C. T., & Dameron, J. D. (1977). How mature women students cope with life situations. *Texas Personnel and Guidance Association Journal, 5*(1), 17–26.

Albrecht, S. L., Bahr, H. M., & Chadwick, B. A. (1979). Changing family and sex roles: An assessment of age differences. *Journal of Marriage and the Family, 41*(1), 41–50.

Antill, J. K., & Cotton, S. (1988). Factors affecting the division of labor in households. *Sex Roles, 18,* 531–553.

Antill, J. K., Cotton, S., & Tindale, S. (1983). Egalitarian or traditional: Correlates of the perception of an ideal marriage. *Australian Journal of Psychology, 35*(2), 245–257.

Atkinson, J., & Huston, T. L. (1984). Sex role orientation and division of labor early in marriage. *Journal of Personality and Social Psychology, 46*(2), 330–345.

Barnett, R. C., & Baruch, G. K. (1987). Determinants of fathers' participation in family work. *Journal of Marriage and the Family, 49,* 29–40.

Baruch, G. K., & Barnett, R. C. (1981). Fathers' participation in the care of their preschool children. *Sex Roles, 7*(10), 1043–1055.

Baruch, G. K., & Barnett, R. C. (1984). *Fathers' participation in family work: Effects on children's sex role attitudes.* (Working Paper No. 126). Wellesley, MA: Wellesley College, Center for Research on Women. (ERIC Document Reproduction Service No. ED 250 080)

Beckman, L. J., & Houser, B. B. (1979). The more you have, the more you do: The relationship between wife's employment, sex-role attitudes, and household behavior. *Psychology of Women Quarterly, 4*(2), 160–174.

Belsky, J., Lang, M., & Huston, T. L. (1986). Sex typing and division of labor as determinants of marital change across the transition to parenthood. *Journal of Personality and Social Psychology, 50*(3), 517–522.

Belsky, J., Spanier, G. B., & Rovine, M. (1983). Stability and change in marriage across the transition to parenthood. *Journal of Marriage and the Family, 45*(3), 567–577.

Berkove, G. F. (1979). Perceptions of husband support by returning women students. *Family Coordinator, 28*(4), 451–457.

Bird, G. W., Bird, G. A., & Scruggs, M. (1984). Determinants of family task sharing: A study of husbands and wives. *Journal of Marriage and the Family*, 46(2), 345–355.

Blood, R. O., Jr., & Wolfe, D. M. (1960). *Husbands and wives: The dynamics of married living*. Glencoe, IL: Free Press.

Brinkderhoff, D. B., & White, L. K. (1978). Marital satisfaction in an economically marginal population. *Journal of Marriage and the Family*, 40(2), 259–267.

Caldwell, M. A., & Peplau, L. A. (1984). The balance of power in lesbian relationships. *Sex Roles*, 10(7/8), 587–599.

Callan, V. J. (1983). Childlessness and partner selection. *Journal of Marriage and the Family*, 45(1), 181–186.

Carlson, B. E. (1984). The father's contribution to child care: Effects on children's perceptions of parental roles. *American Journal of Orthopsychiatry*, 54(1), 123–136.

Chiriboga, D. A., & Thurnher, M. (1980). Marital lifestyles and adjustment to separation. *Journal of Divorce*, 3(4), 379–390.

Condran, J. G., & Bode, J. G. (1982). Rashomon, working wives, and family division of labor: Middletown, 1980. *Journal of Marriage and the Family*, 44(2), 421–426.

Craddock, A. E. (1980). The effect of incongruent marital role expectations upon couples' degree of goal-value consensus in the first year of marriage. *Australian Journal of Psychology*, 32(2), 117–125.

Denmark, F. L., Shaw, J. S., & Ciali, S. D. (1985). The relationship among sex roles, living arrangements, and the division of household responsibilities. *Sex Roles*, 12(5/6), 617–625.

DiCanio, M., & Johnson, G. (1978). *The sex assumption in task allocation*. Unpublished paper, Memphis State University. (ERIC Document Reproduction Service No. ED 185 179)

Ericksen, J. A., Yancey, W. L., & Ericksen, E. P. (1979). The division of family roles. *Journal of Marriage and the Family*, 41(2), 301–313.

Fassinger, P. A., & Schwarzweller, H. (1984). The work of farm women: A midwestern study. In H. Schwarzweller (Ed.), *Research in rural sociology and development* (Vol. 1). Greenwich, CT: JAI Press.

Garza, J. M. (1980). Sex roles within cohabiting relationships. *American Journal of Psychoanalysis*, 40(2), 159–163.

Haas, L. (1981). Domestic role sharing in Sweden. *Journal of Marriage and the Family*, 43(4), 957–967.

Haas, L. (1982). Parental sharing of childcare tasks in Sweden. *Journal of Family Issues*, 3(3), 389–412.

Hartzler, K., & Franco, J. (1985). Ethnicity, division of household tasks and equity in marital roles: A comparison of Anglo and Mexican American couples. *Hispanic Journal of Behavioral Sciences*, 7(4), 333–344.

Hilier, D. V., & Philliber, W. W. (1986). The division of labor in contemporary marriage: Expectations, perceptions, and performance. *Social Problems*, 33(3), 191–201.

Huston-Hoburg, L., & Strange, C. (1986). Spouse support among male and female returning adult students. *Journal of College Student Personnel, 27*, 388–394.

Ichilov, O., & Rubineck, B. (1977). The relationship between girls' attitudes concerning the family and their perception of the patterns existing in the family of origin. *Journal of Marriage and the Family, 39*(2), 417–422.

Keith, P. M. (1981). Sex-role attitudes, family plans, and career orientations: Implications for counseling. *Vocational Guidance Quarterly, 29*(3), 244–252.

Keith, P. M., & Brubaker, T. H. (1977). Sex-role expectations associated with specific household tasks: Perceived age and employment differences. *Psychological Reports, 41*, 15–18.

Keith, P. M., & Brubaker, T. H. (1980). Adolescent perceptions of household work: Expectations by sex, age, and employment situation. *Adolescence, 15*, 171–182.

Keith, P. M., Goudy, W. J., & Powers, E. A. (1981). Employment characteristics and psychological well-being of men in two-job families. *Psychological Reports, 49*, 975–978.

Keith, P. M., & Schafer, R. B. (1980). Role strain and depression in two-job families. *Family Relations, 29*, 483–488.

Koopman-Boyden, P. G., & Abbott, M. (1985). Expectations for household task allocation and actual task allocation: A New Zealand study. *Journal of Marriage and the Family, 47*(1), 211–219.

Krause, N., & Markides, K. S. (1985). Employment and psychological well-being in Mexican American women. *Journal of Health and Social Behavior, 26*, 15–26.

Lee, R. A. (1983). Flexitime and conjugal roles. *Journal of Occupational Behaviour, 4*, 297–315.

Leslie, L. A. (1986). The impact of adolescent females' assessments of parenthood and employment on plans for the future. *Journal of Youth and Adolescence, 15*(1), 29–49.

Levant, R. F., Slattery, S. C., & Loiselle, J. E. (1987). Fathers' involvement in housework and child care with school-aged daughters. *Family Relations, 36*, 152–157.

Lundgren, D. C., Jergens, V. H., & Gibson, J. L. (1980). Marital relationships, evaluations of spouse and self, and anxiety. *Journal of Psychology, 106*, 227–240.

Lynch, J. M., & Reilly, M. E. (1985–86). Role relationships: Lesbian perspectives. *Journal of Homosexuality, 12*(2), 53–69.

Madden, M. E. (1982, April). *Women's and men's marriages: Marital satisfaction, perceived control, and attitudes toward women*. Paper presented at the meeting of the Eastern Psychological Association, Baltimore. (ERIC Document Reproduction Service No. ED 223 932)

Mannheim, B., & Schiffrin, M. (1984). Family structure, job characteristics, rewards and strains as related to work-role centrality of employed and self-employed professional women with children. *Journal of Occupational Behaviour, 5*, 83–101.

Meyer, R. J., & Lewis, R. A. (1976). New wine from old wineskins: Marital power research. *Journal of Comparative Family Studies, 7*(3), 397–407.

Monroe, P. A., Bokemeier, J. L., Kotchen, J. M., & McKean, H. (1985). Spousal response consistency in decision-making research. *Journal of Marriage and the Family, 47*(3), 733–738.

Mukhopadhyay, C. C. (1982, June). *What is an egalitarian family: Reflections from a Los Angeles hospital.* Paper presented at the meeting of the National Women's Studies Association, Arcata, CA. (ERIC Document Reproduction Service No. ED 228 125)

Nicola, J. S., & Hawkes, G. R. (1985). Marital satisfaction of dual-career couples: Does sharing increase happiness? *Journal of Social Behavior and Personality, 1*(1), 47–60.

Nyquist, L., Slivken, K., Spence, J. T., & Helmreich, R. L. (1985). Household responsibilities in middle-class couples: The contribution of demographic and personality variables. *Sex Roles, 12*(1/2), 15–34.

Pavan, B. N. (1987, April). *Sex role stereotyping for household chores by aspiring and incumbent female and male public school administrators.* Paper presented at the meeting of the American Educational Research Association, Washington, DC. (ERIC Document Reproduction Service No. ED 283 303)

Perlmutter, J. C., & Wampler, K. S. (1985). Sex role orientation, wife's employment, and the division of household labor. *Home Economics Research Journal, 13*(3), 237–245.

Perrucci, C. C., Potter, H. R., & Rhoads, D. L. (1978). Determinants of male family-role performance. *Psychology of Women Quarterly, 3*(1), 53–66.

Rachlin, V. C. (1987). Fair vs. equal role relations in dual-career and dual-earner families: Implications for family interventions. *Family Relations, 36*(2), 187–192.

Rathge, R. W., & Swenson, C. L. (1985, August). *An evaluation of use value production of farm women in an agricultural state.* Paper presented at the meeting of the Rural Sociological Society, Blacksburg, VA. (ERIC Document Reproduction Service No. ED 269 213)

Riley, D. (1985, April). *Survey measurement of father involvement in childrearing: A reliability and validity study.* Paper presented at the meeting of the Society for Research in Child Development, Toronto. (ERIC Document Reproduction Service No. Ed 258 692)

Rogler, L. H., & Procidano, M. E. (1986). The effect of social networks on marital roles: A test of the Bott hypothesis in an intergenerational context. *Journal of Marriage and the Family, 48*, 693–701.

Russell, G. (1982). Maternal employment status and fathers' involvement in child care. *Australian and New Zealand Journal of Sociology, 18*(2), 172–179.

Schneider, M. S. (1986). The relationships of cohabiting lesbian and heterosexual couples: A comparison. *Psychology of Women Quarterly, 10*, 234–239.

Scholl, K. K., & Tippett, K. S. (Eds.) (1982). Household production. *Family Economics Review* (special issue 3). (ERIC Document Reproduction Service No. ED 217 187)

Shamir, B. (1986). Unemployment and household division of labor. *Journal of Marriage and the Family, 48*, 195–206.

Shepard, W. (1980). Mothers and fathers, sons and daughters: Perceptions of young adults. *Sex Roles, 6*(3), 421–433.

Spitze, G. (1986). The division of task responsibility in U.S. households: Longitudinal adjustments to change. *Social Forces, 64*, 689–701.

Spitze, G. D., & Huber, J. (1981, August). *The division of household labor*. Paper presented at the meeting of the American Sociological Association, Toronto. (ERIC Document Reproduction Service No. ED 208 193)

Stafford, R., Backman, E., & Dibona, P. (1977). The division of labor among cohabiting and married couples. *Journal of Marriage and the Family, 39*(1), 43–57.

Stephenson, M. J. (1976). *Changing family patterns of married women over thirty who have returned to college*. Unpublished master's thesis, University of Maryland. (ERIC Document Reproduction Service No. ED 186 612)

Szinovacz, M. E. (1977). Role allocation, family structure, and female employment. *Journal of Marriage and the Family, 39*(4), 781–791.

Szinovacz, M. E. (1980). Female retirement: Effects on spousal roles and marital adjustment. *Journal of Family Issues, 1*(3), 423–440.

Tavecchio, L. W., Van Ijzendoorn, M. H., Goossens, F. A., & Vergeer, M. M. (1984). The division of labor in Dutch families with preschool children. *Journal of Marriage and the Family, 46*(1), 231–242.

Thrall, C. A. (1978). Who does what: Role stereotypy, children's work, and continuity between generations in the household division of labor. *Human Relations, 31*(3), 249–265.

Wheeler, C. L., & Arvey, R. D. (1981). Division of household labor in the family. *Home Economics Research Journal, 10*, 10–20.

Willis, F. M. (1976). *Options for life styles of university women*. Unpublished manuscript, American Association of University Women, Washington, DC. (ERIC Document Reproduction Service No. ED 179 119)

Willis, M. L. (1979). *The organization of household work and role problems for employed women and men*. Unpublished manuscript, Pacific Lutheran University, Tacoma, WA. (ERIC Document Reproduction Service No. ED 176 002)

Woods, N. F. (1985). Employment, family roles, and mental ill health in young married women. *Nursing Research, 34*(1), 4–10.

BIBLIOGRAPHY:

Beere, C. A. (1979). *Women and women's issues: A handbook of test and measures* (pp. 269–274). San Francisco: Jossey-Bass.

HOMEMAKING STRESSORS SCALE

AUTHOR: Frederic W. Ilfeld, Jr.

DATE: 1976

VARIABLE: Stress associated with homemaking responsibilities

TYPE OF INSTRUMENT: Summated rating scale

DESCRIPTION: Two separate versions of the Homemaking Stressors Scale have been used. The form for unemployed women contains seven questions asking about various aspects of the homemaking role that might cause stress. Each item is accompanied by four response options: "almost always, much of the time, once in a while, never or almost never." The form for employed women contains three questions asking about potential sources of stress associated with the homemaker role. Response options are "never, once in a while, fairly often, very often."

SAMPLE ITEMS: (unemployed women) How often are you not appreciated for your work in the house?

(employed women) How often do you just have more to do than you can handle?

PREVIOUS SUBJECTS: Married women

APPROPRIATE FOR: Married women

ADMINISTRATION: Self-administered or administered as part of an interview; a couple of minutes

SCORING: Items are scored on a scale from 0 to 3, with 3 assigned to the response showing the greatest stress. Item scores are summed, divided by a number equal to three times the number of items on the scale, and multiplied by 100. This yields a score between 0 and 100, with higher scores reflecting greater stress. Ilfeld (1976a) reported means and standard deviations for two samples of women: one employed sample and one unemployed sample.

DEVELOPMENT: The Homemaking Stressors Scale was designed as part of a larger study in which nine measures of social stressors were developed. Ilfeld (1976a) defined social stressors as "those circumstances or conditions of daily social roles which are generally considered to be problematic or undesirable" (p. 1234). Ilfeld (1976a) further differentiated his definition of social stressors from more common definitions of stressors: "Our stressors are tied to a social role, are usually repeated experiences instead of discrete events, and are commonly regarded as problematic and undesirable" (p. 1234). All nine measures of stress were developed concurrently. Open-ended tape-recorded interviews were conducted with approximately 175 people over a period of about 18 months. The substance of the stressors and the language for expressing them were taken from the information acquired during the interviews.

RELIABILITY: The Homemaking Stressors Scale for unemployed women was completed by 811 women; coefficient alpha was .69. The Homemaking Stressors Scale for employed women was completed by 392 women; coefficient alpha was .74.

VALIDITY: If respondents react differently to the separate measures of stress, it suggests that they are not simply reporting a generalized experience of stress but rather are differentiating among various potential sources of stress in their lives. Low correlations between scores on the Homemaking Stressors Scale and the other measures of stress would provide support for the validity of the Homemaking Stressors Scale. For a sample of employed, married mothers, Ilfeld (1976b) correlated scores on the Homemaking Stressors Scale with scores on other measures of stress: job, financial, parental, neighborhood, and marital stressors. The correlations ranged from .04 (correlation between Homemaking Stressors and neighborhood stressors) to .26 (correlation between Homemaking Stressors and job stressors). For a sample of unemployed, married mothers, Ilfeld (1976b) obtained correlations of .04 with neighborhood stressors, .15 with financial stressors, .26 with parental stressors, and .39 with marital stressors.

For a sample of employed, married mothers Ilfeld (1976b) obtained a correlation of .13 between scores on the Homemaking Stressors Scale and a measure of psychiatric symptoms.

Krause (1983) used the Homemaking Stressors Scale as a measure of dissatisfaction with housework. He obtained evidence to support two hypotheses regarding scores on the Homemaking Stressors Scale. First, he confirmed that "the greater the degree of conflict in a marriage over sex-role expectations for the female role, the more dissatisfied a housewife would be with her housework role" (p. 1122); second, he confirmed that older women are less dissatisfied with housework than are younger women. Contrary to prediction, Krause was unable to find a relationship between educational level and dissatisfaction with housework, though he had predicted that they would be directly related.

NOTES & COMMENTS: (1) Along with developing the Homemaking Stressors Scale, Ilfeld (1976a) developed measures of neighborhood stressors (8 items), job stressors (19 items), financial stressors (9 items), parental stressors (29 items), marital stressors (17 items), stressors from being single (7 items), stressors from being unemployed (7 items), and stressors associated with retirement (8 items).

(2) Ilfeld (1976a) found that 38% of a sample of respondents reported that the most problematic homemaking stressor they experienced had been creating stress for more than 6 years. Only 12% reported that the most problematic homemaking stressor had been creating stress for less than 1 year.

(3) Ilfeld (1976a) performed a regression analysis to determine the ability of five variables—number of children at home, age, marital status, income level, and race—to predict scores on the Homemaking Stressors Scale. He found that number of children at home and age were the strongest predictors; the former had a positive regression coefficient and the latter had a negative one.

AVAILABLE FROM: Ilfeld, 1976a

USED IN:

Ilfeld, F. W., Jr. (1976a). Characteristics of current social stressors. *Psychological Reports*, 39, 1231–1247.

Ilfeld, F. W., Jr. (1976b). Methodological issues in relating psychiatric symptoms to social stressors. *Psychological Reports*, 39, 1251–1258.

Krause, N. (1983). Conflicting sex-role expectations, housework dissatisfaction, and depressive symptoms among full-time housewives. *Sex Roles*, 9(11), 1115–1125.

HOSKINS DOMINANCE-ACCOMMODATION SCALE
AUTHOR: Carol Noll Hoskins
DATE: 1986

VARIABLE: Dominance and accommodation between partners, either married or living together

TYPE OF INSTRUMENT: Summated rating scale

DESCRIPTION: The 48-item Hoskins Dominance-Accommodation Scale consists of two subscales—the first subscale with 32 items measuring dominance-accommodation "characterized by a bipolar quality" (Hoskins, 1986, p. 633) and the second with 16 items measuring "equality and mutual consideration in the relationship" (p. 633). The items on the second subscale relate to "open communication, consideration of the partner's views, and resolution of differences" (p. 633). Each item is accompanied by five response options: "strongly agree, agree, undecided, disagree, strongly disagree."

SAMPLE ITEMS: (Factor 1) If we disagree on what the most important things in life are, it is better in the long run if I go along with my partner's opinions.

(Factor 2) When I make plans with friends, my partner will adjust his (her) schedule.

PREVIOUS SUBJECTS: Persons who are married or living as though married

APPROPRIATE FOR: Persons who are married or living as though married

ADMINISTRATION: Self-administered; about 15 minutes

SCORING: Items are individually scored on a 5-point scale and summed to yield two scores, one on each subscale. High scores indicate a greater tendency to be accommodating; low scores indicate a perceived absence of domination. Total scores can range from 32 to 160 on Factor 1; they can range from 16 to 80 on Factor 2. Hoskins (1986) reported means and standard deviations on each factor.

DEVELOPMENT: The Hoskins Dominance-Accommodation Scale is based on the following description of a dominant person: "Attempts to control his (or her) environment; expresses opinions, preferences or attitudes in a verbal or nonverbal manner that tends to strongly influence or direct the behavior of the partner" (Hoskins, 1986, p. 629). An accommodating person "accepts blame and criticism even when not deserved; tends to be self-effacing; avoids risk of physical or emotional harm; seeks to maximize personal psychological safety, well-being or stability" (p. 630).

Based on the relevant literature, 10 content areas were identified: "sexual relations, relations with friends, how to spend leisure time, demonstration of affection, conventionality (right and wrong conduct), what and when to eat, sleeping and waking patterns, allocation of responsibilities for household tasks, finances, and philosophy of life" (Hoskins, 1986, p. 630). A pool of 100 items was constructed: 10 items from each of the 10 content areas. The item pool was reviewed by an expert in family theory and an expert in educational psychology. Their suggestions for improving the items were implemented. Overall, their assessment of the content and face validity of the items was favorable.

A sample of 119 persons, either married or cohabiting for at least 2 years, completed the 100-item pool along with the Personality Research Form (PRF) (Jackson, 1967). After several different factor analyses were performed, a varimax rotated two-factor analysis was used to identify items for the scale: 8 items were eliminated because they had loadings above .30 on both factors; 32 items with loadings above .30 comprise the first factor; and 16 items with loadings above .30 comprise the second factor.

RELIABILITY: Using responses from a sample of 100 persons, the alpha coefficient was found to be .90 for the first factor and .86 for the second factor.

VALIDITY: Scores from 119 persons who completed the Hoskins Dominance-Accommodation Scale were compared with scores on the PRF. Seven variables on the PRF were expected to relate to the Hoskins scores. The correlations were significant and in the predicted direction, but they were all quite low ($-.29$ to $+.29$). Factor 1 scores on the Hoskins Dominance-Accommodation Scale were positively related to Abasement and Social Recognition on the PRF, and they were negatively related to Aggression, Defendence, and Understanding on the PRF. Factor 2 scores were positively related to Defendence and Harm avoidance on the PRF. Factor 2 scores were also significantly correlated with three other personality variables on the PRF: Affiliation, Exhibition, and Play. These correlations were not anticipated.

NOTES & COMMENTS: (1) Responses from a second sample of 59 persons were factor analyzed to determine the stability of the factor structure. Using a more stringent criterion, that is, a factor loading of .40 on one factor and a loading below .40 on the other factor, 34 items loaded on Factor 1 and 17 items loaded on Factor 2; one item loaded equally on both factors. The results of the factor analysis and an examination of the item content for those items loading on each factor led to a different version of the scale. The new version included 30 items on Factor 1 and 10 items on Factor 2. However, the reliabilities of these two subscales were considerably lower than the reliabilities of the longer subscales. The alpha coefficient for the 30-item Factor 1 was .64; the alpha coefficient for the 10-item Factor 2 was .57.

(2) Because there are differences between the scale that was initially developed using factor analytic techniques and the scale that would have been developed from the second sample, further research is needed to clarify the subscales, their meaning, and the items to be included on them.

AVAILABLE FROM: Hoskins, 1986

USED IN:

Hoskins, C. N. (1986). Measuring perceived dominance-accommodation: Development of a scale. *Psychological Reports, 58,* 627–642.

BIBLIOGRAPHY:
Jackson, D. N. (1967). *Personality Research Form*. Goshen, NY: Research Psychologists Press.

INTERPERSONAL INFLUENCE SURVEY (IIS)
AUTHOR: Jennifer B. Wilson
DATE: 1984
VARIABLE: Male partner's influence on female partner's life decisions
TYPE OF INSTRUMENT: Summated rating scale
DESCRIPTION: There are two versions of the Interpersonal Influence Survey (IIS), one for males and one for females. Each version consists of 60 items covering nine areas in which women make decisions during early and middle adulthood. The areas are community involvement (6 items), family (8 items), friendship (6 items), goals (8 items), leisure (6 items), political involvement (6 items), religious involvement (8 items), residence (6 items), and work/employment (6 items). Each item is a statement of a decision that a woman might make. For each item on the female form, the woman is to indicate the amount of influence she feels her "partner" will have or has had on the outcome of the decision. A "partner" is defined as "a spouse, fiance, or intimate friend" of the opposite sex. There are five response options: "no influence, little influence, fair amount of influence, much influence, very much influence." The items on the male form are essentially equivalent to those on the female form except for minor wording changes for nouns and pronouns. The male is to rate the amount of influence he has had or will have when his partner is faced with each of the decisions listed.
SAMPLE ITEMS: (These items are from the female form.)
   (community involvement) Deciding on the type of community activities in which I will participate.
   (family) Deciding to marry or to live together on a permanent basis.
   (friendship) Determining who *my* friends are.
   (goals) Determining our family goals.
   (leisure) Deciding how much energy I will expend on leisure activities.
   (political involvement) Our allocation of non-monetary family or personal resources for politics.
   (religious involvement) Deciding on our amount of involvement in religious activities.
   (residence) Determining the distance we will live from either set of parents.
   (work/employment) My decision to change occupations.
PREVIOUS SUBJECTS: College students
APPROPRIATE FOR: College students and adults
ADMINISTRATION: Self-administered; about 20–25 minutes
SCORING: Items are individually scored on a 5-point scale, with 5 points

assigned to the end of the continuum reflecting greater influence. Item scores are summed to yield a total score that can range from 60 (no influence) to 300 (very much influence in all areas).

DEVELOPMENT: In developing the IIS, Wilson (1984) used Levinson, Darrow, Klein, Levinson, and McKee's (1978) concept of life decisions. Levinson et al. listed nine areas of critical life decisions: work, family, friendship, residence, leisure, religion, politics, community involvement, and goals. An item pool consisting of 9 items representing each of these nine areas was developed by Wilson. Three faculty members and seven graduate students, divided into two groups, served as judges and independently identified the category placement of each of the 81 items. An item was selected for inclusion on the IIS if a majority of the judges in each group agreed on the critical life decision being measured.

RELIABILITY: A sample of 30 females and their partners completed the IIS on two occasions separated by a 2-week interval. The test-retest reliability coefficient for the female respondents was .84; the test-retest reliability coefficient for the male respondents was .89. Internal consistency was measured using coefficient alpha. For the original test, alpha was .99 for the female respondents, .93 for the male respondents, and .89 for males and females combined. For the retest, coefficient alpha was .96 for the females, .94 for the males, and .89 for the males and females combined (Wilson, 1984).

Another sample of 31 females and their partners completed the IIS on two occasions with a 4- to 6-week interval between testings. The test-retest reliability coefficient was .91 for females and .89 for males. Coefficient alpha was .94 for males, .82 for females, and .96 for males and females combined (Wilson, 1984).

VALIDITY: Content validity was built into the IIS in that items were selected to represent each of the nine critical decision areas, and the judges verified that the items represented the areas they were intended to represent.

The correlation between the male's perceptions and the female's perceptions of the male's influence was .43 ($p < .01$). There were no significant sex differences between mean ratings on any of the nine categories.

NOTES & COMMENTS: Wilson (1986) related males' and females' scores on the IIS to males' scores on the Bem Sex Role Inventory (Bem, 1974) (see separate entry).

AVAILABLE FROM: Order from NAPS c/o Microfiche Publications, P. O. Box 3513, Grand Central Station, New York, NY 10163–3513; NAPS document no. 04708; for microfiche, in U.S. remit $4.00 with order.

USED IN:

Wilson, J. B. (1984). Perceptions of male partner's influences on female partner's life choices. *New Jersey Journal of Professional Counseling*, 47(1), 2–5.

Wilson, J. B. (1986). Perceived influence of male sex role identity on female
    partner's life choices. *Journal of Counseling and Development, 65,* 74–77.
BIBLIOGRAPHY:
Bem, S. L. (1974). The measurement of psychological androgyny. *Journal of Con-
    sulting and Clinical Psychology, 42,* 155–162.
Levinson, D. J., Darrow, C. M., Klein, E. B., Levinson, M. H., & McKee, B.
    (1978). *The seasons of a man's life.* New York: Ballantine Books.

MARRIAGE ROLE EXPECTATION INVENTORY

AUTHOR: Marie S. Dunn

DATE: 1959

VARIABLE: Traditional versus egalitarian marital role orientation

DESCRIPTION: The Marriage Role Expectation Inventory is a 71-item
summated rating scale covering seven aspects of the marital role: authority, homemaking, care of children, personal characteristics, social
participation, education, and financial support and employment. There
are two forms of the scale, a male form and a female form, differing
only in terms of the phrasing, not the substance, of the items.

ARTICLES LISTED IN BEERE, 1979: 24

NOTES & COMMENTS: (1) Some researchers have modified the scale.

(2) The Marriage Role Expectation Inventory is included in *The Ninth
Mental Measurements Yearbook* (entry 655).

AVAILABLE FROM: Dunn, 1960

USED IN:

Antill, J. K., & Cotton, S. (1988). Factors affecting the division of labor in house-
    holds. *Sex Roles, 18,* 531–553.
Craddock, A. E. (1977). Relationships between authoritarianism, marital power
    expectations and marital value systems. *Australian Journal of Psychology,
    29*(3), 211–221.
Craddock, A. E. (1980). Marital problem-solving as a function of couples' marital
    power expectations and marital value systems. *Journal of Marriage and the
    Family, 42,* 185–196.
Dunn, M. S. (1960). Marriage role expectations of adolescents. *Marriage and
    Family Living, 22,* 99–111.
Granvold, D. K., Pedler, L. M., & Schellie, S. G. (1979). A study of sex role
    expectancy and female postdivorce adjustment. *Journal of Divorce, 2*(4),
    383–393.
Knaub, P. K. (1976, October). *Marriage and career role expectations: A longitudinal
    study.* Paper presented at the meeting of the National Council on Family
    Relations, New York. (ERIC Document Reproduction Service No. ED 147
    670)
Larson, J. H. (1984). The effect of husband's unemployment on marital and
    family relations in blue-collar families. *Family Relations, 33*(4), 503–511.

Makosky, V. P., & Roeding, G. M. (1983, August). *Father involvement: Attitudinal and personality correlates for college women.* Paper presented at the meeting of the American Psychological Association, Anaheim. (ERIC Document Reproduction Service No. ED 243 030)

Maxwell, J. W., & Andress, E. L. (1982). Marriage role expectations of divorced men and women. *Journal of Divorce, 5*(4), 55–66.

Weeks, M. O., & Botkin, D. R. (1987). A longitudinal study of the marriage role expectations of college women: 1961–1984. *Sex Roles, 17*, 49–58.

Weeks, M. O., & Gage, B. A. (1984). A comparison of the marriage-role expectations of college women enrolled in a functional marriage course in 1961, 1972, and 1978. *Sex Roles, 11*, 377–388.

BIBLIOGRAPHY:

Beere, C. A. (1979). *Women and women's issues: A handbook of tests and measures* (pp. 291–295). San Francisco: Jossey-Bass.

Mitchell, J. V., Jr. (Ed.). (1985). *The ninth mental measurements yearbook* (Vol. 1). Lincoln: Buros Institute of Mental Measurements, University of Nebraska.

SCANZONI SCALES

AUTHOR: John H. Scanzoni

DATE: 1975 (used 1971)

VARIABLE: Support for traditional or egalitarian marital roles

DESCRIPTION: Beere (1979) described three Scanzoni scales: Social Position of Husband Scale, Social Position of Mother Scale, and Social Position of Wife Scale. The three summated rating scales are described collectively here because researchers frequently use a combination of the scales. The Social Position of Wife Scale consists of two parts: the Traditional-Wife Role portion, with eight items, and the Wife Self-Actualization part, with four items. The Social Position of Husband-Father Scale includes three parts: the Problematic Husband Alterations, with five items; the Institutionalized Equality, with two items; and the Traditional Husband Role, with two items. The Social Position of Mother Scale includes two parts: Religious-Legitimation-of-Mother Role consists of two questions, and the Traditional-Mother Role consists of five questions.

ARTICLES LISTED IN BEERE, 1979: 4

NOTES & COMMENTS: Many of the articles listed below relied on variations or portions of Scanzoni's scales.

AVAILABLE FROM: Scanzoni, 1975, 1976, 1978

USED IN:

Bird, G. W., Bird, G. A., & Scruggs, M. (1984). Determinants of family task sharing: A study of husbands and wives. *Journal of Marriage and the Family, 46*, 345–355.

Bowen, G. L. (1987). Changing gender-role preferences and marital adjustment: Implications for clinical practice. *Family Therapy, 14*, 17–33.

Bowen, G. L., & Neenan, P. A. (1988). Sex-role orientations among married men in the military: The generational factor. *Psychological Reports, 62*, 523–526.

Bowen, G. L., & Orthner, D. K. (1983). Sex-role congruency and marital quality. *Journal of Marriage and the Family, 45*, 223–230.

Burge, P. L. (1983). Triple roles of Appalachian farm women: Household, farm, and wage-earning. *Research in Rural Education, 2*(2), 69–72.

Fox, G. L., & Inazu, J. K. (1979, September). *The impact of mother-daughter communication on daughter's sexual knowledge, behavior and contraceptive use.* Paper presented at the meeting of the American Psychological Association, New York. (ERIC Document Reproduction Service No. ED 194 858)

McKenry, P. C., Hamdorf, K. G., Walters, C. M., & Murray, C. I. (1985). Family and job influences on role satisfaction of employed rural mothers. *Psychology of Women Quarterly, 9*, 242–257.

Rao, V. P., & Rao, V. N. (1985a). Sex-role attitudes: A comparison of sex-race groups. *Sex Roles, 12*, 939–953.

Rao, V. P., & Rao, V. N. (1985b). Sex-role attitudes across two cultures: United States and India. *Sex Roles, 13*, 607–624.

Rao, V. P., & Rao, V. N. (1986). Community size and sex role attitudes of the students in India. *Journal of Comparative Family Studies, 17*, 291–309.

Scanzoni, J. H. (1975). *Sex roles, life-styles, and childbearing: Changing patterns in marriage and the family.* New York: Free Press.

Scanzoni, J. (1976). Sex role change and influences on birth intentions. *Journal of Marriage and the Family, 38*, 43–58.

Scanzoni, J. H. (1978). *Sex roles, women's work, and marital conflict: A study of family change.* Toronto: Lexington Books.

Scanzoni, J. (1979). Sex-role influences on married women's status attainments. *Journal of Marriage and the Family, 41*(4), 793–800.

Scanzoni, J. (1980). Contemporary marriage types: A research note. *Journal of Family Issues, 1*(1), 125–140.

Schaninger, C. M., & Buss, W. C. (1986). The relationship of sex-role norms to couple and parental demographics. *Sex Roles, 15*, 77–94.

Tomeh, A. K. (1978). Sex-role orientation: An analysis of structural and attitudinal predictors. *Journal of Marriage and the Family, 40*, 341–354.

Tomeh, A. K., & Gallant, C. J. (1984). Familial sex role attitudes: A French sample. *Journal of Comparative Family Studies, 15*(3), 389–405.

Van Loo, M. F., & Bagozzi, R. P. (1984). Labor force participation and fertility: A social analysis of their antecedents and simultaneity. *Human Relations, 37*, 941–967.

Walters, C. M., & McKenry, P. C. (1985). Predictors of life satisfaction among rural and urban employed mothers: A research note. *Journal of Marriage and the Family, 47*, 1067–1071.

BIBLIOGRAPHY:
Beere, C. A. (1979). *Women and women's issues: A handbook of tests and measures* (pp. 306–311). San Francisco: Jossey-Bass.

TRADITIONAL FAMILY IDEOLOGY SCALE (TFI)
AUTHOR: Phyllis E. Huffman
DATE: 1950

VARIABLE: Democratic versus autocratic views of the family

DESCRIPTION: The Traditional Family Ideology Scale (TFI) is a summated rating scale consisting of 40 items dealing with four aspects of family life: parent-child relationships and child-rearing techniques, husband and wife roles and relationships, male-female relationships and masculinity/femininity, and general values and aims.

ARTICLES LISTED IN BEERE, 1979: 18

AVAILABLE FROM: Levinson and Huffman, 1955; Shaw and Wright, 1967

USED IN:

Crawford, J. E., & Crawford, T. J. (1978). Development and construct validation of a measure of attitudes toward public exposure to sexual stimuli. *Journal of Personality Assessment, 42*, 392–400.

Edwards, K. J., & Norcross, B. N. (1980). A comparison of two sex-role androgyny measures in a study of sex-role identity for incarcerated delinquent and nondelinquent females. *Sex Roles, 6*, 859–870.

Feinberg, R. A., & Workman, J. E. (1981). Sex-role orientation and cognitive complexity. *Psychological Reports, 49*, 246.

Levinson, D. J., & Huffman, P. E. (1955). Traditional family ideology and its relation to personality. *Journal of Personality, 23*, 251–273.

Richmond-Abbott, M. (1984). Sex-role attitudes of mothers and children in divorced, single-parent families. *Journal of Divorce, 8*, 61–81.

Rodgon, M. M., & Gralewski, C. (1979). Employment status and sex role attitudes in middle-class suburban mothers. *Journal of Applied Social Psychology, 9*, 127–134.

Steinberg, C. L., Teevan, R. C., & Greenfeld, N. (1983). Sex-role orientation and fear of failure in women. *Psychological Reports, 52*, 987–992.

Strong, L. D. (1978). Alternative marital and family forms: Their relative attractiveness to college students and correlates of willingness to participate in nontraditional forms. *Journal of Marriage and the Family, 40*, 493–503.

Vezina, J. P. (1980, October). *Grandmothers, mothers, and daughters: Intergenerational attitude transference among rural women.* Unpublished manuscript, Chadron State College, Nebraska. (ERIC Document Reproduction Service No. ED 243 630)

BIBLIOGRAPHY:

Beere, C. A. (1979). *Women and women's issues: A handbook of tests and measures* (pp. 313–316). San Francisco: Jossey-Bass.

Shaw, M. E., & Wright, J. M. (1967). *Scales for the measurement of attitudes.* New York: McGraw-Hill.

TRADITIONAL SEX ROLE IDEOLOGY SCALE

AUTHOR: Lois Wladis Hoffman

DATE: 1958

VARIABLE: Attitudes regarding men's participation in household tasks

DESCRIPTION: The Traditional Sex Role Ideology Scale is a brief, summated rating scale consisting of five items regarding the role of women

and men in performing household tasks. Items are accompanied by four response options ranging from "agree a lot" to "disagree a lot."
ARTICLES LISTED IN BEERE, 1979: 5
AVAILABLE FROM: Hoffman, 1960
USED IN:
Gaskell, J. (1977–78). Sex-role ideology and the aspirations of high school girls. *Interchange, 8*(3), 43–53.
Hoffman, L.N.W. (1960). Effects of the employment of mothers on parental power relations and the division of household tasks. *Marriage and Family Living, 22,* 27–35.
BIBLIOGRAPHY:
Beere, C. A. (1979). *Women and women's issues: A handbook of tests and measures* (pp. 316–318). San Francisco: Jossey-Bass.

ATTITUDE TOWARD TIMING OF PARENTHOOD (ATOP)
AUTHORS: Joseph W. Maxwell and James E. Montgomery
DATE: 1969
VARIABLE: Support for delayed parenthood
TYPE OF INSTRUMENT: Summated rating scale
DESCRIPTION: The Attitude Toward Timing of Parenthood (ATOP) scale consists of 10 items, most favoring early parenthood. Each item is accompanied by five response options ranging from "strongly agree" to "strongly disagree."
SAMPLE ITEMS: The best time to begin having children is usually within the first two years of marriage.
   A marriage relationship is strengthened if children are born in the early years of marriage.
PREVIOUS SUBJECTS: Married women, ages 21–84; college students
APPROPRIATE FOR: High school students and older
ADMINISTRATION: Self-administered; about 5 minutes
SCORING: Items are individually scored on a 5-point scale, with responses favoring early parenthood assigned 5 points and responses opposing early parenthood assigned 1 point. Item scores are summed to yield a total score that can range from 10 (strongly opposed to early parenthood) to 50 (strongly supportive of early parenthood).
DEVELOPMENT: No information was provided.
RELIABILITY: No information was provided.
VALIDITY: The data obtained from 96 married women were analyzed, and the item responses from the upper quartile were compared with those from the lower quartile. All 10 items discriminated significantly between the two groups (Maxwell & Montgomery, 1969). Maxwell and Montgomery (1969) found that persons who waited longer before having their first child scored lower on the ATOP; that is, their attitudes and their behavior were congruent. Knaub, Eversoll, and Voss (1979, 1981, 1983) reported that the women they tested about 10 years after Maxwell

and Montgomery's research was published, supported delayed parenthood more than did the women tested by Maxwell and Montgomery.

NOTES & COMMENTS: (1) Maxwell and Montgomery (1969) found that scores on the ATOP varied with age (older people scored higher), education (those with more education scored lower), socioeconomic status (those with higher SES scored lower), and number of children (those with more children scored higher).

(2) Researchers generally look at the percentage of respondents agreeing and disagreeing on each item (Eversoll, Voss, & Knaub, 1983; Knaub et al., 1979, 1983; Voss, Knaub, & Eversoll, 1980).

AVAILABLE FROM: Eversoll, Voss, and Knaub, 1983; Knaub, Eversoll, and Voss, 1979, 1983; Maxwell and Montgomery, 1969; Voss, Knaub, and Eversoll, 1980

USED IN:

Eversoll, D. B., Voss, J. H., & Knaub, P. K. (1983). Attitudes of college males toward parenthood timing. *Journal of Home Economics*, *75*(4), 25–29.

Knaub, P. K., Eversoll, D. B., & Voss, J. H. (1979, August). *Contemporary women and their attitudes toward parenthood*. Paper presented at the meeting of the National Council on Family Relations, Boston. (ERIC Document Reproduction Service No. ED 184 023)

Knaub, P. K., Eversoll, D. B., & Voss, J. H. (1981). Student attitudes toward parenthood: Implications for curricula in the 1980s. *Journal of Home Economics*, *73*(4), 34–37.

Knaub, P. K., Eversoll, D. B., & Voss, J. H. (1983). Is parenthood a desirable adult role? An assessment of attitudes held by contemporary women. *Sex Roles*, *9*(3), 355–362.

Maxwell, J. W., & Montgomery, J. E. (1969). Societal pressure toward early parenthood. *Family Coordinator*, *18*(4), 340–344.

Voss, J., Knaub, P. K., & Eversoll, D. (1980, October). *Contemporary women and their attitudes toward parenthood: Extension and replication*. Paper presented at the meeting of the National Council on Family Relations, Portland, OR. (ERIC Document Reproduction Service No. ED 198 461)

BARNETT CHILDBEARING ATTITUDES SCALE

AUTHOR: Larry D. Barnett

DATE: 1969

VARIABLE: Attitudes toward having children

TYPE OF INSTRUMENT: Summated rating scale

DESCRIPTION: The Barnett Childbearing Attitudes Scale consists of 11 items relating to a variety of motives for having children. The items represent four areas: prestige motives (3 items), woman's role obligation motives (3 items), religious motives (3 items), and marital happiness motives (2 items). Each item is accompanied by five response options: "strongly agree, agree, don't know, disagree, strongly disagree."

SAMPLE ITEMS: (prestige motives) The more children a couple has, the greater is their social prestige.

(woman's role obligation motives) A woman's responsibility should be having and rearing children.

(religious motives) If a couple has children, they have also fulfilled a religious duty.

(marital happiness motives) A couple who on purpose don't have children cannot have a good, solid marriage.

PREVIOUS SUBJECTS: Women, ages 18 and older; parents

APPROPRIATE FOR: High school students and older

ADMINISTRATION: Self-administered; about 5 minutes

SCORING: Items are scored on a 5-point scale, with 5 points assigned to the response indicating the least acceptance of the statement as a motive for having children. For all but one item, this was the "strongly disagree" response. Item scores are averaged to yield four subscale scores corresponding to the four areas listed. The lower the mean score is, the greater is the acceptance of the motives listed in the particular area. Kirkpatrick (1978) scored the scale in the exact opposite direction.

DEVELOPMENT: No information was provided other than a statement that the four areas were selected "on an a priori basis to be prevalent in the United States" (Stolka & Barnett, 1969, p. 740).

RELIABILITY: Kirkpatrick (1978) reported a corrected split-half reliability of .73 for persons with one child (n = 160) and a corrected split-half reliability of .69 for persons with more than one child (n = 268). The corrected split-half reliability for the total sample was .71.

VALIDITY: Stolka and Barnett (1969) found that several demographic variables related to scores on the Barnett Childbearing Attitudes Scale. Protestant women compared to Catholic women scored higher (less acceptance) on all four subscales, and women with more education compared to women with less education scored higher (less acceptance) on all four subscales. These relationships were more complex when other variables, such as income, age, and frequency of church attendance, were taken into account.

NOTES & COMMENTS: (1) The subscales form Guttman scales. Stolka and Barnett (1969) reported a coefficient of reproducibility of .95 for the religion subscale and coefficients of reproducibility of .96 for the other three subscales.

(2) Stolka and Barnett (1969) reported that the importance or acceptability of the four motivations is ranked in the following order, from most important to least important to women: woman's role obligation motivations, religious motivations, marital happiness motivations, and prestige motivations.

(3) The purpose of Kirkpatrick's (1978) study "was to develop, with the use of path analysis, and cross-validate a structural model for adjustment to parenthood. Two model states, primaparous and multiparous, were proposed" (p. 53). Kirkpatrick used the Barnett Childbearing

Attitudes Scale to measure one of the many variables used to develop the model.

AVAILABLE FROM: Stolka and Barnett, 1969

USED IN:

Kirkpatrick, S. W. (1978). Adjustment to parenthood: A structural model. *Genetic Psychology Monographs*, *98*, 51–82.

Stolka, S. M., & Barnett, L. D. (1969). Education and religion as factors in women's attitudes motivating childbearing. *Journal of Marriage and the Family*, *31*(4), 740–750.

BELL PARENTHOOD MOTIVATION SCALE

AUTHORS: J. Stephen Bell, John Bancroft, and Alistair Philip

DATE: 1985

VARIABLE: Reasons for and against having children

TYPE OF INSTRUMENT: Summated rating scale

DESCRIPTION: The Bell Parenthood Motivation Scale consists of 27 items representing three factors: 14 items pertain to the perceived advantages of having children, 12 items deal with the perceived disadvantages of having children, and 1 item concerns the importance of career in relation to children. Items are accompanied by five response options.

SAMPLE ITEMS: (perceived advantages) I feel having children makes a couple more stable and responsible.

   (perceived disadvantages) If we had children I should feel tied to the house.

   (career relationship) If I had children it would be less important for me to compete for success in my career.

PREVIOUS SUBJECTS: Husbands and wives in the United Kingdom

APPROPRIATE FOR: Childless, married persons

ADMINISTRATION: Self-administered; about 10 minutes

SCORING: Items are individually scored and summed to yield three factor scores. The agreement end of the continuum is assigned 1 point, and the disagreement end is assigned 5 points. Thus, the maximum score on the first factor is 70, the maximum score on the second factor is 60, and the maximum score on the third factor is 5. In all cases, higher scores mean greater agreement. On the first factor, it means greater agreement with the advantages; on the second factor, it means greater agreement with the disadvantages.

DEVELOPMENT: Based on a review of the relevant research and input acquired during interviews with hospital personnel, a pool of 77 items was generated, with items relating to the benefits as well as the costs associated with parenthood. Each item was accompanied by five response alternatives. This 77-item version of the scale was completed by 150 married couples. A frequency analysis of scores on each item led to the deletion of 17 items that had highly skewed distributions. Responses to the remaining 60 items were factor analyzed. Because there were significant sex differences on only 6 items, the responses of males and females were analyzed jointly. Three factors were extracted, and items with loadings over .40 on only one factor were retained.

RELIABILITY: Based on testing 150 couples, coefficient alpha was .77 for Factor 1 and .83 for Factor 2.

VALIDITY: When scores from infertility patients were compared with scores from persons attending a family planning clinic, it was found that the former group scored significantly lower on the first factor. In other words, the former group saw more advantages to having children. Furthermore, the infertility patients saw fewer disadvantages to having children.

NOTES & COMMENTS: (1) Bell, Bancroft, and Philip (1985) reported a correlation of − .07 between scores on Factor 1 and Factor 2.

(2) When separate factor analyses were performed for males and for females, Bell et al. (1985) concluded that "essentially the same factor structure emerged from both" (p. 117).

AVAILABLE FROM: Bell, Bancroft, and Philip, 1985

USED IN:

Bell, J. S., Bancroft, J., & Philip, A. (1985). Motivation for parenthood: A factor analytic study of attitudes towards having children. *Journal of Comparative Family Studies*, 16(1), 111–119.

HOLAHAN DECISION STRATEGIES

AUTHOR: Carole K. Holahan

DATE: 1983

VARIABLE: Process by which the decision was made to have or not to have children

TYPE OF INSTRUMENT: Summated rating scale

DESCRIPTION: The Holahan Decision Strategies scale is designed to identify the process by which one reaches a decision regarding whether to have a child. The scale consists of 18 items representing five subscales: Active Information Search (5 items), Impact on Goal Attainment (5 items), Nondecision (3 items), Impact on Future Satisfaction (3 items), and Impact on Others (2 items). Each item is accompanied by a 5-point scale ranging from "not at all characteristic of me" to "extremely characteristic of me."

SAMPLE ITEMS: (Active Information Search) I asked couples with children how they felt about their decision to have children.

(Impact on Goal Attainment) I thought about what things in life most mattered to me, and how having or not having children would affect my goals for myself.

(Nondecision) I decided to let fate make the decision.

(Impact on Future Satisfaction) I tried to imagine how I would feel several years from now if I did not have children.

(Impact on Others) I considered what others would be gaining or losing if I did or did not have children.

PREVIOUS SUBJECTS: Voluntarily childless women and mothers, over age 30, in the San Francisco area

APPROPRIATE FOR: Men or women who have made a decision to have or not have children

ADMINISTRATION: Self-administered; about 5–10 minutes

SCORING: Items are individually scored, with 1 point assigned to the "not at all characteristic of me" end of the continuum and 5 points assigned to the "extremely characteristic of me" end of the continuum. Item scores are summed to yield a score on each of the five factors.

DEVELOPMENT: The only information regarding development was that "five scales were constructed from these [18] items based on the results of a principal factor analysis with iteration" (Holahan, 1983, p. 529).

RELIABILITY: Using the responses from 85 women, coefficient alpha was computed for each subscale. The results were: Active Information Search = .77; Impact on Goal Attainment = .81; Nondecision = .67; Impact on Future Satisfaction = .68; and Impact on Others = .48.

VALIDITY: No information was provided.

NOTES & COMMENTS: (1) The internal consistency values were quite low, particularly for the last, very short subscale. Additional work should be done to lengthen the subscales and then determine if they are more reliable.

(2) Holahan (1983) used the scale to examine "the relationship between women's perceptions of the manner in which the decision concerning childbearing was made and present life satisfaction" (p. 528) for two groups of women: mothers and voluntarily childless women.

AVAILABLE FROM: Holahan, 1983

USED IN:

Holahan, C. K. (1983). The relationship between information search in the child-bearing decision and life satisfaction for parents and nonparents. *Family Relations, 32,*(4), 527–535.

INDEX OF PARENTHOOD MOTIVATION (IPM)

AUTHOR: Mary-Joan Gerson

DATE: 1978

VARIABLE: Intensity of the wish for a child

TYPE OF INSTRUMENT: The scale is composed of different item types, including ratings, rankings, and multiple choice items.

DESCRIPTION: The Index of Parenthood Motivation (IPM) consists of six component parts: (1) a question regarding one's eagerness to have children, with the answer recorded on a 9-point scale ranging from "not at all" to "more than anything"; (2) a ranking of the value, the creativity, and the interest associated with child raising relative to nine other activities, such as athletics, political activities, and teaching; (3) a rating of the appeal of six different stages of childbearing and child rearing; (4) five questions, some with two parts, regarding motivations to have children in the light of particular hardships, such as health risks or financial difficulties; (5) a rating of 11 possible role conflicts relating to having or not having children; and (6) a listing of 16 possible reasons for having children and 23 possible problems resulting from having children, each to be rated on a 4-point scale of importance.

SAMPLE ITEMS: (items from the first four components are described above)

(role conflicts) When a woman becomes pregnant she is no longer in control of her own body

(reasons for having children) to feel really useful and needed

(problems from having children) it makes it difficult to pursue a career

PREVIOUS SUBJECTS: Women, ages 18–41; males, ages 25–41; single and married persons

APPROPRIATE FOR: Persons in their childbearing years

ADMINISTRATION: Self-administered; about 30–45 minutes

SCORING: Scoring instructions are provided for each component of the IPM. The component scores are standardized and then summed to yield a total IPM score.

DEVELOPMENT: According to Gerson (1983), many portions of the IPM build on scales developed previously: "Components 1 and 2 were devised by Lott [1973]. The reasons profile of component 6 . . . was based on Kirchner's [1973] early factor-analytic work and the problems profile was Hoffman's and is based on an exploratory study of the parenthood motivation of college undergraduates [Hoffman, 1972]" (Gerson, 1983, p. 215).

RELIABILITY: Based on testing a sample of 184 unmarried college women, coefficient alpha was .85. When Component 5, role conflicts, was omitted, alpha increased to .89. Based on testing another sample of 113 childless women and 75 childless men, coefficient alpha was .89. Component 5 was not included when these persons were tested. For the first sample, the average intercorrelation among the six components was .49; for the second sample, it was .62.

VALIDITY: Gerson (1983) found that IPM scores were significantly related to memories of fathers' and mothers' being nurturing in early childhood and to identification with an organized religion. For college students, there was a significant relationship between IPM scores and Bem Sex Role Inventory (BSRI) (Bem, 1974) femininity scores (see separate entry), but there was not a significant relationship between IPM scores and BSRI masculinity or androgyny scores. Gerson (1983) also found a high positive correlation between desired number of children and IPM scores.

Gerson (1980) found that "positive memories of early childhood maternal love, traditional feminine sex-role identification and antifeminist sympathy were the primary unique psychological variables accounting for expressed desire for children" (p. 207). Memories of father's nurturance, perceptions of mother's success at child rearing, and childhood happiness also related to parenthood motivation.

Gerson (1984) found that support for the principles of the feminist movement was negatively related to parenthood motivation. For college women, mother's nurturing ability rather than father's was predictive of parenthood motivation.

Unlike the study just mentioned, Gerson (1986) found that support for the principles of the feminist movement was unrelated to parenthood motivation in a sample of older men and women. "Older" was defined to include persons between the ages of 21 and 42. Differences in men's scores were accounted for by differences in demographic variables.

NOTES & COMMENTS: (1) Gerson (1983) suggested that the evidence is sufficiently strong that Component 5, role conflict, should be eliminated from the scale.

(2) The IPM has the advantage of looking at parenthood motivation from a variety of directions. Most other measures of parenthood motivation involve only rating the various advantages and disadvantages associated with childbearing and child rearing.

AVAILABLE FROM: Mary-Joan Gerson, 27 West 72nd Street, Suite 812, New York, NY 10023

USED IN:

Gerson, M. (1978, August). *Motivations for motherhood*. Paper presented at the meeting of the American Psychological Association, Toronto. (ERIC Document Reproduction Service No. ED 184 010)

Gerson, M. (1980). The lure of motherhood. *Psychology of Women Quarterly*, 5(2), 207–218.

Gerson, M. (1983). A scale of motivation for parenthood: The Index of Parenthood Motivation. *Journal of Psychology, 113,* 211–220.

Gerson, M. (1984). Feminism and the wish for a child. *Sex Roles, 11*(5/6), 389–399.

Gerson, M. (1986). The prospect of parenthood for women and men. *Psychology of Women Quarterly, 10,* 49–62.

BIBLIOGRAPHY:

Bem, S. L. (1974). The measurement of psychological androgyny. *Journal of Consulting and Clinical Psychology, 42,* 155–162.

Hoffman, L. W. (1972). A psychological perspective on the value of children to parents. In J. T. Fawcett (Ed.), *The satisfactions and costs of children: Theories, concepts, methods.* Honolulu: East-West Population Institute.

Kirchner, E. P. (1973). *Reasons for wanting children: Factors and correlates.* Unpub-

lished paper, Institute for Research on Human Resources, Pennsylvania
State University.

Lott, B. E. (1973). Who wants the children? Some relationships among attitudes
toward children, parents and the liberation of women. *American Psychologist, 28*, 573–582.

PARENTHOOD MOTIVATION QUESTIONNAIRE

AUTHORS: W. Burleigh Seaver, Elizabeth P. Kirchner, Margret K.
Straw, and Maria E. Vegega

DATE: 1977

VARIABLE: Perceived costs and benefits of having children

TYPE OF INSTRUMENT: Summated rating scale

DESCRIPTION: There are two forms of the Parenthood Motivation
Questionnaire: a female form and a male form. The female form consists
of 53 positive statements (reasons for having a child) and 50 negative
statements (reasons for not having a child). The positive statements
represent 12 scales: Immortality (4 items), Experiencing the Birth Process
(5 items), Experiencing Love and Life's Fuller Meaning (5 items), Re-
membering and Reexperiencing Own Childhood (3 items), Old Age
Insurance (3 items), Partnership Benefits (2 items), Sculptor (7 items),
Opportunity for Personal Growth (5 items), Deeper Love (2 items), Fulfillment Through Nurturance (9 items), Sex Role Fulfillment (2 items),
and Stimulation and Feelings of Pride (4 items). The negative items
represent 10 scales: Social and Personal Restrictions (11 items), Concern
about Ability to Parent (7 items), Possibility of Defective Child (4 items),
Pessimistic World View (4 items), Financial Considerations (3 items),
Worries and Responsibilities of Rearing Child (4 items), Discomforts of
Childbearing (4 items), Population Concerns (4 items), Emotional Immaturity (4 items), and Education and Career Interference (5 items).

The male form consists of 48 positive statements (reasons for having
a child) and 48 negative statements (reasons for not having a child). The
positive scales are: Immortality (4 items), Experiencing the Birth Process
(3 items), Experiencing Love and Life's Fuller Meaning (10 items), Re-
membering and Reexperiencing Own Childhood (3 items), Old Age
Insurance (3 items), Partnership Benefits (2 items), Sculptor (7 items),
Pragmatism and Normative Behavior (9 items), Desire to be Needed and
Loved (3 items), Adding Interest to Family Life (2 items), and Fun (2
items). The negative scales are: Social and Personal Restrictions (11
items), Concern about Ability to Parent (8 items), Possibility of Defective
Child (4 items), Pessimistic World View (4 items), Financial Consider-
ation (3 items), Worries and Responsibilities of Rearing Child (5 items),
Discomforts of Childbearing (3 items), Population Concerns (4 items),
Emotional Immaturity (4 items), and Dangers of Childbirth (2 items).
On both the positive and negative subscales, each item is accompanied

by eight response options ranging from "extremely unimportant," to "extremely important."

SAMPLE ITEMS: (female form, positive motivation) To pass on my genes to a new generation.

(female form, negative motivation) Because children limit a couple's privacy.

(male form, positive motivation) To carry on the family business.

(male form, negative motivation) Because children would restrict my own growth and development.

PREVIOUS SUBJECTS: Men and women

APPROPRIATE FOR: Ages 16 and older

ADMINISTRATION: Self-administered; each form takes about 30–40 minutes

SCORING: Items are individually scored on an 8-point scale, with the "extremely unimportant" end of the continuum assigned 1 point and the "extremely important" end of the continuum assigned 8 points. Items on a given subscale are summed to yield a subscale score. Then all of the items on the positive subscales are summed to yield a measure of positive motivation or perceived benefits, and all of the items on the negative subscales are summed to yield a measure of negative motivation or perceived costs. A strength of motivation score is obtained by subtracting the negative total from the positive total. (Caution should be exercised in interpreting this difference on the female form because the scale has more positive than negative items.) Seaver, Kirchner, Straw, and Vegega (1977) reported means and standard deviations for each subscale on each form.

DEVELOPMENT: Item pools were generated based on a review of relevant research, previous research by one of the scale's authors, and college students' responses to a questionnaire asking for reasons for having and not having children. The item pools were reduced to 100 positive and 100 negative statements regarding having children. A sample of 245 males and 258 females rated the items on 8-point scales, and their responses were factor analyzed, separately by sex. A total of 18 positive and 12 negative factors were interpreted for females, and 17 positive and 12 negative factors were interpreted for males. The authors decided to include 12 positive and 10 negative motives for a female scale and 11 positive and 10 negative motives for a male scale. In selecting the motives, the results of the factor analysis were used. Single-item factors were deleted, as were factors accounting for less than 2% of the variance. The motives retained had items with higher loadings and higher mean importance ratings.

The following criteria were used to select items for the subscales: inclusion of items with high item-total correlations; selection of items with representative content; elimination of redundant items; elimination of items rated as extremely unimportant or having low variances; selection of items with high factor loadings; elimination of items that loaded above .40 on more than one factor.

RELIABILITY: Using data from 322 couples, Seaver et al. (1977) computed estimates of internal consistency reliability. For females, coefficient alpha was .97 for the positive motivation subscale and .95 for the negative motivation subscale. The subscale estimates ranged from .56 to .96. For males, coefficient alpha was .95 for both the positive and negative motivation subscales, and subscale reliabilities ranged from .58 to .96. For both males and females, the reliabilities of the negative motivation subscales tended to be higher than those for the positive motivation subscales.

VALIDITY: Content validity was built into the scale. Furthermore, Seaver et al. (1977) presented some evidence to support the construct validity of the scale. For both males and females, scores on the positive subscales and the total positive score were positively and significantly correlated with another, very different measure of parenthood motivation. And for both males and females, all but one negative subscale and the total negative score were negatively and significantly correlated with this other measure of parenthood motivation. The composite score on the Parenthood Motivation Questionnaire, obtained by subtracting the total negative score from the total positive score, was substantially related to scores on the second measure of parenthood motivation ($r =$ .70 for females and .65 for males). Seaver et al. reported moderate correlations between scale and subscale scores and several measures of fertility intentions.

NOTES & COMMENTS: (1) The factor analysis performed in conjunction with the scale's development included too few subjects per item to yield stable results.

(2) Some of the subscales are short and have low reliability. Caution should be exercised if these subscale scores are to be used.

(3) DeVellis, Wallston, and Acker (1984) used several measures, including the Parenthood Motivation Questionnaire, to compare voluntarily sterilized, child-free women, voluntarily sterilized women who had borne two children, and women experiencing their first pregnancy and happy about it.

AVAILABLE FROM: Seaver, Kirchner, Straw, and Vegega, 1977
USED IN:

DeVellis, B. M., Wallston, B. S., & Acker, D. (1984). Childfree by choice: Attitudes and adjustment of sterilized women. *Population and Environment*, 7(3), 152–162.

Seaver, W. B., Kirchner, E. P., Straw, M. K., & Vegega, M. E. (1977). Parenthood Motivation Questionnaire: Scales for measuring motivations for and against parenthood. *Catalog of Selected Documents in Psychology*, 7(3), 69. (Ms. No. 1519)

WESTBROOK SCALE OF POSITIVE AND NEGATIVE
ASPECTS OF CHILDBEARING
AUTHOR: Mary T. Westbrook
DATE: 1975
VARIABLE: Attitudes toward childbearing
TYPE OF INSTRUMENT: Summated rating scale
DESCRIPTION: The Westbrook Scale of Positive and Negative Aspects
of Childbearing consists of nine positive and nine negative categories.
The positive categories are: feelings of well-being, satisfaction from the
baby, wider family satisfactions, satisfactions concerning enhancement
of mother's femininity, value satisfactions, satisfactions to the marriage,
future satisfactions, traditional role domestic satisfactions, and growth
of maturity. The negative categories are: rejection, problems in labor,
fear of self, physical problems, problems concerning marriage, upsetting
environments, disturbed way of life, worries, and problems concerning
care of the baby. Each category is represented by some defining stimuli,
exemplars of the category.

To administer the scale, 18 cards are prepared, each displaying the
defining stimuli for one positive or one negative category. The title of
the category is not put on the card. The respondent is first shown each
negative card and told: "These cards list things that some people have
found stressful while they were having a baby or after it was born.
Consider each card as a whole and indicate whether you found them
very stressful, [stressful], slightly stressful, or not at all stressful" (Westbrook, 1979, p. 404). A similar procedure is followed in administering
the positive items, but the respondent is asked to label each one as "very
satisfying, satisfying, slightly satisfying, or not a source of satisfaction."
SAMPLE ITEMS: (positive category—feelings of well-being) Feeling of
physical well-being; the enjoyment of coping with a new experience;
makes you feel complete as a woman

(negative category—rejection) Embarrassment at baby's shortcomings;
disappointment at sex of child; pregnancy unwanted
PREVIOUS SUBJECTS: Australian women who had borne a baby during
the prior year
APPROPRIATE FOR: Women who have borne a baby in the prior year
ADMINISTRATION: The scale has been individually administered, but
it could be self-administered; completion time is about 10 minutes
SCORING: Items are scored on a 4-point scale, with 4 points assigned
to the "very stressful" or "very satisfying" end of the continuum and
1 point assigned to the "not a source of stress" or "not a source of
satisfaction" end of the continuum.
DEVELOPMENT: Westbrook (1975) performed several studies to determine how people classify the positive and negative aspects of childbearing. Using multidimensional scaling techniques, she came up with

the 18 categories used on the Westbrook Scale of Positive and Negative Aspects of Childbearing.
RELIABILITY: No information was provided.
VALIDITY: No information was provided.
NOTES & COMMENTS: (1) The three Westbrook articles listed below report information from the same data set, obtained from a sample of 200 women in Sydney, Australia. All of the women had borne a child within the prior 2 to 7 months. The women completed the Westbrook Scale of Positive and Negative Aspects of Childbearing, as well as several other measures. For example, the women told stories in response to a stimulus picture showing a woman with a baby, and their responses were content analyzed. The articles below analyze 30 experiential variables in terms of three different independent variables: parity (Westbrook, 1978a), quality of marital relationship (Westbrook, 1978b), and socioeconomic status (Westbrook, 1979). The 30 experiential variables include the nine positive and nine negative items of the Westbrook scale.
   (2) Before this scale is used again, its reliability and validity need to be demonstrated.
AVAILABLE FROM: Westbrook, 1978a, 1978b, 1979
USED IN:
Westbrook, M. T. (1978a). The effect of the order of a birth on women's experience of childbearing. *Journal of Marriage and the Family, 40*(1), 165–172.
Westbrook, M. T. (1978b). The reactions to child-bearing and early maternal experience of women with differing marital relationships. *British Journal of Medical Psychology, 51*, 191–199.
Westbrook, M. T. (1979). Socioeconomic differences in coping with childbearing. *American Journal of Community Psychology, 7*(4), 397–412.
BIBLIOGRAPHY:
Westbrook, M. T. (1975). *Analyzing people's experience of events: A study of the childbearing years.* Unpublished doctoral dissertation, Macquarie University, Sydney, Australia.

ALPERT RICHARDSON STRESSFUL EVENTS IN PARENTING
AUTHORS: Judith L. Alpert and Mary Sue Richardson
DATE: 1978
VARIABLE: Sources of stress for new parents
TYPE OF INSTRUMENT: Checklist
DESCRIPTION: The Alpert Richardson Stressful Events in Parenting scale is a listing of 21 events that new parents may experience as stressful. The respondent's task is to check all of the applicable items.
SAMPLE ITEMS: Physical complications within one month after childbirth and related to childbirth (e.g., excessive bleeding, infections, etc.)
   Feeding problems
PREVIOUS SUBJECTS: Parents

APPROPRIATE FOR: Parents of young children

ADMINISTRATION: Self-administered; about 5 minutes

SCORING: Because Alpert, Richardson, and Fodaski (1978) did not present the stressful events as a scale, there is no mention of scoring. They do, however, provide five average weightings for each stressful event. The average weightings refer to the ratings assigned by the total group of 63 parents and by each of the four subgroups: working mothers, nonworking mothers, fathers with working wives, and fathers with nonworking wives.

DEVELOPMENT: Thirty-five parents, all of whom had at least one child below the age of 5, were individually interviewed and asked to list what they found stressful about parenting. They were prompted to list daily events, as well as more dramatic ones. The stressful events they named were listed on cards and sorted into categories based on item content. There were a total of 26 categories, and 21 of them included an event(s) listed by at least 10 of the 35 interviewees. A summary stressful event was derived to represent each of these 21 categories. For example, "some [respondents] indicated that their in-laws were intrusive while others indicated that their in-laws were not helpful. . . . From this category . . . the stressful event 'interference from in-laws related to child' was derived" (Alpert et al., 1978). Another sample of 63 parents with one or more children under age 5 was asked to rank the 21 events in terms of the amount of change the events would produce in an adult's usual way of life. After arranging the cards from most change to least change, the parents were asked to rate each change on a 100-point scale, with 1 meaning "no change" and 100 meaning "total change." The responses from these parents were used to develop weights for each of the stressful events.

RELIABILITY: During the scale development, 63 parents rated the 21 stressful events. The parents represented four groups: working mothers, nonworking mothers, fathers with working wives, and fathers with nonworking wives. Intraclass correlations were computed to determine if there was consistency in the ratings within the four groups. The coefficients ranged from .81 to .92. The intraclass correlation coefficient for the entire group of 63 parents was .85.

VALIDITY: Content validity can be presumed because of the method of scale development that was used.

A nonparametric test was used to determine whether there were any significant differences in the way the four groups of parents ranked the potential stressors. There were significant differences for two items: "frequent conflictual demands between needs for self and child" and "frequent minor illnesses of child."

NOTES & COMMENTS: Although Alpert et al. (1978) suggested that "the list [of stressors] could be used to further research on parenting"

(p. 12), they did not represent their items as a scale. Nevertheless, it seems that the ranked items and associated weightings have potential for assessing stress levels in new parents.

AVAILABLE FROM: Alpert, Richardson, and Fodaski, 1978
USED IN:
Alpert, J. L., Richardson, M. S., & Fodaski, L. (1978). *Onset of parenting and stressful events*. Unpublished paper. (ERIC Document Reproduction Service No. ED 169 452)

CLEMINSHAW-GUIDUBALDI PARENT SATISFACTION SCALE

AUTHORS: John Guidubaldi and Helen K. Cleminshaw
DATE: 1985
VARIABLE: Satisfaction with various aspects of the parenting role
TYPE OF INSTRUMENT: Summated rating scale
DESCRIPTION: The Cleminshaw-Guidubaldi Parent Satisfaction Scale consists of 50 items, with 10 items representing each of 5 factors: Spouse Support, Child-Parent Relationship, Parent Performance, Family Discipline and Control, and General Satisfaction. Each item is accompanied by four response options: "strongly agree, agree, disagree, strongly disagree." Some items are phrased to reflect satisfaction with the parenting role; other items are phrased to reflect dissatisfaction.
SAMPLE ITEMS: (Spouse Support) I feel good about the amount of involvement my spouse has with my children.

   (Child-Parent Relationship) I am satisfied with the way my children treat me.

   (Parent Performance) I wish I did not become impatient so quickly with my children.

   (Family Discipline and Control) All my spouse does is yell at the children which displeases me.

   (General Satisfaction) Being a parent has brought me a lot of work and heartaches.
PREVIOUS SUBJECTS: Fathers and mothers, ages 21 to 71
APPROPRIATE FOR: Parents
ADMINISTRATION: Self-administered; about 20 minutes
SCORING: Items are individually scored on a 4-point scale, with higher scores assigned to the response indicating greater satisfaction. Item scores are summed to yield five factor scores and an overall total score. Guidubaldi and Cleminshaw (1985) reported means and standard deviations for the five factors.
DEVELOPMENT: A pool of 250 items was developed from two sources. First, 100 adults were asked to list three factors that contributed to satisfaction in parenting and three factors that contributed to dissatisfaction in parenting. Their responses were used to develop items. Second, ex-

isting scales were reviewed to identify potentially relevant items. The 250-item pool was administered to a sample of 35 parents. They were asked to react to each item using four response options: "strongly agree, agree, disagree, strongly disagree." They were also asked to indicate how relevant the items were and to provide feedback for improving the wording of the items. In addition, three child and family development experts provided information on the face validity of the items. These procedures led to the deletion of some items and the revision of others. The changes resulted in a 211-item version of the scale.

The scale was administered to 130 parents, and their responses were factor analyzed. Five factors were identified, and 10 items with the highest factor loadings were selected for each factor.

RELIABILITY: Coefficient alpha was computed for each of the subscale scores and the total score. The results were as follows: Spouse Support = .93; Child-Parent Relationship = .86; Parent Performance = .83; Family Discipline and Control = .82; General Satisfaction = .76; and total score = .93.

VALIDITY: Husbands scored higher (more satisfied) than wives on Factor 1, Spouse Support. Married persons also scored higher (more satisfied) than single persons on Spouse Support. The authors concluded that "the spouse support scale nonetheless appears relevant to single parents, as a great deal of diversity exists in parenting arrangements among divorced spouses (i.e., joint custody, visitation privileges, etc.)" (Guidubaldi & Cleminshaw, 1985, p. 297). No significant relationships were found between factor scores and "age, employment status, retirement, years of schooling, income, number of children, years of marriage, remarriage, natural versus adoptive parents status, or religion" (p. 296).

Guidubaldi and Cleminshaw (1985) administered their Parent Satisfaction Scale along with two measures of life satisfaction and two measures of marital satisfaction. As predicted, factor scores and total scores on the Parent Satisfaction Scale were generally significantly related to all four satisfaction measures.

NOTES & COMMENTS: (1) It is not clear how Guidubaldi and Cleminshaw (1985) conducted a factor analysis since it appears that they had 211 items and only 130 subjects.

(2) The factor analytic results do not seem logical. Factor 1 is called Spouse Support, but most of the items pertain to satisfaction with, or approval of, the parenting done by the respondent's spouse. Factor 3 is called Parent Performance, but some of the items pertain directly to discipline, which is a different factor—for example, "I feel uncomfortable with the way I often discipline my children." Factor 4 is called Family Discipline and Control, but it is difficult to see how some of the items pertain to this construct—for example, "My parents gave me good advice on how to be a good parent." Furthermore, several of the items loading

on Factor 4 seem to relate logically to the items on Factor 1, Spouse Support—for example, "I am satisfied with my spouse's childrearing skills" loads on Factor 1, while "I wish my spouse displayed more consistent parenting skills" loads on Factor 4.

(3) The authors reported the intercorrelations among the five subscale scores.

(4) After discussing the implications of their scale development, Guidubaldi and Cleminshaw (1985) concluded: "While showing promise at this stage of development for clinical applications, the scale requires considerable work; therefore, we recommend that clinicians and counselors use it primarily as an experimental research tool.

AVAILABLE FROM: Guidubaldi and Cleminshaw, 1985

USED IN:

Guidubaldi, J., & Cleminshaw, H. K. (1985). The development of the Cleminshaw-Guidubaldi Parent Satisfaction Scale. *Journal of Clinical Child Psychology*, 14(4), 293–298.

TRANSITION DIFFICULTY

AUTHOR: Renee Hoffman Steffensmeier

DATE: 1977

VARIABLE: Degree of difficulty in the transition to parenthood during the first 3 to 6 months after the baby's birth

TYPE OF INSTRUMENT: Multiple choice

DESCRIPTION: The Transition Difficulty scale consists of 25 items that represent three factors. There are 8 items on the Parental Responsibilities and Restrictions factor. These items focus on the impact of the baby's birth on the life-style of the couple; many of the items relate to changes in the parents' daily living arrangements and leisure activities. The Parental Gratifications factor consists of 10 items that relate to the rewards of parenthood and the changes that take place in one's self-concept. There are 7 items on the Marital Intimacy and Stability factor, most relating to worries that spouses have regarding the quality of their relationship in the future. Each of the 25 items on the scale is presented following one of five stems. For example, 7 items follow the stem: "For each item in the list I'm going to read I'd like to know first, how much change there has been since the baby came and how you feel about this change: are you enthusiastic (1), satisfied (2), doesn't matter (3), somewhat dissatisfied (4), or very dissatisfied (5) with the change?" (Steffensmeier, 1982, p. 323).

SAMPLE ITEMS: (All samples follow the stem given above.)

(Parental Responsibilities and Restrictions) Getting together with friends

(Parental Gratifications) Attention you get from mate

(Marital Intimacy and Stability) Understanding you receive from spouse

PREVIOUS SUBJECTS: Married parents of babies 13 to 21 weeks old

APPROPRIATE FOR: Married parents of babies

ADMINISTRATION: Though the scale items were originally part of a large questionnaire administered by a personal interview, the items could be adapted for self-administration. When self-administered, the scale would take about 10 minutes to complete.

SCORING: Steffensmeier (1982) suggested a scoring system that involves weighting each item proportionally to its involvement in a factor pattern and obtaining scores on each of the three factors. She provided the necessary weights. When her scoring model is followed, high scores on Parental Responsibilities and Restrictions reflect greater difficulty or increased responsibilities and restrictions; low scores on Parental Gratifications reflect fewer gratifications; and low scores on Marital Intimacy and Stability reflect more marital problems or less marital intimacy.

DEVELOPMENT: Scale development began with the generation of a large item pool including items adapted from other studies, as well as items constructed specifically for the current study. The items were both objective and subjective in nature; the distinction between the objective and subjective is the difference between noting whether an event occurred (objective) and how the individual perceived the event (subjective). After individual interviews were held to administer the questionnaire to both partners from 54 married couples, the 78 subjective items in the questionnaire were factor analyzed. "Factor analysis was used to delete items that were overlapping and thus highly correlated with each other, items with low communalities, and items with obscure factor loadings" (Steffensmeier, 1982, p. 322). The set of 25 items that remained were factor analyzed, and "after some trial and error, these items were forced into three factors" (p. 322).

RELIABILITY: Steffensmeier (1982) reported coefficient alpha for each factor score: Parental Responsibilities and Restrictions = .75; Parental Gratifications = .82; and Marital Intimacy and Stability = .76.

VALIDITY: Steffensmeier (1982) proposed a model and five hypotheses regarding the relationship between the difficulty in the transition to parenthood and numerous other variables. She concluded that "the proposed model was more successful in explaining the variance in PRR [Parental Responsibilities and Restrictions] than in PG [Parental Gratifications] or MIS [Marital Intimacy and Stability]" (p. 319). A greater percentage of the variance in Parental Gratifications was explained when other variables—planfulness, value of children, and length of marriage—were added to the model.

According to Steffensmeier (1982), sex is consistently related to transition difficulty.

NOTES & COMMENTS: (1) The factor analysis performed in conjunction with the scale's development included too few subjects for the number of items in the analysis.

(2) Correlations between the factor scores were rather low, ranging from −.19 (Parental Responsibilities and Restrictions correlated with Parental Gratifications) to +.16 (Parental Gratifications correlated with Marital Intimacy and Stability) (Steffensmeier, 1982).

(3) Steffensmeier (1982) provided correlations between the three factor scores and numerous other variables, including sex, education, perceived role conflict, role clarity, and anticipatory socialization (preparation for parenting). Furthermore, she examined the relative importance of these variables in predicting the difficulty in transition to parenthood.

(4) Items would be clearer if they were rephrased and not grouped under sentence stems. For example, the first sample item given above could be rewritten as: "Compared to your life before the birth of the baby, how satisfied are you now with how much you get together with friends." Of course, one cannot assume that reliability and validity data for the scale as it currently exists would apply equally to a revised set of items.

(5) Pistrang (1984) used items from the Transition Difficulty scale along with items from several other scales to study the relationships between women's work involvement prior to pregnancy and their experience of new motherhood. Myers-Walls (1984) used the 25 items of the Transition Difficulty scale in a study of women's use of various coping strategies to balance new parenthood with four other roles: outside employment, social life, marriage, and housekeeping. Myers-Walls (1984) obtained "an overall Adjustment to Parenthood score and six subscale scores: (1) Freedom from Changes, (2) Acceptance of Changes, (3) Joys, (4) Marital Satisfactions and Harmony, (5) Freedom from Parental Responsibilities and Restrictions, and (6) Freedom from Childrearing Anxiety" (p. 269). She obtained alpha coefficients ranging from .59 to .82 for the six subscales.

AVAILABLE FROM: Steffensmeier, 1982

USED IN:

Myers-Walls, J. A. (1984). Balancing multiple role responsibilities during the transition to parenthood. *Family Relations, 33*(2), 267–271.

Pistrang, N. (1984). Women's work involvement and experience of new motherhood. *Journal of Marriage and the Family, 46,* 433–447.

Steffensmeier, R. H. (1982). A role model of the transition to parenthood. *Journal of Marriage and the Family, 44*(2), 319–334.

MATERNAL SELF-DEFINITION QUESTIONNAIRE (MSDQ)

AUTHORS: Diane Ruble, Jeanne Brooks-Gunn, Alison Fleming, Garrett Fitzmaurice, Charles Stangor, and Francine Deutsch

DATE: 1981
VARIABLE: Maternal self-definition
TYPE OF INSTRUMENT: Summated rating scale
DESCRIPTION: The Maternal Self-Definition Questionnaire (MSDQ) consists of a list of 27 behaviors and traits reflecting five aspects of mothering: Fun (7 items), Involved Mom (7 items), Traditional Mom (6 items), Protective Mom (3 items), and Knowledgeable Mom (4 items). All of the behaviors and traits are phrased to reflect good mothering qualities. Women rate the extent to which they are likely to exhibit each behavior and attribute; a 5-point rating scale is provided, with endpoints labeled "not at all" and "extremely."
SAMPLE ITEMS: (Fun Mom) Getting enjoyment out of life
   (Involved Mom) Preparing all baby foods at home
   (Traditional Mom) Devoted to homemaking
   (Protective Mom) Protecting the child from harm
   (Knowledgeable Mom) Knowledge of child development
PREVIOUS SUBJECTS: Married women either planning to get pregnant for the first time or currently pregnant for the first time and women who recently gave birth for the first time
APPROPRIATE FOR: Females, ages 16 and older
ADMINISTRATION: Self-administered; about 10–15 minutes
SCORING: Items are individually scored on a 5-point scale and summed to yield scores on each of the five subscales. A single score can also be used.
DEVELOPMENT: A list of 47 behaviors and traits presumed to reflect good mothering was given to a sample of more than 600 prepregnant, pregnant, or postpartum women who rated the items for themselves. Their responses were factor analyzed, and the results of the factor analysis were used to build the scale.
RELIABILITY: Using responses from about 650 women, Ruble et al. (1988) computed coefficient alpha for each of the subscales. The results were: Fun Mom = .71; Involved Mom = .69; Traditional Mom = .68; Protective Mom = .68; and Knowledgeable Mom = .69. Ruble et al. also reported coefficient alpha for three subsets of women: prepregnant, pregnant, and postpartum. The coefficients ranged from .59 to .73.
   A longitudinal study (Ruble et al., 1988) involved testing women during pregnancy and again 3 months postpartum. The correlations between the two testings were significant ($p < .001$) for all five subscales. They ranged from .56 to .78.
VALIDITY: Ruble et al. (1988) found that the covariance structures for the subscales were the same across the different groups of women. The researchers also found that a single higher-order factor, positive aspects of mothering, best described the MSDQ across the childbearing groups.
   When comparing women in the three groups—prepregnancy, preg-

nancy, and postpartum—Ruble et al. (1988) found a significant linear increase in scores on two subscales: Protective Mom and Involved Mom. NOTES & COMMENTS: (1) The alpha coefficients were low, perhaps in part because the subscales are short. Some consideration should be given to lengthening the subscales.

(2) A large sample of women in Toronto, Seattle, and the New York area provided the data for developing the MSDQ and exploring some of its psychometric properties. Deutsch, Ruble, Fleming, Brooks-Gunn, and Stangor (1988) reported research using a portion of these same data to study the self-definitional processes that accompany the transition to motherhood. The researchers were particularly interested in how information-seeking behaviors relate to the development of maternal self-definition.

AVAILABLE FROM: Diane Ruble, Department of Psychology, New York University, Washington Square, New York, NY 10003
USED IN:

Deutsch, F. M., Ruble, D. N., Fleming, A., Brooks-Gunn, J., & Stangor, C. S. (1988). Information-seeking and maternal self-definition during the transition to motherhood. *Journal of Personality and Social Psychology, 55,* 420–431.

Ruble, D. N., Brooks-Gunn, J., Fleming, A. S., Fitzmaurice, G., Stangor, C., & Deutsch, F. (1988). *Comparability of attitude constructs and self-definitional change across phases of childbearing.* Manuscript submitted for publication.

MATERNAL SEPARATION ANXIETY SCALE

AUTHORS: Ellen Hock, M. Therese Gnezda, and Susan McBride
DATE: 1982
VARIABLE: Maternal separation anxiety defined as "an unpleasant emotional state reflecting a mother's apprehension about leaving her child" (Hock, 1984, p. 18)
TYPE OF INSTRUMENT: Summated rating scale
DESCRIPTION: The Maternal Separation Anxiety Scale is composed of 35 items representing three subscales: Subscale 1, titled Maternal Separation Anxiety, consists of 21 items pertaining to the mother's negative feelings associated with leaving her child and her beliefs regarding the importance of exclusive maternal care; Subscale 2, titled Perception of Separation Effects on the Child, consists of 7 items pertaining to the mother's perceptions of her child's ability to adjust when the mother is absent; and Subscale 3, titled Employment-Related Separation Concerns, consists of 7 items dealing with beliefs about the balance between motherhood and career. Each item is accompanied by five response alternatives: "strongly disagree, disagree, somewhat agree, agree, strongly agree."
SAMPLE ITEMS: (Maternal Separation Anxiety) When I am away from my child, I feel lonely and miss him/her a great deal.

(Perception of Separation Effects on the Child) Exposure to many different people is good for my child.

(Employment-Related Separation Concerns) I would resent my job if it meant I had to be away from my child.

PREVIOUS SUBJECTS: Mothers and fathers of children from birth through kindergarten

APPROPRIATE FOR: Mothers of children from birth through kindergarten. With slight modifications in the wording, the scale can also be used with fathers, but the career versus homemaking items on Subscale 3 are not meaningful for fathers.

ADMINISTRATION: Self-administered; about 15 minutes

SCORING: Items are individually scored on a 5-point scale and summed to yield three subscale scores. For Subscale 1, the total is divided by 3. Thus, all subscale scores range from 7 to 35. Higher scores on Subscale 1 reflect more anxiety regarding separation and stronger beliefs about the importance of exclusive maternal care. Higher scores on Subscale 2 reflect the belief that children do not benefit from the separation and will have difficulty adapting to it. Higher scores on Subscale 3 reflect high anxiety about leaving the child in order to pursue outside employment.

DEVELOPMENT: Scale development began by identifying factors that underlie a mother's feelings about leaving her child. Four factors were presumed to influence maternal separation anxiety: the mother's personality traits and needs that lead her to feel sad, fearful, or depressed about leaving her child; the mother's belief that she is uniquely able to provide high-quality care for her child; the mother's perceptions of her child's ability to handle the mother's absence; and the mother's belief about the desired relationship between motherhood and career. A pool of 68 items developed to reflect these various issues relating to maternal anxiety was administered to 620 mothers of firstborn children. Their scores were correlated with scores on two other measures: a measure of generalized anxiety and a measure of the tendency to give socially desirable responses. The correlation between maternal anxiety and generalized anxiety was .34; the correlation between maternal anxiety and social desirability was −.39. The negative correlation with social desirability was predictable. Given that these initial analyses were encouraging, responses to the 68 items were factor analyzed. Three factors were extracted, and the 19 items that failed to load on any of the factors were deleted from the item pool. Item analyses were performed with the remaining 49 items, and an additional 14 items were eliminated from the scale. Responses to the remaining 35 items were factor analyzed, and three factors were extracted. These factors determined the three subscales.

RELIABILITY: A group of over 600 new mothers completed the Maternal

Separation Anxiety Scale while they were still in the maternity ward of the hospital. A sample of 400 women completed the scale a second time, 3 months later. Using the first set of responses obtained from the mothers, coefficient alpha for each of the three subscales was .90, .71, and .79. Coefficient alpha for the full 35-item scale was .88. Using the second set of responses from the mothers, the alpha coefficients for Subscales 1–3 were .91, .72, and .81, respectively. For the full scale, coefficient alpha was .90. Test-retest reliabilities were .73, .58, .72, and .75 for Subscales 1, 2, and 3, and the full scale, respectively.

Hock, DeMeis, and McBride (1988) administered the Maternal Separation Anxiety Scale to a sample of 130 mothers on four occasions: 2 days postpartum, 7 weeks postpartum, 8 months postpartum, and 14 months postpartum. For adjacent administrations (i.e., Time 1 with Time 2, or Time 3 with Time 4) the test-retest correlations were above .70 for Subscale 1, above .55 for Subscale 2, and above .75 for Subscale 3. When scores obtained 7 weeks postpartum were compared with scores obtained when the child was 14 months, the correlations were .67, .52, and .62 for Subscales 1, 2, and 3, respectively.

On two occasions, Pitzer (1985) tested 40 mothers with the Maternal Separation Anxiety Scale. The mothers were first tested when their first-born was 7 months old; they were tested again when their second-born was 7 months old. The correlations between the two testings were .49, .55, and .55 for Subscales 1, 2, and 3, respectively.

VALIDITY: Hock, McBride, and Gnezda (1989) obtained multiple measures of maternal separation anxiety from a sample of 36 new mothers who were not currently employed. Subscale 1 from the Maternal Separation Anxiety Scale provided one measure of maternal separation anxiety. The researchers found significant, positive correlations between Subscale 1 scores and each of the following: Emotional Status Index, which measures "the degree of separation anxiety a mother experiences with respect to a specific brief separation event" (Hock et al., 1989, p. 15) ($r = .77$); an interview measure of maternal separation anxiety ($r = .79$); and a measure rating the mother's behavior with her child when they are reunited ($r = .40$). A measure rating the mother's behavior with her child when she is separating from the child was not significantly correlated with Subscale 1 scores.

Martin-Huff (1983) found that fathers scored similarly to mothers on Subscales 1 and 2. She also found an inverse relationship between mothers' anxiety scores and children's adjustment; that is, mothers with higher Maternal Separation Anxiety scores were more likely to have children with lower adjustment scores.

NOTES & COMMENTS: (1) Hock et al. (1988) reported results from a longitudinal study that examined Maternal Separation Anxiety scores over a period of 3 ½ years and related scores to numerous other variables, including feelings about employment and choice of nonmaternal care.

(2) DeMeis, Hock, and McBride (1986) reported that the factor structure of the Maternal Separation Anxiety Scale was sufficiently stable. Using data collected about 3 months apart, "the coefficients of congruence were 1.0 for Factor 1, .987 for Factor 2, and .996 for Factor 3" (p. 628).

(3) DeMeis et al. (1986) used the Maternal Separation Anxiety Scale as one measure in a study examining how "older, well-educated mothers of infants come to terms with establishing a balance between maternal and career roles" (p. 627).

AVAILABLE FROM: Hock, McBride, & Gnezda (in press)
USED IN:

DeMeis, D. K., Hock, E., & McBride, S. L. (1986). The balance of employment and motherhood: Longitudinal study of mothers' feelings about separation from their first-born infants. *Developmental Psychology, 22*(5), 627–632.

Hock, E. (1984). The transition to day care: Effects of maternal separation anxiety on infant adjustment. In R. Ainslie (Ed.), *The child and the day care setting: Qualitative variations and development.* New York: Praeger.

Hock, E., DeMeis, D., & McBride, S. (1988). Maternal separation anxiety: Its role in the balance of employment and motherhood in mothers of infants. In A. Gottfried & A. Gottfried (Eds.), *Maternal employment and children's development: Longitudinal research* (pp. 191–227). New York: Plenum.

Hock, E., McBride, S., & Gnezda, M. T. (1989). Maternal separation anxiety: Mother-infant separation from the maternal perspective. *Child Development, 60,* 793–802.

Martin-Huff, E. (1983). Parental and contextual influences on children's early adjustment to kindergarten. (Doctoral dissertation, Ohio State University, Columbus, 1982). *Dissertation Abstracts International, 44,* 66A.

Pitzer, M. (1985). A study of maternal separation anxiety in working mothers of second-born infants. (Doctoral dissertation, Ohio State University, Columbus, 1984). *Dissertation Abstracts International, 46,* 88A.

MATERNAL SOCIAL SUPPORT INDEX (MSSI)

AUTHORS: John M. Pascoe, Frank A. Loda, Valerie Jeffries, and Jo Anne Earp

DATE: 1981

VARIABLE: Maternal social support

TYPE OF INSTRUMENT: Structured interview

DESCRIPTION: The Maternal Social Support Index (MSSI) consists of seven items, some with several parts. The first item asks 10 questions about home responsibilities; for example, "Who fixes things around the house?" The answer to each question is coded in terms of three options: no one does the task, only the mother does the task, or the mother and/

or someone else does the task. The second item asks about the number of relatives seen each week and the respondent's satisfaction with this number. The third item includes only 1 question: "How many people can you count on in time of need?" The fourth and fifth items are also single-question items; one relates to neighborhood support for child care, and the other pertains to satisfaction with mate. The sixth item poses 3 questions about other persons, over age 14, in the household. The last item contains 3 questions about participation in religious, social, educational, and political organizations.

PREVIOUS SUBJECTS: Mothers of preschool children

APPROPRIATE FOR: Mothers

ADMINISTRATION: The MSSI is administered by a trained interviewer. The questions might be embedded in a longer structured interview or may be asked alone. If asked alone, it would take about 15–20 minutes to complete the scale.

SCORING: Pascoe, Loda, Jeffries, and Earp (1981) provide instructions for scoring each item. The item scores are summed to yield a total score that can range from 0 (no social support) to 19 (maximum social support).

DEVELOPMENT: Most of the original questions on the MSSI were modifications of questions used on other measures. Items were selected for the MSSI if they appeared to be compatible with another measure, the Inventory of Home Stimulation, and if they related to a recently published social network index (Berkman & Syme, 1979). Regression analysis, regressing Inventory of Home Stimulation items on MSSI items, was used to select the final set of items for the MSSI.

RELIABILITY: No information was provided.

VALIDITY: To obtain evidence of the construct validity of the MSSI, Pascoe, Walsh-Clifford, and Earp (1982) administered the scale to a group of mothers who had involvement with protective services and to a second group of mothers from the same socioeconomic class who were not involved with protective services. As predicted, the mothers who were involved with protective services had lower MSSI scores; that is, they had less social support.

NOTES & COMMENTS: All of the articles listed below studied the relationship between MSSI scores and various indicators of child-rearing ability, particularly provision of a good, stimulating environment.

AVAILABLE FROM: Pascoe, Loda, Jeffries, and Earp, 1981

USED IN:

Adamakos, H., Ryan, K., Ullman, D., Diaz, R., Pascoe, J., & Chessare, J. (1985, May). *Maternal social support as a predictor of mother/child stress and child home stimulation in high risk families.* Paper presented at the meeting of the Midwestern Psychological Association, Chicago. (ERIC Document Reproduction Service No. ED 257 289)

Pascoe, J. M., & Earp, J. A. (1984). The effect of mothers' social support and life changes on the stimulation of their children in the home. *American Journal of Public Health, 74*(4), 358–360.

Pascoe, J. M., Loda, F. A., Jeffries, V., & Earp, J. A. (1981). The association between mothers' social support and provision of stimulation to their children. *Developmental and Behavioral Pediatrics, 2*(1), 15–19.

Pascoe, J. M., Walsh-Clifford, N., & Earp, J. A. (1982). Construct validity of a Maternal Social Support Scale. *Developmental and Behavioral Pediatrics, 3*(2), 122.

Ryan, K., Adamakos, H., Ullman, D., Diaz, R., Pascoe, J., & Chessare, J. (1985, April). *Maternal social support systems moderating levels of mother/child stress and home stimulation.* Paper presented at the meeting of the Ohio Psychological Association. (ERIC Document Reproduction Service No. ED 257 590)

Ryan, K., Ullman, D., Adamakos, H., Diaz, R., Pascoe, J., & Chessare, J. (1985, April). *Environmental correlates of optimal child development: A look at the maternal social support system moderating levels of mother/child stress and home stimulation.* Paper presented at the meeting of the Ohio Psychological Association. (ERIC Document Reproduction Service No. ED 261 771)

BIBLIOGRAPHY:

Berkman, L. F., & Syme, S. L. (1979). Social networks, host resistance, and mortality: A nine-year follow-up study of Alameda County residents. *American Journal of Epidemiology, 109*, 186–204.

MOTHERHOOD INVENTORY

AUTHORS: Rachel T. Hare-Mustin and Patricia C. Broderick

DATE: 1979

VARIABLE: Attitudes toward motherhood and toward selected women's issues

TYPE OF INSTRUMENT: Summated rating scale

DESCRIPTION: The Motherhood Inventory consists of 40 items covering a variety of topics: "decisions about having children, birth control, pregnancy, delivery, breastfeeding, abortion, adoption, single motherhood, sexuality, promiscuity, child-rearing responsibility, and personal fulfillment" (Hare-Mustin & Broderick, 1979). Attitudes are expressed using a 4-point scale with the options "agree strongly, agree mildly, disagree mildly, disagree strongly."

SAMPLE ITEMS: Women should give up their children for adoption if they don't want to raise a child.

Breastfeeding in public should be acceptable even in front of strangers.

PREVIOUS SUBJECTS: College students; mental health professionals

APPROPRIATE FOR: Ages 16 and older

ADMINISTRATION: Self-administered; about 15–20 minutes

SCORING: According to R. Hare-Mustin (personal communication, March 1989), the Motherhood Inventory is a series of items, not truly a scale, and therefore no overall score is computed. However, one article (Hare-Mustin & Lamb, 1984) that reported on the use of the Motherhood

Inventory mentions four subscales: Male-Female Relations, Abortion, Maternal Instinct, and Women's Control Over Reproduction. Two of the four subscales are considered sufficiently homogeneous to use.

DEVELOPMENT: An initial item pool was developed using information from sentence completions to motherhood stems and using information from the literature on gender roles and mothering. Inputs from 12 judges were used to develop the final version of the scale. More specific information on scale development is not provided.

RELIABILITY: Because the Motherhood Inventory is not truly a scale, the authors did not discuss reliability of scores. In fact, the only mention of reliability is in regard to the reliability of two subscales. Coefficient alpha for a 7-item Maternal Instinct subscale was .76. Coefficient alpha for a 5-item Male-Female Relations subscale was .97.

VALIDITY: A sample of about 300 college students completed the Motherhood Inventory and the 25-item version of the Attitudes Toward Women Scale (AWS) (Spence, Helmreich, & Stapp, 1973) (see separate entry). AWS scores were significantly correlated with 32 of the 40 items on the Motherhood Inventory. The strongest correlations were the negative correlations between AWS scores and items of the Motherhood Inventory relating to the idealization of motherhood. That is, respondents who were profeminist as reflected on the AWS were less likely to idealize motherhood.

In another study (Hare-Mustin, Bennett, & Broderick, 1983), college students and adults completed the Motherhood Inventory and the short form of the AWS. When items from the two scales were jointly factor analyzed, the items from the AWS loaded on a different factor than did the items of the Motherhood Inventory.

NOTES & COMMENTS: (1) The item content on the Motherhood Inventory is unusually diverse.

(2) Hare-Mustin et al. (1983) factor analyzed responses to the Motherhood Inventory. They performed a separate factor analysis for each of three groups (younger men, younger women, and older women) and obtained different factor structures from each analysis; however, all sample sizes were small ($n = 98$, $n = 120$, $n = 56$).

(3) Hare-Mustin and Lamb (1984) used the Motherhood Inventory to compare the attitudes of counselors that specialized in family therapy and other nonfamily counselors. Bankart (1989) used the Motherhood Inventory with three groups in Japan: unmarried college men, unmarried college women, and married mothers. Separate factor analyses were performed for each of the three groups.

AVAILABLE FROM: Order from NAPS c/o Microfiche Publications, P. O. Box 3513, Grand Central Station, New York, NY 10163–3513; NAPS document no. 04674; for microfiche, in U.S. remit $4.00 with order.

USED IN:

Bankart, B. (1989). Japanese perceptions of motherhood. *Psychology of Women Quarterly*, *13*, 59–76.

Hare-Mustin, R. T., Bennett, S. K., & Broderick, P. C. (1983). Attitude toward motherhood: Gender, generational, and religious comparisons. *Sex Roles*, *9*(5), 643–661.

Hare-Mustin, R. T., & Broderick, P. C. (1978, August). *The Motherhood Inventory: A questionnaire for studying attitudes toward motherhood*. Paper presented at the meeting of the American Psychological Association, Toronto. (ERIC Reproduction Service No. ED 167 919)

Hare-Mustin, R. T., & Broderick, P. C. (1979). The myth of motherhood: A Study of attitudes toward motherhood. *Psychology of Women Quarterly*, *4*(1), 114–128.

Hare-Mustin, R. T., & Lamb, S. (1984). Family counselors' attitudes toward women and motherhood: A new cohort. *Journal of Marital and Family Therapy*, *10*, 419–421.

BIBLIOGRAPHY:

Spence, J. T., Helmreich, R. L., & Stapp, J. (1973). A short version of the Attitudes Toward Women Scale (AWS). *Bulletin of the Psychonomic Society*, *2*, 219–220.

EVERSOLL FATHER ROLE OPINIONNAIRE (EFRO)

AUTHOR: Deanna Baxter Eversoll

DATE: 1979 (used 1975)

VARIABLE: Attitudes toward five dimensions of the father's role: nurturer, problem solver, provider, societal model, and recreational role

TYPE OF INSTRUMENT: Summated rating scale

DESCRIPTION: The Eversoll Father Role Opinionnaire (EFRO) consists of 30 items, with 6 items representing each of five dimensions of the father's role. The dimensions are defined as follows. Nurturer encompasses "providing for the emotional needs and the physical-care needs of the child" (Eversoll, 1979b, p. 538); problem solver means "providing solutions for problems the family members may encounter" (p. 538); provider refers to "behaviors related to earning income for the family unit" (p. 538); societal model means "developing a child's sense of commitment beyond the family unit to the community at large" (p. 538); and recreational role relates to "providing for family members' leisure-time activities" (p. 538). Each item is accompanied by five response alternatives ranging from "strongly disagree" to "strongly agree." All of the items are prescriptive; that is, they focus on what fathers should or should not do, not on what fathers actually do or fail to do. All but 5 of the items state that fathers "should" perform certain behaviors; 5 items are phrased in the reverse direction, suggesting that fathers "should not" perform certain behaviors.

SAMPLE ITEMS: (nurturer) A father should always be interested in listening to children's ideas and concerns about life.

(problem solver) If a child is having difficulty getting along with a group of peers, a father should talk to the child's playmates and solve the problem.

(provider) A father should not be primarily concerned with the income earning role.

(societal model) A father should take an active part in activities which are aimed at community improvement for future generations.

(recreational role) A father should find time each day for some leisure time.

PREVIOUS SUBJECTS: College students; parents of college men

APPROPRIATE FOR: High school students and older

ADMINISTRATION: Self-administered; about 10–15 minutes

SCORING: Five items must be reversed before being scored. Items are scored on a 5-point scale, with 5 points indicating that the father's role should include this behavior; generally 5 points are assigned to the "strongly agree" response. Six items are summed to comprise each of the five subscale scores. The subscale scores range from 6 to 30. In addition, an overall total score is obtained; this score can range from 30 to 150. Higher scores represent the belief that the father should actively be involved in the particular role.

DEVELOPMENT: Based on a review of relevant research, Eversoll (1979a) identified five dimensions of the father's role. She then generated a pool of 85 items to represent these different dimensions. The items were submitted to five professionals in a department of human development and family. They were asked independently to indicate the dimension associated with each item or to indicate that the item did not represent any of the dimensions. From a list of 53 items for which there was perfect agreement among the judges, a set of 10 items was selected to represent each of the five dimensions. This 50-item version of the scale was administered to a sample of 49 college men and 20 sets of their parents. It was presumed that items with means above 4 and below 2 did not show sufficient variability to discriminate. Therefore, to be included on the final version of the EFRO, an item had to have a mean score between 2 and 4 for all three groups—sons, mothers, and fathers. This led to the selection of 29 items—6 representing each dimension except the nurturer one. So that all subscales had an equal number of items, an item was added to the nurturer scale even though the item had a mean above 4. This produced the current 30-item version of the scale.

RELIABILITY: In a pilot test (Eversoll, undated), split-half reliability was computed using the responses from a sample of 49 college men, 20 of their fathers, and 20 of their mothers. The split-half correlations for the five subscale scores ranged from .93 to .97. The split-half correlation for the total scores was .98.

In a pilot test of college men, their mothers, and their fathers, Eversoll (undated) checked the item-subtotal correlations and the item-total correlations of all items on the scale. All item-subtotal correlations were significant at the .05 level for at least two of the three groups; all item-total correlations were significant at the .01 level for all three groups.

VALIDITY: The use of professionals to judge the role dimension referred to in each item helps to ensure content validity for the scale.

NOTES & COMMENTS: (1) Eversoll (1979a) looked at the EFRO scores from 221 college men and their mothers and fathers. She found that fathers and sons were significantly different in their responses on four of the five subscale scores, and mothers and sons were significantly different on all five subscale scores. Fathers scored significantly higher than their sons on the provider role and the societal model role; they scored significantly lower than their sons on the nurturer role and the recreational role. Mothers scored significantly higher than their sons on the provider role and the societal model role; they scored significantly lower than their sons on the other three roles.

(2) Eversoll (1979b) compared the EFRO scores of 346 college men and 309 college women. She found that males and females did not differ significantly on two of the subscales—societal model and recreational role—but they did differ significantly on the other three roles. College women, compared to college men, put more emphasis on the nurturer role and less emphasis on the problem solver and provider roles. Eversoll pointed out that the two dimensions on which there were no significant differences "measure less stereotyped sex behaviors" (p. 539).

AVAILABLE FROM: Deanna Baxter Eversoll, Evening Programs & Adult Learning Services, Division of Continuing Studies, University of Nebraska–Lincoln, 162 Nebraska Center for Continuing Education, Lincoln, NE 68583—0900.

USED IN:

Eversoll, D. (1979a). A two generational view of fathering. *Family Coordinator*, 28(4), 503–508.

Eversoll, D. (1979b). The changing father role: Implications for parent education programs for today's youth. *Adolescence*, 14, 535–544.

Eversoll, D. (undated). *Methods and procedures for Eversoll Father Role Opinionnaire (EFRO) development*. Unpublished paper, University of Nebraska, Lincoln.

LONE PARENTHOOD SCALES

AUTHORS: Susan Beattie and Linda L. Viney

DATE: 1981

VARIABLE: Positive and negative appraisals of single parenthood and coping strategies for dealing with single parenthood

TYPE OF INSTRUMENT: Summated rating scale

DESCRIPTION: The Lone Parenthood Scales consist of two parts. The first part lists 56 possible effects, both positive and negative, from single parenthood; the second part lists 30 coping strategies that one might use for dealing with single parenthood. The respondent is to consider the first 6-week period following separation from the spouse and rate each item on a 4-point scale: "not at all important, not very important, fairly important, very important." The possible positive effects of single parenthood deal with eight general areas: better relationships with children (6 items), better relationships with peers (5 items), increased self-esteem (4 items), support from others (4 items), mobilization of personal resources (3 items), mobilization of social resources (3 items), new opportunities (3 items), and relief from marital stress (2 items). The possible negative effects of lone parenthood deal with a different group of eight general areas: loss of relationship with partner (4 items), fear of losing family (4 items), personal losses (3 items), children's loss of family life (7 items), pressures from others (3 items), pressures of new roles (3 items), conflict over new roles (3 items), and emotional conflict (4 items). The coping strategies also represent eight general areas: active realism (5 items), passive optimism (6 items), confrontation (6 items), avoidance (3 items), resignation (3 items), reliance on others (5 items), anticipation (3 items), and self-control (2 items). In some cases, an item contributes to more than one area.

SAMPLE ITEMS: (positive effect) You could take up a career.

   (negative effect) Children found it difficult to understand what had happened.

   (coping strategies) Make several alternate plans for the future.

PREVIOUS SUBJECTS: Separated or divorced parents with minor children

APPROPRIATE FOR: Separated or divorced parents with minor children

ADMINISTRATION: Self-administered; about 30 minutes

SCORING: Individual items are scored on a 4-point scale, with 4 points assigned to the "very important" response. Item scores are summed and then divided by the number of items to yield scores on 24 subscales: 8 subscales for each of the three major areas—negative appraisals, positive appraisals, and coping strategies. Thus, all scores are actually average item scores, varying between 1 and 4. Beattie and Viney (1981) provided means and standard deviations based on the responses from 101 persons who completed the Lone Parenthood Scales.

DEVELOPMENT: Three 30-item sets of statements were developed. The 30 positive and 30 negative appraisals were taken from responses to a Parents Without Partners survey that asked members to record the benefits and problems associated with lone parenting. The 30 coping strategy items were taken from Westbrook (1975). The items were given to 95 parents with dependent children. They were asked to take each set of 30 items and reduce it to a smaller number—between 2 and 10—by grouping items that were similar in content. Using the responses from these parents, a nonmetric multidimensional scaling technique was used to identify the major groupings of items. Four negative-effect items were dropped because they reduced the internal consistency of the scales.

RELIABILITY: Internal consistency reliability was .86 for the negative-effect items and for the positive-effect items. For the coping items, internal consistency was .76. For all three domains considered together, internal consistency was .85.

A sample of 17 single parents completed the Lone Parenthood Scales on two occasions, separated by a 1-month interval. The test-retest reliability coefficients ranged from .81 to .92 across the 24 general areas. The one exception was confrontation, a coping strategy, that had a test-retest reliability of .79.

VALIDITY: Beattie and Viney (1981) provided references to the existing literature that support the construct validity of each of the groupings for the negative effects and the positive effects. To support the construct validity of the groupings of coping strategy items, they indicated that the results were similar to those obtained by Westbrook (1975), who tested another group of subjects.

AVAILABLE FROM: Beattie and Viney, 1981

USED IN:

Beattie, S., & Viney, L. L. (1981). Appraisal of lone parenthood after marital breakdown. *Journal of Personality Assessment*, 45(4), 415–423.

BIBLIOGRAPHY:

Westbrook, M. T. (1975). *Analyzing people's experience of events: A study of the childbearing years.* Unpublished doctoral dissertation, Macquarie University, Sydney, Australia.

7

Employee Roles

The 24 scales described in this chapter include 9 scales pertaining to specific careers, 4 dealing with sexual harassment, and 11 dealing with other work role issues. The scales that focus on specific careers look at attitudes or opportunities for persons in cross-sex-typed careers. There are scales dealing with women as university faculty, police officers, managers-executives, army personnel, and scientists. In addition, one scale deals with male nurses. Seven scales are summated rating scales. There is also one true/false measure and one multiple choice measure. The length of these scales varies from 7 to 38 items.

All 9 specific career scales first appeared in the published literature between 1974 and 1983. All 9 scales have evidence of adequate internal consistency reliability; 3 scales have evidence of adequate test-retest reliability. Furthermore, there is some evidence of the validity for all 9 scales. Overall, the scales in this section offer promising instruments for future research.

These scales are intended primarily for adults. Only 3 can be used with persons below college age. The most frequently used scale in this chapter is the Women As Managers Scale (WAMS) (Peters, Terborg, & Taynor, 1974), which I also described in my previous handbook (Beere, 1979). For the current handbook, I identified 31 articles and ERIC documents reporting on the use of the WAMS; none of these overlapped with the 8 articles listed in my previous book. The other 8 scales in this chapter have been used in one to six published studies.

The 9 specific career scales are followed by 4 scales pertaining to sexual harassment. The four scales are fairly new; the oldest was published in 1980. Each is of a different type: a Guttman scale, a checklist, a multiple choice measure, and a summated rating scale. The Guttman scale is the shortest, with only 8 items; the checklist and the multiple choice measures each have 28 items. Two of the scales show evidence of internal consistency reliability and test-retest reliability. The coefficients of reproducibility and scalability for the Guttman scale are adequate. There are no reliability data for the fourth scale. All 4 scales show at least some evidence of validity. There have been factor analytic studies using two of the measures. Each of the four measures has been used in two or three published studies.

The last 11 scales in this chapter cover a variety of topics: attitudes toward vicarious or direct achievement; attitudes toward the employment of married women; knowledge of the female work force experience; importance of a career in one's life; women's work motivation, career salience, work involvement, and work values; affirmative action compliance; and barriers to women's involvement in male-typed careers. A variety of types of measures are included in this section: summated rating scales, a ranking task, a semantic differential, and a survey. One scale, the Awareness of Occupational Experience Scale II (Pedro, 1980), is a true/false measure that has right and wrong answers. The oldest scale in this section first appeared in the literature in 1964; the newest scale first appeared in 1988. Three of the measures were described in my previous handbook (Beere, 1979), and two others have been in use long enough that they could have been included in that handbook. There is evidence regarding the internal consistency reliability for 6 of the 8 scales new to this handbook. However, most of the reliability coefficients are between .70 and .80, which is considered borderline. For one scale, the subscale reliabilities are unacceptably low, although the full-scale reliability is adequate. There is no evidence of the reliability of one scale that is based on factual information, and there is no evidence of the reliability of another scale that reports scores for items rather than scores for persons. In both instances, reliability is not likely to be a problem. There is also some evidence of the validity of all 11 scales in this section. None of the scales in this section is appropriate for persons below high school age; 3 of the scales are appropriate only for females.

Overall, the scales included in this chapter should prove useful to future researchers. Several described here have not been used extensively, but I include them because they measure a variable not measured by the other scales or they provide a good foundation for the development of other scales. Unfortunately, the number of scales in the chapter is not particularly large, and researchers may not find a measure to satisfy their specific purpose. The explanation is simple: there are not many measures that deal specifically with work roles or employee roles *as they relate to gender*, and I did not include measures that relate to employees or work in general. For example, my search did not include measures of job satisfaction, employee relations, or career selection, though these measures can and have been used to compare males and females, thus increasing our knowledge of employee roles as they relate to gender. The comparable chapter in my previous handbook was also short; it contained only 16 scales. Four of those 16 measures are described briefly in this chapter; the remaining 12 scales have not been used again since I wrote my previous book, and so they are not included here. Researchers unable to find an appropriate measure in this chapter should also consult Chapter 8, which includes scales dealing with multiple roles, and Chapter 9, which includes scales measuring attitudes toward gender role issues.

BIBLIOGRAPHY:

Beere, C. A. (1979). *Women and women's issues: A handbook of tests and measures.* San Francisco: Jossey-Bass.

Pedro, J. D. (1980). Awareness of Occupational Experience Scale II: A measure of knowledge of facts about the female occupational experience. *Catalog of Selected Documents in Psychology, 10,* 14. (Ms. No. 1979)

Peters, L. H., Terborg, J. R., & Taynor, J. (1974). Women as Managers Scale (WAMS): A measure of attitudes toward women in management positions. *Catalog of Selected Documents in Psychology, 4,* 27. (Ms. No. 585)

ACADEMIC SYSTEM BELIEFS SCALE

AUTHOR: Carlotta Joyner Young

DATE: 1977

VARIABLE: Beliefs about equality of opportunity for university faculty

TYPE OF INSTRUMENT: Summated rating scale

DESCRIPTION: The Academic System Beliefs Scale consists of 18 items pertaining to two major issues: 10 items concern "the university as a meritocracy, including standards for merit, allocating responsibility, advancement, and so forth" (Young, MacKenzie, & Sherif, 1980, p. 516), and 8 items concern "the need for and effects of change in the system" (p. 516). Two of these 8 items look at the possibility of reverse discrimination. Ten items are phrased to support current university practices, oppose affirmative action, and show concern that changes in employment practices can harm men. The remaining 8 items are phrased in the opposite direction.

SAMPLE ITEMS: Advertisement of job openings through informal channels of communication (such as colleagues) operates to the disadvantage of women in comparison with men.

Nowadays a woman can get an academic position more easily than a man, even if she is not as well qualified.

PREVIOUS SUBJECTS: Full-time female faculty and staff of academic departments

APPROPRIATE FOR: Faculty, administrators, and academic support staff at a college or university

ADMINISTRATION: Self-administered; about 10 minutes

SCORING: Items are scored on a 5-point scale, with higher scores assigned to responses that reflect support for current university practices, opposition to affirmative action, and concern that employment changes could be harmful to men. Item scores are summed to yield a total score that can range from 18 to 90. Young (1977) reported the mean, standard deviation, and range for a sample of 120 full-time, female faculty.

DEVELOPMENT: No information was provided.

RELIABILITY: The Academic System Beliefs Scale was pretested with a sample of 20 graduate students. Coefficient alpha was .87. Based on a sample of 120 full-time, female faculty, coefficient alpha was .84 (Young, 1977).

VALIDITY: Reid (1987) found that female faculty and female staff obtained significantly different scores on the Academic System Beliefs Scale. Faculty were less likely than staff members to believe that the university operated as a meritocracy.

NOTES & COMMENTS: Young (1977) and Young et al. (1980) used the Academic System Beliefs Scale as one criterion for identifying "token women" in a university setting. The researchers also identified nontoken women and women with conflicting orientations. The three groups were then compared in terms of demographic variables and other variables, such as perceptions of status discrepancies between men and women faculty.

AVAILABLE FROM: Carlotta Joyner Young, 5748 Independence Circle, Alexandria, VA 22312

USED IN:

Reid, P. T. (1987). Perceptions of sex discrimination among female university faculty and staff. *Psychology of Women Quarterly, 11*(1), 123–128.

Young, C. J. (1977). *Token women in academia*. Unpublished master's thesis, Pennsylvania State University.

Young, C. J., MacKenzie, D. L., & Sherif, C. W. (1980). In search of token women in academia. *Psychology of Women Quarterly, 4*(4), 508–525.

ATTITUDES TOWARD FEMALE PROFESSORS SCALE

AUTHOR: William D. Brant

DATE: 1978 (used 1977)

VARIABLE: Attitudes toward female professors

TYPE OF INSTRUMENT: Summated rating scale

DESCRIPTION: The Attitudes Toward Female Professors Scale consists of 20 items—7 positive statements and 13 negative statements. About half of the items ask for general feelings regarding female professors—for example, "Females are not qualified to be college professors." Some items are the opposites of other items; for example, "I have as much respect for my female professors as my male professors" is opposite to "I have less respect for my female professors than my male professors." Items are accompanied by five response options: "disagree strongly, disagree, no opinion, agree, strongly agree."

SAMPLE ITEMS: Women professors only excel in the humanities and arts.

Females are just as capable at college teaching as their male counterparts.

PREVIOUS SUBJECTS: College students

APPROPRIATE FOR: College students

ADMINISTRATION: Self-administered; about 10 minutes

SCORING: Before scoring, responses on the 13 negatively phrased items must be reversed. Then items can be individually scored on a 5-point scale, with higher points assigned to the response reflecting the most positive attitude toward female professors. Item scores are summed to yield a total score that can vary from 20 (very negative attitudes toward female professors) to 100 (very positive attitudes toward female professors).

DEVELOPMENT: A sample of 90 college students responded to 80 attitude statements selected from a larger pool. Each item was accompanied by five response options ranging from "strongly disagree" to "strongly agree." Item-total correlations were computed, and 20 items with the highest correlations were selected for the scale. The item-total correlations for the selected items were all greater than .40, and most were greater than .50.

RELIABILITY: To calculate split-half reliability, the scale was completed by a different sample of 56 college women and 32 college men. The corrected split-half reliability coefficient was .88. Another sample of 59 college women and 34 college men completed the scale on two occasions, with a 5-week interval between the two testings. The test-retest reliability coefficient for this sample was .95.

Brant (1979) reported item-total correlations for all 20 items. The correlations ranged from .42 to .95, with an average correlation of .63.

VALIDITY: The sample of 56 college women and 32 college men completed Rokeach's (1960) short form of the Dogmatism scale in addition to the Attitudes Toward Female Professors Scale. As predicted, there was a significant, negative correlation between the two measures ($r = -.63$, $p < .05$): highly dogmatic persons tended to respond unfavorably toward female professors.

Female respondents compared to male respondents had significantly higher scores, reflecting their more positive attitudes toward female professors. Furthermore, students majoring in traditionally masculine disciplines (e.g., business, science, agriculture, and engineering) had significantly lower, more negative, scores than students majoring in

other areas (e.g., education, home economics, and liberal arts) (Brant, 1978).
AVAILABLE FROM: Brant, 1979
USED IN:
Brant, W. D. (1978). Attitudes Toward Female Professors: A scale with some data on its reliability and validity. *Psychological Reports, 43,* 211–214.
Brant, W. D. (1979). Attitudes Toward Female Professors Scale. *Psychological Reports, 44,* 1310.
BIBLIOGRAPHY:
Rokeach, M. (1960). *The open and closed mind.* New York: Basic Books.

ATTITUDES TOWARD MALE NURSES (ATMN)
AUTHORS: Edward Laroche and Hanoch Livneh
DATE: 1983
VARIABLE: Attitudes toward male nurses
TYPE OF INSTRUMENT: Alternate choice: true/false
DESCRIPTION: The Attitudes Toward Male Nurses (ATMN) scale consists of 21 statements, each pertaining to male nurses alone or to male nurses in comparison with female nurses. Items deal with such topics as the competence of male nurses, the appropriate role for male nurses, the behavior of male nurses, and the traits inherent in male nurses. The respondent reads each item and responds either "true" or "false." Most items are phrased to reflect a negative view of male nurses.
SAMPLE ITEMS: Male nurses are not smart enough to be doctors.
    Nursing is not an appropriate career for men.
PREVIOUS SUBJECTS: Ages 13 and older
APPROPRIATE FOR: Ages 13 and older
ADMINISTRATION: Self-administered; about 10 minutes
SCORING: Items are scored 0 or 1, with 0 assigned to the response reflecting a negative attitude toward male nurses and 1 assigned to the response reflecting a positive attitude. Item scores are summed to yield a total score that can range from 0 (most negative attitude) to 21 (most positive attitude).
DEVELOPMENT: Items were developed based on a review of the literature dealing with males in the nursing profession.
RELIABILITY: The responses from 174 persons were used to compute Kuder-Richardson reliability; a value of .86 was obtained (Laroche & Livneh, 1983).
VALIDITY: Consistent with expectations, the responses from 174 persons showed that attitudes toward male nurses were associated with respondents' educational level. The higher was the educational background, the more positive were the attitudes. Also consistent with expectations, females expressed more positive attitudes toward male nurses than did males.

NOTES & COMMENTS: (1) Laroche and Livneh (1986) reported the results of a factor analytic study of the ATMN using the responses from 169 people. The researchers extracted four factors.

(2) E. Laroche (personal communication, July 20, 1988) has indicated that he and Livneh are undertaking additional research on the validity of the scale, and this research may lead to some alterations in it.

AVAILABLE FROM: Order from NAPS c/o Microfiche Publications, P.O. Box 3513, Grand Central Station, New York, NY 10163–3513; NAPS document no. 04708; for microfiche, in U.S. remit $4.00 with order.

USED IN:

Laroche, E., & Livneh, H. (1983). Regressional analysis of attitudes toward male nurses. *Journal of Psychology*, *113*, 67–71.

Laroche, E., & Livneh, H. (1986). The factorial structure of American attitudes toward male nurses. *Journal of Social Psychology*, *126*(5), 679–680.

ATTITUDES TOWARD POLICEWOMEN

AUTHORS: Esther J. Koenig and Samuel Juni

DATE: 1981

VARIABLE: Attitudes toward policewomen

TYPE OF INSTRUMENT: Alternate choice and multiple choice

DESCRIPTION: The Attitudes Toward Policewomen scale consists of 12 items pertaining to women on the police force. Items relate to "supervision, competence, foot patrol duties, detective and inspector duties, male-female teams, injuries, absenteeism, and effectiveness" (Koenig & Juni, 1981, p. 466). Ten items are accompanied by the response options "agree" and "disagree." Two items have three response options: "less effective, as effective, more effective" and "less policewomen, no change, more policewomen" (p. 468). The former item refers to the effectiveness of policewomen relative to policemen, and the latter item pertains to the change desired in the number of policewomen. Some items are phrased to reflect positive attitudes toward policewomen, and others are phrased to reflect negative attitudes.

SAMPLE ITEMS: It is not good for female officers to supervise male officers.

Policewomen are as competent as policemen.

PREVIOUS SUBJECTS: Adults

APPROPRIATE FOR: High school students and older

ADMINISTRATION: Self-administered; a couple of minutes

SCORING: Scores are expressed on a scale of 0 to 100. The procedure for obtaining the scores is not clear.

DEVELOPMENT: No information was provided.

RELIABILITY: Internal consistency reliability using the responses from 569 adults was .82. For 11 of the 12 items, item-total correlations were statistically significant.

VALIDITY: As expected, female respondents were significantly more positive than male respondents in their attitudes toward policewomen. Males and females differed in their attitudes toward policewomen on 8 of the 12 items. For 3 of the 4 items showing no significant sex differences, the antipolicewomen option was rarely chosen by men or women.

A sample of 569 adults completed the Attitudes Toward Policewomen scale, as well as a measure of general attitudes toward women and a covert measure of attitudes toward policewomen. For males, there were significant correlations between the Attitudes Toward Policewomen scale and both of the other measures. For females, only the correlation between Attitudes Toward Policewomen scores and the attitudes toward women measure was significant.

NOTES & COMMENTS: (1) Koenig and Juni (1981) reported relationships between scores on the Attitudes Toward Policewomen scale and measures of four background variables: political views, dominant father versus mother, history of supervision by a woman, and judgment of rating of past female supervision.

(2) Koenig and Juni (1981) also constructed a covert measure of attitudes toward policewomen. This measure provided a creative and more subtle way of looking at attitudes toward policewomen.

(3) Though the Attitudes Toward Policewomen scale has not been used much in published research, it is included because it provides a measure in an area where no other measure has been identified.

AVAILABLE FROM: Koenig and Juni, 1981
USED IN:

Koenig, E. J., & Juni, S. (1981). Attitudes toward policewomen: A study of interrelationships and determinants. *Journal of Police Science and Administration, 9*(4), 463–474.

COMMUNICATION COMPETENCIES OF WOMEN MANAGERS SCALE (CCWMS)

AUTHOR: Cynthia Berryman-Fink
DATE: 1982
VARIABLE: Perceived communication competencies of women managers
TYPE OF INSTRUMENT: Summated rating scale
DESCRIPTION: The Communication Competencies of Women Managers Scale (CCWMS) consists of 30 statements pertaining to communication skills. Some items pertain to the ability to communicate *to* other persons, and some items pertain to the ability to understand and accept communications *from* other persons. All statements begin, "Women managers . . . " Sixteen items are positive statements about women managers; 14 items are negative statements.
SAMPLE ITEMS: Women managers generally are good listeners.

Women managers generally have difficulty relating to others.
PREVIOUS SUBJECTS: Employed adults
APPROPRIATE FOR: Persons who are or have been employed
ADMINISTRATION: Self-administered; about 10–15 minutes
SCORING: No information was provided other than to indicate that higher scores reflect more positive attitudes. It can be presumed that items are individually scored and summed to yield a single score.
DEVELOPMENT: A group of 101 managers were asked to indicate "(a) communication skills that women possess relative to effective management, and (b) the communication skills on which women managers should receive training to become more effective managers" (Wheeless & Berryman-Fink, 1985, p. 140). The first question elicited the following communication strengths of women managers: "interpersonal competency skills of listening, verbal ability, empathy, receptiveness, nonverbal communication, and flexibility" (p. 140). The second question elicited the following areas of weakness in the communication skills of women managers: "assertiveness, public speaking, credibility, professionalism and emotional control" (p. 140). Based on these general areas, Berryman-Fink generated the 30 items on the CCWMS.
RELIABILITY: Based on the responses from 178 persons employed in a variety of organizations, the internal consistency of the scale was .90.
VALIDITY: As one would expect, women respondents obtained significantly higher (more positive) scores than male respondents. There was no significant difference, however, when the responses from persons who had worked with or for a woman manager were compared with the responses from persons who had not worked with or for a woman manager.

Scores on the CCWMS were correlated with scores on several other measures, including the Positive Regard Scale (Ross & Walters, 1973)(see separate entry), the Women as Managers Scale (WAMS)(Peters, Terborg, & Taynor, 1974)(see separate entry), and the Marlowe-Crowne Social Desirability Scale (Crowne & Marlowe, 1960). The Positive Regard Scale is a 32-item measure of the perceptions of the personality traits, ability, and behavior of women in comparison with men. The WAMS is a 21-item measure of attitudes toward women in managerial roles. The Marlowe-Crowne Scale is a measure of one's tendency to rely on a social desirability response set in answering questions. As expected, correlations with the first two measures were significant: Positive Regard Scale = .62, and WAMS = .53. Because the correlation with Marlowe-Crowne was low and nonsignificant ($r = .05$), it can be presumed that social desirability did not interfere with responding.
NOTES & COMMENTS: Berryman-Fink and Wheeless (1984) did a single factor analysis using responses to three scales: the Positive Regard Scale, the WAMS, and the CCWMS. They extracted three factors. Using a

criterion of a factor loading greater than .40, 20 CCWMS items loaded on the second factor, and this was the only factor where CCWMS items loaded. The remaining 10 CCWMS items had loadings of .28 or higher on this factor. Furthermore, no items from the other two scales had loadings greater than .33 on this factor.

AVAILABLE FROM: Berryman-Fink and Wheeless, 1984; Wheeless and Berryman-Fink, 1985

USED IN:

Berryman-Fink, C., & Wheeless, V. E. (1984, February). *Effects of attitudes toward women and women in management on perceived communication competencies of women managers.* Paper presented at the meeting of the Western Speech Communication Association, Seattle. (ERIC Document Reproduction Service No. ED 241 975)

Wheeless, V. E., & Berryman-Fink, C. (1985). Perceptions of women managers and their communicator competencies. *Communication Quarterly, 33*(2), 137–148.

BIBLIOGRAPHY:

Crowne, D. P., & Marlowe, D. (1960). A new scale of social desirability independent of psychopathology. *Journal of Consulting Psychology, 24,* 349–354.

Peters, L. H., Terborg, J. R., & Taynor, J. (1974). Women as Managers Scale (WAMS): A measure of attitudes toward women in management positions. *Catalog of Selected Documents in Psychology, 4,* 27. (Ms. No. 585)

Ross, S., & Walters, J. (1973). Perceptions of a sample of university men concerning women. *Journal of Genetic Psychology, 122,* 329–336.

MANAGERIAL ATTITUDES TOWARD WOMEN EXECUTIVES SCALE (MATWES)

AUTHORS: Peter Dubno, John Costas, Hugh Cannon, Charles Wankel, and Hussein Emin

DATE: 1979

VARIABLE: Managerial attitudes toward women executives

TYPE OF INSTRUMENT: Summated rating scale

DESCRIPTION: The Managerial Attitudes Toward Women Executives Scale (MATWES) consists of 38 statements pertaining to women executives. Items relate to a variety of topics, such as the competence of women executives, the impact of women executives on male subordinates, and the "right" of women to hold executive positions. About 40% of the items express positive views of women executives; the other items express negative views. Each item is accompanied by five response alternatives ranging from "highly agree" to "highly disagree."

SAMPLE ITEMS: Sex should not play a role in hiring women to executive positions.

Women executives don't understand what their subordinates are doing.

PREVIOUS SUBJECTS: MBA students and PhD students in business schools

APPROPRIATE FOR: College students and older

ADMINISTRATION: Self-administered; about 15 minutes

SCORING: Items are individually scored on a 5-point scale, with 1 point assigned to the response that is more favorable toward women executives.

DEVELOPMENT: About 400 undergraduate and graduate business students, most of them male, were shown a picture of a woman manager observing the work of a male employee. A caption indicated that she was vice-president of marketing observing the testing of a new product. Respondents were asked to write a few sentences expressing the feelings and thoughts of the male employee shown in the picture. A pool of 259 different, relevant statements was produced. After editing the statements for readability, each was typed onto a 3 x 5 index card. The cards were submitted to a panel of 30 women executives, most of whom had experienced "some" or "a considerable amount" of prejudice from male executives. The women were "familiar with affirmative action programs and were well versed and knowledgeable about the problem [of prejudice from male executives]" (Dubno, Costas, Cannon, Wankel, & Emin, 1979, p. 359). The panel members independently sorted the cards into seven piles ranging from "least prejudiced toward women" to "most prejudiced toward women." Six items having low semi-interquartile ranges were selected from each of the seven categories. This item pool was administered to 153 MBA and PhD students in a business school. Four items that failed to correlate significantly with total scores were deleted, leaving 38 items on the MATWES.

RELIABILITY: Item-total correlations were significant at the .05 level for all 38 items; they were significant at the .01 level for 20 of the items. Coefficient alpha was .97 based on testing 153 graduate business students. A subgroup of 65 students completed the MATWES on two occasions with a 4-week interval between testings. The test-retest reliability was .78.

VALIDITY: A sample of 258 graduate business students completed the MATWES and the Women as Managers Scale (Peters, Terborg, & Taynor, 1974) (see separate entry). The correlation between the two scales was .73 (Dubno et al., 1979). Furthermore, the median score for female respondents was significantly different from the median score for male respondents.

Dubno (1985) reported means and standard deviations for samples of male and female MBA students tested in 1975, 1978, and 1983. He found that females' scores on the MATWES reflected consistently more positive attitudes toward women executives than were reflected by the males' scores.

NOTES & COMMENTS: (1) There are inconsistencies in the data reported in Dubno et al. (1979) and Dubno (1985). For example, one article suggested that high scores reflect more positive attitudes, and the other article suggested that low scores reflect more positive attitudes. None of the inconsistencies reduces the value of the scale, however.

(2) Since the development of the MATWES established that the various items represented differing degrees of prejudice against women, it is not clear why the items are not weighted differentially in computing scale scores. In other words, the scale development seemed to follow the procedure known as "the method of equal-appearing intervals" used to develop Thurstone scales (see Edwards, 1957), but summative scoring is not usually used with these scales.

AVAILABLE FROM: Dubno, Costas, Cannon, Wankel, and Emin, 1979
USED IN:
Dubno, P. (1985). Attitudes toward women executives: A longitudinal approach. *Academy of Management Journal, 28*(1), 235–239.
Dubno, P., Costas, J., Cannon, H., Wankel, C., & Emin, H. (1979). An empirically keyed scale for measuring managerial attitudes toward women executives. *Psychology of Women Quarterly, 3*(4), 357–364.
BIBLIOGRAPHY:
Edwards, A. L. (1957). *Techniques of attitude scale construction*. New York: Appleton-Century-Crofts.
Peters, L. H., Terborg, J. R., & Taynor, J. (1974). Women as Managers Scale (WAMS): A measure of attitudes toward women in management positions. *Catalog of Selected Documents in Psychology, 4*, 27. (Ms. No. 585)

SEX ROLE ATTITUDES IN THE ARMY
AUTHORS: John C. Woelfel, Joel M. Savell, Barry E. Collins, and Peter M. Bentler
DATE: 1976
VARIABLE: Attitudes toward women in the U.S. Army
TYPE OF INSTRUMENT: Summated rating scale, multiple choice, and forced choice
DESCRIPTION: There are two versions of the Sex Role Attitudes in the Army scale: a long form with 18 items and a short form with 7 items. On the long form, the items follow a variety of formats: 1 item offers two statements and asks the respondent to select the most appropriate one; 11 items follow a Likert format with the response options being "strongly agree, agree, disagree, strongly disagree"; and 6 items are multiple choice. The authors recommend slightly modified phrasing on some of the items on the short form. Three of those items are multiple choice, and 4 are Likert-type, with five response options: "strongly agree, somewhat agree, no opinion at all, somewhat disagree, strongly disagree." Some items are phrased in a traditional direction; others are phrased in a contemporary direction.

SAMPLE ITEMS: The Army's mission is best carried out: a) by men only, b) mostly by men with some women in support roles, c) mostly by men with some women in combat as well as support roles, d) equally by men and women, e) mostly by women.

If a greater number of women were placed in command positions, the effectiveness of the Army: a) would increase, b) would decrease, c) would not change.

PREVIOUS SUBJECTS: Cadets in the Reserve Officers Training Corps (ROTC), cadets in summer training programs, and soldiers

APPROPRIATE FOR: Persons knowledgeable about the military

ADMINISTRATION: Self-administered; the 7-item version takes a couple of minutes to complete; the 18-item version takes about 10 minutes

SCORING: All items are scored so that higher scores are associated with a contemporary orientation. To score either the long or short form of the scale, respondent's item scores are converted to z scores to adjust for the fact that different items have different numbers of response alternatives. Each z score is multiplied by the appropriate factor loading on Factor I, and then item scores are summed to yield a total score. Woelfel, Savell, Collins, and Bentler (1976) provided means and standard deviations on both the long and short form for the following groups of respondents: men in the Army, women in the Army, Army officers, and enlisted persons.

DEVELOPMENT: The researchers assembled an item pool of 174 items and administered them to 800 soldiers: 75% male and 25% female. The responses were factor analyzed, and 37 items were identified because they showed high loadings on the strongest factor. These 37 items were factor analyzed, and one strong, significant factor was identified. The factor was labeled "traditional/contemporary orientation toward women" (Woelfel et al., 1976, p. 3). Eighteen items that loaded heavily on this factor comprise the long form of the scale. Further factor analysis using responses to the 18 items again led to the conclusion that these items can be explained with a single factor: traditional versus contemporary views of women. A subset of 7 items was selected for the short form of the scale. These items were selected to satisfy two criteria: internal consistency reliability of at least .70 for the set of items and unambiguous phrasing of the individual items. A factor analysis of the 7 items again produced a strong single factor that was described as a traditional versus contemporary orientation toward women.

RELIABILITY: Coefficient alpha for the 18-item version was .88; for the 7-item scale, it was .78 (Woelfel et al., 1976). Adams, Rice, and Instone (1984) used the short form of the scale to test military cadets attending summer training programs. They obtained a coefficient alpha of .79 for one group of cadets and a coefficient alpha of .74 for another group.

VALIDITY: The researchers predicted that scores on both the long and the short forms would correlate with the following variables: respondent's sex, respondent's educational level, self-perception as liberal or conservative, mother's gender role attitude, father's gender role attitude, attitudes of same-sex peers, and attitudes of opposite-sex peers. Their results supported all of the predictions for both the long and the short forms. In fact, except for one correlation, all were significant at the .001 level. The one exception, the correlation between education and the short form, was significant at the .01 level.

Adams et al. (1984) reported significant sex differences, with females scoring as more contemporary than males.

Priest (cited in Adams et al., 1984) reported a correlation of .59 between this scale and the Attitudes Toward Women Scale (Spence & Helmreich, 1972)(see separate entry).

NOTES & COMMENTS: (1) The Sex Role Attitudes in the Army scale is also referred to as the Army Research Institute Attitudes Toward Women in the Military Scale (ARIAWS).

(2) Savell, Woelfel, Collins, and Bentler (1979) reported on the analysis of responses to a portion of the 174 items originally used for scale development. The items they analyzed play only a small role on the final version of the scale.

(3) Adams et al. (1984) and Adams, Rice, Instone, and Hicks (1981) compared scores on the short form of the Sex Role Attitudes in the Army scale to respondents' reactions to male and female leaders. Larwood, Glasser, and McDonald (1980) used five questions from the Sex Role Attitudes in the Army scale, along with several other items, to compare the views of male and female ROTC cadets. Stevens and Gardner (1987) used the same scale to study the attitudes of male Coast Guard cadets.

AVAILABLE FROM: Woelfel, Savell, Collins, and Bentler, 1976

USED IN:

Adams, J., Rice, R. W., & Instone, D. (1984). Follower attitudes toward women and judgments concerning performance by female and male leaders. *Academy of Management Journal*, 27(3), 636–643.

Adams, J., Rice, R. W., Instone, D., & Hicks, J. M. (1981, August). *Follower attributional biases and assessments of female and male leaders' performance*. Paper presented at the meeting of the American Psychological Association, Los Angeles. (ERIC Document Reproduction Service No. ED 209 609)

Larwood, L., Glasser, E., & McDonald, R. (1980). Attitudes of male and female cadets toward military sex integration. *Sex Roles*, 6(3), 381–390.

Savell, J. M., Woelfel, J. C., Collins, B. E., & Bentler, P. M. (1979). A study of male and female soldiers' beliefs about the "appropriateness" of various jobs for women in the Army. *Sex Roles*, 5(1), 41–50.

Stevens, G., & Gardner, S. (1987). But can she command a ship? Acceptance of women by peers at the Coast Guard Academy. *Sex Roles*, 16(3/4), 181–188.

Woelfel, J. C., Savell, J. M., Collins, B. E., & Bentler, P. M. (1976). *A preliminary version of a scale to measure sex-role attitudes in the Army*. (Research Memorandum 76–3). Arlington, VA: Army Research Institute for the Behavioral and Social Sciences. (ERIC Document Reproduction Service No. ED 178 549)
BIBLIOGRAPHY:
Spence, J. T., & Helmreich, R. L. (1972). The Attitudes Toward Women Scale: An objective instrument to measure attitudes toward the rights and roles of women in contemporary society. *Catalog of Selected Documents in Psychology*, 2, 66. (Ms. No. 153)

WOMEN AS MANAGERS SCALE (WAMS)

AUTHORS: Lawrence H. Peters, James R. Terborg, and Janet Taynor
DATE: 1974
VARIABLE: Attitudes toward women as managers in a business organization
DESCRIPTION: The Women as Managers Scale (WAMS) is a summated rating scale consisting of 21 items representing three factors: General Acceptance of Females as Managers (10 items), Feminine Barriers to Full-Time Permanent Employment (5 items), and Personality Traits Usually Ascribed to Managers (6 items). Each item is accompanied by seven response options ranging from "strongly disagree" to "strongly agree."
ARTICLES LISTED IN BEERE, 1979: 8
NOTES & COMMENTS: (1) The Educational Research Service, Inc. (1979, 1981) used the Women as School District Administrators survey, which included modified versions of the items on the WAMS. Jagacinski (1987a, 1987b) selected a subset of seven items from the WAMS and changed the wording to be appropriate to the field of engineering. Garland, Hale, and Burnson (1982) modified the WAMS by replacing the word *business* with the word *management*.

(2) The reliability and dimensionality of the WAMS have been discussed by Crino, White, and DeSanctis (1981) and by Ilgen and Moore (1983). Herbert and Yost (1978) have looked at the fakeability of the WAMS.
AVAILABLE FROM: Peters, Terborg, and Taynor, 1974; Terborg, Peters, Ilgen, and Smith, 1977; Pereira, 1978
USED IN:

Berryman-Fink, C., & Wheeless, V. E. (1984, February). *Effects of attitudes toward women and women in management on perceived communication competencies of women managers*. Paper presented at the meeting of the Western Speech Communication Association, Seattle. (ERIC Document Reproduction Service No. ED 241 975)
Beutell, N. J. (1984). Correlates of attitudes toward American women as managers. *Journal of Social Psychology*, 124(1), 57–63.
Cohen, S. L., & Leavengood, S. (1978). The utility of the WAMS: Shouldn't it

relate to discriminatory behavior. *Academy of Management Journal*, 21(4), 742–748.

Collins, M., Waters, L. K., & Waters, C. W. (1979). Relationships between sex-role orientation and attitudes toward women as managers. *Psychological Reports*, 45(3), 828–830.

Crino, M. D., White, M. C., & DeSanctis, G. L. (1981). A comment on the dimensionality and reliability of the Women as Managers Scales (WAMS). *Academy of Management Journal*, 24(4), 866–876.

Cromie, S. (1981). Women as managers in Northern Ireland. *Journal of Occupational Psychology*, 54(2), 87–91.

Dubno, P., Costas, J., Cannon, H., Wankel, C., & Emin, H. (1979). An empirically keyed scale for measuring managerial attitudes toward women executives. *Psychology of Women Quarterly*, 3(4), 357–364.

Educational Research Service, Inc. (1979). *Survey of attitudes toward women as school district administrators: Summary of responses to a survey of a random sample of superintendents and school board presidents.* Unpublished paper prepared for the American Association of School Administrators by Educational Research Service. (ERIC Document Reproduction Service No. ED 191 926)

Educational Research Service, Inc. (1981). *Survey: Attitudes toward women as school district administrators. Summary of responses to a survey of a random sample of superintendents and school board presidents.* Unpublished paper prepared for the American Association of School Administrators by Educational Research Service. (ERIC Document Reproduction Service No. ED 202 129)

Gackenbach, J. (1978). The effect of race, sex, and career goal differences on sex role attitudes at home and at work. *Journal of Vocational Behavior*, 12(1), 93–101.

Garland, H., Hale, K. F., & Burnson, M. (1982). Attributions for the success and failure of female managers: A replication and extension. *Psychology of Women Quarterly*, 7(2), 155–162.

Hatcher, M. A., & Penner, L. (1983, March). *Beauty and the boss.* Paper presented at the meeting of the Southeastern Psychological Association, Atlanta. (ERIC Document Reproduction Service No. ED 234 329)

Herbert, T. T., & Yost, E. B. (1978). Faking study of scores on the Women as Managers Scale. *Psychological Reports*, 42(2), 677–678.

Ilgen, D. R., & Moore, C. F. (1983). When reason fails: A comment on the reliability and dimensionality of the WAMS. *Academy of Management Journal*, 26(3), 535–540.

Irvine, J. J. (1980, April). *The relationships among sex role orientations, general attitudes toward women, and specific attitudes toward women in a managerial role.* Paper presented at the meeting of the American Educational Research Association, Boston. (ERIC Document Reproduction Service No. ED 184 961)

Irvine, J. J., & Robinson, C. (1982). The relationship among sex role orientations, general attitudes toward women, and specific attitudes toward women in managerial roles. *Journal of Educational Equity and Leadership*, 2(3), 196–204.

Jagacinski, C. M. (1987a). Androgyny in a male-dominated field: The relationship of sex-typed traits to performance and satisfaction in engineering. *Sex Roles, 17,* 529–547.

Jagacinski, C. M. (1987b). Engineering careers: Women in a male-dominated field. *Psychology of Women Quarterly, 11,* 97–110.

Muchinsky, P. M., & Harris, S. L. (1977). The effect of applicant sex and scholastic standing on the evaluation of job applicant resumes in sex-typed occupations. *Journal of Vocational Behavior, 11*(1), 95–108.

Nevill, D. D., Stephenson, B. B., & Philbrick, J. H. (1983). Gender effects on performance evaluation. *Journal of Psychology, 115*(2), 165–169.

Pereira, B. F. (1978). Organizational and personal correlates of attitudes toward women as managers. *Indian Journal of Social Work, 39*(3), 287–296.

Peters, L. H., Terborg, J. R., & Taynor, J. (1974). Women as Managers Scale (WAMS): A measure of attitudes toward women in management positions. *Catalog of Selected Documents in Psychology, 4,* 27. (Ms. No. 585)

Russell, J. E., & Rush, M. C. (1987). A comparative study of age-related variation in women's views of a career in management. *Journal of Vocational Behavior, 30,* 280–294.

Russell, J. E. A., Rush, M., & Herd, A. (1988). An exploration of women's expectations of effective male and female leadership. *Sex Roles, 18*(5/6), 279–287.

Schmidt, V. J., & Scott, N. A. (1986, August). *Home-career conflict: An exploration of the delicate balance.* Paper presented at the meeting of the American Psychological Association, Washington, DC. (ERIC Document Reproduction Service No. ED 283 076)

Stevens, G. E. (1984). Women in business: The view of future male and female managers. *Journal of Business Education, 59*(8), 314–317.

Stevens, G. E., & DeNisi, A. S. (1980). Women as managers: Attitudes and attributions for performance by men and women. *Academy of Management Journal, 23*(2), 355–361.

Terborg, J. R., Peters, L. H., Ilgen, D. R., & Smith, F. (1977). Organizational and personal correlates of attitudes toward women as managers. *Academy of Management Journal, 20,* 89–100.

Welsh, M. C. (1979a). Attitudinal measures and evaluation of males and females in leadership roles. *Psychological Reports, 45*(1), 19–22.

Welsh, M. C. (1979b, March). *Attitudinal measures and evaluation of males and females in leadership roles.* Paper presented at the meeting of the Southeastern Psychological Association, New Orleans. (ERIC Document Reproduction Service No. ED 174 927)

Welsh, M. C., & Hawker, J. (1978, March). *Personality characteristics and evaluation of women's role.* Paper presented at the meeting of the Southeastern Psychological Association, Atlanta. (ERIC Document Reproduction Service No. ED 165 075)

Wheeless, V. E., & Berryman-Fink, C. (1985). Perceptions of women managers and their communicator competencies. *Communication Quarterly, 33*(2), 137–148.

BIBLIOGRAPHY:

Beere, C. A. (1979). *Women and women's issues: A handbook of tests and measures* (pp. 342–344). San Francisco: Jossey-Bass.

WOMEN IN SCIENCE SCALE (WiSS)

AUTHORS: Thomas O. Erb and Walter S. Smith

DATE: 1981

VARIABLE: Attitudes toward women in science

TYPE OF INSTRUMENT: Summated rating scale

DESCRIPTION: The Women in Science Scale (WiSS) contains 27 items; 15 items are directly related to women in regard to science and science careers, and 12 relate to women's educational opportunities, parental and marital opportunities and responsibilities, and the issue of combining marriage and career. According to Erb and Smith (1984), the items represent three dimensions: "women possess characteristics which enable them to be successful in science careers" (8 items); "women's roles as mother and wife are compatible with successful science career pursuits" (9 items); and "women and men ought to have equal opportunities to prepare for and pursue science careers" (10 items)(p. 393). Twelve items reflect contemporary, egalitarian views; the other 15 items reflect traditional views. Each item is judged on a 6-point response scale ranging from "strongly agree" to "strongly disagree." There is not a neutral choice on the response scale.

SAMPLE ITEMS: Women should have the same educational opportunities as men.

Women can be as good in science careers as men can.

PREVIOUS SUBJECTS: Ages 10–18

APPROPRIATE FOR: Erb and Smith recommended the scale for ages 10–15

ADMINISTRATION: Self-administered; about 15 minutes

SCORING: Items are individually scored on a 6-point scale, with 6 points assigned to the contemporary, egalitarian end of the scale. Item scores are summed to yield a total score that can range from 27 to 162. Erb and Smith (1984) provided means and standard deviations for over 600 boys and over 600 girls; they also provided means and standard deviations by age for each year from 10 to 16 years of age.

DEVELOPMENT: A 30-item version of the WiSS was administered to 25 fifth graders. As a result of this pretest, 3 items were deleted and replaced with 3 new items, and 7 items were reworded. This revised 30-item version of the WiSS was administered to a sample of 612 adolescents, ages 10 to 16. Item-total correlations were computed, and 3 items were deleted due to low or negative correlations. The remaining 27 items, with item-total correlations of .35 or higher, comprise the scale.

RELIABILITY: Responses from a cross-validation sample of 612 adolescents, ages 10 to 16, were used to estimate reliability. Coefficient alpha was .92. A subset of 202 students completed the scale a second time, 2 months after they were first tested. Test-retest reliability was .82.

VALIDITY: Erb and Smith (1984) found a significant difference between the WiSS scores of 611 girls, ages 10–16, and 613 boys in the same age range. As expected, girls expressed more positive attitudes toward women in science.

To obtain further evidence of the construct validity of the WiSS, Erb and Smith (1984) correlated WiSS scores from over 1,200 adolescents with their scores on five other measures: Attitudes Toward Scientists, Attitudes Toward Science, Preference for Science Careers, Preference for Business Careers, and Preference for Service Careers. As predicted, correlations between WiSS scores and Attitudes Toward Scientists were significant and positive for both girls ($r = .44$) and boys ($r = .46$), and correlations between WiSS scores and Attitudes Toward Science scores were significant and positive for both girls ($r = .20$) and boys ($r = .29$). Correlations with the career preference scales were also consistent with predictions. Significant positive correlations were found between WiSS scores and Preference for Science Careers ($r = .18$ for boys and $r = .20$ for girls) and nonsignificant, near-zero correlations were found between WiSS scores and the other two preference scores.

Smith and Erb (1986) used the WiSS as a pretest and posttest in a study designed to determine whether exposure to women role models can change the attitudes of early adolescents. The researchers found a significant change in the predicted direction. Smith and Erb also replicated the finding of a significant sex difference; girls again had more positive attitudes toward women in science.

NOTES & COMMENTS: Erb and Smith (undated) recommended labeling the scale "Science Attitude Inventory" when it is administered to students.

AVAILABLE FROM: Erb and Smith, 1984

USED IN:

Erb, T. O. (1981). Attitudes of early adolescents toward science, women in science, and science careers. In T. O. Erb (Ed.), *Middle school research: Selected studies 1981*. Columbus, OH: National Middle School Association.

Erb, T. O., & Smith, W. S. (undated). *Women in Science Scale*. Unpublished paper, University of Kansas, Lawrence.

Erb, T. O., & Smith, W. S. (1984). Validation of the Attitude Toward Women in Science Scale for early adolescents. *Journal of Research in Science Teaching*, 21(4), 391–397.

Smith, W. S., & Erb, T. O. (1986). Effect of women science career role models on early adolescents' attitudes toward scientists and women in science. *Journal of Research in Science Teaching*, 23(8), 667–676.

PADGITT SEXUAL HARASSMENT SCALE

AUTHOR: Janet S. Padgitt

DATE: 1983

VARIABLE: Definition of sexual harassment and judgment of particular behaviors as offensive

TYPE OF INSTRUMENT: Guttman scale
DESCRIPTION: The Padgitt Sexual Harassment Scale is actually a list
of eight categories of behavior, each accompanied by some specific examples of behaviors that fall into that category. The eight categories are:
sexist comments, undue attention, verbal sexual advances, body language, invitations, physical advances, explicit sexual propositions, and
sexual bribery. The items have been used in two ways. First, respondents
have been asked to indicate which of the eight categories of behavior
are offensive, and second, they have been asked which constitute sexual
harassment. In judging the items, the respondents were asked to imagine that the behavior was being directed at a student by a faculty member.
SAMPLE ITEM: Physical advances: kissing, hugging, pinching, fondling
PREVIOUS SUBJECTS: Undergraduate and graduate college students
APPROPRIATE FOR: High school students and older; the scale could
be used to make judgments about behaviors exhibited in the workplace,
as well as in educational settings.
ADMINISTRATION: Self-administered; about 5 minutes
SCORING: Padgitt did not discuss scale scoring but did point out that
the items form a Guttman scale. Adams, Kottke, and Padgitt (1983)
provided results by behavioral category and respondent's sex based on
responses from 372 college students.
DEVELOPMENT: Items for the scale were selected from a review of legal
cases relating to sexual harassment. Criminal behaviors, such as rape
and sexual assault, were omitted so as to limit the scale to civil offenses.
Guttman scalogram analysis was used to analyze the anonymous responses of 372 college students. When the Guttman analysis was applied
to the judgments of the offensiveness of the behavior, the eight behaviors
constituted a Guttman scale for women but not for men. When two
items were omitted (sexist comments and body language), the remaining
six items constituted an acceptable Guttman scale for both men and
women. When the respondents judged whether each of the eight behaviors constituted sexual harassment, neither the responses from men
nor the responses from women formed an acceptable Guttman scale.
Three items that accounted for most of the inconsistencies were deleted
(sexist comments, body language, and invitations), and the remaining
five items were found to constitute an acceptable Guttman scale for both
men and women.
RELIABILITY: Considering the six items that formed a Guttman scale
for the offensiveness of the behaviors, the coefficient of reproducibility
was .95 for women and .92 for men, and the coefficient of scalability
was .62 for women and .74 for men. Looking at the five items that
formed a Guttman scale for judging behavior as sexual harassment, the

coefficient of reproducibility was .98 for women and .97 for men, and the coefficient of scalability was .85 for women and .79 for men.

VALIDITY: Women judged harassing behavior as offensive behavior. Men were more inconsistent, sometimes seeing harassing behavior as not offensive. After offering several explanations for this, the authors concluded: "The evidence, however, indicates that, in general, the behaviors relative to each other did systematically convey meaning to both male and female students" (Padgitt & Padgitt, 1986, p. 37).

NOTES & COMMENTS: (1) The six-item offensiveness scale had a percentage improvement of .08 for women and .23 for men. The five-item harassment scale had a percentage improvement of .11 for women and .11 for men.

(2) This scale provides a hierarchy of sexually harassing behaviors, which may be useful in further research on the subject of sexual harassment.

AVAILABLE FROM: Adams, Kottke, and Padgitt, 1983
USED IN:

Adams, J. W., Kottke, J. L., & Padgitt, J. S. (1983). Sexual harassment of university students. *Journal of College Student Personnel*, 24(6), 484–490.

Padgitt, S. C., & Padgitt, J. S. (1986). Cognitive structure of sexual harassment: Implications for university policy. *Journal of College Student Personnel*, 27(1), 34–39.

RADECKI JENNINGS SEXUAL DOMINANCE SCALE

AUTHORS: Catherine Radecki and Joyce Jennings (Walstedt)
DATE: 1980
VARIABLE: Use of dominance and sexual intimacy behaviors in the work setting
TYPE OF INSTRUMENT: Checklist
DESCRIPTION: The Radecki Jennings Sexual Dominance Scale consists of 28 items: 12 dominance behaviors and 16 sexual intimacy behaviors. The behaviors on the checklist are sustaining behaviors, verbal behaviors, and physical behaviors. Sustaining behaviors are "those social behaviors which keep interactions flowing smoothly . . . such behaviors as eye contact and forms of address" (Radecki & Jennings, 1980, p. 72). When Radecki and Jennings administered the scale, they asked respondents to complete the checklist four times; respondents checked behaviors *they exhibited toward* (1) opposite-sex coworkers and (2) opposite-sex superiors, and they checked behaviors *they experienced from* (1) opposite-sex coworkers and (2) opposite-sex superiors. Coworkers were defined as persons with whom they worked but who were not their boss or supervisor. Superiors were defined as those who were their boss or had a higher work status.

SAMPLE ITEMS: (dominance behaviors) First name address; apologizing for things done

(sexual intimacy behaviors) Commenting on looks and appearance; brushing up against body

PREVIOUS SUBJECTS: Employees of corporations and higher education institutions

APPROPRIATE FOR: Employed persons working in a setting where there is an opportunity to interact with opposite-sex coworkers and superiors

ADMINISTRATION: Self-administered; about 10 minutes

SCORING: The score is equal to the number of items checked. Four scores were obtained by Radecki and Jennings (1980): dominance toward coworkers, dominance from coworkers, dominance toward superiors, and dominance from superiors.

DEVELOPMENT: The dominance behaviors selected for the Radecki Jennings Sexual Dominance Scale were based on the dominance and submission research of Henley (1977) and others. Three categories of behaviors were selected: sustaining movements (defined above); non-linguistic speech, which "includes amount of self-disclosure, teasing and sexual joking" (Radecki & Jennings, 1980, p. 73); and proxemics, which "includes not only posture, body orientation, and personal space invasion, but also physical contact" (p. 73).

RELIABILITY: No information was provided.

VALIDITY: Radecki and Jennings (1980) obtained completed scales from 69 men and 88 women employed in higher education. As predicted, the researchers were able to demonstrate that the dominance and sexual intimacy behaviors could be expressed on a single continuum. Guttman scalogram analysis yielded a coefficient of reproducibility greater than .91.

As predicted, sex was a salient factor in influencing responses to the scale; however, not all of the differences were in the predicted direction, and some predicted differences did not occur. Therefore, these results provide equivocal evidence of the scale's validity (see NOTES & COMMENTS).

NOTES & COMMENTS: (1) Radecki and Jennings (1980) suggested that males' responses to the scale may be influenced by a social desirability response set. "Men, in reporting that women directed as much dominance behavior toward them as they themselves did toward women, may have been reporting reciprocity to fit a conscious perception that they treat females fairly" (Radecki & Jennings, 1980, p. 82). The researchers therefore concluded that "more refined measures must be developed for future research in this area" (p. 82).

(2) Der-Karabetian and Rico (1983) and Der-Karabetian and Angel (1985) reported using the Radecki Jennings Sexual Dominance Scale. In

both studies, the authors obtained separate scores for dominance and for intimacy, but they reported that each subscale had 14 items when in fact there are 12 dominance items and 16 sexual intimacy items. It is not clear whether they varied the scale or classified some items differently from the way in which Radecki and Jennings (1980) classified them. Regardless, Der-Karabetian and Rico (1983) found a nonsignificant correlation of .28 between the two subscale scores when the scale was completed by 82 female employees; and Der-Karabetian and Angel (1985) found a relatively low but significant correlation of .33 ($p < .05$) between the two subscale scores when the scale was completed by 375 female employees of a major corporation. They concluded that the findings "suggest the possibility that experiences of intimacy gestures happen independently of the dominance experiences" (Der-Karabetian & Angel, 1985, p. 9).

(3) Radecki and Jennings (1980) looked at scores on the Radecki Jennings Sexual Dominance Scale in relation to sex, occupation, age, marital status, and education. Der-Karabetian and Rico (1983) looked at scale scores in relation to age and marital status. Der-Karabetian and Angel (1985) looked at scores in relation to age, marital status, length of employment, religious affiliation, and attitudes toward feminism. The last two studies asked respondents only to indicate which behaviors were exhibited toward them by their coworkers.

AVAILABLE FROM: Radecki and Jennings, 1980
USED IN:

Der-Karabetian, A., & Angel, D. (1985, April). *Intimacy and dominance gestures in the work place*. Paper presented at the meeting of the Western Psychological Association, San Jose, CA. (ERIC Document Reproduction Service No. ED 260 337)

Der-Karabetian, A., & Rico, E. (1983). Reported intimacy and dominance gestures by women in a corporate setting. *Psychological Reports, 52,* 1007–1010.

Radecki, C., & Jennings, J. (1980). Sex as a status variable in work settings: Female and male reports of dominance behavior. *Journal of Applied Social Psychology, 10*(1), 71–85.

BIBLIOGRAPHY:
Henley, N. (1977). *Body politics: Power, sex and nonverbal communication*. Englewood Cliffs, NJ: Prentice-Hall.

SEXUAL EXPERIENCES QUESTIONNAIRE (SEQ)/SEXUAL EXPERIENCES QUESTIONNAIRE 2 (SEQ2)

AUTHORS: Louise F. Fitzgerald and Sandra L. Shullman
DATE: 1985
VARIABLE: The Sexual Experiences Questionnaire (SEQ) measures sexual harassment of college students; the Sexual Experiences Questionnaire 2 (SEQ2) measures sexual harassment in the workplace.
TYPE OF INSTRUMENT: Multiple choice: never/once/more than once

DESCRIPTION: The SEQ is intended for use with college students and consists of 28 items: 7 items relate to gender harassment defined as "generalized sexist remarks and behavior"; 5 items relate to seductive behavior defined as "inappropriate and offensive, but essentially sanction-free sexual advances"; 4 items relate to sexual bribery defined as "solicitation of sexual activity or other sex-linked behavior by promise of rewards"; 4 items relate to sexual coercion defined as "coercion of sexual activity by threat of punishment"; and 7 items relate to sexual assault defined as "gross sexual imposition or assault" (Fitzgerald, Shullman et al., 1988, p. 157). The final item on the SEQ states: "I have been sexually harassed" (Fitzgerald, Shullman et al., 1988, p. 158). All items on the SEQ are phrased in behavioral terms, and the phrase *sexual harassment* is avoided until the last item. Each item is accompanied by three response alternatives—"never, once, more than once"—for the respondents to indicate the extent to which they have experienced the named behavior. For items answered "once" or "more than once," respondents are to indicate whether the person involved was a man, a woman, or both. The "both" response is used when the behavior had been exhibited more than once, and sometimes it involved a man and sometimes a woman.

The SEQ2, intended for use in the workplace, is similar to the SEQ except that the wording of some items was modified, and 5 items were added to the scale: 4 items were added to seductive behavior, and 1 item was added to sexual assault.

SAMPLE ITEMS: (gender harassment) Have you ever been in a situation where a professor made crudely sexual remarks, either publicly in class, or to you privately?

(seduction) Have you ever been in a situation where a professor or instructor made unwanted attempts to draw you into a discussion of personal or sexual matters (e.g., attempted to discuss or comment on your sex life)?

(sexual bribery) Have you ever been in a situation where a professor or instructor *directly* offered you some sort of reward for being sexually cooperative?

(sexual coercion) Have you ever felt that you were being subtly threatened with some sort of "punishment" for not being sexually cooperative with a professor or instructor (e.g., lowering your grade, failing an exam, etc.)?

(sexual imposition) Have you ever been in a situation where a professor or instructor made unwanted attempts to touch or fondle you (e.g., stroking your leg or neck, touching your breast, and so forth)?

PREVIOUS SUBJECTS: SEQ has been used with college students; SEQ2 has been used with female employees of a university, including faculty, administrators, clerical workers, and other staff

APPROPRIATE FOR: SEQ is appropriate for college students; SEQ2 is appropriate for employees

ADMINISTRATION: Self-administered; about 10–15 minutes

SCORING: Since the purpose of the SEQ and the SEQ2 is to assess the prevalence of sexual harassment, scores are not assigned to persons; rather scores are assigned to items. Fitzgerald, Shullman et al. (1988) recommended combining the "once" and "more than once" responses. Thus, an item is assigned a score equal to the number of persons responding "once" or "more than once."

DEVELOPMENT: The development of the SEQ rested on the work of Till (1980), who identified five levels of sexual harassment: gender harassment, seductive behavior, sexual bribery, sexual coercion, and sexual assault. Items were generated to reflect each of these areas. A pool of 30 items was administered to 468 college students. The students responded to the items and also commented on the wording and relevance of the items. Based on inputs from the students, some wording changes were made, and 2 items were deleted from the scale. The remaining 28 items comprise the final form of the SEQ.

To develop the SEQ2, two groups of 8 to 10 faculty and staff women reviewed the SEQ. Their review and discussion led to wording changes for some items and the addition of 5 items.

RELIABILITY: Based on testing a sample of 1,395 college students, Fitzgerald, Shullman et al. (1988) obtained a coefficient alpha for the SEQ of .92. A subset of 46 college students completed the SEQ on two occasions, 1 week apart. The test-retest reliability was .86. Corrected split-half coefficients for the five "scales" averaged .75 (range of .62 to .86).

For the SEQ2, Fitzgerald, Shullman et al. (1988) reported a coefficient alpha of .86.

VALIDITY: Fitzgerald, Shullman et al. (1988) pointed out that content validity of the SEQ was built into the scale by the way in which it was constructed. They also reported that all but three items correlated significantly with the criterion item, "I have been sexually harassed."

Men reported experiencing less sexual harassment on the SEQ than did women. The SEQ was able to discriminate among the patterns of sexual harassment at different universities and for different levels of students (i.e., undergraduate versus graduate students).

Factor analyses failed to confirm the five factors described by Till (1980). Instead a three-factor solution was identified in which one factor included bribery and threat, a second factor included seduction and sexual imposition items, and a third factor included the gender harassment items.

NOTES & COMMENTS: (1) Fitzgerald, Shullman et al. (1988) indicated that some rarely endorsed items could be dropped from the scale without diminishing the value of the measure. In particular, they suggested dropping items dealing with rape and attempted rape since respondents usually use the "comments" section to volunteer information on these extreme forms of sexual harassment.

(2) Since Fitzgerald, Shullman et al. (1988) suggested that the institution, not the individual, should be the unit of analysis, it is not clear why they reported reliabilities for individuals. It is not necessary that coefficient alpha across individuals be high; in fact, it is surprising that it is so high. If the scale is to be used to draw conclusions about institutions, then the reliability of the measure for institutions is important.

(3) Fitzgerald, Weitzman, Gold, and Ormerod (1988) used a subset of items from the SEQ to assess male faculty members' perceptions of their own behavior. To encourage faculty to feel comfortable in admitting to sexually harassing behaviors, other items were included to ask about whether students exhibited comparable behaviors toward the faculty member. To encourage honest responding, 7 distractor items were included—for example, "Have you ever made your personal library available to students for their personal use?" "Have you ever established what you considered to be a friendship with a student?" The Faculty Experience Questionnaire (FEQ), as they called the scale, contained 22 items. It was completed by 235 male faculty members from a single university.

AVAILABLE FROM: Order from NAPS c/o Microfiche Publications, P.O. Box 3513, Grand Central Station, New York, NY 10163–3513; NAPS document no. 04708; for microfiche, in U.S. remit $4.00 with order.

USED IN:

Fitzgerald, L. F., Shullman, S. L., Bailey, N., Richards, M., Swecker, J., Gold, Y., Ormerod, M., & Weitzman, L. M. (1988). The incidence and dimensions of sexual harassment in academia and the workplace. *Journal of Vocational Behavior, 32*, 152–175.

Fitzgerald, L. F., Weitzman, L. M., Gold, Y., & Ormerod, M. (1988). Academic harassment: Sex and denial in scholarly garb. *Psychology of Women Quarterly, 12*, 329–340.

BIBLIOGRAPHY:

Till, F. (1980). *Sexual harassment: A report on the sexual harassment of students.* Washington, DC: National Advisory Council on Women's Educational Programs.

TOLERANCE FOR SEXUAL HARASSMENT INVENTORY

AUTHORS: Bernice Lott, Mary Ellen Reilly, and Dale R. Howard

DATE: 1980

VARIABLE: Tolerance for sexual harassment

TYPE OF INSTRUMENT: Summated rating scale

DESCRIPTION: The Tolerance for Sexual Harassment Inventory consists of 10 statements pertaining to sexual harassment. Each item is accom-

panied by five response alternatives ranging from "strongly agree" to "strongly disagree."
SAMPLE ITEMS: Most women who are sexually insulted by a man provoke his behavior by the way they talk, act, or dress.

An attractive woman has to expect sexual advances and should learn how to handle them.
PREVIOUS SUBJECTS: College students
APPROPRIATE FOR: College students and adults
ADMINISTRATION: Self-administered; about 5 minutes
SCORING: Items are individually scored on a 5-point scale, with 5 points assigned to "strongly disagree" and 1 point assigned to "strongly agree." Scoring for two items must be reversed before the item scores are totaled to yield a score for tolerance of sexual harassment. Total scores can range from 10 to 50, with higher scores meaning less tolerance for sexual harassment.
DEVELOPMENT: No information was provided.
RELIABILITY: Reilly, Lott, and Gallogly (1986) administered the scale to 393 college students. The alpha coefficient was .78, and the split-half reliability coefficient was .83.
VALIDITY: The Tolerance for Sexual Harassment Inventory was completed by 171 college men and 218 college women (Reilly et al., 1986). Males were significantly more tolerant than females on all 10 items and on the total scale score. When responses from younger students (ages 22 and younger) were compared with responses from older students (ages 23 and older), significant differences were found on 6 items and on the total scale score. Younger students were more tolerant of sexual harassment than were older students.

Lott, Reilly, and Howard (1982) obtained scores from 514 college women and 354 college men. They found significant sex differences on all 10 items and the total scale score. Again, men were more tolerant of sexual harassment than were women. They also found that younger persons were more accepting of sexual harassment than were older persons.
NOTES & COMMENTS: (1) Reilly et al. (1986) factor analyzed the responses from 393 students. They extracted three factors: "flirtations are natural" (4 items), "provocative behavior" (4 items), and "feminist beliefs" (2 items). "All items in each factor had strong loadings and no item appeared in more than one factor" (Reilly et al., 1986, p. 350).

(2) The Tolerance for Sexual Harassment Inventory has been used as part of a larger questionnaire to study sexual harassment of college students (Lott & Reilly, 1980; Lott et al., 1982; Reilly et al., 1986).
AVAILABLE FROM: Lott and Reilly, 1980; Lott, Reilly, and Howard, 1982; Reilly, Lott, and Gallogly, 1986

USED IN:

Lott, B., & Reilly, M. E. (1980, August). *Assessment of sexual harassment within the University of Rhode Island community*. Paper presented at the conference of the Association for Women in Psychology, Boston. (ERIC Document Reproduction Service No. ED 212 918)

Lott, B., Reilly, M. E., & Howard, D. R. (1982). Sexual assault and harassment: A campus community case study. *Signs*, *8*(2), 296–319.

Reilly, M. E., Lott, B., & Gallogly, S. M. (1986). Sexual harassment of university students. *Sex Roles*, *15*(7/8), 333–358.

ACHIEVEMENT ORIENTATION SCALE II

AUTHOR: Joan Daniels Pedro

DATE: 1980

VARIABLE: Attitudes toward vicarious or direct achievement

TYPE OF INSTRUMENT: Summated rating scale

DESCRIPTION: The Achievement Orientation Scale II consists of 25 statements, many of which pertain to educational and work aspirations in regard to self and spouse. Twelve items are phrased to reflect the desire for direct achievement, and 13 items are phrased to reflect the desire for vicarious achievement. Items are accompanied by five response options ranging from "strongly agree" to "strongly disagree."

SAMPLE ITEMS: If I were married it would be important for me to achieve job success.

I would rather help responsible people do their jobs than take on serious responsibility myself.

PREVIOUS SUBJECTS: High school females

APPROPRIATE FOR: High school and college females

ADMINISTRATION: Self-administered; about 10–15 minutes

SCORING: Items are individually scored on a 5-point scale, with more points assigned to the response reflecting a desire for direct achievement and fewer points assigned to the response reflecting a desire for vicarious achievement. Pedro (1980) reported means, standard deviations, and ranges for two groups of 11th-grade females. She also provided means and standard deviations for the individual items.

DEVELOPMENT: A pool of 50 statements was generated based on Lipman-Blumen and Leavitt's (1977) theory of vicarious and direct achievement. The item pool was submitted to six judges for editing. The edited items were administered to 10 high school students, who were also asked to comment on the phrasing of the items. After the statements were revised, they were administered to 129 high school girls and 83 high school boys. The item pool was reduced to 25 items using the following previously established criteria: items were retained if all five response options were used, items that showed male-female differences in the predicted direction were retained, and items were selected to create a balance between present and future content. Item weighting was also taken into account in selecting items for the scale.

RELIABILITY: Internal consistency reliability was computed for several groups of high school girls. For one group of 11th-grade females, the reliability was .79; for a different group of 11th-grade females, the reliability was .82. Other values for the reliability fell between those two limits.

VALIDITY: Pedro (1982) reported a strong and significant correlation (r = .50) between scores on the Achievement Orientation Scale II and the career planning involvement of high school girls. Career planning involvement was measured by the Self-Rating of Planning Involvement Scale (American College Testing Program, 1974). The measure is "designed to gain information on students' career guidance needs and to assess outcomes of career guidance programs" (Pedro, 1982, p. 246).

Pedro also found significant correlations between scores on the Achievement Orientation Scale II and a measure of occupational information, a career maturity attitude measure, and knowledge of women's occupational experience.

NOTES & COMMENTS: Pedro (1980) reported the results of a factor analysis of responses to the Achievement Orientation Scale II. She reported information about seven factors.

AVAILABLE FROM: Pedro, 1980

USED IN:

Pedro, J. D. (1980). Achievement Orientation Scale II: A measure of an individual's attitude toward vicarious or direct achievement. *Catalog of Selected Documents in Psychology, 10,* 14. (Ms. No. 1980)

Pedro, J. D. (1982). Career maturity in high school age females. *Vocational Guidance Quarterly, 30,* 243–251.

BIBLIOGRAPHY:

American College Testing Program. (1974). *Assessment of career development handbook, user's guide, and report of research.* Boston: Houghton Mifflin.

Lipman-Blumen, J., & Leavitt, H. (1977). Vicarious and direct achievement patterns in adulthood. In N. Schlossberg & A. Entine (Eds.), *Counseling adults.* Belmont, CA: Wadsworth.

ATTITUDES TOWARD EMPLOYMENT
AUTHOR: Ingrid Waldron

DATE: 1964

VARIABLE: Attitudes toward the employment of married women

TYPE OF INSTRUMENT: Summated rating scale

DESCRIPTION: The Attitudes Toward Employment scale is a short scale consisting of only nine statements, each pertaining to advantages or disadvantages that might accrue to the individual or family when a married woman is in the work force. Items alternate between statements that are supportive of married women working and items that oppose married women being in the labor force. Each item is accompanied by five response options ranging from "strongly agree" to "strongly disagree."

SAMPLE ITEMS: Modern conveniences permit a wife to work without neglecting her family.

A woman's place is in the home, not in the office or shop.

PREVIOUS SUBJECTS: Middle-aged married women

APPROPRIATE FOR: High school students and older

ADMINISTRATION: Self-administered; about 5 minutes

SCORING: Items are individually scored on a 5-point scale with +2 points assigned to the response that reflects a positive attitude towards married women working and −2 points assigned to the response that opposes married women working. Total scores can thus range from −18 (very opposed to married women working) to +18 (very supportive of married women working). Waldron and Herold (1986) considered scores in the range of −18 to +4 as indicative of opposition to married women working; they considered scores in the range of +5 to +18 to be supportive of married women working.

DEVELOPMENT: The nine-item survey was part of a large research project, the National Longitudinal Surveys of Labor Market Experience. No other information was provided.

RELIABILITY: When the scale was administered to over 3,000 married women in 1972, coefficient alpha was .76. When the scale was administered to a somewhat smaller subset of married women in 1977, coefficient alpha was .75.

VALIDITY: Waldron and Herold (1986) found that women whose labor force participation was consistent with their attitudes were likely to have better health. That is, women who were working and had positive attitudes toward married women working and women who were not working and had negative attitudes toward married women working were more likely to report better health than were women whose behavior and attitudes were inconsistent with each other.

In a longitudinal study, Waldron and Herold (1986) found that "women who expressed favorable attitudes toward employment in 1972 [as measured by the Attitudes Toward Employment scale] were more likely to join the labor force by 1977" (p. 96). Thus, they concluded that the scale has predictive validity.

NOTES & COMMENTS: Though there is not a lot of published information regarding this measure and it has not been included in many published studies, I describe it here for two reasons: item responses are still likely to show considerable variability, and it is a short scale and thus may be useful as a quick measure of attitudes.

AVAILABLE FROM: Waldron and Herold, 1986

USED IN:
Waldron, I., & Herold, J. (1986). Employment, attitudes toward employment, and women's health. *Women and Health*, *11*(1), 79–98.

AWARENESS OF OCCUPATIONAL EXPERIENCE SCALE II
AUTHOR: Joan Daniels Pedro
DATE: 1980
VARIABLE: Knowledge of the female work force experience
TYPE OF INSTRUMENT: Alternate Choice: true/false
DESCRIPTION: The Awareness of Occupational Experience Scale II consists of 25 statements covering three areas: "(1) patterns of work force participation of women; (2) . . . differences in the occupational experiences of men and women; and (3) . . . legislative protection which can aid the work force participation of women" (Pedro, 1980, p. 1). The respondent is to indicate if each item on the scale is true or false.
SAMPLE ITEMS: (patterns of work force participation) One third of families headed by females live on poverty level incomes.

(differences in male-female experiences) Men are more likely than women to seek jobs near their homes.

(legislative protection) An affirmative action program stresses the hiring and promotion of white males.
PREVIOUS SUBJECTS: 11th-grade females
APPROPRIATE FOR: High school students and older
ADMINISTRATION: Self-administered; about 10 minutes
SCORING: One point is counted for each item answered consistently with the key. The maximum score is 25. Pedro (1980) reported means, standard deviations, and ranges for two samples of high school females.
DEVELOPMENT: A pool of 50 items was generated based on a 1977 Department of Labor monograph. About one-third of the items represented each of the three areas included on the scale: patterns of work force participation, work experience of males and females, and legal assistance for female employees. Six experienced counselors provided inputs that were used for editing the 50 items. The items were then administered to 10 adolescents, who provided further suggestions for modifying the items. A sample of 202 high school students, primarily juniors, completed the scale. Various statistical procedures were used to select the 25 items for the final version of the scale: "(1) items which had the highest beta weights were retained; (2) items which had X_{50} scores which permitted a spread across the ability criterion were retained; (3) items which had highest reliability were retained" (Pedro, 1980, p. 2). Care was taken to ensure that the three content areas were equally represented.
RELIABILITY: Using the data from 129 11th-grade females on whom the

scale was developed, the internal consistency reliability of the 25-item version of the scale was .77.

VALIDITY: The author claimed content validity for the scale because of the procedures used to develop it.

NOTES & COMMENTS: (1) Before using the scale, the researcher must check whether any items need to be updated. Since these items have right and wrong answers, it is possible that some will be obsolete.

(2) Four items on the scale contain the word *should*, but no indication is given as to the criterion to be used in judging the item. For example, one item states, "Girls and boys should have equal opportunities in all areas of their high school and/or college education." The statement is keyed "true," although it is a matter of opinion.

(3) Pedro (1982) used the Awareness of Occupational Experience Scale II as one of five career-related instruments to study the career planning involvement of high school females.

AVAILABLE FROM: Pedro, 1980

USED IN:

Pedro, J. D. (1980). Awareness of Occupational Experience Scale II: A measure of knowledge of facts about the female occupational experience. *Catalog of Selected Documents in Psychology, 10*(1), 14. (Ms. No. 1979)

Pedro, J. D. (1982). Career maturity in high school age females. *Vocational Guidance Quarterly, 30*(3), 243–251.

CAREER SALIENCE INVENTORY

AUTHOR: Jeffrey H. Greenhaus

DATE: 1970

VARIABLE: Importance of a career in one's life

TYPE OF INSTRUMENT: Summated rating scale with one ranking item

DESCRIPTION: The Career Salience Inventory consists of 27 Likert-type items and 1 ranking item. Seventeen of the Likert-type items are positively worded, and 10 are negatively worded. Most of the items represent one of three rationally derived subscales: Relative Importance (7 items), Planning and Thinking (8 items), and General Attitudes Toward Work (9 items). The Likert-type items are each accompanied by five response options ranging from "strongly agree" to "strongly disagree." The 1 ranking item lists six aspects of life (e.g., family relationships, leisure-time recreational activities, and religious beliefs and activities) and asks respondents to rank the activities "in terms of how much satisfaction you expect they will give you in your life" (Greenhaus, 1970, p. 160).

SAMPLE ITEMS: (Relative Importance) I intend to pursue the job of my choice even if it cuts deeply into the time I have for my family.

(Planning and Thinking) I enjoy thinking about and making plans about my future career.

(General Attitudes Toward Work) Work is one of the few areas in life where you can gain real satisfaction.
PREVIOUS SUBJECTS: College students, working women, married couples, members of dual career couples
APPROPRIATE FOR: Ages 16 and older
ADMINISTRATION: Self-administered; about 10–15 minutes
SCORING: Items are individually scored on a 5-point scale, with 5 points assigned to the response reflecting greater career salience. Item scores can be summed to yield three subscale scores and a total score. The total score can range from 27 to 135. Higher scores reflect higher degrees of career salience. Greenhaus (1970) reported means and standard deviations for the three subscale scores and the total score for two different samples of college students.
DEVELOPMENT: Because Greenhaus (1970) felt that career salience had been ill defined, he identified separate dimensions of career salience for inclusion on his scale. His notion of the "Relative Importance" dimension of career salience was based on the work of George (1965), and 7 items measuring this dimension were taken from George, with the wording slightly changed. The dimension of "Planning and Thinking" is related to the work of Super and Overstreet (1960), and the Planning and Thinking dimension is similar to Super's idea of vocational maturity.

The original version of the Career Salience Inventory was pretested on a sample of 10 graduate students. The students' feedback led to revisions, additions, and deletions of items. The new version of the inventory was administered to 12 social workers. Apparently this administration did not lead to any changes.
RELIABILITY: Greenhaus (1970) reported alpha coefficients for two samples of college students. For the first sample of 228 college students, the values of alpha were: Relative Importance = .64, Planning and Thinking = .49, and General Attitudes = .63. Alpha for the total score was .78. For the second sample of 149 college students, the values of alpha were: Relative Importance = .72, Planning and Thinking = .51, and General Attitudes = .69. For this sample, alpha for the total score was .84.

Greenhaus (1971) tested 104 college males and 273 college females. He reported alpha coefficients of .81 for both male and female college students. Fannin (1979) tested 147 college women and reported an alpha coefficient of .85. Beutell and Greenhaus (1982) tested 126 married women and 115 married men. They reported alpha coefficients of .83 for women and .90 for men.
VALIDITY: Greenhaus (1970) reported moderate correlations between scores on the Career Salience Inventory and a measure of self-esteem. Greenhaus did not find the anticipated relationship between sex and Career Salience scores, although the correlations were in the predicted direction. Only one correlation was statistically significant, and it too

was rather low. As expected, however, Greenhaus did find that career salience was consistently related to educational aspiration. Furthermore, career salience was positively related to career prestige and highly related to self-ratings of ambition. Greenhaus reported that a variety of other measures were significantly related to Career Salience scores: effort, self-ratings of performance, perception of impact of school success on future success, and several personality traits (persuasiveness, self-confidence, scholarliness, creativity, aggression, and wittiness). These findings tended to replicate the findings of Masih (1967), who measured career salience through an interview procedure.

Greenhaus (1971) reported that males scored significantly higher than females on the Career Salience Inventory.

NOTES & COMMENTS: (1) The subscale reliabilities are unacceptably low. Unless the reliability coefficients are increased, the use of subscale scores should be avoided.

(2) Greenhaus (1970) reported intercorrelations among the three subscale scores. All of the intercorrelations were statistically significant. The highest correlation was between the Planning and Thinking score and the General Attitudes score. Furthermore, of the three subscale scores, the General Attitudes score was most highly correlated with total score.

(3) Greenhaus (1970) reported the results of two factor analytic studies, each based on responses from a different sample. In both cases, eight factors were identified and labeled. Four factors seem to be similar in the two analyses. These could be labeled "Relative Importance," "Leisure-Interpersonal," "Planning-Source of Satisfaction," and "Breadth of Interest."

(4) Greenhaus (1970, 1971) studied the relationship between scores on the Career Salience Inventory and occupational choice, as well as occupational satisfaction.

(5) Many researchers in addition to Greenhaus have used the Career Salience Inventory. Fannin (1979) used it in a study "designed to ascertain whether the relations among sex-role attitude, work-role salience, atypicality of college major, and self-esteem would combine to differentiate ego-identity status in college women" (p. 12). Illfelder (1980) used the Career Salience Inventory as one of several measures in a study examining the relationship among career salience, fear of success, gender role attitudes, and trait anxiety in college women. Hardesty and Betz (1980) studied marital adjustment in dual career couples. They related marital adjustment scores to several different variables, including career salience, attitudes toward women, and several demographic and family characteristics. Beutell and Greenhaus (1982) studied married women's interrole conflict and its relationship to several variables including career salience. Marshall and Wijting (1982) studied the dimensions of women's career orientation using a variety of measures, including the Career

Salience Inventory. They collected data from both working women and college women. Fassinger (1985) developed a model of women's career choice that she tested with several measures, including the Career Salience Inventory. DeMeis, Hock, and McBride (1986) conducted a longitudinal study to examine "how older, well-educated mothers of infants come to terms with establishing a balance between maternal and career roles" (p. 627). One of the measures they used was the Career Salience Inventory.

AVAILABLE FROM: Greenhaus, 1970

USED IN:

Beutell, N. J., & Greenhaus, J. H. (1982). Interrole conflict among married women: The influence of husband and wife characteristics on conflict and coping behavior. *Journal of Vocational Behavior, 21,* 99–110.

DeMeis, D. K., Hock, E., & McBride, S. L. (1986). The balance of employment and motherhood: Longitudinal study of mothers' feelings about separation from their first-born infants. *Developmental Psychology, 22*(5), 627–632.

Fannin, P. M. (1979). The relation between ego-identity status and sex-role attitude, work-role salience, atypicality of major, and self-esteem in college women. *Journal of Vocational Behavior, 14,* 12–22.

Fassinger, R. E. (1985). A causal model of college women's career choice. *Journal of Vocational Behavior, 27,* 123–153.

Greenhaus, J. H. (1970). Self-esteem and career salience as influences on vocational choice and vocational satisfaction. (Doctoral dissertation, New York University, 1970). *Dissertation Abstracts International, 31,* 6966B.

Greenhaus, J. H. (1971). An investigation of the role of career salience in vocational behavior. *Journal of Vocational Behavior, 1,* 209–216.

Hardesty, S. A., & Betz, N. E. (1980). The relationships of career salience, attitudes toward women, and demographic and family characteristics to marital adjustment in dual-career couples. *Journal of Vocational Behavior, 17,* 242–250.

Hock, E., DeMeis, D., & McBride, S. (1988). Maternal separation anxiety: Its role in the balance of employment and motherhood in mothers of infants. In A. Gottfried & A. Gottfried (Eds.), *Maternal employment and children's development: Longitudinal research* (pp. 191–227). New York: Plenum.

Illfelder, J. K. (1980). Fear of success, sex role attitudes, and career salience and anxiety levels of college women. *Journal of Vocational Behavior, 16,* 7–17.

Marshall, S. J., & Wijting, J. P. (1982). Dimensionality of women's career orientation. *Sex Roles, 8*(2), 135–146.

BIBLIOGRAPHY:

George, P. M. (1965). Occupational choice of college students: Centrality of occupation, and evaluative-cognitive congruence. (Doctoral dissertation, University of North Carolina, 1965). *Dissertation Abstracts International, 27,* 252A.

Masih, L. K. (1967). Career saliency and its relation to certain needs, interests, and job values. *Personnel and Guidance Journal, 45,* 653–658.

Super, D. E., & Overstreet, P. L. (1960). *The vocational maturity of ninth-grade boys.* New York: Bureau of Publications, Teachers College, Columbia University.

DESIRE TO WORK SCALE
AUTHOR: Lorraine Dittrich Eyde
DATE: 1962
VARIABLE: Women's work motivation
DESCRIPTION: The Desire to Work Scale asks women to indicate how much they would like to work under each of 17 conditions. The conditions vary in terms of the woman's marital status, the number and ages of her children, and her husband's salary. For each item, the respondent uses a 5-point scale to indicate whether she would or would not want to work under the condition described.
ARTICLES LISTED IN BEERE, 1979: 8
AVAILABLE FROM: Eyde, 1962
USED IN:
Barry, T. E., Gilly, M. C., & Doran, L. E. (1985). Advertising to women with different career orientations. *Journal of Advertising Research*, 25(2), 26–35.
Eyde, L. D. (1962). *Work values and background factors as predictors of women's desire to work*. Bureau of Business Research Monograph 108. Columbus: Ohio State University.
Marshall, S. J., & Wijting, J. P. (1982). Dimensionality of women's career orientation. *Sex Roles*, 8, 135–146.
Orcutt, M. A., & Walsh, W. B. (1979). Traditionality and congruence of career aspirations for college women. *Journal of Vocational Behavior*, 14, 1–11.
BIBLIOGRAPHY:
Beere, C. A. (1979). *Women and women's issues: A handbook of tests and measures* (pp. 322–324). San Francisco: Jossey-Bass.

MARINO MEASURE OF AFFIRMATIVE ACTION COMPLIANCE
AUTHOR: Kenneth E. Marino
DATE: 1980
VARIABLE: Evaluation of the importance of activities that can be undertaken by an employer to comply with affirmative action requirements
TYPE OF INSTRUMENT: Summated rating scale
DESCRIPTION: The Marino Measure of Affirmative Action Compliance contains a list of 34 actions that an employer might undertake in order to comply with the government's requirements for affirmative action. The items represent six factors: Seeking Community Support (11 items), Informing the Employees (8 items), Internalizing the Equal Employment Opportunity (EEO) Policy (4 items), Enhancing Advancement Opportunities (3 items), Increasing Minority Applicant Flow (3 items), and Demonstrating Top Management Support (5 items). (Some items load heavily on more than one factor, but each item was counted only once in the accounting given here.) In completing the scale, respondents rate each item in terms of "its importance in evaluating the contractor's

compliance effort" (Marino, 1980, p. 347). Each item is rated on a 7-point scale ranging from "relatively unimportant" to "very important." SAMPLE ITEMS: (Seeking Community Support) Inclusion of predominantly minority colleges and universities in the contractor's campus recruitment activities.

(Informing the Employees) Display of contractor's EEO policy statement in work areas.

(Internalizing the EEO Policy) Evidence that the contractor has encouraged minority employees to refer other minorities to the contractor for possible employment.

(Enhancing Advancement Opportunities) Institution of minority oriented training programs.

(Increasing Minority Applicant Flow) Personal contact, by the EEO coordinator, with employment referral agencies such as the Urban League or Job Corps.

(Demonstrating Top Management Support) Evidence that the CEO [chief executive officer] or plant manager is seriously committed to EEO policy.

PREVIOUS SUBJECTS: EEO compliance officers

APPROPRIATE FOR: Business persons familiar with EEO requirements and EEO terminology

ADMINISTRATION: Self-administered; about 15 minutes

SCORING: Items are individually scored on a 7-point scale, with 1 point assigned to the "unimportant" end of the continuum and 7 points assigned to the "important" end of the continuum. Marino (1980) made no mention of factor scores or total scores. He did, however, report means and standard deviations for each item, based on the responses from 50 EEO compliance officers.

DEVELOPMENT: A pool of 39 items was developed based on (1) interviews with individuals who were experienced in evaluating affirmative action programs and (2) a review of selected documents issued by the U.S. Department of Labor. The items were pretested using the same individuals who participated in the interviews. After minor modifications, the measure was completed by 50 EEO compliance officers. Their responses led to the elimination of five items that were redundant with other items on the scale. Furthermore, their responses were factor analyzed, and nine factors were identified. Three trivial factors were eliminated, leaving the six factors mentioned.

RELIABILITY: No information was provided.

VALIDITY: The method of scale construction suggests that the measure has content validity. In fact, when the scale was pretested, respondents were given the opportunity to add relevant activities that were not already on the scale. According to Marino (1980), "no new evaluative criteria were identified" (p. 347).

NOTES & COMMENTS: (1) Marino (1980) correctly pointed out that the number of respondents relative to the number of scale items led to a factor structure of questionable stability.

(2) Marino (1980) stated, "These results can be employed in the construction of a measurement instrument" (p. 350). Obviously, he did not believe that this is already a finished measure. However, it is included here because nothing similar was identified from the literature search conducted for this book. The uniqueness of the measure increases its potential value to researchers.

AVAILABLE FROM: Marino, 1980

USED IN:

Marino, K. E. (1980). A preliminary investigation into the behavioral dimensions of affirmative action compliance. *Journal of Applied Psychology*, 65(3), 346–350.

OCCUPATIONAL ASPIRATION SCALE FOR FEMALES (OAS-F)

AUTHORS: Lawrence Hotchkiss, Evans Curry, Archibald O. Haller, and Keith Widaman

DATE: 1979

VARIABLE: Occupational aspirations of female adolescents

TYPE OF INSTRUMENT: Multiple choice

DESCRIPTION: The Occupational Aspiration Scale for Females (OAS-F) consists of eight questions, each followed by a unique set of 10 occupational titles. Thus, 80 different occupations are listed on the scale. The eight questions pertain to occupational aspirations. They vary according to time frame (when schooling is over, and by the age of 30) and degree of realism (realistic job choice and idealistic job choice). Crossing these two variables gives four questions (two time frames by two degrees of realism), and each of the four questions is repeated twice, to produce eight questions. All 10 occupational choices that follow each question are appropriate for females (male stereotyped occupational titles are avoided), and they vary in prestige. Each set of 10 choices is presented in random order, not rank ordered by prestige. The respondent's task is to select one answer for each question.

SAMPLE ITEM: Of the jobs listed in this question, which is the BEST ONE you are REALLY SURE YOU CAN GET when your SCHOOLING IS OVER? [The question is followed by 10 occupational titles that range in prestige from Federal Court Judge to Professional Babysitter.]

PREVIOUS SUBJECTS: Black and white 10th-grade females

APPROPRIATE FOR: High school females

ADMINISTRATION: Self-administered; about 5–10 minutes

SCORING: Each occupational choice has a prestige ranking assigned to it. The respondent's score is the sum of the rank scores for the eight items selected.

DEVELOPMENT: The Occupational Aspiration Scale (OAS) (Haller & Miller, 1971) was developed "to provide a short instrument to measure levels of occupational aspirations (LOA) in an occupational prestige hierarchy . . . among teenage youth" (Hotchkiss, Curry, Haller, & Widaman, 1979, p. 95). It was designed to be easy to administer, easy to take, and easy to score. Since the scale was developed on a male sample, used many stereotypically male job titles, and raised some doubts regarding the scale's usefulness with females, an alternate form of the scale was developed for use with females. The occupational titles on the female form of the scale avoid any male stereotyping. Occupational titles were selected to match the prestige rankings of those on the original OAS. Whereas the National Opinion Research Center (NORC) study of occupational prestige (Reiss, 1961) provided the prestige rankings for the occupations on the original OAS, a study by Siegel (1971) provided the prestige rankings for the occupational titles on the OAS-F. Within each set of 10 occupations, the correlations between the prestige rankings of the items on the original OAS and the OAS-F were very high; all eight correlations were above .93, and three correlations were .99.

RELIABILITY: Coefficient alpha for a sample of about 100 white female 10th graders was .72; for a sample of about 100 black female 10th graders, it was .71.

VALIDITY: Hotchkiss et al. (1979) predicted that scores on the OAS-F would correlate with nine variables: realistic occupational aspiration, realistic educational aspiration, high school freshman grade point average, intelligence, father's occupational status, father's educational achievement, mother's educational achievement, father's occupational expectation for his daughter, and mother's occupational expectation for her daughter. For black female sophomores, seven of the nine correlations were significant; only father's occupational status and father's educational level were not. For white female sophomores, six of the nine correlations were significant. Again father's occupational status and father's educational level were not significant; additionally, mother's educational level was not significant. Although 13 of the 18 correlations were significant, all tended to be rather low, with the significant correlations ranging from .19 to .51.

NOTES & COMMENTS: (1) Hotchkiss et al. (1979) used a variety of procedures to factor analyze responses to the OAS-F. Their results were largely inconclusive, though it was clear that the test is not unidimensional.

(2) After reviewing the positive aspects of the OAS-F, Hotchkiss et al. (1979) cautioned that "much work remains before one can be highly confident of the accuracy of measurement of youth's occupational as-

pirations. . . . Efforts to improve the reliability and clarify the factor struc-
ture of the scale should be emphasized" (p. 116).
AVAILABLE FROM: Hotchkiss, Curry, Haller, and Widaman, 1979
USED IN:
Hotchkiss, L., Curry, E., Haller, A. O., & Widaman, K. (1979). The Occupational
       Aspiration Scale: An evaluation and alternate form for females. *Rural
       Sociology*, 44(1), 95–118.
BIBLIOGRAPHY:
Haller, A. L., & Miller, I. W. (1971). *The Occupational Aspiration Scale: Theory,
       structure and correlates*. Cambridge, MA: Schenkman Publishing.
Reiss, A. J., Jr. (1961). *Occupations and social status*. New York: Free Press.
Siegel, P. M. (1971). *Prestige in the American occupation structure*. Unpublished
       doctoral dissertation, University of Chicago.

RANKED WORK VALUES SCALE
AUTHOR: Lorraine Dittrich Eyde
DATE: 1962
VARIABLE: Women's work values
DESCRIPTION: The Ranked Work Values Scale is a ranking scale that
requires a woman to rank order six items in each of 14 sets. Within a
given set, there is one item reflecting each of the following values: dom-
inance-recognition, economic, independence, interesting activity/vari-
ety, mastery-achievement, and social.
ARTICLES LISTED IN BEERE, 1979: 5
AVAILABLE FROM: Eyde, 1962
USED IN:
Eyde, L. D. (1962). *Work values and background factors as predictors of women's desire
       to work*. Bureau of Business Research Monograph 108. Columbus: Ohio
       State University.
Glogowski, D., & Lanning, W. (1976). The relationship among age category,
       curriculum selected, and work values for women in a community college.
       Vocational Guidance Quarterly, 25, 119–125.
BIBLIOGRAPHY:
Beere, C. A. (1979). *Women and women's issues: A handbook of tests and measures*
       (pp. 332–334). San Francisco: Jossey-Bass.

SITUATIONAL ATTITUDE SCALE FOR WOMEN (SASW)
AUTHORS: Michele H. Herman and William E. Sedlacek
DATE: 1973
VARIABLE: Attitudes toward women in nontraditional gender roles
DESCRIPTION: The Situational Attitude Scale for Women (SASW) is a
semantic differential scale in which 10 single-sentence descriptions of
situations are each followed by 10 semantic differential scales. Nine of
the 10 descriptions relate to employment situations in which sex might
be a variable affecting the way a person responds to the situation. There

are two forms of the scale—one in which the sex of the person in the situation is unspecified and one in which the sex is given.

ARTICLES LISTED IN BEERE, 1979: 6

NOTES & COMMENTS: (1) Shueman and Sedlacek (1976) described a different version of the scale: the Situational Attitude Scale for Women–4 (SASW–4), a 49-item inventory with seven semantic differential scales accompanying brief descriptions of each of seven situations. Again, there are two forms of the scale, differing only in terms of the sex of the person in the situation.

(2) Knight and Sedlacek (1983) used the Situational Attitude Scale for Women in Occupations.

AVAILABLE FROM: Herman and Sedlacek, 1973; for the SASW–4, see Shueman and Sedlacek (1976); for the Situational Attitude Scale for Women in Occupations, see Knight and Sedlacek (1983).

USED IN:

Albury, R. M., Chaples, E. A., & Stubbs, K. (1977). Sexism among a group of Sydney tertiary students. *Australian and New Zealand Journal of Sociology*, 13, 133–136.

Herman, M. H., & Sedlacek, W. E. (1973). *Sexist attitudes among male university students*. Unpublished paper, University of Maryland. (ERIC Document Reproduction Service No. ED 074 421)

Hirt, J., Hoffman, M. A., & Sedlacek, W. E. (1983). Attitudes toward changing sex-roles of male varsity athletes versus nonathletes: Developmental perspectives. *Journal of College Student Personnel*, 24(1), 33–38.

Knight, G. D., & Sedlacek, W. E. (1983). *Sex-role identity and attitudes toward women in traditional and non-traditional occupations*. Unpublished paper, University of Maryland. (ERIC Document Reproduction Service No. ED 248 335)

Minatoya, L. Y., & Sedlacek, W. E. (1981). *The SASW: A measure of sexism among university freshmen*. Unpublished paper, University of Maryland. (ERIC Document Reproduction Service No. ED 217 346)

Minatoya, L. Y., & Sedlacek, W. E. (1983). The Situational Attitude Scale—Women (SASW): A means to measure environmental sexism. *Journal of the National Association of Women Deans and Counselors*, 47(1), 25–30.

Shueman, S. A., & Sedlacek, W. E. (1976). *Measuring sexist attitudes in a situational context*. Unpublished manuscript, University of Maryland. (ERIC Document Reproduction Service No. ED 157 929)

BIBLIOGRAPHY:

Beere, C. A. (1979). *Women and women's issues: A handbook of tests and measures* (pp. 338–340). San Francisco: Jossey-Bass.

SURVEY OF WOMEN'S ATTITUDES ABOUT CAREERS

AUTHORS: Hollie B. Thomas, Leo Christie, Kay Calvin, and Karen Denbroeder

DATE: 1980

VARIABLE: Barriers to women's entry into male-dominated occupations

TYPE OF INSTRUMENT: Summated rating scale

DESCRIPTION: The Survey of Women's Attitudes About Careers was developed to identify the barriers that discourage women from entering male-dominated occupations. It consists of 200 items arranged into 21 sets. Each item set contains a sentence stem followed by a series of endings for the stem. Each complete statement (stem plus ending) is a potential barrier that might discourage women from entering male-dominated occupations. For each ending, the respondent expresses her degree of agreement using five response options ranging from "strongly agree" to "strongly disagree." Following are the item stems and the number of items associated with each stem: "A woman may decide *not* to enter careers that are usually held by men because . . . " (8 items); "Information about careers usually held by men . . . " (5 items); "If a woman seeks information about non-traditional occupations (those usually held by men) she may find that . . . " (6 items); "A woman who attempts to get training in a male dominated field is likely to feel that persons offering the training programs . . . " (10 items); "A woman who makes plans to enter a career usually sought only by men is likely to feel that her friends think that . . . " (8 items); "A woman may be reluctant to seek training for a career usually held by men because . . . " (11 items); "Women who hold jobs in traditional female fields find it difficult to leave their jobs to acquire jobs traditionally held by men because . . . " (6 items); "Women have traditionally remained in certain jobs and professions because they believe that . . . " (9 items); "A woman may not prepare for *any* career because . . . " (6 items); "A woman may have difficulty getting qualified and staying qualified for jobs traditionally held by men because . . . " (16 items); "A woman may feel that if she is successful in an occupation typically held only by men that . . . " (9 items); "An employed woman may not be willing to risk seeking a job usually held by men because . . . " (5 items); "College education for a woman . . . " (6 items); "A woman may be reluctant to pursue a career in a field dominated by men because . . . " (20 items); "Women may have difficulty getting jobs usually held by men because . . . " (5 items); "Women do not seek the same careers as do men because . . . " (12 items); "A woman who obtains a job in an area dominated by men may find it difficult to cope with . . . " (11 items); "A woman who works in jobs usually held by men . . . " (7 items); "A woman is likely to choose to enter a 'female' career (those usually dominated by women) because . . . " (11 items); "A woman's family may affect her career decision by . . . " (13 items); and finally, "A woman may not go into a non-traditional or previously male dominated career because . . . " (16 items) (Denbroeder & Thomas, 1980, p. 12).

SAMPLE ITEMS: (Information about careers usually held by men) May be difficult to relate to for a woman.

May never be sought by women.

PREVIOUS SUBJECTS: Teachers, nurses, secretaries; females enrolled in community college

APPROPRIATE FOR: High school students and older

ADMINISTRATION: Self-administered; about an hour

SCORING: Items are individually scored on a 5-point scale, with higher points assigned to the "strongly disagree" end of the continuum. Thus, total scores can range from 200 (very strong belief in many barriers) to 1000 (belief in no barriers).

DEVELOPMENT: A sample of 50 women including secretaries, nurses, and teachers who had at one time considered entering a male-dominated occupation were interviewed and asked about the deterrents they experienced that had kept them from entering the occupations they had originally considered. Similar items were grouped together, and redundant items were changed or deleted. This procedure resulted in the 200 items that comprise the scale.

RELIABILITY: Thomas (1981) reported a coefficient alpha of .98.

VALIDITY: Though the details are not provided, Thomas (1981) stated: "Evidence of content and construct validity was provided by a Q-sort and a factor analysis of the items" (p. 34).

NOTES & COMMENTS: (1) Denbroeder and Thomas (1980) and Thomas (1981) reported the results of the same study. The Survey of Women's Attitudes About Careers was completed by 256 women—secretaries, teachers, and nurses. Comparisons were made of the responses of those who had seriously considered a male-dominated occupation, those who had given slight consideration to a male-dominated occupation, and those who had not considered a male-dominated occupation.

(2) Thomas, Christie, Calvin, and Denbroeder (1980) used a modification of the Survey of Women's Attitudes About Careers in a pretest/posttest design to look at the impact of a short-term educational program designed to help junior college women overcome barriers to entry in male-dominated occupations. They modified the scale, shortening it from 200 items to 123 items by applying two criteria. First, they selected items for which 40% or more of the respondents in an earlier study had responded "strongly agree" or "agree"; second, they ensured that each of 17 orthogonal factors identified in an earlier factor analysis was represented by at least three items. If the 40% rule resulted in a factor's being underrepresented, the highest loading items on that factor were added to the revised scale. The internal consistency reliability of the resulting scale was .97. Test-retest reliability was computed using data from a control group tested on two occasions, with an interval of about 5 weeks between testings. The average item test-retest reliability was .39 (range was −.29 to .75); for 17 factor scores,

the average test-retest reliability (interval unspecified) was .45 (range .29 to .65).

AVAILABLE FROM: Denbroeder and Thomas, 1980
USED IN:

Denbroeder, K. L., & Thomas, H. B. (1980, April). *Barriers to entry into non-traditional occupations for women: A study to determine the ability to discriminate among groups.* Paper presented at the meeting of the American Educational Research Association, Boston. (ERIC Document Reproduction Service No. ED 186 637)

Thomas, H. B. (1981). Barriers to entry into non-traditional careers and training programs perceived by women. *Journal of Industrial Teacher Education,* 18(2), 32–42.

Thomas, H. B., Christie, L., Calvin, K., & Denbroeder, K. (1980, April). *Impact of an educational program designed to assist women overcome the deterrents to entering non-traditional occupations.* Paper presented at the meeting of the American Educational Research Association, Boston. (ERIC Document Reproduction Service No. ED 186 636)

WORK INVOLVEMENT INDEX

AUTHORS: Josephine A. Ruggiero and Louise C. Weston
DATE: 1988
VARIABLE: Extent of work involvement in women
TYPE OF INSTRUMENT: Survey
DESCRIPTION: The Work Involvement Index is not an instrument per se; rather it is a coding scheme for determining the extent of work involvement in women. The Index consists of four indicators: Work Continuity, divided into three scoring categories (1 = no breaks more than 1 year; 2 = no breaks more than 3 years; and 3 = out more than 3 years, not employed; no full-time work since 1970); Work Status, also divided into three scoring categories (1 = full-time work only; 2 = full-time and part-time work; and 3 = part-time work only); Current/Most Recent Occupation, divided into two categories (1 = professional; 2 = nonprofessional); and Educational Achievement, divided into three scoring categories (1 = PhD/professional degree; 2 = MA; and 3 = BA only). In assessing Work Continuity, vocational training and/ or graduate school count as work; thus, a woman who works 2 years, attends graduate school for 2 years, and then returns to working would be coded as "1, No breaks more than 1 year."
PREVIOUS SUBJECTS: Female college graduates
APPROPRIATE FOR: Female college graduates
ADMINISTRATION: The information necessary to complete the Work Involvement Index can be obtained from a paper-and-pencil questionnaire or from an interview.

SCORING: The scores assigned to the four indicators are summed to yield a total score that can range from 4 (highest possible work involvement) to 11 (lowest work involvement). According to Ruggiero and Weston (1988), women scoring in the 4 to 6 range are categorized as having "high" work involvement; women scoring in the 7 to 8 range are categorized as having "moderate" work involvement; and women scoring in the 9 to 11 range are categorized as having "low" work involvement.

DEVELOPMENT: Though Ruggiero and Weston (1988) did not describe the development of the Work Involvement Index, they did define "work involvement": "Work involvement refers to the occupational choices that respondents made since they graduated from college and to the education they have acquired in order to pursue these choices" (p. 495).

RELIABILITY: No information was provided. However, since the Index is based primarily on factual items, it is likely that the test-retest reliability would be quite high.

VALIDITY: Scores on the Work Involvement Index were related to responses to a single-item question asking about "present major activity." As expected, "women classified as high on our work involvement index tended to mention either graduate or professional school . . . or work . . . as their present major activity . . . the moderates most typically mentioned work . . . the lows tended to be fairly evenly distributed among mentions of family . . . , work . . . , or work and family" (Ruggiero & Weston, 1988, p. 498).

NOTES & COMMENTS: Ruggiero and Weston (1988) used the Work Involvement Index to identify the level of women's work commitment. They then looked at various life-style, family, and work variables to see how they related to level of work involvement.

AVAILABLE FROM: Ruggiero and Weston, 1988

USED IN:

Ruggiero, J. A., & Weston, L. C. (1988). Work involvement among college-educated women: A methodological extension. *Sex Roles*, *19*, 491–507.

8

Multiple Roles

This chapter looks at 30 scales dealing with men and/or women in regard to more than a single role. The roles are generally the marital and parental roles and the employee role. The first 11 scales deal primarily with role conflict or role strain. The next 3 scales pertain specifically to dual career couples, and the final 16 scales deal with a variety of multiple role issues.

I did not describe any of the 11 role conflict/role strain measures in my previous handbook (Beere, 1979), though one of the scales is old enough to have been included. Most of the scales focus on the conflict between demands from the employee role and demands from the marital/parental roles. Many of the scales are intended to measure the *experience* of role conflict, and therefore they are appropriate for use only with employed married adults. Two of the scales have a slightly different focus. The Sage Loudermilk Role Conflict Scale (Sage & Loudermilk, 1979) deals with the role conflict experienced by female athletes, and the Sex Role Conflict Scale (Chusmir & Koberg, 1986) deals with the experience of conflict between the way a person is treated and the way the person wishes to be treated.

Most of the role conflict/role strain measures are summated rating scales, though there is also an alternate choice measure and a projective measure. These scales vary in length from 4 to 60 items.

Reliability is a problem for the scales in this section. There are data on the test-retest reliability of only two scales, and although there are data regarding the internal consistency reliability of most of the scales, those data often suggest that the scales are not sufficiently reliable. There is at least some discussion of the validity of each of the scales in this section.

The most frequently used role conflict/role strain scale is Holahan and Gilbert's (1978) Role Conflict Scales, which first appeared in the literature in 1978. This measure has been used in 11 published studies and ERIC documents. Another scale used in several studies is the Nevill Damico Role Conflict Questionnaire (Nevill & Damico, 1974). Six of the 11 measures in this section have been used by only one researcher, though most of the 6 have been written about in more than one article.

The role conflict/role strain scales are followed by three scales that focus on dual career couples. One scale is for the wives/mothers in dual career couples; one scale is for both partners of the dual career marriage; and one scale can be used with persons of at least high school age. The three scales each follow a different format: a Guttman scale, a summated rating scale, and a multiple choice measure. The multiple choice measure is very brief and can be completed in less than 10 minutes. It consists of two job-seeking simulations, each followed by some questions. The summated rating scale is rather lengthy, consisting of 49 statements and requiring about 20–25 minutes to complete. Although all three scales are promising for researchers, none is strong in terms of reliability, *and* validity, *and* frequency of use by other researchers.

The 16 remaining scales in this chapter cover a variety of topics. Their common element is that they all look at more than a single role, generally the marital/parental roles and the employee role. Seven of these scales were included in my previous handbook, but none has been used extensively since its publication. Of the 9 scales new to this handbook, factor analysis has been used with 5 of the measures. Eleven of the scales in this section are summated rating scales, ranging in length from 15 to 70 items. As was the case with the role conflict/role strain scales, reliability is a problem with some of these scales. Either there is no evidence of the scale's internal consistency reliability or the evidence shows that the scale is not sufficiently reliable. There is no evidence regarding the test-retest reliability of any of the 16 measures.

The most commonly used measure in this section is the Work and Family Orientation Questionnaire (WOFO) developed by Helmreich and Spence (1978), which measures achievement motivation and attitudes toward family and career. WOFO has been used in 34 published articles and ERIC documents. It is appropriate for persons who are at least of high school age and has been used in a number of countries, including France, Tunisia, Mexico, and Fiji.

Of the 20 measures included in the "Multiple Roles" chapter of my previous handbook, 13 of the measures have not been used again; however, they have been replaced by other scales. Overall, there are more scales available for multiple roles research today than 10 years ago.

BIBLIOGRAPHY

Beere, C. A. (1979). *Women and women's issues: A handbook of tests and measures.* San Francisco: Jossey-Bass.

Chusmir, L. H., & Koberg, C. S. (1986). Development and validation of the Sex Role Conflict Scale. *Journal of Applied Behavioral Science, 22*(4), 397–409.

Helmreich, R. L., & Spence, J. T. (1978). The Work and Family Orientation Questionnaire: An objective instrument to assess components of achievement motivation and attitudes toward family and career. *Catalog of Selected Documents in Psychology, 8*, 35. (Ms. No. 1677)

Holahan, C. K., & Gilbert, L. A. (1978, August). *Interrole conflict for dual career couples: The effects of gender and parenthood.* Paper presented at the meeting of the American Psychological Association, Toronto. (ERIC Document Reproduction Service No. ED 172 102)

Nevill, D., & Damico, S. (1974). Development of a role conflict questionnaire for women: Some preliminary findings. *Journal of Consulting and Clinical Psychology, 42*, 743.

Sage, G. H., & Loudermilk, S. (1979). The female athlete and role conflict. *Research Quarterly, 50*(1), 88–96.

CAREER/MARITAL STRESS OF WOMEN INVENTORY (CMSWI)

AUTHORS: Sandra Thomas, Sandra Shoun, and Kay Albrecht

DATE: 1981

VARIABLE: "Perceptions of both husband and wife regarding the developmental progress of the wife's career, with emphasis on stress factors, coping strategies, and spousal support" (Thomas, Albrecht, & White, 1984, p. 515).

TYPE OF INSTRUMENT: A variety of item types

DESCRIPTION: Intended for use with couples in dual career marriages, there are two forms of the Career/Marital Stress of Women Inventory (CMSWI)—one to be completed by the wife and the other by her husband. Both husband and wife answer the questions in terms of the wife's career progress and her stressors. The first section of the CMSWI asks 12 questions seeking demographic information on age, family size, education, occupation, income, race, and so on. The second section, "Initial Career Plans," has 6 items, some with several parts. These questions focus on the woman's initial career goals, commitment to the goals, and support of these goals from parents, relatives, and spouse. Some ask about the husband's and wife's success in achieving their career goals. Sections III and IV each include 15 items asking about stress factors. Section III looks at stress factors in the marital/family sphere. Section IV looks at work-related stress factors. Three pieces of information are requested for each of the stressors listed: a rating of how much effect the stressor has had on the woman's life ("no, little, moderate, or much"), a brief description of the strategy employed to contend with the stressor, and a rating of the outcome of employing the strategy (positive, negative, or neutral). Section V asks for ratings of the husband's supportiveness during stressful times. Ratings are made in four areas: emotional support, financial support, support in child rearing, and support in household management. A 4-point scale is provided for recording the ratings: "unsupportive, somewhat supportive, moderately supportive, very supportive." Section VI contains 6 questions pertaining to the woman's "current career status." Items pertain to such factors as work satisfaction, work commitment, and various aspects of husband's responses to his wife's work. The last section, Section VII, has 3 "semiprojective" questions regarding the advice the couple would give to their daughter about her own career planning and asking what the woman would or should have done differently in her dealings with stressors that affected her career development.

SAMPLE ITEMS: (Section III—marital/family stress) Home management tasks; conflict with spouse

(Section IV—work-related stress) Discriminatory management practices; financial compensation

PREVIOUS SUBJECTS: Husbands and wives in dual career marriages

APPROPRIATE FOR: Husbands and wives in dual career marriages

ADMINISTRATION: Self-administered; about 45 minutes

SCORING: Scores are obtained on five subscales: Career Adjustment, Work Environment, Resource Management, Dyadic Interaction, and Family Crisis. Further information regarding scoring was not provided.

DEVELOPMENT: According to Thomas et al. (1984), "The instrument was carefully scrutinized by three university faculty members who conduct research on stress, women's issues, and family problems" (p. 515). Additionally, the measure was reviewed by 20 graduate students in child and family studies, who suggested changes, additions, and deletions. The measure was then administered to 10 couples, who made further suggestions for improving the measure.

RELIABILITY: Coefficient alpha for four subscale scores ranged from .64 to .77. For a fifth subscale, Family Crisis, coefficient alpha was .35, a very low value. Thomas et al. (1984) explained the lack of internal consistency on this variable by stating: "Internal consistency for this scale was lower since couples experiencing one type of crisis are not necessarily experiencing others" (p. 515).

VALIDITY: Thomas et al. (1984) presumed content validity because the scale development process included review by faculty and graduate students.

NOTES & COMMENTS: (1) Thomas et al. (1984) used the CMSWI in a study of marital quality in dual career couples.

(2) White, Mascalo, Thomas, and Shoun (1986) found that in three areas—Dyadic Interaction, Management, and Career Adjustment—

wives reported experiencing greater stress than their husbands thought they had. In the remaining two areas, Family Crisis and Work Environment, there were no significant differences between the perceptions of the husbands and the experiences of their wives.

AVAILABLE FROM: Order from NAPS c/o Microfiche Publications, P.O. Box 3513, Grand Central Station, New York, NY 10163–3513; NAPS document no. 04674; for microfiche, in U.S. remit $4.00 with order.

USED IN:

Thomas, S., Albrecht, K., & White, P. (1984). Determinants of marital quality in dual-career couples. *Family Relations, 33*(4), 513–521.

Thomas, S., Shoun, S., & Albrecht, K. (1981). *Career/Marital Stress of Women Inventory.* Unpublished test, University of Tennessee, Center for Nursing Research, Knoxville.

White, P., Mascalo, A., Thomas, S., & Shoun, S. (1986). Husbands' and wives' perceptions of marital intimacy and wives' stresses in dual-career marriages. *Family Perspective, 20*(1), 27–35.

GERSON ROLE GRATIFICATION AND ROLE STRAIN SCALES

AUTHOR: Judith M. Gerson

DATE: 1985

VARIABLE: Role gratification, role strain, and net role gratification defined as role gratification minus role strain

TYPE OF INSTRUMENT: Alternate choice

DESCRIPTION: There are two parts to the Gerson Role Gratification and Role Strain Scales. The Role Gratification portion consists of 12 positive items—statements about ways in which the respondent's life has improved. The Role Strain portion consists of 12 negative items—statements about stressors or ways in which the respondent's life has deteriorated. Although Gerson (1985) did not specify the response options, "true" and "false" are appropriate for each item and consistent with Gerson's scoring procedures.

SAMPLE ITEMS: (Role Gratification) I have more respect for myself now.
  (Role Strain) I do not have enough time to do things.

PREVIOUS SUBJECTS: Mothers between the ages of 30 and 50 who returned to college; housewives

APPROPRIATE FOR: Adults

ADMINISTRATION: Self-administered; about 10 minutes

SCORING: The Role Gratification score is the sum of the endorsed items on the Role Gratification scale. Similarly, the Role Strain score is the sum of the endorsed items on the Role Strain scale. A net gratification score is obtained by subtracting the Role Strain score from the Role Gratification score. Thus, higher scores indicate greater role gratification, greater role strain, and greater net gratification.

DEVELOPMENT: The Role Gratification items were generated by developing three statements to represent each of Sieber's (1974) four role benefits: "role privileges, overall status security, resources for status enhancement and role performance, and personality enrichment and ego gratification" (Gerson, 1985, p. 82). Similarly, the Role Strain items were generated by developing three statements to represent each of Goode's (1960) dimensions of role strain: "intrusion on personal freedom; competing demands of time, place, or resources; inconsistent norms; and competing pressures from role sets" (Gerson, 1985, p. 82). RELIABILITY: Coefficient alpha for the Role Gratification scale was .74. Coefficient alpha for the Role Strain scale was .67.

VALIDITY: As expected, mothers who returned to college experienced greater role gratification and greater role strain than did housewives. When differences on the individual items were analyzed, Gerson (1985) found significant differences on 8 of the 12 items on the Role Gratification scale and 6 of the 12 items on the Role Strain scale.

NOTES & COMMENTS: (1) Gerson (1985) found that Role Gratification scores and Role Strain scores were essentially independent. The correlation for mothers returning to school was .003; the correlation for housewives was −.128.

(2) Gerson (1985) reported correlations among the three role scores—Role Gratification, Role Strain, and Net Gratification—and measures of family income, housework, child care, extradomestic roles, feminism, and self-esteem. The pattern of correlations was different for mothers returning to school and for housewives.

(3) Gerson's (1985) study compared housewives with women who returned to college. Unfortunately the study did not include employed women. It is likely that comparing the Role Gratification, Role Strain, and Net Gratification scores of working women and housewives would reveal greater differences than the comparison of housewives and women who returned to college. As Gerson (1985) pointed out, "The student role is a potential source of status enhancement, one not yet realized" (p. 84).

AVAILABLE FROM: Gerson, 1985

USED IN:

Gerson, J. M. (1985). Women returning to school: The consequences of multiple roles. *Sex Roles*, 13(1/2), 77–92.

BIBLIOGRAPHY:

Goode, W. J. (1960). A theory of role strain. *American Sociological Review*, 25, 483–496.

Sieber, S. D. (1974). Toward a theory of role accumulation. *American Sociological Review*, 39, 567–578.

HOME-CAREER CONFLICT MEASURE

AUTHOR: Helen S. Farmer

DATE: 1977

VARIABLE: Home-career conflict in college women

TYPE OF INSTRUMENT: Projective test

DESCRIPTION: A home-career conflict occurs for women "when they value both homemaking and career roles and at the same time view these roles as incompatible" (Farmer, Rooney, & Lyssy, 1982, p. 3). To measure home-career conflict, women are given 4 minutes to respond to each of four verbal Thematic Apperception Test–type cues. The directions specify: "You are going to read a series of verbal leads or cues and your task is to tell a story that is suggested by each cue. Try to imagine what is going on in each. Then tell what the situation is, what led up to the situation, what the people are thinking, and feeling, and what they will do" (Farmer et al., 1982, p. 6). The four cues describe a scene involving a woman and her child. Cues 1,2, and 3 contain only a woman and her child; Cue 4 involves a man, a woman, and her child. Each cue is followed by a page listing specific questions and providing space for the written responses. The questions are: "(1) What is happening? Who are the persons? (2) What has led up to this situation? That is, what has happened in the past? (3) What is being thought? What is wanted? By whom? (4) What will happen? What will be done?"

SAMPLE ITEM: (sample cue) Judy is arriving home in the middle of the afternoon. Her child is waiting for her.

PREVIOUS SUBJECTS: College women; married mothers; married mothers enrolled in college

APPROPRIATE FOR: High school females and older

ADMINISTRATION: Self-administered; total testing time is 20 minutes

SCORING: Each story is scored on three variables: affect, events, and activity. The Affect score can be $+2$, $+1$, -2, -1 or 0, and reflects whether the affect is positive, negative, or mixed or whether no affect is evident in the story. The Events score is similar in that the same numerical scores are possible; the score reflects whether the events are positive, negative, or mixed or whether no positive or negative events are apparent in the story. The Activity score refers to the activity of the woman outside the home. Three scores are possible: $+2$, $+1$, and -2. A trained judge scores the stories; the process requires the judge to read the story three times. Numerous examples to assist in scoring are provided by Farmer et al. (1982).

After the responses to the individual cues are scored, several composite scores are obtained. The Affect scores from Cues 1, 2, and 3 are summed to yield Affect 1; the Affect score from Cue 4 is labeled Affect 2; the Activity scores from Cues 1, 2, and 3 are summed to yield Activity 1; the Activity score from Cue 4 is labeled Activity 2; the Event scores from Cues 2 and 3 are combined to yield an Event score. The Event scores from Cues 1 and 4 are not used.

DEVELOPMENT: The initial version of the Home-Career Conflict Measure consisted of four verbal cues: three original ones and one taken from Alper (1974). The scale was administered to 163 college women, and their stories were scored using four categories: negative consequences, denial, neutral, and positive consequences. The data were examined, and revisions were made in both the cues and the story categories. The revised cues specified that the child in the cue was the child of the woman in it. That is, unlike the first version of the scale, there was no ambiguity about the relationship between the woman and the child. The new scoring categories were affect, events, activity, and denial. The revised scale was administered to 50 women enrolled in engineering programs and 50 female student teachers. When their responses were analyzed with the new categories, no "denial" themes were found, so the scoring category was eliminated. Further analysis produced the most meaningful combinations of scores to produce five home-career conflict indexes from the scale.

RELIABILITY: Interrater reliability for the original version of the scale was .92 for three raters who independently scored the responses from 163 college women. Interrater reliability for the newer version was .93 for three raters who independently scored responses from 100 college women.

Internal consistency reliability was computed for the multiple item subscales: for Affect 1 (3 items), the reliability was .37; for Activity 1 (3 items), it was .39; and for Events (2 items), it was .23.

VALIDITY: In the study of 50 women enrolled in engineering programs and 50 student teachers, two alternative measures were used to measure home-career conflict. One measure was a multiple choice version of the Home-Career Conflict Measure, and the other included eight Likert-type items. The former measure was intended to assess affect about combining home and work; the latter was designed to assess activity related to home and career roles. When results from the first measure were correlated with the Affect 1 and Affect 2 scores from the Home-Career Conflict Measure, the correlations were both significant though not particularly high ($r = .33$ and $r = .22$). When the latter measure was correlated with the Activity 1 score, the correlation was .20, again low but significant.

Discriminant analysis comparing the responses from engineering majors and student teachers showed that "traditional majors wrote stories depicting more mothers as primarily homemakers and described more negative affect in their stories. The reverse is the case for the engineering students" (Farmer, 1984, p. 672).

In a study involving the first version of the scale, it was found that "high negative Affect scores on the H-C [Home-Career Conflict] measure predicted low Career Motivation scores" (Farmer, 1984, p. 673).

NOTES & COMMENTS: (1) Farmer (1984) suggested the need for more validation research to determine how the Home-Career Conflict Scale can be used to differentiate between women who have difficulty with home-career conflict and women who do not.

(2) Internal consistency reliabilities for the subscale scores are extraordinarily low. This problem must be addressed before the measure is used in other research.

(3) Farmer (1977) used the original version of the Home-Career Conflict Measure in a study designed to investigate the relationship among home-career conflict, fear of success, career motivation, and need for achievement in women of differing gender role orientations. Farmer (1978) and Farmer and Fyans (1983) also used the original version of the Home-Career Conflict Measure. In this study of married mothers who returned to college, home-career conflict was one of seven predictor variables; the two criterion variables were achievement motivation and career motivation.

AVAILABLE FROM: Farmer, Rooney, and Lyssy, 1982

USED IN:

Farmer, H. S. (1977). *The relationship of home-career conflict, fear of success, and sex-role orientation to achievement and career motivation given different levels of perceived environmental support.* Unpublished paper, University of Illinois, Urbana. (ERIC Document Reproduction Service No. ED 154 294)

Farmer, H. S. (1978). *Career and family present conflicting priorities for married women today.* Unpublished paper, University of Illinois, Urbana. (ERIC Document Reproduction Service No. ED 177 284)

Farmer, H. S. (1984). Development of a measure of home-career conflict related to career motivation in college women. *Sex Roles, 10,* 663–675.

Farmer, H. S., & Fyans, L. J., Jr. (1983). Married women's achievement and career motivation: The influence of some environmental and psychological variables. *Psychology of Women Quarterly, 7*(4), 358–372.

Farmer, H. S., Rooney, G., & Lyssy, K. (1982). A Home-Career Conflict Measure. *Catalog of Selected Documents in Psychology, 12*(4), 48. (Ms. No. 2511)

BIBLIOGRAPHY:

Alper, T. (1974). Achievement motivation in women: Now-you-see-it-now-you-don't. *American Psychologist, 28,* 194–203.

JOB TIME-DEMAND SCALE

AUTHOR: Phyllis J. Johnson

DATE: 1982

VARIABLE: Extent to which job time-demands conflict with family responsibilities

TYPE OF INSTRUMENT: Summated rating scale

DESCRIPTION: The Job Time-Demand Scale was developed to measure "the time required in employment that could coincide or conflict with time for family responsibilities" (Johnson, 1982, p. 1087). The scale consists of 13 items representing three factors: Flexibility in Work Schedule

(7 items), Family-Work Schedule Conflicts (3 items), and Irregular Work Demands (3 items). Each item is accompanied by five response options ranging from "almost always" to "never."

SAMPLE ITEMS: (Flexibility in Work Schedule) Do you work different hours day-to-day?

(Family-Work Schedule Conflicts) Do serious consequences result from your being late for or absent from work?

(Irregular Work Demands) Do you have to bring work home to finish it?

PREVIOUS SUBJECTS: Divorced mothers

APPROPRIATE FOR: Employed adults

ADMINISTRATION: Self-administered; about 5 minutes

SCORING: Items are scored on a 5-point scale, with higher scores being assigned to the response that reflects greater job time demands. Scores can be obtained for each of the three subscales (factors) and for the total scale.

DEVELOPMENT: A pool of 18 items was generated and submitted to a panel of 10 judges, including specialists from Family Relations and Human Development, Home Management and Housing, Administrative Sciences, and Human Resources at Ohio State University. The items were evaluated in terms of their "appropriateness for employed people with dependent children at home and for measuring time-demands of the job in relation to family responsibilities" (Johnson, 1982, p. 1089). Based on inputs from the panel members, 1 item was added, 4 items were deleted, and several items were reworded. A 15-item scale resulted from these modifications. Four response options, ranging from "almost always" to "never or almost never," accompanied each item. The scale was pretested with 28 divorced mothers who had custody of children under the age of 13. The analysis of the data from the 28 mothers showed that one item was negatively correlated with the total score; it was deleted. Coefficient alpha for the remaining items was .77. Since many persons chose the option "almost never or never," it was divided into two choices: "rarely" and "never." The 14-item version of the scale, having five response options for each item, was administered to 574 divorced women with a child younger than age 13. Their responses were factor analyzed, and three factors were extracted; the three factors explained 55% of the variance. One item loaded on two factors, and its loadings on both factors were quite low (.23 and .22); the item was deleted from the scale. The remaining 13 items comprise the scale.

RELIABILITY: Using the responses from the 574 divorced women, the following values were found for coefficient alpha: Flexibility in Work Schedule = .82; Family-Work Schedule Conflicts = .73; Irregular Work Demands = .66; and total scale = .80.

VALIDITY: The 574 respondents were divided into two groups: those who said their jobs created problems for them in terms of managing family responsibilities and those who said their jobs did not create these problems. As expected, the first group scored significantly higher on the scores for Flexibility in Work Schedule and Family-Work Schedule Conflicts. The expected difference was not found for Irregular Work Demands. The author explained this by noting that "the factor includes the item, 'Do you have to bring work home to finish it?' Apparently, this item is not viewed as increasing job time-demands or creating difficulties in management of family responsibilities" (Johnson, 1982, p. 1092).

Correlations were computed between hours worked and scores on each of the three factors and the total scale. All correlations were negligible, suggesting that the Job Time-Demand Scale is not simply reflecting the number of hours the woman works.

When respondents were divided into professional-managerial employees and clerical-technicians, there was a significant difference in scores on only one factor: Irregular Work Demands.

NOTES & COMMENTS: (1) Johnson (1982) offered several suggestions for future refinement and use of the scale. She recommended that the role of "autonomy in scheduling employment hours and responsibilities" (p. 1093) be considered as a factor affecting employment and home responsibility conflict. Johnson also suggested that research is needed to clarify whether working different hours on different days improves or intensifies the conflict between employment and home responsibilities. As a further recommendation, Johnson suggested that the scale might be administered to men who are responsible for both employment and home responsibilities.

(2) The items are phrased as questions, and the responses are given in terms of frequency. They do not seem to go together. If the questions were rephrased to read "How often do you . . . ?" they would mesh better with the responses.

AVAILABLE FROM: Johnson, 1982
USED IN:
Johnson, P. J. (1982). Development of a measure of job time-demands. *Psychological Reports*, *51*, 1087–1094.

JOB-FAMILY ROLE STRAIN SCALE
AUTHORS: Halcyone H. Bohen and Anamaria Viveros-Long (with the help of an advisory committee including Mary Jo Bane, Urie Bronfenbrenner, John Demos, Jerome Kagan, Sheila B. Kamerman, Rosabeth Moss Kanter, Robert K. Leik, Joseph Pleck, Mary Sue Richardson, and Isabel V. Sawhill)
DATE: 1981
VARIABLE: Role strain created by job and family demands

TYPE OF INSTRUMENT: Summated rating scale

DESCRIPTION: "The [Job-Family] Role Strain Scale seeks to tap the kind of stress related to internalized values and emotions—such as self-doubt, worry, guilt, and pressure—but also feelings of contentment, fulfillment, self-respect, and balance in regard to job and family obligations" (Bohen & Viveros-Long, 1981, p. 233). The scale consists of 19 statements, 11 of which can be answered by both parents and non-parents and 8 of which can be answered only by parents. The items represent the following areas defined by Komarovsky (1977): ambiguity about norms (3 items), socially structured insufficiency of resources for role fulfillment (3 items), low rewards for role conformity (3 items), conflict between normative phenomena (4 items), and overload of role obligations (6 items). Each item is accompanied by the response options "always, most of the time, some of the time, rarely, never," as well as "not applicable."

SAMPLE ITEMS: (ambiguity about norms) I worry that other people at work think my family interferes with my job.

(socially structured insufficiency of resources for role fulfillment) I worry about how my kids are while I'm working.

(low rewards for role conformity) I feel more respected than I would if I didn't have a job.

(conflict between normative phenomena) My job keeps me away from my family too much.

(overload of role obligations) I feel I have more to do than I can handle comfortably.

PREVIOUS SUBJECTS: Employees in corporations and government agencies

APPROPRIATE FOR: Employed adults with families that include a spouse or children or both

ADMINISTRATION: Self-administered; although the scale has been used as part of a much larger questionnaire, it would only take about 10 minutes to complete just the items on this scale

SCORING: Items are individually scored on a 5-point scale, with higher scores assigned to the response indicating greater job-family role strain. Two overall scores are suggested: the mean of the item scores for those items than can be answered by both parents and nonparents (Adult part) and the mean of all item scores (Total). It is advisable to omit the three items pertaining to "low rewards for role conformity" because of their impact on scale reliability. (See RELIABILITY.)

DEVELOPMENT: Komarovsky's (1977) delineation of six modes of role strain provided a framework for item construction for the Job-Family Role Strain Scale. Items representing five of the six modes are included on the scale; items were not written for the mode "lack of congruity between an individual's personality and a particular social role" because "the scope and design of the study could not adequately take account of personality variables" (Bohen & Viveros-Long, 1981, p. 232). Items for the Job-Family Role Strain Scale were generated concurrently with items for a Family Management Scale. Two sources were used to stimulate item generation. First, a series of relevant research studies published during the 1970s were reviewed. Second, fathers, mothers, and children from 10 families were interviewed and asked to describe the kinds of role strains they (or their parents) experienced. Finally, the items generated were shown to two groups of federal employees, who discussed their reactions to the items. The scale was pretested by administering it to 50 federal employees. Based on the employees' responses to the items, some minor changes were made in the scale.

RELIABILITY: Coefficient alpha, based on the pretesting of 50 federal employees, was .71. When the final scale was administered to 481 persons, coefficient alpha was .65 for the Adult scale and .55 for the Total scale. When the three items relating to "low reward for role conformity" were eliminated, coefficient alpha increased to .72 for the Adult scale and .71 for the Total scale. (Note: .71 is the number reported in the text, but a chart shows coefficient alpha as .603 [Bohen & Viveros-Long, 1981, p. 238]).

VALIDITY: Bohen and Viveros-Long (1981) claimed content validity for the scale on the grounds that there was "a review of the items by a panel of six judges (two psychologists, a sociologist, and three federal personnel experts . . .) who rated the items according to how well they tapped the content designated for the scale" (p. 236).

The authors established concurrent validity for the scale by correlating scores with scores on predictor variables. As expected, scores on the Job-Family Role Strain Scale were positively related to "the number of hours worked by the respondent, the length of time spent commuting, and the number of hours worked by the respondent's spouse" (Bohen & Viveros-Long, 1981, p. 237). When the final version of the scale was used, scores were related to age (younger respondents experienced more role strain), sex (women reported more role strain), home responsibilities (those with more home responsibilities experienced more role strain), and time demands (those who worked and commuted more hours experienced more role strain). Furthermore, those who had greater work-family interference and those who had greater responsibility for the home and children also reported greater role strain.

NOTES & COMMENTS: (1) One should be cautious about using the Job-Family Role Strain Scale since the scale reliabilities tend to be somewhat low.

(2) Bohen and Viveros-Long (1981) factor analyzed the responses from over 400 respondents. One factor accounted for 87% of the variance for the Adult score on the Job-Family Role Strain Scale. This factor was "overload of role obligations" and corresponded to one of Komarovsky's

(1977) modes. A second factor corresponding to another of Komarovsky's modes, "conflicts between normative phenomena," accounted for the balance of the variance. For the Total score on the Job-Family Role Strain Scale, four factors were identified.

(3) Burden (1986) reported using the Job-Family Role Strain Scale in a study of how combined work and family responsibilities affect single parent employees. Because she reported the scale as having 13 "adult" items and 7 "child-related" items, it appears that she made some changes from Bohen and Viveros-Long's scale. Burden reported a coefficient alpha of .78 for the adult items and .64 for the child-related items.

AVAILABLE FROM: Bohen and Viveros-Long, 1981
USED IN:
Bohen, H. H., & Viveros-Long, A. (1981). *Balancing jobs and family life*. Philadelphia: Temple University Press.
Burden, D. S. (1986). Single parents and the work setting: The impact of multiple job and homelife responsibilities. *Family Relations, 35*(1), 37–43.
BIBLIOGRAPHY:
Komarovsky, M. (1977). *Dilemmas of masculinity*. New York: Norton.

KEITH SCHAFER WORK-FAMILY ROLE STRAIN

AUTHORS: Pat M. Keith and Robert B. Schafer

DATE: 1980

VARIABLE: Amount of role strain created by the combined responsibilities of work and family

TYPE OF INSTRUMENT: Summated rating scale

DESCRIPTION: Respondents are presented with four situations and asked to indicate the frequency with which they are bothered by each situation. The four situations are: "feeling that their job outside the home may interfere with their family life; feeling that family life may interfere with the job outside the home; thinking that the amount of work they have to do may interfere with how well it gets done; and feeling that others in the family will not do household tasks as well as they would do them" (Keith & Schafer, 1980, p. 485). Each item is accompanied by five response options ranging from "never" to "very often."

PREVIOUS SUBJECTS: Employed husbands and wives, employed single-parent mothers, employed husbands whose wives were employed, and employed husbands whose wives were not employed

APPROPRIATE FOR: Employed adults with families that include a spouse or children or both

ADMINISTRATION: Self-administered although the scale has been used as part of an interview; a couple of minutes

SCORING: Items are scored on a 5-point scale, with 5 points assigned to the response "very often." Items are summed to yield a total score that can range from 4 (no work-family role strain) to 20 (high work-family role strain).

DEVELOPMENT: No information was provided.

RELIABILITY: Coefficient alpha was .65 (Keith & Schafer, 1982). This low value is not surprising given the brevity of the scale. Still, steps must be taken to improve the scale's reliability.

VALIDITY: Keith and Schafer (1980) examined the factors associated with work-family role strain and depression in 135 two-job families. They found that women in two-job families, compared to men in two-job families, experienced significantly more work-family role strain. They also found that the number of hours per week spent at work was the most significant factor in explaining work-family role strain, and this variable was more important for men ($r = .33$) than for women ($r = .17$). Work-family role strain was greater for younger adults and for those with more children living at home. The amount of time the spouse worked was a significant factor in women's work-family role strain, but this was not true for men's work-family role strain. They also found that depression was significantly related to work-family role strain for men ($r = .32$) but not for women. For both men and women, no significant relationship was found between involvement in masculine or feminine tasks and work-family role strain.

Keith and Schafer (1982) studied a variety of possible correlates of depression in single, employed mothers. The two researchers found that work-family role strain was significantly related to depression ($r = .26$). Although this finding appears to contradict Keith and Schafer (1980), the earlier study involved women with husbands, while this study involved single mothers.

In a study comparing husbands whose wives were employed with husbands whose wives were not employed, Keith and Schafer (1984) found no significant difference in the work-family role strain experienced by the two groups of men. There were, however, differences in the variables that related to work-family role strain in the two groups. For husbands whose wives were not employed, the two strongest correlates of work-family role strain were age ($r = -.24$) and education ($r = .24$); in other words, younger men and men with more education experienced more work-family role strain. For men with employed wives, the strongest correlate of work-family role strain was level of occupation ($r = .30$), with higher-level occupations associated with greater role strain. The next highest correlate was education ($r = .25$), but a regression analysis showed that the beta weight was not significant. For husbands in both single-paycheck and dual-paycheck marriages, work-family role strain was significantly related to role conflict ($r = .51$ for men in single-paycheck marriages; $r = .32$ for men in dual-paycheck marriages).

NOTES & COMMENTS: (1) This is a very brief and easy-to-administer scale, but the reliability is quite low.

(2) Walters and McKenry (1985) used the Keith Schafer Work-Family

Role Strain scale as one of several measures in a study comparing the predictors of life satisfaction for rural and urban employed mothers.
AVAILABLE FROM: Keith and Schafer, 1980, 1982, 1984
USED IN:

Keith, P. M., & Schafer, R. B. (1980). Role strain and depression in two-job families. *Family Relations, 29*, 483–488.

Keith, P. M., & Schafer, R. B. (1982). Correlates of depression among single parent, employed women. *Journal of Divorce, 5*(3), 49–59.

Keith, P. M., & Schafer, R. B. (1984). Role behavior and psychological well-being: A comparison of men in one-job and two-job families. *American Journal of Orthopsychiatry, 54*(1), 137–145.

Walters, C. M., & McKenry, P. C. (1985). Predictors of life satisfaction among rural and urban employed mothers: A research note. *Journal of Marriage and the Family, 47*(4), 1067–1071.

NEVILL DAMICO ROLE CONFLICT QUESTIONNAIRE

AUTHORS: Dorothy Nevill and Sandra Damico
DATE: 1974 (used 1971)
VARIABLE: Role conflict in women
TYPE OF INSTRUMENT: Summated rating scale
DESCRIPTION: The Nevill Damico Role Conflict Questionnaire consists of eight items, each stating an area of potential conflict for women and giving a specific example of the conflict area. Each item ends with a question asking how much conflict is created in this area. Response options range from "1, not at all" to "7, extremely." Respondents also have the option of marking "0, does not apply."
SAMPLE ITEM: Many women find that the demands on their time are difficult to meet. For example, how does one find time to satisfy needs for privacy, household obligations, and social commitments? To what degree do you experience time conflicts?
PREVIOUS SUBJECTS: Women faculty of a university and university secretaries; members of women's service clubs, church groups, and community organizations; fertile and infertile women
APPROPRIATE FOR: Women
ADMINISTRATION: Self-administered; about 5 minutes
SCORING: Nevill and Damico (1974, 1975a, 1975b) reported means for each item rather than reporting scores for individuals. This enabled Nevill and Damico to rank order the conflict areas across women.
DEVELOPMENT: A sample of 30 women, approximately half of them married and some with children, independently listed the role conflicts they faced. Their lists produced 252 problems, which were then categorized by three judges. The judges were instructed to use no more than 10 categories. After categories having fewer than 3 items were eliminated, 8 categories remained: "Time Management, Relations with Husband, Household Management, Financial, Child Care, Expectations

for Self, Expectations of Others, and Guilt" (Nevill & Damico, 1974, p. 743). Each of these 8 categories is represented by one item on the Nevill Damico Role Conflict Questionnaire. To ensure that all significant topics were covered, 87 undergraduates were asked to complete the questionnaire and add conflicts they felt were omitted. No new categories were added by the students.

RELIABILITY: No information was provided.

VALIDITY: Nevill and Damico (1975b) found a significant difference in mean scores on six of the eight conflict areas as a function of marital status. Nevill and Damico (1975a) found that Child Care and Relations with Husband were the two conflict areas most affected by children. Nevill and Damico (1978) found that a woman's occupational status was a significant variable affecting role conflict in six of the eight areas. Women in professional occupations and housewives reported the least amount of role conflict.

NOTES & COMMENTS: (1) Mertensmeyer and Coleman (1987) modified the Nevill Damico Role Conflict Questionnaire. The modified version contained 11 items, each accompanied by six response options. A total score was obtained by summing the item scores. Thus, the total score ranged from 11 (never feel conflict) to 66 (always feel conflict). Berkowitz and Perkins (1984) modified the Questionnaire for use with farm women. Their modified version contained 10 items.

(2) Allison (1979) used the Nevill Damico Role Conflict Questionnaire to compare the role conflicts of infertile women with the role conflicts experienced by women without a history of infertility. Pyke and Kahill (1983) used the Questionnaire to compare the role conflicts experienced by male and female physicians.

AVAILABLE FROM: Dorothy Nevill, Psychology Department, University of Florida, Gainesville, FL 32611

USED IN:

Allison, J. R. (1979). Roles and role conflict of women in infertile couples. *Psychology of Women Quarterly, 4,* 97–113.

Berkowitz, A. D., & Perkins, H. W. (1984). Stress among farm women: Work and family as interacting systems. *Journal of Marriage and the Family, 46,* 161–166.

Mertensmeyer, C., & Coleman, M. (1987). Correlates of inter-role conflict in young rural and urban parents. *Family Relations, 36,* 425–429.

Nevill, D., & Damico, S. (1974). Development of a role conflict questionnaire for women: Some preliminary findings. *Journal of Consulting and Clinical Psychology, 42,* 743.

Nevill, D., & Damico, S. (1975a). Family size and role conflict in women. *Journal of Psychology, 89,* 267–270.

Nevill, D., & Damico, S. (1975b). Role conflict in women as a function of marital status. *Human Relations, 28,* 487–498.

Nevill, D., & Damico, S. (1978). The influence of occupational status on role conflict in women. *Journal of Employment Counseling, 15,* 55–61.

Pyke, S. W., & Kahill, S. P. (1983). Sex differences in characteristics presumed relevant to professional productivity. *Psychology of Women Quarterly, 8,* 189–192.

REILLY ROLE OVERLOAD SCALE
AUTHOR: Michael D. Reilly
DATE: 1982
VARIABLE: Role overload for wives
TYPE OF INSTRUMENT: Summated rating scale
DESCRIPTION: The Reilly Role Overload Scale consists of 13 statements, each reflecting that the respondent feels pressured and overloaded with responsibilities. Items are accompanied by five response options ranging from "strongly agree" to "strongly disagree."
SAMPLE ITEMS: I have to do things which I don't really have the time and energy for.
   I seem to have more commitments to overcome than some of the other wives I know.
PREVIOUS SUBJECTS: Wives
APPROPRIATE FOR: Wives
ADMINISTRATION: Self-administered; about 5–10 minutes
SCORING: Items are scored on a 5-point scale, with 5 points assigned to the "strongly agree" end of the continuum. Item scores are summed to yield a total score that ranges from 13 (no role overload) to 65 (extensive role overload).
DEVELOPMENT: The Reilly Role Overload Scale was modeled after role-conflict and role-ambiguity scales developed by House and Rizzo (1972). An item pool developed by Reilly and three doctoral students was administered to a sample of 106 married women. After items with low item-total correlations were eliminated, 13 items remained. These items comprise the Reilly Role Overload Scale.
RELIABILITY: Coefficient alpha was .88. Two items were administered twice in the final scale. The correlation for these two items was .74. Reilly (1982) reported item-total correlations for the 13 items. The correlations ranged from .50 to .80, with half of the correlations above .63.
VALIDITY: Reilly (1982) developed a model to predict the amount of convenience foods served and the number of time-saving durable goods that are owned. The model included wife's educational level, wife's work involvement, family social status, wife's earnings, total family income, and role overload. Reilly tested his model using the Reilly Role Overload Scale to measure role overload. He found that both of the predicted variables were positively but weakly related to role overload. The correlation with time-saving durables was significant; the correlation with convenience food use was not. Reilly concluded: "In both cases, the

relationship might be expected to be weak to the extent that convenience consumption is effective in reducing role overload" (p. 414).

NOTES & COMMENTS: The Reilly Role Overload Scale gives a global indication of the amount of role overload but provides no information on the source of that overload: work responsibilities, children, nonwork activities outside the home, or other commitments.

AVAILABLE FROM: Reilly, 1982

USED IN:

Reilly, M. D. (1982). Working wives and convenience consumption. *Journal of Consumer Research, 8*, 407–418.

BIBLIOGRAPHY:

House, R. J., & Rizzo, J. R. (1972). Role conflict and ambiguity as critical variables in a model of organizational behavior. *Organizational Behavior and Human Performance, 7*, 467–505.

ROLE CONFLICT SCALES

AUTHORS: Carole K. Holahan and Lucia A. Gilbert

DATE: 1978

VARIABLE: Conflict among four roles: professional, spouse, parent, and self as a self-actualizing person

TYPE OF INSTRUMENT: Summated rating scale

DESCRIPTION: There are six Role Conflict Scales, each including three or four items relating to a conflict between two of the following four roles: Professional (worker), Spouse, Parent, and Self as a self-actualizing person. Each item is a phrase expressing a possible conflict between the demands of two roles, and each item is accompanied by five response options: "causes no internal conflict, slight internal conflict, some internal conflict, moderate internal conflict, high internal conflict." The respondent can circle "na" if the item does not pertain to her.

SAMPLE ITEMS: (Professional vs. Self) Wanting to be recognized at a high level in terms of your work versus wanting to maximize your personal development.

(Professional vs. Parent) Supporting your child's recreational activities versus spending time on your career development.

(Spouse vs. Parent) Taking a long vacation with only your spouse versus being with your child.

(Spouse vs. Self) Attending social functions which support your spouse's career versus attending functions congruent with your own interests.

(Parent vs. Self) Giving priority to your family versus giving priority to yourself.

(Professional vs. Spouse) Putting yourself first in terms of your work versus your spouse putting himself first in terms of his work.

PREVIOUS SUBJECTS: Dual career couples; career and noncareer work-

ing women; first-time mothers; women in South Africa; fathers in South
Africa

APPROPRIATE FOR: Persons who experience the parental, spouse, and
employee roles

ADMINISTRATION: Self-administered; about 10 minutes

SCORING: Items are scored on a 5-point scale, with 5 points assigned
to the response "high internal conflict" and 1 point assigned to the
response "causes no internal conflict." The items contributing to each
scale are summed to yield six scale scores. Higher scores represent
greater role conflict. Since some scales include four items and others
only three items, scale scores cannot be compared unless item averages
rather than item totals are used as scale scores.

DEVELOPMENT: No information was provided.

RELIABILITY: Based on testing 28 couples, Holahan and Gilbert (1979a,
1979b) reported the following values for coefficient alpha: Professional
versus Spouse = .81; Professional versus Parent = .81; Professional
versus Self = .86; Spouse versus Parent = .82; Spouse versus Self =
.75; and Parent versus Self = .88.

Majewski (1986) slightly modified the Role Conflict Scales so that they
would be equally applicable to women in jobs as well as women in
careers. Using the measure with first-time mothers, Majewski obtained
the following values for coefficient alpha: Worker versus Spouse = .68;
Worker versus Parent = .68; Worker versus Self = .66; Spouse versus
Parent = .60; Spouse versus Self = .55; and Parent versus Self = .75.

Schmidt and Scott (1986) reported a full-scale coefficient alpha of .95
based on testing 83 employees of a large health insurance company.
Frone and Rice (1987) used two subscales from the Role Conflict Scales.
Testing a sample of 141 adults, they obtained a coefficient alpha of .64
for the Professional versus Parent conflict and a coefficient alpha of .62
for the Professional versus Spouse conflict.

VALIDITY: Holahan and Gilbert (1979a) administered the Role Conflict
Scales to a sample of 28 dual career couples. One of their objectives was
to test the hypothesis that there would be differences in the Role Conflict
scores obtained by men and by women. Their hypothesis was not supported.

Based on correlational analysis, Holahan and Gilbert (1979a) concluded that, in general, "lower conflict in both genders generally tended
to be correlated with higher self-esteem, more profeminist attitudes,
higher satisfaction from the major life roles, working fewer hours, higher
spouse support, and higher career commitment" (p. 459).

Holahan and Gilbert (1979b) compared the Role Conflict scores from
career and noncareer working women. Contrary to expectation, the noncareer group reported greater role conflict than did the career group.
Knaub (1985) studied professional women and found that those who

had brief career interruptions, 2 years or less, were more likely to experience role conflict.

Working in Johannesburg, South Africa, Barling and Barenbrug (1984) used the Role Conflict Scales to compare the role conflicts of women employed full time in an organization with flexitime and women employed full time in an organization without flexitime. Women in flexitime organizations suffered less role conflict on only two of the scales (Parent versus Spouse and Parent versus Self).

NOTES & COMMENTS: (1) Holahan and Gilbert (1979b) reported intercorrelations among the subscales of the Role Conflict Scales ranging from .22 to .64; the median intercorrelation was .44. As would be expected, subscales with overlapping roles showed higher intercorrelations.

(2) The reliabilities of the subscales are marginal. Users of the scale should ensure that the scale is reliable for their sample.

(3) Greenglass (1985) used the Role Conflict Scales in a study looking at the effects of stress on managerial women. Greenglass and Burke (1988) used the Role Conflict Scales to look at the relationship between role conflict and burnout in teachers. Majewski (1986) used a slightly modified version of the Role Conflict Scales in a study of 86 first-time mothers. Majewski examined the relationships among role conflict, employment status, marital satisfaction, employment role attitudes, and ease of transition to the parental role. Schmidt and Scott (1986) used the Role Conflict Scales to test some hypotheses regarding role conflict and its relationship to "career commitment, commitment to family roles, number of roles, marital status, parental status, spouse support, attitudes toward women, and family configuration" (p. 2). Suchet and Barling (1986) used the Role Conflict Scales to study the relationships among role conflict, marital communication, spouse support, and marital satisfaction in a sample of 64 mothers, employed full-time. Barling (1986) used the Role Conflict Scales to study role conflict and marital adjustment in a sample of 73 fathers. Frone and Rice (1987) used a portion of the Role Conflict Scales to look at the relationships among job involvement, family involvement, and role conflict in a sample of 141 nonteaching, professional employees of a university.

AVAILABLE FROM: Order from NAPS c/o Microfiche Publications, P.O. Box 3513, Grand Central Station, New York, NY 10163–3513; NAPS document no. 04708; for microfiche, in U.S. remit $4.00 with order.

USED IN:

Barling, J. (1986). Interrole conflict and marital functioning amongst employed fathers. *Journal of Occupational Behaviour*, 7, 1–8.

Barling, J., & Barenbrug, A. (1984). Some personal consequences of "flexitime" work schedules. *Journal of Social Psychology*, 123, 137–138.

Frone, M. R., & Rice, R. W. (1987). Work-family conflict: The effect of job and family involvement. *Journal of Occupational Behaviour*, 8, 45–53.

Greenglass, E. R. (1985). Psychological implications of sex bias in the workplace. *Academic Psychology Bulletin, 7,* 227–240.

Holahan, C. K., & Gilbert, L. A. (1978, August). *Interrole conflict for dual career couples: The effects of gender and parenthood.* Paper presented at the meeting of the American Psychological Association, Toronto. (ERIC Document Reproduction Service No. ED 172 102)

Holahan, C. K., & Gilbert, L. A. (1979a). Conflict between major life roles: Women and men in dual career couples. *Human Relations, 32*(6), 451–467.

Holahan, C. K., & Gilbert, L. A. (1979b). Interrole conflict for working women: Careers versus jobs. *Journal of Applied Psychology, 64*(1), 86–90.

Knaub, P. K. (1985). Professional women perceive family strengths. *Journal of Home Economics, 77,* 52–55.

Majewski, J. L. (1986). Conflicts, satisfactions, and attitudes during transition to the maternal role. *Nursing Research, 35*(1), 10–14.

Schmidt, V. J., & Scott, N. A. (1986, August). *Home-career conflict: An exploration of the delicate balance.* Paper presented at the meeting of the American Psychological Association, Washington, DC. (ERIC Document Reproduction Service No. ED 283 076)

Suchet, M., & Barling, J. (1986). Employed mothers: Interrole conflict, spouse support and marital functioning. *Journal of Occupational Behaviour, 7,* 167–178.

BIBLIOGRAPHY:

Greenglass, E. R., & Burke, R. J. (1988). Work and family precursors of burnout in teachers: Sex differences. *Sex Roles, 18,* 215–229.

SAGE LOUDERMILK ROLE CONFLICT SCALE

AUTHORS: George H. Sage and Sheryl Loudermilk

DATE: 1979 (used 1976)

VARIABLE: Role conflict of female athletes

TYPE OF INSTRUMENT: Summated rating scale

DESCRIPTION: The Sage Loudermilk Role Conflict Scale is a 20-item scale consisting of two 10-item sections. The first section measures role conflict perception (RCP). The directions for this part state: "Regardless of your personal experiences with these problems, will you please indicate whether you see them as actual problems for female athletes in general, and if so, how important you believe them to be." Each item in the first part is accompanied by five response options ranging from "not a problem at all" to "a problem of very great importance." The second section contains the same 10 items, but the focus is on role conflict experience (RCE). The directions state: "Indicate . . . whether any of these problems has caused you any personal concern (i.e., that you have *experienced* this problem and been to some extent troubled by it)." Each item in the second part is accompanied by five response options ranging from "not at all" to "to a very great extent." Item content focuses primarily on the conflict between what is expected from a successful athlete and what is expected from a "successful" female.

SAMPLE ITEMS: Because American society traditionally places little value on girls' participation in sports, the female athlete receives little recognition for her skills and accomplishments.

Girls are usually expected to have low levels of sports skills, but athletes must develop their skills to a high level.

PREVIOUS SUBJECTS: Female college athletes; female high school athletes

APPROPRIATE FOR: The RCP items are appropriate for high school students and older; the RCE items are appropriate only for female athletes in high school or older.

ADMINISTRATION: Self-administered; about 10 minutes

SCORING: Items are scored on a 5-point scale, with higher points assigned to the response reflecting greater role conflict. Separate total scores are obtained for the RCP and the RCE items. For each portion, total scores can range from 10 to 50.

DEVELOPMENT: The Sage Loudermilk Role Conflict Scale was based on a model of role conflict developed by Grace (1972) and later expanded by Massengale and Locke (1976). Role conflict questions were generated from literature on sex stereotypes, literature regarding athletic role expectations, and discussions with female athletes and coaches. The conflict areas that Sage and Loudermilk (1979) chose to include were not intended to be a representative sample of potential conflicts; rather they were "selected because cultural sex-role prescriptions and previous research led to a theoretical expectation that they would be appropriate" (p. 91).

RELIABILITY: Sage and Loudermilk (1979) reported interitem correlations as an indication of the scale's internal consistency. There were 45 intercorrelations for each of the two sets of 10 items. For the RCP items, 41 of the intercorrelations were significant at the .05 level; for the RCE items, all 45 intercorrelations were significant at the .05 level. Sage and Loudermilk did not provide the values for the intercorrelations; they only indicated their significance.

Sage and Loudermilk (1979) administered the Sage Loudermilk Role Conflict Scale to a sample of 24 female college-age athletes on two occasions, 2 to 3 weeks apart. Test-retest reliability for the RCP scores was .72; test-retest reliability for the RCE scores was .76.

VALIDITY: As one indication of construct validity, Sage and Loudermilk (1979) reported item-total correlations for the two portions of the scale. For both portions, mean item-total correlations were above .60. More specific information regarding the item-total correlations for the individual items was not provided.

Sage and Loudermilk (1979) administered the Sage Loudermilk Role Conflict Scale and the short form of the Attitudes Toward Women Scale (AWS) (Spence, Helmreich, & Stapp, 1973) (see separate entry) to 268 female college athletes. The RCP scores of 15 respondents scoring above the 60th percentile on the AWS were compared with the RCP scores of 15 respondents scoring below the 60th percentile on the AWS. As expected, there was a significant difference between the two groups. Sage and Loudermilk did not explain their rationale for selecting 15 respondents for each group or for using the 60th percentile as the dividing point on the AWS.

NOTES & COMMENTS: (1) Some of the procedures Sage and Loudermilk (1979) used to establish the reliability and validity of the scale were rather atypical.

(2) Sage and Loudermilk (1979) found that, in general, female college athletes do not experience extreme role conflict nor do they believe it is extremely prevalent. On the RCP items, 44% of the responses were either "not at all" or "of little importance." On the RCE items, 56% of the responses were either "not at all" or "of little importance." However, 26% of the RCP responses and 20% of the RCE responses were "great" or "very great," suggesting serious role conflict for some female athletes.

(3) Anthrop and Allison (1983) looked at Sage and Loudermilk Role Conflict scores for a sample of female high school athletes. Desertrain and Weiss (1988) also administered the scale to female high school athletes; they compared the Role Conflict scores to scores on the Personal Attributes Questionnaire (Spence, Helmreich, & Stapp, 1974), a measure of gender role orientation (see separate entry).

AVAILABLE FROM: George H. Sage, Department of Kinesiology, University of Northern Colorado, Greeley, CO 80639

USED IN:

Anthrop, J., & Allison, M. T. (1983). Role conflict and the high school female athlete. *Research Quarterly for Exercise and Sport, 54*(2), 104–111.

Desertrain, G. S., & Weiss, M. R. (1988). Being female and athletic: A cause for conflict? *Sex Roles, 18*(9/10), 567–582.

Sage, G. H., and Loudermilk, S. (1979). The female athlete and role conflict. *Research Quarterly, 50*(1), 88–96.

BIBLIOGRAPHY:

Grace, G. R. (1972). *Role conflict and the teacher*. London: Routledge & Kegan.

Massengale, J. D., & Locke, L. F. (1976, April). *The teacher/coach in conflict: A selective analysis of perceived and experienced dysfunction within the occupational role*. Paper presented at the meeting of the American Alliance for Health, Physical Education and Recreation, Milwaukee.

Spence, J. T., Helmreich, R. L., & Stapp, J. (1973). A short version of the Attitudes Toward Women Scale (AWS). *Bulletin of the Psychonomic Society, 2*, 219–220.

Spence, J. T., Helmreich, R. L., & Stapp, J. T. (1974). The Personal Attributes Questionnaire: A measure of sex-role stereotypes and masculinity-femininity. *Catalog of Selected Documents in Psychology, 4*, 43–44. (Ms. No. 617)

SEX ROLE CONFLICT SCALE (SRCS)

AUTHORS: Leonard H. Chusmir and Christine S. Koberg

DATE: 1986

VARIABLE: Gender role conflict defined as "the degree of conflict expressed between an individual's (1) treatment based on gender versus that person's desired treatment as an individual (intrarole or interrole incongruity) and (2) private self-concept of the person's sex role versus the self-concept defined by one's society and work organization (intrapersonal incongruity)" (Chusmir & Koberg, 1986, p. 398).

TYPE OF INSTRUMENT: Summated rating scale

DESCRIPTION: The Sex Role Conflict Scale (SRCS) consists of 17 items, each beginning with the word "if" or "when" and describing a situation in which a person may or may not experience conflict. The set of items is preceded with the phrase, "How much conflict do you feel, if any . . . " It is necessary to have separate forms of the SRCS for men and for women since the wording of some of the items must be altered to make it appropriate for the other sex. (See SAMPLE ITEMS.) Each item is accompanied by five response options: "absolutely no conflict, not very much conflict, a little conflict, quite a lot of conflict, a great deal of conflict."

SAMPLE ITEMS: When the men (women) in your company are uncomfortable working with you because of your gender?

When you often have to work on unnecessary things because you are a woman (man)?

PREVIOUS SUBJECTS: Employed adults

APPROPRIATE FOR: Employed adults

ADMINISTRATION: Self-administered; about 5–10 minutes

SCORING: Items are scored on a 5-point scale and summed to yield an overall score. Total scores can range from 17 (no conflict in any of the situations) to 85 (maximum conflict in all of the situations).

DEVELOPMENT: A pool of 60 items was constructed based on a search of the relevant literature. The items pertained to intrarole, interrole, and intrapersonal incongruity. After being checked for "content or face validity, relevance, clarity, and simplicity" (Chusmir & Koberg, 1986, p. 401) by a panel of four faculty members, the items were administered to 102 employed adults who were also enrolled in an MBA program. In responding to the items, the adults were to select one of five response options ranging from "absolutely no conflict" to "a great deal of conflict." Item-total correlations were computed for each of the 60 items, and the data were subjected to factor analysis. Using the results of these two analyses, the scale was reduced to 17 items.

RELIABILITY: Using the data obtained from the 102 respondents on whom the scale was developed, Chusmir and Koberg (1986) obtained alpha coefficients of .91 for women and .89 for men using data for the 17 items; for both sexes combined, coefficient alpha was .90 for the 17 items. Using data obtained from another sample of 556 working persons, Chusmir and Koberg obtained alpha coefficients of .94 for men and .93 for women; coefficient alpha for both sexes combined was .94. Split-half reliability was .73 for the initial sample of 102 respondents and .82 for the second group of 556 respondents. A sample of 34 persons completed the scale a second time, 2 weeks after the first data were collected. The test-retest reliability coefficient was .96.

VALIDITY: In order to assess the construct validity of the SRCS, Chusmir and Koberg (1986) correlated SRCS scores with measures of role conflict, job satisfaction, job involvement, and propensity to leave a job. For both the initial and the second sample, all of the correlations were in the predicted direction and all but one were significant. However, none of the correlations was very high, suggesting that the SRCS is related to but still different from the measures it was being compared to.

NOTES & COMMENTS: (1) Factor analysis using the data from the second sample of 556 working persons led to a factor structure similar to that obtained using data from the 102 persons whose data were used for scale development. Items 1 to 10 load on Factor 1, which accounted for 85.8% of the total variance in the second sample. It was labeled "treatment based on gender versus treatment as an individual" (Chusmir & Koberg, 1986, p. 406). Items 11 to 17 load on Factor 2, which accounted for 14.2% of the variance for the second sample. This factor was labeled "private self-concept versus socially and work-defined self-concept" (p. 406).

(2) Five items on the SRCS are adapted from Rizzo, House, and Lirtzman's (1970) measure of role ambiguity and conflict.

(3) Chusmir and Koberg (1987) used the SRCS to look at the relationship between age and gender role conflict in a sample of 556 working women and men.

AVAILABLE FROM: Chusmir and Koberg, 1986

USED IN:

Chusmir, L. H., & Koberg, C. S. (1986). Development and validation of the Sex Role Conflict Scale. *Journal of Applied Behavioral Science*, 22(4), 397–409.

Chusmir, L. H., & Koberg, C. S. (1987). Role of age in sex-role conflict. *Psychological Reports*, 61, 337–338.

BIBLIOGRAPHY:

Rizzo, J. R., House, R. J., & Lirtzman, S. I. (1970) Role conflict and ambiguity in complex organizations. *Administrative Science Quarterly*, 15, 150–163.

DUAL-CAREER FAMILY SCALES

AUTHORS: Brian F. Pendleton, Margaret M. Poloma, and T. Neal Garland

DATE: 1980 (used 1977)

VARIABLE: Six aspects of dual-career marriages: Marriage Type, Domestic Responsibility, Satisfaction with Roles, Self-Image, Career Salience, and Career Line

TYPE OF INSTRUMENT: Guttman scale

DESCRIPTION: The original Dual-Career Family Scales contain 31 items representing six scales. Six items pertain to Marriage Type. These items deal with child care and the husband's importance compared to the wife's importance within the family. They can be thought of as measuring egalitarian versus traditional marriage relationships. Three items pertain to Domestic Responsibility. These items pertain to the husband's and wife's relative responsibility for household tasks. Three items pertain to Satisfaction. There is one item pertaining to satisfaction from family, one to satisfaction from children, and one to satisfaction from career. Four items pertain to Self-Image. These items relate to self-concept regarding career, spouse, and mother. Eight items pertain to Career Salience. These items deal with the importance of the wife's career relative to her roles as wife and mother. The final seven items pertain to Career Line. These items deal with the wife's ability to commit herself fully to a career in light of the demands from home and family. Each scale is a Guttman scale in which the first item is the easiest to agree with and the last item is the most difficult to agree with.

Gaddy, Arnkoff, and Glass (1985) modified the Dual-Career Family Scales by adding 13 items. The revised scale contains 6 items regarding Marriage Type, 5 items regarding Domestic Responsibility, 4 items regarding Satisfaction, 4 items regarding Self-Image, 19 items regarding Career Salience, and 6 items regarding Career Line. These new items "were designed to improve the scales by balancing the number of items that reflected each bipolar end of the scaled dimension" (p. 121). On both the original and revised versions of the Dual-Career Family Scales, the respondent answers "true" or "false" for each statement.

SAMPLE ITEMS: (Marriage Type) I would not attend a professional convention if it inconvenienced my husband.

(Domestic Responsibility) Although my husband may assist me, the responsibility for homemaking tasks is primarily mine.

(Satisfaction) I would be a less fulfilled person without my experience of family life.

(Self-Image) I spend (spent) as much or more actual time with my children as my non-working neighbors who are active in community affairs.

(Career Salience) I view my work more as a job that I enjoy than as a career.

(Career Line) A married woman's career goals tend to be more modest than those of her male colleagues.

PREVIOUS SUBJECTS: Mothers in dual career marriages
APPROPRIATE FOR: Mothers in dual career marriages
ADMINISTRATION: Self-administered; about 10–15 minutes for the original version; about 15–20 minutes for the expanded version
SCORING: In discussing scoring, Pendleton, Poloma, and Garland (1980) stated: "Guttman scale scores can be assigned to each wife on the basis of the number of items she and her colleagues are in agreement on" (p. 273). Scores are obtained on the six short scales but not on the full scale.
DEVELOPMENT: The theoretical basis for the development of the Dual-Career Family Scales derived from the work of Garland (1969, 1971), Poloma (1970), Poloma and Garland (1971a, 1971b, 1978), Theodore (1971), Michel (1971), and Safilios-Rothschild (1972). The first phase of the research that eventually led to scale development was conducted in 1969. Interviews were conducted with couples in which the wife was an attorney, college professor, or physician. Information obtained through the interviews provided the basis for developing the questions included on the 1977 questionnaire.

In expanding the Dual-Career Family Scales, Gaddy et al. (1985) added some items from the original item pool used to develop the scales, and they developed some new items based on a search of the relevant literature.
RELIABILITY: Pendleton et al. (1980) reported coefficient alpha for each of the six scales, based on testing 45 women. The values of alpha were: Marriage Type = .67, Domestic Responsibility = .42, Satisfaction = .50, Self-Image = .73, Career Salience = .57, and Career Line = .76.

Gaddy et al. (1985) administered the expanded version of the Dual-Career Family Scales to 70 married women, each of whom had a child below the age of 12. They obtained the following values for coefficient alpha: Marriage Type = .64, Domestic Responsibility = .39, Satisfaction = .29, Self-Image = .38, Career Salience = .62, and Career Line = .74. Although Gaddy et al. used a larger sample size and increased the length of five of the six scales, they obtained lower values for coefficient alpha for all scales except Career Salience.
VALIDITY: Pendleton et al. (1980) raised the issue of the scale's validity and stated: "The validity of these scales is extremely difficult to establish both because of the ambiguity of what 'validity' is . . . and because of the often needed 'test-retest' design for validity" (p. 271). The authors suggested that the intercorrelations between the subscales provided evidence of the scale's validity. Five of the 15 intercorrelations were significant at the .01 level, and 6 of the intercorrelations were totally independent. Four of the significant correlations were between Career Salience and each of the following: Career Line, Satisfaction, Domestic Responsibilities, and Marriage Type.
NOTES & COMMENTS: (1) Guttman analyses performed by Pendleton

et al. (1980) yielded coefficients of reproducibility of .81 for Marriage Type, .85 for Domestic Responsibility, .97 for Satisfaction, .98 for Self-Image, .78 for Career Salience, and .76 for Career Line. Scalability results were .40 for Marriage Type, .53 for Domestic Responsibility, .20 for Satisfaction, .23 for Career Salience, and .43 for Career Line. Three of the six scales—Domestic Responsibility, Satisfaction, and Self-Image—satisfied the criterion that reproducibility be at least .85. Four scales—Marriage Type, Domestic Responsibility, Self-Image, and Career Line—satisfied the criterion of a coefficient of scalability of at least .40.

(2) Internal consistency was very low for the scales.

(3) Pendleton et al. (1980) reported interitem correlations for each subscale. Gaddy et al. (1985) reported interscale correlations.

(4) Gaddy et al. (1985) compared scores on the Dual-Career Family Scales with scores on the PRF ANDRO (Berzins, Welling, & Wetter, 1978), which measures masculinity, femininity, and self-esteem (see separate entry).

(5) Pendleton, Poloma, and Garland (1982) reported the development of a different set of dual-career scales. These scales cover "family and career interface, personal satisfaction with trend setting, career support of the traditional wife-mother role, trend breaking, trend maintenance, and compensatory factors" (p. 69). This set of scales was developed from the same data pool used for the Dual-Career Family Scales, and there is overlap in the items on the two sets of scales.

(6) Gaddy, Glass, and Arnkoff (1983) used two scales from the Dual-Career Family Scales; they combined the Marriage Type scale and the Domestic Responsibility scale and added two more items. This 11-item scale was used to measure marital egalitarianism.

AVAILABLE FROM: The original version is in Pendleton, Poloma, and Garland, 1980; the expanded version is in Gaddy, Arnkoff, and Glass, 1985

USED IN:

Gaddy, C. D., Arnkoff, D. B., & Glass, C. R. (1985). A study of the scales for investigation of the dual-career family. *Measurement and Evaluation in Counseling and Development, 18*, 120–127.

Gaddy, C. D., Glass, C. R., & Arnkoff, D. B. (1983). Career involvement of women in dual-career families: The influence of sex role identity. *Journal of Counseling Psychology, 30*(3), 388–394.

Pendleton, B F., Poloma, M. M., & Garland, T. N. (1980). Scales for investigation of the dual-career family. *Journal of Marriage and the Family, 42*, 269–276.

Pendleton, B. F., Poloma, M. M., & Garland, T. N. (1982). An approach to quantifying the needs of dual-career families. *Human Relations, 35*(1), 69–82.

BIBLIOGRAPHY:

Berzins, J. I., Welling, M. A., & Wetter, R. E. (1978). A new measure of psychological androgyny based on the Personality Research Form. *Journal of Consulting and Clinical Psychology, 46*, 126–138.

Garland, T. N. (1969). Comment on Orden and Bradburn's "working wives and marriage happiness." *American Journal of Sociology, 75,* 412–413.

Garland, T. N. (1971). Husbands of professional women: The forgotten men. (Doctoral dissertation, Case Western Reserve University, 1971). *Dissertation Abstracts International, 32,* 4734A.

Michel, A. (1971). *Family issues of employed women in Europe and America.* Leiden, Netherlands: J. J. Brill.

Poloma, M. M. (1970). The married professional woman: An empirical examination of three myths. (Doctoral dissertation, Case Western Reserve University, 1970). *Dissertation Abstracts International, 32,* 564A.

Poloma, M. M., & Garland, T. N. (1971a). The married professional woman: A study in the tolerance of domestication. *Journal of Marriage and the Family, 33,* 531–540.

Poloma, M. M., & Garland, T.N. (1971b). The dual profession family. *National Business Woman, 52,* 6–8.

Poloma, M. M., & Garland, T. N. (1978). Two sides of the coin: An investigation of the dual-career family. In J. R. Eshleman & J. N. Clarke (Eds.), *Intimacy, commitment, and marriage* (pp. 236–246). Boston: Allyn & Bacon.

Safilios-Rothschild, C. (1972). *The sociology of women.* Lexington, MA: Xerox Publishing.

Theodore, A. (1971). *The professional woman.* New York: Schenkman.

DUAL EMPLOYED COPING SCALES (DECS)

AUTHORS: Denise A. Skinner and Hamilton McCubbin

DATE: 1982 (used 1981)

VARIABLE: Coping behaviors and patterns of dual employed families

TYPE OF INSTRUMENT: Summated rating scale

DESCRIPTION: The Dual Employed Coping Scales (DECS) consist of 49 items representing four factors. Factor 1, "Maintaining, Restructuring, and Strengthening the Family System," consists of 16 items dealing with coping behaviors that focus on family matters. Factor 2, "Procurement of Support to Maintain Family Roles," consists of 7 items dealing with coping behavior that focus on securing outside help and support. Factor 3, "Modifying Roles and Standards to Maintain a Work/Family Balance," consists of 15 items dealing with behaviors that adjust work to family and family to work. Factor 4, "Maintaining a Positive Perspective on the Lifestyle and Reducing Tensions and Strains," consists of 11 items that focus on satisfying individual needs and maintaining an optimistic perspective. Each item is a coping behavior that one might adapt to deal with the problems and stresses of a dual career marriage.

SAMPLE ITEMS: (Factor 1) Planning for various family relations to occur at a certain regular time each day or week (e.g., "from the time we get home until their bedtime, is the 'children's time' ").

(Factor 2) Relying on extended family members for childcare help.

(Factor 3) Limiting job involvement in order to have time for my family.

(Factor 4) Believing that, overall, there are more advantages than dis-advantages to our lifestyle.

PREVIOUS SUBJECTS: Dual career couples

APPROPRIATE FOR: Dual career couples

ADMINISTRATION: Self-administered; about 20–25 minutes

SCORING: Items are individually scored on a 5-point scale. The response options and the details for scoring are not provided; however, it is clear that item scores are summed to yield scores on the four factors and an overall score. Higher scores indicate greater use of the coping strategies. Skinner and McCubbin (1982) provided means and standard deviations separately for husbands and wives, based on the results from 69 dual career couples.

DEVELOPMENT: Originally the DECS contained 58 items. When it was administered to 69 couples and the results were factor analyzed, four factors were identified. The 49 items loading on these factors comprise the current version of the DECS.

RELIABILITY: Based on responses from 69 couples, coefficient alpha was .72, .74, .78, and .76 for Factors 1, 2, 3, and 4, respectively. Coefficient alpha for the full scale was .86.

VALIDITY: In a sample of 69 dual career couples, the wives scored significantly higher than the husbands on the total score and on two of the four factor scores.

Skinner and McCubbin (1982) reported that DECS correctly classified the sex of 91.3% of the respondents in a sample of 69 dual career couples.

NOTES & COMMENTS: (1) Skinner and McCubbin (1982) provided the factor loadings for all 49 items. They also provided the intercorrelations between the factor scores.

(2) Skinner and McCubbin (1982) related scores on the DECS to scores on the Family Adaptability and Cohesion Scales (Olson, Bell, & Portner, 1978), a measure of family adaptation.

AVAILABLE FROM: Skinner and McCubbin, 1982

USED IN:

Skinner, D. A., & McCubbin, H. (1982, October). *Coping in dual-employed families: Spousal differences*. Paper presented at the meeting of the National Council on Family Relations, Washington, DC. (ERIC Document Reproduction Service No. ED 227 422)

BIBLIOGRAPHY:

Olson, D. H., Bell, R., & Portner, J. (1978). *Family Adaptability and Cohesion Scale*. Unpublished paper, University of Minnesota, St. Paul.

WALLSTON JOB SEEKING SIMULATIONS

AUTHORS: Barbara Strudler Wallston, Martha A. Foster, and Michael Berger

DATE: 1978 (used 1974)

VARIABLE: The use of egalitarian versus nonegalitarian decision-making rules in accepting employment for dual career couples
TYPE OF INSTRUMENT: Multiple choice
DESCRIPTION: The Wallston Job Seeking Simulations scale consists of two hypothetical situations in which the partners in a dual career marriage must make a decision regarding job offers. "In simulation one, form one, a male had an outstanding job offer where his wife was unable to locate a position, while both had moderately attractive offers elsewhere. . . . Simulation two presented the wife with a very good offer before her husband had anything definite (form one)" (Wallston, Foster, & Berger, 1978, p. 13). In the first part of Simulation 2, there is no time pressure on the couple; in the second part, there is time pressure. Each simulation is followed by several response options. Some options are considered traditional (e.g., Bob accepts the more attractive offer and Sue comes along, hoping to find something), and others are considered nontraditional (e.g., Mary accepts the job, and Frank pursues his possibilities, with the chance that they'll live separately for the time being). There are two forms of the measure. The second form reverses the gender of the persons in the simulations. Respondents are given only one of the two forms.
PREVIOUS SUBJECTS: Recent PhDs in psychology and biological sciences and their spouses
APPROPRIATE FOR: High school students and older
ADMINISTRATION: Self-administered; about 10 minutes
SCORING: There are no scores per se. Rather, decisions are classified as nontraditional (egalitarian) or traditional (nonegalitarian). Data are analyzed for groups of respondents.
DEVELOPMENT: No information was provided.
RELIABILITY: No information was provided.
VALIDITY: In situations where there were no external constraints, such as few available positions or time pressure, males and females who self-labeled as feminists were significantly more likely than nonfeminists to select egalitarian responses. When there was the constraint of few available positions, only females who self-labeled as feminists were significantly more likely than nonfeminists to select egalitarian responses. When the constraint of time pressure was added, there were no differences between the responses of feminists and nonfeminists for either males or females. These differing patterns of response suggest that respondents did differentiate between the different situations; that is, they did not simply give lip-service to what might be considered the more socially desirable response—the egalitarian response.
NOTES & COMMENTS: (1) The Wallston Job Seeking Simulations is not a scale in the same sense as most of the other measures in this handbook.

It does, however, provide a standardized approach to assessing persons' responses to the complex questions dual career couples face.

(2) The three references listed below describe the same research study.

AVAILABLE FROM: Wallston, Foster, and Berger, 1978

USED IN:

Berger, M., Foster, M., Wallston, B. S., & Wright, L. (1977). You and me against the world: Dual-career couples and joint job seeking. *Journal of Research and Development in Education*, 10(4), 31–37.

Foster, M. A., Wallston, B.S., & Berger, M. (1980). Feminist orientation and job-seeking behavior among dual-career couples. *Sex Roles*, 6(1), 59–65.

Wallston, B.S., Foster, M. A., & Berger, M. (1978). I will follow him: Myth, reality, or forced choice—job-seeking experiences of dual-career couples. *Psychology of Women Quarterly*, 3(1), 9–21.

ATTITUDES TOWARD WORKING MOTHERS SCALE (AWM)

AUTHORS: Toby J. Tetenbaum, Jessica Lighter, and Mary Travis

DATE: 1983

VARIABLE: Attitudes toward working mothers

TYPE OF INSTRUMENT: Summated rating scale

DESCRIPTION: The Attitudes Toward Working Mothers Scale (AWM) consists of 32 statements, most of which pertain to the working mother's impact on her children. All of the items are phrased in the same direction; that is, all express negative attitudes about working mothers or positive attitudes about nonworking mothers. Items are accompanied by seven response options: "disagree strongly, disagree moderately, disagree slightly, neither agree nor disagree, agree somewhat, agree moderately, agree strongly."

SAMPLE ITEMS: Mothers should be home when their children return from school.

Working mothers can't be as close to their children as non-working mothers.

PREVIOUS SUBJECTS: Graduate students, teachers, counselors, school psychologists, school administrators, and pupil personnel workers; undergraduate students; high school students in grades 11 and 12

APPROPRIATE FOR: High school students and older

ADMINISTRATION: Self-administered; about 15 minutes

SCORING: Items are individually scored on a 7-point scale, with 7 points assigned to "agree strongly" and 1 point assigned to "disagree strongly." Item scores are summed to yield a total score that can range from 32 (very positive attitude toward working mothers) to 224 (very negative attitude toward working mothers). Tetenbaum, Lighter, and Travis (1983) reported average item scores rather than total scores. They reported means and standard deviations separately for males and females for the following groups: urban educators, suburban educators, urban high school students, suburban high school students, secretaries, members of the National Organization for Women (NOW), and members of a Right to Life group.

DEVELOPMENT: The first version of the AWM contained 45 statements that "assessed attitudes toward women's role and the perceived effects of this role on the woman and/or her family" (Tetenbaum et al., 1983, p. 71). This version was administered to 526 graduate students, and separate factor analyses were performed for the 329 females and the 182 males. The results for males and females were quite similar. A single factor was extracted that accounted for more than 55% of the variance. The data for the two sexes were combined. The 32 items with factor loadings greater than .40 were retained for the final scale.

RELIABILITY: Coefficient alpha for a sample of 329 adult females was .94; similarly for a sample of 182 adult males, coefficient alpha was .95 (Tetenbaum et al., 1983).

Item-total correlations were computed for the 32 items. The correlations ranged from .48 to .74; more than half the items had item-total correlations greater than .60.

VALIDITY: Tetenbaum, Lighter, and Travis (1981) administered the AWM scale to teachers, school psychologists/guidance counselors, and administrators. They found that teachers and administrators did not differ from each other in their attitudes, but psychologists/guidance counselors had significantly higher scores, reflecting more positive attitudes than those expressed by the teachers and administrators. Furthermore, Tetenbaum et al. (1981) found that within each of the three groups, females expressed significantly more positive attitudes than did males. The researchers also found that younger teachers expressed more positive attitudes than older teachers. However, no age differences were found for the administrators or for the psychologists/guidance counselors.

As predicted, a sample of 81 members of NOW (a feminist organization) scored significantly higher, demonstrating more positive attitudes toward working women, than a sample of 73 members of a Right to Life group (an anti-abortion, presumably conservative organization) (Tetenbaum et al., 1983). It was also predicted that women who work would have more positive attitudes toward working mothers than would women who do not work. The researchers compared women in NOW who worked with women in the same group who did not work; they also compared women in the Right to Life group who worked with women in that group who did not work. For both groups, they found that their prediction was supported: working women had higher scores than nonworking women on the AWM scale.

In order to demonstrate that the AWM measures a construct different from feminism or attitudes toward women and to demonstrate that a social desirability response set does not unduly influence responses, 60 students completed the AWM and the following scales: the FEM Scale (Smith, Ferree, & Miller, 1975) (see separate entry), the short form Attitudes Toward Women Scale (Spence, Helmreich, & Stapp, 1973) (see separate entry), the Feminism II Scale (Dempewolff, 1974) (see separate entry), and the Marlowe-Crowne Social Desirability Scale (Crowne & Marlowe, 1964). Though the AWM was significantly correlated with two of the scales—the FEM Scale and the Feminism II Scale—the highest correlation was − .25, indicating that only 6% of the variance was shared by the two measures (Tetenbaum et al., 1983).

As predicted, females scored significantly higher than males on the AWM, demonstrating that females have more positive attitudes toward working mothers than do males (Tetenbaum et al., 1983).

NOTES & COMMENTS: Etaugh and Gilomen (1986) administered the AWM along with a biographical questionnaire to 96 college women and 96 college men. The researchers used regression analysis to identify the most effective predictors of attitudes toward women. Lighter, Tetenbaum, and Travis (1981) administered the AWM to 246 adolescent girls in the 11th and 12th grades. They then used regression analysis to examine the relationship between AWM scores and the following predictors: "maternal employment status, maternal power within the family, division of labor, maternal attitude toward her employment status, adolescent satisfaction with the mothering received, and paternal attitudes toward women working" (p. 8).

AVAILABLE FROM: Toby J. Tetenbaum, School of Education at Lincoln Center, 113 West 60th Street, Box 132, Fordham University, New York, NY 10023-7478

USED IN:

Etaugh, C., & Gilomen, G. (1986, August). *Demographic predictors of college students' attitudes toward working mothers*. Paper presented at the annual meeting of the American Psychological Association, Washington, DC. (ERIC Document Reproduction Service No. ED 281 131)

Lighter, J. R., Tetenbaum, J. B., & Travis, M. (1981, April). *Predicting career orientation in adolescent females: A look at some forgotten family variables*. Paper presented at the meeting of the American Educational Research Association, St. Louis. (ERIC Document Reproduction Service No. ED 203 044)

Tetenbaum, T. J., Lighter, J., & Travis, M. (1981). Educators' attitudes toward working mothers. *Journal of Educational Psychology, 73*(3), 369–375.

Tetenbaum, T. J., Lighter, J., & Travis, M. (1983). The construct validation of an Attitudes Toward Working Mothers Scale. *Psychology of Women Quarterly, 8*(1), 69–78.

BIBLIOGRAPHY:

Crowne, D. P., & Marlowe, D. (1964). *The approval motive*. New York: Wiley.

Dempewolff, J. (1974). Development and validation of a feminism scale. *Psychological Reports, 34*, 651–657.

Smith, E. R., Ferree, M. M., & Miller, F. D. (1975). A short scale of attitudes toward feminism. *Representative Research in Social Psychology*, 6, 51–56.

Spence, J. T., Helmreich, R. L., & Stapp, J. (1973). A short version of the Attitudes Toward Women Scale (AWS). *Bulletin of the Psychonomic Society*, 2, 219–220.

BELIEFS ABOUT THE CONSEQUENCES OF MATERNAL EMPLOYMENT FOR CHILDREN (BACMEC)

AUTHORS: Ellen Greenberger, Wendy A. Goldberg, Thomas J. Crawford, and Jean Granger

DATE: 1988

VARIABLE: Beliefs about the effects of a mother's employment on her children

TYPE OF INSTRUMENT: Summated rating scale

DESCRIPTION: The Beliefs About the Consequences of Maternal Employment for Children (BACMEC) consists of 24 items: 11 items are phrased as costs or disadvantages affecting the child of a working mother, and 13 items are phrased as benefits or advantages that accrue to a child whose mother works. In describing the content of 22 of the items, Greenberger, Goldberg, Crawford & Granger (1988) listed: "physical health and safety (2 items); negative psychosocial impacts, such as emotional insecurity (6 items); positive psychosocial items, such as greater independence and adaptability (6 items); impacts on sex-role conceptions (5 items); and effects on learning and school performance (3 items)." Items are accompanied by six response options ranging from "agree very strongly" to "disagree very strongly."

SAMPLE ITEMS: (Costs) Children are less likely to form a warm and secure relationship with a mother who is working full time.

   (Benefits) Children whose mothers work are more independent and able to do things for themselves.

PREVIOUS SUBJECTS: College students, university staff, child development experts, adult women

APPROPRIATE FOR: Ages 16 and older

ADMINISTRATION: Self-administered; about 10–15 minutes

SCORING: Each item on the BACMEC is scored on a 6-point scale, with the "disagree very strongly" end of the continuum assigned 1 point and the "agree very strongly" end of the continuum assigned 6 points. Two scores are obtained from the BACMEC. The Benefits score is the sum of the scores on the 13 benefit items; the Costs score is the sum of the scores on the 11 cost items. On both subscales, higher scores reflected greater belief in that area—that is, greater belief in the costs and greater belief in the benefits of maternal employment. An overall total score is obtained by reversing the scoring on the benefits items and then totaling all 24 items. Thus, a higher total score reflects a belief that maternal employment has negative consequences for children.

DEVELOPMENT: An item pool was generated including items written by the scale's authors and items submitted by undergraduate psychology students. The pool was reduced to 55 nonoverlapping items: 27 regarding costs of maternal employment and 28 regarding benefits from maternal employment. The 55 items were completed by a sample of college students, who also responded to 11 general statements about maternal employment. Using item analysis data, correlations with the general statements, and correlations with child's age when mother should begin work, the item pool was reduced to the 24 items that comprise the BACMEC.

RELIABILITY: Greenberger et al. (1988) administered the BACMEC to five samples: university staff employees, child development experts, adult women, and two groups of university students. They reported alpha coefficients for the subscales and the total scale for each of the five groups. For the Costs subscale, coefficient alpha ranged from .88 to .94; for the Benefits subscale, coefficient alpha ranged from .83 to .91; and for the total scale, coefficient alpha ranged from .89 to .94. Item-total correlations and item-subscale correlations were reported for two samples. Item-total correlations were at least .50 for over two-thirds of the items for both samples. Item-subscale correlations were at least .60 for over three-quarters of the items.

VALIDITY: As would be expected, the correlation between the two subscales was negative and significant for each of the five samples; the correlations ranged from −.39 to −.66.

Greenberger et al. (1988) presented various findings supporting the validity of the BACMEC. Total and subscale scores were all significantly correlated with attitudes toward maternal employment. The Costs subscale was significantly correlated with scores on the 15-item, short form of the Attitudes Toward Women Scale (Spence & Helmreich, 1978) (see separate entry). Total and subscale scores were significantly correlated with beliefs about the child's age when maternal employment is appropriate and with the respondent's employment status. When age and sex differences existed, they were in the expected direction: That is, younger respondents and females, compared to older respondents and males, were likely to see more benefits and fewer costs associated with maternal employment. BACMEC scores were not significantly correlated with social desirability nor were they significantly correlated with educational level.

NOTES & COMMENTS: Greenberger et al. (1988) suggested several research areas in which it would be appropriate to use the BACMEC.

AVAILABLE FROM: Greenberger, Goldberg, Crawford, and Granger, 1988

USED IN:
Greenberger, E., Goldberg, W. A., Crawford, T. J., & Granger, J. (1988). Beliefs
    About the Consequences of Maternal Employment for Children. *Psychology of Women Quarterly*, 12, 35–59.
BIBLIOGRAPHY:
Spence, J. T., & Helmreich, R. L. (1978). *Masculinity and femininity: Their psychological dimensions, correlates, and antecedents*. Austin: University of Texas
    Press.

CONSEQUENCES OF WORKING AND NOT WORKING FOLLOWING CHILDBIRTH

AUTHOR: Cherlyn Skromme Granrose

DATE: 1984

VARIABLE: Attitudes toward working following childbirth

TYPE OF INSTRUMENT: Rating scale

DESCRIPTION: The scale to measure Consequences of Working and
Not Working Following Childbirth consists of 34 items, though only 29
are scored. There are three parts to the scale. In the first part, respondents are asked to consider each item and rate it on its importance in
their lives. The instructions state, "Please consider how much you would
like each item to be a part of your life." A 5-point response scale is
provided, with the endpoints labeled "extremely undesirable" and "extremely desirable." For the second and third parts of the scale, respondents are given the same list of 34 items and asked to rate the likelihood
that the item will occur if they *do* work during the first 3 years after the
birth of their child (second part) and if they *do not* work during the first
3 years after the birth of their child (third part). For both the second and
third parts, a 5-point response scale is provided, with the endpoints
labeled "very unlikely" and "very likely."

SAMPLE ITEMS: Have fun

   A sense of accomplishment

   Feel tied down

PREVIOUS SUBJECTS: Upper-class college women

APPROPRIATE FOR: College women and older who have not yet had
children

ADMINISTRATION: Self-administered; about 20–30 minutes

SCORING: For each item, the likelihood of its occurring if the woman
does not work is subtracted from the likelihood of its occurring if she
does work. Both "likelihood" responses are scored on 5-point scales,
with the "very likely" end of the continuum assigned 5 points. The
difference score is then multiplied by the importance attached to the
item (obtained from the answer to Section 1 of the questionnaire); the
importance score is also expressed on a 5-point scale, with the "extremely
desirable" end of the continuum assigned 5 points. These values are
summed across the 29 items.

DEVELOPMENT: College students were asked to list all of the consequences that might occur if a woman went to work within the first 3 years following childbirth and all of the consequences that might occur if she did not work within these first 3 years. Based on content analysis of their responses, a list of 44 consequences was prepared. The measure was pretested with 20 college students. As a result, "Ten consequences were eliminated because subjects objected to the length of the instrument and because these items overlapped with included items or were rated as equally probable to occur whether or not a mother worked" (Granrose 1981, p. 32). When the responses from 202 college women were analyzed, it was found that five items were not strongly correlated with the other items on the scale. These items were not deleted from the scale, but they are not scored.

RELIABILITY: Using the responses from 202 college women, coefficient alpha was found to be .88.

VALIDITY: No information was provided.

NOTES & COMMENTS: (1) Granrose (1984, 1985, 1987) reported using the scale of Consequences for Working and Not Working Following Childbirth to test a model of labor force participation intentions.

(2) A factor analysis of the scale led to the identification of three factors. However, several items loaded on more than one factor, and factor scores would be highly intercorrelated. Therefore, Granrose (1984) concluded that the use of factor scores would not be useful.

AVAILABLE FROM: The 29 items are available in Granrose, 1984.

USED IN:

Granrose, C. S. (1981). Pathways to intention: a model of college women's intention to remain in the labor force following childbirth. (Doctoral dissertation, Rutgers University, 1981). *Dissertation Abstracts International, 42,* 1633B.

Granrose, C. S. (1984). A Fishbein-Ajzen model of intention to work following childbirth. *Journal of Vocational Behavior, 25*(3), 359–372.

Granrose, C. S. (1985). Anticipating the decision to work following childbirth. *Vocational Guidance Quarterly, 33*(3), 221–230.

Granrose, C. S. (1987). Intentions to work after childbirth of single and partnered college women. *The Career Development Quarterly, 36,* 66–80.

DUAL ROLE SCALE

AUTHORS: Lorraine Walker and S. Thomas Friedman

DATE: 1977

VARIABLE: Professional women's attitudes toward combining career and family roles

TYPE OF INSTRUMENT: Summated rating scale

DESCRIPTION: The Dual Role Scale consists of 15 items representing three factors: Career as Enriching Family Life (7 items), Role Equality (6 items), and Primary Role Priority (2 items). Each item is accompanied by a 7-point scale ranging from "strongly agree" to "strongly disagree." Ten items are phrased to reflect a supportive attitude toward a dual role for women; 5 items are phrased to reflect a more traditional attitude toward a dual role for women.

SAMPLE ITEMS: (Career as Enriching Family Life) A woman with a career is a better companion to her husband and children.

(Role Equality) A husband and wife should spend equal time in raising the children when they both work.

(Primary Role Priority) If her child is sick, a woman's first responsibility is to her child, not her job.

PREVIOUS SUBJECTS: Faculty members of a school of nursing

APPROPRIATE FOR: High school students and older

ADMINISTRATION: Self-administered; about 5–10 minutes

SCORING: Items are individually scored on a 7-point scale, with 7 points assigned to the response that is most favorable toward a dual role for women. Item scores are summed to yield three scores—one score for each factor. Using data obtained from 84 nursing faculty, Walker and Friedman (1977) provided percentile norms for each of the three factor scores.

DEVELOPMENT: Using items generated by the authors, a 19-item version of the scale was constructed and administered to 84 women on the faculty of three nursing schools. Their responses were factor analyzed, and three factors were extracted. The 15 items with factor loadings greater than .35 were retained for the scale.

RELIABILITY: Using the responses from the 84 nursing faculty, coefficient alpha was computed for each of the three factors: Career as Enriching = .79; Role Equality = .64; and Primary Role Priority = .59.

VALIDITY: The Feminine Interest Questionnaire (Miller, 1977) (see separate entry) measures modern versus traditional female role orientation. Walker and Friedman (1977) administered the Dual Role Scale and the Feminine Interest Questionnaire to 84 nursing faculty. Scores on the Feminine Interest Questionnaire were significantly correlated with two of the three factor scores on the Dual Role Scale: Career as Enriching (r = .30, $p < .01$) and Role Equality (r = .64, $p < .01$).

NOTES & COMMENTS: (1) Walker and Friedman (1977) reported the intercorrelations between the three factor scores: Career as Enriching with Role Equality = .28 ($p < .05$); Career as Enriching with Primary Role Priority = .24 ($p < .05$); and Role Equality with Primary Role Priority = .09 (ns).

(2) Walker and Friedman (1977) compared the Dual Role Scale factor scores with a variety of demographic and other variables: number of children at home, age of youngest child at home, age of oldest child at home, age of subject, marital status, full-time/part-time employment status, graduate student status, perceived flexibility in work schedule,

perceived spouse supportiveness of career, satisfaction with amount of time for family, perceived equality in mate's sharing housework, and region of the country. Since each of these 12 variables was compared with three factor scores, there were 36 comparisons. Only 2 were significant, and it is possible these differences were due to chance.

(3) This scale can be criticized on several grounds. The percentile norms are of little value given that they are based on a small sample tested over a decade ago. For a factor analytic study, the sample size was small relative to the number of items. With only 2 items on the Primary Role Priority factor, it is not surprising that the reliability of this score is low and the factor score does not correlate significantly with three of the four other scores with which it was compared.

AVAILABLE FROM: Walker and Friedman, 1977
USED IN:
Walker, L., & Friedman, S. T. (1977). Professional women's attitudes toward the dual role of women. *Psychological Reports, 41,* 327–334.
BIBLIOGRAPHY:
Miller, W. B. (1977). *Manual for description of instruments used in a research project on the psychological aspects of fertility behavior in women.* Unpublished manuscript, American Institutes for Research, Palo Alto, CA.

FEMININE INTEREST QUESTIONNAIRE
AUTHOR: Warren B. Miller
DATE: 1977
VARIABLE: Modern versus traditional female role orientation
DESCRIPTION: The Feminine Interest Questionnaire is a summated rating scale consisting of 31 items, most of which pertain to women in regard to marital, maternal, or career roles. Each item is accompanied by four response options ranging from "agree completely" to "disagree completely."
ARTICLES LISTED IN BEERE, 1979: 2
NOTES & COMMENTS: (1) Researchers sometimes use only a portion of the scale.

(2) There is also a Masculine Interest Questionnaire authored by Warren B. Miller.
AVAILABLE FROM: Warren B. Miller, 669 Georgia Avenue, Palo Alto, CA 94306
USED IN:
Abrahams, B., Feldman, S. S., & Nash, S. C. (1978). Sex role self-concept and sex role attitudes: Enduring personality characteristics or adaptations to changing life situations? *Developmental Psychology, 14,* 393–400.
Baber, K. M., & Dreyer, A. S. (1986). Gender-role orientations in older child-free and expectant couples. *Sex Roles, 14,* 501–502.
Barber, B. L. (1982, October). *Motherhood after 28: Career women who waited.* Paper

presented at the meeting of the National Council on Family Relations,
Washington, DC. (ERIC Document Reproduction Service No. ED 243 020)

Nash, S. C., & Feldman, S. S. (1978). *Responsiveness to babies: Life-situation specific sex differences in adulthood.* Unpublished paper, Stanford University. (ERIC Document Reproduction Service No. ED 184 660)

Nash, S. C., & Feldman, S. S. (1980). Responsiveness to babies: Life-situation specific sex differences in adulthood. *Sex Roles, 6,* 751–758.

Walker, L., & Friedman, S. T. (1977). Professional women's attitudes toward the dual role of women. *Psychological Reports, 41,* 327–334.

BIBLIOGRAPHY:

Beere, C. A. (1979). *Women and women's issues: A handbook of tests and measures* (pp. 352–354). San Francisco: Jossey-Bass.

HOME AND EMPLOYMENT ROLE SCALES (HER)

AUTHORS: Glenys Parry and Peter Warr

DATE: 1980

VARIABLE: Attitude toward present domestic and child care work, attitude toward present paid employment, and strain of coping with both roles

TYPE OF INSTRUMENT: Summated rating scale

DESCRIPTION: Three 12-item subscales comprise the Home and Employment Role Scales (HER): the Home Role Attitude scale (HRA), the Employment Role Attitude scale (ERA), and the Interaction Strain scale (IS). The HRA is intended to measure "mother's overall attitude to her present domestic and child-care work"; the ERA is intended to measure a "mother's overall attitude to her present paid employment"; and the IS is intended to measure "the strain experienced by an employed mother in coping with both domestic and paid work" (Parry & Warr, 1980, p. 245). Each item is accompanied by three response alternatives: "Yes, true; No, untrue; Don't know." Of the 36 items on the three scales, about half are phrased positively, and half are phrased negatively.

SAMPLE ITEMS: (Home Role Attitude) My family really shows that they appreciate all I do for them.

(Employment Role Attitude) People where I work are very friendly.

(Interaction Strain) The hours I work make it very difficult to look after the children.

PREVIOUS SUBJECTS: Married women with children below age 14; married women with an infant between 5 and 18 months of age

APPROPRIATE FOR: Married, employed women with children living at home

ADMINISTRATION: Self-administered; about 15 minutes

SCORING: Items are individually scored on a 3-point scale. Scores on each of the three scales can range from 12 to 36. On the HRA and the ERA, higher scores reflect more positive attitudes; on the IS, higher scores reflect greater role strain.

DEVELOPMENT: A search of the relevant literature and interviews with mothers of young children provided the information for developing the initial item pool. A sample of 27 persons responded to the items, and their data were used to revise the items. The 48-item version of the scale that resulted from the first pretesting was completed by 185 women with children. The pool was reduced to include 12 items on each of the three scales by applying the following criteria: high interitem and item-total correlations, item mean near the middle of the distribution, and large item standard deviation. In addition, redundant items were eliminated, and items were selected to represent a broad range of content.

RELIABILITY: Based on testing 185 women, the values for coefficient alpha were: HRA = .71, ERA = .78, and IS = .75. Majewski (1986) used the ERA with 86 first-time mothers. She obtained a coefficient alpha of .72.

VALIDITY: Parry and Warr (1980) used the HER along with measures of positive affect, negative affect, social supports, and life satisfaction to test four hypotheses. The first hypothesis was that IS scores would be higher for full-time employed mothers compared to part-time employed mothers, but there would be no difference between the two groups in terms of HRA and ERA scores. This hypothesis was supported. The second hypothesis was that IS scores but not ERA scores would be correlated with social supports. This hypothesis was also supported. The third hypothesis was that HRA scores would be more highly correlated with life satisfaction than would ERA scores. The correlations were consistent with the prediction, but the differences were not statistically significant. The last hypothesis was that HRA scores would be more highly correlated with negative affect than would ERA scores, and ERA scores would be more highly correlated with positive affect than would HRA scores. This hypothesis was supported.

Parry and Warr (1980) reported the intercorrelations between the scale scores. After life satisfaction scores were partialed out, the correlations showed that IS scores were significantly related to ERA and HRA scores, as would be expected, and ERA scores and HRA scores were not significantly related to each other.

NOTES & COMMENTS: Majewski (1986) used the ERA as one of several measures in a study designed to examine the relationship between employment status, role conflict, marital satisfaction, employment role attitude, and ease of transition to the maternal role for 86 first-time mothers.

AVAILABLE FROM: Parry and Warr, 1980

USED IN:

Majewski, J. L. (1986). Conflicts, satisfactions, and attitudes during transition to the maternal role. *Nursing Research*, 35(1), 10–14.

Parry, G., & Warr, P. (1980). The measurement of mothers' work attitudes. *Journal of Occupational Psychology*, 53, 245–252.

KING-MCINTYRE-AXELSON THREAT FROM WORKING WIVES SCALE

AUTHORS: Karl King, Jennie McIntyre, and Leland J. Axelson

DATE: 1968 (used 1963)

VARIABLE: Perception of whether a working wife is a threat to a marital relationship

DESCRIPTION: The King-McIntyre-Axelson Threat from Working Wives Scale is a Guttman scale consisting of five items. Each item suggests that a working wife threatens the marital relationship. Respondents indicate whether they agree or disagree with each statement.

ARTICLES LISTED IN BEERE, 1979: 4

AVAILABLE FROM: King, McIntyre, and Axelson, 1968

USED IN:

King, K., Abernathy, T. J., Jr., & Chapman, A. H. (1978). Do adolescents believe the employment of wives is a threat to marital relationships? *Family Coordinator, 27*, 231–235.

King, K., McIntyre, J., & Axelson, L. J. (1968). Adolescents' views of maternal employment as a threat to the marital relationship. *Journal of Marriage and the Family, 30*, 633–637.

BIBLIOGRAPHY:

Beere, C. A. (1979). *Women and women's issues: A handbook of tests and measures* (pp. 357–539). San Francisco: Jossey-Bass.

LIFE ROLE SALIENCE SCALES (LRSS)

AUTHORS: Ellen S. Amatea, E. Gail Cross, Jack E. Clark, and Carol L. Bobby

DATE: 1986 (for current version)

VARIABLE: Work and family role expectations

TYPE OF INSTRUMENT: Summated rating scale

DESCRIPTION: The Life Role Salience Scales (LRSS) were designed to measure work and family role expectations of men and women who are already engaged in occupational, marital, and parental life roles or who anticipate those roles. It consists of 40 items, with 5 items representing each of eight factors. The eight factors are a "role reward value" factor and a "role commitment" factor for each of four roles: occupational, parental, marital, and home care roles. Thirty of the items are phrased in the same direction; 10 items are reversed. Each item is accompanied by five response options: "disagree, somewhat disagree, neither agree nor disagree, somewhat agree, agree."

SAMPLE ITEMS: (Occupational Role Reward Value) Having work/a career that is interesting and exciting to me is my most important life goal.

(Occupational Role Commitment) I want to work, but I do not want to have a demanding career.

(Parental Role Reward Value) Although parenthood requires many sacrifices, the love and enjoyment of children of one's own are worth it all.

(Parental Role Commitment) It is important to me to have some time for myself and my own development rather than have children and be responsible for their care.

(Marital Role Reward Value) My life would seem empty if I never married.

(Marital Role Commitment) I expect to commit whatever time is necessary to making my marriage partner feel loved, supported, and cared for.

(Homecare Role Reward Value) It is important to me to have a home of which I can be proud.

(Homecare Role Commitment) I expect to leave most of the day-to-day details of running a home to someone else.

PREVIOUS SUBJECTS: College students; female college faculty; married couples

APPROPRIATE FOR: College students and older

ADMINISTRATION: Self-administered; about 15–20 minutes

SCORING: Items are scored on a 5-point scale, with higher scores reflecting agreement with an item; scores on 10 items must be reversed. Eight subscale scores are obtained by summing the 5 items on the subscale. The subscale scores can range from 5 (strong disagreement with the particular value or with commitment to the role) to 25 (strong agreement with the particular value or with commitment to the role). Amatea, Cross, Clark, and Bobby (1986) reported mean scores for each of the eight subscales. The means are based on responses from 150 married couples.

DEVELOPMENT: The LRSS was developed over a period of several years; in its original form, it was called the Life Roles Expectation Scales. The original scale was developed by writing items relating to six areas: reward value of occupational, marital, and parental roles and commitment to occupational, marital, and parental roles. A search of relevant literature led to the generation of 15 items for each of these six areas. The pool of 90 items was administered to 143 college students, and items were deleted from the scale if their mean score was above 4.0 or below 2.0 (too extreme) or if their standard deviation was below .50 (too little variability). From this pilot study, a set of 60 items—10 items for each of the six subscales—was selected. This set of 60 items comprised the Life Roles Expectation Scales and was administered to two different samples, college students and female university faculty. Their responses were factor analyzed. The factor structures from the two different samples were fairly similar and tended to support the original six subscales, so the 6 items that loaded most strongly on each subscale were selected for the subscale. Alpha coefficients were computed for each sample, as were test-retest reliabilities using responses from 60 students tested on two occasions. The results for two subscales, Marital Role Commitment and Occupational Role Commitment, were unacceptably low, so these two subscales were substantially revised. Existing items were revised and new items added. Furthermore, two new scales suggested by an earlier factor analysis were added: Homecare Role Reward Value and Homecare Role Commitment. Altogether 28 new or revised items were added to the 24 items retained on the scale. This 52-item version of the scale was administered to 150 married couples, and their responses were subjected to both item analysis and factor analysis. On the basis of the item analysis, 4 items with low discriminatory power were deleted. The factor analysis of the remaining items led to eight factors; "the five strongest-loading items on each of the eight factors were then selected to comprise the items in each scale" (Amatea et al., 1986, p. 836).

RELIABILITY: Alpha coefficients are reported based on responses from 150 married couples. For the eight subscale scores, alpha ranged from .79 to .94.

VALIDITY: No information was provided.

NOTES & COMMENTS: (1) The Life Roles Expectation Scales, which preceded the LRSS, were used by Amatea and Clark (1984), Clark (1985), and Reading and Amatea (1986).

(2) Amatea et al. (1986) reported the intercorrelations among the eight subscales. The values ranged from −.20 to +.40, with an average of +.29. Of the 28 correlation coefficients, 13 are statistically significant.

AVAILABLE FROM: Amatea, Cross, Clark, and Bobby, 1986

USED IN:

Amatea, E. S., & Clark, J. E. (1984). A dual career workshop for college couples: Effects of an intervention program. *Journal of College Student Personnel, 25,* 271–272.

Amatea, E. S., Cross, E. G., Clark, J. E., & Bobby, C. L. (1986). Assessing the work and family role expectations of career-oriented men and women: The Life Role Salience Scales. *Journal of Marriage and the Family, 48,* 831–838.

Clark, J. E. (1985). A validation study of the Life Role Expectations Scales. (Doctoral dissertation, University of Florida, 1984). *Dissertation Abstracts International, 45,* 1990A.

Reading, J., & Amatea, E. S. (1986). Role deviance or role diversification: Reassessing the psychosocial factors affecting the parenthood choice of career-oriented women. *Journal of Marriage and the Family, 48,* 255–260.

LIFE STYLE INDEX

AUTHOR: Shirley S. Angrist

DATE: 1970 (used 1964)

VARIABLE: Level of women's career aspirations

DESCRIPTION: The Life Style Index is a multiple choice measure consisting of 11 questions. The questions concern future educational and occupational plans. Each item is accompanied by five or six response options that vary depending on the question.

ARTICLES LISTED IN BEERE, 1979: 9

AVAILABLE FROM: Angrist, 1971–72

USED IN:

Angrist, S. S. (1971–72). Measuring women's career commitment. *Sociological Focus, 5*, 29–39.

Komarovsky, M. (1982). Female freshmen view their future: Career salience and its correlates. *Sex Roles, 8*, 299–314.

Lentz, L. P. (1984). *Graduate women's career salience, aspirations, and involvement.* Unpublished paper, Oakland University, Rochester, MI. (ERIC Document Reproduction Service No. ED 249 833)

BIBLIOGRAPHY:

Beere, C. A. (1979). *Women and women's issues: A handbook of tests and measures* (pp. 359–361). San Francisco: Jossey-Bass.

LIFE STYLES FOR WOMEN SCALE

AUTHOR: Marie Susan A. Burns

DATE: 1974

VARIABLE: Attitudes toward different life-styles for women

DESCRIPTION: The Life Styles for Women Scale is a summated rating scale consisting of 20 items. Item content deals with marital, maternal, and career roles of women. Each item is accompanied by five response options ranging from "strongly agree" to "strongly disagree."

ARTICLES LISTED IN BEERE, 1979: 2

AVAILABLE FROM: Burns, 1974

USED IN:

Burns, M. S. A. (1974). Life Styles for Women: An attitude scale. *Psychological Reports, 35*, 227–230.

Chasia, S., & Eyo, I. E. (1977). Locus of control and traditional/nontraditional sex-role orientations in a sample of British female undergraduates. *Psychological Reports, 41*(3), 1015–1019.

BIBLIOGRAPHY:

Beere, C. A. (1979). *Women and women's issues: A handbook of tests and measures* (pp. 361–363). San Francisco: Jossey-Bass.

MATERNAL ATTITUDES TOWARD EMPLOYMENT

AUTHOR: Anita M. Farel

DATE: 1979

VARIABLE: Attitudes of mothers toward maternal employment

TYPE OF INSTRUMENT: Summated rating scale

DESCRIPTION: The Maternal Attitudes Toward Employment scale consists of 18 items, with 3 items representing each of six subscales: "Working makes a better mother," "Working makes a poorer mother," "Children have a negative attitude toward working mothers," "Mothers with preschool-age children should not work," "Intrinsic motivation to work for personal satisfaction," and "Intrinsic motivation to work—other" (Farel, 1981, p. 12). Items alternate. An item expressing a positive view of working is followed by an item expressing a negative view of working. Respondents express their approval or disapproval of each item by selecting one of five response options: "strongly disagree, disagree, not sure, agree, strongly agree."

SAMPLE ITEMS: Having a job outside the home is (would be) satisfying for me.

Children feel less close to working mothers.

PREVIOUS SUBJECTS: Mothers of kindergarten children; other adult women

APPROPRIATE FOR: The wording of the items is such that only women can respond to them, and the scale was developed specifically for mothers.

ADMINISTRATION: The scale is intended for administration by an interviewer, who reads the words in parentheses for women who are not working at the time they respond to the items and who omits those words for women currently working.

SCORING: Items are scored on a 5-point scale. After some item scores are reversed, they are summed to yield scores on the six subscales.

DEVELOPMENT: In pilot testing, a sample of 51 mothers completed an attitude measure consisting of 85 items on 16 scales. The scales pertained to "motivation to work, attitudes about the needs of young children and sex role stereotyping" (Farel, 1981, p. 1); there was considerable emphasis on the maternal needs of young children. Means, standard deviations, and internal consistency reliability coefficients were computed for each scale; interitem correlations were computed for the items within each scale; and the 16 scale scores were factor analyzed. It is not clear how the results of these analyses were used to develop the final version of the scale. Farel (1981) stated: "Seven scales measuring attitudes toward work and the maternal role were selected from the pilot study" (p. 4). Two of the scales were combined to form a new scale, "mothers with preschool-age children should not work." Thus, there were six scales; three items were selected from the pilot testing to represent each of the six scales.

RELIABILITY: Using data from the pilot study, internal reliability coefficients were computed. For the six scales, the reliabilities ranged from .62 to .82. The final version of the scale was completed by 212 mothers of kindergarten children. The internal consistency reliabilities ranged from .67 to .84, with three of the six values being greater than .80.

VALIDITY: No information was provided.

NOTES & COMMENTS: (1) A factor analysis of the data from the 212 mothers of kindergarten children produced four factors: "Working is bad for the child," "Intrinsic motivation to work," "Mothers of pre-school-age children should not work," and "Working is good for the child" (Farel, 1981, p. 7).

(2) Farel (1980) tested the hypothesis that "mothers whose attitudes toward work and whose employment status are congruent have children who are more competent and show better adjustment to school than the children of mothers with incongruent work attitudes and work behavior" (p. 1179).

AVAILABLE FROM: Farel, 1981
USED IN:

Farel, A. M. (1979). *Effects of preferred maternal roles and maternal employment on school adjustment and competence.* Unpublished doctoral dissertation, University of North Carolina, Chapel Hill.

Farel, A. M. (1980). Effects of preferred maternal roles, maternal employment, and sociodemographic status on school adjustment and competence. *Child Development, 51,* 1179–1186.

Farel, A. M. (1981). Assessment of maternal attitudes toward employment: Test instrument and implications. *Catalog of Selected Documents in Psychology, 11,* 47. (Ms. No. 2282)

MOTIVATIONS FOR CHILDREN AND WORK QUESTIONNAIRE

AUTHOR: Linda J. Beckman
DATE: 1977
VARIABLE: Perceptions of rewards and costs of children and rewards and costs of employment
TYPE OF INSTRUMENT: Summated rating scale
DESCRIPTION: The original version of the Motivations for Children and Work Questionnaire contains four sections: (1) 20 pleasures (rewards) that one might derive from children; (2) 20 drawbacks (costs) that one might experience from children; (3) 10 positive aspects (rewards) of working; and (4) 10 negative aspects (costs) of working. In responding to the rewards and costs associated with children, the respondent is to report "how important each of these factors is in your thinking at this time about having children (or more children)." For the positive and negative aspects of working, the directions state: "We would like to know how important each is to you at the present time." Responses are reported on a 7-point scale that has three anchor points: 1—of no importance; 4—moderately important; and 7—extremely important. If the item does not apply, an "X" is recorded; if the respondent disagrees with the statement, a "D" is recorded.

A revised version of the scale contains 20 rewards of parenthood, 18 costs of parenthood, 15 rewards of employment, and 12 costs of employment (Beckman & Houser, 1979). The revised scale also includes 25 rewards and 22 costs associated with having additional children; these include the rewards and costs associated with parenthood in general, plus 5 rewards and 4 costs associated with having additional children. SAMPLE ITEMS: (rewards of children) I want to be able to observe the growth and changes that occur in my child.

(costs of children) I do not want to contribute to the population explosion by having children.

(positive aspects of working) Working adds to my sense of self-esteem.

(negative aspects of working) I dislike some of the tasks that I have to do on my job.

PREVIOUS SUBJECTS: Employed women in their late childbearing years; married women; 11th- and 12th-grade females completed a modified scale.

APPROPRIATE FOR: In its current form, the scale is best used with married women of childbearing age.

ADMINISTRATION: The original form of the scale was self-administered; completion time was about 15 minutes. The newer version of the scale was administered by an interviewer. The items pertaining to having additional children are not administered to women without children because they are not appropriate for them.

SCORING: Beckman (1979) computed three summary indexes for the scale. MOT-AC was an index of motivation for additional children; it was calculated by totaling the ratings assigned to the rewards from additional children and subtracting the total of the ratings assigned to the costs of additional children. SAT-P was a summary index for parenthood; it was calculated by totaling the ratings assigned to the rewards of children and subtracting the total of the ratings assigned to the costs of children. The SAT-E score is a summary index for employment; it was found by totaling the ratings assigned to the employment rewards and subtracting the ratings assigned to the employment costs.

DEVELOPMENT: The original form of the scale was developed by selecting items with face validity. In revising the scale, items that had low average importance ratings were deleted, and items were added to represent the responses that women had given to open-ended questions regarding the rewards and costs of parenthood and employment. Some further revisions were made as a result of administering the scale to a sample of 30 currently married women.

RELIABILITY: No information was provided.

VALIDITY: Beckman (1977) hypothesized that motivation for parenthood (measured as the difference between the rewards and the costs) would decrease as the number of children increased. In general, this hypothesis was supported except that professional women with small families were more highly motivated for parenthood than were professional women with no children.

Beckman (1979), using the newer version of the Motivations for Children and Work Questionnaire, found that the "index of motivation for additional children was positively related to preference for a/another child and negatively related to future employment intentions" (p. 147). She also found that mothers who were more satisfied with parenthood and saw more rewards associated with parenthood were more likely to have more children.

NOTES & COMMENTS: (1) Beckman (1979) reported the following correlations: satisfaction with parenthood and motivation for parenthood = .45; rewards of parenthood and rewards of additional children = .48; costs of parenthood and costs of additional children = .60; satisfaction with employment and satisfaction with parenthood = −.05; and satisfaction with employment and motivation for parenthood = −.02.

(2) In two articles, Beckman (1977, 1978) reported data from the same study of 123 currently married, employed women in their late childbearing years. Similarly, Beckman (1979) and Beckman and Houser (1979) reported data from the same study of married women between the ages of 18 and 49; they used the revised form of the scale.

(3) Leslie (1986) modified the scale for administration to 11th- and 12th-grade females. Items regarding "additional children" were omitted, and several other items were rephrased in the future tense. She used the revised scale to study "adolescent females' assessments of the rewards and costs of employment and parenthood, and the impact of these assessments on their plans for organizing their adult lives" (Leslie, 1986, p. 29).

AVAILABLE FROM: Beckman, 1979, and Beckman and Houser, 1979, provide the substance, though not the exact wording, of the items on the newer version of the scale.

USED IN:

Beckman, L. J. (1977). Exchange theory and fertility-related decision-making. *Journal of Social Psychology, 103,* 265–276.

Beckman, L. J. (1978). The relative rewards and costs of parenthood and employment for employed women. *Psychology of Women Quarterly, 2*(3), 215–234.

Beckman, L. J. (1979). Fertility preferences and social exchange theory. *Journal of Applied Social Psychology, 9*(2), 147–169.

Beckman, L. J. (1984). Husbands' and wives' relative influence on fertility decisions and outcomes. *Population and Environment, 7,* 182–197.

Beckman, L. J., & Houser, B. B. (1979). Perceived satisfactions and costs of motherhood and employment among married women. *Journal of Population, 2*(4), 306–327.

Leslie, L. A. (1986). The impact of adolescent females' assessments of parenthood and employment on plans for the future. *Journal of Youth and Adolescence, 15*(1), 29–49.

ROLE PERCEPTION SCALE
AUTHORS: Mary Sue Richardson and Judith Landon Alpert
DATE: 1980
VARIABLE: Perceptions of five roles: work, marriage, parent, work-marriage, and work-parent
DESCRIPTION: The Role Perception Scale is a combination projective-objective test, but only the objective portion is scored. It is based on the assumption that the projective portion of the measure elicits deeper aspects of the personality, and this affects responses to the objective portion of the scale.

The Role Perception Scale consists of five verbal cues, one representing each of five roles: work, marriage, parent, work-marriage, and work-parent. The gender and names of the characters in the cues are reversed when the scale is administered to males compared to females. Standard Thematic Apperception Test instructions are given for responding to the cues, and 5 minutes are provided for writing a story. After the 5 minutes, respondents are to complete one set of 40 true/false items: 10 true/false items for each of four subscales (innovation, involvement, affectivity, and competition). The items from the four subscales are intermingled, and each refers to the main figure in the projective story. Identical sets of true/false statements follow each of the projective cues.
ARTICLES LISTED IN BEERE, 1979: 4
NOTES & COMMENTS: (1) The combination of projective-objective methodology is unique compared to the format of most other scales included in this handbook.

(2) For each sex, Richardson and Alpert (1980) compared role engagement scores across roles and competition scores across roles.

(3) Richardson and Alpert (1980) reported the results from factor analyses performed separately for each sex using the responses from 88 college women and 46 college men. The results confirmed that "each of the four subscales loaded predominantly on different factors, with three factors highly intercorrelated and one factor orthogonal to the rest" (p. 788).
AVAILABLE FROM: Richardson and Alpert, 1980
USED IN:
Richardson, M. S., & Alpert, J. L. (1980). Role perceptions: Variations by sex and roles. *Sex Roles, 6*(6), 783–793.
BIBLIOGRAPHY:
Beere, C. A. (1979). *Women and women's issues: A handbook of tests and measures* (pp. 369–371). San Francisco: Jossey-Bass.

SCALE OF ATTITUDES TOWARD A DUAL ROLE FOR WOMEN
AUTHORS: Julia I. Dalrymple, Phyllis K. Lowe, and Helen Y. Nelson
DATE: 1971

VARIABLE: Attitudes toward a dual role—homemaker and wage earner—for women

DESCRIPTION: The Scale of Attitudes Toward a Dual Role for Women is a summated rating scale consisting of 25 items covering four areas: how a mother's working affects children, financial benefits from a working wife, home and family relationships, and societal implications of working women. Items are accompanied by five response options ranging from "strongly disagree" to "strongly agree."

ARTICLES LISTED IN BEERE, 1979: 1

AVAILABLE FROM: Dalrymple, Lowe, and Nelson, 1971

USED IN:

Dalrymple, J. I., Lowe, P. K., & Nelson, H. Y. (1971). *Preparation for a dual role: Homemaker-wage earner, with adaptations to inner-city youth.* Unpublished report, Cornell University, Ithaca, NY. (ERIC Document Reproduction Service No. ED 058 464)

Stuckey, M. F., McGhee, P. E., & Bell, N. J. (1982). Parent-child interaction: The influence of maternal employment. *Developmental Psychology, 18,* 635–644.

BIBLIOGRAPHY:

Beere, C. A. (1979). *Women and women's issues: A handbook of tests and measures* (pp. 375–376). San Francisco: Jossey-Bass.

STUDENT ATTITUDE SCALE

AUTHORS: Elizabeth G. French and Gerald S. Lesser

DATE: 1964

VARIABLE: Value placed on intellectual goals and women's role goals

DESCRIPTION: The Student Attitude Scale consists of 65 true/false items, with 34 items pertaining to intellectual attainment and 31 items pertaining to various aspects of the woman's role. The items refer to college, and so the scale is useful only with college students.

ARTICLES LISTED IN BEERE, 1979: 5

AVAILABLE FROM: Gerald S. Lesser, Larson Hall, Appian Way, Cambridge, MA 02138

USED IN:

Beedle, S. L., Jordan-Viola, E. P., & Cross, H. J. (1979). Sex-role orientations of high school and college students. *Sex Roles, 5,* 363–364.

Ingram, B. L., & Berger, S. E. (1977). Sex-role orientation, defensiveness, and competitiveness in women. *Journal of Conflict Resolution, 21,* 501–518.

BIBLIOGRAPHY:

Beere, C. A. (1979). *Women and women's issues: A handbook of tests and measures* (pp. 379–381). San Francisco: Jossey-Bass.

WORK AND FAMILY ORIENTATION QUESTIONNAIRE (WOFO)

AUTHORS: Robert L. Helmreich and Janet T. Spence

DATE: 1978

VARIABLE: Achievement motivation and attitudes toward family and career

TYPE OF INSTRUMENT: Summated rating scale

DESCRIPTION: The Work and Family Orientation Questionnaire (WOFO) consists of 32 items: 23 items concern achievement motivation; the remaining 9 items "assess concerns with educational aspirations, pay, prestige, and advancement, attitudes toward spouse employment, relative importance of marriage vs. career and number of children desired" (Helmreich & Spence, 1978, p. 1). The 23 motivational items represent four factors: Work, which pertains to a "desire to work hard" (6 items); Mastery, which pertains to a "desire for intellectual challenge" (8 items); Competitiveness, which refers to a "desire to succeed in competitive, interpersonal situations" (5 items); and Personal Unconcern, which "measures attitudes about the possible negative interpersonal consequences of achievement and is conceptually related to the notion of Fear of Success" (4 items). Of the 32 items on the scale, 29 are Likert-type items with five response options ranging from "strongly agree" to "strongly disagree." The remaining 3 items are multiple choice items with five options per item. Six of the Likert-type items are keyed "strongly disagree," and 23 are keyed "strongly agree."

SAMPLE ITEMS: (Work) It is important for me to do my work as well as I can even if it isn't popular with my co-workers.

(Mastery) I would rather do something at which I feel confident and relaxed than something which is challenging and difficult.

(Competitiveness) I enjoy working in situations involving competition with others.

(Personal Unconcern) I feel that good relations with my fellow workers are more important than performance on a task.

(Other) Assuming that I get (or am) married, I would like my husband or my wife to have a job or career that pays well.

PREVIOUS SUBJECTS: High school and college students; psychologists, scientists, engineers; athletes, female distance runners; junior high school students, senior high school students and college students in France, Tunisia, and Mexico; students in Fiji; married couples; West Point cadets; gifted and talented female adolescents; women school administrators

APPROPRIATE FOR: High school students and older

ADMINISTRATION: Self-administered; about 10–15 minutes

SCORING: The 23 achievement motivation items are scored on a 5-point scale ranging from 0 to 4. A scoring key indicates, for each item, which end of the response continuum is coded 4. Item scores are summed to yield scores on each of the four subscales (factors). Higher scores represent more of the named attribute. Helmreich and Spence (1978) provided normative information for college students, by sex. The normative information includes subscale means, standard deviations, medians, modes, skewness, and kurtosis, as well as percentile scores for each subscale. Helmreich and Spence also provided response distributions, means, and standard deviations for each of the 9 items that are not part of the subscale scores.

DEVELOPMENT: The WOFO currently used is the third version of the scale. The first version consisted of 22 items: 19 items dealing with work and achievement-related situations and 3 items dealing with educational goals, importance of marriage relative to vocation, and number of children desired. Some of the achievement-related items were adapted from Mehrabian's (1969) Achievement Scales. Based on factor analyzing responses from high school students, six scales were developed: "Work Orientation, Mastery, Competitiveness, Effort, Job Concerns, and Spouse Career Aspirations" (Spence & Helmreich, 1978, p. 39). The researchers felt that the factor structure of this version of the WOFO showed that the concept of competitiveness was not being adequately measured. A second version of the WOFO was developed in which "items dealing with the pay and prestige of jobs for self and spouse were dropped, while five new items dealing with mastery and competition were added" (Spence & Helmreich, 1978, p. 40). The revised 14-item WOFO was administered to high school students and older individuals. Their responses were factor analyzed, and four scales were derived: "Work Orientation, Mastery, Competitiveness, and Personal Unconcern." Research with the second version of the scale was encouraging and led to a further revision of the WOFO. The third version of the scale is the current version. Responses were factor analyzed from 851 college women and 607 college men who completed the 23 motivational items. The factor structure was similar for males and females. Four factors were identified: Mastery, Work Orientation, Competitiveness, and Personal Unconcern. The results of the factor analysis determined the structure of the four subscales; each item was assigned to the factor on which it had the highest loading.

RELIABILITY: Using the responses from 851 college women and 607 college men, Helmreich and Spence (1978) computed coefficient alpha, by sex, for each subscale. For females, the coefficients were .62, .63, .72, and .50 for Mastery, Work, Competitiveness and Personal Unconcern, respectively. For males, the comparable coefficients were .61, .66, .76, and .50.

Adams, Priest, and Prince (1985) tested almost 4,000 West Point cadets with the WOFO. They obtained the following alpha coefficients for male respondents: .62, .74, .64, and .45 for Mastery, Work, Competitiveness, and Personal Unconcern, respectively. The comparable alpha coefficients for female respondents were .56, .65, .64, and .43. On the basis of the low alpha coefficients on Personal Unconcern, obtained in both this study and Helmreich and Spence's (1978) study, Adams et al. concluded that the Personal Unconcern subscale should be revised or eliminated.

Farmer (1985) used six items from the Mastery subscale in a study involving 9th- and 12th-grade students. Farmer obtained a coefficient alpha of .59.

VALIDITY: Research with earlier versions of the WOFO showed that college students had higher scores on Work and Mastery than did high school students. Furthermore, scientists compared to college students were higher on Mastery, Work, and Personal Unconcern but lower on Competitiveness (Helmreich & Spence, 1978).

Using the current version of the WOFO, Helmreich and Spence (1978) compared scores from male scientists, male athletes, and a general sample of college men. Scientists scored highest on Mastery and Work; athletes were second highest, and college men were lowest. On Competitiveness, athletes scored highest, college men were second, and scientists were lowest. On Personal Unconcern, scientists' scores were highest and athletes' scores were lowest. When female scientists were compared with college students, the scientists scored higher on Work and Mastery and lower on Competitiveness. Interestingly, women with PhDs scored significantly higher on Work than any other group tested.

Helmreich and Spence (1978) offered some further support of the construct validity of the WOFO by showing the relationship between WOFO scores and college grade point average and the relationship between WOFO scores and income.

NOTES & COMMENTS: (1) Alpha coefficients for the subscales tend to be low, and therefore one needs to be cautious about how the scores are used.

(2) Helmreich and Spence (1978) reported intercorrelations of the four subscale scores and seven other items. They compared subscale scores for males and females and related subscale scores to masculinity and femininity scores on the Personal Attributes Questionnaire (Spence, Helmreich, & Stapp, 1975) (see separate entry).

(3) Several researchers have related scores on the WOFO to masculinity and femininity (Adams et al., 1985; Babladelis, Deaux, Helmreich, & Spence, 1983; Basow, 1984, 1986; Gaeddert, 1983, 1985; Harris & Jennings, 1977; Hawkins, Turell, & Jackson, 1983; Helmreich & Spence, 1978; Olds, 1979; Olds & Shaver, 1980; Spence & Helmreich, 1979).

(4) Researchers have looked at scores on the WOFO in other countries including Fiji (Basow, 1984, 1986), and France, Tunisia, and Mexico (Almeida Acosta & Sanchez de Almeida, 1983; Almeida Acosta, Rodriguez de Arizmendi, Mercado Corona, Rivero Weber, & Sanchez de Almeida, 1983).

(5) Adams et al. (1985) factor analyzed WOFO responses from 3,727

West Point cadets. For the most part, their findings replicated the findings of Helmreich and Spence (1978). Adams et al. found the same four factors and concluded that achievement motivation is a multidimensional construct. Gill (1986) also factor analyzed responses to the WOFO and basically confirmed the factors described by Helmreich and Spence (1978).

(6) The list of published studies that has used the WOFO is too long for all of them to be summarized here.

AVAILABLE FROM: Gill, 1986; Helmreich and Spence, 1978

USED IN:

Adams, J. (1984). Women at West Point: A three-year perspective. *Sex Roles, 11*(5/6), 525–541.

Adams, J., Priest, R. F., & Prince, H. T., II. (1985). Achievement motive: Analyzing the validity of the WOFO. *Psychology of Women Quarterly, 9*(3), 357–370.

Almeida Acosta, E., Rodriguez de Arizmendi, G., Mercado Corona, D., Rivero Weber, M., & Sanchez de Almeida, M. E. (1983). Psychological characteristics of male and female students and the status of women in Mexico. *International Journal of Psychology, 18*, 67–81.

Almeida Acosta, E., & Sanchez de Almeida, M. E. (1983). Psychological factors affecting change in women's roles and status: A cross-cultural study. *International Journal of Psychology, 18*, 3–35.

Babladelis, G., Deaux, K., Helmreich, R. L., & Spence, J. T. (1983). Sex-related attitudes and personal characteristics in the United States. *International Journal of Psychology, 18*, 111–123.

Basow, S. A. (1984). Ethnic group differences in educational achievement in Fiji. *Journal of Cross Cultural Psychology, 15*, 435–451.

Basow, S. A. (1986). Correlates of sex-typing in Fiji. *Psychology of Women Quarterly, 10*, 429–442.

Falbo, T. (1981). Relationships between birth category, achievement, and interpersonal orientation. *Journal of Personality and Social Psychology, 41*(1), 121–131.

Farmer, H. S. (1985). Model of career and achievement motivation for women and men. *Journal of Counseling Psychology, 32*(3), 363–390.

Fassinger, R. E. (1985). A causal model of college women's career choice. *Journal of Vocational Behavior, 27*, 123–153.

Gaeddert, W. P. (1983, April). *Sex and sex role effects on achievement strivings: An examination of four explanations.* Paper presented at the meeting of the Eastern Psychological Association, Philadelphia. (ERIC Document Reproduction Service No. ED 248 418)

Gaeddert, W. P. (1985). Sex and sex role effects on achievement strivings: Dimensions of similarity and difference. *Journal of Personality, 53*(2), 286–305.

Gill, D. L. (1986). Competitiveness among females and males in physical activity classes. *Sex Roles, 15*(5/6), 233–247.

Harris, D. V., & Jennings, S. E. (1977). Self-perceptions of female distance runners. In P. Milvy (Ed.), *The marathon: Physiological, medical, epidemiological, and psychological studies* (pp. 808–815). New York: New York Academy of Sciences.

Hawkins, R. C., II, Turell, S., & Jackson, L. J. (1983). Desirable and undesirable masculine and feminine traits in relation to students' dieting tendencies and body image dissatisfaction. *Sex Roles, 9*(6), 705–718.

Helmreich, R. L., Beane, W., Lucker, G. W., & Spence, J. T. (1978). Achievement motivation and scientific attainment. *Personality and Social Psychology Bulletin, 4,* 222–226.

Helmreich, R. L., & Spence, J. T. (1978). The Work and Family Orientation Questionnaire: An objective instrument to assess components of achievement motivation and attitudes toward family and career. *Catalog of Selected Documents in Psychology, 8,* 35. (Ms. No. 1677)

Helmreich, R. L., Spence, J. T., Beane, W. E., Lucker, G. W., & Matthews, K. A. (1980). Making it in academic psychology: Demographic and personality correlates of attainment. *Journal of Personality and Social Psychology, 39*(5), 896–908.

Hollinger, C. L., & Fleming, E. S. (1984). Internal barriers to the realization of potential correlates and interrelationships among gifted and talented female adolescents. *Gifted Child Quarterly, 28,* 135–139.

Hollinger, C. L., & Fleming, E. S. (1985). Social orientation and the social self-esteem of gifted and talented female adolescents. *Journal of Youth and Adolescence, 14*(5), 389–399.

Johnson, C. H. (1984, March). *Effects of personality correlates on achievement motivation in traditional and reentry college women.* Paper presented at the meeting of the Southeastern Psychological Association, New Orleans. (ERIC Document Reproduction Service No. ED 250 646)

Lester, P., & Chu, L. (1979). *Women administrators: Feminine, masculine, or androgynous?* Unpublished paper, New Mexico State University. (ERIC Document Reproduction Service No. ED 181 107)

Lester, P., & Chu, L. (1980). *Personality factors and achievement motivation of women in higher education administration.* Unpublished paper, New Mexico State University. (ERIC Document Reproduction Service No. ED 197 663)

Lester, P., & Chu, L. (1981). Women administrators: Feminine, masculine or androgynous? *Journal of Educational Equity and Leadership, 1*(3), 171–179.

Nyquist, L., Slivken, K., Spence, J. T., & Helmreich, R. L. (1985). Household responsibilities in middle-class couples: The contribution of demographic and personality variables. *Sex Roles, 12*(1/2), 15–34.

Olds, D. E. (1979, September). *Masculinity, femininity, achievement conflicts and health.* Paper presented at the meeting of the American Psychological Association, New York. (ERIC Document Reproduction Service No. ED 180 865)

Olds, D. E., & Shaver, P. (1980). Masculinity, femininity, academic performance, and health: Further evidence concerning the androgyny controversy. *Journal of Personality, 48*(3), 323–341.

Rooney, G. S. (1984, August). *Sex differences in career and achievement motivation.* Paper presented at the meeting of the American Psychological Association, Toronto. (ERIC Document Reproduction Service No. ED 250 629)

Spence, J. T., & Helmreich, R. L. (1978). *Masculinity and femininity: Their psychological dimensions, correlates, and antecedents.* Austin: University of Texas Press.

Spence, J. T., & Helmreich, R. L. (1979). On assessing "androgyny." *Sex Roles*, 5(6), 721–738.

Spence, J. T., Helmreich, R. L., & Sawin, L. L. (1980). The Male-Female Relations Questionnaire: A self-report inventory of sex role behaviors and preferences and its relationships to masculine and feminine personality traits, sex role attitudes, and other measures. *Catalog of Selected Documents in Psychology*, 10(4), 87. (Ms. No. 2123)

Sztaba, T. I., & Colwill, N. L. (1988). Secretarial and management students: Attitudes, attributes, and career choice considerations. *Sex Roles*, 19, 651–665.

Thomas, C. C. (1985, August). *Social power: Effect on spouses' quality of personal life*. Paper presented at the meeting of the American Psychological Association, Los Angeles. (ERIC Document Reproduction Service No. ED 269 682)

Thorbecke, W., & Grotevant, H. D. (1982). Gender differences in adolescent interpersonal identity formation. *Journal of Youth and Adolescence*, 11(6), 479–492.

BIBLIOGRAPHY:

Mehrabian, A. (1969). Measures of achieving tendency. *Educational and Psychological Measurement*, 29, 445–451.

Spence, J. T., Helmreich, R. L., & Stapp, J. (1975). Ratings of self and peers on sex-role attributes and their relation to self-esteem and conceptions of masculinity and femininity. *Journal of Personality and Social Psychology*, 32, 29–39.

9

Attitudes Toward Gender Role Issues

This chapter contains scales that measure attitudes toward men, toward women, toward both men and women, and toward a variety of issues particularly associated with men and/or women. Overall, a diversity of topics is covered in this chapter. Though factor analyses may suggest that some of the scales are unidimensional, an examination of the measures shows that item content tends to be quite diverse.

This chapter contains more scales than any other chapter in this handbook, and it contains a larger number of scales that were developed over a decade ago. Specifically, this chapter includes descriptions of 56 measures, 19 of which I described in my previous book (Beere, 1979). The scales in this chapter are arranged first according to their major focus: men, women, or both men and women. Within each of these three sections, scales are arranged alphabetically by scale name. There are 6 scales that measure attitudes toward men; none was available at the time I wrote my previous book. Next, there are 24 scales that measure attitudes toward women and women's issues; 11 were described in my previous book. Finally, there are 26 scales that focus on attitudes regarding both males and females; 8 of these were in my previous book. Two of the scales in this last group focus on gender role attitudes regarding children.

Two notable facts are apparent from comparing this chapter with the comparable chapter in my previous handbook. First, over half of the 41 scales in that handbook have not been used again in a published study. Second is the relatively new focus on attitudes toward men. Whereas my 1977 literature search failed to locate a single measure of attitudes toward men, the literature search for this handbook located six measures of attitudes toward men. Two of the measures were described in articles published in 1978; the remaining four were described in articles published after 1980. Obviously the study of attitudes toward men and men's issues is relatively recent.

Beyond a doubt, the most common type of instrument to measure gender role attitudes is the summated rating scale. Fifty of the 56 measures in this chapter are summated rating scales, yet they differ from each other in several ways. They differ in the number of response options they offer; researchers use anywhere from two to seven options. A larger number of options, such as seven, is likely to produce a more reliable scale, but having as many as seven options may prove confusing and frustrating for some respondents. The wording of the options may vary, but the most common options are variations on the words *agree* and *disagree*. The summated rating scales also differ in terms of whether they offer a middle or "neutral" option. Some researchers use an odd number of choices and include a neutral response, and others omit the middle response and force respondents to agree or disagree with the statement. The summated rating scales vary in length. The shortest scale contains 6 items, the longest 120. The median length is 25, and the modal length is 20.

In addition to summated rating scales, this chapter includes two Thurstone scales, one forced-choice scale, a checklist, and two alternate choice measures. One of the summated rating scales is also a Guttman scale.

Based on item content, the majority of scales in this chapter can be used with persons who range in age from high school students through senior citizens; however, researchers must determine whether a particular scale is understandable to their prospective subjects and whether it is reliable and valid for them.

There are alternate forms of only two scales in this chapter: the Chatterjee Puhan Attitude Scale (Chatterjee & Puhan, 1980), a measure of attitudes toward male-female roles and relationships that is intended for use in India; and the Sex-Role Egalitarianism Scale (SRE) (Beere, King, Beere, & King, 1984), a 95-item measure of attitudes toward equality between the sexes. Parallel short forms of the SRE, with 25 items each, have also been developed (King & King, 1986).

The majority of measures in this chapter yield a single, overall score, but subscale scores are computed for some of the scales. Unfortunately, the subscales are sometimes based on very few items, and their reliabilities are often unacceptably low. Before accepting an author's recommendation that subscales can be used, a researcher needs to evaluate carefully the psychometric properties of the subscales.

A few of the scales in this chapter have been developed for special populations or for other countries. Sherman, Koufacos, and Kenworthy (1978) developed two scales for use with mental health therapists: the

Therapists' Attitude Toward Women Scale and the Therapists' Information About Women Scale. Galambos, Petersen, Richards, and Gitelson (1985) developed the Attitudes Toward Women Scale for Adolescents, a modification of the Attitudes Toward Women Scale (Spence & Helmreich, 1972). The Women's Social Freedom Scale (Bhushan, 1981) and the Chatterjee Puhan Attitude Scale (Chatterjee & Puhan, 1980) have been developed for use in India and would not be appropriate in cultures that are quite different from India's. The Fine-Davis Attitudes Toward the Role and Status of Women (Fine-Davis, 1976) was developed in Ireland, and the Attitudes Toward Women Scale— British Version (Parry, 1983) was developed in England. Though originally developed in the United States, the Feminism Survey (Takooshian & Stuart, 1983) has been translated into Spanish, Armenian, and Chinese. The Attitudes Toward Women Scale (Spence & Helmreich, 1972) has been used in England, Japan, Canada, Yugoslavia, Australia, Fiji, Ireland, and Trinidad.

There is considerable variability in the extent to which the scales described here have already been used by researchers. Most scales in this chapter have been used in research reported in one (13 scales), two (11 scales), or three (9 scales) journal articles or ERIC documents. Of course, these figures would change considerably if the use of scales in doctoral dissertations were considered. Not surprisingly, the scales that appeared in my previous book have, on the average, been used more during the past decade than have the newer scales. This may simply reflect the fact that those scales have been available longer; it may not indicate superior quality.

The most commonly used measure of gender role attitudes is Spence and Helmreich's (1972) Attitudes Toward Women Scale. It has been used over 400 times, not considering its use in unpublished doctoral dissertations. No other attitude scale has been used nearly as often. Of the six scales measuring attitudes toward men, the most commonly used has been the Attitude Toward Masculinity Transcendence Scale (Moreland & Van Tuinen, 1978).

A review of the scales in this chapter shows that many of them suffer from some common problems: weak evidence of validity, questionable use of factor analysis, low subscale reliabilities, inclusion of factual items among the attitude items, susceptibility to response bias, and fakeability. Though it is easy to list these problems, some of them are very difficult to solve.

First, consider the problem of weak evidence of validity. As is frequently the case in attitude measurement, most of the scales have not been validated against behavioral criteria. In fact, for many of the scales, the validity data are scant, with the only evidence of validity being that the use of the scale produced results consistent with expectations. For some scales, however, there is also evidence of concurrent validity, and some authors provided evidence of convergent and discriminant validity.

Factor analysis was a significant part of the development of several of the scales; for other scales, factor analysis was sometimes used to understand the scale further. Unfortunately, many researchers used far too few subjects in their factor analytic studies. In order to produce stable results, the number of subjects must be large relative to the number of items in the analysis. As a rule of thumb, Nunnally (1978) suggested using 10 subjects for each item in the analysis.

The problem of low subscale reliabilities has been discussed. It should be emphasized, however, that the problem of low reliabilities also applies to some of the full scale scores. Because computers handle the computations, many researchers during the past decade have reported coefficient alpha. Sometimes, however, the researchers ignore their own findings and proceed to use the scale even when the value of alpha is too low. Furthermore, scale authors frequently overlook the fact that coefficient alpha considers only one aspect of reliability: homogeneity. Too few authors provide evidence of test-retest reliability.

Some authors included factual items along with the attitude items on their scales. This leads to ambiguous results. Respondents may well know that the "facts" are different from their own opinions, but they do not know whether to answer in terms of their own views or in terms of what is factually accurate. Furthermore, what is the difference between "agreeing" and "strongly agreeing" with a factual item? Do persons strongly agree because they are very certain of their answers or because they have strong views on the subject? Do some persons overlook that a factual item has a right and wrong answer and instead give their own views on the subject; and do other persons answer from a right/wrong perspective? The ambiguity produced by factual statements can easily be eliminated by avoiding the use of factual items on an attitude measure.

Much has been written about the subject of response bias in regard to attitude measures. Suffice it to say that scale authors would be wise to vary the phrasing of the items so that a person with a particular viewpoint will disagree with some items and agree with others. For most scales in this chapter, the scale authors followed this guideline. Occasionally, however, an author phrased all questions in the same direction.

In general, attitude measures tend to be quite fakeable; that is, respondents can portray themselves as having a particular attitude if they so choose. Jean and Reynolds (1984) demonstrated this with the Bias in Attitudes Survey and the Attitudes Toward Women Scale. It is likely that every scale included in this chapter can be faked, if respondents choose to present themselves in a particular light. Similarly, attitude scales are often susceptible to a social desirability response bias. Respondents do not intend to give misleading answers; they are just attracted to the socially desirable response.

In summary, this chapter contains a wide array of measures, many of which should prove quite valuable to researchers. Another source for potentially relevant measures is Beere (in press), which contains descriptions of approximately 200 other scales relating to sex and gender issues.

BIBLIOGRAPHY:

Beere, C. A. (1979). *Women and women's issues: A handbook of tests and measures.* San Francisco: Jossey-Bass.

Beere, C. A. (in press). *Sex and gender issues: A handbook of tests and measures.* Westport, CT: Greenwood.

Beere, C. A., King, D. W., Beere, D. B., & King, L. A. (1984). The Sex-Role Egalitarianism Scale: A measure of attitudes toward equality between the sexes. *Sex Roles, 10*(7/8), 563–576.

Bhushan, L. I. (1981). Development of Women's Social Freedom Scale: A report. *Asian Journal of Psychology and Education, 7*(2), 34–38.

Chatterjee, B. B., & Puhan, B. N. (1980). A Thurstone scale for measuring attitude towards sex. *Indian Psychological Review, 19*(2), 1–8.

Fine-Davis, M. (1976). *Structure, determinants and correlates of attitudes toward the role and status of women in Ireland, with particular reference to employment status of married women.* Unpublished doctoral dissertation, Trinity College, University of Dublin.

Galambos, N. L., Petersen, A. C., Richards, M., & Gitelson, I. B. (1985). The Attitudes Toward Women Scale for Adolescents (AWSA): A study of reliability and validity. *Sex Roles, 13*, 343–356.

Jean, P. J., & Reynolds, C. R. (1984). Sex and attitude distortion: Ability of females and males to fake liberal and conservative positions regarding changing sex roles. *Sex Roles, 10*, 805–815.

King, L. A., & King, D. W. (1986, May). Development of alternate short forms to measure sex-role egalitarian attitudes. Paper presented at the meeting of the Midwestern Psychological Association, Chicago.

Moreland, J., & Van Tuinen, M. (1978, July). *The Attitude Toward Masculinity Transcendence Scale.* Paper presented at Ohio State University, Columbus, OH.

Nunnally, J. C. (1978). *Psychometric theory.* New York: McGraw-Hill.

Parry, G. (1983). A British version of the Attitudes Toward Women Scale (AWS-B). *British Journal of Social Psychology, 22*, 261–263.

Sherman, J., Koufacos, C., & Kenworthy, J. A. (1978). Therapists: Their attitudes and information about women. *Psychology of Women Quarterly, 2*(4), 299–313.

Spence, J. T., & Helmreich, R. L. (1972). The Attitudes Toward Women Scale: An objective instrument to measure attitudes toward the rights and roles of women in contemporary society. *Catalog of Selected Documents in Psychology, 2*, 66. (Ms. No. 153)

Takooshian, H. A., & Stuart, C. R. (1983). Ethnicity and feminism among American women: Opposing social trends? *International Journal of Group Tensions*, *13*, 100–105.

ATTITUDES TOWARD MALES IN SOCIETY (AMS)
AUTHORS: Steven D. Falkenberg, C. Douglas Hindman, and Donald Masey
DATE: 1983
VARIABLE: Attitudes toward men
TYPE OF INSTRUMENT: Summated rating scale
DESCRIPTION: The Attitudes Toward Males in Society (AMS) scale is a relatively brief measure consisting of 14 items, each of which overtly compares men and women and indicates that men are superior to women in traditional ways. For each item, respondents select one of four response options: "agree strongly, agree mildly, disagree mildly, disagree strongly."
SAMPLE ITEMS: Men are naturally better drivers than women.

Because men are strong and women are weak, it is only right that this is a man's world.
PREVIOUS SUBJECTS: College students and adults
APPROPRIATE FOR: High school students and older
ADMINISTRATION: Self-administered; about 5–10 minutes
SCORING: Items are individually scored on a 4-point scale, with 4 points assigned to the "disagree strongly" response. Total scores can range from 14 to 56; lower scores indicate more traditional attitudes.
DEVELOPMENT: Forty newly generated items stimulated by a review of the literature, personal experiences, and discussion among males were combined with the 45 items on Doyle and Moore's (1978) Attitudes Toward the Male's Role Scale (see separate entry). The items were administered to 61 college men and 123 college women. Their responses were factor analyzed, and a total of 23 factors were identified. The first factor accounted for 19.4% of the variance. Fourteen items with factor loadings over .30 on this factor and factor loadings below .30 on all other factors in these analyses and in Doyle and Moore's (1978) analyses were selected for the AMS scale.
RELIABILITY: No information was provided.
VALIDITY: The scores of college women were significantly more liberal than the scores of college men. This finding was consistent with previously published results obtained with scales measuring attitudes toward women.

Although there was no significant age effect on the scores of men, there was a significant age effect for women: older women had more liberal attitudes than did younger women.
NOTES & COMMENTS: (1) Although the item pool for the development of this scale was considerably broader than just the items on Doyle and

Moore's (1978) Attitudes Toward the Male's Role Scale, the final 14 items on the AMS scale appear on Doyle and Moore's scale, and in fact, all load on the first factor of Doyle and Moore's scale.

(2) The factor analysis performed to develop this scale was based on a small number of subjects relative to the number of items. Thus, the results of the factor analysis are not likely to be very stable.

AVAILABLE FROM: Falkenberg, Hindman, and Masey, 1983
USED IN:

Falkenberg, S. D., Hindman, C. D., & Masey, D. (1983, March). *Measuring attitudes toward males in society*. Paper presented at the meeting of the Southeastern Psychological Association, Atlanta. (ERIC Document Reproduction Service No. ED 233 287)

BIBLIOGRAPHY:

Doyle, J. A., & Moore, R. J. (1978). Attitudes Toward the Male's Role Scale (AMR): An objective instrument to measure attitudes toward the male's sex role in contemporary society. *Catalog of Selected Documents in Psychology, 8*(2), 35. (Ms. No. 1678)

ATTITUDES TOWARD MEN SCALE (AMS)

AUTHORS: A. Chris Downs and Steven A. Engleson
DATE: 1982 (used 1981)
VARIABLE: Attitudes toward men
TYPE OF INSTRUMENT: Summated rating scale
DESCRIPTION: The Attitudes Toward Men Scale (AMS) consists of 34 items covering a variety of topics. Twenty items directly compare men and women; the other 14 items do not mention women. Twenty-nine items are phrased in a traditional direction; 5 items are phrased in a nontraditional direction. Respondents express their views by selecting one of four response options: "agree strongly, agree mildly, disagree mildly, disagree strongly."
SAMPLE ITEMS: When a man takes a job traditionally done by a woman, such as nursing, he has sacrificed some of his masculinity.

Women are better at housekeeping than men.
PREVIOUS SUBJECTS: College students, elementary school teachers
APPROPRIATE FOR: High school students and older
ADMINISTRATION: Self-administered; about 15 minutes
SCORING: Items are individually scored on a 4-point scale, with 4 points assigned to the nontraditional view. Total scores range from 34 (very traditional) to 136 (very nontraditional).
DEVELOPMENT: Based on a review of the literature and suggestions from colleagues, Downs and Engleson developed a pool of 165 items. Eliminating redundant items reduced the pool to 83 items that related to "sexual relationships and orientation, occupational interests, domestic skills, relationships with women, power-seeking, athletic interests, artistic abilities, parenting skills, emotionality, intellectual performance,

and relationships with men" (Downs & Engleson, 1982, p. 2). The item pool was administered to 56 college men and 57 college women on two occasions about 2 weeks apart. Items were eliminated if they did not show significant item-total correlations or if their test-retest reliability coefficients were not significant. Thirty-four of the items satisfying these two criteria were selected to represent all of the various content areas covered in the original item pool. These 34 items comprise the AMS.

RELIABILITY: Reliability data were computed for four samples: 21 male K–12 teachers, 66 female K–12 teachers, 235 male college students, and 295 female college students. Alpha coefficients for the four groups were .90, .85, .89, and .86, respectively. Test-retest reliabilities were computed for the two groups of K–12 teachers who completed the AMS on two occasions about 2 weeks apart. Test-retest reliability for the total test score was .94 for males and .90 for females. Test-retest reliability coefficients for the individual items ranged from .61 to .92, and all item reliability coefficients were statistically significant.

VALIDITY: As would be expected, females scored as significantly more nontraditional than males in both the sample of K–12 teachers and the sample of college students. Furthermore, the younger undergraduates scored as more traditional than the older K–12 teachers. This finding was also consistent with predictions.

The K–12 teachers completed the Attitudes Toward Women Scale (Spence & Helmreich, 1972) (see separate entry) after they completed the AMS. For males, the correlation between scores on the two measures was .84; for females, the correlation was .57. Both values were statistically significant.

A subgroup of 75 college men and 125 college women who completed the AMS also completed Villemez and Touhey's (1977) Macho Scale (see separate entry) and Doyle and Moore's (1978) Attitudes Toward the Male's Role Scale (see separate entry). The correlation between the AMS and the Attitudes Toward the Male's Role Scale was .67; the correlation between the AMS and the Macho Scale was .66.

NOTES & COMMENTS: (1) A factor analysis using the responses from the college students produced seven meaningful factors. The first factor accounted for 42.3% of the variance and appeared to measure vocational and recreational interests. The second factor accounted for 13.4% of the variance and related to intellectual abilities. The remaining five factors each accounted for less than 10% of the variance.

(2) College students completed a measure of self-esteem, and their scores on the AMS were related to their self-esteem scores. For men, there was a significant relationship: self-esteem scores were higher for men reporting nontraditional attitudes toward men. The relationship between AMS scores and self-esteem scores was not significant for women.

AVAILABLE FROM: Downs and Engleson, 1982

USED IN:
Downs, A. C., & Engleson, S. A. (1982). The Attitudes Toward Men Scale
    (AMS): An analysis of the role and status of men and masculinity. *Catalog
    of Selected Documents in Psychology, 12*(4), 45. (Ms. No. 2503)
BIBLIOGRAPHY:
Doyle, J. A., & Moore, R. J. (1978). Attitudes Toward the Male's Role Scale
    (AMR): An objective instrument to measure attitudes toward the male's
    sex role in contemporary society. *Catalog of Selected Documents in Psychol-
    ogy, 8*(2), 35. (Ms. No. 1678)
Spence, J. T., & Helmreich, R. L. (1972). The Attitudes Toward Women Scale:
    An objective instrument to measure attitudes toward the rights and roles
    of women in contemporary society. *Catalog of Selected Documents in Psy-
    chology, 2*, 66. (Ms. No. 153)
Villemez, W. J., & Touhey, J. C. (1977). A measure of individual differences in
    sex stereotyping and sex discrimination: The "Macho" Scale. *Psychological
    Reports, 41*(2), 411–415.

ATTITUDES TOWARD MEN SCALE (AMS)
AUTHOR: Anthony Iazzo
DATE: 1983
VARIABLE: Attitudes toward men in four domains: Marriage and Par-
enthood, Sexuality, Work, and Physical and Personality Attributes
TYPE OF INSTRUMENT: Summated rating scale
DESCRIPTION: The Attitude Toward Men Scale (AMS) contains 32 items
relating to four areas: Marriage and Parenthood (13 items), Sexuality (7
items), Work (4 items), and Physical and Personality Attributes (8 items).
Each Item is accompanied by four response options: "agree strongly,
agree mildly, disagree mildly, disagree strongly." About half of the items
are phrased so that agreement with the statement represents a positive
view of men and the other half reflect a negative view of men.
SAMPLE ITEMS: (Marriage and Parenthood) Men consider marriage a
trap.
    (Sexuality) Men want only "one thing" from a woman.
    (Work) It is important to a man that he provide for his family.
    (Physical and Personality Attributes) An athletic man is to be admired.
PREVIOUS SUBJECTS: Male and female college students; female adults
APPROPRIATE FOR: High school students and older
ADMINISTRATION: Self-administered; about 15 minutes
SCORING: Items are individually scored on a 4-point scale, with 4 points
assigned to the end of the continuum representing a positive view of
men. Item scores are totaled to yield an overall score that can range from
32 (very negative view of men) to 128 (very positive view of men). For
a sample of 104 women from a variety of settings and covering a wide
age span, the mean total score was 89.92 (standard deviation of 9.56).
Scores can be obtained for each of the four subscales by summing the

items on the subscale. Iazzo (1983) reported subscale means and standard deviations for a sample of 104 women.

DEVELOPMENT: A pool of 63 items representing the four content areas (Marriage and Parenthood, Sexuality, Work, and Physical and Personality Attributes) was given to 10 graduate students with instructions to rate the degree to which each item was relevant to men. Based on their ratings, 11 items were deleted, and the remaining 52 items were administered to 104 women from a variety of settings. Their responses were factor analyzed, and four factors were extracted. Items that met the theme of the factor and had a loading of at least .30 were retained for the final version of the scale. Thirty-two items were thus retained.

RELIABILITY: Coefficient alpha for the total scale was .79. For the four subscale scores, alpha coefficients were: Marriage and Parenthood = .85, Sexuality = .73, Work = .60, and Physical and Personality Attributes = .69.

VALIDITY: Scores on the AMS were correlated with scores on the Marlowe-Crowne Social Desirability Scale (Crowne & Marlowe, 1960) to determine whether responding to the AMS was significantly affected by a social desirability response bias. The correlation between the two measures was .02.

The scores from four groups of women—battered wives, rape victims, feminists, and lesbians—were predicted to be lower than the scores of women-in-general. Iazzo (1983) tested persons from these four groups and found that for each group, the predicted relationship was obtained.

NOTES & COMMENTS: (1) A portion of the scale development was based on factor analysis, but with 52 items and only 104 subjects, the factor analytic results cannot be presumed stable.

(2) Because some of the subscales are quite short, it is not surprising that their internal consistency reliabilities are low. Given these low reliabilities, however, one must question the wisdom of using subscale scores.

(3) Schneider and Dearing (1986) administered the AMS and several other measures to 88 male and 88 female college students. They found no relationship between AMS scores and a measure of psychological distress. They did find that males were significantly more positive than females on the Sexuality subscale, and females were more positive than males on the Work subscale.

AVAILABLE FROM: Iazzo, 1983

USED IN:

Iazzo, A. N. (1983). The construction and validation of Attitudes Toward Men Scale. *Psychological Record*, 33(3), 371–378.

Schneider, L. J., & Dearing, N. (1986, April). *Personality and career concomitants of life stress in college students*. Paper presented at the meeting of the Southwestern Psychological Association, Ft. Worth. (ERIC Document Reproduction Service No. ED 272 793)

BIBLIOGRAPHY:
Crowne, D. P., & Marlowe, D. (1960). A new scale of social desirability independent of psychopathology. *Journal of Consulting Psychology*, 24, 349–354.

ATTITUDE TOWARD MASCULINITY TRANSCENDENCE SCALE

AUTHORS: John Moreland and Mark Van Tuinen

DATE: 1978

VARIABLE: Attitudes toward men's gender roles

TYPE OF INSTRUMENT: Summated rating scale

DESCRIPTION: The Attitude Toward Masculinity Transcendence Scale consists of 54 items covering a variety of issues relating to men and masculinity. The items were selected to represent four factors: "Dominance Transcendence, Homophobia Transcendence, Non-traditional Roles, Male-Female Relationships." Some items are phrased to reflect transcendence and others to reflect traditional attitudes. Information on the specific response options was not provided. There is also a 46-item version of the scale that omits 8 items with low item-total correlations.

SAMPLE ITEMS: (Dominance Transcendence) In male-female relationships, the man should make most of the important decisions.

(Homophobia Transcendence) I think men should feel free to have sex with each other.

(Non-traditional Roles) Men should be encouraged to do volunteer work in their children's classrooms.

(Male-Female Relationships) In general, a man should be more assertive than a female companion.

PREVIOUS SUBJECTS: College students

APPROPRIATE FOR: High school students and older

ADMINISTRATION: Self-administered; about 20–30 minutes

SCORING: Little information on scoring was available, but it can be presumed that items are individually scored and summed to yield a total score. Higher scores are assigned to the more liberal or transcendent responses. Because the factor analytic results could not be replicated (see DEVELOPMENT), it is recommended that factor scores not be used.

DEVELOPMENT: Before developing items, Moreland and Van Tuinen (1978) specified 11 "situations or themes in which a sex-role transcendent male might behave differently than a stereotypically masculine man": "men and achievement and status, men and work, male-male relationships, men and emotionality, men and dominance in heterosexual relationships, men and marriage, men and the 'new women,' men and children, men and sexuality/sensuality, men and play, men and stereotypic courtesies" (p. 2). They then arrived at a four-dimensional model of the male gender role: "dominance, non-emotionality, status achievement, and . . . no-sissy stuff" (p. 2). The 11 themes and four dimensions were represented in the 160-item pool that was generated. The item pool was administered to 590 college students, and an item analysis was performed using their responses. Low variability in responses led to the elimination of 37 items. Responses to the remaining 123 items were factor analyzed, and the authors selected a four-factor solution as most meaningful. The four factors were: "Dominance Transcendence, Homophobia Transcendence, Non-traditional Activities, Attitudes toward the New Woman" (p. 3). Four rules were then followed for selecting the 54 items on the final version of the scale. First, items with factor loadings of at least .40 on one factor and less than .30 on the other factors were retained. Second, items on the Dominance Transcendence and Homophobia Transcendence factors were reworded so that half of the items reflected transcendence and half reflected a traditional attitude. Third, redundant items were eliminated. And finally, items on the fourth factor, "Attitudes Toward the New Woman," were reworded to be more descriptive of "the impact of women's behavior on men" (Moreland & Van Tuinen, 1978, p. 4). These procedures produced the 54-item version of the scale.

The 54-item version was completed by 293 college men and 287 college women. Separate factor analyses were performed for each sex, and two conclusions were drawn: "1. Items loading on a given factor in the original factor analysis did not load on similar factors in the second study. 2. Although the four factor rotations for males and females in the original sample were very similar, the factor structures in the second sample were dissimilar" (Moreland & Van Tuinen, 1978, p.5). Since the scale was changed considerably after the first factor analysis, it is not surprising that the second factor analysis produced different results.

Item analysis of the 54-item scale led to the elimination of 8 items, with item-total correlations less than .25 for both males and females.
RELIABILITY: Alpha coefficients were computed separately for each sex. For the 54-item version of the scale, coefficient alpha was .92 for college women and .89 for college men. For the 46-item version of the scale, completed by a different sample of 176 college women and 230 college men, coefficient alpha was .95 for men, .94 for women, and .95 for men and women considered together.

Buhrke (1988) administered the 54-item version of the Attitude Toward Masculinity Transcendence Scale to 184 college students and computed the alpha coefficients for the total score as well as for four subscales. For the total score, alpha was .95. The following results were obtained for the subscales: Dominance Transcendence = .89, Homophobia Transcendence = .86, Nontraditional Activities = .81, and Attitudes Toward the New Woman = .73.
VALIDITY: Harren and Kass (1977) gave 578 college students several

measures, including the Attitudes Toward Women Scale (AWS) (Spence, Helmreich, & Stapp, 1973) (see separate entry), the Bem Sex Role Inventory (BSRI) (Bem, 1974) (see separate entry), and the Attitude Toward Masculinity Transcendence Scale. Correlations among the scales suggest that the Attitude Toward Masculinity Transcendence Scale was not measuring masculinity/femininity ($r = .05$ for masculinity on the BSRI, $r = .16$ for femininity on the BSRI, and $r = .14$ for androgyny on the BSRI), but there was a substantial relationship between what was measured by the Attitude Toward Masculinity Transcendence Scale and what was measured by the AWS ($r = .61$). Harren (1979, as cited by Tinsley, Kass, Moreland, & Harren, 1983) tested 713 college students and reported correlations among the same three scales. Again, the Attitude Toward Masculinity Transcendence Scale was substantially correlated with the AWS Scale ($r = .57$) but only slightly correlated with the BSRI ($r = .12$).

Buhrke (1988) administered the Attitude Toward Masculinity Transcendence Scale and three other gender role attitude scales to 184 college students: the AWS, the Sexist Attitudes Toward Women Scale (Benson & Vincent, 1980) (see separate entry), and the Sex-Role Ideology Scale (Kalin & Tilby, 1978) (see separate entry). Additionally, Buhrke administered   the Marlowe-Crowne Social Desirability Scale (Crowne & Marlowe, 1964). The correlation between the Attitude Toward Masculinity Transcendence and the other scales were: Sex-Role Ideology Scale = .75; AWS = .80; and Sexist Attitudes Toward Women Scale = $-.85$. Buhrke also reported all of the subscale intercorrelations. The correlation between the Attitude Toward Masculinity Transcendence Scale and the Marlowe-Crowne Social Desirability Scale was .05. Buhrke obtained significant correlations between the Attitude Toward Masculinity Transcendence Scale and several single-item scales expected to correlate with the scores. NOTES & COMMENTS: (1) Moreland and Van Tuinen (1978) reported item-total correlations separately for males and females and for both sexes combined.

(2) Though the scale was developed over 10 years ago, the items are still current.

(3) Several articles (Harren, 1979; Harren & Kass, 1977; Harren, Kass, Tinsley, & Moreland, 1978, 1979; Kass, Tinsley, Harren, & Moreland, 1978; Tinsley et al., 1983) pertain to research looking at the effects of gender role attitudes, as measured by the Attitude Toward Masculinity Transcendence Scale, and other variables on college students' career decision-making. Harren and Biscardi (1980) described research in which scores on the Attitude Toward Masculinity Transcendence Scale were one of several factors used to predict membership in Holland's (1973)

six personality categories: realistic, investigative, artistic, social, enterprising, and conventional. These personality categories are part of Holland's theory of vocational choices.

(4) Burda and Vaux (1987) used the Attitude Toward Masculinity Transcendence Scale to test the hypothesis that "the strength with which men hold traditional masculine beliefs will be negatively related to various social support variables from their network resources" (p. 33).

(5) Buhrke (1988) factor analyzed the subscale scores from several sex role ideology measures. She included the subscale scores from the Attitude Toward Masculinity Transcendence in the factor analysis.

AVAILABLE FROM: John Moreland, 4237 Salisbury Road, Suite 411, Bldg. 4, Jacksonville, FL 32216

USED IN:

Buhrke, R. A. (1988). Factor dimensions across different measures of sex role ideology. *Sex Roles, 18*, 309–321.

Burda, P. C., & Vaux, A. C. (1987). The social support process in men: Overcoming sex-role obstacles. *Human Relations, 40*(1), 31–44.

Harren, V. A. (1979, February). *The influence of sex roles and cognitive styles on the career decision-making of college men and women*. Unpublished manuscript. (ERIC Document Reproduction Service No. ED 189 265)

Harren, V. A., & Biscardi, D. L. (1980). Sex roles and cognitive styles as predictors of Holland typologies. *Journal of Vocational Behavior, 17*(2), 231–241.

Harren, V. A., & Kass, R. A. (1977, August). *The measurement and correlates of career decision making*. Paper presented at the meeting of the American Psychological Association, San Francisco. (ERIC Document Reproduction Service No. ED 147 733)

Harren, V. A., Kass, R. A., Tinsley, H. E., & Moreland, J. R. (1978). Influence of sex role attitudes and cognitive styles on career decision making. *Journal of Counseling Psychology, 25*(5), 390–398.

Harren, V. A., Kass, R. A., Tinsley, H. E., & Moreland, J. R. (1979). Influence of gender, sex-role attitudes, and cognitive complexity on gender-dominant career choices. *Journal of Counseling Psychology, 26*(3), 227–234.

Kass, R. A., Tinsley, H.E.A., Harren, V. A., & Moreland, J. R. (1978, August). *Cognitive and attitudinal influences on career decision making*. Paper presented at the meeting of the American Psychological Association, Toronto. (ERIC Document Reproduction Service No. ED 197 273)

Moreland, J., & Van Tuinen, M. (1978, July). *The Attitude Toward Masculinity Transcendence Scale*. Paper presented at Ohio State University, Columbus.

Tinsley, H.E.A., Kass, R. A., Moreland, J. R., & Harren, V. A. (1983). A longitudinal study of female college students' occupational decision making. *Vocational Guidance Quarterly, 32*(2), 89–102.

BIBLIOGRAPHY:

Bem, S. L. (1974). The measurement of psychological androgyny. *Journal of Consulting and Clinical Psychology, 42*, 155–162.

Benson, P. L., & Vincent, S. (1980). Development and validation of the Sexist Attitudes Toward Women Scale (SATWS). *Psychology of Women Quarterly, 5*, 276–291.

Crowne, D. P., & Marlowe, D. (1964). *The approval motive*. New York: Wiley.

Holland, J. L. (1973). *Making vocational choices: A theory of careers.* Englewood Cliffs, NJ: Prentice-Hall.

Kalin, R., & Tilby, P. J. (1978). Development and validation of a sex-role ideology scale. *Psychological Reports, 42,* 731–738.

Spence, J. T., & Helmreich, R. L. (1972). The Attitudes Toward Women Scale: An objective instrument to measure attitudes toward the rights and roles of women in contemporary society. *Catalog of Selected Documents in Psychology, 2,* 66. (Ms. No. 153)

Spence, J. T., Helmreich, R. L., & Stapp, J. (1973). A short version of the Attitudes Toward Women Scale (AWS). *Bulletin of the Psychonomic Society, 2,* 219–220.

ATTITUDES TOWARD THE MALE'S ROLE SCALE (AMR)

AUTHORS: James A. Doyle and Robert J. Moore

DATE: 1978

VARIABLE: Attitudes toward men and men's issues

TYPE OF INSTRUMENT: Summated rating scale

DESCRIPTION: The Attitudes Toward the Male's Role Scale (AMR) consists of 45 items pertaining to the following topics: "(a) male dominance; (b) general interests, vocational pursuits, and skills; (c) sexuality; (d) emotionality; (e) courtesies toward women; and (f) interpersonal relations" (Doyle & Moore, 1978, p.[i]). The items load on five factors: stereotypic sex role behavior, appropriate male behavior, chivalry, male role in the family and occupation, and attitudes toward homosexuality. Each item is accompanied by four response options: "agree strongly, agree mildly, disagree mildly, disagree strongly." Thirty-five items are phrased so that agreement is the conservative response; 10 items are phrased so that agreement is the nontraditional response.

SAMPLE ITEMS: It is only right that men should show courtesies to women like holding open a door or helping her on with her coat.

The political and moral leadership of a community should remain largely in the hands of men.

PREVIOUS SUBJECTS: High school students, college students, adults

APPROPRIATE FOR: High school students and older

ADMINISTRATION: Self-administered; about 20–25 minutes

SCORING: Items are individually scored on a 4-point scale, with 4 points assigned to the nontraditional end of the continuum and 1 point assigned to the most conservative response. Total scores vary from 45 (very conservative) to 180 (very nontraditional). According to Doyle and Moore (1978), scores above 113 indicate "an increasing liberal or nontraditional attitude toward the male sex role" (p. 2). Doyle and Moore reported means and standard deviations by sex for several different groups, including adults, college students, and high school students. In addition to the total score, four factor scores can be computed (see NOTES & COMMENTS).

DEVELOPMENT: By combining items gleaned from relevant research and adding original items developed by Doyle and Moore, a pool of 135 items was compiled. Redundant and ambiguous items were deleted, thereby reducing the pool to 75 items that were administered to 200 college students. Item discrimination analysis was used to determine which items successfully discriminated between top and bottom scorers on the scale, and item-total correlations were computed. A total of 45 items that successfully discriminated between top and bottom scorers and that showed significant item-total correlations was retained for the final scale.

RELIABILITY: Doyle and Moore (1978) tested 327 adult men, 373 adult women, 474 college men, 499 college women, 490 high school girls, and 528 high school boys. Coefficient alpha was .92 for both the adult men and the adult women. For the college men, coefficient alpha was .93, and for the college women, it was .91. Coefficient alpha was .88 for high school boys and .89 for high school girls. For all groups combined, coefficient alpha was .92 for males and .91 for females.

Doyle and Moore (1978) tested 89 male and 91 female college students on two occasions, separated by 13 weeks. Test-retest reliabilities were .89 for males and .85 for females.

VALIDITY: Within each of the three age groups tested by Doyle and Moore (1978), males, as expected, scored as more traditional than females.

Doyle and Moore (1978) tested 170 males attending a conference on "men in transition." These men were expected to be less traditional than the men in the normative groups tested earlier. The prediction was confirmed. Furthermore, as expected, homosexual men attending the conference were less traditional than heterosexual men attending the conference.

A group of 44 male and 51 female college students completed the Attitudes Toward Women Scale (Spence & Helmreich, 1972) (see separate entry) in addition to the AMR. The correlations between scores on the two measures were .76 for females and .64 for males.

Downs and Engleson (1982) administered the AMR and the Attitudes Toward Men Scale (see separate entry) to a group of 200 college students. The correlation between the two scales was .67. They also administered Villemez and Touhey's (1977) Macho Scale (see separate entry) to the same students and obtained a correlation of .72 between the AMR and the Macho Scale.

NOTES & COMMENTS: (1) Doyle and Moore (1978) factor analyzed scale responses and identified seven factors, five of which were interpretable. The first factor, stereotyping sex role behavior, accounted for 27% of the variance; the remaining factors each accounted for less than 5% of the variance. The researchers then identified items that loaded .30 on one factor and did not load any higher on other factors. These items comprise factor scores. Factor Score 1 has 17 items; Factor Score

2 has 11 items; Factor Score 3 has 5 items; Factor Score 4 has 8 items; and there were no items on the fifth factor that satisfied the two criteria. The alpha coefficients for the factor scores were: Factor 1 = .90; Factor 2 = .77; Factor 3 = .61; and Factor 4 = .84.

Falkenberg, Hindman, and Masey (1983) also factor analyzed data obtained with the AMR. They identified 11 factors, 9 of which were interpretable. Four factors identified in this study closely resembled 4 of the factors identified by Doyle and Moore (1978).

(2) Whitley (1987) used a modification of the AMR created by combining items from the AMR with items from Spence and Helmreich's (1972) Attitudes Toward Women Scale. Overlapping items were deleted, and 23 items with the highest part-whole correlations were selected from each scale. The correlation between the two revised scales was .74 for 135 college women and .80 for 107 college men. Whitley also related scores on the revised AMR to attitudes toward homosexuality.

AVAILABLE FROM: Doyle and Moore, 1978

USED IN:

Downs, A. C., & Engleson, S. A. (1982). The Attitudes Toward Men Scale (AMS): An analysis of the role and status of men and masculinity. *Catalog of Selected Documents in Psychology, 12*(4), 45. (Ms. No. 2503)

Doyle, J. A., & Moore, R. J. (1978). Attitudes Toward the Male's Role Scale (AMR): An objective instrument to measure attitudes toward the male's sex role in contemporary society. *Catalog of Selected Documents in Psychology, 8*(2), 35. (Ms. No. 1678)

Falkenberg, S. D., Hindman, C. D., & Masey, D. (1983, March). *Measuring attitudes toward males in society.* Paper presented at the meeting of the Southeastern Psychological Association, Atlanta. (ERIC Document Reproduction Service No. ED 233 287)

Gackenbach, J. I., & Auerbach, S. M. (1985). Sex-role attitudes and perceptual learning. *Journal of Social Psychology, 125*(2), 233–243.

Whitley, B. E., Jr. (1987). The relationship of sex-role orientation to heterosexuals' attitudes toward homosexuals. *Sex Roles, 17*(1/2), 103–113.

BIBLIOGRAPHY:

Spence, J. T., & Helmreich, R. L. (1972). The Attitudes Toward Women Scale: An objective instrument to measure attitudes toward the rights and roles of women in contemporary society. *Catalog of Selected Documents in Psychology, 2*, 66. (Ms. No. 153)

Villemez, W. J., & Touhey, J. C. (1977). A measure of individual differences in sex stereotyping and sex discrimination: The "Macho" Scale. *Psychological Reports, 41*(2), 411–415.

BRANNON MASCULINITY SCALE

AUTHORS: Robert Brannon and Samuel Juni

DATE: 1982

VARIABLE: Approval of the traditional male gender role

TYPE OF INSTRUMENT: Summated rating scale

DESCRIPTION: The Brannon Masculinity Scale is based on Brannon's four-component model of the male role, which suggests that the major dimensions of the male role are: "(1) strong avoidance of everything viewed as feminine, including emotional expressiveness; (2) a need to be respected and 'looked up to'; (3) a style communicating toughness, confidence, self-reliance, seriousness, determination, and related instrumental traits; and (4) a propensity for aggressive, violent, competitive, daring, and adventuresome actions" (Brannon & Juni, 1984, p. 1). The Brannon Masculinity Scale includes 110 items on seven separate subscales representing these four dimensions of the male role. The first dimension is represented by two subscales: Avoiding Femininity (16 items) and Concealing Emotions (16 items). The second dimension is represented by two subscales: The Breadwinner (15 items) and Admired and Respected (16 items). The third dimension is also represented by two subscales: Toughness (16 items) and The Male Machine (16 items). The fourth dimension is represented by one subscale: Violence and Adventure (15 items). Each item is accompanied by a 7-point scale ranging from "strongly disagree" to "strongly agree." Of the 110 items on the scale, 16 are phrased in the reverse direction from the other items.

A short form of the Brannon Masculinity Scale contains 58 items: 9 items from Avoiding Femininity, 8 items from Concealing Emotions, 9 items from The Breadwinner, 8 items from Admired and Respected, 8 items from Toughness, 8 items from The Male Machine, and 8 items from Violence and Adventure. Brannon and Juni (1984) cautioned that subscale scores should not be obtained for the short form of the scale.

SAMPLE ITEMS: (Avoiding Femininity) It bothers me when a man does something that I consider feminine.

(Concealing Emotions) I like the kind of guy who doesn't complain or carry on much when he gets hurt.

(The Breadwinner) Success in his work has to be a man's central goal in this life.

(Admired and Respected) I like the kind of man that is given the best seat in a crowded restaurant without asking for it.

(Toughness) It disgusts me when a man comes across as weak.

(The Male Machine) I always like a man who's totally sure of himself.

(Violence and Adventure) Having wild adventures and doing exciting things brings out the glamour and manliness of a man.

PREVIOUS SUBJECTS: College students; mothers and fathers

APPROPRIATE FOR: High school students and older

ADMINISTRATION: Self-administered; about 40–45 minutes for the full-length scale; about 20–25 minutes for the short version

SCORING: Items are individually scored on a 7-point scale. Item scores are totaled to yield 7 subscale scores and a total score. For the short form of the Brannon Masculinity Scale, only a total score is obtained.

DEVELOPMENT: An initial pool of 228 items written by 75 college undergraduates was administered to 210 college men and 210 college women. Items that correlated most heavily with other items on the same factor were retained, and those that correlated highly with items on other factors were eliminated. The wording of most of the 144 retained items was revised, and 35 new items were added to the pool. These items were administered to 150 college men and 150 college women. The item analysis procedures were repeated, and 110 items were retained on seven subscales.

To select items for the short form of the scale, 58 items having the highest correlations with subscale and full scale totals were retained.
RELIABILITY: The 110-item scale was administered to 144 college students on two occasions with a 4-week interval between testings. The test-retest reliability was .92.

Coefficient alpha was computed for each subscale. The results were as follows: Avoiding Femininity = .87; Concealing Emotions = .84; The Breadwinner = .77; Admired and Respected = .81; Toughness = .79; The Male Machine = .77; and Violence and Adventure = .79.
VALIDITY: Brannon and Juni (1984) looked at the intercorrelations among the subscale scores. The three highest intercorrelations were between the pairs of subscales that are supposed to be measuring the same dimension in Brannon's theory of the male role; that is, between Avoiding Femininity and Concealing Emotion ($r = .65$), between The Breadwinner and Admired and Respected ($r = .64$), and between Toughness and The Male Machine ($r = .69$).

Brannon and Juni (1984) asked 150 males who completed the Brannon Masculinity Scale to indicate whether they had participated in each of 10 activities during the preceding 5 years (e.g., watched boxing on TV; done some sewing; lifted barbells and weights). Correlations between item responses and both subscale and full scale scores on the Brannon Masculinity Scale provided some evidence of the validity of the Brannon scale. The responses to 9 of the 10 activity items correlated in the expected direction with the full-scale score on the Brannon. There were 70 correlations between subscale scores and activity items (7 x 10 = 70). Forty of the 70 correlations were significant, all in the predicted direction.

Based on a sample of 300 respondents, the correlation between the short form of the scale and the full-length scale was .89, suggesting that the short form yields results quite similar to the full-length form. No comparisons between subscale scores were made because Brannon and Juni (1984) were quite clear in stating that subscale scores should not be computed on the short form; there are too few items on each subscale.
NOTES & COMMENTS: (1) Brannon and Juni (1984) reported subscale intercorrelations as well as subscale-total correlations. The correlations between subscale scores and total scores were quite substantial, ranging

from a low of .65 for Violence and Adventure to a high of .86 for Toughness. With the exception of the intercorrelations already mentioned (see VALIDITY), the intercorrelations between the subscale scores were moderate, ranging from .22 to .57 (excluding the intercorrelations between subscales measuring the same dimension).

(2) Thompson, Grisanti, and Pleck (1985) tested college men and compared their attitudes on the short form of the Brannon Masculinity Scale with measures of homophobia, Type A behavior, self-disclosure, and decision-making power within an intimate relationship.

(3) In a study designed to examine fathers' participation in family responsibilities and the relationship between this participation and the development of children's sex role attitudes, the short form Brannon Masculinity Scale was administered to the fathers and mothers of 160 children in kindergarten and fourth grade (Barnett & Baruch, 1987; Baruch & Barnett, 1983, 1984, 1986).

(4) Thompson and Pleck (1986) factor analyzed responses from over 200 college men. They identified three factors from which they created three subscales: Status Norm Scale (11 items), Toughness Norm Scale (8 items), and Anti-Femininity Norm Scale (7 items).

AVAILABLE FROM: Brannon and Juni, 1984
USED IN:

Barnett, R. C., & Baruch, G. K. (1987). Determinants of fathers' participation in family work. *Journal of Marriage and the Family*, 49(1), 29–40.

Baruch, G. K., & Barnett, R. C. (1983). *Correlates of fathers' participation in family work: A technical report* (Working Paper No. 106). Wellesley, MA: Wellesley College, Center for Research on Women. (ERIC Document Reproduction Service No. ED 262 859)

Baruch, G. K., & Barnett, R. C. (1984). *Fathers' participation in family work: Effects on children's sex role attitudes* (Working Paper No. 126). Wellesley, MA: Wellesley College, Center for Research on Women. (ERIC Document Reproduction Service No. ED 250 080)

Baruch, G. K., & Barnett, R. C. (1986). Fathers' participation in family work and children's sex-role attitudes. *Child Development*, 57(5), 1210–1223.

Brannon, R., & Juni, S. (1984). A scale for measuring attitudes about masculinity. *Psychological Documents*, 14(1), 6. (Ms. No. 2612)

Thompson, E. H., Jr., Grisanti, C., & Pleck, J. H. (1985). Attitudes toward the male role and their correlates. *Sex Roles*, 13(7/8), 413–427.

Thompson, E. H., & Pleck, J. H. (1986). The structure of male role norms. *American Behavioral Scientist*, 29, 531–543.

ATTITUDES TOWARD EQUAL RIGHTS AMENDMENT SCALE

AUTHORS: Gerald D. Gibb and James R. Bailey
DATE: 1983

VARIABLE: Attitudes toward the equal rights amendment (ERA)
TYPE OF INSTRUMENT: Thurstone scale
DESCRIPTION: The Attitudes Toward Equal Rights Amendment Scale contains 21 statements pertaining to the advantages and disadvantages of the ERA and the sources of support for the amendment. The task for the respondent is to respond "true" or "false" to each item. Nine of the statements are phrased in the reverse direction from the remainder of the items, so that 12 items are keyed true and 9 items are keyed false.
SAMPLE ITEMS: The major support of ERA lies in career-oriented women.

  ERA will serve *no* purpose in society.
PREVIOUS SUBJECTS: Ages 15–76 years
APPROPRIATE FOR: High school students and older
ADMINISTRATION: Self-administered; about 10 minutes
SCORING: Though no directions are given for scoring the scale, it can be presumed that standard Thurstone scoring procedures are followed. That is, the score would be the median of the scale values for those items endorsed by the respondent. Gibb and Bailey (1983) provide the scale value for each item.
DEVELOPMENT: Using the Thurstone technique for scale development, 67 undergraduate students sorted a pile of 200 attitude statements into 11 categories reflecting the degree of positiveness or negativeness inherent in the statement. For the final scale, the authors selected 21 statements that had low interquartile ranges and scale values covering the entire 11-point continuum.
RELIABILITY: No information was provided.
VALIDITY: The scale was administered by mail to 119 men and 163 women, ages 15 to 76 years. As expected, women had a significantly more positive attitude toward the ERA. The correlation between age and attitude was not significant for men, but there was a significant negative correlation for women: older women had less positive attitudes.

  A sample of 34 college men and 37 college women completed the scale, along with an additional item that asked, "What are your feelings toward the actual Equal Rights Amendment as proposed?" (Gibb & Bailey, 1983, p. 806). A 7-point scale was provided for responding to the item. Correlations between scale scores and responses to this one item were .78 for men and .84 for women, both statistically significant.
NOTES & COMMENTS: Some of the items on the scale are factual; that is, regardless of one's own opinion, the statement is either true or false— for example, "ERA is equally supported by men and women." Responses to factual items may reflect knowledge of the facts rather than attitudes.
AVAILABLE FROM: Gibb and Bailey, 1983

USED IN:
Gibb, G. D., & Bailey, J. R. (1983). Attitude Toward Equal Rights Amendment Scale: An objective measurement tool of attitudes toward equal rights legislation. *Psychological Reports*, 53(3), 804–806.

ATTITUDES TOWARD THE FEMALE ROLE QUESTIONNAIRE

AUTHORS: Pauline Slade and F. A. Jenner
DATE: 1978
VARIABLE: Attitudes toward women and men
TYPE OF INSTRUMENT: Summated rating scale
DESCRIPTION: The Attitudes Toward the Female Role Questionnaire consists of 25 statements regarding women, men, or both women and men. About half of the items pertain directly to women in regard to the working world. Eighteen items are phrased so that disagreement with the statement reflects a more egalitarian attitude, and 7 items are phrased in the reverse direction. Four response options are provided: "strongly disagree, mildly disagree, mildly agree, strongly agree." There is intentionally no "neutral" response, so that persons are forced to express an opinion in one direction or the other.
   SAMPLE ITEMS: A good mother would not go out to work whilst she had a child under 5.
   The only really satisfying role for a woman is as a wife and mother.
PREVIOUS SUBJECTS: British women; Dutch and Indian adults
APPROPRIATE FOR: High school students and older
ADMINISTRATION: Self-administered; about 10–15 minutes
SCORING: Items are individually scored with 0, 1, 3, or 4 points; 4 points are assigned to the most egalitarian response. Item scores are summed to yield a total score that can range from 0 (very traditional) to 100 (very egalitarian).
DEVELOPMENT: Very little information was provided. "Thirty-five statements were prepared and tested on domestic, secretarial and professional workers. Twenty-five items showed discrimination apparently due to personal attitudes. Other items depended on religion (abortion) or seemed to be contaminated by factual knowledge (women drivers . . .)" (Slade & Jenner, 1978, p. 352).
RELIABILITY: Slade and Jenner (1978) administered the scale to 20 British women. They obtained a corrected, split-half reliability coefficient of .92. Of the original sample, 17 were retested 10 days later; the test-retest reliability coefficient was .94.
   Gupta and Murthy (1984) tested 92 adults in India and obtained a corrected split-half reliability coefficient of .88. They also computed the Kuder-Richardson reliability, which was .86. Van Ijzendoorn (1984)

tested 175 college students in the Netherlands and obtained a coefficient alpha of .87.

Gupta and Murthy (1984) computed item-total correlations using data from bank employees in India. Every item was significantly correlated with the total score; the item-total correlations ranged from a low of .24 to a high of .69.

VALIDITY: Slade and Jenner (1978) compared responses from women in traditional occupations (i.e., nurses and secretaries) with responses from women in nontraditional occupations (i.e., university lecturers). As predicted, the women in traditional occupations obtained significantly lower scores. Slade and Jenner also compared responses from a random sample of female undergraduates with responses from the University Women's Liberation Group and again obtained the predicted significant difference.

Gupta and Murthy (1984) administered the Attitudes Toward the Female Role Questionnaire to Indian bank employees, along with Bhadra and Girija's (1976) Attitudes Toward Women Scale. The correlation between scores on the two scales was .69.

Hubbard, Van Ijzendoorn, and Tavecchio (1982) performed an item discrimination analysis and reported significant differences on every item when the results from the top-scoring individuals were compared with the results from the bottom-scoring individuals.

NOTES & COMMENTS: (1) Slade (1981) compared scores of fertile and infertile women on the Attitudes Toward the Female Role Questionnaire. She found no significant differences between the two groups. Slade and Jenner (1980) related menstrual symptomatology to scores on the Attitudes Toward the Female Role Questionnaire. There were no significant correlations between scores and symptom factors. When they looked at correlations with "deviation from the mean attitude score for the group," Slade and Jenner found that persons scoring at the two ends of the scale had greater menstrual symptomatology.

(2) Hubbard et al. (1982) used the Attitudes Toward the Female Role Questionnaire with 728 persons, ages 16 to 65 years, in the Netherlands. Using an "optimal scaling method" (p. 492), they deleted 5 items from the scale. Coefficient alpha for the remaining 20 items was .92. Test-retest reliability, with 10 days between successive testings and a sample of 25 students, was .84. Like Slade and Jenner (1978), Hubbard et al. found significant differences between the responses of women in traditional and in nontraditional occupations. The prediction that persons with higher educational levels would score in the more nontraditional direction was only partially supported. Based on their data analysis, Hubbard et al. also concluded that scale weights of 0, 1, 2, and 4 yielded more valid results than the original weights of 0, 1, 3, and 4.

(3) Some of the phrasing on the Attitudes Toward the Female Role

Questionnaire would be perceived as unusual if the scale were administered to persons in the United States. For example, the first item uses the word *whilst*, and the directions tell respondents to put a "tick" to indicate their choice of answers. Different wording could correct this problem.

(4) Nederhof (1983) used the Attitudes Toward the Female Role Questionnaire in a study focused on increasing response rates for mailed surveys. The subject matter of the survey was not of importance to Nederhof.

AVAILABLE FROM: Slade and Jenner, 1978
USED IN:
Gupta, G. R., & Murthy, V. N. (1984). Attitudes Toward the Female Role Questionnaire: Its Usefulness for an Indian sample. *Psychological Studies, 29*(2), 189–191.
Hubbard, F.O.A., Van Ijzendoorn, M. H., & Tavecchio, L. W. (1982). Validation of a questionnaire measuring attitudes toward females' social roles for a Dutch population. *Psychological Reports, 51*(2), 491–498.
Nederhof, A. J. (1983). Effects of repetition and consistency of personalization treatments on response rate in mail surveys. *Social Science Research, 12*, 1–9.
Slade, P. (1981). Sexual attitudes and social role orientations in infertile women. *Journal of Psychosomatic Research, 25*(3), 183–186.
Slade, P., & Jenner, F. A. (1978). Questionnaire measuring attitudes to females' social roles. *Psychological Reports, 43*(2), 351–354.
Slade, P., & Jenner, F. A. (1980). Attitudes to female roles, aspects of menstruation and complaining of menstrual symptoms. *British Journal of Social and Clinical Psychology, 19*(2), 109–113.
Van Ijzendoorn, M. H. (1984). Answers without questions: A note on response style in questionnaires. *Perceptual and Motor Skills, 59*(3), 827–831.
BIBLIOGRAPHY:
Bhadra, B. R., & Girija, P. R. (1976). A scale for the measurement of attitudes towards women. *Asian Journal of Psychology and Education, 1*, 41–44.

ATTITUDES TOWARD FEMINIST ISSUES SCALE (ATFI)
AUTHORS: Patricia B. Elmore, Annette M. Brodsky, and Nancy Naffziger
DATE: 1975
VARIABLE: Attitudes toward nine feminist issues
DESCRIPTION: The Attitudes Toward Feminist Issues Scale (ATFI) is a summated rating scale consisting of 120 statements representing nine areas: human reproduction, child care, politics and legislation, employment, overcoming self-denigration, marriage and family, consciousness raising in media, religion, and education. Items are accompanied by five response options ranging from "strongly agree" to "strongly disagree."
ARTICLES LISTED IN BEERE, 1979: 3
AVAILABLE FROM: Elmore, Brodsky, and Naffziger, 1975

USED IN:
Elmore, P. B., Brodsky, A. M., & Naffziger, N. (1975, March). *The Attitudes Toward Feminist Issues Scale: A validation study*. Paper presented at the meeting of the American Personnel and Guidance Association, New York. (ERIC Document Reproduction Service No. ED 109 544)

Elmore, P. B., & Vasu, E. S. (1979, April). *Math anxiety: Its impact on graduate level statistics achievement*. Paper presented at the meeting of the American Educational Research Association, San Francisco. (ERIC Document Reproduction Service No. ED 178 331)

Elmore, P. B., & Vasu, E. S. (1980). Relationship between selected variables and statistics achievement: Building a theoretical model. *Journal of Educational Psychology*, 72, 457–467.

Elmore, P. B., & Vasu, E. S. (1986). A model of statistics achievement using spatial ability, feminist attitudes and mathematics-related variables as predictors. *Educational and Psychological Measurement*, 46, 215–222.
BIBLIOGRAPHY:
Beere, C. A. (1979). *Women and women's issues: A handbook of tests and measures* (pp. 388–389). San Francisco: Jossey-Bass.

FINE-DAVIS ATTITUDES TOWARD THE ROLE AND STATUS OF WOMEN

AUTHOR: Margret Fine-Davis
DATE: 1976
VARIABLE: Attitudes toward the role and status of women
TYPE OF INSTRUMENT: Summated rating scale
DESCRIPTION: The Fine-Davis Attitudes Toward the Role and Status of Women scale consists of 33 items, with 28 of the items loading on eight factors: Traditional Sex Role Orientation (6 Items), Positive Attitude to Contraception (4 items), Belief in Equal Opportunity (2 items), Positive Attitude to Maternal Employment (5 items), Belief in Equal Pay (3 items), Belief in Higher Tax for Married Women (2 items), Perception of Females as Inferior (4 items), and Perception of Limitations in Housewife Role (2 items). The remaining 5 items do not load on any of the factors listed. Of the 28 items loading on eight factors, 10 items are phrased in a liberal direction, and 18 items are phrased in a conservative direction. Each item is accompanied by six response alternatives ranging from "strongly agree" to "strongly disagree."
SAMPLE ITEMS: (Traditional Sex Role Orientation) Some equality in marriage is a good thing, but by and large the husband ought to have the main say in family matters.

(Positive Attitude to Contraception) The sale of contraceptives should be legalised [sic] in Ireland.

(Belief in Equal Opportunity) People should be employed and promoted strictly on the basis of ability, regardless of sex.

(Positive Attitude to Maternal Employment) A woman who has a job she enjoys is likely to be a better wife and mother, because she has an interest and some fulfillment outside the home.

(Belief in Equal Pay) Even if it means financial difficulties for some companies, equal pay for equal work should be given immediately.

(Belief in Higher Tax for Married Women) It is only fair that a married couple (both working) pay more tax than two single people.

(Perception of Females as Inferior) Generally speaking women think less clearly than men.

(Perception of Limitations in Housewife Role) Housework is basically dull and boring.

PREVIOUS SUBJECTS: Adults in Ireland

APPROPRIATE FOR: Ages 16 and older in Ireland

ADMINISTRATION: Self-administered; about 15 minutes

SCORING: Items are individually scored on a 6-point scale, with higher scores assigned to the end of the continuum that agrees with the factor name. That is, for Traditional Sex Role Orientation, higher scores are assigned to responses that support Traditional Sex Role Orientation; for Positive Attitude to Contraception, higher scores are assigned to responses that reflect positive attitudes, and so forth. Item scores are averaged, after selected ones are reversed, to yield scores on each of the eight factors. An overall average score can be obtained. Thus all scores range from 1 to 7.

DEVELOPMENT: An item pool was created with many items selected from the Attitudes Toward Women Scale (AWS) (Spence & Helmreich, 1972) (see separate entry), the Traditional Family Ideology Scale (Levinson & Huffman, 1955) (see separate entry), and the Belief Pattern Scale for Measuring Attitudes Toward Feminism (Kirkpatrick, 1936) (see separate entry). In order to make the items appropriate and relevant for Irish culture, some items were modified, and new items were written. A sample of 122 adults in Dublin completed the 60-item version of the scale. Their responses were factor analyzed, and the results led to the selection of items for the final version of the scale: "In general, items were selected on the basis of having high loadings on the resulting factors; however, in some cases an item was retained because of the interest and importance of its content even if it was not among the highest loading items" (Fine-Davis, 1983, p. 115).

RELIABILITY: No information was provided.

VALIDITY: Fine-Davis (1979b) examined the relationship between scores on the Fine-Davis Attitudes Toward the Role and Status of Women and several other variables. Many of her findings provide support for the validity of the measure. For example, employed married women had less traditional gender role attitudes than did nonemployed married women, and employed married women were more supportive of changes in the direction of greater equality for women.

Furthermore, older married women compared to younger married women were more traditional in their attitudes and less supportive of social change. Women with dependent children compared to women without dependent children were more supportive of maternal employment.

Fine-Davis (1979a) obtained other data supportive of the validity of the measure. She found that religiosity related to scores on the Fine-Davis Attitudes Toward the Role and Status of Women. More religious persons were more supportive of traditional gender roles, less likely to support the legalization of contraception, more opposed to the employment of women, particularly those with children, more opposed to equal pay, more supportive of higher taxes for married women, saw fewer drawbacks to the housewife role, and were more likely to perceive women as inferior.

Fine-Davis (1983) compared factor scores based on respondents' sex, marital status, age, and socioeconomic status. She found significant sex differences on six factors: men were more supportive of traditional gender role orientation, had a more positive attitude to contraception, were less likely to believe in equal opportunity and equal pay, were more likely to perceive females as inferior, and were more likely to perceive limitations in the housewife role. Fine-Davis found significant marital status differences on three factors: married persons had more positive attitudes toward maternal employment, were less likely to support higher taxes for married women, and were more likely to perceive limitations in the housewife role. There were five significant differences between age groups: younger respondents were less supportive of traditional gender role orientations, had a more positive attitude toward contraception and a more positive attitude toward maternal employment, were more supportive of equal pay, but less likely to support higher taxes for married women. Fine-Davis found three significant differences between the low and high socioeconomic groups; the low socioeconomic group was more supportive of traditional gender role orientation, had a less positive attitude to maternal employment, and was more likely to perceive females as inferior.

NOTES & COMMENTS: (1) Given that some factors are comprised of few items, it is important that evidence be obtained to demonstrate that the factor scores are reliable.

(2) Fine-Davis (1983) reported intercorrelations between the factor scores. However, some of the factor scores were not based on all of the items loading on that factor. The highest intercorrelations were between Traditional Sex Role Orientation and Positive Attitude to Maternal Employment ($r = -.43$) and between Traditional Sex Role Orientation and Belief in Equal Pay ($r = -.43$). Of the 56 correlations, 20 were statistically significant ($p < .01$).

AVAILABLE FROM: Fine-Davis, 1976; items that load on eight factors are also in Fine-Davis, 1983.

USED IN:

Fine-Davis, M. (1976). *Structure, determinants and correlates of attitudes toward the role and status of women in Ireland, with particular reference to employment status of married women.* Unpublished doctoral dissertation, Trinity College, University of Dublin.

Fine-Davis, M. (1979a). Personality correlates of attitudes toward the role and status of women in Ireland. *Journal of Personality, 47,* 379–396.

Fine-Davis, M. (1979b). Social-psychological predictors of employment status of married women in Ireland. *Journal of Marriage and the Family, 41,* 145–158.

Fine-Davis, M. (1983). A society in transition: Structure and determinants of attitudes toward the role and status of women in Ireland. *Psychology of Women Quarterly, 8*(2), 113–132.

BIBLIOGRAPHY:

Kirkpatrick, C. (1936). The construction of a belief-pattern scale for measuring attitudes toward feminism. *Journal of Social Psychology, 7,* 421–437.

Levinson, D. J., & Huffman, P. E. (1955). Traditional family ideology and its relation to personality. *Journal of Personality, 23,* 251–273.

Spence, J. T., & Helmreich, R. L. (1972). The Attitudes Toward Women Scale: An objective instrument to measure attitudes toward the rights and roles of women in contemporary society. *Catalog of Selected Documents in Psychology, 2,* 66. (Ms. No. 153)

ATTITUDES TOWARD WOMEN SCALE (AWS)

AUTHORS: Janet T. Spence and Robert Helmreich

DATE: 1972

VARIABLE: Attitudes toward women

DESCRIPTION: There are three versions of the Attitudes Toward Women Scale (AWS): a 55-item version, a 25-item version, and a 15-item version. The items on the 55-item version pertain to six theme areas: vocational, educational, and intellectual roles; freedom and independence; dating, courtship, and etiquette; drinking, swearing, and dirty jokes; sexual behavior; and marital relations and obligations. The 25-item version contains a subset of the items on the longer version, and the 15-item version contains an even smaller subset of items. In general, items pertain to the rights, roles, and privileges of women. On all three versions, items are accompanied by four responses ranging from "agree strongly" to "disagree strongly."

NOTES & COMMENTS: (1) The AWS is the most commonly used measure of attitudes toward women. The literature search for this handbook identified almost 270 published studies and 52 ERIC documents that used the AWS. None of these references overlaps the 101 references listed in Beere (1979). The 270 published studies are listed at the end of this description.

(2) The two shorter versions of the AWS are strongly correlated with

the 55-item version. Spence, Helmreich, and Stapp (1973) looked at the correlations between the 55-item version and the 25-item version. They obtained the following correlations: .97 for college men, .97 for college women, .96 for mothers of college students, and .96 for fathers of college students. Spence and Helmreich (1978) reported a correlation of .91 between the 55-item version and the 15-item version. They also reported a coefficient alpha of .89 for the 15-item version.

(3) College students were the subjects in a large number of studies using the AWS. In addition the scale has been administered to men convicted of rape, murder, or property offenses; varsity athletes; U.S. Air Force, Army, Coast Guard, and Navy cadets; women awaiting trial; junior and senior high school students; school administrators; pregnant and sterilized women; medical and dental students; firefighters and police officers; fathers and mothers; abused wives, bulimics; jail and prison inmates; tennis players; nursing students; clients of a mental health clinic; grandmothers; physical educators; union members; professional and career women; mental health professionals; lesbians; staff and residents of a drug rehabilitative program; counseling students; and alcoholics and opiate addicts. The AWS has been administered to Hispanics and Cuban-Americans in the United States. In addition it has been used in England, Japan, Canada, Yugoslavia, Australia, Fiji, Ireland, and Trinidad.

(4) Some researchers have used "informal" modifications of the AWS; that is, they have varied the items in some way or used a nonstandard subset of the items. Other researchers have developed more formal modifications of the AWS. For example, Parry (1983) developed the Attitudes Toward Women Scale—British Version (see separate entry), a modification for use in Great Britain, and Galambos, Petersen, Richards, and Gitelson (1985) developed the Attitudes Toward Women Scale for Adolescents (see separate entry).

(5) The diversity of research involving the AWS is too broad to summarize here. However, some articles that focus on the psychometric properties of the AWS warrant special mention. Smith and Bradley (1980) administered the 55-item version of the AWS to tennis players. They also scored the scale for the 25-item version in order to correlate scores on the two versions and study the reliability of each version. Yoder, Rice, Adams, Priest, and Prince (1982) used the 25-item version of the AWS with freshmen at a U.S. military academy. The focus of their research was to confirm the reliability of the scale. Daugherty and Dambrot (1986) conducted a study of the reliability of all three versions of the AWS. Borges, Levine, and Naylor (1982) asked subjects to complete the AWS three times: once for themselves, once as their typical female classmate would complete it; and once as their typical male classmate would complete it. Helmreich, Spence, and Gibson (1982) looked at

scores on the AWS for the years 1972 through 1980. Buhrke (1988) compared four measures of sex role ideology: the AWS, the Attitude Toward Masculinity Transcendence Scale (Moreland & Van Tuinen, 1978) (see separate entry), the Sexist Attitudes Toward Women Scale (Benson & Vincent, 1980) (see separate entry), and the Sex-Role Ideology Scale (Kalin & Tilby, 1978) (see separate entry).

ARTICLES LISTED IN BEERE, 1979: 101

AVAILABLE FROM: The 55-item version is in Spence and Helmreich, 1972. The 25-item version is in Spence, Helmreich, and Stapp, 1973. The 15-item version is in Spence and Helmreich, 1978.

USED IN:

Adams, J. (1984). Women at West Point: A three-year perspective. *Sex Roles, 11,* 525–541.

Adams, K. A., & Landers, A. D. (1978). Sex differences in dominance behavior. *Sex Roles, 4*(2), 215–223.

Ajdukovic, D., & Kljaic, S. (1984). Personal attributes, self-esteem, and attitude towards women: Some cross-cultural comparisons. *Studia Psychologia, 26*(3), 193–198.

Alyn, J. H., & Becker, L. A. (1984). Feminist therapy with chronically and profoundly disturbed women. *Journal of Counseling Psychology, 31*(2), 202–208.

Argentino, C. M., Kidd, A. H., & Bogart, K. (1977). The effects of experimenter's sex and subject's sex on the attitudes toward women of fraternity, sorority, and mixed-dormitory residents. *Journal of Community Psychology, 5*(2), 186–188.

Atkinson, J., & Huston, T. L. (1984). Sex role orientation and division of labor early in marriage. *Journal of Personality and Social Psychology, 46*(2), 330–345.

Auerbach, S. M., Kilmann, P. R., Gackenbach, J. I., & Jullian, A., III. (1980). Profeminist group experience: Effects of group composition on males' attitudinal affective response. *Small Group Behavior, 11*(1), 50–63.

Baker, D. D., & Terpstra, D. E. (1986). Locus of control and self-esteem versus demographic factors as predictors of attitudes toward women. *Basic and Applied Social Psychology, 7*(2), 163–172.

Bankart, B. B. (1985). Japanese attitudes toward women. *Journal of Psychology, 119*(1), 45–51.

Baranowski, T., Rassin, D. K., Richards, C. J., & Brown, J. P. (1986). The study of "why?": Reasons vs. factors. *Journal of Developmental and Behavioral Pediatrics, 7*(6), 376–377.

Barnett, R. C. (1981). Parental sex-role attitudes and child-rearing values. *Sex Roles, 7*(8), 837–846.

Baruch, G. K., & Barnett, R. C. (1981). Fathers' participation in the care of their preschool children. *Sex Roles, 7*(10), 1043–1055.

Basow, S. A. (1984). Ethnic group differences in educational achievement in Fiji. *Journal of Cross Cultural Psychology, 15*(4), 435–451.

Basow, S. A. (1986). Correlates of sex-typing in Fiji. *Psychology of Women Quarterly, 10*(4), 429–442.

Basow, S. A., & Howe, K. G. (1979). Model influence on career choices of college students. *Vocational Guidance Quarterly, 27*(3), 239–243.

Basow, S. A., & Howe, K. G. (1980). Role-model influence: Effects of sex and sex-role attitude in college students. *Psychology of Women Quarterly*, 4(4), 558–572.

Baucom, D. H., & Sanders, B. S. (1978). Masculinity and femininity as factors in feminism. *Journal of Personality Assessment*, 42(4), 378–384.

Beauvais, C., & Spence, J. T. (1987). Gender, prejudice, and categorization. *Sex Roles*, 16(1/2), 89–100.

Bebeau, M. J., & Loupe, M. J. (1984). Masculine and feminine personality attributes of dental students and their attitudes toward women's roles in society. *Journal of Dental Education*, 48(6), 309–314.

Belk, S. S., & Snell, W. E., Jr. (1986). Beliefs about women: Components and correlates. *Personality and Social Psychology Bulletin*, 12(4), 403–413.

Benson, P. L., & Vincent, S. (1980). Development and validation of the Sexist Attitudes Toward Women Scale (SATWS). *Psychology of Women Quarterly*, 5(2), 276–291.

Berman, M. R., Gelso, C. J., Greenfeig, B. R., & Hirsch, R. (1977). The efficacy of supportive learning environments for returning women: An empirical evaluation. *Journal of Counseling Psychology*, 24(4), 324–331.

Bernard, M. L., & Gilliland, B. E. (1981). Sex bias in counseling: An examination of certain counselor characteristics and their effect on counseling behavior. *School Counselor*, 29(1), 34–40.

Beutell, N. J., & Greenhaus, J. H. (1983). Integration of home and nonhome roles: Women's conflict and coping behavior. *Journal of Applied Psychology*, 68(1), 43–48.

Blackman, S. (1986). The masculinity-femininity of women who study college mathematics. *Sex Roles*, 15, 33–41.

Blakemore, J. E. (1985). Interaction with a baby by young adults: A comparison of traditional and feminist men and women. *Sex Roles*, 13, 405–411.

Borges, M. A., Levine, J. R., & Naylor, P. A. (1982). Self-ratings and projected ratings of sex role attitudes. *Psychology of Women Quarterly*, 6(4), 406–414.

Bowman, P. C., & Auerbach, S. M. (1978). Measuring sex-role attitudes: The problem of the well-meaning liberal male. *Personality and Social Psychology Bulletin*, 4(2), 265–271.

Bowman, P. R. (1982). An analog study with beginning therapists suggesting bias against "activity" in women. *Psychotherapy Theory, Research and Practice*, 19(3), 318–324.

Brattesani, K., & Silverthorne, C. P. (1978). Social psychological factors of menstrual distress. *Journal of Social Psychology*, 106(1), 139–140.

Brenner, O. C., & Tomkiewicz, J. (1986). Race difference in attitudes of American business school graduates toward the role of women. *Journal of Social Psychology*, 126(2), 251–253.

Bridges, J. S. (1978). Correlates of sex role and attitudes toward women. *Psychological Reports*, 43(3), 1279–1282.

Briere, J. (1987). Predicting self-reported likelihood of battering: Attitudes and childhood experiences. *Journal of Research in Personality*, 21, 61–69.

Brown, J. J., & Hart, D. H. (1977). Correlates of females' sexual fantasies. *Perceptual and Motor Skills*, 45(3), 819–825.

Buhrke, R. (1988). Factor dimensions across different measures of sex role ideology. *Sex Roles, 18*(5/6), 309–321.

Byers, E. S., & Wilson, P. (1985). Accuracy of women's expectations regarding men's responses to refusals of sexual advances in dating situations. *International Journal of Women's Studies, 8*(4), 376–387.

Calway, F. N., Wallston, B. S., & Gabel, H. (1979). The relationship between attitudinal and behavioral measures of sex preference. *Psychology of Women Quarterly, 4*(2), 274–280.

Caron, S. L., Carter, D. B., & Brightman, L. A. (1985). Sex-role orientation and attitudes towards women: Differences among college athletes and non-athletes. *Perceptual and Motor Skills, 61*(3), 803–806.

Cash, T. F., Rissi, J., & Chapman, R. (1985). Not just another pretty face: Sex roles, locus of control, and cosmetics use. *Personality and Social Psychology Bulletin, 11*(3), 246–257.

Cheatham, H. E. (1984). Integration of women into the U.S. military. *Sex Roles, 11*, 141–153.

Clark, M. L. (1986). Predictors of scientific majors for black and white college students. *Adolescence, 21*, 205–213.

Colker, R., & Widom, C. S. (1980). Correlates of female athletic participation: Masculinity, femininity, self-esteem, and attitudes toward women. *Sex Roles, 6*(1), 47–58.

Cooper, K., Chassin, L. A., & Zeiss, A. (1985). The relation of sex-role self-concept and sex-role attitudes to the marital satisfaction and personal adjustment of dual-worker couples with preschool children. *Sex Roles, 12*, 227–241.

Corder, J., & Stephan, C. W. (1984). Females' combination of work and family roles: Adolescents' aspirations. *Journal of Marriage and the Family, 46*(2), 391–402.

Costin, F. (1985). Beliefs about rape and women's social roles. *Archives of Sexual Behavior, 14*(4), 319–325.

Craig, J. M., & Jacobs, R. R. (1985). The effect of working with women on male attitudes toward female firefighters. *Basic and Applied Social Psychology, 6*(1), 61–74.

Crawford, J. D. (1978). Career development and career choice in pioneer and traditional women. *Journal of Vocational Behavior, 12*(2), 129–139.

Crouter, A. C., Perry-Jenkins, M., Huston, T. L., & McHale, S. M. (1987). Processes underlying father involvement in dual-earner and single-earner families. *Developmental Psychology, 23*(3), 421–440.

Dambrot, F. H., Papp, M. E., & Whitmore, C. (1984). The sex-role attitudes of three generations of women. *Personality and Social Psychology Bulletin, 10*(3), 469–473.

Daugherty, C. G., & Dambrot, F. H. (1986). Reliability of the Attitudes Toward Women Scale. *Educational and Psychological Measurement, 46*(2), 449–453.

DeFleur, L. B., Gillman, D., & Marshak, W. (1978). Sex integration of the U.S. Air Force Academy: Changing roles for women. *Armed Forces and Society, 4*(4), 607–622.

DeGregoria, B. (1987). Sex role attitude and perception of psychological abuse. *Sex Roles, 16*, 227–35.

Deitz, S. R., Blackwell, K. T., Daley, P. C., & Bentley, B. J. (1982). Measurement of empathy toward rape victims and rapists. *Journal of Personality and Social Psychology*, 43(2), 372–384.

Deitz, S. R., Littman, M., & Bentley, B. J. (1984). Attribution of responsibility for rape: The influence of observer empathy, victim resistance, and victim attractiveness. *Sex Roles*, 10, 261–280.

del Rey, P. (1977). In support of apologetics for women in sport. *International Journal of Sport Psychology*, 8(3), 218–224.

del Rey, P., & Russell, D. S. (1978). Some proof that women's studies courses can 'raise consciousness.' *Phi Delta Kappan*, 59(10), 716–717.

Demare, D., Briere, J., & Lips, H. M. (1988). Violent pornography and self-reported likelihood of sexual aggression. *Journal of Research in Personality*, 22, 140–153.

DeVellis, B. M., Wallston, B. S., & Acker, D. (1984). Childfree by choice: Attitudes and adjustment of sterilized women. *Population and Environment Behavioral and Social Issues*, 7(3), 152–162.

Devine, R. C., & Stillion, J. M. (1978). An examination of locus of control and sex role orientation. *Journal of Psychology*, 98(1), 75–79.

Downs, A. C., & Engleson, S. A. (1982). The Attitudes Toward Men Scale (AMS): An analysis of the role and status of men and masculinity. *Catalog of Selected Documents in Psychology*, 12(4), 45. (Ms. No. 2503)

Doyle, J. A. (1977). Incoming college males' choice of major and attitudes toward women. *Psychological Reports*, 40, 630.

Doyle, J. A., & Shahade, R. (1977). College males' academic field and attitudes toward women. *Psychological Reports*, 40(3), 1089–1090.

Durning, K. P. (1978). Women at the Naval Academy: An attitude survey. *Armed Forces and Society*, 4(4), 569–588.

Edwards, V. J., & Spence, J. T. (1987). Gender-related traits, stereotypes, and schemata. *Journal of Personality and Social Psychology*, 53(1), 146–154.

Erickson, V. L. (1977). Beyond Cinderella: Ego maturity and attitudes toward the rights and roles of women. *Counseling Psychologist*, 7(1), 83–88.

Espin, O. M., & Warner, B. (1982). Attitudes towards the role of women in Cuban women attending a community college. *International Journal of Social Psychiatry*, 28(3), 233–239.

Etaugh, C., & Spandikow, D. B. (1981). Changing attitudes toward women: A longitudinal study of college students. *Psychology of Women Quarterly*, 5(4), 591–594.

Fannin, P. M. (1979). The relation between ego-identity status and sex-role attitude, work-role salience, atypicality of major, and self-esteem in college women. *Journal of Vocational Behavior*, 14(1), 12–22.

Fassinger, R. E. (1985). A causal model of college women's career choice. *Journal of Vocational Behavior*, 27(1), 123–153.

Feild, H. S. (1978). Attitudes toward rape: A comparative analysis of police, rapists, crisis counselors, and citizens. *Journal of Personality and Social Psychology*, 36(2), 156–179.

Fischer, G. J. (1986a). College student attitudes toward forcible date rape: Changes after taking a human sexuality course. *Journal of Sex Education and Therapy*, 12(1), 42–46.

Fischer, G. J. (1986b). College student attitudes toward forcible date rape: I. Cognitive predictors. *Archives of Sexual Behavior*, 15(6), 457–466.

Fischer, G. J. (1987). Hispanic and majority student attitudes toward forcible date rape as a function of differences in attitudes toward women. *Sex Roles*, 17(1/2), 93–101.

Fitzpatrick, J. L. (1978). Academic underachievement, other-direction, and attitudes toward women's roles in bright adolescent females. *Journal of Educational Psychology*, 70(4), 645–650.

Foss, C. J., & Slaney, R. B. (1986). Increasing nontraditional career choices in women: Relation of attitudes toward women and responses to a career intervention. *Journal of Vocational Behavior*, 28(3), 191–202.

Furnham, A., & Singh, A. (1986). Memory for information about sex differences. *Sex Roles*, 15(9/10), 479–486.

Furnham, A. F., & Karani, R. (1985). A cross-cultural study of attitudes to women, just world, and locus of control beliefs. *Psychologia: An International Journal of Psychology in the Orient*, 28, 11–20.

Gackenbach, J. (1978a). The effect of race, sex, and career goal differences on sex role attitudes at home and at work. *Journal of Vocational Behavior*, 12(1), 93–101.

Gackenbach, J. I. (1978b). A perceptual defense approach to the study of gender sex related traits, stereotypes, and attitudes. *Journal of Personality*, 46(4), 645–676.

Gackenbach, J. I., & Auerbach, S. M. (1985). Sex-role attitudes and perceptual learning. *Journal of Social Psychology*, 125(2), 233–243.

Galambos, N. L., Petersen, A. C., Richards, M., & Gitelson, I. B. (1985). The Attitudes Toward Women Scale for Adolescents (AWSA): A study of reliability and validity. *Sex Roles*, 13, 343–356.

Garcia, L. T. (1986). Exposure to pornography and attitudes about women and rape: A correlational study. *Journal of Sex Research*, 22(3), 378–385.

Gayton, W. F., Sawyer, B. L., Baird, J. G., & Ozmon, K. L. (1982). Further validation of a new measure of machismo. *Psychological Reports*, 51(3), 820–822.

Gerdes, E. P., & Kelman, J. H. (1981). Sex discrimination: Effects of sex-role incongruence, evaluator sex, and stereotypes. *Basic and Applied Social Psychology*, 2(3), 219–226.

Ghaffaradli-Doty, P., & Carlson, E. R. (1979). Consistency in attitude and behavior of women with a liberated attitude toward the rights and roles of women. *Sex Roles*, 5(4), 395–404.

Gilbert, L. A. (1981). Perceptions of sex roles: The influences of client gender and student-counselor attitudes. *Counselor Education and Supervision*, 21(1), 57–62.

Gilbert, L. A., & Waldroop, J. (1978). Evaluation of a procedure for increasing sex-fair counseling. *Journal of Counseling Psychology*, 25(5), 410–418.

Goff, D. H., Goff, L. D., & Lehrer, S. K. (1980). Sex-role portrayals of selected female television characters. *Journal of Broadcasting*, 24(4), 467–478.

Goldberg, P. A., Katz, J. F., & Rappeport, S. (1979). Posture and prediction on the Attitudes Toward Women Scale. *Psychology of Women Quarterly*, 3(4), 403–406.

Greenberg, R. P., & Zedlow, P. B. (1977). Personality characteristics of men with liberal sex-role attitudes. *Journal of Psychology, 97*(2), 187–190.

Greenberger, E., Goldberg, W. A., Crawford, T. J., & Granger, J. (1988). Beliefs about the consequences of maternal employment for children. *Psychology of Women Quarterly, 12,* 35–50.

Gregson, J. F., & Colley, A. (1986). Concomitants of sport participation in male and female adolescents. *International Journal of Sport Psychology, 17*(1), 10–22.

Hall, E. R., Howard, J. A., & Boezio, S. L. (1986). Tolerance of rape: A sexist or antisocial attitude? *Psychology of Women Quarterly, 10*(2), 101–117.

Hall, J. A., Braunwald, K. G., & Mroz, B. J. (1982). Gender, affect, and influence in a teaching situation. *Journal of Personality and Social Psychology, 43*(2), 270–280.

Hall, J. R., & Black, J. D. (1979). Assertiveness, aggressiveness, and attitudes toward feminism. *Journal of Social Psychology, 107*(1), 57–62.

Hardesty, S. A., & Betz, N. E. (1980). The relationships of career salience, attitudes toward women, and demographic and family characteristics to marital adjustment in dual-career couples. *Journal of Vocational Behavior, 17*(2), 242–250.

Hare-Mustin, R. T., Bennett, S. K., & Broderick, P. C. (1983). Attitude toward motherhood: Gender, generational, and religious comparisons. *Sex Roles, 9*(5), 643–661.

Hare-Mustin, R. T., & Broderick, P. C. (1979). The myth of motherhood: A study of attitudes toward motherhood. *Psychology of Women Quarterly, 4*(1), 114–128.

Hare-Mustin, R. T., & Lamb, S. (1984). Family counselors' attitudes toward women and motherhood: A new cohort. *Journal of Marital and Family Therapy, 10*(4), 419–421.

Harmon, L. W. (1981). The life and career plans of young adult college women: A follow-up study. *Journal of Counseling Psychology, 28*(5), 416–427.

Harren, V. A., & Biscardi, D. L. (1980). Sex roles and cognitive styles as predictors of Holland typologies. *Journal of Vocational Behavior, 17*(2), 231–241.

Harren, V. A., Kass, R. A., Tinsley, H. E., & Moreland, J. R. (1979). Influence of gender, sex-role attitudes, and cognitive complexity on gender-dominant career choices. *Journal of Counseling Psychology, 26*(3), 227–234.

Harrison, B. G., Guy, R. F., & Lupfer, S. L. (1981). Locus of control and self-esteem as correlates of role orientation in traditional and nontraditional women. *Sex Roles, 7*(12), 1175–1188.

Helmreich, R. L., Spence, J. T., & Gibson, R. H. (1982). Sex-role attitudes: 1972–1980. *Personality and Social Psychology Bulletin, 8*(4), 656–663.

Helmreich, R. L., Spence, J. T., & Holahan, C. K. (1979). Psychological androgyny and sex role flexibility: A test of two hypotheses. *Journal of Personality and Social Psychology, 37*(10), 1631–1644.

Henkin, B., & Fish, J. M. (1986). Gender and personality differences in the appreciation of cartoon humor. *Journal of Psychology, 120*(2), 157–175.

Hess, E. P., & Bornstein, P. H. (1979). Perceived sex role attitudes in self and other as a determinant of differential assertiveness in college males. *Cognitive Therapy and Research, 3*(2), 155–159.

Hoferek, M. J. (1982). Sex-role prescriptions and attitudes of physical educators. *Sex Roles, 8*(1), 83–98.

Holms, V. L., & Esses, L. M. (1988). Factors influencing Canadian high school girls' career motivation. *Psychology of Women Quarterly, 12,* 313–328.

Howard, J. A. (1984a). The "normal" victim: The effects of gender stereotypes on reactions to victims. *Social Psychology Quarterly, 47*(3), 270–281.

Howard, J. A. (1984b). Societal influences on attribution: Blaming some victims more than others. *Journal of Personality and Social Psychology, 47*(3), 494–505.

Howells, K., Shaw, F., Greasley, M., Robertson, J., Gloster, D., & Metcalfe, N. (1984). Perceptions of rape in a British sample: Effects of relationship, victim status, sex, and attitudes to women. *British Journal of Social Psychology, 23*(1), 35–40.

Illfelder, J. K. (1980). Fear of success, sex role attitudes, and career salience and anxiety levels of college women. *Journal of Vocational Behavior, 16*(1), 7–17.

Irvine, J. J., & Robinson, C. (1982). The relationships among sex role orientations, general attitudes toward women, and specific attitudes toward women in managerial roles. *Journal of Educational Equity and Leadership, 2*(3), 196–204.

Jacobson, M. B., & Insko, W. R. (1984). On the relationship between feminism and use of "Ms." *Psychological Reports, 54*(2), 388–390.

Jacobson, M. B., & Insko, W. R. (1985). Use of nonsexist pronouns as a function of one's feminist orientation. *Sex Roles, 13,* 1–7.

Jacobson, M. B., Popovich, P. M., Biers, D. W. (1980). The Feminist Attitudes Toward Rape Scale. *Catalog of Selected Documents in Psychology, 10,* 88. (Ms. No. 2140).

Jean, P. J., & Reynolds, C. R. (1984). Sex and attitude distortion: Ability of females and males to fake liberal and conservative positions regarding changing sex roles. *Sex Roles, 10,* 805–815.

Johnson, R. W., Doiron, D., Brooks, G. P., & Dickinson, J. (1978). Perceived attractiveness as a function of support for the feminist movement: Not necessarily a put-down of women. *Canadian Journal of Behavioural Science, 10*(3), 214–221.

Kabacoff, R. I., Marwit, S. J., & Orlofsky, J. L. (1985). Correlates of sex role stereotyping among mental health professionals. *Professional Psychology Research and Practice, 16*(1), 98–105.

Kahn, S. E. (1982). Sex-role attitudes: Who should raise consciousness? *Sex Roles, 8*(9), 977–985.

Katz, P. A., & Boswell, S. (1986). Flexibility and traditionality in children's gender roles. *Genetic, Social and General Psychology Monographs, 112*(1), 103–147.

Kelley, K. (1985). The effects of sexual and/or aggressive film exposure on helping, hostility, and attitudes about the sexes. *Journal of Research in Personality, 19*(4), 472–483.

Kern, J. M., Cavell, T. A., & Beck, B. (1985). Predicting differential reactions to males' versus females' assertions, empathic-assertions, and nonassertions. *Behavior Therapy, 16*(1), 63–75.

King, L. A., & King, D. W. (1986). Validity of the Sex-Role Egalitarianism Scale: Discriminating egalitarianism from feminism. *Sex Roles*, *15*(3/4), 207–214.

Kingery, D. W. (1985). Are sex-role attitudes useful in explaining male/female differences in rates of depression? *Sex Roles*, *12*, 627–636.

Kirkpatrick, C. S. (1980). Sex roles and sexual satisfaction in women. *Psychology of Women Quarterly*, *4*(4), 444–459.

Klentz, B., Beaman, A. L., Mapelli, S. D., & Ullrich, J. R. (1987). Perceived physical attractiveness of supporters and nonsupporters of the women's movement: An attitude-similarity-mediated error (AS-ME). *Personality and Social Psychology Bulletin*, *13*(4), 513–523.

Koblinsky, S. A., & Palmeter, J. G. (1984). Sex-role orientation, mother's expression of affection toward spouse, and college women's attitudes toward sexual behaviors. *Journal of Sex Research*, *20*(1), 32–43.

Koffman, S., & Lips, H. M. (1980). Sex differences in self-esteem and performance expectancies in married couples. *Social Behavior and Personality*, *8*(1), 57–63.

Komarovsky, M., & Mayer, E. R. (1984). Consistency of female gender attitudes: A research note. *Social Forces*, *62*(4), 1020–1025.

Koss, M. P. (1985). The hidden rape victim: Personality, attitudinal, and situational characteristics. *Psychology of Women Quarterly*, *9*(2), 193–212.

Koss, M. P., Leonard, K. E., Beezley, D. A., & Oros, C. J. (1985). Nonstranger sexual aggression: A discriminant analysis of the psychological characteristics of undetected offenders. *Sex Roles*, *12*, 981–992.

Kozma, C., & Zuckerman, M. (1983). An investigation of some hypotheses concerning rape and murder. *Personality and Individual Differences*, *4*(1), 23–29.

Kranau, E. J., Green, V., & Valencia-Weber, G. (1982). Acculturation and the Hispanic woman: Attitudes toward women, sex-role attribution, sex-role behavior, and demographics. *Hispanic Journal of Behavioral Sciences*, *4*(1), 21–40.

Kremer, J., & Curry, C. (1987). Attitudes toward women in Northern Ireland. *Journal of Social Psychology*, *127*(5), 531–533.

Kurdek, L. A., & Blisk, D. (1983). Dimensions and correlates of mothers' divorce experiences. *Journal of Divorce*, *6*(4), 1–24.

Lammers, H. B., & Wilkinson, M. L. (1980). Attitudes toward women and satisfaction with sex roles in advertisements. *Psychological Reports*, *46*(3), 690.

Lasley, J., Kuhl, A. F., & Roberg, R. R. (1985). Relationship of nontraditional sex-role attitudes to severity of women's criminal behavior. *Psychological Reports*, *56*(1), 155–158.

Lester, P., & Chu, L. (1981). Women administrators: Feminine, masculine or androgynous? *Journal of Educational Equity and Leadership*, *1*(3), 171–179.

Levant, R. F., Slattery, S. C., & Loiselle, J. E. (1987). Fathers' involvement in housework and child care with school-aged daughters. *Family Relations*, *36*(2), 152–157.

Leventhal, G. (1977). Female criminality: Is "women's lib" to blame? *Psychological Reports*, *41*(3), 1179–1182.

Leventhal, G., & Matturo, M. (1981). Males' attitudes towards women: What they say and what they do. *Psychological Reports*, *48*(1), 333–334.

Levine, R., Gillman, M. J., & Reis, H. (1982). Individual differences for sex differences in achievement attributions? *Sex Roles*, 8(4), 455–466.

Levine, R. V., & West, L. (1979). Attitudes toward women in the United States and Brazil. *Journal of Social Psychology*, 108(2), 265–266.

Loeffler, D., & Fiedler, L. (1979). Woman—A sense of identity: A counseling intervention to facilitate personal growth in women. *Journal of Counseling Psychology*, 26(1), 51–57.

Logan, D. D., & Kaschak, E. (1980). The relationship of sex, sex role, and mental health. *Psychology of Women Quarterly*, 4(4), 573–580.

Loo, R. (1983). Nursing students: Personality dimensions and attitudes toward women. *Psychological Reports*, 52(2), 504–506.

Loo, R., & Logan, P. (1982). Personality correlates of the Attitudes Toward Women Scale. *Personality and Individual Differences*, 3(3), 329–330.

MacKinnon, C. E., Stoneman, Z., & Brody, G. H. (1984). The impact of maternal employment and family form on children's sex-role stereotypes and mothers' traditional attitudes. *Journal of Divorce*, 8(1), 51–60.

Maier, R. A., & Lavrakas, P. J. (1981). Some personality correlates of attitudes about sports. *International Journal of Sport Psychology*, 12(1), 19–22.

Maier, R. A., & Lavrakas, P. J. (1984). Attitudes toward women, personality rigidity, and idealized physique preferences in males. *Sex Roles*, 11, 425–433.

Marcotte, D. B., & Logan, C. (1977). Medical sex education: Allowing attitude alteration. *Archives of Sexual Behavior*, 6(2), 155–162.

Mark, M. M., & Miller, M. L. (1986). The effects of sexual permissiveness, target gender, subject gender, and attitude toward women on social perception: In search of the double standard. *Sex Roles*, 15(5/6), 311–322.

Matheson, K., & Kristiansen, C. M. (1987). The effect of sexist attitudes and social structure on the use of sex-biased pronouns. *Journal of Social Psychology*, 127(4), 395–398.

Mazelan, P. M. (1980). Stereotypes and perceptions of the victims of rape. *Victimology*, 5, 121–132.

McCormick, N. B. (1979). Come-ons and put-offs: Unmarried students' strategies for having and avoiding sexual intercourse. *Psychology of Women Quarterly*, 4(2), 194–211.

McCormick, N., Izzo, A., & Folcik, J. (1985). Adolescents' values, sexuality, and contraception in a rural New York county. *Adolescence*, 20, 385–395.

McHale, S. M., & Huston, T. L. (1984). Men and women as parents: Sex role orientations, employment, and parental roles with infants. *Child Development*, 55(4), 1349–1361.

McIntire, W. G., Drummond, R. J., & Carter, C. E. (1977). The HIM-B as a family interaction assessment technique. *Small Group Behavior*, 8(3), 361–368.

McKinney, K. (1987). Age and gender differences in college students' attitudes toward women: A replication and extension. *Sex Roles*, 17(5/6), 353–358.

Mezydlo, L. S., & Betz, N. E. (1980). Perceptions of ideal sex roles as a function of sex and feminist orientation. *Journal of Counseling Psychology*, 27(3), 282–285.

Michael, M. E., Gilroy, F. D., & Sherman, M. F. (1984). Athletic similarity and attitudes towards women as factors in the perceived physical attractiveness and liking of a female varsity athlete. *Perceptual and Motor Skills, 59*(2), 511–518.

Moore, T. E., Griffiths, K., & Payne, B. (1987). Gender, attitudes toward women, and the appreciation of sexist humor. *Sex Roles, 16*(9/10), 521–531.

Muehlenhard, C. L., Friedman, D. E., & Thomas, C. M. (1985). Is date rape justifiable? The effects of dating activity, who initiated, who paid, and men's attitudes toward women. *Psychology of Women Quarterly, 9*(3), 297–309.

Muehlenhard, C. L., & Hollabaugh, L. C. (1988). Do women sometimes say no when they mean yes? The prevalence and correlates of women's token resistance to sex. *Journal of Personality and Social Psychology, 54*, 872–879.

Muehlenhard, C. L., & Linton, M. A. (1987). Date rape and sexual aggression in dating situations: Incidence and risk factors. *Journal of Counseling Psychology, 34*(2), 186–196.

Murphy, L., & Rollins, J. H. (1980). Attitudes toward women in co-ed and all female drug treatment programs. *Journal of Drug Education, 10*(4), 319–323.

Nirenberg, T. D., & Gaebelein, J. W. (1979). Third party instigated aggression: Traditional versus liberal sex role attitudes. *Personality and Social Psychology Bulletin, 5*(3), 348–351.

Notar, M., & McDaniel, S. A. (1986). Feminist attitudes and mother-daughter relationships in adolescence. *Adolescence, 21*, 11–21.

O'Connor, K., Mann, D. W., & Bardwick, J. M. (1978). Androgyny and self-esteem in the upper-middle class: A replication of Spence. *Journal of Consulting and Clinical Psychology, 46*(5), 1168–1169.

O'Neil, J. M., Ohlde, C., Barke, C., Gelwick, B. P., & Garfield, N. (1980). Research on a workshop to reduce the effects of sexism and sex role socialization on women's career planning. *Journal of Counseling Psychology, 27*(4), 355–363.

Ordman, A. M., & Kirschenbaum, D. S. (1985). Cognitive-behavioral therapy for bulimia: An initial outcome study. *Journal of Consulting and Clinical Psychology, 53*(3), 305–313.

Orlofsky, J. L. (1981). Relationship between sex role attitudes and personality traits and the Sex Role Behavior Scale—1: A new measure of masculine and feminine role behavior. *Journal of Personality and Social Psychology, 40*(5), 927–940.

Orlofsky, J. L. (1982). Psychological androgyny, sex-typing, and sex-role ideology as predictors of male-female interpersonal attraction. *Sex Roles, 8*(10), 1057–1073.

Orlofsky, J. L., Cohen, R. S., & Ramsden, M. W. (1985). Relationship between sex-role attitudes and personality traits and the Revised Sex-Role Behavior Scale. *Sex Roles, 12*, 377–391.

Orlofsky, J. L., & O'Heron, C. A. (1987a). Development of a short-form Sex Role Behavior Scale. *Journal of Personality Assessment, 51*(2), 267–277.

Orlofsky, J. L., & O'Heron, C. A. (1987b). Stereotypic and nonstereotypic sex role trait and behavior orientations: Implications for personal adjustment. *Journal of Personality and Social Psychology, 52*(5), 1034–1042.

Parry, G. (1983). A British version of the Attitudes Toward Women Scale (AWS-B). *British Journal of Social Psychology*, 22(3), 261–263.

Petersen, A. C. (1984). The early adolescence study: An overview. *Journal of Early Adolescence*, 4(2), 103–106.

Phillips, S. D., & Johnston, S. L. (1985). Attitudes toward work roles for women. *Journal of College Student Personnel*, 26(4), 334–338.

Pines, A. (1979). The influence of goals on people's perceptions of a competent woman. *Sex Roles*, 5(1), 71–76.

Pistrang, N. (1984). Women's work involvement and experience of new motherhood. *Journal of Marriage and the Family* 46(2), 433–447.

Pomerantz, S., & House, W. (1977). Liberated versus traditional women's performance satisfaction and perceptions of ability. *Journal of Psychology*, 95, 205–11.

Post, R. D. (1981). Causal explanations of male and female academic performance as a function of sex-role biases. *Sex Roles*, 7(7), 691–698.

Potts, C., Plant, W. T., & Southern, M. L. (1978). Conventional sex differences in personality: Does sex or verbal ability level account for more variance? *Psychological Reports*, 43(3), 931–936.

Pryor, J. B. (1987). Sexual harassment proclivities in men. *Sex Roles*, 17(5/6), 269–290.

Rakowski, S. L., & Farrow, J. M. (1979). Sex-role identification and goal orientation in teenage females. *Psychological Reports*, 44(2), 363–366.

Redfering, D. L. (1979). Relationship between attitudes toward feminism and levels of dogmatism, achievement, and anxiety. *Journal of Psychology*, 101(2), 297–304.

Reviere, R., & Posey, T. B. (1978). Correlates of two measures of fear of success in women. *Psychological Reports*, 42(2), 609–610.

Rice, R. W., Bender, L. R., & Vitters, A. G. (1980). Leader sex, follower attitudes toward women, and leadership effectiveness: A laboratory experiment. *Organizational Behavior and Human Performance*, 25(1), 46–78.

Richardson, D., Vinsel, A., & Taylor, S. P. (1980). Female aggression as a function of attitudes toward women. *Sex Roles*, 6(2), 265–271.

Robinson, E. A., & Follingstad, D. R. (1985). Development and validation of a behavioral sex-role inventory. *Sex roles*, 13, 691–713.

Rollins, J., & White, P. N. (1982). The relationship between mothers' and daughters' sex-role attitudes and self-concepts in three types of family environment. *Sex Roles*, 8(11), 1141–1155.

Rose, S., & Roades, L. (1987). Feminism and women's friendships. *Psychology of Women Quarterly*, 11(2), 243–254.

Rosenbaum, A., & O'Leary, K. D. (1981). Marital violence: Characteristics of abusive couples. *Journal of Consulting and Clinical Psychology*, 49(1), 63–71.

Ross, J., & Kahan, J. P. (1983). Children by choice or by chance: The perceived effects of parity. *Sex Roles*, 9(1), 69–77.

Rossi, S. R., & Rossi, J. S. (1985). Gender differences in the perception of women in magazine advertising. *Sex Roles*, 12, 1033–1039.

Rowland, R. (1977). Australian data on the Attitude Toward Women Scale: Norms, sex differences, reliability. *Australian Psychologist*, 12(3), 327–331.

Rozsnafszky, J., & Hendel, D. D. (1977). Relationship between ego development and attitudes toward women. *Psychological Reports, 41*(1), 161–162.

Russell, M. (1986). Teaching feminist counseling skills: An evaluation. *Counselor Education and Supervision, 25*(4), 321–30.

Salisbury, J., & Passer, M. W. (1982). Gender-role attitudes and participation in competitive activities of varying stereotypic femininity. *Personality and Social Psychology Bulletin, 8*(3), 486–493.

Sattem, L., Savells, J., & Murray, E. (1984). Sex-role stereotypes and commitment of rape. *Sex Roles, 11*, 849–860.

Schneider, L. J. (1985). Feminist values in announcements of professional services. *Journal of Counseling Psychology, 32*(4), 637–640.

Scott, R. L., & Tetreault, L. A. (1987). Attitudes of rapists and other violent offenders toward women. *Journal of Social Psychology, 127*(4), 375–380.

Segal, Z. V., & Marshall, W. L. (1985). Self-report and behavioral assertion in two groups of sexual offenders. *Journal of Behavior Therapy and Experimental Psychiatry, 16*(3), 223–229.

Segal, Z. V., & Stermac, L. (1984). A measure of rapists' attitudes towards women. *International Journal of Law and Psychiatry, 7*, 437–440.

Shank, J. W. (1986). An exploration of leisure in the lives of dual career women. *Journal of Leisure Research, 18*(4), 300–319.

Shea, G. A. (1983). Voluntary childlessness and the Women's Liberation Movement. *Population and Environment, 6*(1), 17–26.

Shotland, R. L., & Goodstein, L. (1983). Just because she doesn't want to doesn't mean it's rape: An experimentally based causal model of the perception of rape in a dating situation. *Social Psychology Quarterly, 46*(3), 220–232.

Skelton, C. A., & Burkhart, B. R. (1980). Sexual assault: Determinants of victim disclosure. *Criminal Justice and Behavior, 7*(2), 229–235.

Slane, S., & Morrow, L. (1981). Race differences in feminism and guilt. *Psychological Reports, 49*(1), 45–46.

Slaney, R. B., & Caballero, M. (1983). Changing male attitudes toward women's career development: An exploratory study. *Journal of Counseling Psychology, 30*(1), 126–129.

Slevin, K. F., & Wingrove, C. R. (1983a). Real vs. perceived differences in how three intra-family generations of women view their roles in society. *Perceptual and Motor Skills, 56*(3), 959–970.

Slevin, K. F., & Wingrove, C. R. (1983b). Similarities and differences among three generations of women in attitudes toward the female role in contemporary society. *Sex Roles, 9*(5), 609–624.

Smith, A. D., Resick, P. A., & Kilpatrick, D. G. (1980). Relationships among gender, sex-role attitudes, sexual attitudes, thoughts, and behaviors. *Psychological Reports, 46*(2), 359–367.

Smith, R. L., & Bradley, D. W. (1979). Factor validation and refinement of the sex-role questionnaire and its relationship to the Attitudes Toward Women Scale. *Psychological Reports, 44*(3), 1155–1174.

Smith, R. L., & Bradley, D. W. (1980). In defense of the Attitudes Toward Women Scale: An affirmation of validity and reliability. *Psychological Reports, 47*(2), 511–522.

Spence, J. T., & Helmreich, R. L. (1972). The Attitudes Toward Women Scale:

An objective instrument to measure attitudes toward the rights and roles of women in contemporary society. *Catalog of Selected Documents in Psychology, 2,* 66. (Ms. No. 153)

Spence, J. T., & Helmreich, R. L. (1978). *Masculinity and femininity: Their psychological dimensions, correlates, and antecedents.* Austin: University of Texas Press.

Spence, J. T., & Helmreich, R. L. (1979a). Comparison of masculine and feminine personality attributes and sex-role attitudes across age groups. *Developmental Psychology, 15*(5), 582–583.

Spence, J. T., & Helmreich, R. L. (1979b). On assessing androgyny. *Sex Roles, 5*(6), 721–738.

Spence, J. T., Helmreich, R. L., & Sawin, L. L. (1980). The Male-Female Relations Questionnaire: A self-report inventory of sex role behaviors and preferences and its relationships to masculine and feminine personality traits, sex role attitudes, and other measures. *Catalog of Selected Documents in Psychology, 10,* 87. (Ms. No. 2123)

Spence, J. T., Helmreich, R. L., & Stapp, J. (1973). A short version of the Attitudes Toward Women Scale (AWS). *Bulletin on the Psychonomic Society, 2,* 219–220.

Stafford, I. P. (1984). Relation of attitudes toward women's roles and occupational behavior to women's self-esteem. *Journal of Counseling Psychology, 31*(3), 332–338.

Stake, J. E. (1979). Women's self-estimates of competence and the resolution of the career/home conflict. *Journal of Vocational Behavior, 14*(1), 33–42.

Stein, S. L., & Weston, L. C. (1982). College women's attitudes toward women and identity achievement. *Adolescence, 17,* 895–899.

Stephan, C. W., & Corder, J. (1985). The effects of dual-career families on adolescents' sex-role attitudes, work and family plans, and choices of important others. *Journal of Marriage and the Family, 47*(4), 921–929.

Stermac, L. E., & Quinsey, V. L. (1986). Social competence among rapists. *Behavioral Assessment, 8*(2), 171–185.

Stevens, G., & Gardner, S. (1987). But can she command a ship? Acceptance of women by peers at the Coast Guard Academy. *Sex Roles, 16*(3/4), 181–188.

Sztaba, T. I., & Colwill, N. L. (1988). Secretarial and management students: Attitudes, attributes, and career choice considerations. *Sex Roles, 19,* 651–665.

Tan-Willman, C. (1979). Prospective teachers' attitudes toward the rights and roles of contemporary women in two cultures. *Psychological Reports, 45*(3), 741–742.

Terpstra, D. E., & Baker, D. D. (1986). Psychological and demographic correlates of perception of sexual harassment. *Genetic, Social and General Psychology Monographs, 112*(4), 459–478.

Tetenbaum, T. J., Lighter, J., & Travis, M. (1983). The construct validation of an Attitudes Toward Working Mothers Scale. *Psychology of Women Quarterly, 8*(1), 69–78.

Thompson, E. H., & Pleck, J. H. (1986). The structure of male role norms. *American Behavioral Scientist, 29,* 531–543.

Thornton, B., & Linnstaedter, L. (1980). The influence of physical attractiveness and sex-role congruence on interpersonal attraction. *Representative Research in Social Psychology, 11*(1), 55–63.

Thornton, B., Ryckman, R. M., & Robbins, M. A. (1982). The relationships of observer characteristics to beliefs in the causal responsibility of victims of sexual assault. *Human Relations, 35*(4), 321–330.

Tinsley, H. E., Kass, R. A., Moreland, J. R., & Harren, V. A. (1983). A longitudinal study of female college students' occupational decision making. *Vocational Guidance Quarterly, 32*(2), 89–102.

Tipton, R. M. (1976). Attitudes towards women's roles in society and vocational interests. *Journal of Vocational Behavior, 8*(2), 155–165.

Tomkiewicz, J., & Brenner, O. C. (1982). Organizational dilemma: Sex differences in attitudes toward women held by future managers. *Personnel Administrator, 27*(7), 62–65.

Topol, P., & Reznikoff, M. (1979). Achievers and underachievers: A comparative study of fear of success, education and career goals, and conception of woman's role among high school seniors. *Sex Roles, 5*(1), 85–92.

Towson, S. M., Zanna, M. P., & MacDonald, G. (1985). Self-fulfilling prophecy: Sex role stereotypes as expectations for behavior. *Imagination, Cognition and Personality, 4*(2), 149–160.

Travis, C. B., & Seipp, P. H. (1978). An examination of secondary reinforcement, operant conditioning, and status envy hypotheses in relation to sex-role ideology. *Sex Roles, 4*(4), 525–538.

Uguccioni, S. M., & Ballantyne, R. H. (1980). Comparison of attitudes and sex roles for female athletic participants and nonparticipants. *International Journal of Sport Psychology, 11*(1), 42–48.

Ullman, L. P., Freedland, K. E., & Warmsun, C. H. (1978). Sex and ethnic group effects on attitudes toward women. *Bulletin of the Psychonomic Society, 11*(3), 179–180.

Vance, B. K., & Green, V. (1984). Lesbian identities: An examination of sexual behavior and sex role attribution as related to age of initial same-sex sexual encounter. *Psychology of Women Quarterly, 8*(3), 293–307.

Vanfossen, B. E. (1977). Sexual stratification and sex-role socialization. *Journal of Marriage and the Family, 39*(3), 563–574.

Vaughn, L. S., & Wittig, M. A. (1980). Occupation, competence, and role overload as evaluation determinants of successful women. *Journal of Applied Social Psychology, 10*(5), 398–415.

Vedovato, S., & Vaughter, R. M. (1980). Psychology of women courses changing sexist and sex-typed attitudes. *Psychology of Women Quarterly, 4*(4), 587–590.

Wallston, B. S., DeVellis, B. M., & Wallston, K. (1983). Licensed practical nurses' sex role stereotypes. *Psychology of Women Quarterly, 7*(3), 199–208.

Ward, C. (1978). Methodological problems in attitude measurement: Sex roles, social approval and the bogus pipeline. *Representative Research in Social Psychology, 9*(1), 64–68.

Ward, C. (1980). Psychological androgyny and attitudes toward women. *Representative Research in Social Psychology, 11*(1), 44–47.

Weathers, C., & Billingsley, D. (1982). Body image and sex-role stereotype as features of addiction in women. *International Journal of the Addictions*, *17*(2), 343–347.

Weidner, G., & Griffitt, W. (1983). Rape: A sexual stigma? *Journal of Personality*, *51*(2), 152–166.

Weidner, G., & Griffitt, W. (1984). Abortion as a stigma: In the eyes of the beholder. *Journal of Research in Personality*, *18*(3), 359–371.

Weitzman, N., Birns, B., & Friend, R. (1985). Traditional and nontraditional mothers' communication with their daughters and sons. *Child Development*, *56*(4), 894—898.

Welsh, M. C. (1979). Attitudinal measures and evaluation of males and females in leadership roles. *Psychological Reports*, *45*(1), 19–22.

Wheeler, C. L., & Arvey, R. D. (1981). Division of household labor in the family. *Home Economics Research Journal*, *10*(1), 10–20.

White, G. L. (1981). Some correlates of romantic jealousy. *Journal of Personality*, *49*(2), 129–147.

Whitley, B. E., Jr. (1987). The relationship of sex-role orientation to heterosexuals' attitudes toward homosexuals. *Sex Roles*, *17*(1/2), 103–113.

Widom, C. S. (1979). Female offenders: Three assumptions about self-esteem, sex-role identity, and feminism. *Criminal Justice and Behavior*, *6*(4), 365–382.

Wilson, J., & Daniel, R. (1981). The effects of a career-options workshop on social and vocational stereotypes. *Vocational Guidance Quarterly*, *29*(4), 341–349.

Wingrove, C. R., & Slevin, K. F. (1982). Age differences and generational gaps: College women and their mothers' attitudes toward female roles in society. *Youth and Society*, *13*(3), 289–330.

Yanico, B. J. (1981). Sex-role self-concept and attitudes related to occupational daydreams and future fantasies of college women. *Journal of Vocational Behavior*, *19*(3), 290–301.

Yoder, J. D., Rice, R. W., Adams, J., Priest, R. F., & Prince, H. T. II. (1982). Reliability of the Attitudes Toward Women Scale (AWS) and the Personal Attributes Questionnaire (PAQ). *Sex Roles*, *8*(6), 651–657.

Zeldow, P. B., & Greenberg, R. P. (1979). Attitudes toward women and orientation to seeking professional psychological help. *Journal of Clinical Psychology*, *35*(2), 473–476.

Zeldow, P. B., & Greenberg, R. P. (1980). Who goes where: Sex-role differences in psychological and medical help seeking. *Journal of Personality Assessment*, *44*(4), 433–435.

Zuckerman, D. M. (1978). Retrospective study of interests and abilities that predict life goals and sex-role attitudes of college women. *Psychological Reports*, *43*(3), 1151–1157.

Zuckerman, D. M. (1979). The impact of education and selected traits on sex-role related goals and attitudes. *Journal of Vocational Behavior*, *14*(2), 248–254.

Zuckerman, D. M. (1980). Self-esteem, self-concept, and the life goals and sex-role attitudes of college students. *Journal of Personality*, *48*(2), 149–162.

Zuckerman, D. M. (1981a). Family background, sex-role attitudes, and life goals of technical college and university students. *Sex Roles*, *7*(11), 1109–1126.

Zuckerman, D. M. (1981b). Sex-role related goals and attitudes of minority students: A study of black college women and reentry students. *Journal of College Student Personnel, 22*(1), 23–30.
BIBLIOGRAPHY:
Beere, C. A. (1979). *Women and women's issues: A handbook of tests and measures* (pp. 390–398). San Francisco: Jossey-Bass.
Kalin, R., & Tilby, P. J. (1978). Development and validation of a sex-role ideology scale. *Psychological Reports, 42,* 731–738.
Moreland, J. R., & Van Tuinen, M. (1978, July). *The Attitude Toward Masculinity Transcendence Scale.* Paper presented at Ohio State University, Columbus.

ATTITUDES TOWARD WOMEN SCALE—BRITISH VERSION (AWS-B)

AUTHOR: Glenys Parry

DATE: 1983

VARIABLE: Attitudes toward women

TYPE OF INSTRUMENT: Summated rating scale

DESCRIPTION: The Attitudes Toward Women Scale—British Version (AWS-B) consists of 21 items pertaining to the rights, roles, and responsibilities of women. About half of the items reflect a contemporary, egalitarian view of women; the other half reflect a traditional view. Each item is accompanied by five response alternatives ranging from "disagree strongly" to "agree strongly."

SAMPLE ITEMS: If a woman goes out to work her husband should share the housework; such as washing dishes, cleaning and cooking.

Girls earning as much as their boyfriends should pay for themselves when going out with them.

PREVIOUS SUBJECTS: Working-class mothers in England; middle-class professional women in England; adolescents in London; men and women in the United States

APPROPRIATE FOR: Ages 14 and older

ADMINISTRATION: Self-administered; about 10 minutes

SCORING: Items are scored on a 5-point scale ranging from 0 to 4. Higher scores are assigned to the contemporary responses; lower scores are assigned to the traditional responses.

DEVELOPMENT: The AWS-B was developed from the 25-item short form of the Attitudes Toward Women Scale (AWS) (Spence & Helmreich, 1972) (see separate entry). Twenty-two items from the short form of the AWS "were simplified and Anglicized" (Parry, 1983, p. 261). Three items that were not easily simplified were omitted. Later, an additional item was omitted because it was ambiguous and did not seem to fit with the other items.

RELIABILITY: For a sample of 104 working-class mothers in England, item-total correlations ranged from .24 to .63. For these women, coefficient alpha was .77. Coefficient alpha for a sample of middle-class women was .85 (Parry, 1983). For a slightly modified AWS-B adminis-tered to 278 men and women, Nelson (1988) obtained a coefficient alpha of .84.

VALIDITY: As predicted, middle-class women, compared to working-class mothers, scored as consistently more liberal on the AWS-B (Parry, 1983).

NOTES & COMMENTS: (1) Item means and standard deviations for two samples of women are available from the British Lending Library, file number SUP 90069.

(2) Furnham and Singh (1986) used the AWS-B to test a selective recall hypothesis that persons with pro-female attitudes would be more likely to remember pro-female information and less likely to remember anti-female information.

(3) Nelson (1988) referred to the scale as the AWS-S on the grounds that there is nothing inherently British about the scale. AWS-S stands for AWS, short form; however, this can lead to confusion since there are other short forms of the AWS.

(4) Nelson (1988) modified the AWS-B by adding an item about equal rights in a divorce, simplifying the wording of some of the items, and making a few additional wording changes. Nelson administered the scale to 117 women and 161 men. She reported means and standard deviations for different social classes, sexes, and age groups. Alpha coefficients for these subgroups ranged from .78 to .85. Nelson found that more liberal attitudes were expressed by females, by younger persons, and by those of higher social status.

AVAILABLE FROM: Parry, 1983; Nelson, 1988
USED IN:

Furnham, A., & Singh, A. (1986). Memory for information about sex differences. *Sex Roles, 15*, 479–486.
Nelson, M. C. (1988). Reliability, validity, and cross-cultural comparisons for the simplified Attitudes Toward Women Scale. *Sex Roles,18*, 289–296.
Parry, G. (1983). A British version of the Attitudes Towards Women Scale (AWS-B). *British Journal of Social Psychology, 22*, 261–263.
BIBLIOGRAPHY:
Spence, J. T., & Helmreich, R. L. (1972). The Attitudes Toward Women Scale: An objective instrument to measure attitudes toward the rights and roles of women in contemporary society. *Catalog of Selected Documents in Psychology, 2*, 66. (Ms. No. 153)

ATTITUDES TOWARD WOMEN SCALE FOR ADOLESCENTS (AWSA)
AUTHORS: Nancy L. Galambos, Anne C. Petersen, Maryse Richards, and Idy B. Gitelson
DATE: 1985 (used 1977)
VARIABLE: Attitudes toward women

TYPE OF INSTRUMENT: Summated rating scale

DESCRIPTION: The Attitudes Toward Women Scale for Adolescents (AWSA) consists of 12 items, with about two-thirds of the items relating to girls or girls and boys. The remaining items deal with adults. Seven items are phrased to reflect a traditional view of females, and 5 items are phrased to reflect a contemporary view of females. Each item is accompanied by four response options ranging from "agree strongly" to "disagree strongly."

SAMPLE ITEMS: Swearing is worse for a girl than for a boy.

On a date, the boy should be expected to pay all expenses.

PREVIOUS SUBJECTS: Adolescents in grades 6 through 12

APPROPRIATE FOR: Ages 12 and older

ADMINISTRATION: Self-administered; about 5–10 minutes

SCORING: Items are individually scored on a 4-point scale, with 4 points assigned to the response that reflects a more contemporary attitude and 1 point assigned to the traditional response. Item scores are summed to yield a total score than can range from 12 to 48.

DEVELOPMENT: The items on the AWSA are based on items included on the short form of the Attitudes Toward Women Scale (AWS) (Spence, Helmreich, & Stapp, 1973) (see separate entry).

RELIABILITY: Galambos, Petersen, Richards, and Gitelson (1985) administered the AWSA to four different samples of adolescents in grades 6 through 12. They reported alpha coefficients for each group. For males, the coefficients ranged from .71 to .86 (average of .78); for females, the coefficients ranged from .62 to .85 (average of .72). Galambos et al. also reported item-total correlations separately for each sex within each group. One item had a low item-total correlation and was later replaced.

Test-retest reliabilities were estimated separately for boys and girls. Testings occurred once a year for a period of 3 years. For boys, the test-retest reliability was .73 between 6th and 7th grades and .60 between 7th and 8th grades. For girls, the test-retest reliability was .54 between 6th and 7th grades and .46 between 7th and 8th grades. Given the lengthy interval between successive testings, the correlation coefficients may be reflecting the fact that real changes in attitudes take place over the long time span. Interestingly, for girls, the test-retest correlation with a 2-year time span between testings (i.e., the correlation between 6th and 8th grade scores) was .62, higher than either of the correlations obtained with 1 year between testings.

VALIDITY: Galambos et al. (1985) found that girls, compared to boys, consistently expressed more contemporary views. They also found that for both boys and girls, respondents from a rural, lower-class community endorsed more conservative attitudes.

Galambos et al. (1985) looked at the relationships between AWSA

scores and Bem Sex Role Inventory scores (Bem, 1974) (see separate entry), scores on a measure of self-image and a measure of self-esteem, and attitudes toward division of labor and work plans. Many of their findings provided further support for the validity of the scale.
AVAILABLE FROM: Galambos, Petersen, Richards, and Gitelson, 1985
USED IN:
Galambos, N. L., Petersen, A. C., Richards, M., & Gitelson, I. B. (1985). The Attitudes Toward Women Scale for Adolescents (AWSA): A study of reliability and validity. *Sex Roles, 13*, 343–356.
BIBLIOGRAPHY:
Bem, S. L. (1974). The measurement of psychological androgyny. *Journal of Consulting and Clinical Psychology, 42*, 155–162.
Spence, J. T., Helmreich, R., & Stapp, J. (1973). A short version of the Attitudes Toward Women Scale (AWS). *Bulletin of the Psychonomic Society, 2*, 219–220.

AUTONOMY FOR WOMEN
AUTHOR: Catherine Cameron Arnott
DATE: 1971
VARIABLE: Attitude toward self-determination for women
DESCRIPTION: The Autonomy for Women scale is a summated rating scale consisting of 10 items, half reflecting a positive attitude toward self-determination for women and half reflecting a negative attitude. Items are accompanied by four response options ranging from strong agreement to strong disagreement.
ARTICLES LISTED IN BEERE, 1979: 5
AVAILABLE FROM: Arnott, 1972; Greenhouse and Rosenthal, 1974
USED IN:
Arnott, C. C. (1972). Husbands' attitude and wives' commitment to employment. *Journal of Marriage and the Family, 34*, 673–684.
Greenhouse, P., & Rosenthal, E. (1974). Attitudes toward women's rights to self-determination. *Journal of Family Counseling, 2*, 64–70.
Hertsgaard, D., & Light, H. K. (1984). Junior high girls' attitudes toward the rights and roles of women. *Adolescence, 19*, 847–853.
Light, H. K., Martin, R. E., & Hertsgaard, D. (1983). Farm women's attitudes toward change in work and family roles. *Research in Rural Education, 2(2)*, 59–64.
Martin, R. E., & Light, H. K. (1984). Education: Its positive impact on women. *College Student Journal, 18*, 401–405.
Venkatesh, A. (1980). Changing roles of women: A life-style and analysis. *Journal of Consumer Research, 7*, 189–197.
BIBLIOGRAPHY:
Beere, C. A. (1979). *Women and women's issues: A handbook of tests and measures* (pp. 401–402). San Francisco: Jossey-Bass.

BELIEF PATTERN SCALE FOR MEASURING ATTITUDES TOWARD FEMINISM
AUTHOR: Clifford Kirkpatrick
DATE: 1936

VARIABLE: Attitudes toward feminism

DESCRIPTION: The Belief Pattern Scale for Measuring Attitudes Toward Feminism is a checklist consisting of 80 items, with 10 profeminist and 10 antifeminist items in each of four areas: economic, domestic, political-legal, and conduct and social status.

ARTICLES LISTED IN BEERE, 1979: 22

NOTES & COMMENTS: Researchers often shorten or modify the Belief Pattern Scale for use in their research. Several researchers refer to using a 1973 modification by Lott.

AVAILABLE FROM: Kirkpatrick, 1936; Shaw and Wright, 1967, p. 280

USED IN:

Biaggio, M. K., Mohan, P. J., & Baldwin, C. (1981, August). *Relationships among attitudes toward children, women's liberation, and personality*. Paper presented at the meeting of the American Psychological Association, Los Angeles. (ERIC Document Reproduction Service No. ED 215 253)

Biaggio, M. K., Mohan, P. J., & Baldwin, C. (1985). Relationships among attitudes toward children, women's liberation, and personality characteristics. *Sex Roles, 12*, 47–62.

Gold, D., & Andres, D. (1978a). Comparisons of adolescent children with employed and nonemployed mothers. *Merrill Palmer Quarterly, 24*, 243–254.

Gold, D., & Andres, D. (1978b). Developmental comparisons between ten-year-old children with employed and nonemployed mothers. *Child Development, 49*, 75–84.

Kirkpatrick, C. (1936). The construction of a Belief-Pattern Scale for Measuring Attitudes Toward Feminism. *Journal of Social Psychology, 7*, 421–437.

Lott, B. E. (1973). Who wants the children? Some relationships among attitudes toward children, parents, and the liberation of women. *American Psychologist, 28*, 573–582.

Priestnall, R., Pilkington, G., & Moffat, G. (1978). Personality and the use of oral contraceptives in British university students. *Social Science and Medicine, 12*, 403–407.

Rosen, R. H., & Martindale, L. J. (1978). Sex role perceptions and the abortion decision. *Journal of Sex Research, 14*, 231–245.

Rosen, R. H., & Martindale, L. J. (1980). Abortion as "deviance": Traditional female roles vs. the feminist perspective. *Social Psychiatry, 15*, 103–108.

BIBLIOGRAPHY:

Beere, C. A. (1979). *Women and women's issues: A handbook of tests and measures* (pp. 403–406). San Francisco: Jossey-Bass.

Shaw, M. E., & Wright, J. M. (1967). *Scales for the measurement of attitudes*. New York: McGraw-Hill.

FEMINISM II SCALE

AUTHOR: Judith Ann Dempewolff

DATE: 1972

VARIABLE: Attitudes toward women

DESCRIPTION: The Feminism II Scale is a summated rating scale consisting of 28 items, each repeated a second time in the opposite direction;

that is, an item phrased to support feminism is rephrased to oppose feminism. Each of the 56 items is accompanied by four response options: "agree very much, agree a little, disagree a little, disagree a lot."
ARTICLES LISTED IN BEERE, 1979: 12
NOTES & COMMENTS: Some researchers use all 56 items; others use 28 items.
AVAILABLE FROM: Dempewolff, 1972; Tests in Microfiche, Test Collection, Educational Testing Service, Princeton, NJ 08541 (order #008695)
USED IN:

Berg, C. M. (1979). *Dental hygiene students' perceptions of themselves and their professional role in regard to feminism*. Unpublished paper, Old Dominion University. (ERIC Document Reproduction Service No. ED 197 692)

Dempewolff, J. A. (1972). Feminism and its correlates. (Doctoral dissertation, University of Cincinnati, 1972). *Dissertation Abstracts International, 33*, 3913–3914.

Gerson, M. (1978, August). *Motivations for motherhood*. Paper presented at the meeting of the American Psychological Association, Toronto. (ERIC Document Reproduction Service No. ED 184 010)

Gerson, M. (1980). The lure of motherhood. *Psychology of Women Quarterly, 5*, 207–218.

Gerson, M. (1983). A scale of motivation for parenthood: The Index of Parenthood Motivation. *Journal of Psychology, 113*, 211–220.

Gerson, M. (1984). Feminism and the wish for a child. *Sex Roles, 11*, 389–399.

Gerson, M. (1986). The prospect of parenthood for women and men. *Psychology of Women Quarterly, 10*, 49–62.

Orcutt, M. A., & Walsh, W. B. (1979). Traditionality and congruence of career aspirations for college women. *Journal of Vocational Behavior, 14*, 1–11.

Rapin, L. S., & Cooper, M. A. (1978, August). *Images of men and women: Comparing feminists and nonfeminists*. Paper presented at the meeting of the American Psychological Association, Toronto. (ERIC Document Reproduction Service No. ED 177 390)

Rapin, L. S., & Cooper, M. A. (1980). Images of men and women: A comparison of feminists and nonfeminists. *Psychology of Women Quarterly, 5*, 186–194.

Steiger, J. C. (1981). The influence of the feminist subculture in changing sex-role attitudes. *Sex Roles, 7*, 627–633.

Tetenbaum, T. J., Lighter, J., & Travis, M. (1983). The construct validation of an attitudes toward working mothers scale. *Psychology of Women Quarterly, 8*, 69–78.

Usher, S., & Fels, M. (1985). The challenge of feminism and career for the middle-aged woman. *International Journal of Women's Studies, 8*, 47–57.

Wenige, L. O. (1979). Preschool children's classification of adult apparel as related to parents' mode of dress and attitudes toward adult gender roles. *Psychological Reports, 45*, 209–210.

BIBLIOGRAPHY:
Beere, C. A. (1979). *Women and women's issues: A handbook of tests and measures* (pp. 420–423). San Francisco: Jossey-Bass.

FEMINISM SURVEY

AUTHOR: Harold Takooshian

DATE: 1983 (used 1980)

VARIABLE: Attitudes toward women

TYPE OF INSTRUMENT: Summated rating scale

DESCRIPTION: Takooshian defined feminism as perceived social and psychological equality for women and men (H. Takooshian, personal communication, November, 1988). The Feminism Survey consists of 15 statements covering a wide variety of issues relating to equality for men and women. Each item is accompanied by three response options: "agree, no opinion, disagree." The response options are represented by a single letter, A, N, or D, placed to the left of each item. The profeminist response is "disagree" for 12 items and "agree" for the other 3 items. Takooshian used an unusual layout in that the profeminist response, sometimes A and sometimes D, is always the response furthest to the left. H. Takooshian (personal communication, March 1989) claimed that this layout has a twofold purpose: to help break people's response set and to speed hand scoring (which takes about 10 seconds per form). Five items measuring authoritarianism are interspersed with the feminism items. The scale is available in English, Spanish, Chinese, and Armenian.

SAMPLE ITEMS: Women who do the same work as men should *not* necessarily get the same salary.

A woman should have more responsibility than a man in caring for a child.

PREVIOUS SUBJECTS: The English version has been completed by college and adult women in New York; the Spanish version has been completed by women in Chile; and the Armenian version has been completed by women in the Armenian Soviet Socialist Republic.

APPROPRIATE FOR: High school students and older in countries where they speak English, Spanish, Chinese, or Armenian.

ADMINISTRATION: Self-administered; about 10 minutes

SCORING: Items are individually scored, with 2 points assigned to the feminist response, 1 point assigned to the neutral response, and 0 points assigned to the antifeminist response. If more than three items are omitted, H. Takooshian (personal communication, November 1988) recommended discarding the survey for that respondent. Total scores can range from 0 (very antifeminist) to 30 (strongly feminist).

DEVELOPMENT: In 1972, Takooshian, along with two doctoral students, developed a 12-item structured interview schedule to profile the average woman's attitudes toward feminist issues. Emphasis was on content validity, with items drawn from topics addressed in *Ms.* magazine and literature obtained from the National Organization for

Women. Early results using the instrument serendipitously found it highly sensitive to ethnic differences, with white ethnic women scoring lower on the scale than nonethnic women. In 1980, the Feminism Survey was thoroughly revised by Takooshian. It was expanded to 20 items based on a correlational item analysis using newly collected data and embedding 5 items measuring authoritarianism; it was converted to a self-administered survey; and the item wording was slightly revised so that it could be answered by men as well as women. (One item, however, is still worded so that only women can easily answer it.) In 1984, the scale was translated into Spanish by a professional translator so that it could be understood by different Spanish dialects in Latin America and the Caribbean. In 1987, the Communist Party Youth magazine *Garun* translated the scale into Eastern-dialect Armenian.

RELIABILITY: Based on responses from 383 persons, coefficient alpha was .78. Using responses from 233 women, Takooshian and Stuart (1983) reported a split-half reliability of .63. Test-retest reliability was computed using responses from 22 college students who completed the survey on two occasions, separated by a 2-week interval. The reliability was .90. Alternate form reliability was estimated by comparing the responses from bilingual students. A group of 10 bilingual students completed the Spanish and English versions, about 1 to 2 weeks apart. The correlation between testings was .75. Another sample of 10 students and faculty completed the Armenian and English versions; the testings were 1 to 3 weeks apart. The correlation between testings was .79.

VALIDITY: Feminism scores correlated significantly with women's age: younger women showed greater support for equality. Feminism scores also correlated significantly with authoritarianism: greater authoritarianism was associated with less support for feminism. Feminism also correlated significantly with ethnicity, education, and being born overseas.

An open-ended question—"What is your general feeling about the feminism movement?"—was included along with the Feminism Survey. According to H. Takooshian (personal communication, November 1988), feminism scores seemed to match women's responses to this question.

A sample of 27 women completed the Feminism Survey and a 5-item version of Singleton and Christiansen's (1977) FEM scale (see separate entry). The correlation between the two scales was .64.

NOTES & COMMENTS: (1) H. Takooshian (personal communication, November 1988) recommended that the title at the top of the survey be "Opinion Survey" rather than "Feminism Survey." He noted that more conservative women, particularly at ethnic gatherings, would resist cooperating when they saw the title "Feminism Survey."

(2) Takooshian and Stuart (1983) compared the Feminism Survey

scores of women from five ethnic groups: Polish, Italian, Armenian, Cuban, and Irish.

AVAILABLE FROM: Order from NAPS c/o Microfiche Publications, P.O. Box 3513, Grand Central Station, New York, NY 10163–3513; NAPS document no. 04708; for microfiche, in U.S. remit $4.00 with order.

USED IN:

Takooshian, H. H., & Stuart, C. R. (1983). Ethnicity and feminism among American women: Opposing social trends? *International Journal of Group Tensions, 13,* 100–105.

BIBLIOGRAPHY:

Singleton, R., & Christiansen, L. (1977). The construct validation of a short form Attitudes Toward Feminism scale. *Sociology and Social Research, 61,* 294–303.

HAWLEY SEX ROLE SCALE

AUTHOR: Peggy Hawley

DATE: 1968

VARIABLE: Attitudes toward women

DESCRIPTION: The Hawley Sex Role Scale is a summated rating scale consisting of 35 items equally representing each of five factors: Woman as Partner, Woman as Ingenue, Woman as Homemaker, Woman as Competitor, and Woman as Knower. Each item is accompanied by six response alternatives ranging from "very strongly agree" to "very strongly disagree."

ARTICLES LISTED IN BEERE, 1979: 8

AVAILABLE FROM: Hawley, 1977; Barta, Halliburton, & Kiser, 1979; Young, Boser, and Layne, 1982.

USED IN:

Barta, S., Halliburton, C., & Kiser, L. (1979). *Project SERVES. Sexism in education: Reducing vocational education stereotypes.* Unpublished paper, Ames Community Schools, Ames, IA. (ERIC Document Reproduction Service No. ED 181 213)

Boser, J., Young, D., & Anderson, S. (1983, April). *Maximizing students' educational and career choices: Results of a two-year equity project.* Paper presented at the meeting of the American Educational Research Association, Montreal. (ERIC Document Reproduction Service No. ED 233 103)

Hawley, P. (1977). *Attitudes Toward Sex Roles Scale. Revised edition.* Unpublished paper, San Diego State University. (ERIC Document Reproduction Service No. ED 185 115)

Hawley, P., & Even, B. (1982). Work and sex-role attitudes in relation to education and other characteristics. *Vocational and Guidance Quarterly, 31,* 101–108.

Lynch, M. V. (1979). *Summary of results and handbook of ideas to reduce sex stereotyping in vocational education in students' career choices.* Unpublished paper,

Shawsheen Valley Regional Vocational-Technical High School, Billerica, MA. (ERIC Document Reproduction Service No. ED 187 893)

Regan, S. D. (1983, March). *Mandated multicultural education: Boon or boondoggle*. Paper presented at the meeting of the American Personnel and Guidance Association, Washington, DC. (ERIC Document Reproduction Service No. ED 239 155)

Verma, R. K., & Ghadially, R. (1985a). Effect of mother's sex role attitudes on need for achievement and expectancy for success in children. *Psychological Studies, 30*, 1–4.

Verma, R. K., & Ghadially, R. (1985b). Mother's sex-role attitudes and demands for independence training in boys and girls. *Indian Journal of Social Work, 46*, 105–111.

Yonge, G. D., & Regan, M. C. (1978). Female sex-role expectations and authoritarianism. *Psychological Reports, 43*, 415–418.

Yonge, G. D., & Regan, M. C. (1979). Females' sex-role expectations and major field of study. *Psychological Reports, 44*, 783–786.

Young, D., Boser, J., & Layne, B. (1982, March). *Reducing stereotypic attitudes: A prerequisite to educational equity*. Roundtable discussion at the meeting of the American Educational Research Association, New York. (ERIC Document Reproduction Service No. ED 218 382)

BIBLIOGRAPHY:

Beere, C. A. (1979). *Women and women's issues: A handbook of tests and measures* (pp. 428–430). San Francisco: Jossey-Bass.

LYSON SEX ROLE ATTITUDES SCALE

AUTHORS: Thomas A. Lyson and Susan S. Brown

DATE: 1982 (used 1977)

VARIABLE: Attitudes toward women

TYPE OF INSTRUMENT: Summated rating scale

DESCRIPTION: The Lyson Sex Role Attitudes Scale consists of nine items, most of which pertain to roles and responsibilities of women. Each item is accompanied by five response options ranging from "strongly agree" to "strongly disagree." A traditional view of women is expressed by agreeing with five items and disagreeing with four.

SAMPLE ITEMS: Women in college are more concerned with getting a husband than with preparing for a career.

The husband and wife should be equal partners in a marriage.

PREVIOUS SUBJECTS: College students

APPROPRIATE FOR: High school students and older

ADMINISTRATION: Self-administered; about 5 minutes

SCORING: Items are individually scored on a 5-point scale, with 5 points assigned to the feminist end of the continuum and 1 point assigned to the traditional end of the continuum. Total scores can range from 9 (very traditional) to 45 (very nontraditional). Scores can also be obtained on two factors: Appropriate Role Scale and Equality Scale. Lyson (1986) provided normative data, by race and sex, based on testing 1,426 black females, 754 black males, 1,737 white females, and 1,833 white males.

DEVELOPMENT: The items on the Lyson Sex Role Attitudes Scale were embedded in a larger scale used by the U.S. Department of Agriculture in a study of college students majoring in agriculture and home economics. No information was provided on the source of the items.

RELIABILITY: Lyson (1986) reported alpha coefficients for four groups based on sex and race. The results were: black females = .567; black males = .574; white females = .689; and white males = .720.

VALIDITY: Lyson (1986) found that males and females scored differently on every item on the scale, as well as on total scores. Females were consistently more nontraditional in their responses than were males.

NOTES & COMMENTS: (1) Lyson and Brown (1982) factor analyzed responses from a large group of college women majoring in agriculture or home economics. They extracted two factors. "The first factor loaded most heavily on items that reflect the primacy of work or family roles in a woman's life and is labeled 'appropriate role.' The second factor loaded most heavily on items that reflect issues of sexual [e]quality at home and in the work place and is labeled 'equality' " (Lyson & Brown, 1982, p. 371). According to Lyson and Brown, both scales had "acceptable reliability levels."

(2) Using responses from over 4,500 college students, Lyson (1986) performed a discriminant analysis and identified two statistically significant functions—one separating respondents along gender lines and the other separating respondents along racial lines.

AVAILABLE FROM: Lyson, 1986; Lyson and Brown, 1982

USED IN:

Lyson, T. A. (1986). Race and sex differences in sex role attitudes of southern college students. *Psychology of Women Quarterly, 10*(4), 421–428.

Lyson, T. A., & Brown, S. S. (1982). Sex role attitudes, curriculum choice, and career ambition: A comparison between women in typical and atypical college majors. *Journal of Vocational Behavior, 20*(3), 366–375.

NADLER OPEN SUBORDINATION OF WOMEN SCALE

AUTHORS: Eugene B. Nadler and William R. Morrow

DATE: 1957

VARIABLE: Attitudes toward women

DESCRIPTION: The Nadler Open Subordination of Women Scale is a summated rating scale consisting of 20 items pertaining to the following areas: social policies that restrict women and encourage their subordination to men; inferiority of women; narrowness of women's outlook; and offensiveness of women. All items are phrased to reflect a negative view of women. Items are accompanied by six response options ranging from "strongly agree" to "strongly disagree."

ARTICLES LISTED IN BEERE, 1979: 3
AVAILABLE FROM: Nadler and Morrow, 1959; Shaw and Wright, 1967, p. 459
USED IN:

Ayers, J. B., Rohr, M. E., & Rohr, E. M. (1977, March). *Attitudes toward women, college major and authoritarianism.* Paper presented at the meeting of the Mid-South Educational Research Association, Birmingham. (ERIC Document Reproduction Service No. ED 157 927)

Ayers, J. B., Rohr, M. E., & Rohr, E. M. (1978). College major, authoritarianism and attitudes toward women. *College Student Journal, 12,* 236–239.

Leventhal, G. (1977). Female criminality: Is "women's lib" to blame? *Psychological Reports, 41*(3), 1179–1182.

Nadler, E. B., & Morrow, W. R. (1959). Authoritarian attitudes toward women and their correlates. *Journal of Social Psychology, 49,* 113–123.

Sattem, L., Savella, J., & Murray, E. (1984). Sex-role stereotypes and commitment of rape. *Sex Roles, 11,* 849–860.

BIBLIOGRAPHY:

Beere, C. A. (1979). *Women and women's issues: A handbook of tests and measures* (pp. 446–447). San Francisco: Jossey-Bass.

Shaw, M. E., & Wright, J. M. (1967). *Scales for the measurement of attitudes.* New York: McGraw-Hill.

POSITIVE REGARD SCALE

AUTHORS: Shirley Ross and James Walters
DATE: 1973
VARIABLE: Positive regard for women
DESCRIPTION: The Positive Regard Scale is a summated rating scale consisting of 32 items regarding the personality traits, ability, and behavior of women in comparison to men. About one-third of the items are phrased to reflect a positive regard for women; the remaining items reflect a negative regard for women. Items are accompanied by five response options ranging from "strongly agree" to "strongly disagree."
ARTICLES LISTED IN BEERE, 1979: 1
AVAILABLE FROM: Ross and Walters, 1973
USED IN:

Berryman-Fink, C., & Wheeless, V. E. (1984, February). *Effects of attitudes toward women and women in management on perceived communication competencies of women managers.* Paper presented at the meeting of the Western Speech Communication Association, Seattle. (ERIC Document Reproduction Service No. ED 241 975)

Ross, S., & Walters, J. (1973). Perceptions of a sample of university men concerning women. *Journal of Genetic Psychology, 122,* 329–336.

Wheeless, V. E., & Berryman-Fink, C. (1985). Perceptions of women managers and their communicator competencies. *Communication Quarterly, 33*(2), 137–148.

BIBLIOGRAPHY:
Beere, C. A. (1979). *Women and women's issues: A handbook of tests and measures* (pp. 188–189). San Francisco: Jossey-Bass.

SEXIST ATTITUDES TOWARD WOMEN SCALE (SATWS)

AUTHORS: Peter L. Benson and Steven Vincent

DATE: 1980 (used 1974)

VARIABLE: Tendency toward, and support for, discrimination against women

TYPE OF INSTRUMENT: Summated rating scale

DESCRIPTION: The Sexist Attitudes Toward Women Scale (SATWS) contains 40 items with at least 4 items from each of six content areas described below (see DEVELOPMENT). Sixteen items are phrased in a nonsexist direction; the other 24 are phrased in a sexist direction. Each item is accompanied by seven response options ranging from "strongly agree" to "strongly disagree."

SAMPLE ITEMS: If I had a daughter, I would discourage her from working on cars.

I get angry at women who complain that American society is unfair to them.

PREVIOUS SUBJECTS: High school students, college students, and adults

APPROPRIATE FOR: High school students and older

ADMINISTRATION: Self-administered; about 15–20 minutes

SCORING: Items are individually scored on a 7-point scale, with the nonsexist end of the continuum assigned the low scores (1, 2, 3) and the sexist end of the continuum assigned the high scores (5, 6, 7). Item scores are summed to yield a total score that can range from 40 (very nonsexist) to 280 (very sexist).

Benson and Vincent (1980) provided score ranges, means, and standard deviations, separately by sex, for high school students, college students, and adults. For the adult sample, they also provided score ranges, means, and standard deviations, by sex, for different age groups, and for different educational levels.

DEVELOPMENT: Benson and Vincent (1980) began by defining sexist attitudes toward women as "attitudes which function to place females in a position of relative inferiority to males by limiting women's social, political, economic, and psychological development" (p. 278). They then established the following seven components of sexism: "1. Attitudes that women are genetically inferior (biologically, emotionally, intellectually) to men. 2. Support for the premise that men should have greater rights and power than women. 3. Support for sex discrimination (antifemale) practices in education, work, and politics. 4. Hostility toward women who engage in traditionally masculine roles and behaviors or who fail to fulfill traditional female roles. 5. Lack of support and empathy for women's liberation movements and the issues involved in such movements. 6. Utilization of derogatory labels and restrictive stereotypes in describing women. 7. Evaluation of women on the basis of physical attractiveness information and willingness to treat women as sexual objects" (p. 278). A pool of 141 items was compiled, with 20 or 21 statements measuring each of these components. About half of the statements were phrased in a sexist direction; the other half were phrased in a nonsexist direction. Each item was accompanied by seven response options ranging from "strongly disagree" to "strongly agree." The item pool was administered to 402 adults and 484 college students, and their responses were used to reduce the size of the item pool.

Items were deleted if "(a) one of the response categories was higher than 50%; (b) more than three of the seven categories had less than a 10% response rate; and (c) the middle response category (neither agree nor disagree) was above 30%" (Benson & Vincent, 1980, p. 279). Applying these criteria, the item pool was left with 91 items, but one of the original seven categories was left with only 5 items. There was very little variability in the responses to these 5 items, and so two categories— (2) and (3) above—were combined into "belief for the premise that men are entitled to greater power, prestige, and social advantage" (p. 279). There were thus six categories, and 10 items were selected for each category. Response variability and a response frequency of at least 10% for at least five of the seven response options were the criteria for item selection.

Using data from the original sample of 886 subjects, scale intercorrelations were calculated. The intercorrelations ranged from .63 to .86, which led Benson and Vincent (1980) to conclude that there was little point in retaining separate subscales. They therefore combined the six areas, retained 40 items that had the highest intercorrelations with the other items on the scale, and used this as the final version of the scale. The 40 items included at least 4 items from each of the six areas defined. RELIABILITY: Using the data from the original sample on whom the scale was developed, Benson and Vincent (1980) calculated coefficient alpha for the 40-item scale to be .91. Administering the test to other samples, they found coefficient alpha to be .90 for college students and .93 for adults.

Buhrke (1988) administered the SATWS to 184 college students and obtained a coefficient alpha of .94. Buhrke also reported alpha coefficients for several subscales: Attitudes of Women's Inferiority to Men = .86; Support for Sex Discrimination = .79; Hostility Toward Women in Nontraditional Roles = .57; Lack of Support for the Women's Movement = .65; Use of Derogatory Labels = .72; and Objectification of Women = .88.

VALIDITY: The SATWS and the Marlowe-Crowne Social Desirability Scale (Crowne & Marlowe, 1960) were administered to 58 adults. The correlation between scores was − .03, indicating that the SATWS was not measuring a general tendency to respond in socially desirable ways.

Benson and Vincent (1980) asked a sample of 58 adults to complete the SATWS along with eight other measures that they expected to correlate with the SATWS scores. Briefly, these eight measures were: ratings of attractive and unattractive females, ratings of artwork attributed to male/female artists, evaluation of sexist jokes, Spence and Helmreich's (1972) Attitudes Toward Women Scale (see separate entry), a measure of sex-role stereotypes, a measure of support for the women's movement, ratings of magazines, and a self-report of driving frequency relative to partner/spouse/lover. The SATWS was significantly correlated with every one of these measures; the range of correlations was .29 to .76.

In another series of four studies, each using a different sample, Benson and Vincent (1980) further confirmed the construct validity of the scale. They found a significant correlation ($r = -.75$) between SATWS scores and support for the equal rights amendment; they found that persons participating in a consciousness-raising group were significantly less sexist than nonparticipants; they found, as predicted, that scores on the SATWS were not related to scores on a creativity measure ($r = -.12$); and they found, as predicted, that scores on the SATWS were not related to scores on a measure of social responsibility ($r = .08$).

Buhrke (1988) administered the SATWS and three other gender role attitude scales to 184 college students. The other scales were the Attitudes Toward Women Scale (Spence & Helmreich, 1972), the Attitude Toward Masculinity Transcendence Scale (Moreland & Van Tuinen, 1978) (see separate entry), and the Sex-Role Ideology Scale (Kalin & Tilby, 1978) (see separate entry). Additionally, Buhrke administered the Marlowe-Crowne Social Desirability Scale (Crowne & Marlowe, 1960). The correlation between the SATWS and the other scales were as follows: the Sex-Role Ideology Scale = − .74; the Attitudes Toward Women Scale = − .81; and the Attitude Toward Masculinity Transcendence Scale = − .85. Buhrke also reported all of the subscale intercorrelations. The correlation between the SATWS and the Marlowe-Crowne Social Desirability Scale was − .06. Buhrke obtained significant correlations between the SATWS and several single-item scales expected to correlate with SATWS scores.

Jones and Jacklin (1988) tested 244 college women and 161 college men with the SATWS. As expected, they found that males were more sexist in their attitudes than were females.

NOTES & COMMENTS: (1) The psychometric properties of this scale suggest it has potential value. Internal consistency is excellent; content validity was assured by the method of scale development; and criterion-

related validity was amply demonstrated. No data were provided regarding test-retest reliability, but this could be easily assessed. The items
are still appropriate, though it has been a long time since they were first
used. What is not clear is why this scale has not been used by other
researchers.

(2) Buhrke (1988) factor analyzed the subscores from several sex role
ideology measures. She included subscale scores she defined from the
SATWS in the factor analysis.

(3) Jones and Jacklin (1988) used the SATWS as a pretest and posttest
measure to study the impact of a gender studies course on the attitudes
of college men and women. They also related scores on the SATWS to
scores on the Bem Sex Role Inventory (Bem, 1974) (see separate entry).

AVAILABLE FROM: Benson and Vincent, 1980

USED IN:

Benson, P. L., & Vincent, S. (1980). Development and validation of the Sexist
    Attitudes Toward Women Scale (SATWS). *Psychology of Women Quarterly*,
    5(2), 276–291.
Buhrke, R. A. (1988). Factor dimensions across different measures of sex role
    ideology. *Sex Roles*, 18, 309–321.
Jones, G. P., & Jacklin, C. N. (1988). Changes in sexist attitudes toward women
    during introductory women's and men's studies courses. *Sex Roles*, 18(9/
    10), 611–622.

BIBLIOGRAPHY:

Bem, S. L. (1974). The measurement of psychological androgyny. *Journal of Con-
    sulting and Clinical Psychology*, 42, 155–162.
Crowne, D. P., & Marlowe, D. (1960). A new scale of social desirability inde-
    pendent of psychopathology. *Journal of Consulting Psychology*, 24, 349–354.
Kalin, R., & Tilby, P. J. (1978). Development and validation of a sex-role ideology
    scale. *Psychological Reports*, 42, 731–738.
Moreland, J. R., & Van Tuinen, M. (1978, July). *The Attitude Toward Masculinity
    Transcendence Scale*. Paper presented at Ohio State University, Columbus.
Spence, J. T., & Helmreich, R. L. (1972). The Attitudes Toward Women Scale:
    An objective instrument to measure attitudes toward the rights and roles
    of women in contemporary society. *Catalog of Selected Documents in Psy-
    chology*, 2, 66. (Ms. No. 153)

SOCIAL ORDER SCALE (SOS)

AUTHORS: Leonard Worell and Judith Worell

DATE: 1977

VARIABLE: Attitudes regarding the issues raised by the feminist movement

DESCRIPTION: The Social Order Scale (SOS) is a summated rating scale
consisting of 14 items regarding feminist issues. The first 7 items are
statements relating to feminist issues. The statements are accompanied
by six response alternatives ranging from "strongly agree" to "strongly
disagree." The remaining 7 items are phrases related to feminist issues.

Each phrase is accompanied by six response options ranging from "strongly approve" to "strongly disapprove."
ARTICLES LISTED IN BEERE, 1979: 1
AVAILABLE FROM: Judith Worell, Department of Educational Psychology, University of Kentucky, Lexington, KY 40506
USED IN:
Abbott, M. W., & Koopman-Boyden, P. G. (1981). Expectations and predictors of the division of labour within marriage. *New Zealand Psychologist, 10,* 24–32.
Koopman-Boyden, P. G., & Abbott, M. (1985). Expectations for household task allocation and actual task allocation: A New Zealand study. *Journal of Marriage and the Family, 47,* 211–219.
BIBLIOGRAPHY:
Beere, C. A. (1979). *Women and women's issues: A handbook of tests and measures* (pp. 462–463). San Francisco: Jossey-Bass.

THERAPISTS' ATTITUDE TOWARD WOMEN SCALE (TAWS)
AUTHORS: Julia Sherman, Corinne Koufacos, and Joy Anne Kenworthy
DATE: 1978
VARIABLE: Attitudes toward women regarding the goals and/or process of psychotherapy
TYPE OF INSTRUMENT: Summated rating scale
DESCRIPTION: The Therapists' Attitude Toward Women Scale (TAWS) consists of 32 items that can be classified as follows: 10 items pertain to psychoanalytic theory but are not consistent with current views; 13 items portray traditional gender role attitudes; 3 items deal with sexuality; 4 items reflect sexist attitudes; and 2 items deal directly with therapists. All of the items relate directly or indirectly to the process or goals of therapy for women or to standards of women's mental health. Each item is accompanied by five response options: "strongly agree, agree, neither agree nor disagree, disagree, strongly disagree." Fifteen items are phrased so that "strongly agree" expresses a feminist attitude; the remaining 17 items are phrased so that a feminist attitude is expressed by the "strongly disagree" response.
SAMPLE ITEMS: Dependency should not be considered more characteristic of a healthy woman than of a healthy man.
   The cure of frigidity is an important goal for women clients.
PREVIOUS SUBJECTS: Social workers, psychologists, psychiatrists, and psychiatric residents
APPROPRIATE FOR: Experienced therapists or persons training to be therapists
ADMINISTRATION: Self-administered; about 15 minutes
SCORING: Items are individually scored on a 5-point scale. The response keyed most liberal is assigned 1 point, and the response keyed most

traditional is assigned 5 points. Total scores can range from 32 (very liberal) to 160 (very traditional).

DEVELOPMENT: Little information was provided other than the authors' statement that "all items were original, and final selection for inclusion in the scales was made after consultation with several colleagues" (Sherman, Koufacos, & Kenworthy, 1978, p. 303).

RELIABILITY: When the TAWS was completed by 184 therapists, coefficient alpha was .86.

VALIDITY: Female therapists were significantly more liberal than male therapists on the total scores and on 10 individual items.

NOTES & COMMENTS: (1) Sherman et al. (1978) administered the TAWS along with the Therapists' Information About Women Scale (TIWS) (see separate entry); the correlation between the two measures was .57 for all therapists participating in the research. For some subgroups, however, the correlation was considerably lower; for example, for male social workers, the correlation was .29.

(2) Stark-Adamec, Graham, and Adamec (1985) combined the items from the TAWS with the items from the TIWS and added seven other items. They administered the expanded scale to faculty and residents associated with a department of psychiatry and found that their sample "responded with a generally liberal orientation" (p. 493).

(3) Stark-Adamec et al. (1985) suggested the following 10 groupings for the 32 items on the TAWS: "Therapy Goals, Therapeutic Styles/Attitudes/Approaches, Sex and Therapy, Marriage/Family/Career, The Mentally Healthy Female, Female Personality Traits, Feminist Therapy, Freudian Theory and Female Mental Health, Feminist Philosophy, Abortion Decisions" (p. 494).

AVAILABLE FROM: Sherman, Koufacos, and Kenworthy, 1978
USED IN:

Sherman, J., Koufacos, C., & Kenworthy, J. A. (1978). Therapists: Their attitudes and information about women. *Psychology of Women Quarterly*, 2(4), 299–313.

Stark-Adamec, C., Graham J. M., & Adamec, R. E. (1985). Clients and therapists: Women and men. *International Journal of Women's Studies*, 8(5), 490–503.

THERAPISTS' INFORMATION ABOUT WOMEN SCALE (TIWS)

AUTHORS: Julia Sherman, Corinne Koufacos, and Joy Anne Kenworthy
DATE: 1978
VARIABLE: Knowledge of the personality traits and biological functioning of women
TYPE OF INSTRUMENT: Summated rating scale
DESCRIPTION: The Therapists' Information About Women Scale

(TIWS) consists of 24 items: "(1) five items with empirical support but contrary to some aspect of psychoanalytic theory, (2) seven items related to unique female biological functioning, (3) four sexual items, (4) two items regarding therapists, and (5) six miscellaneous items" (Sherman, Koufacos, & Kenworthy, 1978, p. 303). Each item is accompanied by five response options ranging from "strongly disagree" to "strongly agree." Though the items resemble attitude statements, particularly because of the response choices, there is, in fact, a correct answer to each item. Eleven items are true, so the correct answer is "agree" or "strongly agree"; 13 items are false, so the correct answer is "disagree" or "strongly disagree."

SAMPLE ITEMS: People tend to regard women as incompetent until proven competent, while men are regarded as competent until proven incompetent.

Women have a less strict conscience than men.

PREVIOUS SUBJECTS: Social workers, psychologists, psychiatrists, and psychiatric residents

APPROPRIATE FOR: Experienced therapists or persons training to be therapists

ADMINISTRATION: Self-administered; about 10–15 minutes

SCORING: The items are individually scored on a 5-point scale. When the statement is true, "strongly agree" is assigned 1 point, "agree" is assigned 2 points, "neutral" is assigned 3 points, "disagree" is assigned 4 points, and "strongly disagree" is assigned 5 points. Scoring is reversed on items where the statement is false. Total scores can range from 24 (all correct) to 120 (all incorrect).

DEVELOPMENT: No information was provided other than the authors' statement that "all items were original, and final selection for inclusion in the scales was made after consultation with several colleagues" (Sherman et al., 1978, p. 303).

RELIABILITY: When the responses from 184 therapists were analyzed, coefficient alpha was .62, which is too low.

VALIDITY: As expected, the study of therapists revealed significant sex differences in that female therapists were more knowledgeable overall than were male therapists. Furthermore, there were significant sex differences on seven of the individual items.

NOTES & COMMENTS: (1) Sherman et al. (1978) acknowledged wording problems with some of the items. Using suggestions from therapists, they offered alternative wording for five items.

(2) Given that there is a correct answer to each item, it is difficult to know the difference between endorsing the correct answer or strongly endorsing the correct answer. Does "strongly agree" or "strongly disagree" mean that a person is more certain of the correctness of the choice,

or do people select the "strongly" response when they have stronger feelings about the subject, or are some people more inclined to select the "strongly" answer than are other people?

(3) Stark-Adamec, Graham, and Adamec (1985) combined the items from the TIWS with the items from the Therapists' Attitude Toward Women Scale (Sherman et al., 1978) (see separate entry) and added seven other items. They administered the scale to faculty and residents associated with a department of psychiatry and found that their sample "responded with a generally liberal orientation" (p. 493).

(4) Stark-Adamec et al. (1985) noted that the 24 items on the TIWS can be combined into seven groupings: "Menstruation/Menopause, Pregnancy/Motherhood, Women as Clients, Female Social Status, Personality Dynamics, Female Sexual Response, Rape Victims" (p. 494).

AVAILABLE FROM: Sherman, Koufacos, and Kenworthy, 1978

USED IN:

Sherman, J., Koufacos, C., & Kenworthy, J. A. (1978). Therapists: Their attitudes and information about women. *Psychology of Women Quarterly*, 2(4), 299–313.

Stark-Adamec, C., Graham, J. M., & Adamec, R. E. (1985). Clients and therapists: Women and men. *International Journal of Women's Studies*, 8(5), 490–503.

TRAVIS SEIPP SEX-ROLE IDEOLOGY SCALE

AUTHORS: Cheryl Brown Travis and Patricia Hudspeth Seipp

DATE: 1978

VARIABLE: Attitudes toward women

TYPE OF INSTRUMENT: Summated rating scale

DESCRIPTION: The Travis Seipp Sex-Role Ideology Scale is a brief measure consisting of six items. Five are statements, and one is phrased as a question. Two items pertain to "educational and occupational equality" for women; two deal with "the possibility of expanding the traditional female role"; one pertains to "sexual freedom for females"; and one asks about women's emotionality in regards to men's. Information on response options is not provided other than to indicate that a 15-point Likert-type scale was used.

SAMPLE ITEMS: A woman is most happy and most fulfilled when she devotes her energies to caring for her children.

A woman should be able to pursue her educational and occupational goals regardless of whether or not she is married.

PREVIOUS SUBJECTS: College students and adults; husbands and wives

APPROPRIATE FOR: High school students and older

ADMINISTRATION: Self-administered; less than 5 minutes

SCORING: Information is not provided for obtaining scale scores. However, Travis and Seipp (1978) indicated that they used scores to classify persons as traditional (one standard deviation below the mean), contemporary (one standard deviation above the mean), or moderate (within one standard deviation of the mean).

DEVELOPMENT: Travis and Seipp provided no information other than to say that they wrote the items.

RELIABILITY: Coefficient alpha for a sample of 635 persons was .83.

VALIDITY: A sample of 48 persons completed the Travis Seipp Sex-Role Ideology Scale along with the Wellesley Role Orientation Questionnaire (Alper, 1973) (see separate entry) and the Attitudes Toward Women Scale (AWS) (Spence & Helmreich, 1972) (see separate entry), both of which are considerably longer measures of attitudes. The correlation between the Travis Seipp Sex-Role Ideology Scale and the Wellesley Role Orientation Questionnaire was .53; the correlation between the Travis Seipp Sex-Role Ideology Scale and the AWS was .73.

Travis and Seipp (1978) stated: "Each item discriminated clearly and significantly (at the .01 level or better) between the contemporary and traditional subjects" (p. 529).

NOTES & COMMENTS: (1) An item analysis by Travis and Seipp (1978) showed that every item was significantly correlated with the other items on the measure, and every item was significantly correlated with the total score.

(2) Haskell (1979) used the Travis Seipp Sex-Role Ideology Scale with 35 husbands and wives and compared their scores with results on a marital satisfaction scale.

AVAILABLE FROM: Travis and Seipp, 1978

USED IN:

Haskell, S. D. (1979, March). *Marital adjustment correlates in young couples.* Paper presented at the meeting of the Southeastern Psychological Association, New Orleans. (ERIC Document Reproduction Service No. ED 174 897)

Travis, C. B., & Seipp, P. H. (1978). An examination of secondary reinforcement, operant conditioning, and status envy hypotheses in relation to sex-role ideology. *Sex Roles, 4*(4), 525–538.

BIBLIOGRAPHY:

Alper, T. (1973). The relationship between role orientation and achievement motivation in college women. *Journal of Personality, 41,* 9–31.

Spence, J. T., & Helmreich, R. L. (1972). The Attitudes Toward Women Scale: An objective instrument to measure attitudes toward the rights and roles of women in contemporary society. *Catalog of Selected Documents in Psychology, 2,* 66. (Ms. No. 153)

WOMEN IN SOCIETY QUESTIONNAIRE (WSQ)

AUTHORS: Virginia Lewis and Norma Grieve

DATE: 1986

VARIABLE: Attitudes toward women in contemporary society

TYPE OF INSTRUMENT: Summated rating scale

DESCRIPTION: The Women in Society Questionnaire (WSQ) consists of two 6-item subscales: Work Roles, containing items concerning financial astuteness, advancement of women's careers and abilities for job success, and Social Roles, with items concerning social roles or issues. Each item is accompanied by six response options ranging from "agree strongly" to "disagree strongly."

SAMPLE ITEMS: (Work Roles) A woman should be less willing than a man to accept a career promotion that requires a family to move interstate.

(Social Roles) A man is as entitled to expect doors to be opened for him as a woman is.

PREVIOUS SUBJECTS: Ages 16 and older

APPROPRIATE FOR: High school students and older

ADMINISTRATION: Self-administered; about 10 minutes

SCORING: Items are individually scored on a 6-point scale, with 6 points assigned to the egalitarian end of the continuum. Total scores can range from 12 (very traditional) to 72 (very egalitarian).

DEVELOPMENT: A pool of 60 items was constructed to represent five content areas: personal relations, paid labor issues, stereotypes about women, the ideology of equality, and attitudes to the assignment of parental and domestic responsibility. The initial item pool was administered to 77 persons, ages 17 to 39, attending a weekend Christian camp. The pool was reduced to 28 items by eliminating items with item-total correlations below .30 and retaining representation from all five content areas. With further testing, Lewis and Grieve discovered that the 28-item version had satisfactory internal consistency ($r = .89$), correlated significantly ($r = .80$) with a 15-item version of the Attitudes Toward Women Scale (AWS) (Spence & Helmreich, 1978) (see separate entry), and discriminated between members of known groups: a women's church group, two women's political activist groups (one more radical than the other), policemen, a soccer club, gay-rights groups, and college students.

Lewis and Grieve selected 22 of the 28 items for further investigation. The items selected were representative of the five content areas and "loaded maximally on to the first function in the discriminant analysis" (Lewis, Grieve, Bell, & Bartlett, 1988, p. 12).

The 22 items were administered to 453 college students. Using results from exploratory and confirmatory factor analyses and the partial credit Rasch model of analysis of rating scales, Lewis and Grieve reduced the scale to 12 items, including two 6-item subscales.

RELIABILITY: The internal consistency reliability of the 12-item scale was .85. For the Work Roles subscale, the reliability was .80; for the Social Roles subscale, the reliability was .71.

VALIDITY: The correlation between the 12-item version of the scale and the 22-item version of the scale was .96. The correlation between the two subscale scores was .67.

Based on testing 453 college students, there were significant and predictable sex differences on both subscale scores and on the total score. NOTES & COMMENTS: According to Lewis and Grieve (1987): "The WSQ was conceived as a replacement for Spence and Helmreich's AWS which has been criticized for the dated content of its items. The strength of the WSQ is that the data was [sic] found to fit the partial credit Rasch model of rating scales. This indicates that the WSQ has the properties of item and sample independence which allow generalization of measurement, including comparison of different populations over time" (V. Lewis & N. Grieve, personal communication, December 11, 1988). In the same communication, Lewis and Grieve also reported that "the AWS was submitted to latent trait analysis and found not to fit the partial credit model."
AVAILABLE FROM: Virginia Lewis or Norma Grieve, Department of Psychology, University of Melbourne, Parkville, Victoria, 3052, Australia
USED IN:
Lewis, V. J. (1988). *Measuring attitudes to women: Development of the Women in Society Questionnaire (WSQ)*. Unpublished master's thesis.
Lewis, V. J., & Grieve, N. (1987). *Measuring attitudes to women*. Paper presented at the Australian Social Psychology Conference, Canberra, Australia.
Lewis, V., Grieve, N., Bell, R., & Bartlett, W. (1988, August). *Measuring attitudes to women: Development of the Women in Society Questionnaire (WSQ)*. Paper presented at the International Congress of Psychology, Sydney, Australia.
BIBLIOGRAPHY:
Spence, J. T., & Helmreich, R. L. (1978). *Masculinity and femininity: Their psychological dimensions, correlates, and antecedents*. Austin: University of Texas Press.

WOMEN'S LIBERATION IDEOLOGY SCALE
AUTHORS: Jean Goldschmidt, Mary M. Gergen, Karen Quigley, and Kenneth J. Gergen
DATE: 1974
VARIABLE: Attitudes toward issues advocated by the feminist movement
DESCRIPTION: The Women's Liberation Ideology Scale is a summated rating scale consisting of 12 items dealing with feminist issues. Each item is accompanied by five response options ranging from "strongly agree" to "strongly disagree."
ARTICLES LISTED IN BEERE, 1979: 3
AVAILABLE FROM: Goldschmidt, Gergen, Quigley, and Gergen, 1974

USED IN:

Goldschmidt, J., Gergen, M. M., Quigley, K., & Gergen, K. J. (1974). The women's liberation movement: Attitudes and action. *Journal of Personality, 42,* 601–617.

Jones, W. H., Chernovetz, M. E., & Hansson, R. O. (1978). The enigma of androgyny: Differential implications for males and females? *Journal of Consulting and Clinical Psychology, 46,* 298–313.

BIBLIOGRAPHY:

Beere, C. A. (1979). *Women and women's issues: A handbook of tests and measures* (pp. 467–468). San Francisco: Jossey-Bass.

WOMEN'S LIBERATION SCALE (WLS)

AUTHOR: Carlos Goldberg

DATE: 1975

VARIABLE: Attitudes toward positions advocated by the feminist movement

DESCRIPTION: The Women's Liberation Scale (WLS) is a summated rating scale consisting of 14 items relating to feminist issues. All items are phrased to reflect feminist attitudes. The response options are altered in that sometimes the response "strongly agree" is the first option, and sometimes the response "strongly disagree" is the first option.

ARTICLES LISTED IN BEERE, 1979: 2

AVAILABLE FROM: Goldberg, 1976

USED IN:

Baucom, D. H., & Sanders, B. S. (1978). Masculinity and femininity as factors in feminism. *Journal of Personality Assessment, 42,* 378–384.

Goldberg, C. (1976). Women's Liberation Scale (WLS): A measure of attitude toward positions advocated by women's groups. *Catalog of Selected Documents in Psychology, 6,* 13. (Ms. No. 1187)

BIBLIOGRAPHY:

Beere, C. A. (1979). *Women and women's issues: A handbook of tests and measures* (pp. 469–470). San Francisco: Jossey-Bass.

WOMEN'S SOCIAL FREEDOM SCALE (WSFS)

AUTHOR: L. I. Bhushan

DATE: 1981

VARIABLE: Women's desire for social freedom in India

TYPE OF INSTRUMENT: Alternate choice: agree/disagree

DESCRIPTION: The author defined "social freedom" as "women's desire to be free from social taboos, conventions, rituals and roles which provide them with lower status in society" (Bhushan, 1987, p. 5). The Women's Social Freedom Scale (WSFS) consists of 24 statements that pertain to whether women should or should not have freedom in a variety of spheres of life: "Freedom from control or interference of parents and husband"; "Freedom from social taboos, customs and rituals

which impose conventional roles and restrictions on girls/women";
"Freedom concerning sex and marriage"; and "Economic freedom and
social equality" (Bhushan, 1987, p. 5). Most items express support for
the social freedom of women; eight items are phrased in the opposite
direction. Each item is accompanied by two responses: agree and disagree.

SAMPLE ITEMS: Marriage or selection of the life-partner should be
based on the choice of girls.

If the wife wishes to take up a job, the interference of her husband
is absolutely improper.

PREVIOUS SUBJECTS: College and adult women in India

APPROPRIATE FOR: Persons in India, ages 14 and older

ADMINISTRATION: Self-administered; about 10–15 minutes

SCORING: For the items phrased in the positive direction, agreement
is scored 1, and disagreement is scored 0. Scoring for the eight negative
items is reversed. Item scores are summed to yield a total score that can
range from 0 (strongly opposed to social freedom for women) to 24
(strongly supportive of social freedom for women). In the test manual,
Bhushan (1987) provides percentile equivalents based on responses from
500 females.

DEVELOPMENT: Open-ended interviews were held with 30 college
women in India. Based on their responses, six specific areas of social
freedom were identified: "Freedom from parental control, Freedom from
interference or control of husband, Freedom from social customs and
rituals, Freedom from social taboos and control on girls, Freedom from
marriage bondage, Economic freedom and equality" (Bhushan, 1981b,
p. 240). A pool of 60 items relating to these areas was developed and
given to 10 judges to rate whether each statement was related to one of
the six areas and to indicate whether there was overlap among any of
the items. The judges agreed that 52 items related to the six content
areas, but 2 of these items were dropped because of overlapping content.
The remaining 50 items were administered to college women in India,
and an item analysis was performed on their responses. Those with the
highest 30% of the scores were compared with those with the lowest
30% of the scores to determine which items discriminated between the
two groups. As a result of this analysis, 24 items were found to discriminate, and these 24 items were retained for the scale.

RELIABILITY: A sample of 100 college women completed the test in
India. The odd-even, split-half reliability for the sample was .86; the first
half–second half, split-half reliability was .90. Eighty of these college
women completed the scale a second time after a 4-week interval. The
test-retest reliability was .79.

VALIDITY: As predicted, married women and housewives were less
supportive of social freedom for women than were unmarried college

women. Furthermore, there was a positive, significant correlation between scores on the WSFS scale and a measure of radicalism.

NOTES & COMMENTS: (1) The scale was written in Hindi and administered in Hindi. It has been translated into English, and the manual is available in English.

(2) The content of some items is definitely inappropriate for persons in the United States.

(3) There are no data to suggest how men would respond to the items.

AVAILABLE FROM: L. I. Bhushan, PhD, Bhagalpur University, Department of Psychology, Bhagalpur, 812007 India

USED IN:

Bhushan, L. I. (1981a). Development of Women's Social Freedom Scale: A report. *Asian Journal of Psychology and Education, 7*(2), 34–38.

Bhushan, L. I. (1981b). Women Social Freedom Scale. *Psychologia, 24*(4), 239–243.

Bhushan, L. I. (1987). *Manual for Women Social Freedom Scale (WSFS)*. Agra, India: National Psychological Corporation.

BELIEFS ABOUT EQUAL RIGHTS SCALE (BAERS)

AUTHORS: Leonard I. Jacobson, Carole L. Anderson, Mark S. Berletich, and Kenneth W. Berdahl

DATE: 1976

VARIABLE: Beliefs about equal rights for men and women

DESCRIPTION: The Beliefs About Equal Rights Scale (BAERS) consists of 28 true/false items. Twelve items express a positive attitude toward equality between men and women, and 16 items express a negative attitude.

ARTICLES LISTED IN BEERE, 1979: 1

AVAILABLE FROM: Jacobson, Anderson, Berletich, and Berdahl, 1976

USED IN:

Daniel, D. G., Abernethy, V., & Oliver, W. R. (1984). Correlations between female sex roles and attitudes toward male sexual dysfunction in 30 women. *Journal of Sex and Marital Therapy, 10*, 160–169.

Daniel, D. G., Abernethy, V., & Oliver, W. R. (1984). The relationship between beliefs about men's and women's roles in society and views on male sexual dysfunction in 135 women. *Social Psychiatry, 19*(3), 127–133.

Jacobson, L. I., Anderson, C. L., Berletich, M. S., & Berdahl, K. W. (1976). Construction and initial validation of a scale measuring beliefs about equal rights for men and women. *Educational and Psychological Measurement, 36*, 913–918.

Scher, D., Nevo, B., & Beit-Hallahmi, B. (1979). Beliefs about equal rights for men and women among Israeli and American students. *Journal of Social Psychology, 109*, 11–15.

BIBLIOGRAPHY:

Beere, C. A. (1979). *Women and women's issues: A handbook of tests and measures* (pp. 407–408). San Francisco: Jossey-Bass.

BIAS IN ATTITUDES SURVEY (BIAS)

AUTHORS: Paula J. Jean and Cecil R. Reynolds

DATE: 1980

VARIABLE: Attitudes toward men and women with a focus on "interpersonal and social issues" (Jean & Reynolds, 1980, p. 271)

TYPE OF INSTRUMENT: Summated rating scale

DESCRIPTION: The Bias in Attitudes Survey (BIAS) includes 35 items pertaining to males and/or females. The items cover a variety of content areas, and a few are factual items. Each item is accompanied by four response options: "strongly disagree, disagree, agree, strongly agree." All but 2 items are phrased in the same direction; that is, a person with a traditional attitude would answer "agree."

SAMPLE ITEMS: Men and women are better suited to different kinds of occupations due to factors other than physical strength.

It is important for a woman to satisfy her husband even though her sex desires may be less than his.

PREVIOUS SUBJECTS: Graduate and undergraduate college students

APPROPRIATE FOR: High school students and older

ADMINISTRATION: Self-administered; about 15–20 minutes

SCORING: Items are individually scored on a 4-point scale. Except for 2 items that must be reversed for scoring purposes, items are scored with 4 points for the "strongly agree" response and 1 point for the "strongly disagree" response. Item scores are totaled to yield an overall score that ranges from 35 (egalitarian attitudes) to 140 (traditional attitudes). Jean and Reynolds (1980, 1984) reported separate means and standard deviations for females and males.

DEVELOPMENT: A pool of 89 statements—factual statements and beliefs about personality differences—was administered to college students. Item means and item-total correlations were computed for each item. Thirty-five items with item means between 1.4 and 3.6 and item–total correlations of at least .35 were selected for the scale.

RELIABILITY: Jean and Reynolds (1980) reported a coefficient alpha equal to .91. Phifer and Plake (1983) administered the BIAS to 508 undergraduate students. For the total sample, coefficient alpha was .90; for males alone, the coefficient was .85; and for females alone, the coefficient was .86. Jean and Reynolds (1984) tested another sample of college students and obtained a coefficient alpha of .94.

VALIDITY: As would be expected, Jean and Reynolds (1980) found that scores from college men were significantly higher, that is, more conservative, than scores for college women. Also expected was the finding that younger students were more conservative than older students. Jean and Reynolds also found, unexpectedly, that divorced students were more conservative than single and married students.

NOTES & COMMENTS: (1) Phifer and Plake (1983) factor analyzed the responses from 508 college students who completed a slightly modified version of the BIAS. The students were given five response options for each item: the standard four options provided in the original BIAS plus a "neutral" option. The researchers extracted two factors that accounted for 68% of the variance when the data for males and females were analyzed together.

(2) In order to distract subjects from the purpose of the study, researchers (Major & Plake, 1983; Powers-Alexander, Galvin, Lambert, Speth, & Plake, 1983; Smith, Bukacek, Parker, Phifer, & Plake, 1983) have interspersed the items from the BIAS with items from the College Self-Expression Scale (Galassi, DeLo, Galassi, & Bastien, 1974), a measure of assertiveness. They then looked at how gender role attitudes related to perceptions of applicants for traditional and nontraditional educational programs and how they related to attributions for the applicants' predicted success in those fields.

(3) Jean and Reynolds (1984) compared the ability of college students to present themselves intentionally as liberal or conservative on the BIAS and on the Attitudes Toward Women Scale (AWS) (Spence & Helmreich, 1972) (see separate entry). Jean and Reynolds concluded: "Results suggest that, when asked to do so, females are able to present themselves as liberal or conservative on either scale. Males can manipulate the concepts of the AWS as directed, but are less able to do so with the concepts on the BIAS" (Jean & Reynolds, 1984, p. 805).

AVAILABLE FROM: Jean and Reynolds, 1980

USED IN:

Jean, P. J., & Reynolds, C. R. (1980). Development of the Bias in Attitudes Survey: A sex-role questionnaire. *Journal of Psychology, 104*(2), 269–277.

Jean, P. J., & Reynolds, C. R. (1984). Sex and attitude distortion: Ability of females and males to fake liberal and conservative positions regarding changing sex roles. *Sex Roles, 10*(9/10), 805–815.

Major, H., & Plake, B. S. (1983, April). *Gender-linked perceptions and causal attributions of female/male competencies.* Paper presented at the meeting of the American Educational Research Association, Montreal. (ERIC Document Reproduction Service No. 227 170)

Phifer, S. J., & Plake, B. S. (1983). The factorial validity of the Bias in Attitude Survey Scale. *Educational and Psychological Measurement, 43*(3), 887–891.

Powers-Alexander, S., Galvin, G. A., Lambert, D. J., Speth, C. A., & Plake, B. S. (1983, April). *Attribution of success in college women: Effort or luck?* Paper presented at the meeting of the American Educational Research Association, Montreal. (ERIC Document Reproduction Service No. ED 227 173)

Smith, E. P., Bukacek, S. E., Parker, C. S., Phifer, S. J., & Plake, B. S. (1983, April). *Role appropriateness of educational fields: Bias in selection.* Paper presented at the meeting of the American Educational Research Association, Montreal. (ERIC Document Reproduction Service No. ED 227 169)

BIBLIOGRAPHY:
Galassi, J., DeLo, J., Galassi, M., & Bastien, S. (1974). The College Self-Expression Scale: A measure of assertiveness. *Behavior Therapy*, 5, 165–171.
Spence, J. T., & Helmreich, R. L. (1972). The Attitudes Toward Women Scale: An objective instrument to measure attitudes toward the rights and roles of women in contemporary society. *Catalog of Selected Documents in Psychology*, 2, 66. (Ms. No. 153)

BROWN-MANELA SEX ROLE ATTITUDES SCALE

AUTHORS: Prudence Brown and Roger Manela

DATE: 1978

VARIABLE: Attitudes toward men and women

TYPE OF INSTRUMENT: Summated rating scale

DESCRIPTION: The Brown-Manela Sex Role Attitudes Scale is a brief measure consisting of 11 items representing three factors: Women in the Home (5 items), Traditional Family Role (3 items), and Job Inequality (3 items). Each item is accompanied by four response options: "strongly disagree, disagree, agree, strongly agree." A traditional gender role ideology is expressed by agreeing with 6 items and disagreeing with the other 5 items.

SAMPLE ITEMS: (Women in the Home) It should be the husband's duty to support his wife and family.

(Traditional Family Roles) Fathers can be just as warm and affectionate with children as mothers are.

(Job Inequality) It's fine for women to earn more money than their husbands.

PREVIOUS SUBJECTS: Women seeking a divorce

APPROPRIATE FOR: High school ages and older

ADMINISTRATION: Self-administered; about 5–8 minutes

SCORING: Items are individually scored on a 4-point scale, with 4 points assigned to the end of the continuum representing a traditional gender role orientation. Scores can be obtained for each of the three factors, and a total score can be computed. Total scores range from 11 (very contemporary) to 44 (very traditional).

DEVELOPMENT: The scale originally consisted of 18 items that were administered on two occasions to a sample of 253 women seeking divorce. Their responses were factor analyzed, and three factors were identified. The 11 items that loaded at least .40 on a factor and that loaded the same way at both testing times were retained for the scale.

RELIABILITY: No information was provided.

VALIDITY: As would be expected, Brown and Manela (1978) found that younger women and women with more education reported more nontraditional gender role ideology.

NOTES & COMMENTS: (1) Brown and Manela (1978) correlated the three factor scores. For both testing times, the correlations ranged from

.06 to .46, suggesting that the factors are independent of each other to some extent.

(2) Evidence of the reliability of the subscales and the full scale is needed before further use of the scale.

(3) Brown and Manela (1978) studied women seeking divorces and compared their scores on the various factors of the scale with their scores on measures of self-esteem, internal/external control, distress, well-being, and personal growth.

(4) Kurdek and Blisk (1983) combined the 11 items from this scale with 25 items from the Attitudes Toward Women Scale (Spence & Helmreich, 1978) (see separate entry) to form a 36-item measure. When this 36-item measure was administered to 25 divorced women, coefficient alpha was .87.

AVAILABLE FROM: Brown and Manela, 1978

USED IN:

Brown, P., & Manela, R. (1978). Changing family roles: Women and divorce. *Journal of Divorce*, 1(4), 315–328.

Kurdek, L. A., & Blisk, D. (1983). Dimensions and correlates of mother's divorce experiences. *Journal of Divorce*, 6(4), 1–24.

BIBLIOGRAPHY:

Spence, J. T., & Helmreich, R. L. (1978). *Masculinity and femininity: Their psychological dimensions, correlates, and antecedents*. Austin: University of Texas Press.

CHATTERJEE PUHAN ATTITUDE SCALE

AUTHORS: B. B. Chatterjee and B. N. Puhan

DATE: 1980

VARIABLE: Attitudes toward male-female roles and relationships

TYPE OF INSTRUMENT: Thurstone scale

DESCRIPTION: There are two forms of the Chatterjee Puhan Attitude Scale, each with 15 statements pertaining to male-female relationships. Item content focuses on a variety of issues, including intimacy, cross-sex friendships, and employment opportunities for women. The respondents' task is to check each item they endorse. For Form A, the scale values range from 2.02 to 8.75, with a mean of 5.42 and a median of 5.17. For Form B, the scale values range from 2.10 to 8.67, with a mean of 4.94 and a median of 5.18. Many of the items are extremely conservative relative to life-styles in the West.

SAMPLE ITEMS: (Form A) There can be just one relation between males and females—sex.

(Form B) Some married couples sit together in public places which does not look nice.

PREVIOUS SUBJECTS: College students in India

APPROPRIATE FOR: College students and older in India; the scale may also be useful in other countries where the type of male-female relations are similar to those in India

ADMINISTRATION: Self-administered; about 5–10 minutes

SCORING: Though Chatterjee and Puhan (1980) did not discuss scoring, Thurstone scales are typically scored by finding the mean or the median scale value of the items endorsed by the respondent.

DEVELOPMENT: An item pool was developed by searching for relevant statements in "books, journals, periodicals, newspapers, novels, and shortstories" (Chatterjee & Puhan, 1980, p. 2) and by interviewing colleagues of the scale's authors. After editing the pool, 141 items remained. Consistent with Thurstone scale development procedures, the items were rated by judges. Seventy-eight master's-level psychology students served as the judges. Using a 9-point scale, the judges rated the degree of favorableness or unfavorableness in each item. The data analysis involved finding the interquartile range and the median of the ratings for each item. Two criteria were used for selecting items for the scale: (1) the items had to have a low semi-interquartile range, and (2) items were selected with median scores covering as broad a range as possible. Thirty items were selected to create two forms of the scale.

RELIABILITY: When the two forms were administered to a sample of 41 college students in India, the correlation between the parallel forms was .81.

VALIDITY: No information was provided.

NOTES & COMMENTS: (1) The items on this scale are inappropriate in Western countries and may not be appropriate in urban areas of India, but the scale is included here for two reasons. First, the item content provides a striking contrast with attitude measures used in the Western world, and second, researchers interested in doing work in other countries, such as India, may find this scale useful.

(2) Though Chatterjee and Puhan (1980) suggested that they are measuring attitudes toward sex, they are not using the term *sex* as it is commonly used in the United States. Thus, the title of their article is quite misleading.

AVAILABLE FROM: Chatterjee and Puhan, 1980

USED IN:

Chatterjee, B. B., & Puhan, B. N. (1980). A Thurstone scale for measuring attitude towards sex. *Indian Psychological Review*, 19(2), 1–8.

CHILD-REARING SEX ROLE ATTITUDE SCALE

AUTHOR: Penny L. Burge

DATE: 1981

VARIABLE: Gender role attitudes related to children and child-rearing practices

TYPE OF INSTRUMENT: Summated rating scale

DESCRIPTION: The Child-Rearing Sex Role Attitude Scale consists of

28 statements pertaining to boys and/or girls. Item content compares boys and girls on a variety of topics, including prescribed behaviors, emotional expression, activities, and career goals. Each item is accompanied by five response options ranging from "strongly agree" to "strongly disagree." Seven items are phrased so that agreement reflects an egalitarian attitude toward child rearing; 21 items are phrased so that agreement reflects more traditional attitudes.

SAMPLE ITEMS: Both boys and girls really need to develop social skills.
   Only boys should be permitted to play competitive sports.

PREVIOUS SUBJECTS: Adults

APPROPRIATE FOR: High school students and older

ADMINISTRATION: Self-administered; 5–10 minutes

SCORING: Items are individually scored on a 5-point scale, with 1 point assigned to the response reflecting the more traditional attitude. Item scores are summed to yield a total score that can range from 28 (very traditional) to 140 (very egalitarian).

DEVELOPMENT: Scale development began with a literature review regarding sex stereotypes in child rearing. A pool of 50 items was developed and submitted to seven judges knowledgeable about child-rearing issues. Based on their feedback, items were revised, and the 28 items were selected for the scale. Specific details on the criteria for final item selection were not provided. The scale was pilot tested with a sample of 25 persons.

RELIABILITY: Coefficient alpha for the pilot test was .83. When the scale was used with a sample of 94 adults, coefficient alpha was .92.

VALIDITY: Scores on the Child-Rearing Sex-Role Attitude Scale were correlated with scores on the Osmond-Martin Sex Role Attitude Scale (see separate entry), which measures "social issue sex-role attitudes" (Burge, 1981, p. 194). For a group of 94 adults, the correlation between the two scales was .69, significant at the .001 level. As would be expected, men scored significantly lower than women on the Child-Rearing Sex-Role Attitude Scale, indicating that men had more traditional attitudes.

NOTES & COMMENTS: (1) The average interitem correlation was .30.
   (2) A major reason for including this scale, which has not been used in more than one published study, is that item content is quite different from what is typically found on gender role attitude scales.

AVAILABLE FROM: Burge, 1981

USED IN:

Burge, P. (1981). Parental child-rearing sex-role attitudes related to social issue sex-role attitudes and selected demographic variables. *Home Economics Research Journal, 9*(3), 193–199.

CLARK LANE SEX ROLE ATTITUDE QUESTIONNAIRE
AUTHORS: Shirley Clark and Mary Kay Lane
DATE: 1977

VARIABLE: Support for traditional or liberated gender role concepts
TYPE OF INSTRUMENT: Summated rating scale
DESCRIPTION: The Clark Lane Sex Role Attitude Questionnaire consists
of 10 items embedded in a 22-item questionnaire. The 10 items are statements referring to women's careers, marriage, educational rights, appearance, and social behaviors (including swearing and sexual
experiences). Each item is accompanied by three response options:
"agree, uncertain, disagree." Half of the items are phrased so that agreement reflects a traditional viewpoint, and half are phrased so that agreement expresses a liberated viewpoint.
SAMPLE ITEMS: The career ambitions of a woman should not be cur-
tailed because they interfere with family responsibilities.

Although education is becoming increasingly important for girls, one
of the most valuable things a mother can do for her daughter is to prepare
her to be a good wife and mother.
PREVIOUS SUBJECTS: Canadian college students
APPROPRIATE FOR: High school students and older
ADMINISTRATION: Self-administered; about 10 minutes
SCORING: A key is provided to indicate the traditional answers and
the liberated answers. Seven traditional answers classify the respondent
as "traditional"; seven liberated answers classify the respondent as "liberated." Because the scale has been used only to identify extreme scorers,
the authors did not provide guidelines for interpreting scores between
the extremes.
DEVELOPMENT: A pool of 73 items was constructed based on issues
raised in the writings of the popular radical feminists of the 1960s and
1970s. The item pool was administered to two groups of women: women
who operated a drop-in center for the women's movement and members
of the Junior League. The former group attracts women who are likely
to be very liberal in their views of gender roles, and the latter group
attracts women who are likely to be traditional in their views of gender
roles. Membership in Junior League is by invitation only, and women
invited to join "endorse conformity to social norms, dedication to family
life and [are] engaged in community volunteer work" (M. K. Lane, personal communication, August 1988). The responses of the two groups
were compared, and 22 items were identified as discriminating between
them. These items were administered to members of two other organizations. One organization was a collective that printed a radical feminist newspaper, and the other was an exclusive club supportive of
traditional family life. The responses from these two groups were used
to select the 10 items for the scale.
RELIABILITY: No information was provided.
VALIDITY: The Clark Lane Sex Role Attitude Questionnaire was used
to identify a group of liberated women and a group of traditional women

in order to test the assumption that "traditionalist women in the West view a male as a superior, whereas liberated women do not" (Clark & Lane, 1978, p. 81). Using a somewhat unusual research method, blood pressure readings were the dependent measure. The findings supported the assumption that traditionalist women view a male as a superior and also showed that liberated women view a female as a superior.

NOTES & COMMENTS: Given the age of this scale, some may question its applicability to women today; however, M. K. Lane (personal communication, August 1988) reported: "I have administered this scale to both high school and university students periodically over the years and have been appalled by the fact that the distribution of scores has remained virtually the same."

AVAILABLE FROM: Order from NAPS c/o Microfiche Publications, P.O. Box 3513, Grand Central Station, New York, NY 10163–3513; NAPS document no. 04708; for microfiche, in U.S. remit $4.00 with order.

USED IN:

Clark, S., & Lane, M. K. (1978). Women's behavioral manifestations of traditionalist and liberated role concepts. *Journal of Psychology, 98*, 81–89.

ELLIS-BENTLER TRADITIONAL SEX-DETERMINED ROLE STANDARDS SCALE

AUTHORS: Linda J. Ellis and Peter M. Bentler

DATE: 1973

VARIABLE: Attitudes toward traditional gender role standards

DESCRIPTION: The Ellis-Bentler Traditional Sex-Determined Role Standards Scale is a forced choice measure consisting of 38 pairs of statements relating to gender role standards in a variety of areas: social, sexual, legal, educational, and economic. Each pair of statements includes an item reflecting support for traditional gender role standards and an item reflecting support for egalitarian gender role standards.

ARTICLES LISTED IN BEERE, 1979: 6

AVAILABLE FROM: Peter Bentler, Department of Psychology, Franz Hall, University of California, 405 Hilgard Ave., Los Angeles, CA 90024

USED IN:

Andres, D., Gold, D., Berger, C., Kinch, R., & Gillett, P. (1983). Selected psychosocial characteristics of males: Their relationship to contraceptive use and abortion. *Personality and Social Psychology Bulletin, 9*(3), 387–396.

Gackenbach, J. I., & Auerbach, S. M. (1983). Sex-role attitudes and situations: Female behavioral predictors in a learning task. *Journal of Psychology, 115*, 33–37.

Gackenbach, J. I., & Auerbach, S. M. (1985). Sex-role attitudes and perceptual learning. *Journal of Social Psychology, 125*, 233–243.

Newcomb, M. D. (1986). Notches on the bedpost: Generational effects of sexual experience. *Psychology: A Quarterly Journal of Human Behavior, 23*(2/3), 37–46.

BIBLIOGRAPHY:
Beere, C. A. (1979). *Women and women's issues: A handbook of tests and measures.* (pp. 220–221). San Francisco: Jossey-Bass.

FEM SCALE

AUTHORS: Eliot R. Smith, Myra Marx Ferree, and Frederick D. Miller

DATE: 1975

VARIABLE: Attitudes toward feminism

DESCRIPTION: The FEM Scale is a summated rating scale with 20 items pertaining to a variety of issues, including marital roles, maternal roles, and stereotyped views of women's personality traits. Each item is accompanied by five response options ranging from "strongly agree" to "strongly disagree."

ARTICLES LISTED IN BEERE, 1979: 3

AVAILABLE FROM: Smith, Ferree, and Miller, 1975

USED IN:

Baker, C. A., & Annis, L. V. (1980). Sex-role stereotyping and the feminism of education undergraduates. *Southern Journal of Educational Research, 14,* 79–87.

Banziger, G., & Hooker, L. (1979). The effects of attitudes toward feminism and perceived feminism on physical attractiveness ratings. *Sex Roles, 5,* 437–442.

Borges, M. A., & Laning, B. (1979). Relationships between assertiveness, achievement motivation, feminist attitudes, and locus of control in the college population. *Psychological Reports, 44,* 545–546.

Branscombe, N. R., Deaux, K., & Lerner, M. S. (1985). Individual differences and the influence of context on categorization and prejudice. *Representative Research in Social Psychology, 15,* 25–35.

Der-Karabetian, A., & Angel, D. (1985, April). *Intimacy and dominance gestures in the work place.* Paper presented at the meeting of the Western Psychological Association, San Jose, CA. (ERIC Document Reproduction Service No. ED 260 337)

Epperson, D. L., & Lewis, K. N. (1987). Issues of informed entry into counseling: Perceptions and preferences resulting from different types and amounts of pretherapy information. *Journal of Counseling Psychology, 34,* 266–275.

Feinberg, R. A., & Workman, J. E. (1981). Sex-role orientation and cognitive complexity. *Psychological Reports, 49,* 246.

Haussmann, M. J. (1981, March). *Women's roles and vulnerability to depression.* Paper presented at the meeting of the Association for Women in Psychology, Boston. (ERIC Document Reproduction Service No. ED 216 250)

Jensen, I. W., & Gutek, B.A. (1982). Attributions and assignment of responsibility in sexual harassment. *Journal of Social Issues, 38*(4), 121–136.

Korman, S. K. (1983a). Nontraditional dating behavior: Date-initiation and date expense-sharing among feminists and nonfeminists. *Family Relations, 32,* 575–581.

Korman, S. K. (1983b). The feminist: Familial influences on adherence to ideology and commitment to a self-perception. *Family Relations, 32,* 431–439.

Korman, S. K., & Leslie, G. R. (1982). The relationship of feminist ideology and date expense sharing to perceptions of sexual aggression in dating. *Journal of Sex Research, 18,* 114–129.

Krulewitz, J. E., & Kahn, A. S. (1983). Preferences for rape reduction strategies. *Psychology of Women Quarterly, 7,* 301–312.

Krulewitz, J. E., & Nash, J. E. (1980). Effects of sex role attitudes and similarity on men's rejection of male homosexuals. *Journal of Personality and Social Psychology, 38,* 67–74.

Krulewitz, J. E., & Payne, E. J. (1978). Attributions about rape: Effects of rapist force, observer sex and sex role attitudes. *Journal of Applied Social Psychology, 8,* 291–305.

Miller, F., Sadd, S., & Zietz, B. (1978, March). *Sex roles, feminism, and achievement conflicts.* Paper presented at the meeting of the Eastern Psychological Association, Washington, DC. (ERIC Document Reproduction Service No. ED 163 309)

Pryor, J. B. (1987). Sexual harassment proclivities in men. *Sex Roles, 17,* 269–290.

Slane, S., & Morrow, L. (1981). Race differences in feminism and guilt. *Psychological Reports, 49,* 45–46.

Smith, E. R., Ferree, M. M., & Miller, F. D. (1975). A short scale of attitudes toward feminism. *Representative Research in Social Psychology, 6,* 51–56.

Taylor, S. E., & Falcone, H. (1982). Cognitive bases of stereotyping: The relationship between categorization and prejudice. *Personality and Social Psychology Bulletin, 8,* 426–432.

Tetenbaum, T. J., Lighter, J., & Travis, M. (1983). The construct validation of an Attitudes Toward Working Mothers Scale. *Psychology of Women Quarterly, 8,* 69–78.

Ullman, L. P., Freedland, K. E., & Warmsun, C. H. (1978). Sex and ethnic group effects on attitudes toward women. *Bulletin of the Psychonomic Society, 11,* 179–180.

Valdez, R. L. (1985, April). *Self-blame and sex-role beliefs in domestic violence victims.* Paper presented at the meeting of the Western Psychological Association, San Jose, CA. (ERIC Document Reproduction Service No. ED 261 272)

BIBLIOGRAPHY:

Beere, C. A. (1979). *Women and women's issues: A handbook of tests and measures* (pp. 416–418). San Francisco: Jossey-Bass.

FEMININE EXPECTATIONS SCALE (FES)/MASCULINE EXPECTATIONS SCALE (MES)

AUTHORS: Stephen Norland, Jennifer James, and Neal Shover

DATE: 1978

VARIABLE: Gender role expectations for females and for males

TYPE OF INSTRUMENT: Summated rating scales

DESCRIPTION: The Feminine Expectations Scale (FES) and the Masculine Expectations Scale (MES) each include five items, each accompanied by five response options ranging from "strongly agree" to "strongly disagree." Each item is a statement about gender role expectations, and each is phrased in the first person.

SAMPLE ITEMS: (FES) If I marry, I would expect to move to another city if my spouse changed jobs.

(MES) If I marry, I would expect to provide most of the income for my family.

PREVIOUS SUBJECTS: Students in grades 8–12

APPROPRIATE FOR: Eighth graders and older

ADMINISTRATION: Self-administered; each scale takes a few minutes

SCORING: Individual items are scored on a 5-point scale, with 5 being assigned to the "strongly agree" response. Item scores are totaled to yield a score on each scale. Total scores can range from 5 to 25.

DEVELOPMENT: A pool of 60 behaviorally descriptive items was developed based on a review of the relevant literature and discussions with students in public school classrooms. In order to determine which statements were perceived as gender specific, the item pool was administered to a sample of 368 students in grades 8 through 12. Half of the students were asked to use a 5-point scale to rate how feminine the item was, and the others were asked to rate how masculine the item was. For example, the "feminine" raters were told, "Mark each of the following statements according to how strongly you believe that fifty years ago it was the kind of thing you would have expected feminine persons to do" (Norland, James, & Shover, 1978, p. 547). Thirteen items were rated as "Probably Masculine" or "Definitely Masculine" by at least 75% of the "masculine" raters, and 12 items were rated as "Probably Feminine" or "Definitely Feminine" by at least 75% of the "feminine" raters. From this pool of 25 items, interitem correlations and item-total correlations were used to reduce the item pool to 5 items on the MES. The final set of 5 items on the FES was selected from the remaining pool of 8 feminine items in such a way as to maximize reliability.

RELIABILITY: The responses from the 368 students used for scale development were also used to compute an alpha coefficient. For the FES, alpha was .69; for the MES, alpha was .81. It is important to note that these were the highest reliability coefficients that could be obtained; that is, the items were selected to maximize coefficient alpha, and the reliability estimates were not confirmed on another sample of respondents.

VALIDITY: To determine whether the FES and the MES could differentiate in the predicted direction, the scales were administered to high school students attending a Mormon church and to high school students attending a Unitarian church. It was predicted that the Mormon females would be more traditional than the Unitarian females on the FES and the Mormon males would be more traditional than the Unitarian males on the MES. Significant differences were found in the predicted direction.

NOTES & COMMENTS: Norland et al. (1978) used the FES and MES to test whether masculinity and femininity are bipolar. They hypothesized

that "if the bipolarity assumption is valid, we would expect that the association between the scale scores would be strongly negative" (p. 549). Testing a different sample of 184 high school students, they found that the correlation, though negative and statistically significant ($r = -.13$), was really quite low.
AVAILABLE FROM: Norland, James, and Shover, 1978
USED IN:
Norland, S., James, J., & Shover, N. (1978). Gender role expectations of juveniles. *The Sociological Quarterly, 19*(4), 545–554.

INDEX OF SEX-ROLE ORIENTATION (ISRO)
AUTHORS: Nancy A. Dreyer, Nancy Fugate Woods, and Sherman A. James
DATE: 1981
VARIABLE: Women's gender role attitudes
TYPE OF INSTRUMENT: Summated rating scale
DESCRIPTION: The Index of Sex-Role Orientation (ISRO) consists of 16 attitude statements, each accompanied by a 5-point response scale ranging from "strongly disagree" to "strongly agree." The items pertain to women's work, marital roles, and parental roles. Ten items are phrased so that a woman with a feminist orientation would disagree with the item; six items are phrased in the reverse direction.
SAMPLE ITEMS: Women should take care of running their homes and leave running the country up to men.
    Most women who want a career should not have children.
PREVIOUS SUBJECTS: Women graduate students, adult women
APPROPRIATE FOR: Ages 13 and older
ADMINISTRATION: Self-administered; about 10 minutes
SCORING: Items are individually scored on a 5-point scale, with a score of 5 assigned to the "feminist" end of the continuum and a score of 1 assigned to the "traditional" end of the continuum. Item scores are totaled to yield a single score, ranging from 16 (most traditional) to 80 (most feminist).
DEVELOPMENT: Dreyer, Woods, and James (1981) defined traditional gender role orientation as being "dictated primarily by rules and rituals derived from past generations, only slightly modified by the current movement toward equality for men and women" (p. 174). For a traditional woman, a major source of satisfaction derives from her husband and children. The modern woman, on the other hand, encourages social changes that will lead to equality between men and women, and she derives much of her satisfaction from her own achievements. In developing the ISRO, Dreyer et al. (1981) began with a pool of 19 items, with most selected from previous gender role research. One item was eliminated because it did not contribute to the factor analytic structure; 2

other items were eliminated because they did not differentiate between traditional and feminist groups.

RELIABILITY: Dreyer et al. (1981) looked at responses from 26 members of feminist organizations, 22 members of traditional women's groups, and 15 graduate nursing students. The 16-item scale had a corrected, split-half reliability of .92. In addition, Dreyer et al. administered the scale to 32 graduate students in public health. These respondents completed the ISRO on two occasions about a month apart. The test-retest correlation was .62.

VALIDITY: There were significant differences between the members of the feminist organizations and the members of the traditional women's groups on all 16 items of the ISRO (Dreyer et al., 1981). Furthermore, when a median split procedure was used to identify "feminist" (above the median) and "traditional" (below the median) women, 96.2% of the feminist group sample were correctly identified as feminist, and 95.5% of the traditional group sample were correctly identified as traditional.

Woods (1985a) tested 144 married women between the ages of 20 and 40. As predicted, she found a significant relationship between ISRO scores and mental health; women who were more traditional on the ISRO were more likely to suffer from mental ill health.

NOTES & COMMENTS: (1) Dreyer et al. (1981) factor analyzed the responses from 63 women and identified three independent factors: "male-female division of labor in the home; child rearing/career conflicts; and sex-role issues involving work outside the home" (p. 180).

(2) A regression analysis indicated that high feminist scores are associated with more education, younger age at first marriage, high income, little importance to religion, single status, and being currently employed (Dreyer et al., 1981).

(3) Clarke and Kleine (1984) administered a slightly modified version of the ISRO to 60 college women. They compared the women's scores on the ISRO with results on an identity status measure and an indicator of their identification with their parents. Woods (1985b) compared the ISRO scores of 179 adult women with measures of menstrual symptomatology, stressful life events, and menstrual attitudes. Only the last measure was significantly related to ISRO scores.

AVAILABLE FROM: Dreyer, Woods, and James, 1981

USED IN:

Clarke, P., & Kleine, P. F. (1984, April). *Parental identification, traditionality, and identity status in adolescent females.* Paper presented at the meeting of the American Educational Research Association, New Orleans. (ERIC Document Reproduction Service No. ED 246 351)

Dreyer, N. A., Woods, N. F., & James, S. A. (1981). ISRO: A scale to measure sex-role orientation. *Sex Roles, 7*(2), 173–182.

Woods, N. F. (1985a). Employment, family roles, and mental ill health in young married women. *Nursing Research, 34*(1), 4–10.

Woods, N. F. (1985b). Relationship of socialization and stress to perimenstrual symptoms, disability, and menstrual attitudes. *Nursing Research, 34*(3), 145–149.

INVENTORY OF FEMININE VALUES/INVENTORY OF MASCULINE VALUES

AUTHOR: Alexandra Botwinik Fand (revised by Anne Steinmann)

DATE: 1955 (revised 1968)

VARIABLE: Attitudes toward the feminine role; attitudes toward the masculine role

DESCRIPTION: The Inventory of Feminine Values contains 34 statements dealing with the needs, rights, and responsibilities of women in regard to men, children, and life in general. Similarly, the Inventory of Masculine Values contains 34 statements dealing with the needs, rights, and responsibilities of men in regard to women, children, and life in general. On each version, about half of the items deal with a family-oriented person and the other half with a self-oriented person. The scale can be answered in terms of self-perception, perceptions of an ideal person, or beliefs about others' perceptions regarding the ideal person.

ARTICLES LISTED IN BEERE, 1979: 80

NOTES & COMMENTS: (1) Stevens, Gardner, and Barton (1984) reported the results of a factor analytic study.

(2) The research articles listed below report using the Fand Inventory, the Inventory of Feminine Values, the Inventory of Masculine Values, or the Maferr Inventories, all variations of the same scale.

(3) Both the Inventory of Masculine Values and the Inventory of Feminine Values are available for two levels; the Developmental Inventories are for junior and senior high school students; the Adult inventories are for college students and adults.

(4) Both Inventories are listed in the *Ninth Mental Measurements Yearbook* (entries 641 and 642) and in *Tests in Print III* (entries 1357 and 1358).

AVAILABLE FROM: Steinmann, 1979; the inventories can be purchased from the Maferr Foundation, Inc., 9 East 81st St., New York, NY 10028

USED IN:

Allison, J. R. (1979). Roles and role conflict of women in infertile couples. *Psychology of Women Quarterly, 4*, 97–113.

Bedeian, A. G., & Zarra, M. J. (1977). Sex-role orientation: Effect on self-esteem, need achievement and internality in college females. *Perceptual and Motor Skills, 45*, 712–714.

Bergquist, D. K., Borgers, S. B., & Tollefson, N. (1985). *Women's attitudes and educational aspirations.* Unpublished paper, University of Kansas, 1985. (ERIC Document Reproduction Service No. ED 277 904)

Berryman, C. L., & Wilcox, J. R. (1977, December). *Attitudes toward male and female speech: Experiments on the effects of sex-typical language.* Paper presented at the meeting of the Speech Communication Association, Washington, DC. (ERIC Document Reproduction Service No. ED 151 873)

Bloom, B. L., & Clement, C. (1984). Marital sex role orientation and adjustment to separation and divorce. *Journal of Divorce, 7*, 87–98.

Brown, R. (1983). Locus of control and sex role orientation of women graduate students. *College Student Journal, 17*, 10–12.

Burlew, A. K. (1982). The experience of black females in traditional and nontraditional professions. *Psychology of Women Quarterly, 6*, 312–326.

Caldwell, R. A., Bloom, B. L., & Hodges, W. F. (1983). Sex differences in separation and divorce: A longitudinal perspective. *Issues in Mental Health Nursing, 5*, 103–120.

Crovitz, E., & Steinmann, A. (1980). A decade later: Black-white attitudes toward women's familial role. *Psychology of Women Quarterly, 5*, 170–176.

Hansen, J. C., & Putnam, B. A. (1978). Feminine role concepts of young women. *Sex Roles, 4*, 127–130.

Hipple, J. L., & Hipple, L. (1980). Concepts of ideal woman and ideal man. *Social Work, 25*, 147–149.

Hoar, C. H. (1983). Women alcoholics—are they different from other women? *International Journal of the Addictions, 18*, 251–270.

Huth, C. M. (1978). Married women's work status: The influence of parents and husbands. *Journal of Vocational Behavior, 13*, 272–286.

Konstam, V., & Gilbert, H. B. (1978). Fear of success, sex-role orientation, and performance in differing experimental conditions. *Psychological Reports, 42*, 519–528.

Mika, K., & Bloom B. L. (1980). Adjustment to separation among former cohabiters. *Journal of Divorce, 4*, 45–66.

Nielsen, E. C., & Edwards, J. (1982). Perceived feminine role orientation and self-concept. *Human Relations, 35*, 547–558.

Ory, J. C., & Helfrich, L. M. (1978). A study of individual characteristics and career aspirations. *Vocational Guidance Quarterly, 27*, 43–49.

Pettit, E. J., & Bloom, B. L. (1984). Whose decision was it? The effects of initiator status on adjustment to marital disruption. *Journal of Marriage and the Family, 46*, 587–595.

Pierce, N. F. (1981, March). *Comparison of sex-role orientation and personality variables in traditional women and college re-entry women.* Paper presented at the Southeastern Psychological Association, Atlanta. (ERIC Document Reproduction Service No. ED 206 945)

Ridley, S. E., & Bayton, J. A. (1980). Personality needs, social status, and preferences for an "ideal woman" in black and white college males. *Journal of Negro Education, 49*, 165–172.

Rimmer, S. M., & Loesch, L. C. (1980). Another look at college students' sex role perceptions. *College Student Journal, 14*, 394–398.

Skrapec, C., & MacKenzie, K. R. (1981). Psychological self-perception in male transsexuals, homosexuals, and heterosexuals. *Archives of Sexual Behavior, 10*, 357–370.

Steinmann, A. (1975). Studies in male-female sex role identification. *Psychotherapy Theory, Research and Practice, 12*, 412–417.

Steinmann, A. (1979a). *Maferr Inventory of Feminine Values: Specimen set and manual series for the interpretation of the Maferr Inventory of Feminine Values (MIFV).* Unpublished manuscript, Maferr Foundation, New York. (ERIC Document Reproduction Service No. ED 194 626)

Steinmann, A. G. (1979b). *Maferr Inventory of Masculine Values: Specimen set and manual for the interpretation of the Maferr Inventory of Masculine Values (MIMV).* Unpublished manuscript, Maferr Foundation, New York. (ERIC Document Reproduction Service No. ED 194 627)

Stevens, G., Barton, E., & Gardner, S. (1983). The illusion of change: Twenty years of wish-fulfillment in research of gender stereotypes. *International Journal of Group Tensions, 13,* 91–99.

Stevens, G., Gardner, S., & Barton, E. (1984). Factor analyses of two "attitude toward gender role" questionnaires. *Journal of Personality Assessment, 48,* 312–316.

Touliatos, J., & Lindholm, B. W. (1977). Correlates of attitudes toward the female sex role and achievement, affiliation, and power motivation of college women. *Adolescence, 12,* 461–470.

Voss, J. (1980). Concepts of self, ideal self, and ideal woman held by college men and women: A comparison study. *Journal of College Student Personnel, 21,* 50–57.

Welsh, M. C., & Hawker, J. (1978, March). *Personality characteristics and evaluation of women's role.* Paper presented at the meeting of the Southeastern Psychological Association, Atlanta. (ERIC Document Reproduction Service No. ED 165 075)

BIBLIOGRAPHY:

Beere, C. A. (1979). *Women and women's issues: A handbook of tests and measures* (pp. 432–442). San Francisco: Jossey-Bass.

Mitchell, J. V., Jr. (Ed.). (1985). *The ninth mental measurements yearbook* (Vol. 1). Lincoln: Buros Institute of Mental Measurements, University of Nebraska.

Mitchell, J. V., Jr. (Ed.). (1983). *Tests in print III.* Lincoln: Buros Institute of Mental Measurements, University of Nebraska.

MACHO SCALE

AUTHORS: Wayne J. Villemez and John C. Touhey

DATE: 1977

VARIABLE: Tendency to engage in gender role stereotyping and sex discrimination

TYPE OF INSTRUMENT: Summated rating scale

DESCRIPTION: The Macho Scale consists of 28 items covering a variety of topics relating to attitudes toward men and women. Item content relates to work roles, family roles, and personality characteristics. Several items reflect stereotyped views of men and women. Each item is accompanied by five response options: "strongly agree, agree, neutral or undecided, disagree, strongly disagree." Most items are phrased so that agreement reflects a sexist or discriminatory attitude; 7 items are phrased in the reverse direction.

SAMPLE ITEMS: Parents usually maintain stricter control over their daughters than their sons, and they should.

For the most part, it is better to be a man than to be a woman.

PREVIOUS SUBJECTS: College students and adults

APPROPRIATE FOR: High school students and older

ADMINISTRATION: Self-administered; 15 minutes

SCORING: Items are individually scored, with the positively keyed items given 4 points for the "strongly agree" end of the continuum. Scoring is reversed for the seven negatively keyed items. Total scores can range from 0 (profeminist) to 112 (chauvinistic). Villemez and Touhey (1977) reported means and standard deviations separately and combined for college students and adults.

DEVELOPMENT: Villemez and Touhey (1977) prepared a pool of 162 statements that "were intended to measure expressions of sexist and equalitarian beliefs, behaviors, and feelings in both sexes" (p. 412). The item pool and several personality measures were administered to 67 college students with instructions to mark each item as "true" or "false." Items were retained if they met two criteria: discriminated between highest- and lowest-scoring respondents and statistically independent from two measures of social desirability (Crowne & Marlowe, 1960; Edwards, 1957). About half of the items were retained and administered to another sample of college students. Using the same criteria, 42 items were retained from the second phase of testing. The pool of 42 items was administered to another sample, but this time the items were given in a Likert rather than a true/false format. Again the same criteria were applied, and the 28 items that survived the analysis comprise the final form of the scale.

RELIABILITY: Test-retest reliability (interval unspecified) was reported for one sample of college students and two samples of adults. The coefficients were .91 for the students and .94 and .89 for the adult groups.

VALIDITY: Villemez and Touhey (1977) tested a sample of undergraduate students and showed that scores on the Macho Scale were not related to a variety of personality measures including "Taylor's (1953) Manifest Anxiety Scale, Mehrabian's (1969) measure of achievement motivation, Rotter's (1966) I-E Scale, or Christie and Geis' (1970) Machiavellianism Scale" (p. 414). Though the correlation between the Macho Scale and the California F Scale (Adorno, Frenkel-Brunswik, Levinson, & Sanford, 1950) was significant for a sample of 122 college students, the magnitude of the correlation was rather low ($r = .22$).

Andersen (1978) tested 65 college students with the Macho Scale and with the Bem Sex Role Inventory (Bem, 1974) (see separate entry). She found that masculine-typed males compared to androgynous or feminine-typed males were more likely to be sexist on the Macho Scale, but sex typing did not relate to Macho scores for female subjects.

Gayton, Sawyer, Baird, and Ozmon (1982) tested college students and compared their scores on the Macho Scale with scores on the Attitudes Toward Women Scale (AWS) (Spence & Helmreich, 1978) (see separate entry) and a measure of attitudes toward cross-sex behavior in children. Gayton et al. obtained a correlation of − .57 between Macho scores and AWS scores, thereby supporting the expectation that persons more conservative on the AWS were also more chauvinistic on the Macho Scale. Scores on the measure of attitudes toward cross-sex behavior in children also correlated significantly with scores on the Macho Scale.

In developing the Attitudes Toward Men Scale (see separate entry), Downs and Engleson (1982) tested a sample of 200 college students with the Macho Scale, the Attitudes Toward Men Scale, and the Attitudes Toward the Male Role Scale (Doyle & Moore, 1978) (see separate entry). Downs and Engleson obtained a correlation of .72 between the Macho Scale and the Attitudes Toward the Male Role Scale and a correlation of .66 between the Macho Scale and the Attitudes Toward Men Scale.

NOTES & COMMENTS: (1) Gayton et al. (1982) obtained mean scores quite different from the means reported by Villemez and Touhey (1977). The mean of 57.03 obtained by Gayton et al. is substantially higher than means of 37.88, 34.58, and 49.17 reported by Villemez and Touhey.

(2) Touhey (1979) identified very high and very low scorers on the Macho Scale. He then had these extreme scorers rate their liking for an attractive or unattractive person of the opposite sex. Touhey found that high scorers on the Macho Scale were more likely to be influenced by the attractiveness of the stimulus person.

AVAILABLE FROM: Villemez and Touhey, 1977.

USED IN:

Andersen, S. M. (1978). Sex-role typing as related to acceptance of self, acceptance of others, and discriminatory attitudes toward women. *Journal of Research in Personality*, 12(4), 410–415.

Downs, A. C., & Engleson, S. A. (1982). The Attitudes Toward Men Scale (AMS): An analysis of the role and status of men and masculinity. *Catalog of Selected Documents in Psychology*, 12(4), 45. (Ms. No. 2503)

Gayton, W. F., Sawyer, B. L., Baird, J. G., & Ozmon, K. L. (1982). Further validation of a new measure of machismo. *Psychological Reports*, 51(3), 820–822.

Touhey, J. C. (1979). Sex-role stereotyping and individual differences in liking for the physically attractive. *Social Psychology Quarterly*, 42(3), 285–289.

Villemez, W. J., & Touhey, J. C. (1977). A measure of individual differences in sex stereotyping and sex discrimination: The "Macho" Scale. *Psychological Reports*, 41(2), 411–415.

BIBLIOGRAPHY:

Adorno, T. W., Frenkel-Brunswik, E., Levinson, D. J., & Sanford, R. N. (1950). *The authoritarian personality*. New York: Harper.

Bem, S. L. (1974). The measurement of psychological androgyny. *Journal of Consulting and Clinical Psychology*, 42, 155–162.

Christie, R., & Geis, F. L. (1970). *Studies in Machiavellianism*. New York: Academic Press.

Crowne, D. P., & Marlowe, D. (1960). A new scale of social desirability independent of psychopathology. *Journal of Consulting Psychology*, 24, 349–354.

Doyle, J. A., & Moore, R. J. (1978). Attitudes Toward the Male's Role Scale (AMR): An objective instrument to measure attitudes toward the male's sex role in contemporary society. *Catalog of Selected Documents in Psychology*, 8(2), 35. (Ms. No. 1678)

Edwards, A. L. (1957). *The social desirability variable in personality assessment and research*. New York: Dryden.

Mehrabian, A. (1969). Measures of achieving tendency. *Educational and Psychological Measurement*, 29, 445–451.

Rotter, J. (1966). Generalized expectancies for internal versus external control of reinforcement. *Psychological Monographs*, 80, No. 1 (Whole No. 609).

Spence, J. T., & Helmreich, R. L. (1978). *Masculinity and femininity*. Austin: University of Texas Press.

Taylor, J. A. (1953). A personality scale of manifest anxiety. *Journal of Abnormal and Social Psychology*, 48, 285–290.

OSMOND-MARTIN SEX ROLE ATTITUDE SCALE

AUTHORS: Marie Withers Osmond and Patricia Yancey Martin

DATE: 1975 (used 1972)

VARIABLE: Gender role attitudes

DESCRIPTION: The Osmond-Martin Sex Role Attitude Scale is a summated rating scale with 32 items covering four areas: familial roles, extrafamilial roles, stereotypes of males and females, and social change issues related to gender roles. Items are accompanied by five response options varying from "strongly agree" to "strongly disagree."

ARTICLES LISTED IN BEERE, 1979: 1

AVAILABLE FROM: Osmond and Martin, 1975

USED IN:

Burge, P. L. (1981). Parental child-rearing sex-role attitudes related to social issue sex-role attitudes and selected demographic variables. *Home Economics Research Journal*, 9, 193–199.

Cunningham, D. L., & Burge, P. L. (1983). Secondary counselors and vocational directors: Sex-role attitudes and attitudes toward teenage parents. *Journal of Vocational Education Research*, 8, 31–41.

Cunningham, D. L., Martin, B. B., & Miller, W. R. (1982). Sex-role attitudes of vocational educators. *Journal of Studies in Technical Careers*, 4, 241–252.

Eversole, J. A. (1977). *Relationship between sex role attitudes of Pennsylvania vocational educators and their stated beliefs about their own sex-role orientation*. Unpublished master's thesis, Pennsylvania State University. (ERIC Document Reproduction Service No. ED 147 515)

Hansen, S. L., & Hicks, M. W. (1980). Sex role attitudes and perceived dating-mating choices of youth. *Adolescence*, 15, 83–90.

Morgan, M. Y. (1987). The impact of religion on gender-role attitudes. *Psychology of Women Quarterly*, 11, 301–310.

Osmond, M. W., & Martin, P. Y. (1975). Sex and sexism: A comparison of male and female sex role attitudes. *Journal of Marriage and the Family, 37,* 744–758.

Rosen, D. L., & Granbois, D. H. (1983). Determinants of role structure in family financial management. *Journal of Consumer Research, 10,* 253–258.

Schmidt, B. J. (1971, April). *Sex-role attitudes of business educators and their perceptions of office education recruitment materials.* Paper presented at the meeting of the American Educational Research Association, Los Angeles. (ERIC Document Reproduction Service No. ED 200 818)

BIBLIOGRAPHY:

Beere, C. A. (1979). *Women and women's issues: A handbook of tests and measures* (pp. 448–449). San Francisco: Jossey-Bass.

ROMBOUGH VENTIMIGLIA ATTITUDES TOWARD SEX ROLES

AUTHORS: Shirley Rombough and Joseph C. Ventimiglia

DATE: 1981 (used 1978)

VARIABLE: Gender role attitudes

TYPE OF INSTRUMENT: Used as a summated rating scale or Guttman scale

DESCRIPTION: The Rombough Ventimiglia Attitudes Toward Sex Roles scale consists of 20 items that measure gender role attitudes in three domains: "internal familial division of labor [8 items], external (economic) division of labor [6 items], and perceived sex differences [6 items]" (Rombough & Ventimiglia, 1981, p. 747). Items are accompanied by five response options: "strongly agree, agree, no opinion, disagree, strongly disagree." Fourteen items are phrased so that "agree" reflects a sexist response; 6 items are phrased in the reverse direction.

SAMPLE ITEMS: (internal familial division of labor) It's all right for the woman to have a career and the man to stay home with the children.

(external division of labor) The job of plumber is equally suitable for men and women.

(perceived sex differences) Women are more envious than men.

PREVIOUS SUBJECTS: College students, working and professional people, members of church and social clubs

APPROPRIATE FOR: High school students and older

ADMINISTRATION: Self-administered; about 10 minutes

SCORING: For summated rating scores, items are individually scored on a 5-point scale, with higher points assigned to the sexist responses. Item scores are totaled to yield four scores: external division of labor, internal division of labor, sex differences, and a total score. Total scores can range from 20 (very egalitarian) to 100 (very sexist). To facilitate use of the scale as a Guttman scale, Rombough and Ventimiglia (1981) provided a table for determining scores.

DEVELOPMENT: An item pool of 197 items was compiled by conducting a search of the literature, selecting items with high face validity, and eliminating items that were redundant. Ambiguous items were rewritten. The items fell into a number of categories: "innate qualities, social behavior, sexual behavior, family activities, economic activity, political activity, education, and military activity" (Rombough & Ventimiglia, 1981, p. 750). The item pool was administered to a sample of college students, working adults, and members of social and church clubs, and their responses were factor analyzed. Two factors were extracted. The first factor included 20 items with 10 items from the original category of economic activity and 10 items from the original category of family activities; the second factor included 7 items representing three of the original categories. Rombough and Ventimiglia did not explain how this 27-item version of the scale was reduced to the final 20-item version.

RELIABILITY: Rombough and Ventimiglia (1981) reported the following alpha coefficients: sex differences = .73, internal division of labor = .88, external division of labor = .85, and total scale = .94. A Guttman analysis produced the following results: reproducibility coefficients of .93 for external division of labor, .90 for internal division of labor, and .92 for sex differences; and scalability coefficients of .60 for sex differences, .56 for internal division of labor, and .71 for external division of labor.

VALIDITY: To establish validity, Rombough and Ventimiglia (1981), expecting that males would be more sexist than females, compared responses from males and females. There were significant sex differences on 17 of the 20 items.

Lawson (1982) also checked for significant sex differences on each of the 20 items. He found that 1 item should be scored in the opposite direction. Using a two-tailed test, 3 other items showed nonsignificant sex differences. Using a one-tailed test, 2 items showed nonsignificant sex differences.

Using data from college students, Faulkender (1985) found that scores from college men showed more sexism than did scores from college women.

NOTES & COMMENTS: (1) Rombough and Ventimiglia (1981) provided subscale intercorrelations, all of them quite high. The correlation between external and internal division of labor was .71; the correlation between external division of labor and sex differences was .68; and the correlation between internal division of labor and sex differences was .71.

(2) Faulkender (1985) related scores on the Rombough-Ventimiglia scale to sex role classification based on the Bem Sex Role Inventory (Bem, 1974) (see separate entry).

AVAILABLE FROM: Rombough and Ventimiglia, 1981; Lawson, 1982
USED IN:
Faulkender, P. J. (1985). Relationship between Bem Sex-Role Inventory groups and attitudes of sexism. *Psychological Reports, 57,* 227–235.

Lawson, E. D. (1982). The Rombough-Ventimiglia Scale: A replication. *Replications in Social Psychology*, 2(2), 27–29.

Rombough, S., & Ventimiglia, J. C. (1981). Sexism: A tri-dimensional phenomenon. *Sex Roles*, 7(7), 747–755.

BIBLIOGRAPHY:

Bem, S. L. (1974). The measurement of psychological androgyny. *Journal of Consulting and Clinical Psychology*, 42, 155–162.

SCOTT SEX ROLE INVENTORY

AUTHORS: Judith Scott and John C. Brantley

DATE: 1983

VARIABLE: Knowledge of sex differences and attitudes toward sex role stereotyping

TYPE OF INSTRUMENT: Summated rating scale

DESCRIPTION: There are two parts to the Scott Sex Role Inventory. The first part consists of 20 attitude statements covering a variety of areas pertaining to girls, boys, women, and men. The second part consists of 17 statements that are labeled as "knowledge" items; these items have right and wrong answers. Both the attitude statements and the knowledge items are accompanied by five response options ranging from "strongly agree" to "strongly disagree." For the knowledge items, respondents are told to indicate whether they agree with the statement; they are not told to indicate whether the statement is factually accurate. Of the 37 items, 22 items are phrased in one direction, and 15 items are phrased in the opposite direction.

SAMPLE ITEMS: (attitudes) It's natural to attach more power and prestige to the male role.

(knowledge) Girls begin school as better achievers than boys, but fall behind as they become socialized.

PREVIOUS SUBJECTS: Teachers

APPROPRIATE FOR: High school students and older

ADMINISTRATION: Self-administered; about 20 minutes

SCORING: Individual items are scored on a 5-point scale, with 5 points assigned to the sexist end of the scale. Twenty-two items are scored in one direction, and 15 items are reverse scored. Item scores are totaled to yield two scores: an attitude score and a knowledge score.

DEVELOPMENT: The first step in scale development was to review the literature to identify appropriate content categories. This step led to six categories: "(1) student/teacher relationships, (2) education and curriculum, (3) employment and adult roles, (4) physical and behavioral characteristics, (5) child rearing, and (6) knowledge about research in the area of sexism" (Scott & Brantley, 1983, p. 343). The authors stated, "One hundred and fifty items were then selected as representing these categories" (p. 343), but they provided no information regarding how the items were selected or from where they were selected. Two experts in test development reviewed the items, and as a result, some items were deleted and some were revised. Again, no details were provided, so there is no way of knowing whether the "experts in test development" were the authors of the scale, what criteria were used for deletion, or what kinds of revisions were made. The resulting 86-item questionnaire was administered to 139 teachers. Their responses were factor analyzed and an item analysis was performed. The factor analysis yielded 10 factors with eigenvalues above 1.0; 7 of those factors contained items loading above .55. Of the 7 factors, 3 contained only a single item. The item analysis looked at the item discrimination index for each item. To perform the item analysis, responses from the highest-scoring 27% of the teachers were compared with responses from the lowest-scoring 27% of the teachers. The authors stated: "By examining both the results of the factor analysis and the indices of discrimination, the attitude section was shortened to 20 items; all knowledge items were retained" (Scott & Brantley, 1983, p. 346). It is not clear how these analyses were used since it appears that all of the items loading above .55 on the 7 factors were retained. It is not at all clear why the factor analysis played such an important role in item selection since there does not seem to be any relationship between the initial plans for the scale and the results of the factor analysis.

RELIABILITY: The odd-even reliability for the attitude items was .90, and for the knowledge items, it was .70. A different sample of respondents was used for estimating test-retest reliability. A sample of 22 teachers from a private school completed the Scott Sex Role Inventory on two occasions, separated by 2 weeks. The test-retest reliability for the full scale was .82; the test-retest reliability for the knowledge items was .69. The authors did not report the test-retest for the attitude items alone, nor did they explain why a full scale, test-retest reliability was computed.

VALIDITY: Scott and Brantley (1983) claimed that content validity was ensured by the method of scale development. Unfortunately, their scale development procedures did not include sufficient detail to evaluate the accuracy of this statement.

As evidence of construct validity, Scott and Brantley (1983) pointed to the factor analysis and the determination of internal consistency. However, they never related the results of the factor analysis to the original plan for scale development. As evidence of internal consistency, they reported the intercorrelations between the factors and between the factors and the total scale. They did not, however, report coefficient alpha for the two parts of the scale, nor did they suggest factor scores should be used. In other words, the usefulness of the data they did present is not clear.

Scott and Brantley (1983) correlated scores on the Scott Sex Role Inventory with scores on another stereotyping measure: Woolever's (1976) adaptation of the Sex Role Stereotype Questionnaire (Rosenkrantz, Bee,

Vogel, Broverman, & Broverman, 1968). Thirty-two teachers from the United States and 15 staff members from an Australian school completed both scales. Since the two scales are scored in opposite directions, negative correlations were expected. For the U.S. teachers, the correlation with the attitude items was $-.43$, and the correlation with the knowledge items was $-.22$. The correlation with the total score was $-.78$. For the Australian sample, the three correlations were $-.72$ (attitude items), $-.65$ (knowledge items), and $-.83$ (total score).

Scott and Brantley (1983) reported no differences in scores between male and female respondents. This is unusual since females generally stereotype less than males.

NOTES & COMMENTS: (1) At the outset, Scott and Brantley (1983) stated: "It was assumed that an inventory yielding several subtest scores based on different areas of sex bias would be more valuable" (p. 343). There is no evidence that they succeeded in developing a scale with valuable subtest scores based on content areas.

(2) Though the Scott Sex Role Inventory was designed for use with teachers, there is little to suggest that the items, particularly those on the attitude portion, are more relevant for teachers than for anyone else. Only 4 of the 20 items on the attitude portion could be construed as directly relating to teaching or schools, and these items can easily be answered by persons other than teachers. A greater proportion of the knowledge items (9 out of 20) relate to education, but these items can be answered by other persons. Since the scale development used teachers, there are no data regarding the psychometric properties of the scale for persons other than teachers.

(3) Three of the factors contain only a single item.

(4) Seventeen items on the scale are factual items. What is the difference between "agreeing" and "strongly agreeing" with a factual statement? Does strong agreement reflect greater confidence in one's knowledge of the facts, or does it reflect a stronger feeling about the item content?

AVAILABLE FROM: Scott and Brantley, 1983

USED IN:

Scott, J., & Brantley, J. C. (1983). Development of an inventory of teachers' attitudes towards sex-role stereotyping and knowledge of sex differences. *Sex Roles*, 9(3), 341–353.

BIBLIOGRAPHY:

Rosenkrantz, P., Vogel, S., Bee, H., Broverman, I., & Broverman, D. M. (1968). Sex-role stereotypes and self-concepts in college students. *Journal of Consulting and Clinical Psychology*, 32(3), 287–295.

Woolever, R. (1976). Expanding elementary pupils' occupational and social roles perception: An examination of teacher attitudes and behavior in pupil attitude change. (Doctoral dissertation, University of Washington, 1976). *Dissertation Abstracts International*, 37, 1394A.

SEX ROLE DIFFERENCES SCALE
AUTHOR: Joseph W. Critelli
DATE: 1979
VARIABLE: Support for gender role differences
TYPE OF INSTRUMENT: Summated rating scale
DESCRIPTION: The Sex Role Differences Scale contains 10 items to measure whether one supports separate and distinct roles for men and women or whether one believes there should be no differences in the gender roles of men and women. Six items reflect support for distinct gender roles; the other 4 items reflect support for equal roles. Eight of the 10 items deal with marital roles; the other 2 items refer to children. Items are accompanied by five response options: "disagree, tend to disagree, neither agree nor disagree, tend to agree, agree."
SAMPLE ITEMS: If a husband and wife both have full-time jobs the husband should devote just as much time to housekeeping as the wife should.

In marriage, the husband should take the lead in decision making.
PREVIOUS SUBJECTS: College students
APPROPRIATE FOR: High school students and older
ADMINISTRATION: Self-administered; about 5 minutes
SCORING: Items are individually scored on a 5-point scale, with higher scores reflecting greater support for separate, distinct gender roles. A total score is obtained by summing the 10 item scores. Critelli (1979) provided means and standard deviations by sex for each item and for the total score for two groups of respondents.
DEVELOPMENT: A pool of 37 items was developed by selecting items from existing measures and by writing some original items. A sample of 225 college men and 180 college women responded to the items in the pool and completed the Marlowe-Crowne Social Desirability Scale (Crowne & Marlowe, 1964), a one-item measure of political conservatism, and a one-item measure of attitudes toward the women's movement. Items were selected for the Sex Role Differences Scale if they had item-remainder correlations of at least .30; correlated with the Marlowe-Crowne Social Desirability Scale at a level no greater than .20; had face validity; and correlated more highly with the other items in the pool than with the one-item measure of political conservatism. Items were intentionally selected to obtain a balance between support for separate roles and support for equal roles. Applying these criteria, 10 items were selected for the scale.
RELIABILITY: For the sample of 405 college students on whom the scale was developed, coefficient alpha was .86. For a sample of 123 dating couples, coefficient alpha was .89.
VALIDITY: Scores on the Sex Role Differences Scale showed moderate correlations with political conservatism ($r = .33$ for males and $r = .42$

for females), with politically conservative students more likely to favor differences in gender roles. Correlations between Sex Role Differences scores and attitudes toward the women's movement were significant (r = $-.53$ for males, r = $-.63$ for females), with those who supported the women's movement less likely to favor differences in gender roles. Males were significantly more likely to favor gender role differences than were females.

Scores on the Sex Role Differences Scale were not correlated with Marlowe-Crowne Social Desirability scores, age, grade point average, or parental income.

NOTES & COMMENTS: Critelli, Myers, and Loos (1986) used the Sex Role Differences Scale as a measure of gender role traditionalism. For a sample of 123 dating couples, they found a relationship between gender role traditionalism and type of love experienced: "traditionals [are] characterized by romantic dependency and romantic compatibility, while nontraditionals emphasized communicative intimacy" (p. 354). They also found that the correlation between the scores of male and female dating partners was .49.

AVAILABLE FROM: Critelli, 1979

USED IN:

Critelli, J. W. (1979). The measurement of attitudes toward sex role differences. *Catalog of Selected Documents in Psychology, 9*(2), 29. (Ms. No. 1844)

Critelli, J. W., Myers, E. J., & Loos, V. E. (1986). The components of love: Romantic attraction and sex role orientation. *Journal of Personality, 54*(2), 354–370.

BIBLIOGRAPHY:

Crowne, D. P., & Marlowe, D. (1964). *The approval motive.* New York: Wiley.

SEX-ROLE EGALITARIANISM SCALE (SRE)

AUTHORS: Carole A. Beere, Daniel W. King, Donald B. Beere, and Lynda A. King

DATE: 1984 (used 1980)

VARIABLE: Attitudes toward equality between the sexes

TYPE OF INSTRUMENT: Summated rating scale

DESCRIPTION: There are two forms of the Sex-Role Egalitarianism Scale (SRE): Form B and Form K. Each consists of 95 items including 19 items representing each of five domains: marital roles, parental roles, employment roles, social-interpersonal-heterosexual roles, and educational roles. All of the items explicitly or implicitly compare women and men. Each item is accompanied by five response options: "strongly agree, agree, neutral or undecided or no opinion, disagree, strongly disagree." On Form B, 39 items are keyed "agree," and 56 items are keyed "disagree." On Form K, 40 items are keyed "agree," and 55 items are keyed "disagree."

King and King (1986a) developed short forms of the SRE. (See NOTES & COMMENTS).

SAMPLE ITEMS: (marital roles) Working husbands and wives should equally sacrifice their careers for the sake of home duties.

(parental roles) It is just as important for fathers to attend their children's school functions as it is for mothers to attend.

(employment roles) There are many jobs in which women should be given preference over men in being hired.

(social-interpersonal-heterosexual roles) Women are typically better listeners than men are.

(educational roles) Business courses are more appropriate for male students than for female students.

PREVIOUS SUBJECTS: College students; police officers; senior citizens

APPROPRIATE FOR: High school students and older

ADMINISTRATION: Self-administered; about 30–40 minutes

SCORING: Items are individually scored on a 5-point scale, with the egalitarian response assigned 5 points. Subscale scores, ranging from 19 (not at all egalitarian) to 95 (very egalitarian), can be obtained for each of the five domains. The overall total score ranges from 95 to 475, with higher scores representing more egalitarian attitudes. Beere, King, Beere, and King (1984) provided means and standard deviations for each subscale and for the total score. Separate data were provided for each of the two forms.

DEVELOPMENT: Before developing the scale, Beere et al. (1984) defined sex role egalitarianism as "an attitude that causes one to respond to another individual independently of the other individual's sex" (p. 564). With this definition in mind, the authors constructed a pool of 524 items that were submitted to five judges. The judges independently sorted the items into the five domains: marital roles, parental roles, employment roles, social-interpersonal-heterosexual roles, and educational roles. Items were eliminated if there was not unanimous agreement on the domain classification. From the remaining items, a set of 40 to 42 items was selected to represent each domain. The items selected for each domain included an equal number of "radical feminine bias" items and "radical masculine bias" items. Radical feminine bias (RFB) was defined as a bias that "would lead a respondent to indiscriminately assert that women can do everything in every way 'better' than men." Similarly, radical masculine bias (RMB) "would lead a respondent to indiscriminately assert that men can do everything in every way 'better' than women" (Beere et al., 1984, p. 565). The item pool, which now included 204 items, was administered to 530 persons with instructions to respond to each item on a 5-point scale. Item analyses were performed on the responses, and the resulting data were used to build alternate forms of the scale. Care was taken to ensure that the number of RMB and RFB items was equal for a given domain on both forms of the scale. For example, for the marital domain, there are six RFB and six RMB items on each form of the scale.

RELIABILITY: Beere et al. (1984) tested large groups of respondents—college students, police officers, and senior citizens—and used their data to compute three types of reliability: split-half, test-retest, and alternate form. Corrected split-half coefficients for the subscales ranged from .84 to .89. For the total score, the correct split-half coefficient was .97 for each form. Test-retest coefficients were computed for both forms of the scale; the interval between testings ranged from 3 to 4 weeks. For the subscale scores, the test-retest coefficients ranged from .81 to .88. The test-retest coefficients for the total score were .88 for Form B and .91 for Form K. Alternate form reliabilities were computed for the subscale scores; they ranged from .84 to .88. For the total score, alternate form reliability was .93.

King and King (1983a) performed a generalizability analysis on responses to the SRE. From this, they concluded that "an investigator may pool a group of subjects, some of whom completed Form B and some of whom completed Form K, and then treat them as if they all completed the same measure" (p. 440).

VALIDITY: Beere et al. (1984) tested about 80 persons with both the SRE and with Edwards's (1957) Social Desirability Scale. The correlations between the SRE subscale scores and the Edwards score ranged from − .03 to .19; the correlations between the Edwards score and each of the two total scores were .17 and .09. These low correlations suggest that the SRE is not measuring social desirability.

As predicted, on both forms of the scale and on every domain, women consistently scored higher—more egalitarian—than did men. It was also predicted that psychology students would be more egalitarian than business students, and college students would be more egalitarian than police officers and senior citizens. Both of these predictions were supported (Beere et al., 1984). The significant sex differences were replicated in research by King and King (1985).

King and King (1986b) administered the SRE Form K, the Attitudes Toward Women Scale (AWS) (Spence & Helmreich, 1972) (see separate entry), and a variety of other measures to a sample of 108 college students. The relationship between SRE and AWS scores was, as hypothesized, curvilinear. After analyzing all of the data, King and King (1986b) concluded: "The results of this study provide evidence for the notion that sex role egalitarianism has an existence separate from feminist attitudes" (p. 213).

NOTES & COMMENTS: (1) Beere et al. (1984) reported the intercorrelations between the different subscores. All of the correlations were quite high, indicating that the subscales were not independent. Beere et al. also reported performing a factor analysis of the domain scores; the analysis showed that all items loaded on a single factor, leading them to conclude "the scale is unidimensional" (p. 575).

(2) King and King (1983a) reported results of a generalizability analysis of the five domains of the SRE. They provided considerable information on the variance components and concluded that "the researcher interested in the SRE Scale may directly use these data to decrease measurement error and thereby increase precision" (p. 447).

(3) King and King (1983b) examined the impact that gender role egalitarian attitudes have on the evaluation of males and females. In one study, subjects were required to evaluate the qualifications of male and female job applicants; in the other study, subjects had to agree or disagree with decisions made by a school board.

(4) King and King (1986a) developed two short forms of the SRE: Form BB and Form KK. Each short form includes 25 items, with 5 items representing each of the five domains from the full-length versions. To develop the short forms, King and King selected the 5 items from each domain with the highest item-total correlations. The correlation between the two short forms was .91. Internal consistency for Form BB was .91. Internal consistency for Form KK was .94. With an interval of 3 to 6 weeks between testings, the correlation between scores on Form B and Form BB was .75. The correlation between Form K and Form KK was .85.

(5) Rosenfeld and Jarrard (1985, 1986) used the short forms of the SRE to measure college students' perceptions of their professors' gender attitudes.

AVAILABLE FROM: Lynda King, Department of Psychology, Central Michigan University, Mt. Pleasant, MI 48859

USED IN:

Beere, C. A., King, D. W., Beere, D. B., & King, L. A. (1984). The Sex-Role Egalitarianism Scale: A measure of attitudes toward equality between the sexes. *Sex Roles, 10*(7/8), 563–576.

Honeck, S. M. (1981). *An exploratory study of the Beere-King Sex-Role Egalitarianism Scale, the MacDonald Sex Role Survey, and Spence and Helmreich's Attitudes Toward Women Scale.* Unpublished master's thesis, Central Michigan University, Mt. Pleasant.

King, D. W., & King, L. A. (1982). Sex-role stereotyping in evaluations of job applicants: Egalitarian attitude as a moderator variable. In N. Weiner & R. Klimoski (Eds.), *Proceedings of the Midwest Academy of Management.* Columbus: Ohio State University.

King, D. W., & King, L. A. (1983a). Measurement precision of the Sex-Role Egalitarianism Scale: A generalizability analysis. *Educational and Psychological Measurement, 43,* 435–447.

King, D. W., & King, L. A. (1983b). Sex-role egalitarianism as a moderator variable in decision-making: Two validity studies. *Educational and Psychological Measurement, 43,* 1199–1210.

King, L. A, Beere, D. B., King, D. W., & Beere, C. A. (1981, April). *A new measure*

of sex-role attitudes. Paper presented at the meeting of the Midwestern
Psychological Association, Detroit. (ERIC Document Reproduction Service No. ED 205 863)

King, L. A., & King, D. W. (1985). Sex-role egalitarianism: Biographical and
personality correlates. *Psychological Reports, 57*, 787–792.

King, L. A., & King, D. W. (1986a, May). *Development of alternate short forms to
measure sex-role egalitarian attitudes*. Paper presented at the meeting of the
Midwestern Psychological Association, Chicago.

King, L. A., & King, D. W. (1986b). Validity of the Sex-Role Egalitarianism Scale:
Discriminating egalitarianism from feminism. *Sex Roles, 15*(3/4), 207–214.

Krueger, H. K., & Bornstein, P. H. (1987). Depression, sex-roles, and family
variables: Comparison of bulimics, binge-eaters, and normals. *Psychological Reports, 60*, 1106.

Rosenfeld, L. B., & Jarrard, M. W. (1985). The effects of perceived sexism in
female and male college professors on students' descriptions of classroom
climate. *Communication Education, 34*, 205–213.

Rosenfeld, L. B., & Jarrard, M. W. (1986). Student coping mechanisms in sexist
and nonsexist professors' classes. *Communication Education, 35*, 157–162.

BIBLIOGRAPHY:

Edwards, A. L. (1957). *The social desirability variable in personality assessment and
research*. New York: Dryden.

Spence, J. T., & Helmreich, R. L. (1972). The Attitudes Toward Women Scale:
An objective instrument to measure attitudes toward the rights and roles
of women in contemporary society. *Catalog of Selected Documents in Psychology, 2*, 66. (Ms. No. 153)

SEX-ROLE IDEOLOGY SCALE

AUTHORS: Rudolf Kalin and Penelope J. Tilby

DATE: 1978

VARIABLE: Gender role prescriptions

TYPE OF INSTRUMENT: Summated rating scale

DESCRIPTION: The Sex-Role Ideology Scale consists of 30 items covering five broad content areas: "(1) work roles of men and women, 6
items; (2) parental responsibilities of men and women, 5 items; (3) personal relationships between men and women; friendship, courtship and
sexual, 7 items; (4) special role of women, and "pedestal" concept, 8
items; (5) motherhood, abortion, and homosexuality, 4 items" (Kalin &
Tilby, 1978, p. 734). Each item is a statement regarding how things
"should" be for women and/or for men. Half of the items are phrased
in a feminist direction, and half are phrased in a traditional direction.
A 7-point response scale accompanies each item.

SAMPLE ITEMS: The husband should be regarded as the legal representative of the family group in all matters of law.

A woman should have exactly the same freedom of action as a man.

PREVIOUS SUBJECTS: College students, health professionals, mental health professionals; women identified as feminist and as traditional; married couples; teachers; persons in Ireland, England, the United States, and Canada, including French-speaking Canada.

APPROPRIATE FOR: High school students and older; most research using this scale has been done in Canada

ADMINISTRATION: Self-administered; about 15 minutes

SCORING: Items are individually scored, with 7 points assigned to the feminist end of the continuum, so half of the items must be reversed before total scores are obtained. Omitted items are assigned the mean score obtained on the other items. Totals can range from 30 (very traditional) to 210 (very strongly feminist).

DEVELOPMENT: An item pool was developed including some items taken from Kirkpatrick's Belief Pattern Scale for Measuring Attitudes Toward Feminism (Kirkpatrick, 1936) (see separate entry). The item pool included a variety of items including ones relevant to women only (e.g., items relating to abortion or contraception) and ones that suggest a positive view of the traditional female role. A version of the scale with 82 items was administered to three samples: a feminist sample, a student sample, and a traditional sample. Based on the results from these samples, 30 items were selected for the final scale by using the following criteria: (1) selected items discriminated among the three groups; that is, there was a large difference between the feminist and traditional groups, and the student group fell in between; (2) selected items had high item-total correlations; (3) selected items represented a variety of content areas and pertained to issues judged as important; (4) a few selected items represented the ends of the traditional-feminist continuum; and (5) an equal number of items were phrased in a traditional direction and in a feminist direction.

Scores on the 30-item final version of the scale were correlated with scores on the full 82-item version. For all samples taken together, the correlation was .98. For the three samples individually, the correlations were: traditional group = .79, students = .95, and liberated group = .94.

RELIABILITY: Kalin and Tilby (1978) computed split-half reliability for several groups not used in the scale development. They obtained coefficients ranging from .57 to .84 in homogeneous samples to .91 in heterogeneous samples. They also looked at test-retest reliability by retesting a sample of college students after a 3-week interval. The reliability coefficient was .87.

Kalin, Heusser, and Edwards (1982) computed split-half reliabilities for several samples of students. For two Canadian samples, the reliability coefficients were .79 and .84; for an English sample, the reliability was

.82; and for an Irish sample, the reliability was .71. Milo, Badger, and Coggins (1983) tested physicians, patients, and college students and calculated coefficient alpha. They obtained a reliability of .82.

Buhrke (1988) administered the Sex-Role Ideology Scale to 184 college students and obtained a coefficient alpha of .88. Buhrke also reported coefficient alpha for several subscales: Work Roles of Men and Women = .55; Parental Responsibilities = .66; Personal Relationships Between Men and Women = .67; Special Role of Women = .66; and Motherhood, Abortion, and Homosexuality = .42. These subscale reliabilities are unacceptably low, but Kalin and Tilby never recommended computing subscale scores.

VALIDITY: Kalin and Tilby (1978) compared responses from male and female college students. The scores were significantly different, with females scoring as more feminist. Kalin and Tilby also compared responses from several groups not involved in the original scale development. Like the scale development samples, the new groups included a feminist group, a student sample, and a traditional sample. The item discrimination results for these three groups were quite similar to those obtained from the groups on whom the scale was developed. Also, on all items, the traditionalists and the feminists scored differently from each other.

Kalin et al. (1982) tested students in Canada, England, and Ireland. The researchers consistently found that females were more feminist than males. Leichner and Kalin (1981) found that among psychiatrists and psychiatric residents, women were significantly more feminist than men. Furthermore, within these groups, as well as within groups of university students, traditional women, and feminist women, Leichner and Kalin found that older respondents were more traditional than younger respondents.

Buhrke (1988) administered the Sex-Role Ideology Scale and three other gender role attitude scales to 184 college students. The other scales were the Attitudes Toward Women Scale (Spence & Helmreich, 1972) (see separate entry), the Attitude Toward Masculinity Transcendence Scale (Moreland & Van Tuinen, 1978) (see separate entry), and the Sexist Attitudes Toward Women Scale (Benson & Vincent, 1980) (see separate entry). Additionally, Buhrke administered the Marlowe-Crowne Social Desirability Scale (Crowne & Marlowe, 1964). The correlation between the Sex-Role Ideology Scale and the other scales was: Sexist Attitudes Toward Women Scale = −.74; Attitudes Toward Women Scale = .73; and Attitude Toward Masculinity Transcendence Scale = .75. Buhrke also reported all of the subscale intercorrelations. The correlation between the Sex-Role Ideology Scale and the Marlowe-Crowne Social Desirability Scale was .04. Buhrke obtained significant correlations between the Sex-Role Ideology Scale and several single-item scales expected to correlate with the scores.

NOTES & COMMENTS: (1) Kalin and Tilby (1978) offered a clear distinction between feminist and traditional ideology: "Traditional ideology starts with the notion of basic differences between the sexes and relegates women to the roles of housewife and mother. Women are viewed as weak, vulnerable, in need of protection and deserving of a special respect. For traditional ideology, man is the actor, provider, and final authority" (p. 732).

(2) Kalin et al. (1982) sought to determine whether the Sex Role Ideology Scale was appropriate for use in Ireland and England. From their research, they concluded that the scale was appropriate in both countries.

(3) Milo et al. (1983) tested physicians, patients, and students in the United States and factor analyzed their responses. They extracted four factors that did *not* conform to the content areas suggested by Kalin and Tilby. Two of the factors were reliable. From their research, Milo et al. concluded: "We suspect that perhaps the Sex-Role Ideology Scale measures not a position on sex-roles but the degree of acceptance or rejection of two relatively distinct phenomena, the political individual-rights ideology of the women's movement and the pragmatic norms of a traditional family-oriented sex-role division" (p. 144).

(4) Tilby and Kalin (1979, 1980) compared Sex-Role Ideology scores with scores on measures of gender stereotyping. In their 1979 study, they reported a correlation of $-.18$; in their 1980 study, they reported a value of $-.27$. Both results showed that the two scales are essentially measuring different constructs.

(5) Buhrke (1988) factor analyzed the subscale scores from several sex role ideology measures. She included subscale scores she derived from the Sex-Role Ideology Scale in the factor analysis.

(6) A variety of research has been conducted using the Sex-Role Ideology Scale. Kalin and Lloyd (1985) looked at the relationship of gender role identity, gender role ideology, and marital adjustment for both respondents and their spouses. Some researchers have looked at whether gender role ideology affects persons' evaluations of gender role–congruent and gender role–incongruent behavior (Subich, 1984; Tilby & Kalin, 1980). The gender role ideology of persons from a variety of professions, all of whom were doing psychotherapy, has been studied (Harper, Leichner, & McCrimmon, 1985; McNevin, Leichner, Harper, & McCrimmon, 1985). Sex Role Ideology scores have also been looked at in regard to self-esteem (de Man & Benoit, 1982; Mintz & Betz, 1986).

AVAILABLE FROM: Kalin and Tilby, 1978; Milo, Badger, and Coggins, 1983

USED IN:

Buhrke, R. A. (1988). Factor dimensions across different measures of sex role ideology. *Sex Roles, 18*, 309–321.

Byers, E. S. (1988). Effects of sexual arousal on men's and women's behavior in sexual disagreement situations. *Journal of Sex Research, 25*(2), 235–254.

de Man, A. F., & Benoit, R. (1982). Self-esteem in feminist and nonfeminist French-Canadian women and French-Canadian men. *Journal of Psychology, 111*(1), 3–7.

Harper, D. W., Leichner, P. P., & McCrimmon, E. (1985). Sex-role ideology among self-identified psychotherapists. *Canadian Journal of Psychiatry, 30*(6), 422–425.

Kalin, R., Heusser, C., & Edwards, J. (1982). Cross-national equivalence of a Sex-Role Ideology Scale. *Journal of Social Psychology, 116*(1), 141–142.

Kalin, R., & Lloyd, C. A. (1985). Sex role identity, sex-role ideology and marital adjustment. *International Journal of Women's Studies, 8*(1), 32–39.

Kalin, R., & Tilby, P. J. (1978). Development and validation of a sex-role ideology scale. *Psychological Reports, 42*, 731–738.

Leichner, P., & Kalin, R. (1981). Sex-role ideology among practicing psychiatrists and psychiatric residents. *American Journal of Psychiatry, 138*(10), 1342–1345.

McNevin, S. H., Leichner, P., Harper, D., & McCrimmon, E. (1985). Sex role ideology among health care professionals. *Psychiatric Journal of the University of Ottawa, 10*(1), 21–23.

Milo, T., Badger, L. W., & Coggins, D. R. (1983). Conceptual analysis of the Sex-role Ideology Scale. *Psychological Reports, 53*(1), 139–146.

Mintz, L. B., & Betz, N. E. (1986). Sex differences in the nature, realism, and correlates of body image. *Sex Roles, 15*(3/4), 185–195.

Subich, L. M. (1984). Ratings of counselor expertness, attractiveness, and trustworthiness as a function of counselor sex role and subject feminist orientation. *Sex Roles, 11*(11/12), 1033–1043.

Tilby, P. J., & Kalin, R. (1979). Effects of sex role deviance in disturbed male adolescents on the perception of psychopathology. *Canadian Journal of Behavioural Science, 11*(1), 45–52.

Tilby, P. J., & Kalin, R. (1980). Effects of sex-role deviant life-styles in otherwise normal persons on the perception of maladjustment. *Sex Roles, 6*(4), 581–592.

BIBLIOGRAPHY:

Benson, P. L., & Vincent, S. (1980). Development and validation of the Sexist Attitudes Toward Women Scale (SATWS). *Psychology of Women Quarterly, 5*, 276–291.

Crowne, D. P., & Marlowe, D. (1964). *The approval motive.* New York: Wiley.

Kirkpatrick, C. (1936). The construction of a belief-pattern scale for measuring attitudes towards feminism. *Journal of Social Psychology, 7*, 421–437.

Moreland, J. R., & Van Tuinen, M. (1978, July). *The Attitude Toward Masculinity Transcendence Scale.* Paper presented at Ohio State University, Columbus.

Spence, J. T., & Helmreich, R. L. (1972). The Attitudes Toward Women Scale: An objective instrument to measure attitudes toward the rights and roles of women in contemporary society. *Catalog of Selected Documents in Psychology, 2,* 66. (Ms. No. 153)

SEX ROLE ORIENTATION SCALE

AUTHORS: Donna Brogan and Nancy G. Kutner

DATE: 1976

VARIABLE: Gender role ideology

DESCRIPTION: The Sex Role Orientation Scale is a summated rating scale consisting of 36 items that measure attitudes toward traditional, sex-based division of labor in marriage; attitudes toward a traditional, sex-based power structure; attitudes toward traditional and nontraditional employment of men and women; attitudes toward the political status of women; support for the traditional gender role socialization of children; and endorsement of stereotypes of gender role related behavior. Items are accompanied by six response alternatives ranging from "strongly agree" to "strongly disagree."

ARTICLES LISTED IN BEERE, 1979: 1

NOTES & COMMENTS: Most researchers use the entire Sex Role Orientation Scale, but some use a subset of the items. For example, Hansen (1982a, 1982b, 1985a, 1985b) used a 10-item subset, and Levy, Faulkner, and Dixon (1984) used a 12-item subset.

AVAILABLE FROM: Brogan and Kutner, 1976

USED IN:

Brogan, D., & Kutner, N. G. (1976). Measuring sex role orientation: A normative approach. *Journal of Marriage and the Family, 38,* 31–40.

Feinberg, R. A., & Workman, J. E. (1981). Sex-role orientation and cognitive complexity. *Psychological Reports, 49,* 246.

Fitzpatrick, M. A., & Indvik, J. (1982). The instrumental and expressive domains of marital communication. *Human Communication Research, 8,* 195–213.

Gardner, K. E., & LaBrecque, S. V. (1986). Effects of maternal employment on sex role orientation of adolescents. *Adolescence, 21,* 875–885.

Grimes, M. D., & Hansen, G. L. (1984). Response bias in sex-role attitude measurement. *Sex Roles, 10,* 67–72.

Hansen, G. L. (1982a). Androgyny, sex-role orientation, and homosexism. *Journal of Psychology, 112,* 39–45.

Hansen, G. L. (1982b). Reactions to hypothetical, jealousy producing events. *Family Relations, 31,* 513–518.

Hansen, G. L. (1985a). Dating jealousy among college students. *Sex Roles, 12,* 713–721.

Hansen, G. L. (1985b). Perceived threats and marital jealousy. *Social Psychology Quarterly, 48,* 262–268.

Henderson, K. A. (1984, March). *Women in leisure services: The Wisconsin data.* Paper presented at the meeting of the American Alliance for Health, Physical Education, Recreation, and Dance, Anaheim, CA (ERIC Document Reproduction Service No. ED 243 857)

Keith, P. M. (1981). Sex-role attitudes, family plans, and career orientations: Implications for counseling. *Vocational Guidance Quarterly, 29,* 244–252.

Krampen, G., & von Eye, A. (1984). Generalized expectations of drug-delinquents, other delinquents, and a control sample. *Addictive Behaviors, 9,* 421–423.

Krausz, S. L. (1986). Sex roles within marriage. *Social Work, 31,* 457–464.

Kutner, N. G., & Brogan, D. R. (1981). Problems of colleagueship for women entering the medical profession. *Sex Roles, 7,* 739–746.

Larsen, K. S., & Long, E. (1988). Attitudes toward sex-roles: Traditional or egalitarian? *Sex Roles, 19,* 1–12.

Levy, D. E., Faulkner, G. L., & Dixon, R. D. (1984). Work and family interaction: The dual career family of the flight attendant. *Humboldt Journal of Social Relations, 11,* 67–86.

Rice, J. K. (1979). Self esteem, sex-role orientation, and perceived spouse support for a return to school. *Adult Education, 29,* 215–233.

Rollins, J., & White, P. N. (1982). The relationship between mothers' and daughters' sex-role attitudes and self-concepts in three types of family environment. *Sex Roles, 8,* 1141–1155.

Swatos, W. H., & McCauley, C. (1984). Working-class sex-role orientation. *International Journal of Women's Studies, 7,* 136–143.

BIBLIOGRAPHY:

Beere, C. A. (1979). *Women and women's issues: A handbook of tests and measures* (pp. 456–458). San Francisco: Jossey-Bass.

SEX ROLE SURVEY (SRS)

AUTHOR: A. P. MacDonald, Jr.

DATE: 1973

VARIABLE: Attitudes regarding equality between the sexes

DESCRIPTION: The Sex Role Survey (SRS) is a summated rating scale consisting of 63 items, most of which pertain to equality between the sexes in one of the following areas: employee roles, marital and parental roles, and social and domestic roles. Each item is accompanied by six response options ranging from "I agree very much" to "I disagree very much."

ARTICLES LISTED IN BEERE, 1979: 5

NOTES & COMMENTS: MacDonald (1974) recommended using a 53-item version of the scale. Some researchers have used MacDonald's 20-item version, which is based on factor loadings and interitem correlations.

AVAILABLE FROM: MacDonald, 1974; Tests in Microfiche, Test Collection, Educational Testing Service, Princeton, NJ 08541 (order #007496)

USED IN:

Lieblich, A., & Friedman, G. (1985). Attitudes toward male and female homosexuality and sex-role stereotypes in Israeli and American students. *Sex Roles, 12,* 561–570.

MacDonald, A. P., Jr. (1974). Identification and measurement of multidimensional attitudes toward equality between the sexes. *Journal of Homosexuality, 1*, 165–182.

McDonald, G. J., & Moore, R. J. (1978). Sex-role self-concepts of homosexual men and their attitudes toward both women and male homosexuality. *Journal of Homosexuality, 4*, 3–14.

Millham, J., & Smith, L. E. (1981). Sex-role differentiation among black and white Americans: A comparative study. *Journal of Black Psychology, 7*, 77–90.

Ross, M. W. (1983). Societal relationships and gender role in homosexuals: A cross-cultural comparison. *Journal of Sex Research, 19*, 273–288.

Sauter, D., Seidl, A., & Karbon, J. (1980). The effects of high school counseling experience and attitudes toward women's roles on traditional or nontraditional career choice. *Vocational Guidance Quarterly, 28*, 241–249.

Weinberger, L. E., & Millham, J. (1979). Attitudinal homophobia and support of traditional sex roles. *Journal of Homosexuality, 4*, 237–246.

BIBLIOGRAPHY:

Beere, C. A. (1979). *Women and women's issues: A handbook of tests and measures* (pp. 458–460). San Francisco: Jossey-Bass.

SEX-ROLE TRADITIONALISM SCALE

AUTHORS: Zick Rubin and Letitia A. Peplau

DATE: 1973

VARIABLE: Gender role attitudes

DESCRIPTION: The Sex-Role Traditionalism Scale is a 10-item summated rating scale with six response options accompanying each item. Items deal with parental roles, marital roles, women and work, social etiquette, and the women's movement.

ARTICLES LISTED IN BEERE, 1979: 6

AVAILABLE FROM: Peplau, 1973

USED IN:

Caldwell, M. A., & Peplau, L. A. (1984). The balance of power in lesbian relationships. *Sex Roles, 10*(7/8), 587–599.

Cochran, S. D., & Peplau, L. A. (1985). Value orientations in heterosexual relationships. *Psychology of Women Quarterly, 9*(4), 477–488.

Hall, J. A., Braunwald, K. G., & Mroz, B. J. (1982). Gender, affect, and influence in a teaching situation. *Journal of Personality and Social Psychology, 43*(2), 270–280.

Peplau, L. A. (1973). *The impact of fear of success, sex role attitudes, and opposite-sex relationships on women's intellectual performance.* Unpublished doctoral dissertation, Harvard University.

Peplau, L. A., Padesky, C., & Hamilton, M. (1982). Satisfaction in lesbian relationships. *Journal of Homosexuality, 8*(2), 23–35.

Risman, B. J., Hill, C. T., Rubin, Z., & Peplau, L. A. (1981). Living together in college: Implications for courtship. *Journal of Marriage and the Family, 43*(2), 77–83.

Rubin, Z., Hill, C. T., Peplau, L. A., & Dunkel-Schetter, C. (1980). Self-disclo-

sure in dating couples: Sex roles and the ethic of openness. *Journal of Marriage and the Family*, 42(2), 305–317.
BIBLIOGRAPHY:
Beere, C. A. (1979). *Women and women's issues: A handbook of tests and measures* (pp. 228–229). San Francisco: Jossey-Bass.

SEXUAL IDEOLOGY INSTRUMENT (SII)
AUTHOR: Ilsa L. Lottes
DATE: 1985 (used 1983)
VARIABLE: Attitudes regarding gender roles, sexuality, and gender role related issues
TYPE OF INSTRUMENT: Summated rating scale
DESCRIPTION: The Sexual Ideology Instrument (SII) consists of 72 items representing 15 subscales that cover a variety of attitudes regarding gender roles, sexuality, and gender role–related issues. Developed to test Reiss's (1981) theories regarding sexual ideologies, the SII contains subscales measuring each of the following: Gender Role Equality (8 items); Body-Centered Sexuality, four subscales (3, 3, 3, and 2 items); Power of Sexual Emotions, three subscales (2, 2, and 6 items); the importance of Coital Focus in sexual relations (9 items); Love Need in Sex (meaning the importance of love for satisfactory sexual relations), with two subscales (9 and 15 items); attitudes toward Abortion (3 items); belief that Gender Differences are Genetic (3 items); attitudes toward Pornography (3 items); and attitudes toward Homosexuality (3 items). Three areas—Body-Centered Sexuality, Power of Sexual Emotions, and Love Need in Sex—require that beliefs about males and females be compared. Therefore, there are 15 pairs of parallel items on the SII. One item in the pair asks about males/men, and the other item in the pair poses the same statement about females/women. About half of the 72 items on the SII are phrased to reflect a contemporary view; the other half are phrased in the opposite direction. Each item is accompanied by a 5-point response scale ranging from "strongly agree" to "strongly disagree."
SAMPLE ITEMS: (Gender Role Equality) I am in favor of the Equal Rights Amendment being added to the United States Constitution.

(Body-Centered Sexuality, Scale 1) It is acceptable for a 16–17 year-old unmarried female to have sexual intercourse.

(Power of Sexual Emotions, Scale 1) If women yield to their sexual feelings, these feelings will probably disrupt and dominate their lives in destructive ways.

(Coital Focus) A mature man and woman should get their greatest sexual pleasure from intercourse rather than from some other sexual activity.

(Love Need in Sex, Scale 1) Having a physical attraction to someone would be sufficient for me to enjoy sex with that person.

(Abortion) The Supreme Court ruling making abortions legal should be reversed.

(Genetic Gender Differences) Men are generally more interested in sex than women.

(Pornography) Pornography influences men to commit sexual crimes including rape.

(Homosexuality) Homosexuals should NOT be teaching school. It is too risky to allow the possibility of such a teacher taking advantage of or influencing the sexual orientation of even one student.

PREVIOUS SUBJECTS: College students and adults

APPROPRIATE FOR: College students and adults

ADMINISTRATION: Self-administered; about 30–40 minutes

SCORING: Items are individually scored on a 5-point scale. Scores on 43 items must be reversed before item scores are combined. On all subscales, high scores indicate support for a modern naturalistic view; low scores sometimes reflect support for a traditional romantic view and sometimes reflect support for an abstinence perspective. In some areas, such as Body-Centered Sexuality and Power of Sexual Emotions, subscales must be compared with each other to interpret the results. For example, on the Body-Centered Sexuality subscales, low scores on all three subscales indicate support for the abstinence perspective, and low scores on Subscales 1 and 3, along with a high score on Subscale 2, indicate support for the traditional romantic view (i.e., body-centered sexuality is acceptable for men but it is not acceptable for women).

DEVELOPMENT: The development of the SII is based on Reiss's (1981) theories regarding sexual ideologies. Reiss proposed three ideologies: Modern Naturalistic, Traditional Romantic, and Abstinence. Within these ideologies, he suggested five specific beliefs, called tenets. The tenets concern Gender Role Equality, Body-Centered Sexuality, the Power of Sexual Emotions, the importance of Coital Focus, and the Need for Love in Sex. An example of the interface of the ideologies and the tenets is the following statement of the beliefs of the Traditional Romantic in terms of Gender Role Equality: "Gender roles should be distinct and interdependent, with the male gender role as dominant" (Lottes, 1985, p. 407). Reiss (1981) also suggested that adherents to each of the ideologies would have predictable attitudes in each of the following areas: abortion, genetic gender differences, pornography, and homosexuality. The various subscales of the SII are directly related to the ideas Reiss proposed. Some of the items on the SII were adapted from existing scales. For example, four items were taken from surveys done by the National Opinion Research Center (1980).

The SII originally contained 92 items. Based on responses from 395 college students and adults, some items were deleted.

RELIABILITY: Lottes (1988) reported alpha coefficients ranging from .46

(Scale 1 of Powerful Sexual Emotions, a 2-item measure) to .86 (Scale 2 of Love Need in Sex, a 9-item measure). The average for the alpha coefficients was .67. Since 10 of the subscales include only two or three items, it is not surprising that the alpha coefficients were low overall.

VALIDITY: According to Lottes (1985), "The construct validity of the scales was generally supported by both interscale correlations and factor analysis" (p. 413). One exception was that Body-Centered Sexuality and Love Need in Sex had high interscale correlations, and this information, combined with factor analytic data, suggested that the two scales were measuring the same construct.

By looking at correlation coefficients and testing for significant differences between the means, Lottes (1985) found further evidence of construct validity. For example, women were more supportive of Gender Role Equality and Love Need in Sex, and they were less supportive of Body-Centered Sexuality and Pornography; nonreligious adults were more likely to support the Modern Naturalistic views; younger adults were more supportive of Body-Centered Sexuality, more positive toward Pornography and Homosexuality, less supportive of Coital Focus and Love Need in Sex, and less likely to believe in Genetic Gender Differences. In general, results in terms of age, sex, and religiosity were consistent with predictions.

NOTES & COMMENTS: (1) The SII was originally developed to test Reiss's (1981) theories regarding sexual ideologies. The data, examined with cluster analysis, were partially supportive of Reiss's ideas.

(2) The SII is a long, time-consuming scale, and as such, it may not be as useful as a shorter, more focused scale. While it may be tempting to use only a portion of the measure, a researcher should be cautious about using the subscales, which have low reliabilities.

AVAILABLE FROM: Lottes, 1988

USED IN:

Lottes, I. L. (1985). The use of cluster analysis to determine belief patterns of sexual attitudes. *Journal of Sex Research, 21*(4), 405–421.

Lottes, I. L. (1988). A sexual ideology instrument. In C. M. Davis, W. L. Yarber, & S. L. Davis (Eds.), *Sexuality-related measures: A compendium* (pp. 177–181). Syracuse: Editors.

BIBLIOGRAPHY:

National Opinion Research Center. (1980). *General social surveys, 1972–1980: Cumulative codebook.* Chicago: University of Chicago Press.

Reiss, I. L. (1981). Some observations on ideology and sexuality in America. *Journal of Marriage and the Family, 43,* 271–283.

SMITH ATTITUDINAL INVENTORY

AUTHORS: M. Dwayne Smith and George D. Self

DATE: 1980

VARIABLE: Gender role attitudes

TYPE OF INSTRUMENT: Summated rating scale

DESCRIPTION: The Smith Attitudinal Inventory consists of 21 items pertaining to "attitudes toward political and sexual equality, stereotypical beliefs about women, and relationships with men" (Smith & Self, 1980, p. 106). Each item is accompanied by four response options: "strongly agree, agree, disagree, strongly disagree." There is no neutral response. For 10 items, the agree response indicates a more contemporary view; for the other 11 items, the disagree response indicates the more contemporary view. The last item, "I consider myself a feminist," has been used to classify respondents into two groups (Smith & Self, 1981).

SAMPLE ITEMS: The achievements of women in history have not been emphasized as much as those of men.

Women are by nature more emotional than men.

PREVIOUS SUBJECTS: High school girls, college women, and adult women

APPROPRIATE FOR: High school students and older

ADMINISTRATION: Self-administered; 10 minutes

SCORING: Items are individually scored on a 4-point scale, with 4 points assigned to the contemporary response. Item scores can be summed or averaged to yield an overall score.

DEVELOPMENT: No information was provided.

RELIABILITY: No information was provided.

VALIDITY: Using responses to the item "I consider myself a feminist," Smith and Self (1981) divided their respondents into two groups: 124 "feminists" and 155 "traditionalists." As expected, they found that feminists generally scored higher on the items on the scale; the difference was significant for 17 of the 20 items (the analysis excluded the item used to divide the group into two subgroups). Somewhat surprisingly, however, they found that although the traditionalists generally scored below the feminists, they still scored in the profeminist direction on most items; that is, they had a mean score above 2.5 on 16 of the 20 items. On 1 item, the traditionalists actually had a higher mean than the feminists, though the difference was not statistically significant.

The correlations between traditionalist-feminist classification and item scores were often rather low. For six items, the correlations were below .20; on only six items were the correlations above .30 (Smith & Self, 1981).

NOTES & COMMENTS: (1) Smith and Self (1981) factor analyzed scores and identified five factors: labor (4 items), male/female differences (5 items), domestic roles (4 items), relations with men (3 items), and politics (4 items).

(2) Smith and Self (1981) found that feminists showed a more consistent ideology than traditionalists, who generally "support egalitarianism

in the labor market and political arena, but are reluctant to alter existing norms concerning interpersonal relationships with men" (p. 187). This suggested that a scale that focuses on male/female relationships might be a better discriminator of traditionalists and feminists.

(3) Smith and Self (1980) compared scores of college students and their mothers to assess the influence of maternal attitudes on the attitudes of their daughters. Weeks, Wise, and Duncan (1984) conducted a similar study using high school girls and their mothers.

AVAILABLE FROM: Smith and Self, 1980, 1981

USED IN:

Smith, M. D., & Self, G. D. (1980). The congruence between mothers' and daughters' sex-role attitudes: A research note. *Journal of Marriage and the Family*, 42(1), 105–109.

Smith, M. D., & Self, G. D. (1981). Feminists and traditionalists: An attitudinal comparison. *Sex Roles*, 7(2), 183–188.

Weeks, M. O., Wise, G. W., & Duncan, C. (1984). The relationship between sex-role attitudes and career orientations of high school females and their mothers. *Adolescence*, *19*, 595–607.

SRD/PE ATTITUDE INVENTORY

AUTHOR: Agnes Chrietzberg

DATE: 1979

VARIABLE: Attitudes toward differential treatment of boys and girls in secondary school physical education programs

TYPE OF INSTRUMENT: Summated rating scale

DESCRIPTION: The SRD/PE Attitude Inventory consists of 42 statements, most of them directly relevant to physical education. Items pertain to a variety of topics, including the types of skills boys and girls should be encouraged to learn, the skills they can be expected to learn, the advisability of using sexist materials or allowing sexist behaviors in the classroom, and the appropriate roles for male and female physical education teachers. About half of the items are phrased to reflect a liberal or egalitarian attitude, and the other half are phrased to reflect a conservative or sexist viewpoint. Items are accompanied by five response alternatives: "strongly disagree, disagree, neutral, agree, strongly agree."

SAMPLE ITEMS: Equal money should be spent on intramurals and other physical education activities for boys and girls.

Girls should be taught combative activities like judo and wrestling.

PREVIOUS SUBJECTS: Secondary-level physical education teachers and teacher trainees

APPROPRIATE FOR: High school students and older

ADMINISTRATION: Self-administered; about 15–20 minutes

SCORING: Items are individually scored on a 5-point scale, with 5 points assigned to the most liberal attitude and 1 point assigned to the most conservative attitude. Item scores are totaled to yield one score that can range from 42 (strong support for differentiating between the sexes) to 210 (no support for differentiating on the basis of sex). Chrietzberg (1981) provided normative data, including percentile scores, based on responses from 241 secondary-level physical education teachers and teacher trainees.

DEVELOPMENT: Item development was based on a search of the relevant literature and results of interviews held with persons directly involved with or interested in physical education. A pool of 58 items was developed and administered to 64 physical education teacher trainees. Item analysis procedures and feedback from the respondents led to the revision of the scale. Next, a revised 44-item inventory was administered to 241 physical education teachers. For reasons not explained, 2 items were deleted, leaving a 42-item scale.

RELIABILITY: Internal consistency reliability, based on the responses from 241 teachers, was .88. Test-retest reliability, based on testings 4 to 8 weeks apart, was .73. Since an instructional intervention occurred between the two testings, it is difficult to know how to interpret this test-retest reliability.

VALIDITY: As expected, mean scores for women were higher—more liberal—than mean scores for men. The overall findings were that educators were only moderately liberal in their attitudes toward gender role differentiation. This finding was consistent with other research (e.g., Silver, Podemski, & Engin, 1977).

An item analysis was performed to compare the item scores for those whose total scores were in the top 25% and those whose total scores were in the bottom 25%. Significant differences were found between the item means on all 42 items.

NOTES & COMMENTS: (1) Chrietzberg (1981) provided the following information for each of the 42 items: mean, standard deviation, correlation with total score, and internal consistency reliability if the item were deleted from the scale.

(2) Chrietzberg, Leslie, Neikirk, and Uhlir (1979) used the SRD/PE Attitude Inventory as a measure of the effectiveness of a package of eight instructional modules. The modules are for use in preservice or inservice education to encourage equal opportunity and decrease gender role differentiation in physical education classes.

AVAILABLE FROM: Chrietzberg, 1981; Tests in Microfiche, Test Collection, Educational Testing Service, Princeton, NJ 08541 (order #013539)

USED IN:

Chrietzberg, A. (1981). SRD/PE Attitude Inventory: A measure of attitude towards sex role differentiation in physical education. *Catalog of Selected Documents in Psychology, 11*(4), 87. (Ms. No. 2379)

Chrietzberg, A., Leslie, M. D., Neikirk, M. M., & Uhlir, A. (1979). *Teacher ed-*

ucation modules: Reduction of sex bias in coeducational instruction and program operation for physical education, secondary level, January, 1978-August, 1979. Unpublished paper, Eastern Kentucky University Richmond College of Health, Physical Education, Recreation, and Athletics. (ERIC Document Reproduction Service No. ED 194 658)

BIBLIOGRAPHY:

Silver, P. F., Podemski, R. S., & Engin, A. W. (1977). Attitudes toward sex role differentiation in education: Implications for Title IX implementation. *Journal of Research and Development in Education, 10,* 26–35.

TRADITIONAL-EGALITARIAN SEX ROLE SCALE (TESR)

AUTHORS: Knud S. Larsen and Ed Long

DATE: 1988

VARIABLE: Attitudes toward traditional-egalitarian beliefs about gender roles

TYPE OF INSTRUMENT: Summated rating scale

DESCRIPTION: The Traditional-Egalitarian Sex Role Scale (TESR) consists of 20 items, 8 phrased to reflect an egalitarian view and 12 phrased to reflect a traditional view. Twelve items explicitly compare men and women; of the remaining items, half deal with males and half with females. Item content covers a variety of areas, including education, parental roles, marital roles, and personality traits.

SAMPLE ITEMS: It is just as important to educate daughters as it is to educate sons.

Women should be more concerned with clothing and appearance than men.

PREVIOUS SUBJECTS: College students

APPROPRIATE FOR: High school students and older

ADMINISTRATION: Self-administered; about 10 minutes

SCORING: Larsen and Long (1988) did not provide information regarding scoring; however, since this is a straightforward summated rating scale, it can be presumed that items are scored on a 5-point scale and summed to yield one total score. Higher scores reflect a more egalitarian attitude.

DEVELOPMENT: An item pool was initially constructed by generating items based on feminist speeches and relevant literature. Using inputs from students enrolled in an attitude methodology class, the pool of 120 items was reduced to 75 nonoverlapping, relevant items. The item pool was administered to 104 college students. Item-total correlations were computed, and 20 items with correlations greater than .48 were selected for the scale.

RELIABILITY: When the TESR was completed by 83 college students, split-half reliability was .85; applying the Spearman-Brown formula yielded a reliability of .91.

VALIDITY: To test the concurrent validity of the TESR, 83 college students completed the TESR and Brogan and Kutner's (1976) Sex Role Orientation Scale (see separate entry) which is a measure of attitudes toward women and women's roles. The correlation between the two scales was .79.

Larsen and Long (1988) reported that, as predicted, college women compared to college men scored as significantly more egalitarian. Larsen and Long (1988) administered seven scales in addition to the TESR to a sample of 51 college men and 43 college women. Scores on six of the seven scales were significantly correlated with scores on the TESR. In particular, TESR was significantly correlated with a 4-item measure of authoritarianism (Lane, 1955) ($r = .36$), a 6-item measure of religious orthodoxy (Putney & Middleton, 1961) ($r = .31$), a 6-item measure of religious fanaticism (Putney & Middleton, 1961) ($r = .30$), a 20-item same-sex touching scale (Larsen & LeRoux, 1984) ($r = .44$) (see Beere, in press), the Rape Myth Acceptance Scale (Burt, 1980) (r = .49) (see Beere, in press), and Feild's (1978) Attitudes Toward Rape Scale ($r = .49$) (see Beere, in press). The relationship between the TESR and a 22-item birth control scale (Wilke, 1934) was nonsignificant.

Larsen and Long (1988) found a correlation of .42 between TESR scores and scores on a divorce attitude scale (Hardy, 1957). They found a correlation of .84 between TESR scores and a modified fascism scale (Edwards, 1941), and a correlation of .47 between TESR scores and scores on a conservative attitudes toward sexuality scale (Kerr, 1946).

NOTES & COMMENTS: (1) Larsen and Long (1988) factor analyzed responses from 94 college students. They identified two factors. Sixteen of the items had their highest loadings on Factor 1; the remaining 4 items had their highest loadings on Factor 2. However, some of the items on Factor 2 had higher loadings on Factor 1 than did some of the items assigned to Factor 1. Larsen and Long did not comment on the fact that one item had a negative loading. They did, however, conclude that "there is little support for a complex factorial structure, and the scale should be used as a unit" (Larsen & Long, 1988, p. 7).

(2) In defending the need for another measure of egalitarianism, Larsen and Long (1988) suggested that existing measures of attitudes were not addressing issues in such a way as to reflect the changes that have taken place in the last several decades. However, the item content on the TESR is not significantly different from the item content on other measures of attitudes toward gender role equality.

AVAILABLE FROM: Larsen and Long, 1988

USED IN:

Larsen, K. S., & Long, E. (1988). Attitudes toward sex-roles: Traditional or egalitarian? *Sex Roles*, *19*(1/2), 1–12.

BIBLIOGRAPHY:

Beere, C. A. (in press). *Sex and gender issues: A handbook of tests and measures*. Westport, CT: Greenwood.

Brogan, D., & Kutner, N. G. (1976). Measuring sex role orientation: A normative approach. *Journal of Marriage and the Family, 38*, 31–40.

Burt, M. R. (1980). Cultural myths and supports for rape. *Journal of Personality and Social Psychology, 38*(2), 217–230.

Edwards, A. L. (1941). Unlabeled fascist attitudes. *Journal of Abnormal and Social Psychology, 36*, 579–582.

Feild, H. S. (1978). Attitudes toward rape: A comparative analysis of police, rapists, crisis counselors, and citizens. *Journal of Personality and Social Psychology, 36*, 156–179.

Hardy, K. R. (1957). Determinants of conformity and attitude change. *Journal of Abnormal and Social Psychology, 54*, 289–294.

Kerr, W. A. (1946). *Liberal and conservative manual of instructions.* Chicago: Psychometric Affiliates.

Lane, R. (1955). Four-item I scale in "Political Personality and Electoral Choice." *American Science Review, 49*, 173–190.

Larsen, K. S., & LeRoux, J. (1984). A study of same-sex touching attitudes: Scale development and personality predictors. *Journal of Sex Research, 20*(3), 264–278.

Putney, S., & Middleton, R. (1961). Dimensions and correlates of religious ideologies. *Social Forces, 39*, 285–290.

Wilke, W. H. (1934). An experimental comparison of the speech, the radio, and the printed page as propaganda devices. *Archives of Psychology*, No. 169.

TRADITIONAL-LIBERATED CONTENT SCALE

AUTHOR: Martin S. Fiebert

DATE: 1983

VARIABLE: Men's gender role attitudes

TYPE OF INSTRUMENT: Summated rating scale

DESCRIPTION: The Traditional-Liberated Content Scale consists of two parts: Scale I, with 15 items that focus on traditional attitudes, and Scale II, with 14 items that reflect liberal attitudes. The items on Scale I are phrased so that a traditional man will disagree with all but 2 of the items; the items on Scale II are phrased so that a traditional man will disagree with 4 of the items. Each item is accompanied by a 7-point scale ranging from "very strongly agree" to "very strongly disagree."

SAMPLE ITEMS: (Scale I) Financial status does not define a man.

   (Scale II) Hugging another man makes me feel uncomfortable.

PREVIOUS SUBJECTS: College and adult men

APPROPRIATE FOR: Males of high school age and older

ADMINISTRATION: Self-administered; about 15 minutes

SCORING: Items are individually scored on a 7-point scale. The authors did not specify the direction for scoring (i.e., which end of the continuum is assigned the high scores), but they did indicate that 2 items on Scale

I and 4 items on Scale II need to be reversed before totals are obtained. A total score is computed, as well as scores for each of the two subscales. DEVELOPMENT: An item pool of 108 items was developed to cover four content areas: men's relationships with women, men's relationships with children, men's relationships with other men, and men's involvements at work. The item pool was administered to 277 men, including college students from a variety of disciplines, older relatives and co-workers of the student participants, and engineers and management personnel. The men's ages ranged from 20 to over 50. A factor analysis of the responses led to the identification of six factors with eigenvalues greater than one. Items were selected from Factor I to comprise Scale I of the Traditional-Liberated Content Scale; similarly, items were selected from Factor II to comprise Scale II. Selected items had factor loadings of at least .35 and item-total correlations of at least .30. In selecting items, preference was given to items with greater variability. In interpreting these factor analytic results, it is important to remember that the number of subjects was very low relative to the number of items.

RELIABILITY: A sample of 70 college men completed the scale on two occasions separated by a 3-week interval. The test-retest correlation was .85 for Scale I (the traditional factor); the test-retest correlation was .92 for Scale II (the liberated factor).

VALIDITY: Essentially no information was provided. Fiebert (1983) reported no significant differences relating to age, marital status, or parental status except for a small effect of age on Scale I scores. These findings, however, neither support nor refute the validity of the scale.

NOTES & COMMENTS: (1) Seven items on Scale I and three items on Scale II use the word *not*. It is easier for a respondent to answer an item when it is phrased in the affirmative; the word *not* can lead to confusion in reading and understanding the meaning of the item.

(2) Biggs and Fiebert (1984) reported the results of a factor analytic study of the same set of data used to develop the Traditional-Liberated Content Scale. Though it appears that Biggs and Fiebert used the same method of factor analysis as Fiebert (1983), they extracted 16 factors, rather than 6 factors, with eigenvalues greater than one, and judged that 7 of the factors should be interpreted. They labeled the factors: breaking the stereotype, working women, loss of power, emotional control, appearance of masculinity, women at home, and toughness. Given that the scale had 108 items and the sample included only 277 men, little confidence should be placed in the results of the factor analysis.

AVAILABLE FROM: Fiebert, 1983

USED IN:

Biggs, P., & Fiebert, M. S. (1984). A factor-analytic study of American male attitudes. *Journal of Psychology*, 116(1), 113–116.

Fiebert, M. S. (1983). Measuring traditional and liberated males' attitudes. *Perceptual and Motor Skills, 56*(1), 83–86.

Fiebert, M. S., & Vera, W. (1985). Test-retest reliability of a male sex-role attitude survey: The Traditional-Liberated Content Scale. *Perceptual and Motor Skills, 60*(1), 66.

Index of Scale Titles

Index of Scale Authors

Index of Variables Measured by Scales

Index of Scale Users

This index is based on all entries in the sections headed USED IN.